THE JEWISH WAY

Living the Holidays

Rabbi Irving Greenberg

A TOUCHSTONE BOOK
Published by Simon & Schuster
New York   London   Toronto   Sydney   Tokyo   Singapore

TOUCHSTONE
Simon & Schuster Building
Rockefeller Center
1230 Avenue of the Americas
New York, New York 10020

5   7   9   10   8   6

Library of Congress Cataloging-in-Publication Data is available.

ISBN 0-671-87303-2

To Blu
who taught me the meaning of covenantal love

Preface

At the prospect of publication of this, my first book, my heart is filled with joy and gratitude. I have been sustained and nurtured by other people and have been shaped by their models, influence, and help. This book, in particular, reflects the ongoing impact of others on me. I would like in this small way to acknowledge my debt of gratitude to them.

This book bears the imprint of two people, above all. One is Rabbi Joseph B. Soloveitchik, the master philosopher/poet of halacha (Jewish law) of our time. Even with the perspective of thirty-five years, it is hard to overstate the electrifying impact on me of the initial encounter with Rabbi Soloveitchik's model and mode of thinking. I was twenty years old, emotionally open and intellectually absorbent, on my maiden flight out of the warm, loving cocoon of the East European refugee yeshiva in which I had studied and been ordained. I had been raised to study and observe all the traditions and rules of halacha; Rabbi Soloveitchik opened my eyes to the patterns of meaning therein. In his analysis the halacha became more than the sum of its thousands of observances and details. It was a system by which to live humanly, a way to seize life whole, a confrontation with the dilemmas and anxieties of existence. The details were the products of divine revelation and an ongoing historic confrontation, love affair, and partnership between God and the Jewish people. Under the light of his illumination, every detail—even those that appeared obscure or mechanical—turned out to be an articulation of a psychological or moral state or an attempt to induce the individual to give deeply human responses to life situations.

If that was not enough of a contribution, Rabbi Soloveitchik went on to show a personal model of open encounter with modern culture and a willingness to influence and be influenced by it. In his Bible and classic text study groups, he brought out the deeply human qualities of those God-intoxicated figures. He showed how to ask questions of the tradition that others didn't dare ask and, thus, to get the sources to yield remarkable answers that otherwise would not have been heard. He combined all this with a deeply spiritual approach to life and a poetic temperament, leavened by humor that always bubbled near the surface, and a winning warmth. I did not study full time with him, but I did have the privilege of hearing his sheurim, of spending individual personal time with him, and of reading his writings over the years. Yet only when I put pen to paper did the full extent of his impact emerge clearly; the manuscript revealed how he had shaped my thinking on Jewish observance, both conceptually and in myriad details. This is not to imply that Rabbi Soloveitchik would agree with all the views expressed in this book; I take full responsibility for this writing. However, I acknowledge with deep gratitude his extraordinary impact on my understanding all these years. My only regret is that he is now too ill for me to be able to express these thanks to him personally.

The other person whose signature is to be found on every page is my father, Rabbi Eliyahu Chayim Greenberg   ל״צז .   More than any other individual, he shaped me, challenged me, taught me. In a sense, my father shaped the primordial structures of my thought at the level before ideas are grasped or put in words. Thus my father's influence is less overt, less quoted by name but more universally present in this book. His passion for justice and desire to help the underdog, his love for Jews and his demand that they be defended and justified, his conviction that the Jewish people can be trusted and that they are endowed with profound spiritual judgment marked all halachic decisions and guidance that he gave to countless others. His great thirst for learning and his belief that, properly used, Torah must be an instrument of life and love overwhelmed all who studied or lived with him.

My father's ardor for stories and storytelling in sacred sources balanced his fervor for halacha in all its details. His wit and ability to see humor in the most solemn texts continue to shape my ways of perceiving everything I read and study. I am sorry that most of the original jokes in this book were removed by the various editors and readers whose judgment I respect, although perhaps this is appropriate since my father's style of humor, like mine, was more oral than written. I miss him; how I wish I could have given him the nachas of this book in his lifetime.

One reason that I so internalized the Jewish tradition is that I grew up in a nurturing family. My wonderful mother, Sonia Greenberg, זצ״ל , was the rock of that family. With her quiet strength and unceasing selflessness she labored all her life for her children's benefit with no thought for herself. Her elemental piety, her continuous conversation with God filled the house with the light of faith. My sisters, Gertrude and Lillian, and my brother, Aharon, were like an extra set of parents in their constant giving to me. I identify the way of life with all that kindness and love.

I thank Arthur Samuelson, who as editor of Summit Books commissioned this work; Peg Parkinson, who did the first editing; my dear friend David Scheinfeld, who never lost faith in the book and who stepped in to help when I needed it; Dominick Anfuso, the new senior editor at Summit, whose editing—done graciously when he had no obligation to do so—improved many passages. Bambi Marcus typed and retyped with unfailing good spirit and intelligence. Rabbi Shalom Carmy gave me the benefit of a thorough and complete reading and made many constructive suggestions. Rabbi Natan Greenberg critiqued three chapters from the extraordinary spiritual perspective of a Bratslaver. He left me wishing that I knew more about mysticism or that he would some day write a book incorporating the mystical interpretations of the holidays. Rabbi David Harbater graciously checked many footnotes and citations for me. Deborah Greenberg, in accordance with her usual talents and helpfulness, labored intensively and under deadline of galleys to produce a most thorough index.

The germ of this book started as a pamphlet on the High Holy Days for the congregants at Riverdale Jewish Center. My warm feelings for them, for their love of tradition and their response to my ideas remain unabated. Two good friends influenced my thought over the years— Zev (Willy) Frank of blessed memory and David Hartman. Their model and inspiration continue to resonate in my mind and heart.

Approximately half of this book originally appeared in a different form, in a series of holiday guides authored for CLAL—The National Jewish Center for Learning and Leadership. The encounter through CLAL's programs with the lay leadership of American Jewry had a profound effect on my life and thinking. The challenge of making the tradition meaningful to them and of incorporating their insights and values into meaningful tradition is always with me. I owe an extraordinary debt of friendship and gratitude to CLAL's supporters, founders, and primary leaders.

I would like to express special thanks to Ben Leuchter, founding chairman, friend, and helper; Irvin Frank, who saved CLAL and sustained me in difficult days with his quiet strength, deep feeling and thought; Herschel Blumberg, whose incisive thinking reshaped CLAL —and made a substantial contribution to the chapter on Yom Ha'Atzmaut; Aaron Ziegelman, whose own initiative, vision, and constructive approaches helped all of us to go forward; and Bob Loup, warm friend, who encouraged me to concentrate more on writing and teaching and thus speeded up the completion of this book. All my colleagues at CLAL have earned my thanks for their model of devotion to learning and teaching. However, I must thank especially Paul Jeser and David Elcott for the joy and privilege of working with them. Paul's professional leadership in tandem with lay leaders turned CLAL into a vital organization and relieved me of a thousand pressures and cares. David took over the educational program and developed a remarkable scholarly staff. Without the two of them, I never could have found the peace of mind and heart to complete this book.

My extraordinary parents-in-law, Rabbi Sam and Sylvia Genauer, powerfully affected our family's religious life. Our children, Moshe, David and his wife, Mindy, Deborah, J.J., and Goody have been my patient listeners, challenging questioners, favorite students and teachers; they have been an unfailing source of love and joy all these years.

My wife, Blu, has been intellectual companion and best friend, inspiration and early warning system, source of constant appreciation and most honest critic. I have learned to depend on her judgment and to ignore her wisdom only at my peril. Her humanness and love, her religious model, her ability to juggle the contradictions of life without self-pity or resentment have been the anchor of my life for more than thirty years. The dedication of this book to her is but a grain of sand on the shores of a boundless sea.

Irving Greenberg
Riverdale, New York
Nissan 5748
April 1988

Contents

A Word to the Reader

THE FOCUS OF THIS BOOK is on Judaism as it expresses itself in the Jewish holidays. Through these days Judaism is most visible and most easily accessible. But this is meant to be more than a book about the holidays; rather, it is a book about the Jewish way through life and history. To celebrate the holidays is to relive by reliving the Jewish way. Over the centuries Jewish thought and values have been crystallized in religious behavior. Judaism's underlying structures of meaning—the understanding of the world, the direction of history, the values of life—have come to their classic expression in the holidays. This book seeks to uncover those patterns.

All halachic behaviors are dramatic/mimetic gestures articulating a central metaphor of living. Grasping the metaphor adds depth to action and joy to life. Entering into the holidays with this understanding widens the range of emotion and brings a whole new set of roles and personae into even the most conventional life. Living the Jewish way calls for a highly developed capacity for fantasy and playacting. If you will, one must be a bit of a ham to be a kosher Jew. I hope that by pointing out the roles we are summoned to play, this book will help release the creative imagination for religious living present in every person.

This is not to suggest that practice of the Jewish faith is all play, all fun and games. There have been times when this religion has brought painful memories, moral problematic conflicts with others, oppressive minutiae, and obligations so great I felt guilty no matter what I accomplished. Yet on balance the overwhelming effect has been to fill my life with a sense of Divine Presence and human continuity, bondedness, joy, textured living experiences full of love that make everything worthwhile. No wonder that over the course of history millions of Jews were willing to die, if necessary, for this faith. Through this book, I hope to show others why it is worth living for this faith.

This book is written for different types of readers: nonobservant Jews who seek new experiences to deepen their Jewish identity; observant Jews who wish to avoid the pitfall of practicing the details while missing the overarching goal; those lacking Jewish education who search for more information and learned Jews who search for new insights; and non-Jews who wish to understand the underlying visions of Judaism and who may find that it resonates in their own religious living.

It is a privilege to be able to write at such a unique moment in our people's history. The age of self-evident identity and of no alternative in values is over. The age of exclusion and stereotyping by Gentiles is drawing to a close. "Jewish flight" to achieve success or integration in the broader society is declining. Many observant Jews have put aside the fear that tradition cannot stand up in the presence of choice. Thus, this is one of those rare moments when we can open a dialogue between Jews and the tradition, between Jews and Jews, between Jews and non-Jews, between the people and its God.

To those readers who come to this subject with a fixed mind, I would like to say a special word:

In human history, freedom and awareness of alternatives generally have led to higher-level choices, more mature faith, and stronger commitment. This book is predicated on those optimistic assumptions. Respectful awareness of alternatives, deep consciousness of choices made along the Jewish way, and trust in the wisdom of both partners in the covenant can only deepen our appreciation for the courage and love of those who lived the endless chain of life that has brought the Torah to us to this moment.

This is the heroic age of the Jewish people, an age of resurrection and rebirth. It is simultaneously an age of awakening and new hope for humanity. Bliss it is to be alive in this dawn, but to be committed is the very heaven. May this book help some find that meaning in deeper involvement.

PART ONE:

◣◣◢◢

The Vision
and the Way

THE HOLY DAYS are the unbroken master code of Judaism. Decipher them and you will discover the inner sanctum of this religion. Grasp them and you hold the heart of the faith in your hand.

The holy days are the quintessential Jewish religious expression because the main teachings of Judaism are incorporated in their messages. Recurrent experience of these days has sustained the Jews on their long march through history. By interpreting and reinterpreting the holidays and by applying their lessons to daily life, the Jewish people have been continuously guided along the Jewish way.

There are thousands of details and practices associated with each Jewish festival. Though customs have grown and changed over millennia, and each community and every age has added its own special flavor and detail, each holiday has one central metaphor that orchestrates myriad details into one coherent whole. By understanding a few key models one can hear and interpret the central messages of Judaism and its development over the course of history.

What makes decoding even more of an adventure is that the pattern is not fixed; it is still unfolding. Judaism itself is a pattern of meaning and direction for human history. Every time there is a major new event or a decisive turn on the road through history, new insights and patterns emerge. These are marked and inserted into the record by adding a new Jewish holiday to the calendar. Thus, the sacred days are the register of Judaism in history. And just as Judaism and the Jewish people are not finished, neither is the role of the holidays. Out of the twentieth century, in response to the two momentous historical events of a new era in Jewish history, two holy days—Yom Hashoah (Holocaust Commemoration Day) and Yom Ha'Atzmaut (Israel Independence Day)—are struggling to be born.

As in a brilliant kaleidoscope, emergent patterns often give new coherence and constellation to already existing ones. In the same way each new Jewish holiday has affected the meaning of all the others. Each holiday pattern projects its own central image and also reflects additional highlights in relation to every other holiday. As each new holiday has refocused the understanding of the existing holidays and thus has shed light on the Jewish way in general, so will Yom Hashoah and Yom Ha'Atzmaut color the fundamental understanding of all of Judaism.

What, then, is the key to Judaism's cipher? Is there some fundamental, unifying principle underlying all the Jewish holidays?

The central paradigm of Jewish religion is redemption. According to the Bible, the human being is created in the image of God. According to the Rabbis this means that every single person is unique and equal, endowed with the dignity of infinite value. But in history most humans have been degraded or denied their due. Judaism affirms that this condition should never be accepted; it must and will be overcome.

The Jewish religion is founded on the divine assurance and human belief that the world *will* be perfected. Life will triumph over its enemies—war, oppression, hunger, poverty, sickness, even death. Before we are done, humanity will achieve the fullest realization of the dignity of the human being. In that messianic era, the earth will become a paradise and every human being will be recognized and treated as an image of God. In a world of justice and peace, with all material needs taken care of, humans will be free to establish a harmonious relationship with nature, with each other, with God.

Jewish tradition has dreams, not illusions. It knows that the world is not now a Garden of Eden. Redemption is a statement of hope. The Torah offers a goal worthy of human effort, to be realized over the course of history. Through the Jewish way of life and the holidays, the Torah seeks to nurture the infinite love and unending faith needed to sustain people until perfection is achieved. It becomes even more necessary to develop staying power—for beyond Judaism's incredible statement that life will totally triumph, it makes an even more remarkable claim. The final, ideal state will not be bestowed upon humans by some miraculous divine fiat. According to classic Judaism, God alone is the divine ground of life but God has chosen a partner in the perfection process. The ultimate goal will be achieved through human partic-ipation. The whole process of transformation will take place on a human scale. Human models, not supernatural beings, will instruct and inspire humankind as it works toward the final redemption. Real-ization of perfection will come not through escape from present reality to some idealized utopia but by improving this world, one step at a time. Universal justice will be attained by starting with the natural love and responsibility for one's family, then widening the concern to in-clude one's people, and eventually embracing the whole world.

The perfect world can be reached only by an endless chain of human effort. The actions of any one people or any single generation are not enough. It would almost seem futile to begin the work unless others could be counted on to complete the work. According to the Bible, God set this process in motion first by covenanting with all human-kind (the children of Noah) and then by singling out one people (the children of Israel). The Jews were charged with the mission of being the vanguard of humanity as it walks through history toward the mes-sianic end goal. The Bible teaches that the Jews have pledged their lives, their fortunes, their sacred honor to make this hope finally come true. By their acceptance of the Torah, the Jews promised not to settle or stop short of that goal. This is the Jewish covenant. Jews have given their word to go on living as a people in a special way so that their lives testify to something greater than themselves. With that testimony they bear witness to a final, universal redemption.

Thus, the Torah—the distinctive way of life of the Jewish people—is part of a covenant with all people. This particular people has com-mitted to journey through history, exploring paths and modeling moments of perfection. But the testimony and example are for the sake of humanity. The Jewish witness affects all people and is affected by them. When the final messianic redemption is achieved, the Jewish testimony will be complete. All humans will live in a divine/human perfection.

The messianic dream is the great moving force of Jewish history and of the Jewish role in the world. It is the natural unfolding and univer-sal application of the Exodus experience. The central biblical event—the overthrow of tyranny, the redemption of the Jewish slaves, and the gift of freedom and dignity—will become the experience of all human-kind in the future kingdom of God. This idea has proven to be one of the most fertile and dynamic concepts of all time. The lesson that humans are entitled to a better life has unleashed a thousand libera-tion movements—spiritual, political, and social. By communicating its dream of redemption to others, Jewry has shaken and moved human-ity. Setting in motion a subversive discontent, creating an explosive tension between the ideal and the real, Judaism has transformed the world again and again. And in Christianity, Islam, and modern secular messianic movements, the redemptive seed cast by Judaism has borne fruit yet again.

The above claim expresses a fundamental Jewish self-understanding. By some astonishing divine grace and by the peculiar experiences of their history, a people—the Jews—have become a key vehicle for the realization of the perfect world. Their task is to enter deeply into present reality while holding fast to the vision of the end days that far surpass it. And through their lives, Jews are to lead the way to a unification that will overcome the tormenting gap between the present and the final messianic perfection.

This is not to claim that the Jews are a super race. As the record shows, the Jews are all too human. Jewish history and religious development reflect the interaction of a people and its mission—sometimes living up to the ideal, sometimes failing miserably. Often, the people are divided over the proper direction to go. Yet somehow they manage to go on. But in their flawed humanness and through their recurrent displays of limitations and greatness, Jews prove the possibilities for all finite humans to reach for infinite life and freedom. These people who often "dwell alone" point the way for all humanity.

To ensure the fulfillment of the Jewish role is a staggering pedagogical challenge. How to inspire the people with the vision of the final perfection? How to supply the strength to persevere for millennia on the road to redemption without selling out? How to prevent the extraordinary range of experiences along the path from turning the Jewish way into a set of discontinuous events experienced by unrelated communities? How to undergo the radical transformations of condition over the course of history without losing the continuity of vision essential to completing the mission? The answer to all these questions is one and the same. The key is found in the *halacha*, the Jewish Way (of life), and its primary pedagogical tools: the Jewish calendar and the Jewish holidays.

Orthodox Jews believe that the halacha and its principles and methods were revealed to Moses at Sinai. In modern times, others may dispute the claim that it all began at Sinai, but all Jews acknowledge that the process did not stop at Sinai. Halacha includes law, custom, institution; it is a strategy for getting through history. Above all, halacha is what the name literally means: the walking, or the way. Add together a set of memories and values with commandments and goals, and you have the halacha, a total life-style that sustained the Jews even as it guided them toward the final goal.

Building on biblical commandments and modes of living, the halacha took every aspect of life—food, dress, sex, names, parenting—and oriented them to affirm Jewish distinctiveness. To make it through history intact, Jews needed to maintain themselves, so the halacha developed boundary practices and group rewards to keep them going. Special obligations were placed on Jews to care for Jews; special penalties were placed on Jews who betrayed Jews; special efforts were required to save Jews. The halacha constantly reminded the downtrodden Jews that, whatever their external circumstances, they were still royalty in God's kingdom of priests.

The crucial factor in Jewish perseverance was that, against the risks of being Jewish, the halacha also provided the rewards of being Jewish. Alongside the sense of overarching purpose, the halacha offered seasons of joy, strong bonds of family, a sense that the others cared, a system of justice and law, and the hope that sustained people even on days of despair.

Many of the halacha's messages were communicated through the distinctive Hebrew calendar that Jews live by, a lunar one. The solar New Year occurs in January; the lunar New Year generally comes in September or October. The solar day begins after midnight, the morning comes before the evening. In the Hebrew lunar calendar, evening precedes morning and the day begins with the night before. The solar calendar knows the variation of the length of days and the seasons of the sun's distance from the earth; the lunar calendar knows the rhythm of the moon's waxing and waning in a monthly cycle. Thus, dates and anniversaries and time locations reinforce the Jewish sense of otherness. Since Jews lived amid a Gentile majority, in the realm of physical space Jewish identity was "deviant." By contrast, the calendar provided a framework of Jewish time that enveloped the Jews. It was a "total institution" into which the Jew entered. In this way, personality and identity were reworked in light of Jewish memory and Jewish values. The calendar was a vehicle of Jewish solidarity. For example, on Shabbat, when non-Jews worked, Jews stayed home and went to their own institutions. When weekdays coincided with holy days, Jews withdrew from society and came together to share the Jewish past.

The Talmud contains stories of the coincidence of Jewish festivals with Roman mourning days and ways in which anti-Semites sought to exploit the contradiction in order to harm the Jews. In America, the Fourth of July falls, in one out of three years, during the three-week period when Jews mourn the darkest days of ancient loss of national independence. The effect is jarring, and it tends to lift traditional Jews out of the present. Through such juxtapositions, the Jewish calendar guides the Jews through history even as it guides each individual through life. As long as people live in the consciousness and rhythm of the Jewish calendar, they will go on living as Jews.

This does not mean that the march of time in the Jewish community is paced by a totally different beat. Judaism's message is dialectical—Jews are distinctive yet are part of society. In this spirit, the Hebrew lunar calendar was intercalated so as not to tear loose from the seasons of the solar year. Passover was always to occur in the spring (see Exodus 13:4) and Sukkot in the fall (Exodus 34:22). Since the lunar year is only 354 days long, an unadjusted lunar calendar would wander eleven days per year—further and further away from the original seasons. (This is what happens in the Islamic lunar calendar.) Such a calendrical arrangement would have separated Jews totally from the flow of time in their host societies—except for the later Moslem culture in which their calendar would be totally congruent with local practice. Instead, by the mandated insertion of an extra month a year (in seven out of every nineteen years), the Jewish calendar was permanently synchronized with the solar one. Thus, the Hebrew calendar remained distinctive yet integrated in all the host cultures. The Jews walked on the path of their own elected mission even as they remained in step with the general society.

The Jewish year has an inner logic of its own. The joy of Passover in the spring is linked through seven weeks of counting to the ascent of Sinai on Shavuot and the climax of the Jewish covenantal commitment to live by the Torah. In late summer, the year dips to its low point as the community retells and reenacts the greatest tragedy of its early history: the destruction of the Temple and the exile of the people. Thirty days later, at the onset of the sixth month, a new cycle begins: the awakening to self-renewal and repentance—individual and national. This builds up to the thunderous climax of judgment on Rosh Hashanah and Yom Kippur. (Because life and death hang in the balance of these days, this period is also called the Days of Awe.) Then, on the heels of the High Holy Days, comes the joyous celebration of Exodus and the harvest that is the holiday of Sukkot. Months later come the two winter holidays—Hanukkah and Purim—that celebrate deliverances along the historic Jewish way.

So the calendar constantly shapes and deepens group memory. Individual Jews might have absorbed, through cultural osmosis, contemporary values, role models, and heroes from the street, but from the calendar and the holy days, Jewish values and ideal types enter the bloodstream. In an annual cycle, every Jew lives through all of Jewish history and makes it his or her personal experience.

Through the power of the calendar and the community, each individual life is linked to a cause that transcends it. Each action is given cosmic significance. Redemption is steeped in little acts that finally add up to a new heaven and a new earth. Judaism plucks eternity in a flower (or a palm branch) and holds infinity in a grain of sand (or a pinch of maror). Even the passion of a young man for his beloved, unleashed by the arrival of spring, became a paradigm of divine-human love (Song of Songs—Passover). Not only the heroic love and self-sacrifice of a widow but also the petty self-interest of the anonymous cousin who could not see beyond momentary advantage and refused to marry the future mother-ancestor of the Messiah (Book of Ruth—Shavuot), and even the world-weariness of a cynical old man whose experience pointed out the limitations of materialism (Kohelet —Sukkot) were woven by human effort and divine plan into the warp and woof of the tapestry of final perfection.

Thus, the experiences garnered from the sacred days made every day a special day. That sense of being special sustained the Jews and gave them the strength to carry the burden of the covenantal way.

CHAPTER ONE

The Holidays
as the
Jewish Way

THE JEWISH RELIGION affirms the life that is the here and now. At the same time, Jewish tradition insists that the final goal of paradise regained is equally worthy of our loyalty and effort. Judaism is the Jewish way to get humanity from the world as it is now to the world of final perfection. To get from here to there, you need both the goal and a process to keep you going over the long haul of history. In Judaism, the holidays supply both.

In the face of widespread evil and suffering, the holy days teach the central idea of redemption. They keep the idea real by restaging the great events of Jewish history that validate the hope. In their variety, the holidays incorporate rich living experiences that sustain the human capacity to hold steadfast on course. Sacred days give sustenance to spiritual life and a dimension of depth to physical life. The holy days provide a record of the struggle to be faithful to the covenant. While chronicling the history, they distill the lessons learned along the way. And because they are popular, the holidays make the dream and the process of realization the possession of the entire people.

THE HOLIDAYS OF THE VISION

The Exodus is the core event of Jewish history and religion. The central moment of Jewish religious history is *yetziat mitzrayim*, exodus from Egypt. In this event, a group of Hebrew slaves were liberated. The initiative for freedom had to come from God, for the slaves were so subjugated that they accepted even the fate of genocide. Moses, called by God, came to Pharaoh with a request that the slaves be given a temporary release to go and worship in the desert. Then, step by step, the power of Pharaoh was broken; step by step, the temporary release escalated into a demand for freedom. Thus, the Torah makes its point that the entry of God into history is also a revelation of human dignity and right to freedom and foreshadows the end of absolute human power with all its abuses.

The Exodus inaugurated the biblical era of the Jewish people's history. In Judaism's teaching, the Exodus is not a one-time event but a norm by which all of life should be judged and guided. The Exodus is an "orienting event"—an event that sets in motion and guides the Jewish way (and, ultimately, humanity's way) toward the Promised Land—an earth set free and perfected. And as they walk through local cultures and historical epochs, people can gauge whether they have lost the way to freedom by charting their behavior along the path against the Exodus norms. An analogy: A rocket fired into space navigates by a star such as Canopus; it even makes a mid-course correction by measuring its relationship to the celestial marker. So does the Exodus serve as the orienting point for the human voyage through time and for mid-course corrections on the trajectory toward final redemption.

The Exodus is brought into life and incorporated into personal and national values through the classic Jewish behavior model—reenactment of the event. The basic rhythm of the year is set through the reenactment of the Exodus (Passover), followed by the covenant acceptance (Shavuot), and then by restaging of the exodus *way* (Sukkot). For the Israelite living in biblical times, the holidays were concentrated in two months: the first month, Aviv, in later times renamed Nissan, which incorporated the seven days of Passover; and the seventh month, Eytanim, in later times renamed Tishrei, with one day of Rosh Hashanah, one day of Yom Kippur, seven days of Sukkot, and an eighth day of closure (Shemini Atzeret). Both months were dominated by the Exodus holidays. The only other annual holiday was Shavuot, which occurred on one day in the third month.

Passover, marking the liberation, and Sukkot, commemorating the journey, are the alpine events in the Hebrew calendar. Shavuot is the link between the two major Exodus commemorations, marking the transformation of Exodus from a one-time event into an ongoing commitment.

Forty-nine days after the Exodus, the people of Israel stood before Sinai. There, in the desert, on the fiftieth day, the Israelites accepted a covenant with God. Shavuot marks the second great historical experience of the Jews as a people—the experience of revelation. Shavuot is the closure of the Passover holiday. On this day the constitution of the newly liberated people, the Torah, was promulgated.

In the land of Israel, both holidays had strong agricultural foundations—Passover linked to the spring and Shavuot to the summer. From Passover to Shavuot, the holiday of freedom leads to the historical conclusion of liberation—the establishment of the covenant at Sinai. From Passover to Shavuot, sowing the seed in the spring culminates in the summer harvest.

Each year on Shavuot, the Jewish people reenact the heart-stopping, recklessly loving moment when they committed themselves to an open-ended, covenantal mission. Through song and story, Torah study and Torah reading, the congregation of Israel is transported to Sinai and stands together again under the mountain of the Lord.

The third core holiday, Sukkot, celebrates the redemption way itself. Sukkot reconstructs the wilderness trek, the long journey to the Promised Land. The festival explores the psychology of wandering, the interplay of mobility and rootedness, and the challenge of walking the way. By reliving the Exodus in a distinctive way (focusing on the process rather than the event), Sukkot ensures that encounter with the Exodus will bracket the Jewish year. Thus, the three core holidays combine to communicate powerfully the origins and vision of the Jewish religion. If, as the prophet said, in the absence of vision a people perishes, then the halacha can truly affirm that in the constant presence of vision, a people lives on eternally.

How can the great redemption events be brought so powerfully into the present? Part of the answer lies in the brilliant pedagogy and rich variety of observances in each holiday. The primary thrust of the holidays is to make the event so vivid and so present that all of current life and the direction of the future will be set by its guidelines. Telling the story and living through these events, liturgically recreated, Jews experience them as *happenings in their own lives*. The Exodus is tasted (matzah, maror, festive seder, Paschal lamb), narrated (haggadah), and celebrated (Psalms 114–18). On Shavuot, the covenant is proclaimed (reading the Book of Exodus, Ten Commandments/Sinai portion), studied (all night), accepted (symbolically), and explored. On Sukkot, the Exodus way is walked, its huts erected (Sukkah), its bounty shared (with the poor), and its exhilaration danced (the Rejoicing of the Water Drawing). Through repetition, the Exodus became so real that the Israelites remained faithful to its message in the face of an indifferent world—even in the face of oppression or defeat.

Beyond this answer there is a deeper Jewish teaching as well. The past is not over; by tapping into the deeper layers of time, the Jew brings the past revelation event into life now. The Sh'ma prayer states:

"And these words which I command you today shall be on your heart" (Deuteronomy 6:6). Say the Rabbis: They are commanded *today* —every day.* In a mystical sense, under the surface of normal time there courses a parallel stream of sacred time. In it, the Sinai revelation and other great events are carried in tandem with present existence. This is the meaning of the rabbinic dictum: "Every day a voice goes out from Horeb (Sinai)."† Ritual calls up that voice into the life of the present-day believer. Energized by that voice, Jews persist on the road to redemption.

A people does not live by vision alone. After communicating the goal, the Torah turns to the next key challenge: how to develop the incredible human capacities needed to carry the burden of the mission. Judaism places this nurturing of human capability at the center of its religious life. Experiencing the event through reenactment gives one the strength to assume the burden of being both witness and trail-blazer and enables one to wrestle with the unrelenting, ratcheting pulls of dream and reality without releasing either.

By summoning the future into the present reality, Judaism cultivates the fundamental quality of hope in humans. In certain liturgical moments, the believer encounters the future and draws its strength into life today. The entire Shabbat experience anticipates the future messianic redemption and gives human beings a foretaste of the kingdom. One can view this layering of time in which past, present, and future coexist from the perspective of God before whom there is no passage of time but only eternity. Or one can view this conception from the perspective of human psychology. Other animals have only the present and the past remembered through instinct or conditioning. Such experiences program the animal and shape its response to stimuli in the present. Uniquely, the human being can anticipate the future redemption and bring it closer. Thus, an event that has not yet occurred can have a profound impact on the present, an impact strong enough to overcome even powerful past conditioning. Beaten, tormented, and totally ground down, human beings, inspired by the future, have arisen and reversed all the conditioning of despair. The human is a future-oriented creature to whom hope is life-giving.

The focus on developing human capacity is particularly exemplified in the Sabbath and Days of Awe, the primary holy days that nurture personal life along the way. The Shabbat, on a weekly basis, and Rosh Hashanah and Yom Kippur, annually, are the key periods of individual and family renewal. These holidays accomplish their goals primarily

---

*Sifre on Deuteronomy 6:6.
†R. Travers Herford, editor, *Ethics of the Fathers* (New York: Schocken Books, 1962) pages 150–51, chapter 6, Mishnah 2.

by lifting the individual out of the routine that controls and, too often, deadens daily life.

The central metaphor which shapes the pattern of Shabbat observance is that of creating a "messianic reality" for a day. In the course of that day, one enters into a preenactment of the world's final state of perfection. The core paradigm of Rosh Hashanah–Yom Kippur is that of being on trial for one's life. In the course of that trial one moves from life through death to renewed life.

Shabbat offers total release from work and daily routine; it brings the family together in relaxed intimacy and mutual support. Although the greatest event of redemption anticipated by Judaism—the universal messianic redemption—has not yet occurred, on Shabbat the future event is made manifest through imagination, liturgy, and ritual. For more than twenty-four hours community space is transformed into the messianic realm. The vivid glimpse of perfection combines with the delights and peace of the day to restore the soul. The Shabbat experience gives the strength to go on for another week . . . and another.

The dialectical interplays of ideal and reality that run through the Sabbath day are matched by the striking juxtapositions of death and life, of guilt and forgiveness, in the Rosh Hashanah–Yom Kippur period. Shaking people out of their routines, shattering the crusts of arrogance and complacency, these days of awe lead to fundamental self-renewal. Those who have encountered their own death have a different perspective on life's choices. Moved, the individual removes the detritus of evil deeds and guilt; afterward, a reborn person walks the Jewish way.

The first five holidays—Passover, Shavuot, Sukkot, Shabbat, and Days of Awe—present a stationary model of Judaism, coherent, revealed, structured. Equipped with these biblical paradigm holidays, the Jewish people set out on their journey through history.

THE HOLIDAYS ON THE WAY

Judaism is intrinsically open to history. It looks forward to a future event—the messianic redemption—that will dwarf the importance of the Exodus. By wagering its truth on the claim that the real world will be transformed, Judaism opens itself to further historical events that can challenge or confirm its message. And whenever an event has truly challenged or confirmed the covenantal way, that event has become another "orienting event" for Judaism. The orienting events have become the nuclei of new holidays.

History is full of the unexpected. Through changing societies, locations, circumstances, and through countless cultures, the people of

Israel wended their way. Wherever they stopped, they took root. In each host country, within each population, they participated, yet remained distinct—their eyes set upon the final goal. At times, Jewish life flourished; at others, it flickered close to extinction. Sometimes the people gloried in their role; sometimes they stumbled like an ignorant army on a darkling plain. There were times when the Jews turned chosenness into self-seeking complacency, and slept away a kingdom. There were times when the people were surprised and even unprepared for what happened to them. How does one deal with experiences that do not fit—nay, challenge—one's categories of meaning? The agony of working them through is part of the record of Jewish spiritual heroism. Each culture, each major crisis of victory or tragedy, of loyalty or betrayal, became part of a record that guided the next and future generations. Those hard-won understandings are codified in the later holidays that were added to the first five.

Around the fifth century B.C.E., as told in the Book of Esther, a decreed genocide of the Jews of the Persian empire was narrowly averted by the heroic actions of an unlikely pair—a queen hitherto known for her shyness and beauty (rather than for her initiative) and a hanger-on in the king's courtyard, a man of controversial reputation. The incident brought the Jews face-to-face with the absurdity and randomness that (contrary to the idealized moral universe of much of Jewish theology) determined life or death in the Persian empire. The highly integrated Jewish community suddenly was confronted with the vulnerability of Diaspora existence. The pattern of meaning that emerged was eventually spelled out in the holiday of Purim, a holiday that tickled the risibility of the masses who created it but baffled the scholars and theologians. In time, Purim was absorbed into the cycle of the year and proved to be a turning point in Jewish understanding of life in the Exile and of God's actions in history.

In the second century B.C.E., a civil war in the house of Israel almost tilted the balance of Jewish history into assimilation and disappearance. A great power intervened and ended up invading the sacred precincts of Israel. The Jewish revolt that followed barely triumphed—or, rather, partially triumphed—only long enough to save the religious way. The event was incorporated into the calendar as Hanukkah, the festival of lights. Hanukkah is actually a case study of three Jewish strategies in response to a dynamic external culture: separation, acculturation, and assimilation. Each of the groups that pursued these policies alone proved inadequate to take charge of Jewish destiny. The shifting alliances and interactive development among the three groups led to the defeat of the assimilators. The coalition that saved Judaism did not last long enough to forge the course of its future development. The victorious ruling group received relatively short shrift in later rabbinic Jewish sources. Yet, by saving Judaism, the Maccabees enabled the rabbinic tradition to emerge triumphant. The effect on world history was even greater, for Christianity also grew out of those groups saved by the Maccabean victory.

As the holiday cycle expanded, tragedies, in particular, proved to be central to the maturation of Judaism, beginning with the destruction of the First Holy Temple, the principal sanctuary of God, by a Babylonian army in 586 B.C.E. The surviving Jews had to face the question of whether the covenant was invalidated by this defeat of unparalleled proportions. They found consolation and a sense of Divine Presence in Babylonia by studying the Scriptures and the story of the Exodus. They intensified prayer. They expressed in words what heretofore had been manifest primarily in sacrifice. They learned to feel the presence of the Lord in subtler, more hidden forms. People placed greater stress on studying the Torah. Personal participation in religious activity was stepped up. After the destruction of the Second Temple in the first century C.E., these tendencies blossomed. After that catastrophe, following past models, the event and its lessons were incorporated into the calendar of holy days in the form of four permanent fast days. The chief fast day of the four was Tisha B'Av, the anniversary date of the great destructions.

Tisha B'Av taught Jews how to deal with tragedy and catastrophe, how to give way to sorrow while yet incorporating it into the round of holy days, thereby purging grief and emphasizing renewal. The four fast days served as spiritual buffers, absorbing repeated tragedy and diverting the shock waves of defeat so they would not crush the inner resources of the people. Strengthened by these days and by rabbinic theological interpretation, the surviving Jews did not yield to despair or to political *force majeure*. Rather, they grew more religiously faithful than before. They became more participatory and more able to discern God's presence in every aspect of life, including the divine sharing of the state of Exile.

Nor did the process of growth stop in the first century. The twentieth century is one of the great generations of revelation and transformation in Jewish history. Two historical events of extraordinary magnitude have occurred in this century: the Holocaust, which is as great a crisis for Judaism as was the destruction of the Temple, and the recreation of the State of Israel, which can only be compared to the Exodus.

It is easy to look back thousands of years, with reenactment and liturgical patterns of the Bible and Talmud in hand, and see the overarching vision of Judaism. It is more difficult in the midst of crisis and rebirth to predict what will emerge. Many faithful Jews have tried to go on without confronting these events. Some great spiritual leaders have opposed incorporating their observances out of fear that they will dominate the religion and distort its message. In particular, many have argued that by entering the Holocaust into the Jewish sacred calendar the Jewish people will fixate on death and thereby defeat the message of redemption.

Yet the events of Holocaust and Israel reborn are too massive and too challenging for us to go on as if nothing has happened. Jewish faith and loyalty are deep enough to cope with these events. "Leave it to the people, Israel—if they themselves are not prophets, then they are the children of prophets."* The people—without asking permission from theologians and halachists—already have begun to respond.

One guesses that the covenant and the Jewish people's role in it—as well as the understanding of holiness and secularity—will be renewed before all is done. The Jewish people will be preceded, in the next stage of their journey, by the cloud of smoke and pillar of fire that are the Holocaust and Israel. Therefore, though it may not complete the work, this generation is not exempt from taking up the task of interpreting their lessons for the covenantal way. This will inevitably lead to adding new holy days to the calendar.

One final feature of the Jewish holidays needs highlighting: These celebrations are oriented toward human needs. The operating assumptions of each special day incorporate a fundamental affirmation of the dignity of humans. Although flawed and fallible, every human being is nevertheless precious to God and central to the divine plan. In the words of Abraham Joshua Heschel: God is in search of man. Some religions seek to escape from our all-too-mortal daily round of life to the eternal presence of God. Judaism, conversely, seeks to draw the Divine into the world. In a thousand little details of the holidays, the presence of the Divine is made manifest.

The very human texture of Judaism is evident in the way holy days focus on family and the simple delights of shared pleasure. Coming back home to be together for special days; advance shopping and cooking with each person's favorite foods in mind; talking or singing together at the table—all contribute to the ambience of holy days. Festival meals are occasions for collective nostalgia, for exchanging family news and community doings, for catching up with one another, for welcoming guests. This is how Jews bring a perfect world closer.

Just as the holidays provide the community with spiritual suste-

*Babylonian Talmud, Tosefta Pesachim, chapter 4, Mishnah 11.

nance, so their dialectical nature expands the individual soul. The burden of redemption is so heavy that it threatens to undermine the ability to get through the demands of daily life; then comes the Shabbat as a corrective, a day of release and family time. The acceptance of gradualism and of everyday reality is so powerful in Jewish tradition that the culture could easily raise a conformist, materialistic, don't-rock-the-boat generation. The countervailing force is the Sabbath, with its foretaste of redemption. The Shabbat atmosphere creates a counter reality; it generates a human appetite for *paradise now* so the individual will not settle for less.

When complacency and self-congratulation threaten, the holiday cycle responds with the radical self-criticism and guilt of Yom Kippur. When depression looms, it is opposed with the balm of hope on Passover. The chastening experience of Rosh Hashanah, with its vision of cosmic Lord and universal judgment, corrects hubris and excessive self-sufficiency. The halacha punctures pompousness with the satire and playfulness of Purim. The ritual drunkenness of Purim challenges repression. Yet the tradition also prevents drunkards by inculcating moderation in drink in the kiddush and Havdalah of the Sabbath and festivals. Just when the individual is overwhelmed by the sense of being puny, a mere sport for great historical forces, the tradition tells the tale of Hanukkah, the triumph of few over many, the story of the handful of loyalists who defied a world empire and won. Yet, when unbridled messianism takes over, the cycle retorts with Tisha B'Av, the story of revolutionaries who overreached and brought catastrophe down on the nation. To those who would like to forget, it offers reenactment of the tragedy. To those who can never forget it offers the High Holy Days' forgiveness of sins and renewal of the past.

In short, the holy days nurture extraordinary dialectical capacities in the individual and the community. Trust in God, but help yourself; demand justice, but take it one step at a time; save the world, but start with your own family; bleed for humanity, but be sure to preserve your own group because "all of Israel are responsible one for the other."*

The vision of messianic perfection generated the need for a community that combined faith with action, hope with realism, universalism with particularism so that it could work persistently toward the final goal. No other people has faced so unrelenting a pattern of hostility and destruction while continuing to preach the ultimate triumph of life. Some argue that anti-Semitism and persecution have kept the Jews Jewish, but that claim grossly simplifies Jewish history. A people

---

*Babylonian Talmud, Shavuot 39A.

continuously defined by its enemies would end up internalizing the hatred and committing mass suicide. And no people could carry the burden of a mission to bring perfection without being eaten up by the strain and guilt of the task. Without the holidays, the Jews would never have lasted. "Were not your Torah my delight, I would have perished in my oppression" (Psalms 119:2).

Living the Jewish way means dreaming a dream of total perfection so vivid that you can almost touch it, while affirming and working with what *is* in order to make the dream come true. The life-style designed to teach the hope and pass it on—the specific acts and images needed to nurture the people who must live out this challenging way—is what this book on the Jewish holidays is all about.

CHAPTER TWO

Judaism as an Exodus Religion:
Passover

THE OVERWHELMING MAJORITY of earth's human beings have always lived in poverty and under oppression, their lives punctuated by sickness and suffering. Few escape damaging illness; even fewer dodge the ravages of old age (except by untimely death); and no one, to date, has avoided death. Most of the nameless and faceless billions know the world as indifferent or hostile. Statistically speaking, human life is of little value. The downtrodden and the poor accept their fate as destined; the powerful and the successful accept good fortune as their due. Power, rather than justice, seems always to rule.

Jewish religion affirms otherwise: Judaism insists that history and the social-economic-political reality in which people live will eventually be perfected; much of what passes for the norm of human existence is really a deviation from the ultimate reality.

How do we know this? From an actual event in history—the Exodus. Mark the paradox: The very idea that much of history—present reality itself—is a deviation from the ideal and that redemption will overcome this divergence comes from a historic experience. That experience was the liberation of the Hebrew slaves, the Exodus from Egypt.

Around the middle of the second millennium B.C.E., the central Israelite family/tribe went down from Canaan to Egypt to escape from famine. Although they were initially well received, the Hebrews later were reduced to slavery. Most of them sank into the apathy and exhaustion of servitude. Even a cruel decision by the Egyptians to destroy the people by killing all male infants stirred no action among the Israelites.

Then came a man named Moses, a Hebrew adopted and raised in the Egyptian court. He brought a message from the God of the Hebrew ancestors, calling the people to worship and to freedom. In a remarkable series of reversals, the Israelites were freed. When the Egyptians later pursued them, the Hebrews were miraculously saved and the Egyptian army destroyed.

On one level, this is a very specific incident in the particular history of a small Middle Eastern tribe. The entire event was so obscure at the time that no independent record of the liberation exists outside of the chronicle of this people. (It happens this people, brought into being by this particular event, went on to transform human consciousness. And its chronicle turned out to be the Bible, the single most influential book in human history.)

On another level, however, the entire experience is highly paradigmatic. Slavery is merely an exaggerated version of the reality endured by most human beings. Oppression and deprivation are not that dissimilar. The most devastating effect of slavery, ultimately, is that the slave internalizes the master's values and accepts the condition of slavery as his proper status. People who live in chronic conditions of poverty, hunger, and sickness tend to show similar patterns of acceptance and passivity. As with slaves, their deprivation derives from their political and economic status and then becomes moral and psychological reality. It is this reality that was overthrown in the Exodus.

The freeing of the slaves testified that *human beings are meant to be free*. History will not be finished until all are free. The Exodus shows that God is independent of human control. Once this is understood by tyrants and their victims then all human power is made relative. Freedom is the inexorable outcome, for only God's absolute power can be morally legitimate.

The Exodus further proves that *God is concerned*. God heard the cries of the Israelites, saw their suffering, and redeemed them. But the God of Israel who acted in the Exodus is the God of the whole world; God's love encompasses all of humankind. God's involvement with Israel is a concrete expression of God's universal mother love. In Jewish history, Exodus morality, from which Jewish ethics and Jewish rituals are derived, was made universal and applied to ever-widening circles of humankind. So the Messiah and the concept of a messianic realm are really implicit in the Exodus model itself. Messianic redemption is the Exodus writ large.

The initial impact of the redemption experience was to *set the Jewish people apart*. The Exodus is the beginning of Jewish existence as a holy (that is, unique) people. After the Exodus, Jewry remains anchored in history; the way of the world goes on with injustice, oppression, suffering. Therefore, there is enormous tension between the Exodus claim and the operational norms of every day. This puts faithful Jews at odds with the world, out of step with reality. It makes Jewish faith a testimony that Jews must give constantly until the rest of the world is persuaded. So the Jews are witnesses, outsiders and challengers, not infrequently the object of fear and anger. Jews and Judaism do compromise with the realities in an unredeemed world, but a special level of ethical behavior is demanded nevertheless—to meet the standards of Exodus.

A case in point: "Because you were outsiders in the land of Egypt" Jews were instructed to treat the widow, the orphan, the stranger, the landless—those who are vulnerable and marginal in every society—with compassion, generosity, and love. The land was distributed to all families. Debts were wiped out at the end of the sabbatical year so that no one need lose his land by foreclosure. If, nevertheless, the land had to be sold, then the family's relatives were commanded to redeem it. Finally, if all else failed, the land was restored to its original possessor in the jubilee year so there would be no permanent landless.

Yet, the redemption experience does not blot out reality. The Bible itself describes at some length how the liberated Jewish slaves carried the moral scars, the dependence, and the despair of slave status with them into freedom. In fact, Pharaoh remained in power and sought to undo the Exodus. This led to the final shattering of Pharaoh's power at the Red Sea. Still, the Bible tells that many other powers remained in the world to carry on policies similar to Pharaoh's—Amalek, Midian, Moab, the Emori, and so on.

No, the Exodus did not destroy evil in the world. What it did was set up an alternative conception of life. Were it not for the Exodus, humans would have reconciled themselves to the evils that exist in the world. The Exodus reestablishes the dream of perfection and thereby creates the tension that must exist until reality is redeemed. This orienting event has not yet been converted into a permanent reality, neither for Jews nor for the whole world, but it points the way to the end goal toward which all life and history must go. Thus, history counts, but it is not normative; it is something to be lived in, yet challenged and overcome.

The Exodus model implies that a partnership between God and humanity will carry out the transformation of the world. Despite the glorification of God and divine power in the biblical accounts, God is, from the beginning, dependent, as it were, on human testimony for awareness of the Divine Presence. The accessibility of God is subject to the behavior of the people of Israel. The Jewish covenant, the people's undertaking to live by the Exodus, points to a mutual dependency. Furthermore, inasmuch as the Exodus occurred in history, so will the messianic age also remain in history. This idea is in contrast to the development of Christian messianism. The early Christians experienced Jesus as the redeemer in their midst. Having experienced the Messiah's "actual presence," the Christians were tormented by the contradictions between his coming, which should have brought the Exodus for all, and the reality of a world that was still unredeemed. One way to resolve this conflict was by denying that the Messiah had come. But for some, the experience of his coming was too strong to deny. Another interpretation was then explored. Somehow the nature of messianic redemption had been misunderstood; the true messiah was not in the external *physical* world but in the internal *spiritual* world. Driven by the dissonance of the continued existence of a suffering world in which abuse of power remained unchecked, Christians ended up changing the very notion of messianism. They translated the concept of messianic redemption into a state of personal salvation, thus removing it from the realm of history. In coming up with this solution, they were acting on the Jewish Exodus model but resolving its tensions in a manner that eventually turned them away from Judaism.

The Jews who remained Jews, who remained faithful to the historical character of the Exodus, continued to insist that redemption could not be fully realized without social, political, and economic liberation as well as spiritual fulfillment.

Where does Israel get the strength—the chutzpah—to go on believing in redemption in a world that knows mass hunger and political exile and boat people? How can Jews testify to hope and human value when they have been continuously persecuted, hated, dispelled, destroyed? Out of the memories of the Exodus! "So that you remember the day you went out of Egypt all the days of your life" (Deuteronomy 16:3). The Jewish tradition takes this biblical ideal literally.

But the more people comprehend the Exodus lessons of human value and love, the greater their pain in experiencing the exploitation routinely encountered in the world. The enormity of human suffering, which continues to exist as if there had been no Exodus, challenges the belief that there *ever was* an Exodus. The world taunts the believer, suggesting that being bound by the Exodus ties one's hands. In a society that accounts personal power supreme, why limit one's gains for a will-o'-the-wisp dream? So the Exodus faith must be renewed continually if Jews are not to surrender its norms.

How can we create a continuing set of Exodus experiences powerful enough to offset the impact of present evil? The challenge is to make the Exodus experience vivid enough in an ongoing way to counter but not blot out the unredeemed experiences of life. The goal is not to flee from reality but to be motivated to perfect it. To cope with contradiction and not to yield easily, the memory must be a "real" experience, something felt in one's bones, tasted in one's mouth. This is why much of Jewish religion consists of reliving the Exodus. "Remember . . . all the days of your life," says the Torah. The Rabbis added that the Exodus should be recounted every night as well. It is as if the hope would crumble if it were not reaffirmed every few hours.

Ceremonial remembrances of the Exodus event are included in the Pentateuchal texts inside the *tefillin* (phylacteries) which are donned every weekday. The Exodus story, complete with the song of redemption at the Red Sea, is recited daily in prayers, shortly before the community gives the affirmation in the Sh'ma prayer that "the Lord our God is the One Lord." The essence of the Exodus event is retold and the blessing for redemption is uttered immediately before Jews rise for the silent central Jewish prayer (Shmoneh Esrei) to ask for their personal and communal needs. The tzitzit—a special fringed undergarment—is worn every day; it reminds of the Exodus. By following a spiritual regimen of choosing and restricting food, Jews remind themselves that God took them out of Egypt to be holy in order to witness to the world. Shabbat becomes *zecher l'yetziat mitzrayim;* Jews live this day in memory of the Exodus. Every week, on the seventh day, Jews assert their Exodus freedom by not working; their servants and even beasts of burden are released from labor on the Sabbath.

The "reliving" model shows the thin line between the sacred and the secular in Judaism. The celebration of Passover, the annual commemoration of Exodus, seems to be all ritual or "sacred" activity: prohibited foods (leavened bread), specially prepared and required foods (unleavened bread, bitter herbs), and holy time when work is prohibited and sacrifice and prayer are required. Yet reliving the Exodus directly translates into political behavior (overthrowing tyrants, freeing slaves), economic behavior (distributing land to all families), legal behavior (justice for strangers and orphans).

The psychological function of religious observance is to confirm and strengthen the conviction that the Exodus happened. But one would be guilty of trivializing to see the "reliving" model in purely psychological terms. Underlying Judaism's ritual system is a metaphysical statement about the nature of reality—specifically, of time. The Exodus teaches us that history is not an eternal recurrence—ever repeating but never progressing—but a time stream with direction. History is not a meaningless cycle but the path along which the Divine-human partnership is operating to perfect the world. Time is linear, not merely circular; all humans are walking toward the end time when the final peace and dignity for humankind will be accomplished.

Throughout the generations this view of history has been an enormous source of hope, galvanizing humans to major efforts to improve their conditions. Especially in modern times, this concept—in secularized forms—has powered liberalism with its promise of progress, and revolutionary radicalism with its expectations of breakthroughs and even of apocalypse. But in modern cultural understanding, time is perceived as only linear; once lived, it is gone. Hence there is a strong tendency to put aside the past as irrelevant. Indeed, many modern movements dismiss sacred time as pure projection, as an opiate of the masses. Yet Judaism insists that the past is available and still normative. Judaism celebrates it as a present channel of access to the Eternal and as a source of hope and renewal for the masses. Through the holiday cycle of the year and other rituals, the past can be summoned up to infuse the present with meaning. Passover, the Exodus, is not some antiquarian past experience: It is present reality. The taste of perfection in a Passover or a Shabbat creates dissatisfaction; that prevents the Jew from slipping into equilibrium with the current reality that he/she inhabits. Thus, in true Jewish dialectical fashion, time is both linear and cyclical. The implied claim of Passover is that in sacred time and ritual, believers can step outside the stream of secular, normal time and *relive the Exodus itself.*

THE REENACTMENT

Passover is the ultimate attempt to involve people in the experience of Exodus. On the yearly anniversary of its occurrence, the entire Exodus from slavery to freedom is recreated in song, story, food, and dress so that it is experienced as an actual happening. Although some models for reenactment are found in the Bible, it is left to every generation and every family to create the total experience. Everyday, homey aspects of life—food, table setting, cooking, dress, conversation, singing—are shaped and fused to create a transcendental reality. What could be frailer than flesh and blood and the gossamer thread of words? Yet together they establish a foundation so powerful that it can carry the weight of the centuries-old drive to perfect the world.

The goal is to go back thousands of years and to experience, first, the crushing bitterness and despair of slavery and, next, the wild, exhilarating release of freedom. The reenactment stretches for seven days, eight days for traditional Diaspora Jews. On the first nights at the festive meal or seder, through use of the haggadah, the family restages the night of the actual exit from Egypt.

Properly staged, the seder is the climax of liberation. On this night oblivion yields up its prey. Pharaoh's tyranny and genocide stalk the land again. But the Jewish people rise up and set out for the Promised Land—slave again, free again, born again.

Two major observances of the Passover holiday are still practiced by most Jews. One is the exclusion of chametz (leavened grain products) and the eating of the matzah (unleavened bread) and associated observances; the other is the retelling of the Exodus story in the haggadah at the seder and in the Torah reading in the synagogue.

In the biblical era there was a third major observance: bringing the Paschal sacrifice, the lamb. The entire family joined in one common sacrifice. The size of the lamb was chosen to suffice the family (or associated families and guests) at that meal. No one ate alone on this evening and nothing was to be left over from the sacrifice. If an individual had no family, he or she joined with friends or another family so there would be a group to share the lamb fully. One of the primary hallmarks of freedom is this capacity for solidarity. A slave thinks only of himself and the next meal. The reassertion of the family unit was the first signal that the Israelites were readying themselves for freedom.

Jewish tradition understood the sacrifice of the lamb to be the first step of liberation. Even when God is the deliverer, freedom cannot simply be bestowed. People must participate in their own emancipation. According to the biblical accounts, on the tenth of the month of Nissan, the Hebrew slaves acted for the first time on their own initiative (Moses' instructions rather than Pharaoh's) and sacrificed a lamb so they could sprinkle its blood on the doorpost and be spared the final plague. Because the lamb was worshiped in Egypt, sacrificing one to Israel's God constituted an act of self-assertion and repudiation of the master.

In biblical times, the Paschal sacrifice was so central that the word Pesach (Passover), simply used, could refer either to the sacrifice or to the holiday. Failure to join in the Passover sacrifice meal meant cutting oneself off from the Jewish people, denying the common destiny and experience of the folk. When the Temple was destroyed, ending all sacrifice, the central ritual act was ripped out of the Passover holiday, so rabbinic Jews expanded every other procedure to focus on communicating the lesson of liberation. What the sacramental Temple sacrifice could not fully accomplish, the participatory seder could.

Today, the Paschal lamb is remembered by the presence of the shank bone (Hebrew *zeroa*) on the seder plate. There is also a tradition not to eat dry roasted meat on the seder night. Since the Paschal lamb was roasted dry, the absence of such meat dramatizes the missing sacrifice. (The holiday Torah reading also incorporates an account of the sacrifice.)

PREPARING FOR FREEDOM

Freedom is not given in a day or reached overnight. The house of bondage is within you; it will accompany you unless you are psychologically ready to be free. It follows that people must prepare themselves, mentally and physically, before they can relive the liberation experience. In Jewish tradition, getting ready for the Exodus begins a month before the holiday itself. It is customary to start studying the laws and procedures of Passover thirty days before the holiday. The other anticipatory step is to begin collecting "money for wheat" (maos chitim), a fund for matzot, wine, and other food necessary for the poor to celebrate Passover properly. All Jewish holidays and celebrations are occasions to share with the needy.

Psychological preparation for emancipation focuses on rejection of *chametz* (bread and other leavened grain products). Bread is a leavened grain product that has undergone fermentation. Fermentation is achieved by adding liquid and/or yeast to dough, then baking, with sufficient time allowed for the fermenting process. The heat and chemical reaction drive air through the dough, causing it to rise. The Bible mentions that in the Exodus the Hebrews had to prepare food hastily, at the last moment. In ancient times the primary food was bread; the Israelites "baked the dough that they took out of Egypt in the form of matzot [that is, unleavened cakes]; it was not leavened because *they could not delay*" (Exodus 12:39). Jews now eat matzah to identify with that liberation. Turning one's back on all forms of leaven (chametz) became a central metaphor for escaping slavery.

Chametz is the Hebrew technical term for any one of five basic types of food grain (wheat, rye, spelt, barley, and oats) that is mixed with water and allowed to ferment. Fermentation generally takes eighteen minutes, assuming that the mixture is not worked or kneaded during this time. In preparation for Passover, traditional Jews totally eliminate chametz—not just bread but any and all forms of leaven—from the house and the diet. This is a symbolic statement of cutting off from the old slave existence and entering the new condition of living as a free person. The decisive break with previous diet is the outward expression of the internal break with slavery and dependence. For the modern celebrant, it is a critical step in the process of liberation that finally leads to freedom.

In an expansion of the metaphor, chametz became a symbol of what is allowed to stand around. Chametz signified staleness and deadening routine; getting rid of it became the symbol of freshness and life growth. Since Passover occurs in the spring, the total cleaning of the house to eliminate leaven was easily expanded to a comprehensive spring cleaning. Throwing out accumulated staleness and the dead hand of winter, cleaning the house and changing utensils became a psychological backdrop for reenacting emancipation. Thus, house-cleaning became part of a cosmic process.

Jewish law not only prohibited eating chametz but forbade its presence during Passover. It was not to be found in the house or even to be seen there at that time.

It may be that the total ban is meant to underscore the stark opposition between the realm where Exodus is the rule and the world according to the status quo. There will be time enough in the Shavuot covenant to temporize with human nature or on the Sukkot journey to compromise with entrenched evil. On this, the breakthrough holiday, the Torah wishes to draw a line in the sand. Choose the God of freedom or choose the Baal of oppression. If you choose the freedom of God, then not a trace of the past servitude is allowed in your life.

The chametz boycott went to great lengths. Not only were bread and cookies forbidden, but whiskey, beer and beverages derived from one of the five types of prohibited grain were also considered chametz. According to Orthodox practice, the shunning is extended to include any product in which chametz is merely an ingredient (ta'arovess chametz). When most other forbidden substances are accidentally mixed with a kosher product, the product may still be eaten if the nonkosher element is less than one part in sixty. But if a product is mixed with even the most minor traces of chametz (less than one part in a thousand!), it may not be used on Passover. Special supervision of manufacturing processes and rabbinical certification that no chametz ingredients have been used are sought for foods that year-round contain admixtures of chametz. In the United States, soda, dried fruits, ground pepper, vinegar, horseradish, and seltzer are among the likely candidates and need reliable supervision. (Since there are numerous complexities in these laws, it is wise to consult with a rabbi if any problem arises.)

Since the emotional dynamic in Passover's special dietary laws is an attempt to act out total avoidance of chametz, Jews of every generation sought additional ways to express the cutoff. In the medieval period, it was noted that grains other than the original five were being ground to obtain flour for food preparation. Although these grains do not undergo fermentation, a flour or breadlike substance could be made from them. Those products resembled chametz products. Thus, in Ashkenazic (north European) Jewish communities, products made from lima beans, kidney beans, peas, rice, corn, peanuts, buckwheat, and mustard were guilty by association and were added to the proscribed list. Because these foodstuffs were not really chametz, only the *eating* of these products was prohibited. Use of non-edible forms (such as cornstarch for pressing shirts) was not banned. Interestingly, Sephardic (Iberian and Mediterranean) Jewish communities never made this association (except for some Turkish communities that shun rice). This explains why devout, observant Sephardim freely eat products on Passover that equally devout Ashkenazic Jews prohibit.

A chametz-free total environment is the Passover goal, so any place where chametz was or might have been used during the year is thoroughly checked and cleaned lest any chametz has been left behind. In devout homes, this search is so detailed that it compares with the need to manufacture computer chips in totally dust-free environments to avoid flaws or failures in operation.

There is a story told about Rabbi Joshua of Kutno, a nineteenth-century east European rabbi considered an expert on the laws of chametz prohibition. His wife cleaned the kitchen surfaces and poured boiling water over them as per various kashering requirements. She took out every book in the library and opened it by the binding so the paper fanned out to release any crumbs of chametz that might possibly have fallen into the books while someone was eating and reading. Then, in an excess of zeal, she took the rabbi's favorite bench, scoured it, and poured boiling water over it. The poor rabbi sat down on a hot, wet bench, leaped up in consternation, and said to her, "Why did you do that? There is no halachic basis for such acts. Why, the Shulchan Aruch [the authoritative Code of Jewish Law] does not require you to ritually cleanse a reading bench!" To which his wife indignantly replied: "Hmph! If I was so lax as to operate by the rules of the Shulchan Aruch alone, this house would be *chametz-dig (chametz-y)!*" The rabbi had the legalities right, but the rebbitzen was expressing the psychology of centuries of Jews who "made" Passover.

In early times, chametz and its products were used up, thrown out, or given away before Passover. But as commercial (or at least large) quantities of chametz grew, forced disposal of them could cause heavy financial losses. A new procedure was developed to reduce the economic burden: A nominal amount of chametz was disposed of by burning, but valuable or irreplaceable chametz was locked out of sight and "sold" to a Gentile so that it was not owned by the Jew on Passover. In time it became convenient to arrange sale through an agent. Today, the process is usually done through the rabbi of the synagogue. The sale must be completed by the sixth hour on the day before Passover.

In *mechirat chametz* (chametz sale), a contract is drawn up stipulating all the possible types of chametz to be sold. The immediate location of the chametz is listed and is leased to the purchaser. In this way, the principle of not having chametz in one's own home is upheld. The seller authorizes the rabbi to act as his agent in selling the chametz on any terms. (The chametz is not being sold *to* the rabbi but *by* the rabbi.) The rabbi pools all the chametz of all the sellers into a master contract (somewhat like a mutual fund) and arranges to sell it to a non-Jew who understands the legal niceties of the contract.

Since the sum value of all the chametz may be quite large, the rabbi typically sells it in a contract that specifies a nominal down payment and a promissory note for the rest. Final and full payment is stipulated for the night following the eighth day of Passover. The rabbi is given a lien on the property. Failure to make the final full payment constitutes default by the buyer. Legal possession of the property is then reclaimed by the rabbi, who transfers it back to those who have appointed the rabbi their agent. Should the buyer decide to make the final payment and collect on the purchase, a problem would arise; mysteriously enough, no Gentile in history has ever made the final payment.

The rabbis were so anti-chametz that if a Jew kept possession of chametz on Pesach, they ruled that chametz should never be used nor should one derive any profit or pleasure from it. Traditional Jews buy new chametz products right after Pesach from a non-Jew or from a Jew who definitely sold his chametz before the holiday. In my childhood in Boro Park, most of the supermarkets were part of such Jewish-owned chains as Food Fair and Waldbaum's. In those days, they did business as usual on Passover. The A&P, then owned by Gentiles, was the great beneficiary of this rule because we bought our cereals there right after Passover. If in doubt about whether a Jewish supermarket's chametz stock was sold, traditional people wait to buy chametz until they can be reasonably certain that a new, post-Pesach delivery of chametz has been made.

In further preparation, refrigerators, sinks, and tables are cleaned thoroughly. Stoves and food preparation surfaces are cleaned and covered with foil or other materials. In Orthodox practice, special Passover pots, dishes, and silverware are used because the year-round utensils may have absorbed trace elements of chametz. Since this shift is not always possible or a family might not be able to afford the extra ware, a process of *kashering* (that is, making fit for kosher use) is used. The principle of kashering is that the process by which a substance is absorbed into a vessel is the same process by which it is removed. After thoroughly cleaning off all visible surface chametz, the chametz residue is removed by cleaning or heating equivalent to the maximum use that may have caused the chametz absorption. The oven, for example, is cleaned thoroughly with chemical cleaners and not used for twenty-four hours. Then it is heated to its maximum temperature, the fire kept burning for several hours or as long as its longest use.

Top burners of the stove are cleaned thoroughly and the flame turned on for at least one hour. (They turn red hot.) In an electric range, the filament is cleaned the same way. Since microwave ovens do not generate much heat during cooking, they are kashered by full cleaning, a twenty-four-hour wait, and then steaming with a pot of boiling water.

Following the same heat purification principle, sinks are kashered by pouring boiling water over all surfaces; racks are then placed on the bottom of the sink for the duration of the holiday period to prevent contact between Passover utensils and a surface that had been in use all year. Year-round utensils directly used on the fire without the intermediation of water (pans, broilers, barbecue spits) require heating to the point where they glow. Pots and flatware are totally immersed in boiling water. Earthenware and china cannot be kashered because they are considered too porous and absorbent for chametz removal. Glassware is kashered by soaking in cold water for seventy-two hours, changing the water every twenty-four hours (the water must overflow the vessel). Glassware with a small neck cannot be kashered, nor can Pyrex dishes that have been used directly on the fire. Beaters and cutters on motor-driven mixers and food processors are replaced; but first the motor housings are opened so that chametz can be brushed off the coils.

If all this sounds like overkill, understand that it was the outgrowth of a fierce desire to really begin a new life.

This whole process of chametz can be likened to preparation for an orbital mission: The goal is a successful liftoff into freedom. The final countdown begins on the day before Passover.

Twenty-four hours to Passover!

On the evening of 14 Nissan, after dark, preferably immediately after the stars come out, the house is given a final check. This is known as Bedikas Chametz, the chametz hunt. Bedikas Chametz is not just a ceremony. Every room in the house is searched thoroughly for chametz, usually by the light of a candle, although the use of a flashlight may be safer. Traditional kits include a candle, a feather to sweep up the chametz, and a bag to deposit it in. (Refer to a haggadah for the full text of the ceremony.) This is an excellent ceremony in which to involve children. One can offer prizes for MVC (Most Valuable Chametz-finder), for the kid-who-did-not-set-fire-to-the-bedspreads-this-year, or straight cash ("find chametz, get bread"). Customarily, some pieces of chametz are "hidden" in advance to ensure that the search will be successful and the blessing not said in vain. Following the search, people set aside any chametz to be eaten before end time, and they disown and renounce any other unsold chametz that may still be in the home. At this point, well-organized families have already put away their year-round utensils. Dishes, silver-ware, and utensils specially dedicated to Passover use are brought out.

Nine hours to go: By the fourth hour of daylight, all eating of cha-metz ceases. Nevertheless, one refrains from eating matzah, so that the first taste of matzah (freedom) at the seder will be fresh and excit-ing. All unsold chametz remaining in the house is disposed of by burning, preferably, or by any other means of annihilation. Following the burning, Kol Chamira—the formula of renunciation—is recited again.

Seven hours to go: Authorization for the rabbi to sell chametz to a Gentile must be given by the sixth hour of daylight because it takes time to consummate the sale. (Similarly, some time is allowed after the holiday for the rabbi to reclaim ownership of the chametz.) In the last hours, it is customary to prepare the seder table and the Passover foods, to shower and change into holiday clothing, and to get into the spirit of Passover. Households are often quite chaotic at this juncture, with all the pressures of a last-minute countdown.

Another custom of emancipation also developed for the day before Passover. Firstborn sons fast until nightfall; a parent can fast on behalf of the firstborn if he is still a child. This act signals gratitude that Jew-ish children were spared when the firstborn of Egypt were decimated in the tenth plague. In lieu of fasting, a tradition has grown for the firstborn to attend a special occasion called a *siyum* (completion). An individual or group completes study of a tractate of the Talmud in public and then invites everyone to participate in a *seudat mitzvah*—the celebration meal that follows. Those who take part are permitted to eat for the rest of the day as well.

THE BREAD OF FREEDOM

Just as shunning chametz is the symbolic statement of leaving slavery behind, so is eating matzah the classic expression of entering freedom.

Matzah was the food the Israelites took with them on the Exodus. "They baked the dough which they took out of Egypt into unleavened cakes [matzot], for it was not leavened, since they were driven out of Egypt and could not delay; nor had they prepared provisions for themselves" (Exodus 12:39). According to this passage, matzah is the hard bread that Jews initially ate in the desert because they plunged into liberty without delaying. However, matzah carries a more com-plex message than "Freedom now!" Made only of flour and water, with no shortening, yeast, or enriching ingredients, matzah recreates the hard "bread of affliction" (Deuteronomy 16:3) and meager food given to the Hebrews in Egypt by their exploitative masters. Like the bitter herbs eaten at the seder, it represents the degradation and suffering of the Israelites.

Matzah is, therefore, both the bread of freedom and the erstwhile bread of slavery. It is not unusual for ex-slaves to invert the very symbols of slavery to express their rejection of the masters' values. But there is a deeper meaning in the double-edged symbolism of matzah. It would have been easy to set up a stark dichotomy: Matzah is the bread of the Exodus way, the bread of freedom; chametz is the bread eaten in the house of bondage, in Egypt. Or vice versa: Matzah is the hard ration, slave food; chametz is the rich, soft food to which free people treat themselves. That either/or would be too simplistic. Freedom is in the psyche, not in the bread.

The halacha underscores the identity of chametz and matzah with the legal requirement that matzah can be made only out of grains that can become chametz—that is, those grains that ferment if mixed with water and allowed to stand. How the human prepares the dough is what decides whether it becomes chametz or matzah. How you view the matzah is what decides whether it is the bread of liberty or of servitude.

The point is subtle but essential. To be fully realized, an Exodus must include an inner voyage, not just a march on the road out of Egypt. The difference between slavery and freedom is not that slaves endure hard conditions while free people enjoy ease. The bread remained equally hard in both states, but the psychology of the Israelites shifted totally. When the hard crust was given to them by tyrannical masters, the matzah they ate in passivity was the bread of slavery. But when the Jews willingly went from green fertile deltas into the desert because they were determined to be free, when they refused to delay freedom and opted to eat unleavened bread rather than wait for it to rise, the hard crust became the bread of freedom. Out of fear and lack of responsibility, the slave accommodates to ill treatment. Out of dignity and determination to live free, the individual will shoulder any burden.

The great Levi Yitzchak of Berditchev, whose analyses always portrayed the people of Israel in a favorable light, insisted that the willingness of the Israelites to enter the desert with hard bread continues to evoke God's love. Levi Yitzchak asked: Why does the Torah continually call Passover *chag hamatzot*—the feast of unleavened bread—while the Jews call it *chag haPesach*—the feast of Passover? Because as lovers they stress each other's goodness. Israel praises God who *passed over* the homes of the Jews when destroying Egypt. God praises the Jews who went so trustingly out of the fertile plain of Egypt into a barren desert with meager food.

Tradition specifically requires eating unleavened bread on the first two nights of Passover. (Dieters will be happy to learn that during the rest of the holiday the only requirement is *not* to eat chametz.) Eating hard bread during the holiday of liberation stimulates appreciation for the flavor of freedom and summons up empathy for those still in need. At the seder, the Exodus retelling opens with the phrase, "This is the bread of affliction which our fathers ate in Egypt." The moral consequence follows immediately: "Let all who are hungry enter and eat; let all who are in need come and join in the Passover with us. This year [we are] slaves. Next year [may the slaves be] free." The hard crust commands us to help the poor, the stranger, the outsider.

The Torah states: "You shall watch over the matzot" (Exodus 12:17). This verse was interpreted as instruction to guard against fermentation during the preparation and matzah-baking process. Since fermentation takes eighteen minutes, properly supervised matzot will be baked within that time frame. All pieces of dough not baked are removed before the next batch is inserted. Only in the past century did machine-made matzot for the most part replace hand-prepared or baked matzot of old—and not without significant resistance.

Among traditional Jews the concept of watching over the matzot was expanded to mean supervising the preparation so that all ingredients are set aside from the very beginning for the express purpose of fulfilling the mitzvah of eating matzah. Some Jews try to obtain—at least for the first two nights of Passover—matzot that have been under continual supervision from the time of cutting the grain until baking. This is known as *matzah shmurah* (that is, specially watched matzah). Since the market is limited, preparation of matzah shmurah is generally in the hands of noncommercial bakers. Like vintage wine, it costs more and has to be specially ordered.

If this tradition discourages you, keep in mind that we are just getting down to fine points and that, as in all things, one can be a "connoisseur" of halacha. (There are two levels of matzah shmurah, for example: machine-made and handmade.) Aficionados insist that different Chasidic groups make matzot of subtly different taste.

Eating shmurah does require intestinal fortitude. Still, if you like to live dangerously, you should arrange to purchase hand-baked matzah shmurah made by various Yeshivot and Chasidic groups. The regular machine-made matzah often seems too pleasant to be truly the bread of affliction, whereas this handmade matzah will give you that old-time flavor of slavery.

RELIVING THE EXODUS:
THE SEDER AS THE EXODUS MEAL

As twilight turns toward night, candles are lit to usher in the holy time of liberation. The two blessings, "to light the holiday candle" and *She-*

hecheyanu ("who has kept us alive . . . until this time"), deepen the sense that redemption is in the air. Then services in the synagogue intensify the mood; in the central Amidah prayer, Passover is described as "the time of our freedom."

But the seder meal is the most powerful vehicle for recreating the Exodus. The seder meal takes place on the first night of Passover (on the first two nights, in traditional communities outside of Israel). The seder is a family meal. This accounts for its great popularity. Over ninety percent of American Jews report attending one annually. But behind a facade of eating and pleasant socializing, a stunning pedagogical drama unfolds. The seder script lays out the actions by which the participants mime the liberation process. In its details and, more important, in its very structure, the seder induces the experience of going from slavery to liberty, and it offers a definition of the nature of freedom.

The family character of the meal is not adventitious; it is a central part of the message. What happens in the seder? In the first phase one reenters the world of slavery through food experiences and story. Then comes a transition-to-freedom phase as the meal gradually turns into the sumptuous feast of the free. Reaching freedom, one has a powerful sense of appreciation and gratitude. The seder, then, teaches that freedom involves making a livelihood and taking care of others, especially one's family. Often such responsibilities create daily frustrations. But compared to slavery . . .

It is the mark of freedom that one can have a family, enjoy a meal with its members, look out for it, and protect it. A slave is unable to maintain a family. The slave woman is available to the master; children's paternity is doubtful. A slave cannot protect the children from being sold, or worse. The ability to sit together as a family at the seder and sing a song of liberation is in itself the most powerful statement of being free.

In the initial phase, the slave often longs to go back to slavery. The taste of freedom is designed to communicate the permanence of freedom. In transition, particularly, the slave often thinks of freedom as the right to be carefree or to abuse others and to lord it over them, as was done to him or her. But true freedom means accepting the ethics of responsibility. Family is a great symbol of that commitment. Freedom does not mean avoiding involvement or being free of cares. Freedom means freely choosing commitment and obligations that bring out the individual's humanity; servitude means carrying out orders dictated by others.

The word *seder* means order, a ritualized progression. It is like a dramatic pageant in which symbolic and ritual acts create a reality to move the actors and the audience through a reappropriation of the Exodus. This is in contrast to most of life's other dramas in which individuals typically are passive consumers. The seder challenges each family to narrate its own version of the Greatest Story Ever Told with each member actively involved. Over the years a script has evolved called the Haggadah, the book of retelling.

No two family seders are alike. Each seder leader is a director who is challenged to fascinate the audience. Over the years I have observed every kind of seder director, from very traditional to very creative. Most lead a standard seder, but some have attained the level of *auteur*. Some can be compared to Alfred Hitchcock striving for mystery, surprises, concrete details that arrest the mind. Some are like Cecil B. De Mille—popular, full of sweep and schmaltz and grandiosity. I have even heard of Woody Allen-type seders—full of self-mocking humor and understatement. (Let's face it. The Exodus wasn't that successful. Look at how many people got their feet wet in the Red Sea, caught cold, and sneezed their way through the Ten Commandments, missing half the lines. "Thou shalt [sneeze!] commit adultery.")

Every detail of the seder is designed to deepen the feeling of well-being and freedom. Traditional Jews recline when eating, recalling an old Persian tradition that masters (free people) reclined on divans while servants waited on them. Many families follow the custom of providing pillows or chair cushions to give participants a sense of being treated like royalty. In some medieval Sephardic communities people enhanced their reenactment by dressing for a journey—with girded loins, sandals on feet, a staff at hand, and packs on their backs.

The centerpiece of the seder is the plate on which traditional symbols of Passover are arranged. The plate includes three matzot used at different times during the meal. In a popular interpretation, they symbolize the three kinds of Jews: Kohanim (priests), Levites and Israelites. One of the tasks of a people seeking independence is to establish its unity of vision and purpose as well as its unity in struggle. Slaves are set one against another. Some are totally subservient to the masters; some try only to save themselves; some try to break out. Jewish unity is as indispensable to survival now as it was then. The three types together symbolize the unity of fate of the Jewish people.

Among the other seder symbols is a remembrance of the Paschal sacrifice, the zeroa. This Hebrew word also recalls the *zeroa netooyah* [outstretched hand] with which the Lord redeemed Israel. The plate also contains an egg, boiled and then roasted, in remembrance of the *chagiga*, the regular holiday sacrifice in the Temple; *maror*—bitter herb (romaine lettuce or horseradish root) to summon up the bitterness of servitude; and *charoset*—a melange of chopped nuts, apples, wine, and cinnamon. In folk imagination, charoset resembles the mortar used by the Israelite slaves building for the Egyptians. At the meal, the maror is dipped in charoset to temper the bitterness of the taste. In addition, there is salt water for dipping and a special cup set aside as the cup of Elijah (reserved for Elijah the Prophet, the bearer of tidings of the coming of the Messiah, that is, of the final redemption).

The preparation of the seder is part of the anticipation and "tuning in" process. All members of the family are encouraged to help prepare (make charoset, set the table, practice reading parts of the haggadah narration, research the history or geography of the Exodus, and so forth). It is traditional to invite others—the poor, the extended family, friends. Sharing or reaching beyond the self is a fundamental mark of free people.

The seder uses games, songs, and special actions to involve everyone. Dialogue, question-and-answer, and text-and-elaboration formats also serve to keep participation high. Parents initiate the story, but children's questions, songs, riddles, and arguments all underscore their key role in fulfilling the biblical instruction to "tell the saga in the hearing of your children and grandchildren . . . and you will know that I am the Lord" (Exodus 10:3).

The unfolding of the story follows a traditional arrangement, immortalized under the following rubrics:

Kadesh (sanctify): Kiddush (the sanctification blessings) is recited after nightfall. This consecrates the holiday. Jewish celebrations and holy days are usually marked by reciting a blessing and drinking a cup of wine. The human being is a union of body and soul. A drop of alcohol as well as good food are part of the celebration for the well-being of the body creates the context for uplift of the soul.

The opening kiddush is the first of four cups of wine drunk on this night to exult in the four types of redemption with which God blessed Israel: God took them out of their burdens and suffering, saved them from hard labor, liberated them with mighty acts, and dedicated them as a holy people. Each of these steps is a different experience; after all, the process of liberation takes struggle and new self-insights. The first stage during the Exodus involved the removal of hard labor, but overthrow of oppression may leave a people empty of meaning. The final stage is the dedication of Israel to a new calling—becoming God's witnesses.

Each cup should have a different effect. (The larger the cup you drink from, the more likely each will have an additional impact.) Tradition suggests that the cup should contain at least three and a half ounces of wine. If you cannot drink wine, dilute it with or even substitute grape juice; in a pinch, you can even dilute grape juice with water.

Although women are generally not obligated to fulfill positive time-bound commandments in the Orthodox tradition, on this occasion women are required to drink four cups as well because "for the sake of righteous women, we are delivered from Egypt." In the egalitarian traditions, women should certainly share this observance.

U'rechatz: Hands are ritually washed; a cup of water is poured over each hand three times. This symbolizes the removal of impurity, the routine of previous activity. For this first washing on the night of Passover, no blessing is recited. Some explain that this extra washing is designed to elicit children's questions. In other words, some behavior on this night should be offbeat, to arouse awareness that something unusual is happening.

Karpas: A vegetable is dipped in salt water. The blessing recited before it is eaten, *"borei pri ha'adamah"* (who creates the fruit of the earth), applies to the maror (bitter herb) eaten later as well. Some say the salt dip is a symbol of the tears of the Jews in Egypt. Others explain that dipping is merely another way to pique the children's interest.

Yachatz: The three matzot are now uncovered, and the middle matzah is split. Poor people who cannot afford whole loaves often eat broken loaves, so the breaking of the matzah expresses the concept of matzah as the bread of affliction. (The whole matzah that is used to make the blessing over the matzah, then, is the symbol of the bread of freedom.) In the early part of the seder, participants relive slavery. The saltwater dip and the broken matzah communicate the tears and deprivation.

The larger part of the broken matzah is hidden to be used as *afikoman*—another routine designed to involve children—while the smaller half is used for the matzah-eating ceremony later in the seder. Traditionally, the children seek out the hidden matzah half, "steal" it, and hold it for ransom at the end of the meal.

Maggid (Telling): The formal narrative of the redemption of Israel from Egypt now begins. The story is embellished, using the imagination and the learning of those present; the significance of the event then and now is dramatized. The commandment to tell of the Exodus is considered to be truly fulfilled only when the story is passed from parent to child in a meaningful manner so that it comes alive for both.

Since the involvement of the child is crucial to learning, the storytelling begins with four questions, traditionally asked by the youngest one present. The child's curiosity has been aroused. In effect, the question is: Why are you acting so strangely tonight? Why *do* Jews act differently? The answer that unfolds is: Something extraordinary has happened. The lives of the Jewish people and of all the people in the world will never be the same. Exodus is the sounding of hope for eternity.

As the story unfolds, the past becomes present, so that old and young relive it together and are united in the experience. Jewish religion grows out of a shared memory; if grandparents or other older persons are at the seder, they tell of their past, the suffering they have experienced, the redemption they have lived through.

The Mishnah, the first stratum of Talmudic material,* states that the central seder experience intended by the rabbis who composed this liturgy was to recapitulate the contrast of earlier Israelite degradation and later dignity. Thus, the narrative initially quotes and elaborates on the biblical account of Israelites' sufferings. The heartbreaking stories of slavery and the drowning of Jewish infants are told. In time, the story shifts to the ten plagues and the breaking of Egyptian power.

In the Talmud there is a debate between two colleagues, Rav and Samuel. What is the essential transformation one should undergo through the seder experience? Samuel teaches that its essence is political—participants should experience the move from slavery to freedom. Rav argues that the key experience is a spiritual transformation—to live through the contrast of the idolatry of our ancestors and the religious liberation of Exodus-Sinai that Jews celebrate. These two interpretations are, in fact, complementary. In Judaism's view, slavery draws legitimacy from idolatry; democracy is ultimately grounded in the God-given dignity of every human being. The God who created and loves us gives us freedom as our right and denies absolute authority to all human governments and systems. Totalitarianism or total worship of any human system is the idolatry of our time. Typically, such absolutism—be it Communism or Fascism or even super patriotism—focuses against the Jews, for it senses that Jewish testimony contradicts these absolute claims. Thus, idolatry and totalitarian enslavement are alike—they deem absolute that which is relative. The Exodus challenges both.

The contemporary contrast of the slavery and genocide of the Holocaust and the redemption of Israel reborn should also be included in the tale. The Exodus is a past and future event. In this generation it has literally occurred again. It is no accident that the most famous ship to bring Jewish survivors of the concentration camps to Israel was called *Exodus '47*.

In consonance with the dynamic character of Jewish tradition, prayers for the martyrs of European Jewry and for Israel have been inserted here in the haggadah by some, and in the later part by others (see Appendix B). The goal of the narrative is to reach the level of involvement at which each person must feel that he/she personally had gone out of Egypt. You will note some of the playful and ingenious ways the Rabbis elaborate: Drops of wine are spilled at the mention of each plague, to express the idea that our joy is diminished by

---

*Babylonian Talmud, Pesachim, chapter 10, Mishnayot 4–10 and following.

the suffering of the erstwhile masters. To dramatize the event by hyperbole, the Rabbis multipled the number of plagues. They also introduced songs of praise such as "Dayenu" to engage all those around the table. The elaboration is long enough to be vivid but not too long because people are hungry. During this section the second cup of wine is drunk.

Rachtzah: The hands are ritually washed again. This time a blessing is recited because the meal is about to begin. In the psychic movement from storytelling to eating, the hands are washed to break the routine of the story and to awaken consciousness of the festive meal. This is also the transition from the dry crust of slavery to the rich, varied feast of free men and women. Thus, feasting and biological pleasure confirm the psychological liberation experience.

Motzi matzah: The two whole matzot and the remaining part of the middle one are lifted and the blessing, *"ha-motzi lechem min haaretz"* (Who brings forth bread from the earth), is recited. The bottom matzah is set down and the blessing, *al acheelat Matzah* (on eating matzah), is recited. Traditionally, each participant eats a minimum of about one-half of a regular matzah during the seder to get a real taste of the bread of affliction.

In many Jewish households a new custom has been established: setting aside an additional matzah as a symbol of the bread of slavery for Jews, wherever they are oppressed, such as in Soviet Russia, Syria, and Ethiopia. A prayer for their deliverance is said at this time. The message is clear: Liberty is indivisible. As long as others remain oppressed, my freedom is diminished. Appropriate readings of letters or statements from Soviet or Ethiopian Jews may be read.

Maror: The bitter herb is dipped into charoset and eaten, reclining. About an ounce of horseradish root (good luck!) or a large leaf of romaine lettuce is eaten after the blessing, *"al acheelat maror,"* is recited.

The maror serves as a reprise of the earlier enslavement theme. The tradition wants to summon up—once more, in a state of freedom—the bitter, wrenching taste of slavery, for there is always a real danger that those who have gone forth into freedom will turn their backs on those still in slavery. The maror and matzah remind participants that though this family may be at ease, it dare not forget that many others —Jews and non-Jews alike—still live in need.

Korech: From portions of the bottom matzah, a sandwich of matzah with maror and charoset is made and eaten while reclining. This is a reenactment of the way Hillel, a leading first-century rabbi, ate the Paschal sacrifice. Our hero Hillel made a sandwich with matzah and maror—the original hero sandwich—to fulfill the biblical instruction that the Paschal lamb be eaten on matzot and with bitter herbs (Exodus 12:8).

Shulchan Orech: The festive meal is eaten. A wide range of seder specialties have been developed in various Jewish communities over the centuries. What is important to remember is that in freedom people can *choose* what to eat. As a result, the seder meal menu varies all over the world and is a culinary guide to Jewish history.

Tzafun: Tzafun means hidden; the reader will recall that one-half of the middle matzah was hidden at the beginning of the seder and "stolen" by the children. Now is the time to ransom the afikoman because the seder cannot proceed without this matzah. This is the moment the young ones have been waiting for. The afikoman is their bargaining chip to obtain their heart's desire. The afikoman game serves to sustain the children's interest since they look forward to "selling" the afikoman.

Many commentators believe that the afikoman is reserved for the end of the meal so that matzah would be the last taste of the celebration. A striking commentary by Rabbi Harold Schulweis suggests that the afikoman is the matzah of the future (messianic) redemption. The matzah is broken because the world is still unredeemed; the matzah is eaten at the end because our hope is still unbroken.

Barech: The grace after meals is recited, followed by drinking the third cup of wine. The fourth cup is now filled, though it is not to be drunk yet; the "cup of Elijah" is also filled.

During the Middle Ages, in an outpouring of anguish and frustration, Jewish tradition inserted here a malediction on those who destroy the Jewish people. It is characteristic of the dialectical nature of Judaism that keening over oppression is linked with the cup of final redemption. Stark reality is faced down with the fullest intensity of yearning for a world free of all torment. In recent times, CLAL, the National Jewish Center for Learning and Leadership, has developed a ritual of remembrance for the Holocaust to be inserted into the haggadah at this point. On this very day, the Nazis began their final liquidation of the Warsaw ghetto; on this very night, those Jews began their incredible revolt.

The message of redemption cannot be reenacted today as if there had never been a Holocaust. Speaking of the Holocaust at the seder does jar the mood of joy, but at the same time, the contrast gives tremendous additional depth to the proclamation of the once and future Exodus. In our generation, the witness to redemption and human dignity is not casual, nor is it based on any illusions about the dangers of such testimony or on any underestimation of the power of evil. This makes the witness all the more heroic and valued.

The ritual of remembrance (see Appendix B) seeks to capture these themes. Beyond the four sons whose varying commitments to Judaism are of such great concern in the haggadah—because the future depends on the new generation's taking up the call—the ritual called "The Fifth Child" summons up the memory of the more than a million children who did not survive to ask any questions. The ritual affirms that silence is the only answer to the question: Why? But the unextinguished hope in the ghettoes and camps expressed in such songs as "Ani Maamin" ("I believe in the coming of the Messiah, even though Messiah tarries") and the "Partisans' Song" ("Never say you go on the final road") is also affirmed. In a concluding ritual act, each seder participant pours some wine into Elijah's cup to express personal determination to bring the Messiah and to work for a final triumph of life.

Hallel: The songs and prayers of praise are completed. This constitutes the outpouring of gratitude as Jews savor the stage of freedom. Following the Hallel, the fourth cup of wine is drunk.

The Fifth Cup: In the Talmud (Pesachim 118) we are told that Rabbi Tarfon used to drink a fifth cup of wine on Passover night. The first four cups stand for four of the five stages of redemption promised in Exodus 6:6–7. Rabbi Tarfon drank a fifth cup to commemorate the fifth stage of redemption: "And I shall bring you into the land which I raised my hand and swore to give to Abraham, Isaac, and Jacob, and I give it to you as an inheritance, I am the Lord" (Exodus 6:8).

Rabbi Menachem M. Kasher, in his *Israel Passover Haggadah*, proposes the adoption of the fifth cup by all Jews: "And now in our own time, when we have been privileged to behold the mercies of the Holy Name, blessed be He, and His salvation over us, in the establishment of the State of Israel which is the beginning of redemption . . . as it is written: And I shall bring you into the land. . . . It is fitting and proper that we observe this pious act, the drinking of the fifth cup, as a form of thanksgiving."*

Jewish tradition is not static. Adding this fifth cup is our testimony that Israel's rebirth is revelation and redemption in our own time. The fifth cup is also a statement of hope and trust that this is a lasting redemption that will not be destroyed again. Our joy and our faith in Exodus is increased because it happened again in this generation.

Of course, drinking all this wine can in itself be a bit much. But the joy is appropriate, and those who can handle it should drink to it.

Nirtzah: The haggadah is now completed. The family expresses its prayer that this service is acceptable and that Zion will be fully established soon. The recitation of the Exodus story is now elaborated and connected to other saving events. Rabbis of old would stay up all night to tell the story. Passover songs such as "Chad Gadya" are sung.

The entire seder is an experience in which normal social and struc-

---

*Menachem M. Kasher, *Israel Passover Haggadah* (New York: Torah Shelaymah Institute, 1957), p. 335.

tural patterns are suspended or transcended. Generation gaps are overcome as the contemporary people of Israel go into freedom alongside those led by Moses, Aaron, and Miriam. The Jewish people are reshaped into a *communitas*, an undifferentiated communion in which neither status nor power rules. All are united in common liberation.

Miraculously, all this is done in the context of family, with eating, talking, and singing, the most natural of human activities. Jewish faith uniquely combines the affirmation that nothing less than fundamental and revolutionary change must take place in history with the assertion that the transformation will be accomplished by human action on a human scale. Not by overriding the normal feelings of family, not by building some Pharaonic—or Stalinist—megaliths and offering up hecatombs of human sacrifices, but by creating community and extending it outward, by recalling the family's liberation and sharing it with all humans will the final triumph of humanity be achieved. On Passover night Jews experience that triumph—not as hope but as event.

FREEDOM'S ROAD

The Season of Freedom: While the liturgical peak of Passover is reached on the night of the Exodus, the rest of the holiday sustains the imagery of the march to freedom. In the prayer liturgy that developed in post-biblical times, the festival is called *zman chayrutaynu* (the season of our freedom). No work is done on the first and last days (first two and last two in Diaspora). In earlier times no secular work was done on the intermediate days, but economic realities of our times have tended to turn these middle days into working days, albeit semi-holidays.

Hallel: Psalms 113–18, songs of praise for the redemption, are chanted every day. Psalm 114 best captures the Exodus exultation:

When Israel went out of Egypt,
The House of Jacob out of a people of foreign speech,
Judah became God's holy one
Israel, God's dominion.

The sea saw—and fled,
Jordan turned and ran backward,
Mountains skipped like rams,
hills like lambs.

What is happening to you, O sea, that you flee?
O Jordan, that you turn and run backward?
Mountains, that you skip like rams,
hills like lambs?

O earth, shiver and shake
Before the Lord, before the God of Israel,
Who turned the rock into a pool of water,
the flinty stone into a water fountain.

On the first two days, the complete Hallel (consisting of six Psalms) is fully recited. Thereafter, parts are omitted—as a mark of mourning for the Egyptians who drowned in the Red Sea. The Egyptians were vicious taskmasters, yet their pursuing army consisted of sons of Egyptian mothers and fathers. Later generations of Jews felt empathy with the pain of their parental loss. The death of any human being is a sorrow.

A special prayer known as the Yaaleh V'yavo, after its opening Hebrew words, is inserted into the Shacharit, Minchah, and Maariv (morning, afternoon, and evening) Amidah prayers as well as in the grace after meals recited throughout the holiday. This same prayer, appropriately adapted to each holiday, is added as well to the Shavuot, Sukkot, Rosh Hashanah, and Yom Kippur liturgies. This prayer adds a flavor of the festival to life several times a day. In the Yaale, petitioners request that God especially remember all Israel and take this occasion to bless and redeem the people.

Crossing the Red Sea: The Bible tells us that Pharaoh regretted letting the Jews go free and set out with an army to recapture his slaves. Pinned down at the Sea of Reeds, the Israelites panicked; but then, under Moses' leadership, they crossed the sea. The Egyptian army, crossing the sea behind them in hot pursuit, drowned. (The Reed Sea location is commonly identified as the Red Sea of today, but the identification is not certain.)

According to tradition, the miraculous rescue at the Reed Sea occurred on the seventh day out of Egypt. Therefore, on the seventh day of Passover, the story of the crossing is recounted in the synagogue in the Torah reading. The song of the Red Sea deliverance is triumphantly chanted before a standing congregation that relives the event.

In furtherance of the reenactment model, Chasidic tradition in the nineteenth century created a ceremony of "crossing the sea." Water is poured on the floor, and the family or group dances across, singing songs of deliverance and joy. (Wall-to-wall carpet fanciers may prefer to put the water in a bucket and then jump over it.) In some Chasidic groups, the men dance, and as they pass by, water is sprinkled on their shoes to represent the lapping of the waves and the wet sea floor as the Israelites marched across to safety.

Marching Toward Sinai, Counting the Omer: The spring harvest begins at Passover time. In biblical times, sheaves of the new crop were brought to Jerusalem and prepared and eaten there in thanksgiving for God's bounty. The Omer (a measure of grain) was brought daily and counted for forty-nine days until the onset of Shavuot. This ceremony is still commemorated in the counting of the Omer (Sefirat HaOmer), a nightly blessing and count for seven full weeks starting from the second night of Passover.

Rabbinic tradition (collectively called *Torah Sheh–B'Al Peh*, the Oral Torah or Law) identified Shavuot as the holiday of Revelation, the anniversary of the giving of the Torah at Sinai. Therefore, each passing day, from the night of Exodus on, is experienced as a day's journey toward Sinai. Sinai was the goal and object of the Exodus. Counting the days becomes the bridge from the social liberation that occurred on Passover to the constitution of freedom accepted and ratified at Sinai. Through the act of counting the Omer, traditional Jews affirm that the purpose of freedom (Passover) is to live the holy life and ethical regimen of the Torah.

THE EXODUS PARADIGM

The Torah places great stress on the fact that Passover occurs in the spring. In biblical times the month in which the holiday fell was called Aviv (spring). During the first exile in Babylon, the months were given Babylonian names. Passover's month was renamed Nissan. Although the name shifted, the Hebrews upheld the Torah's insistence on the link of spring and Passover. Critical scholars believe that the date connects spring festivals (the Feast of Unleavened Bread from pastoral roots and the Paschal lamb from shepherd traditions) that were absorbed into the Passover holiday. In this view, the earlier ritual elements were incorporated and reinterpreted as historical reminders of redemption. Many traditional scholars have objected to any attempt to place the Torah in a cultural context. Some, such as Maimonides, have seen no religious objection to having the Sinaitic revelation transform earlier elements into the Torah's theological/historical pattern, as long as its divinity is upheld.

The Torah stresses both the agricultural and the historical aspects of Passover. There is a strong but subtle relationship of nature and history in the Bible's teachings. The human being is a body/soul fusion. Somatic states affect the mind just as strong emotions—jealousy, anger, lust—rack the body. Because the spiritual and the biological are intertwined, shifts in one dimension translate into shifts in the other. The reward of righteousness is long life; living in harmony with the divine blessing yields prosperity and fertility. Moral evil pollutes the land; cruelty to other humans drives away the Divine. The fullest spiritual development will take place when the people feel secure and rooted in the land. In the messianic age, when humans will "know" God, people will dwell under their own trees and vines in peace and harmony.

Thus, in the Bible, human and natural phenomena are read at two levels simultaneously. The Hebrew Scriptures are this-worldly. Nature is true substance; the world of biological phenomena is not illusion. Yet, while these phenomena are real, they also reflect the divine realm, which transcends nature. The people of Israel are at once a human family with self-interests, sibling rivalries, and daily cares, and also witnesses of Divine Presence in the world. The land of Israel is at once a land of milk and honey, of rain and mountain springs, and the land on which God keeps a divine eye from year's beginning to year's end.

Biblical language and symbol point to spring as the proper season for deliverance. The rebirth of earth after winter is nature's indication that life overcomes death: Spring is nature's analogue to redemption. Life blossoming, breaking winter's death grip, gives great credence to the human yearning for liberation. A correct reading of the spring season would hear its message of breaking out and life reborn at the biological level simultaneously with an Exodus message of good overcoming evil, of love overpowering death, of freedom and redemption. The Bible envisions a world in which moral and physical states coincide, when nature and history, in harmony, confirm the triumph of life. The Exodus paradigm suggests that the outcome of history will be an eternal spring. Read with a historical/theological hermeneutic, spring *is* Exodus.

All great symbols resonate at many levels of meaning. Later kabbalistic tradition, including certain forms of Chasidism, developed an outright mystical interpretation of Judaism and all its symbols. The mystics transposed Exodus from a historical journey into a deeply personal, spiritual one. Passover/Exodus symbolized the struggle of the spirit/soul to break out of the slavery of the material/body. Egypt (in Hebrew, spelled *mtzrm*, pronounced *mitzrayim)* is the same root word as *mitzarim*, which means narrow straits. These are the spiritual straits that the soul must negotiate to avoid being shipwrecked on its voyage to the promised land of spiritual salvation.

To the mystics, all the acts and gestures of Passover were deeply personal and spiritual in their intent. Appropriate spiritual *kavvanot* (intentions) would ensure that each observance played its proper role in nurturing the cosmic forces and unifying the upper world with the lower world. The extreme concentration on eliminating chametz was nothing less than a spiritual purification of the cosmos. Proper preparation of matzot from the moment of cutting the grain to the final baking brought closer the cosmic *tikkun* (perfection) of the world. In the hands of the mystics, the historical experience of the Jewish people became an allegory of the endless spiritual search of the soul for salvation.

Many modern Jews dismiss Christianity as excessively spiritual and otherworldly and argue that such spiritualization is foreign to Judaism. But that view simplifies Judaism and filters out the resonance of the Exodus model. The Exodus paradigm can be interpreted at every level—historical, material, and spiritual. Tendencies toward each of these directions exist within various schools of Jewish thought and religion, and each of these approaches reappears continuously within Jewish history. When two different schools take a polar position within Judaism and push it to an extreme, they end up very far from the initial common ground. They may appear to be foreign to each other, yet a closer look shows that each is the metamorphosis of a commonly held model.

The mystical spiritualization of Passover within the Jewish tradition is methodologically not unlike the systematic spiritual reinterpretation of the Passover/Exodus symbols that ultimately defined Christianity as a separate religion. Of course, the Christians repudiated the physical base of the holidays and its observances, whereas the Jewish mystics upheld the unity of body and soul as they added a layer of spiritual meaning to the commandments.

In the first century, it was relatively easy for the early Christians, operating out of Jewish context, to reinterpret Exodus/Passover as a spiritual paradigm. As the followers of Jesus came to grips with the relatively unchanged political/natural realm after his death, they concluded that the Kingdom of God was not of this world. Jesus had observed Passover. The Last Supper was probably a seder. It was natural for his followers to play off these Jewish models but give them new meaning in the light of Jesus' life and death. Passover was reinterpreted as the season of spiritual liberation. In the new interpretation of redemption, Exodus meant freeing humans from the slavery of sin through love and forgiveness. Represented again as Easter, the Passover holiday celebrated the triumph of life; resurrection broke the shackles of death.

The Christian interpretation can be hermeneutically derived from the Passover/Exodus model by those who experience Jesus as Messiah, as the early Christians did. The vast bulk of Jewry did not accept this experience because God did not intend them to do so. The Jews were and are called to carry forth their covenantal way. The subsequent Christian denial of the legitimacy of the ongoing Jewish covenantal interpretation was an illegitimate annexation of the role of God's people. It was imperialistic to claim exclusive ownership of the very symbols that were revealed and lived out in the Jewish community. Such a claim denied the plain logic that Jewish interpretation was closer to the sources than the Christian commentary. Christianity claimed to know the mind of God exhaustively so that there was room for no other interpretation. It also underestimated God's capacities in its assumption that if God were calling Christians, there was neither logic nor strategy left to use the original people and faith of Israel in any way to achieve the divine goals.

The main Christian tradition went on to put down Judaism as a carnal religion, implying that in the Jewish religion the concept of redemption is arrested at the politico-economic stage instead of shifting to the spiritual level. According to this polemic, the Hebrew Scriptures' call for justice falls short of the New Testament message of love. In actual fact, the Rabbis offered similarly spiritual interpretations of Exodus, spring, and redemption. However, for the most part, rabbinic Judaism stubbornly upheld the inseparability of biological and spiritual redemption. The Rabbis affirmed the interconnection of the natural and the historical triumph of life.

The Rabbis' theology is expressed in their halachic practices, such as in their choice of Torah readings. For the Shabbat of Passover, they selected a Torah portion that includes references to the three pilgrimage holidays but dwells on divine forgiveness in the context of history and human fallibility. The Torah reading deals with the mystery of divine nature and the revelation to Moses that the ultimate truth about God is that "the Lord is a merciful God, full of grace, slow to anger, and abounding in transforming love and truth, conserving mercy for thousands of generations, forgiving iniquity, transgression, and sin . . ."* (Exodus 34:6–7).

Similarly, the Rabbis chose Ezekiel 37, the prophetic vision of resurrection, as the reading from the Prophets for the Shabbat of Passover. Of course, the Rabbis intended a dual message. The past Exodus points to a future redemption in which Israel will be restored to the land. This gives hope to the people of Israel who languish in Exile. But the resurrection imagery ("O my people, I will open your graves and bring you back to the land of Israel!") is deliberately chosen to affirm the final triumph of life as the climax of the spring and redemption motifs of the Exodus holiday.

The Rabbis ordained the reading of *The Song of Songs*. By tradition, this biblical book is read after the seder as well. *The Song of Songs* includes vivid nature poetry: "The winter is over, the rain is past and gone; the flowers appear on the earth; the time of song is come." The

---

*This is where the list of divine attributes cuts off, according to rabbinic interpretation.

book is full of love poetry as well. "I am a rose of Sharon, a lily of the valleys...like an apple tree among the trees of the forest so is my beloved among the youths." "How wonderful are your kisses my [soul] sister, my beloved, your kisses are sweeter than wine, your fragrance better than all perfumes."

Popular wisdom has it that in the spring a young man's fancy turns to thoughts of love. Here again biology and psyche coincide. The rising sap evokes the renewal of human libidinal energy. The Rabbis saw the book as an allegory of the love between God and Israel, the same love affair that leads to Exodus and covenanted love for each other.

Human love is the most apt metaphor for the human-divine encounter. The climactic union of man and woman is the most basic experience of the unity that undergirds all of existence. The Exodus paradigm is driven by love. Divine love validates the value of life; divine love drives the engine of redemption. But human love is the corresponding response of humanity to the intrinsic dignity of life and freedom.

In the spirit of their interpretation of the Exodus paradigm, the Rabbis inserted into the liturgy of the first day of Passover the prayer for dew—the source of moisture that keeps the crops in Israel alive through the dry months ("Give dew to renew the earth and its green"). To make their intentions clear, the Rabbis inserted the dew prayer in the second blessing of the central prayer, the Amidah—that is the blessing that proclaims the resurrection. The dew prayer, "For you are God our Lord who brings the wind and dew drops...for life not death..." is directly connected to "You sustain the living with loving kindness and revive the dead with great mercy....You bring death and restore to life, You make salvation grow. You are trustworthy to revive the dead...." The action of the dew moisture, giving life to dried-out greenery, gives credibility to the promise of future resurrection.

To close the circle of interpretation, on the last day of the holiday the prophetic portion, taken from Isaiah (Chapter 11), articulates the futurist dimension of the Exodus. In that final fulfillment, the Lord will "recover the remnant of God's people and gather the dispersed of Israel...from the four corners of the earth." The ingathering will be a new Exodus. "The Lord will dry up the inlet of the Egyptian sea...so that it can be crossed dry-shod. Then it will be a highway for the remnant of God's people to return." This restoration will be messianic: "A shoot shall grow out of the stump of Jesse [King David is the son of Jesse]". It will be associated with universal justice ("He shall judge the poor with righteousness and decide with justice for the lowly") and universal peace—no more "nature red in tooth and claw." "The calf and the young lion will graze together...the suckling babe will play over a viper's hole.... They shall not harm nor destroy throughout My holy mountain; for the earth shall be filled with knowing the Lord as water covers the sea." Thus will come the Exodus for all people, the future universal Exodus whose source and guarantor is the original Exodus celebrated on Passover.

AFTERWORD

Periodically, scholars survey historians' opinions as to what is the most influential event of all time. In recent decades the Industrial Revolution has often appeared at the top of the list. For the politically oriented, not uncommonly the French Revolution wins; for Marxists, the Russian Revolution. Christians often point to the life and death of Jesus as the single most important event of history. For Moslems, Mohammed's revelations and his hegira have a similar transcendental authority.

Yet when Jews observe Passover they are commemorating what is arguably the most important event of all time—the Exodus from Egypt. If for no other reason than the fact that the Exodus directly or indirectly generated many of the important events cited by other groups, this is *the* event of human history. That it was a Jewish event is an eloquent tribute to the extraordinary role the Jewish people—so minute a fragment of the human race—have played in human history.

The Exodus transformed the Jewish people and their ethic. The Ten Commandments open with the words, "I am the Lord your God who took you out of the land of Egypt, out of the house of bondage." Having no other God means giving no absolute status to other forms of divinity or to any human value that demands absolute commitment. Neither money nor power, neither economic nor political system has the right to demand absolute loyalty. All human claims are relative in the presence of God. This is the key to democracy.

Exodus morality meant giving justice to the weak and the poor. Honest weights and measures, interest-free loans to the poor, leaving part of the crops in the field for the stranger, the orphan, and the widow, treating the alien stranger as a native citizen—these are all applications of the Exodus principle to living in this world. Thus, the Exodus, as articulated at Sinai, transformed the Jewish people and their religious ethical system. Inasmuch as Christianity and Islam adopted the Exodus at their core, almost half the world is profoundly shaped by the aftereffects of the Exodus event.

In modern times, the image of redemption has proven to be the most powerful of all. The rise of productivity and affluence has heightened expectations of the better life. Widely disseminated scientific ideas and conceptions of human freedom carry the same message:

Do not accept disadvantage or suffering as your fate; rather, let the world be transformed! These factors come together in a secular concept of redemption. By now, humans are so suffused with the vision of their own right to improvement that any revolutionary spark sets off huge conflagrations. In a way, humane socialism is a secularized version of the Exodus' final triumph: The liberator is dialectical materialism, and the slaves are the proletariat—but the model and the end goal are the same. Indeed, directly revived images of the Exodus play as powerful a role as Marxism does in the worldwide revolutionary expectations. In South America, the theology of liberation directly touches the hundreds of millions who strive to overcome their poverty.

The secret of the impact of the Exodus is that it does not present itself as ancient history, a one-time event. Since the key way to remember the Exodus is reenactment, the event offers itself as an ongoing experience in human history. As free people relive the Exodus, it turns memory into moral dynamic. The experience of slavery that breaks and crushes slaves does not destroy free people. It evokes feelings of repulsion and determination to help others to escape that state. As participants eat the bitter herb, they remember the heartbreaking tale and the death of the children. They also remember that slavery gradually conditions people to accept servitude as the norm. The Israelites fell into that trap and were delivered, not by their own merit. The lesson is that a slave needs help to get started on liberation.

In the seder ritual, the family also acts as the transmitter of memory. The past is not excised but becomes an active part of the lives of the participants. Parents tell the story to children. At the same time, the children are not merely dependent. They ask questions and participate in the discussion. They must become involved for it is essential that they join in the unfinished work of liberation. This is why when Pharaoh offered to let the adult Jews leave Egypt to worship God if the children were left behind, Moses rejected the offer: "With our youth and our elders we will go." The seder order is deliberately designed to hold the children's attention, to fascinate them with their people's history so that they will feel impelled to take up the covenantal task. Thus, by the magic of shared values and shared story, the Exodus is not some ancient event, however important; it is the ever-recurring redemption. it is the event from ancient times that is occurring tonight; it is the past and future redemption of humanity. The Exodus is the most influential historical event of all time because it did not happen once but recurs whenever people open up and enter into the event again.

CHAPTER THREE

The Covenant
of Redemption:
Shavuot

As WE HAVE LEARNED from the Exodus, the heart of Judaism is a vision of perfection. When tyranny was overthrown, reality's veil parted long enough to show the fullest possibilities of sustaining human value. And, as the prophets spell out, what happened then to the Jewish people will *someday* happen to the rest of the world.

But how can people live by the Exodus now? The world is not yet redeemed. Shall we treat every human being as if he or she is of infinite worth? Inevitably, this would bankrupt the people with good intentions, for present resources cannot cope with all human misery. Shall we disarm as if the world is at peace? This would hand the world over to the wicked, who still abound.

Shall we then act as if the world is nothing more than a jungle? Shall power, not love, govern all relationships? Shall we grab what we may, live for this moment, savor what this life offers, for this life is all we shall ever have? Evil and suffering are entrenched enough to "justify" such a strategy. But to live this way would betray the Exodus experience; to live this way would be to sell the dream for a mess of pottage.

Shall we choose a third alternative: revolution? Driven by the morally outrageous gap between perfection and the present human reality, shall we commit to change the world totally and at once? The twentieth century offers evidence that the power to transform the world is available. But revolution arouses the forces of human and institutional inertia, generating resistance and counterpressures that often defeat the objectives of the revolution. For its part, the revolution bears down on its actual or imputed enemies. Time and again this dynamic turns it into a totalitarian and destructive force.

Hear the witness of a visitor to China in 1982:

> When the romance and urgency of the Communist liberation began to fade, Mao contrived internal revolutions—to keep alive a set of feelings. The Cultural Revolution was only the longest lasting and most murderous of these purgative wars. . . . [In the Cultural Revolution] people were beaten in bags; children denounced their parents; intellectuals were paraded through the streets with human excrement on their heads or forced to crawl on crushed glass in front of enormous crowds. . . . There were instances of people literally crucified against walls, nails driven through their palms, and left to die. . . . According to Chinese figures released since the Cultural Revolution, there were 100 million people persecuted and harassed, and up to 850,000 deaths by beating or suicide. Whole villages were exterminated; people's bodies washed down the rivers and piled up in harbors on incoming tides.*

There is a fourth alternative: to throw ourselves on the mercy of God. Let Almighty God use infinite power directly or through a redeemer to lift humanity up from the mire and place it in an earthly paradise. Only a divine unlimited force can overcome all obstacles. Only divine compassion can absorb all the hatefulness and cruelty and mistaken goodwill of humanity. Or, alternatively: Let humanity discover that this vale of tears is all illusion; let humans become illuminated and escape to the everlasting arms of God in a reality other than this one and thus end all misery.

But this world is not an illusion, says Judaism, nor does God want humans to surrender and let God do it. Nor will some divine fiat bring the final redemption into being. True, God loves humans. But although God yearns for a messianic consummation of history and even promises that it will come to be, God will not force humans to be free. In truth, freedom cannot be given to another. Freedom bestowed is dependency. Freedom must be earned.

THE COVENANT

How then can we reach the goal? Nothing less than a partnership between God and humanity will achieve the dream of perfection. By a

*Annie Dillard, "For the Love of China," *Harvard Magazine*, vol. 85, no. 6 (July–August 1983), pp. 38–44.

process of voluntary self-limitation, God summons humanity to participate in the process of creating a redeemed world. Each partner enters into this treaty of total redemption; each brings a pledge to this binding covenant. God pledges that seeking perfection is not an exercise in futility. God promises to accompany humanity every step of the way. The human partner pledges to start the process of redemption, to go as far as possible in his or her lifetime, to create life and pass on the vision and the responsibility to the next generation—and not to relent or settle until the final goal is reached.

This covenant means that God has accepted human agency. But this leads to a further covenant—the one between God and Israel. The people of Israel take on a binding commitment to teach the message of redemption. Israel promises to walk the way of the Lord. In faithfulness to that commitment, the people of Israel pledge to teach the way of justice and righteousness as best it can; to remain distinctive and unassimilated in the world and thus hold up the message for all people to see; to create a model community showing how the world can go about realizing the dream; and to work alongside others to move society toward the end goal of redemption. Thus, the Jewish covenant mission will be a blessing for all families of the earth. For its part, the Divine is pledged never to abandon Israel, to protect and safeguard the people, to help in the realization of the dream. The divine promise includes the pledge of eternal life to the Jewish people: "You who hold fast to the Lord your God are all alive today"(Deuteronomy 4:4).

The Covenant as Process

The covenant of Israel turns the Exodus into an ongoing process. On Passover, God committed to the covenant by an act of redemption. On Shavuot, standing at Sinai, the Jewish people responded by accepting the Torah. The teaching that guides the way of the Jews, the Torah, became the constitution of the ongoing relationship of God and the Jewish people.

The subjects of the Torah are the stuff of infinity and eternity: a God beyond measurement or dimension, beyond human grasp or ken; a destiny that will outlast history. Such concepts are not commensurate with the limited, fragmented, imperfect world we inhabit. But through the mechanism of the covenant, infinity and eternity are converted into finite, temporal, usable forms—without losing their ground in the absolute. The covenant makes possible Judaism's functioning in history.

Judaism proposes to achieve its infinite goals in finite steps. The covenant makes it possible to move toward ultimate perfection, one step at a time. There are inevitable compromises between the ideal and reality because a push to override all obstacles now would result in all the deformations of the revolutionary method. But is not compromise a sellout? No, covenantal compromises are legitimate because they are not the end of the process. Each generation lives up to the Exodus principles to the extent possible in its generation and tries to advance a bit further, closer to the level of perfection. The next generation will carry on and move even closer to the end goal. As long as there is a constant renewal of the covenantal vision, then the ultimate Exodus principle is *not* betrayed, nor is the status quo fully accepted. Judaism's covenant marries unyielding revolutionary goals with ceaseless evolutionary methods. The ideal and the real are betrothed to each other; this dynamic interaction will go on until paradise is regained.

Here is how the ideal/real interaction works. In the Torah, some of the Exodus principles are practiced at once. The weak, the widow, the orphan, the outsiders are treated kindly and with justice. There is one law for the citizen and the outsider. Human life is precious; murder is the ultimate crime.

On the other hand, Israel, too, must make concessions to reality. The way of Judaism upholds the principles of the ultimate human condition to the extent that is possible now. These concessions are part of the process of redemption. The shortfalls will be overcome ultimately, but, as necessary steps along the way, they are affirmed. Any covenant that respects freedom must allow for process.

Item: Despite the Exodus, slavery was not abolished at once. Hebrew slaves were liberated within six years and treated kindly in the interim. Canaanite slavery continued but with a restriction: If a slave was physically abused, the slave was set free. Over the course of centuries, slavery was further ameliorated and then abolished.

Item: After the Exodus, economic inequality was not abolished. At the entrance to Israel, each family was given land—a source of income. The biblical code built in aids to help each family keep its patrimony and source of income. But when poverty and social disadvantage did develop, these conditions were softened by special help; they were not obliterated.

Item: Human life is in the image of God, so it is sacred. Therefore, anyone who destroys human life deserves the ultimate sanction—to be put to death. In principle, capital punishment for homicide is required because it affirms the seriousness of murder and upholds the sanctity of life. However, death is ultimately contradictory to human value, so capital punishment was steadily restricted. For all practical purposes, capital punishment was abolished by the halacha.

Item: In principle, women are in the image of God: "And God created the human being in God's image—man and woman, God created them" (Genesis 1:27). However, women's secondary, almost chattel-like status is the point of departure. Over the ages, women were steadily moved toward greater dignity and equality.*

Concessions to an imperfect and often unjust status quo were morally tenable because they were *within the framework of a covenant*—a pledge to keep living and working until all these limitations were overcome. The integrity of this pledge depends on a constant infusion of the perfectionist idea so that people will never settle.

The halacha is the mechanism whereby the covenant process is kept in motion. It communicates the contradictions of reality and ideal through its ritual structures even as it formulates reconciling behaviors in its laws and ethics.

To achieve the covenant goals and to model the covenantal process, the Jewish people have formed a community in which the Jewish way is carried on and realized. Thus, the individual overcomes the isolation of the "I" and bonds with all living Jews. In the community, each generation overcomes the isolation of the "now" and links to the generations that have gone before and to those that will come after it. Because the goal of perfection cannot be achieved in one generation, the covenant is, of necessity, a treaty between all the generations. Each generation will have to do its share of the mission and pass it on to the next generation until the redemption is complete. By taking up its task, each generation joins with the past and carries on until the day that the hopes of all will be fulfilled. If one generation rejects the covenant or fails to pass it on to the next generation, then the effort of all the preceding and future generations would be frustrated as well. Each generation knows that it is not operating in a vacuum; the accomplishments of the generations that preceded it make its work possible; and the efforts of its successors will make or break its own mission.

This sense of being part of the chain creates the emotional commitment to Jewish survival even in people and generations who do not know the reason for this drive or indeed the reason for Judaism at all. What appears to be blind sentiment or "tribalism" is really an urgency communicated between generations. This tradition is too important to lose, especially since the efforts of countless people—some of whom gave their very lives for the vision—would be lost along with it.

The covenant is binding, not just because it is juridical (that is, commanded) but because people continually accept its goal and become bound to its process. The present generation is neither the slavish follower of the tradition handed down by past generations nor an autonomous community free to tamper with past practices or to reject past goals. Each generation is a partner entering into the covenantal re-

*See Blu Greenberg, *On Women and Judaism: A View from Tradition* (Philadelphia: Jewish Publication Society of America, 1981), especially chapters 3 and 4.

sponsibility and process and thus joining the transgenerational covenantal community.

This is the basis of the rabbinic tradition that all Jews who ever lived or who ever will live stood at Sinai and heard the proclamation of the covenant. It is that moment—standing before Sinai to accept the covenant—that is symbolically recreated every year on the morning of Shavuot.

THE OPEN COVENANT

Since the covenant links two incommensurables—infinite God and finite humans—it holds within it an exquisite series of dialectics. The Jews were chosen; they experienced the Exodus and tried to live up to the promise of that experience. But the chosenness does not indicate superiority: "You are the least of all the nations" (Deuteronomy 7:7; 8:16–18). Israel does not own God. If it becomes vain or exploits the relationship, it will be rebuked.

God has a special relationship to Israel yet ultimately remains the Lord of all the vast universe, the Lord of Lords. Therefore, the covenant is not restricted to Jews. The covenant was offered before there were Jews in the world. The very first biblical covenant was with Noah and his family, the ancestors of all humankind. All people can and will be redeemed; one need not be Jewish to be saved.

This covenant is potentially a model for an absolute commitment that does not deny the validity of other commitments and religions. It is a model of tremendous importance in this age when the growth of communication and power has created a unitary world in which one has to reconcile absolutes through pluralism or risk all-out collision and destruction.

A special covenant was offered to Abraham. If he and his children would "observe the way of the Lord to do righteousness and justice" (Genesis 18:19), they would guide humankind toward the final redemption and thus "be a blessing to the nations" (Genesis 12:3). The covenant with Abraham was inscribed in his flesh. The rite of circumcision became the sign of commitment. Being circumcised meant that Abraham and those born to his family could not deny what they stood for, could not hide from their role by posing as just ordinary people. By extension, this means that every Jew—believing consciously or not—testifies in and through his or her very being. The statement of his or her life denies every idolatry—for example, every partial or human reality that claims to be perfect—because the existence of the Jews challenges absolutes and speaks to the need for final redemption. This recognition is what led the Nazis to try to kill every single Jew whether the Jew "believed" or not.

Yet again the dialectic of the covenant makes its appearance. Because Abraham's covenant is built on values and concepts—transcendence, redemption, justice—Abraham's is more than a biological family. Were Jewry just a family, one could not join Judaism. Either one is born into a family or one is not. Such a pattern would make Jews a "master race" and turn the Torah into a doctrine of tribal improvement. In fact, the covenant makes it possible to join Abraham's family voluntarily, by conversion which constitutes adoption into the family.

There is another dynamic in this model. Since the covenant is open, it is open to further revelations in history. New redemptive events confirm the covenant and move the world closer to the messianic age. The day will come, says Jeremiah, when people will no longer swear "by the God who took the children of Israel out of Egypt" but will take the oath "by the God who brought the children of the house of Israel . . . from all the lands to which . . . [God] had banished them . . . and . . . [brought them back] to dwell on their own soil" (Jeremiah 23; 7–8). New tragic events challenge the covenant. They test it, bring it into question, and force it to grow in order to overcome tragedy.*

Through the unfolding covenant, many Gentiles are brought into the messianic process and become partners in the covenant of God and humanity. This affirmation in no way undercuts the validity and integrity of the Sinaitic treaty with Israel. After the holocaust and in light of the pluralism of the postmodern world, Christianity and Islam will have to reject their own claims to supersede Judaism. And Jews will, more clearly than before, recognize these religions as outgrowths of the original covenant. Such development, far from disproving Judaism, only shows that the original covenant continues to bear fruit and bring life. If and when this recognition triumphs, then on Shavuot Jews will celebrate not merely their own illumination but the fulfillment of the words of the Mekhilta:

Why was the Torah not given in the Land of Israel? In order that the nations of the world shall not [say:] "Because it was given in Israel's land, we do not accept it." [Lest one group say:] "In my territory, the Torah was given": therefore, the Torah was given in the desert, publicly and openly, in a place belonging to no one. . . . To three things, the Torah was likened: to the desert, to fire, and to water. This is to tell you that just as those three things are free to all who come into

*See Irving Greenberg, "Cloud of Smoke, Pillar of Fire: Judaism, Christianity and Modernity After the Holocaust" in *Auschwitz: Beginning of a New Era?* edited by Eva Fleishner (New York: KTAV, 1977), 7–55.

the world, so also are the words of the Torah free to all who come into the world.*

As the Jewish people and the Torah develop in order to move toward the final goal, everything done to carry out the mission is vested with the authority of the process of perfection itself. The covenant required an ongoing Oral Law through ongoing rabbinic rulings. Since tradition is part of a necessary unfolding and application of the covenant in new situations and circumstances, it is not inferior to the original Scriptures. Tradition draws its authority from the process of perfection. In this way, the Torah is at once eternal yet contemporary in every age. This, too, Jews celebrate when on Shavuot they reenact the biblical proclamation at Sinai. They do it in the synagogue, the premier institution of the Rabbis, using many customs created by the Rabbis.

THE COVENANT THAT BINDS GOD

Many people—some formally religious and some not—agree that an infinite God or power is the source of this vast universe. But some of them are bothered by the Jewish claim that this Divine Being has chosen the Jews to serve as a special vehicle. (As the old anti-Semitic doggerel puts it: "How odd/of God/to choose/the Jews.") Similarly, Judaism's daughter religions, Christianity and Islam, agree that God binds humans to God's covenant. However, theologians of the other monotheistic religions find it somewhat hard to accept Judaism's affirmation that God is not merely the source of the Torah but is also bound by it. Opponents argue that such a statement is incredibility piled on top of paradox. Would an infinite, universal, all-powerful One care enough to intervene in "trivial" human concerns? Would that Being then be held to the terms of that intervention? Yes, says the Bible and later Jewish tradition.

It all stems from the biblical assertion that the human is in the image of God. Like God, humans are endowed with freedom, power, and consciousness. According to Scriptures, God allows for these human qualities. (In biblical language: Adam and Eve sin but are not put to death. Then, after the flood, God self-limits in the first covenant and promises never again to destroy the earth with a deluge.) This means that the process of exercising human freedom, including the doing of evil, is accepted. Perfection may come more slowly, but henceforth it

---

*Commentary on Exodus 20:2 quoted in *Mekhilta de-Rabbi Ishmael* edited by J. Z. Lauterbach (Philadelphia: Jewish Publication Society, 1933), 3 volumes.

will come only in a partnership—a covenant—of humans and God. In this covenant the human will not be overwhelmed and forced to do good.

If goodness will not be imposed by power, then the human must be educated toward perfection. The rabbis conceive of God as teacher and pedagogue—teaching Torah to Israel and to the world. This also explains why, in the words of *Ethics of the Fathers* (chapter 6, Mishnah 2), "the only truly free person is one who studies Torah."*

As teacher, God offers a personal model for human behavior. The imitation of God is the basis for ethics. Parents, however warm or spontaneous, cannot enable children to grow unless the parents are prepared to bind themselves—to be available in some committed, dependable way. To teach successfully, teachers must offer a reliable and consistent model. Then God, as parent and teacher, must bind God's own self to humans.

From this understanding of the divine commitment in the covenant stems Abraham's incredible challenge when God seeks to destroy Sodom: "You dare not! Shall the Judge of all the earth not do justice?" (Genesis 18:25) Out of this comes the Jewish tradition of a *din Torah mit'n Ribbono Shel Olam*— a trial of God. From Moses to Jeremiah and Lamentations through Levi Yitzchak of Berditchev and Elie Wiesel in our time, Jewish religious life has brought forth people who do not fear arraigning even God when there is injustice.

The binding of God in the covenant is the guarantor that redemption is the true fate of humankind. Reality itself does not always seem to operate to ensure the triumph of good. Ultimately, then, it is God's promise that justifies hope. This is the irony and paradox of the "guarantee": It is built on nothing more substantial than the word of God. What could be more ephemeral than a word, especially when the promise of redemption may point to an event hundreds or even thousands of years away? Yet Jews trusted, waited, and worked. The Torah is no easy, ironclad guarantee against fate or suffering, yet it has outlasted empires. The Jews' testimony is that the covenant will outlast even those societies and cultures that deny its existence. On the other hand, the ethics of asking people to depend on God's word implies that God will truly bind God's own self to keep that promise.

Therefore, Shavuot is not a coronation ceremony. On Rosh Hashanah, Jews blow the *shofar* and crown the Lord as ruler of the universe. Shavuot is a more "democratic" holiday. It remembers those who trekked to Sinai to receive the Torah. It celebrates the God who

---

*My translation. *Pirkei Avot* (Ethics of the Fathers), a collection of rabbinic wisdom and ethics, has also been translated by Judah Goldin in *The Living Talmud* (New York: New American Library, 1957).

"descended upon the mountain" and bound the divine self permanently to the Jewish people. A ruler issues decrees of life and death. A covenant rests upon "free negotiations, mutual assumption of duties, and full recognition of the equal rights of both parties."* God also becomes a partner in this covenantal community. God joins in human community and shares in its covenantal existence. As Joseph B. Soloveitchik points out, the whole concept of God suffering along with humanity ("I [God] shall be with him in trouble" [Psalm 91:5]) "can only be understood within the perspective of the covenantal community which involves God in the destiny of his fellow members."†

So Shavuot is the holiday of partnership. The Divine, out of unbounded love, voluntarily puts aside unbounded power; this equalizes the two partners. This idea of partnership has had an immeasurably positive impact on human history even beyond religion. Covenant became the source of morality and ethics, moving humanity away from magical and ritual/mechanical concepts of divine-human interaction. Concern for social justice, compassion for human suffering, and the demand that religious people serve other humans have all flowed from this idea.

Another outgrowth of this covenant concept has been the principle of the rule of laws, not men. If God is bound by the law, then an earthly ruler is not above the law either. This tradition persists in the United States with the supremacy of the Constitution, the right of the individual and the group to legal protection, and the consensus on the need for limits on government.

Finally, one might well say, along with Alfred North Whitehead, that the biblical tradition is entitled to significant credit for the rise of science in the West. The biblical concept of a lawful world operating as the creation of God, by fixed and reliable principles, was the fundamental assumption needed to conceive the laws of nature and utilize them for human benefit. Surely an important ingredient here is the Jewish insistence that even God can be held accountable to established principles of covenant, so the universe itself cannot be incomprehensible or beyond the law of accountability. One wonders whether a distant echo of the covenant idea is not present in Albert Einstein's famous comment when he justified his attempt at a theory to unify all major scientific phenomena in reality: "I do not believe that God plays dice with the universe."

---

*Joseph B. Soloveitchik, "The Lonely Man of Faith," in *Tradition: A Journal of Orthodox Jewish Thought*, vol. 7. no. 21 (Summer 1965), pp. 5–67, especially p. 29.
†Ibid., pp. 28–29.

FROM NATURE TO HISTORY:
FROM THE HARVEST TO THE COVENANT

The dominant motif of Shavuot in the Bible was agricultural. Scripture gives the holiday three names: Chag Ha-katzir, the feast of the harvest, Shavuot, the feast of weeks; and Yom Ha-bikkurim, the day of the first fruits.

"Feast of the harvest" reflects the fact that Shavuot occurs during the summer harvest season in Israel. "Shavuot/weeks" derives from the seven weeks that stretch from Passover to Shavuot. On the second day of Passover, the Omer—a measure of barley, the first crop to ripen—was ritually offered. The Omer was brought and waved daily until Shavuot when the wheat finally ripened. On Shavuot, *lechem ha-bikkurim* (bread) baked from the first cuttings of new wheat was offered in the sanctuary. By starting the seven-week count from the first day after Passover starts—the day when the first barley sheaf was waved in the Temple—the Torah makes clear that the connection between Passover and Shavuot is the connection between a joyous spring harvest festival and a joyful summer harvest holiday.

The ripening first fruits for which Israel is known—wheat, barley, grapes, figs, pomegranates, olive oil, dates, honey—were taken to Jerusalem with great ceremony. The Mishnah describes the occasion:* The inhabitants of the cities of each district marched to Jerusalem. An ox, its horns bedecked with gold and its head crowned with an olive wreath, led the way. A flutist played in front of the marchers, who sang pilgrimage psalms. As they entered Jerusalem, dignitaries and skilled artisans of Jerusalem greeted the farmers. When they entered the Temple, the Levites' choir hailed them jubilantly with the verse, "I will extol you, O Lord, for You have raised me up." (Psalms 30:2). The farmers would then transfer the basket of first fruits to the priest. In the course of the transfer, the priest waved the first fruits, and together they recited the ancient summary of Judaism: "My father was a wandering Aramaean, and he went down to Egypt, and the Egyptians . . . afflicted us . . . and the Lord brought us out of Egypt with a mighty hand . . . and has given us . . . a land flowing with milk and honey" (Deuteronomy 26: 5–9). The rich brought their fruits in baskets overlaid with silver or gold, while the poor used wicker baskets of peeled willow branches. Ultimately the baskets and the first fruits were given to the priest. Then there was feasting, celebrating, and sharing with family, the poor, and the Levites.

*Talmud, Tractate Bikkurim, chapter 3, Mishnayot 2–8.

As the covenant theme became more dominant in Jewish theology and religion, the agricultural dimension of the holiday was subordinated to the historical one: the anniversary of Revelation. The history of this shift is still shrouded in mystery and scholarly controversy. One of the keys may be the argument between the Pharisees and the Sadducees, two conflicting sects within Judaism at the close of the Second Temple period. The Rabbis (and almost all existing Jews) are the descendants of the Pharisees.

The Sadducees were aristocratic, connected to the Temple priesthood and the government. The Pharisees were more rooted in provincial Jewish culture. The Sadducees insisted that only the written Torah was authoritative. The Pharisees affirmed that side by side with the written Torah there was a parallel revelation at Sinai of principles and categories with which humans could interpret, apply, and develop the Law. That body of revelation given over to humans was called the *Torah Sheh–B'Al Peh* (the Oral Torah) by the Pharisees and later Rabbis. The oral law, linked with Scriptures, was equally the will of God. Indeed, the written Torah could only be understood properly through the oral tradition. The Pharisees placed a tremendous stress on learning and on Torah as a way of life. Out of their tradition came the Talmud.

There were many factors—sociological and political as well as theological and legal—in the conflict between the Pharisees and the Sadducees. I believe the heart of the matter was that the sects ended up with two different conceptions of the covenant. To the Sadducees, it was a concluded covenant. The political-sacral form of Judaism in the biblical period was the final form. Reinterpretation was restricted, and there was little room for further development.

In the Pharisees' view, the openness of the covenant meant that it could be further applied and interpreted. The Pharisees stressed a deeper level of meaning in the covenant concept. The biblical teaching that God had self-limited, which could be interpreted narrowly as a divine decision not to overbear human freedom by cataclysmic punishment, was understood by the Pharisees to be a statement of respect for humanity. Through the covenant, God was summoning humans to participate in the process of perfecting the world. To the Pharisees, the revelation of the oral law of Sinai included a mandate for human interpretation, development, and application of the written Torah in further generations. In light of the partnership model, laws derived and adopted by the Rabbis were deemed commanded by God as well.

The Pharisees broadened the application of religious values in all aspects of life. Holiness could be found everywhere: the sacramental Temple was a quintessential but not exclusive locus for Divine-human encounter. The whole world was God's Temple; all of Israel could be "priests"; every home table could be an altar at which food might be served and eaten as an offering before the Lord.

To the Pharisees, the state itself was subordinated to the Torah and the ongoing covenant of Israel to serve God. The Sadducees, on the other hand, were far more dependent on the existence of the Temple and of the state. When the destruction of the Temple and the Exile came to pass in the first century, the Pharisees proved more resilient, more capable of living the Jewish way under the new circumstances.

The clash of Pharisee and Sadducee viewpoints came to a head in the understanding of the holiday of Shavuot. The biblical verse states, "You shall count for yourselves from the day *after the Sabbath* (holy day) . . . seven complete Sabbaths (weeks)" (Leviticus 23:15). The Sadducees interpreted *Sabbath* to mean literally the weekly Sabbath. Therefore, they ruled that counting the Omer started the day after the Sabbath of Passover and ran forty-nine days until Shavuot. Depending on which day of the week the holiday began, the Sabbath of Passover could fall on any day from the second to the seventh day of the holiday. Shavuot's chronological distance from Passover thus varied from year to year. For the Sadducees, Shavuot was not necessarily the day of Sinai; it was related to Passover on a purely agricultural basis. In other words, seven weeks after the first barley offering, be it a few days earlier or a few days later, the second harvest celebration would follow.

The Pharisees, on the other hand, insisted that the central connection between Passover and Shavuot was the march from Egypt to Sinai, the movement from political liberation to spiritual dedication. They ruled that the counting was to start the day after the holiday of Passover began. The oral law interpreted the word *Sabbath*, in the scriptural verse, to mean holy day, that is, Passover itself. Therefore, counting of the Omer always begins on the second day of Passover. Thus, Shavuot invariably comes forty-nine days after Passover.

Stressing Shavuot as the holiday of Revelation was essential to the Rabbis because acceptance of the covenant of the Torah made Israel an eternal people. "When Israel stood at Sinai and received the Torah, the Holy One, the Blessed, said to the Angel of Death, 'You have power over all . . . but not over this people, for they are My portion.' "*Acceptance of the Torah had occurred outside the land of Israel. Holiness could be found everywhere. Through mitzvot and halacha, every aspect of life could be made holy anywhere in the world. While treasuring the geographic holiness of the land of Israel and the sacredness of the Temple, the Pharisees nevertheless were focusing on covenant,

---

*Leviticus Rabba (Vilna: Romm Printers, n.d.; reprint Jerusalem, 1961), chapter 18, section 3.

revelation, and holiness in time. These are religious models that can operate everywhere independent of holy space. Thanks to the Pharisees, the historical dimension of Shavuot became dominant—and none too soon.

The destruction of the Temple and the Roman expulsion of the Jews from Jerusalem abruptly and violently cut Israel off from its main channels of communication with the Divine. Some Jews understood this to be the end of the Jewish religion. Christian Jews concluded that the covenant was broken. In time, of course, they left the Jewish community.

To the Sadducees and others, the destruction had no such normative weight. Since they had no strategy for shifting religious modes, they insisted that the Temple had to be rebuilt so the traditional channels of worship, grace, and forgiveness would be reopened. Over the next two centuries the Jews of Israel and of Diaspora poured enormous efforts into restoring the Temple. These included a worldwide revolt against Rome in 117 C.E. and a major revolt in Judea in 132 C.E. But all was in vain. The Romans tightened their grip. The Jewish revolts were put down with bloody losses. No one could accomplish the recovery of the Temple or the State. The Sadducees disappeared.

The Rabbis also participated with tremendous devotion in the efforts to restore Jerusalem and the Holy Temple. They continued to study and teach the laws of sacrifice and of Temple administration as if it were still standing. They prayed each day for its restoration. Nevertheless, they also concluded that underlying the covenant was a pedagogical model. In this destruction, God, as master pedagogue, was calling the Jews to a new level of covenantal relationship. The Temple had been destroyed, but the Divine Presence was everywhere, yearning for the Jews to uncover it. Wherever people ate and said words of Torah, wherever people sat as a court and gave justice, whenever the sick were visited or the hungry fed, there was the Divine Presence.

After the *churban* (destruction), the Rabbis taught that there would be no further prophecy. God had self-limited again. But through Talmud Torah (study of Torah), God's will could be discerned. Talmud Torah became the central religious act. "Talmud Torah equals all of them [mitzvot]."* "Great is learning because it leads one to [proper] action."† In time, learning became the equivalent to biblical ritual acts: "The [Talmud] Torah of sacrifices is equal in efficacy to the actual bringing of sacrifices."** Shavuot was the holiday of the Torah par excellence. In rabbinic ritual, the holiday's name is "the time of the

---

*Talmud, Peah, chapter 1, Mishnah 1.
†Babylonian Talmud, Kiddushin, 40B.
**Babylonian Talmud, Menachot, 110A.

giving of our Torah." Had the Shavuot holiday been exclusively agricultural, it would have withered on the vine.*

During the Exile, certain agricultural associations were preserved in the synagogue: The Rabbis did not want to break the connection to the land of Israel. They ordained a Shavuot reading of the Book of Ruth, a book whose climactic action occurs in the harvest season. The Rabbis also identified Shavuot as the day on which the fate of the fruit trees is determined, just as human fate is decreed on Rosh Hashanah–Yom Kippur. In later centuries, the agricultural connection was expressed in the practice of decorating synagogues and homes with trees and greenery and of spreading the floor of the synagogues with dried grasses.

Compared to Sukkot and Passover, Shavuot has a relative paucity of religious symbols. Of course, there are two ways of looking at this shortfall. A Jewish folk saying is that Shavuot is the best among the holidays because one can eat whatever one likes, wherever one likes, and whenever one likes—as opposed to Pesach when chametz is prohibited; Sukkot when meals are to be eaten only in the sukkah; Rosh Hashanah when you can eat only after completing the lengthy prayers; and Yom Kippur when you may not eat at all. In the absence of other rituals, the reenactment of Sinai became all the more dominant a religious model.

SINAI: THE REENACTMENT

The covenantal way depends for its effectiveness on the continuing recruitment of new generations to keep the human chain going. As with any transmission of tradition, there is a danger that the freshness and depth of covenantal commitment will be lost. Future descendants may carry the tradition as obligation or even burden—as a fossil law handed on without personal involvement. The work of all the previous generations would be forfeit if an entire generation of relay runners dropped the torch. In a very real sense, the covenant is vulnerable to history and must be ratified again and again.

The holiday of Shavuot is the response to these concerns. Shavuot celebrates and renews the covenant of the Jewish people. In accordance with the classic rabbinic method, Shavuot is the time when Jews recreate the Revelation at Sinai and then reaccept the book of the covenant.

The reenactment of Sinai starts forty-nine days before the event. As

---

*It is noteworthy that the ceremony of bringing first fruits has been revived in modern Israel and is practiced even in many "secular" kibbutzim.

already noted, the countdown begins on the first night after the Exodus. The Omer is counted every night from one to forty-nine, by days and by weeks. According to Maimonides' interpretation, as soon as the Israelites were out of Egypt, they looked forward to receiving the Torah. Maimonides views Sefirat Ha'Omer (Counting of the Omer) as the outcome of the extraordinary anticipation that Jews felt for the moment of Revelation. The Israelites counted every night much like a child who counts the days until his or her birthday.

Earlier rabbinic midrash interprets the weeks between Passover and Shavuot as a passage period from slavery to freedom. The Israelites came out of Egypt saturated with Egyptian values; the forty-nine days enabled them to "remove" the impurities of Egypt and to uncover some primordial Jewish identity and memory.

The Omer count goes on for seven times seven days. Seven is the number/symbol of perfection in biblical language, as evidenced in such facts as the Sabbath is the seventh day, the slave goes free in the seventh year, and so on. The number forty-nine communicates arrival at the pinnacle of perfection. Day by day the individual works on the inner self, striving to attain the level of perfection worthy of receiving the Torah. To the kabbalists, the forty-nine days are seven aspects of the seven *sefirot* (emanations) that make up the divine and human personalities. Each day, one aspect of one *sefirah* is addressed and perfected through meditation, *kavvanot* (directions), and self-renewal.

In biblical times, the entire period between Passover and Shavuot appears to have been a happy time. In the rabbinic era, however, the seven weeks became a period of sadness and mourning. The Talmud speaks of a plague that decimated the students of Rabbi Akiva during this period. It is entirely possible that the plague was, in fact, a Roman purge of Akiva's students for the crime of being involved in the Bar Kochba revolt against Rome. Rabbi Akiva was a major figure in that uprising.

In olden times armies marched during the spring and summer. Over the years the sadness in the Omer period was confirmed by a multitude of enemies and armies who fell upon powerless Jewish communities and inflicted heavy casualties, if not total destruction. In time, the mourning led to a ban during the Omer period on marriages and other specially joyful occasions. Other rituals of grief such as not getting haircuts were introduced. The one exception to this period of mourning was the thirty-third day of the Omer (Lag B'Omer—the numerical value of the Hebrew letters *La*med and *Gim*el, "Lag" equals thirty-three). According to tradition, on this day the plague among Akiva's students stopped.

Another Lag B'Omer tradition in the land of Israel is to celebrate the *yahrzeit* of Rabbi Simeon bar Yochai by visiting his grave at Meron in Galilee and with dancing, feasting, and bonfires. The Zohar (Book of

Splendor), the most influential Jewish kabbalistic work, is attributed to Bar Yochai. Among Chasidic and Sephardic groups, it is customary not to cut a boy's hair until he is three; many parents take their three-year-olds to Meron for the first haircut. The attribution of Bar Yochai's grave and of the occasion of the yahrzeit is uncertain, but folk spirit has preserved these ancient traditions and their association with this day.

All of this appears to be unrelated to the countdown to Sinai, but history has a way of imposing its own experiences. For most of the rabbinic period, a powerless Jewish community suffered repeated devastating blows from its host cultures. The periods of gloom and mourning in the Jewish calendar expanded steadily throughout the historical era. The sadness added to the sobriety and somberness of the pre-Shavuot period, so the Revelation was taken with greater seriousness.

As one approaches the event of Revelation, preparation intensifies. The three days before Shavuot are known as the *shloshet yemay hagbalah*, the three boundary days. In the biblical account, Moses instructed the people to use the three days before the Sinai theophany for purification. The boundary days act out the historical image as if the contemporary Jews are encamped three days from Sinai. People get haircuts and buy new clothes, and mourning ceases in anticipation of the great day. Weddings, another form of covenantal relationship, are scheduled during this period.

The holiday is ushered in at nightfall on the fiftieth day. Since Shavuot occurs in the summertime, the stars come out quite late. Thus, the dictum of the Torah, "You shall count... seven *complete* weeks," is fulfilled.

There is a custom to stay awake the entire night of Shavuot in preparation for the Revelation. The kabbalists saw this as time to prepare the bride's (Israel's) trousseau for the wedding (with God) in the morning. What is the preparation during this long night? It is the study of Torah, preparing a Jew for what he or she is about to receive. In the sixteenth century, kabbalists created a Tikkun Leyl Shavuot (Liturgy of the Night of Shavuot), an anthology that was a symbolic representation of the complete Torah, written and oral. This was to be reviewed before receiving the Sinai Revelation.

Many congregations today carry on the tradition of all-night study by scheduling various classes and study groups to make the learning more meaningful. Good all-night sessions are an exciting, if tiring, off-beat learning experience. Those who stay up all night pray the morning service immediately at daybreak—carrying through the symbolic acting out of "eagerness" and anticipation to receive the Revelation. The service, which is full of joy and celebration, includes the chanting of the complete Hallel as on Passover.

On the morning of Shavuot, the entire congregation gathers to hear the reading of the Ten Commandments. Originally, the Ten Commandments were read daily because they represented the body of Torah or the Sinaitic covenantal moment. But then Christians and other sectarians began to repudiate the other commandments of the Bible while upholding the Ten Commandments as the eternal essence of the revelation. The Rabbis reacted by striking the Ten Commandments from the daily liturgy, their idea being to uphold the entire Torah by undercutting any distinction between the importance of the Ten Commandments and the rest of the Torah. However, on Shavuot, the rabbinic objections were moot. Only one reading could satisfy the liturgy of reenactment, namely, the account of Sinai and the text of the Ten Commandments.

In Jewish tradition, marriage is the peak covenantal moment of personal life. Nothing could be more appropriate as a metaphor for receiving the covenant than a marriage ceremony. Some Sephardic congregations followed through the kabbalistic image of the wedding of God and Israel by reading a simulated wedding or engagement contract between God and Israel. One example of such a document (written in 1688) is a perfect parody of the standard engagement contract used even today by traditional Jews:

> The One who foretells the end from the very beginning
> Will uphold the validity of these conditions of covenanting
> That were agreed between the two sides, all for greater name, praise, glory.
> Party of the first part: One and Unique, the Creator of All, the All-Powerful, the Life and Ground of Existence, Prime Matter, and so forth.
> Party of the second part: The Community of Israel, beautiful as the moon, shining like the sun, and so forth.
> The worthy young man, a mighty one like the cedars, the beloved of the world, the unique groom, the King of Kings, the Holy One blessed be He,
> Will marry—for good *mazel!*—the beauteous maiden, Israel, with canopy and sanctification according to the laws of Moses and Israel.
> The Holy Groom obligated Himself to bring with Him all that He created, shaped, and made—all for her.
> The Holy Bride obligated herself to bring all that she has with her.
> The groom also undertook to give the bride additional presents:
> The holy Sabbath, both spiritual sustenance and bodily sustenance.
> And the wedding will be—with good *mazel!*—on the sixth of

Sivan in the year 5448 (1688 C.E.) to the creation of the world—to be paid for on the Groom's account, who on account of this has issued crack of thunder and lightning.

And all is in effect and valid!

[Signed] the heaven and the highest heavens—first witness
[Signed] the earth and all within it—second witness*

Once upon a time, rose petals and laurel wreaths were flung at the Torah as it was taken out for the grand reenactment. In other congregations, it was customary to hang strings of eggshells with feathers attached, symbolizing hovering birds to fulfill the dictum, "I lifted you up on eagle's wings and brought you to Me" (Exodus 19:4).

It is considered especially meritorious for women to be present at the Torah reading, for the Torah was given both to men and women. The rabbinic midrash teaches us that "thus shall you say to the House of Jacob" refers to the women and "declare to the children of Israel" refers to the men.†

To underscore the drama of Sinai, the reading is preceded by the responsive recitation of a special liturgical hymn—"Akdamot" (The Introduction). Written in Aramaic in the eleventh century, the hymn praises God for the creation and for choosing the people of Israel. Dramatically, it portrays suffering Israel as tempted by the nations to abandon God, but Jewry remains steadfast and is promised a rich reward in the messianic age.

Following "Akdamot," the account of the encampment at Sinai is read. Again, Israel stands as one before its Maker. Again, the people are told: "If you will hearken to My voice and observe My covenant, you shall be My treasured people among the nations. You shall be a kingdom of priests and a holy people to Me." Again, the People answer together: "All that the Lord said we shall do" (Exodus 19:5–8). Again, the mountain shakes and the world is riven by the eternal revelation. The Ten Commandments are chanted with special "trop" (musical notes) to make the reading even more impressive. When the Ten Commandments are read, the entire congregation rises to stand in awe as if it were once again hearing the Voice at Sinai.

The prophetic reading for Shavuot is Ezekiel's vision of the chariot. This is considered the mystic's great text, the source of the most important kabbalistic speculations. Thus, the peak collective Revelation experience is echoed by the peak personal mystical experience. This is another striking example of Judaism's balance of individual and community.

---

*Yom Tov Lewinski, Sefer Hamoadim: Shavuot (Tel Aviv: Ovir, 1968), pp. 98–100.
†Mekhilta de-Rabbi Ishmael on Exodus 19:3.

CELEBRATING THE COVENANT DAY

There is a tradition that every holiday should be celebrated "half and half"—half for God and half for personal pleasure. Rabbi Eliezer says that since Shavuot is the day on which the Torah was given, one must increase joy to show how delighted one is and to balance the Torah's spirituality half with "our" pleasure half.

As always, feasting is a key feature of Jewish celebration. In the case of Shavuot, the tradition of eating dairy meals is strong. Blintzes and cheesecakes are often the special fare. Some attribute this custom to the verse that likens Torah to milk and honey. A folk tradition explains that upon receiving the Torah, the Jews were required to eat kosher meat (that is, meat specially slaughtered and prepared). Since it takes time to prepare meat in this manner, they initially ate dairy after Sinai. The insistence on dairy food may well be a messianic reference. Just as Passover evokes the future universal redemption, so Shavuot evokes the hope of the universal covenant. The prophet predicts that even the carnivorous animals will turn vegetarian ("and the lion, like the ox, shall eat straw"); hence follows the anticipatory dairy meal of Shavuot.

Another custom is to bake two extra-long challahs in remembrance of the two special loaves offered in the Temple on the day of the first fruits. A still later custom is to prepare triangular-shaped latkes or kreplach. The three-sided shapes evoke the old witticism that God gave a three-part Torah (Torah, Prophets, and Writings) to a three-part people (Kohen, Levite, and Israelite) through a third-born son (Moses, youngest sibling to Miriam and Aaron) in the third month (Sivan).

Given the strong association of Shavuot and Talmud Torah, it was customary in traditional French and German Jewish society for young children to begin studying the Torah on this day. To sweeten the experience, parents would coat the first letters that the child was to learn with honey. Licking off the honey, the child would taste the fulfillment of the psalmist's words that the commandments are "more desired than gold...and sweeter than honey" (Psalms 19:11). Still another custom is to bake "Mount Sinai cakes"—honey cakes filled with almonds and raisins—to fulfill the dictum: "Taste and see that God is good" (Psalms 34:9).

All in all, Shavuot is the festival most limited in specific rituals and shortest in duration—one day in Israel, two days in Diaspora in traditional Jewish practice. Samson Raphael Hirsch suggested that the Torah deliberately avoided creating one dominant holiday ritual in connection with the giving of the Torah lest people think that a specific ritual was *the* way to celebrate the Torah. In fact, the Torah should be with all the people at all times and should permeate all actions.

Hirsch's own favorite symbol of the holiday was the two loaves of bread and the *shlamim*—the peace offering—that was brought on Shavuot to the Temple. These represented food and human independence and the state of complete human happiness that was expressed in the shlamim sacrifice, a celebration of inner peace and harmony. "For those who have achieved this inner harmony . . . there is no longer any conflict or chasm between heaven and earth, between time and eternity, between temple and home, altar and table. For heaven and eternity, bliss and supreme happiness have entered the daily, temporal concerns of such people . . . In the presence of God, together with wife and children, they can enjoy eternal values which transform every moment of our fleeting existence on earth into a taste of eternity."*

THE COVENANT OF TOTAL BEING

When Moses completed the covenant ceremony and read the book of the covenant before the Israelites, they responded, "We will do and we will listen" (Exodus 24:7). The expression has always been a source of wonderment and surprise to rabbis and a refutation of the anti-Semitic portrayal of Jews as calculating and self-protective. "We will do and we will listen" implies a commitment to observe the covenant even before the Jews heard its details!

The Talmud tells this story about a Sadducee who once saw Rava so engrossed in learning that he did not attend a wound in his own hand! The Sadducee exclaimed, "You rash people! You put your mouths ahead of your ears [by saying we will do and we will listen]! and you still persist in your recklessness. First, you should have heard out [the covenant details]. If it is within your powers, then accept it. If not, you should have rejected it!" Rava answered: "We walked with our whole being. [Rashi's classic Talmudic commentary: "We walked . . . as those who serve (God) in love. We relied on God not to burden us with something we could not carry."] Of us it is written: 'The wholeness (meaning wholeheartedness) of the righteous shall guide them.' "†

This story captures one other crucial dimension of the covenant commitment—it is open-ended. Like love, it has proven to be a limitless commitment. Why is this so? As Rabbi Joseph B. Soloveitchik has explained, the Torah is a covenant of being, not of doing.** The goal is the completion of being, the full realization of humanness. It is not a utilitarian contract designed for useful ends so that if the advantage is

---

*Samson Raphael Hirsch, *Judaism Eternal* (London: Soncino Press, 1956), volume I, p. 109.
†Babylonian Talmud, Shabbat, 88A.
**Joseph B. Soloveitchik, *The Lonely Man of Faith*, pp. 23–45.

lost, the agreement is dropped. The covenant is a commitment on the part of each partner to be the only one, to be unique to the other. It is a turning of the whole person to the other. The two are bound together in a wholeness that transcends all the particulars of interest and advantage.

When the initial agreement was made, neither side knew its limits. When Israel accepted a mission to the world, it sounded agreeable. But what if the Jews had known then what they know now about the cost of this election? As Elie Wiesel once said, "If God wanted to send us on a mission to redeem the world, that was all right—but God failed to tell us that it was a suicide mission."

Initially, the Jews accepted the covenant out of love and gratitude for redemption. It gave them the strength to commit themselves to what turned out to be an open-ended covenant—very much like a commitment to marriage or to having a child—a commitment in which there was no way of knowing the ultimate cost. As the risk and suffering of Jewish history unfolded, however, the commitment was tested repeatedly. The tests were so extraordinary that they challenged the basic structure of the agreement. In the destruction of the First Temple, the prophets suggested that Israel had not lived up to the covenant. Did the destruction mean that God was angry, so angry as to repudiate the covenant itself? Was it all over? The answer is explored again and again in prophetic literature. God was angry. God would punish. But finally God came to realize that if one loves, one must forgive everything. The ultimate expression of this view is found in Hosea's prophecy. God told Hosea to marry a woman, Gomer. He loved her and she bore his children. Then she whored and betrayed and failed him. In anger and jealousy, he sent her away. But Hosea loved her so that he called her back. Poignantly, he even offered to pay her a harlot's hire to stay with him.

The people of Israel, like Gomer, broke God's heart, as it were, but after the rage, the hurt, the jealousy, the wrestling with rejection comes God's anguished affirmation: "How shall I give up, Ephraim? How can I surrender you, Israel?" (Hosea 11:8) The crisis of the destruction passed. God was committed permanently. In the future it was axiomatic that the Shechinah (Divine Presence) would go into exile with Israel but would never abandon the people or leave the covenant.

In the crisis of the destruction of the Second Temple, Israel again experienced the silence of God. The God who intervened in the Exodus to save Israel at the Red Sea was now the God who self-limited and allowed human freedom even when it meant that the wicked triumphed. The enemy trampled the Temple and all but destroyed the Jewish people. Prophecy ceased, and the Jewish people had to ask themselves whether God's silence and the Jews' suffering meant that the covenant was finished. Again, they came to recognize that it was not. As Rabbi Soloveitchik wrote: "In the bleak autumnal night of dreadful silence unillumined by the vision of God or made homely [*heimish*] by His voice, they refused to acquiesce in this cruel historical reality and would not let the ancient dialogue between God and man come to an end. . . . If God has stopped calling man, they urged, let man call God."*

The concept of prayer and the synagogue was developed by the Rabbis to carry on the covenantal dialogue—now with man speaking and God listening. They discerned God's presence in the hiddenness. The flawed, partial human redemption of Purim was recognized as the new redemption, and the Sinai covenant was reconfirmed. In retrospect, the Rabbis said that Sinai was too grandiose. The Jews were "coerced" into the covenant by the Exodus miracles. Purim was, by contrast, a voluntary renewal, for the covenant was accepted out of discernment and faith and not out of response to awesomeness. The Jews redoubled their commitment and reaffirmed the covenant.

But is there some limit that could break the covenant? The sum of woe inflicted on the Jews as a result of their covenantal witness is truly staggering. Is the suffering worthwhile? This question forces itself into consciousness whenever the holiday of the covenant and the reenactment of Sinai approach. This is why the liturgical climax of Shavuot is the reading of the Book of Ruth.

THE READING OF THE BOOK OF RUTH

Many explanations have been offered for the custom of reading Megillat Ruth (the Scroll of Ruth) on Shavuot. There would be no conversion but for the covenant, which opened up the Jewish people to others who shared its values. Ruth was an ancestor of David, the king; according to tradition, David died on Shavuot. The story of Ruth is set in the harvest season, and Shavuot celebrates the summer harvest.

But none of these reasons touches the deepest levels of the book. Only after the Holocaust can one understand its true message. Despite its surface gentleness Megillat Ruth is suffused with tragedy, with suffering, even with betrayal. The land of Judah suffered famine, and Ruth's husband-to-be and father-in-law abandoned it to save them-

*Ibid., p. 37.

selves. In Moab they died suddenly, without children, unknown on a foreign soil, their lives untimely ended. In this welter of pain the questions arose: Is life absurd? What is the meaning of all this? The answers grew out of the woman named Ruth. She loved her husband even after his death and did not want his name to die with his childless family.

The covenant of love extends beyond the grave. Ruth loved Naomi, her living mother-in-law, and would not let her go away alone and impoverished. Although there was no hope or reason for it and there was no visible redeemer to keep the family name alive, Ruth insisted on going with Naomi. She acted out of *chessed*, a loving kindness that saw not only the bleak reality but the possibilities of redemption that may still break through the harsh surface of an unredeemed world. Ruth remained faithful. She joined Naomi's people and embraced Naomi's God. And incredibly, out of this barren, rocky soil grew hope —an act of kindness, a relative who cared. A marriage followed and a child was born who became the grandfather of David from whom would come the Messiah. Out of faithfulness comes hope; out of suffering comes redemption; out of love comes renewed life.

On the holiday of Shavuot the mind turns to the cruel and bloody record of Jewish history, to the harsh, unyielding evil that all but destroyed the Jewish people in our time. And the questions rise up and afflict the soul: Did it all matter? Was it worth it? Will any good come of it?

Perhaps an even more profound question is posed: You are released from the previous covenant—acceptance—for how can God bind you to it if God will not protect you? What say you now, people of Israel?

Quietly, gently—for one can make no demands on survivors—the story of Ruth is told. The pain is not in vain. The tale is not told by an idiot; it is not full of sound and fury, signifying nothing. Out of the barren, blood-drenched rocks there grows a flower. A flower from the stock of Jesse. One can dream that

> A shoot shall grow out of the stump of Jesse,
>   a twig shall branch off from his stock . . .
> The spirit of the Lord shall alight upon him—
>   a spirit of wisdom and insight . . .
> He shall sense the truth . . .
> He shall judge the poor with equity
>   and decide with justice for the lowly of the land . . .
> The wolf shall dwell with the lamb,
>   the leopard shall lie down with the kid . . .
> With a little boy to herd them . . .
> They shall not hurt nor destroy in My holy mountain
> For the earth shall be full of devotion to the Lord . . . (Isaiah 11)

The answer to the question of whether there is a limit to the covenant commitment has been given by the Jewish people in its post-Holocaust behavior: Since life is infinite, the commitment is infinite. No setback, no loss has proven strong enough to destroy the covenant. By living on as Jews, Jews dare to affirm the final realization and to bring perfection closer.

If we understand and accept the story of Ruth, we understand that we can accept the covenant—again. We understand that suffering is connected to redemption by a love more powerful than death. We understand that messianic possibility is born in the generation in which all is destroyed.

Can there be any question but that Ruth lives in our own time? Or that this generations' response to the creation of Israel means that we stand before Sinai again—all of us: those who died, those who live, those who are as yet unborn?

AFTERWORD

Though Shavuot has the least number of distinguishing rituals as compared to Passover and Sukkot, it is the holiday most in the process of development. It has spawned major new features, more recently, than any of the other traditional Jewish holidays. The Tikkun Leyl Shavuot is a mere four hundred years old. Like the idea of the covenant that it celebrates, the holiday of Shavuot is open to history.

In more recent times, Reform Judaism established a confirmation ceremony, confirming teenagers as adult Jews, as a Shavuot liturgy. Unfortunately, adopting the ceremony was often associated with the dropping of the Bar Mitzvah ceremony, so traditional Jews rejected confirmation. As Reform has become more traditional and recovered Bar Mitzvah, observance of confirmation has weakened somewhat.

The definitive source that Shavuot is the anniversary of Sinai comes to us not from the Torah but from the oral tradition. Rabbi Soloveitchik has made the powerful point that by Scriptures obscuring the direct connection between the date of Shavuot and the giving of the Torah, the supremacy of the oral law is established. The anniversary of the revelation of the written Torah can only be ascertained by direction of the oral Torah. This insight teaches us that Shavuot celebrates not only God's word, the Revelation received passively by the people, but also the Torah of tradition, the one received and unfolded by the Rabbis and the people.

The term "unfolding" is deliberately used. Just as a diamond, when carved out of an unshaped stone, reveals brilliant new facets and lights, so the unfolding of the Word of God reveals dimensions and layers of meaning that were not initially apparent. The oral tradition highlights and shapes the Torah so that its different levels of meaning speak at different times to different people with different cultural models. Some of this unfolding can be grasped by viewing the Falashas' religion in Israel. Separated from the Jewish people before the development of the Talmud, the Beta Israel have preserved the biblical commandments and traditions. Seeing them in action makes one realize that different levels of meaning have unfolded in history.

On the Shabbat, for instance, the Beta Israel have no light or cooked food at all. Their observance of ritual immersion in the *mikvah* is preceded by women going into a separate tent and being almost completely outside of the community during menstruation. Both observances bear the unmistakable tone of taboo. There is much to admire in the Falashas' faithfulness and dedication to Judaism, but there is much less joy, warmth, creativity, and humor in their experience of commandment. Mediated by the models of their culture, the Torah's prohibitions become inscrutable decrees. Human dignity and human partnership are far more central in the rabbinic tradition.

Rabbi Soloveitchik's interpretation makes clear how much false consciousness there is in the modern debate over Jewish religion. Perceiving themselves to be stifled by the blanketing nature of rabbinic tradition, modernists sought to go back to "pristine" biblical patterns. They glorified the written Scripture and argued that the rabbinic adumbrations were petty and legalistic, lacking spiritual depth. From the Falasha record we can see that, on the contrary, a fundamental contribution of the Rabbis and of the oral law is deepening, personalizing, enhancing the spiritual depth of the Jewish way of life.

We also see the utter inadequacy of portraying God as the sole fount of Torah, with the people of Israel mere receivers. In Rabbi Soloveitchik's brilliant articulation, humans are partners in the *Torah Sheh–B'Al Peh*, the Oral Law. Tradition is not a passive category. Its dynamic includes human participation in the creation of Torah as well as in absorbing the ancient traditions through the cultural tools of each era and time. Tradition is the application of the received, and the shaping of every century and every life experience, by the categories of the Torah.

Unfolding brings new understanding and new experiences within the framework of Jewish religion; it constantly uncovers facets of meaning and directional guides that make the Torah a living experience in every generation. "These words which I command you today" means that every day the Torah is new and renewed.

The final implication, then, is that the Torah in its broadest sense is not complete. Continuing and further revelation in this lifetime should be absorbed through the *Torah Sheh–B'Al Peh*. A central task of this generation is to incorporate experiences such as the Holocaust and the rebirth of Israel into the religious understanding of the Jewish way. Shavuot should properly be called the holiday of the Continuous Giving of the Torah. It celebrates "what God and humans have wrought."

Jews today are living in the greatest age of the renewal of the covenant. Coming after the incredible destruction of the Holocaust, the creation of Israel and the rebuilding of Jewish life constitute an unparalleled reacceptance of the covenant. What could be more appropriate than a new dimension of Shavuot celebration focusing on this acceptance?

In the work of CLAL, The National Jewish Center for Learning and Leadership, the tradition of the Covenant Between the Pieces (the covenant passage in which Abraham voluntarily became the first Jew) has been recalled.

A passageway is created, such as between two extended tables or screens. The congregation lines up in dyads (husbands, wives, friends, and so forth) behind each other, or in groups, in two groupings on either side of the passageway facing each other. The passageway is lined with a cleft religious ritual object (such as a very large challah cut in two). The initial dyad carries a Sefer Torah, with joyous song accompanying them through the passage, and places the Torah in the hands of the dyad on the other side. These two carry the Torah back through the passage and pass it on to the counterpart pair. So it continues until every person has gone through the passage. The entire group sings throughout: *Yisrael, v'orayta, kudsha brich hu chad hu. Torah orah. Halleluyah!* The people of Israel, and the Torah, [and] the Holy One the Blessed are one (united)! The Torah is light! *Halleluyah!*

Concluding the ceremony, the entire group forms circles, dances, and sings, "Am Yisrael Chai!" The People of Israel Lives! "Od Aveenu Chai!" Our Parent Lives! and the modern messianic song, "David Melech Yisrael Chai v'Kayam!" David [Future] Ruler of Israel Is Alive and Present!

By passing through, the individuals affirm their willingness to bring together with their lives that duo that is truly one but is currently separated: be it ideal and reality, God and Israel, the Jew and tradition. Thus, symbolically, family and friends together pledge faithfulness and renewed commitment to the covenant of hope of the Jewish people. In the ceremony of the Covenant Between the Pieces both men and women can participate fully.

In this age of the most open and free society in history, it is appropriate to revive/create/unfold a covenant ritual that expresses the voluntary nature of commitment.

Families should have, at least, a covenant meal at home together on Shavuot. People should talk of the content of the covenant. They should summon up memories of generations gone before who carried their share on the covenantal journey and passed the torch on to us. Through Shavuot, Jewish people reaffirm their destiny as the people of the Unfinished Covenant, the carriers of the once and future redemption.

CHAPTER FOUR

Journey to Liberation:

Sukkot

Previously, we described Judaism as a religion of hope for a world redeemed. What distinguishes hope from escapism?

A hope is a dream that has accepted the discipline of becoming a fact. Jewish faith is the communal commitment to work at realizing the hope. Passover states Judaism's goal, which is defined by hope. Shavuot confirms the covenant, which is the commitment to persist until the goal is reached. Sukkot addresses the third dimension of Judaism's religious core: how to get there.

Despite all the good intentions and commitments, there is still an enormous gap between the hope and the reality of the world. The halacha is the primary mechanism of the Jewish struggle. As a system, it converts absolute ends into proximate means. Halacha is the art of the possible, the divine science of the doable. While halacha presents demands that make people stretch, it mediates between what is and what ought to be.

Many religious people think that concessions to human limitations are incompatible with divine law. An eternal truth should not be qualified by socioeconomic realities or cultural norms. Halacha's pragmatism bespeaks a different understanding of Judaism.

When divine power is perceived to be arbitrary and inscrutable, then human devotion takes on the quality of bribery and appeasement. That is how slaves relate to their masters: Divine despotism must be humored and fed; a wrongful action, even an unintentional or innocent failure to deliver, will anger the gods and draw down wrath on insignificant humanity. It is as if the gods are consumers of human services and will be weakened, offended, or shamed by their servants' failures.

In such a system, religious acts always have magical overtones—the exact phrase or ritual, not the substance or validity of the act, is what is important. In magic, if the act is done exactly right, it may coerce, or at least assure, the desired divine response. For a god to be a credible tyrant, humans must be kept powerless. And because their concerns are insignificant, there is no need for the gods to make concessions to their frailties.

But in Judaism, the Divine is both loving and self-limiting out of respect for humankind. Since the perfection of humanity is an essential part of God's purpose, divine demands are made in accordance with human capacity to respond. Human beings have more than an instrumental value in the divine economy.

Religious acts are acts of substance, intended for the benefit of God's creation; they are not made because God "needs" them. The midrash says, "What difference does it make to the Holy Blessed One whether the slaughterer cuts from the front of the neck or the back of the neck? [The law of Kosher slaughter requires the cut be made from the front.] The only purpose of giving the commandments is to perfect [purify] God's creatures."* God places the future of creation into our hands now because humans have infinite value now, and not just when humanity is perfected. The processes of *tikkun olam* (perfecting the world) and *tikkun ha-adam* (perfecting humanity) go on side by side and reinforce each other.

The halacha is willing generally to compromise its ideal demands in a real situation, on condition that if perfection cannot be achieved now, then at least there can be an improvement in the status quo. Judaism's ideal world is vegetarian but, for now, halacha permits eating meat, with restrictions. The regulations include humane slaughter, removal of blood, no wanton killing, no cruelty to live animals, no mixing of milk (the source of life nurture) with meat (the product of killing). Similarly, Judaism insists that nothing less than universal peace must be the ultimate condition of the world, but halacha does not affirm pacifism as the only method to get there. On the contrary, a war of self-defense is labeled a *mitzvah* (righteous act). The system regulates the military tactics used so that they will be morally appro-

*Genesis Rabba, chapter 44, section 1.

priate to the goal and proportionate to the nature of the war. The more elective or marginal the war, the more restrictions on tactics. The process of halachic decision-making is never-ending, for in every culture and every age the moral balance must be struck again.

To keep Jews ever striving to come closer to the ideal, they must continually experience the Exodus. Thus, the Jewish annual calendar is anchored by two total reenactments of the Exodus. The liturgical cycle ensures that Jews do not wait a full year between Exodus encounters. Long delays between such experiences would diminish Exodus consciousness and dissipate its effect on behavior. "Mini" Exodus experiences reinforce Jewish commitments every day, but lest the overall impact fade, the total experience of Exodus is never more than six months away. The first replay, the week-long Passover, comes on 15 Nissan. The second, Sukkot, begins six months later, on 15 Tishrei.

Through the centuries, commentators have puzzled over the rationale of the Sukkot holiday. The actual anniversary of the Exodus is 15 Nissan. Passover comes in the spring when nature is freed from the bonds of winter, just as the Jews were released from the house of bondage in Egypt. Sukkot's date in the fall reflects no anniversary, indeed, no obvious connection to the redemption. Modern scholars have argued that the calendar dates of Passover and Sukkot reflect their roots in agricultural festivals, celebrating the coming of the spring and fall harvests. Two traditional scholars, Maimonides and Jacob ben Asher (a medieval Spanish halachic authority), explain that the Sukkot celebration was deliberately scheduled during an "inappropriate" season. On Sukkot (meaning booths), traditional Jews enter into booths in imitation of the portable homes the Israelites lived in during their wanderings in the desert. Jacob ben Asher reasons that if Jews were to move into open-air booths in the spring during warm weather, it would appear to be less a commemoration of Exodus than a communion with nature. The Torah bade the people of Israel go into the booth in the cool of autumn when it is unusual to live outdoors. Onlookers are prompted to ask: Why do these people dwell in booths at this time? The answer is: to obey the will of the Creator and testify to the Exodus and the subsequent wandering.

But Sukkot is more than an encore of Passover. On Passover, Jews restage the great *event* of liberation. Sukkot celebrates the *way* of liberation—the march across a barren desert to freedom and the Promised Land.

What happens the morning after redemption? It is like the old Hollywood movie: After the ups and downs of courtship, the boy and girl marry. They kiss, fade out, and cut! Presumably they live happily ever after. But that is not the way life works. It is much harder to handle the daily struggle of life than the highs and lows of courtship. The fifty percent American divorce rate is proof enough of that.

The Jews rose to the Exodus occasion with a great act of heroism—departing. But the daily strain of collecting manna and pitching tents and carrying their children through the desert eroded their commitment. Time and again, they were thrown by the prosaic frustrations of no meat, of boring food, of insufficient water.

The real achievement of freedom does not come in one day; there is no quick cure for slavery. The liberated person is the one who learns to accept the daily challenges of existence as the expression of self-fulfillment and responsibility. Sukkot commemorates the maturation of the Israelites, achieved not in crossing the Red Sea but in walking the long way to freedom. It is relatively easy to rise to one peak moment of self-abnegation and courageous commitment. It is more taxing and more heroic to wrestle with everyday obstacles without highs or diversions. True maturity means learning to appreciate the finite rewards of every day along the way. Some parents receive no pleasure from their children because they are overwhelmed by the constant anxieties, conflicts, and potential setbacks of the growing-up process. Parents are far happier—and children feel much better about themselves—when the simple joys of every day are shared and appreciated.

Passover celebrates a brave departure through a festive meal. Sukkot marks the hasty lunches and the endless wandering in the dessert. Sukkot expresses the deeper Exodus—the reflective, gritty days of marching during which a new generation grew up. Freedom came as the end result of pitching tents (booths) and taking them down over the course of 14,600 days. Sukkot honors the forty-three thousand meals prepared on the desert trek, the cleanups, the washing of utensils. Passover celebrates a moment of pure triumph. Sukkot celebrates a seemingly endless forty-year journey. Passover is the holiday of faith; Sukkot is the holiday of faithfulness.

The halacha addresses the challenges of a perpetual journey in Sukkot's sacral structures, but the language is symbolic, the language of ritual. In Judaism, theology, dogma, and values are encapsulated in gestures; ultimate truths are expressed in what appear to be external and everyday acts. The messianic hope of perfection of the world is expressed in a cup of wine at the seder. The grief felt when a close relative dies and the fabric of life is torn is articulated when mourners rip a piece of their clothing. Among the holidays, Sukkot is one of the richest in symbolic language.

Despite its good spirit and feasting, the holiday remains among the most neglected. Perhaps it is because contemporary society has robbed us of the capacity to hear symbolic language. Sukkot has equipped Jewry to deal with certain recurring dilemmas encountered on its millennial Exodus journey, but the language must be translated so the methods can be grasped.

What, then, are the questions posed by the long years of journeying? How can a people persist on an endless march toward a state of universal exodus without its treasury of idealism being nickeled and dimed away at every stop? What is the proper relationship between daily living and eternal calling? Given the enormous gap between the end goal and the present moment, is it proper to enjoy life? Given the widespread suffering of humanity, do ease and affluence not constitute self-indulgence and insensitivity to the plight of others?

These questions boil down to three major challenges to religious integrity and faithfulness. Beyond honoring and reenacting the journey in the desert, the holiday of Sukkot offers living strategies to deal with these universal challenges.

The first challenge is to develop a working method of improving the world. In its present condition, the world cannot sustain the full dignity of human life. This leads some to surrender to passivity. By contrast, a commitment to perfection generates an activist stance toward nature, a determination to transform the world so that it will support a higher standard of human living. But management and technology too easily slip into abuse and degradation of the environment and loss of proper human relationship to nature. How can one navigate successfully between the Scylla of fatalism and the Charybdis of soulless manipulation of natural order?

Second, there is a powerful tendency to become rooted in a specific land and a particular community and culture. Such rootedness is in itself a major source of freedom and dignity for the individual. Yet rootedness leads to total acceptance of the local norms of behavior and value. Many people idolize their land and will stop at nothing to preserve their stake. People who measure themselves by prevailing standards end up absolutizing those norms, thereby betraying the Exodus goal. Yet rootlessness is no answer. Taken to its extreme, rootlessness leads to social pathology and vulnerability. Where is the resolution?

Third, how shall people live with the simple pleasures of life along the Exodus march through history? Poverty is an enemy to be overcome, yet affluence so easily erodes the moral fiber. Like others, Jews have all too often succumbed to ease and acceptance by yielding their roles as gadflies for change. Is wealth also an enemy? Then who or what is a friend? Must Jews exercise repression in every aspect of life in order to reach their goal of perfecting every aspect of life?

Sukkot addresses these dilemmas by offering its own remarkable combinations of experiences. Sukkot rituals pay tribute to the Israelite journeys in a desert while celebrating the produce of the land of Israel. Sukkot rituals affirm the holiness of pleasure, even while they infuse pleasure into the holy. The Sukkot liturgy celebrates material wealth even as it warns that it is "vanity of vanities." In the course of communicating these dialectical truths, Sukkot's central ritual model of the holiday—the reenactment of the journey to liberation—becomes the foreshadowing of the Exodus way through human history to a universal Promised Land.

SUKKOT: THE REENACTMENT OF THE EXODUS JOURNEY

The *sukkah*, the booth, is the central symbol of the ancient Israelites' trust and hope for forty years in the desert. The Hebrews left the protection of man-made thick walls to place themselves under the protection of God. Exposed to dangerous natural conditions and hostile roving bands, they placed their confidence in the divine concern, which is the only true source of security. Their act of faith remains a source of merit for the people of Israel and a continuing support for the covenantal commitment. By eating, learning, and sleeping in the booth so that the sukkah becomes one's home for a week, we reenact their original act of faith.

In the Talmud, Rabbi Akiva states that the sukkot commemorate the actual desert booth dwellings. Rabbi Eliezer maintains that sukkot really symbolize the clouds of glory that hovered over the Jews and led the way through the Sinai. Rabbi Eliezer meant that the miracle and celebration are due not only to God who protects but also to the people of Israel who were willing to expose themselves to the fiercest storms of history with only the intangible, and at times partial, shelter of God's presence.

The halachic requirements for the construction of a sukkah attempt to capture the fragility and openness of the booths. The sukkah may not be too impressive a home; its total height may not exceed twenty cubits—about ten yards. Nor may it be lower than what is reasonably high enough to enter and live in, that is, ten handbreadths or forty inches. Similarly, the sukkah should be built well enough to withstand normal winds but not so solidly that it withstands winds of unusual force. By deliberately giving up solid construction, Jews admit their vulnerability and testify that the ultimate trust is in the divine shelter.

The most important part of the Sukkah, halachically, is the *s'chach*, materials of vegetable origin such as evergreen branches or marsh rushes that form the roof. For support, these coverings may be laid across wooden slats or bamboo poles; heavy boards or beams that offer solid support should not be used, nor should any of the roof materials be nailed down permanently. Though completely covering the top, the materials should be loosely spread so as to be open to the heavens, with the stars visible through. Thus, the s'chach is the perfect expression of divine protection. God is not a mechanical shield that protects from all evil; God is the Presence who gives the strength to persevere, to overcome.

The fragility of sukkah borders on the playful. What is the minimum sukkah one can build? It need not have four walls, that is, be fully enclosed. The minimum is two walls plus part of a third. By legal fiction, the partial walls are projected as if they were complete. Similarly, the vertical walls need not be fully finished from top to bottom. The owner can build a frame or part of a wall and "project" it for completion.

My father, of blessed memory, used to tell a favorite joke: A jerry-built sukkah was broken into by a cossack who stole all the family belongings. The two yeshiva boys who discovered the break-in were totally puzzled by the theft. "How could he even get in?" one asked. "This [incomplete] wall is legally projected to the end; that vertical frame is legally projected to the ground. So where did the cossack find an opening and get in?" To which the other answered: "You see, the cossack is an ignoramus who did not know the law of projection of the wall." Thus, the Jews playfully created shelters of sticks and s'chach— and of humor—in the face of evil. As frail as these were, they outlasted powerful forces that assailed them.

The s'chach is meant to teach something about the true nature of protection. Human beings instinctively strive to build solid walls of security. People shut out life; they heap up treasures and power and status symbols in the hope of excluding death and disaster and even the unexpected. This search for "solid" security all too often leads to idolatry, to the worship of things that give security. People end up sacrificing values and even loved ones to obtain the tangible sources of security. The sukkah urges people to give up this pseudo-safety.

By moving into the sukkah for a week, Jews demythologize solid walls and controllable security. It is not a renunciation of self-protection but a recognition of its limits. One should accept vulnerability and live more deeply, rather than build thick walls that are intended to protect from hurt but end up cutting us off from life. The sukkah does not deny the value of a solid home or of human effort; fifty-one weeks a year Jews are allowed to live in homes and are encouraged to build up the world and increase security and well-being. But the sukkah teaches that builders of homes should be able to give them up or move out if necessary. Renunciation is the secret of mastery. "Who loves money [absolutely] will never have his fill of money" (Ecclesiastes 5:9). People become masters rather than slaves of their achievements when they develop the capacity to let go of their accomplishments, even if only for the moment.

The move into the sukkah is a movement from the certainty of fixed position toward the liberating insecurity of freedom. Participants open up to the world, to the unexpected winds, to the surprise setback as well as the planned gain. The joy of Sukkot is a celebration of the privilege of starting on the road to freedom, knowing that to finish the task is not decisive but failure to start is.

The sukkah provides a corrective to the natural tendency of becoming excessively attached to turf. It instructs Jews not to become overly rooted, particularly not in the exile. For thousands of years Jews built homes in Diaspora. Civilizations of extraordinary richness—culturally, religiously, and at times economically and socially—were created. But, outside of Israel, all such Jewish homes and civilizations have proven thus far to be temporary ones, blown away when a turn of the wheel brought new forces to power. Often, self-deception and the desire to claim permanent roots led Jews to deny what was happening until it was too late to escape.

In 1933 and 1934, there were German Jews who tried to reach Adolf Hitler and plead for the right to stay in Germany. How many Jews would have been saved had they not held on so long because they believed with Alfred Wiener of the Central Verein of German Jewry that "the decisive majority of German Jews nevertheless and in spite of everything remain deeply rooted in the soil of our German homeland."?* It is not that people should not enjoy and care about their homes; if anything, the very consciousness of fragility gives deeper joy to daily rooted existence. But the precious capacity not to deceive oneself when change takes place is made possible by sukkah consciousness.

The Sukkot rituals play with the relationship of rootedness and mobility. In the process, they reach beyond the Jewish experience of exile to address one of humanity's most universal tendencies—idol worship.

The human being is a social animal. Rootedness and connection are as natural and as necessary to humans as water is to fish. Deprived of roots, people get sick; deprived of connectedness, they go mad. Therefore, human beings naturally sink roots wherever they are. They start by loving their home and their time. Then they so invest themselves that they can conceive of no other home or time than the present one. Finally, the present value is reified and projected outside of themselves onto land, possessions, status. This leads to pathological rootedness in which the source of value is perceived as being vested in the place and the time instead of in the individual and in God. The gods of that turf

---

*In *Central Verein Zeitung*, June 1, 1933, quoted in *Hitpatchut Haantishemiut Hanazit Mithelathah Vehateguvah Hayehudit Aleha* [The Development of Nazi Anti-Semitism from Its Beginning and the Jewish Response to It] by A. Margaliot (Jerusalem: Hebrew University, 1975], p. 82.

are accepted as if they were the gods of the universe. If the local deity is Moloch, who demands that a child be sacrificed, then that is the price that will be paid. This idolatrous act, in turn, sucks the value out of the individual, resulting in a loss of worth by the worshiper.

All of this reinforces idolatry because it leaves the individual feeling ever more dependent on the deity and more likely to yield to further demands. By contrast, when a believer has given up something of value to the One God, he or she is given it back with greater value. Therefore, Judaism fights the gods of space as idolatrous. The ability to move on, as represented by the sukkah, derives from rootedness in the one God who loves a particular place and people but who is everywhere and loves all of humanity at the same time.

Mobility undercuts idolatry. Wandering weakens fixed categories, challenging the belief that there is a measurable way to program (read: control) divine behavior. The variety of experiences and settings makes the local gods relative. The wanderer sees how each group considers its own god and worship methods to be absolute. Yet the nomad, out of firsthand experience, learns that assumptions about the nature of divinity differ markedly from one area to another. Such insight leads to the breakdown of the local cults. This happened in the Greco-Roman period. The gods of Olympus steadily lost their credibility in the face of new philosophical and religious encounters engendered by the cultural openness of the empire. The result was a growing atheism or a search for a universal deity who transcended tribal ownership. Thus, people discovered the God who is everywhere.

When human society is one's exclusive reference point, the individual believes its values absolute. The next step is to perceive the society as the source of personal validity. The individual feels alone, worthless, and dependent on society to bestow personal dignity. Under the circumstances, the desire for acceptance often overrides individual conscience. By contrast, Jewish tradition moved the reference point to the God who *was* before the world was created and who *will be* long after particular human civilizations have vanished into the eons.

In the sacred system of idolatry, there are specific holy places where a god's presence and power are to be found exclusively. When a god has dominion over a particular locale, there are other places where the god is not found. As Jews moved into exile, they understood what the sukkah had always taught them: God is not fixed; God is everywhere. One can go elsewhere and find God present there. After the Exodus, Israel went into the desert to meet its Lord. Later, the favor was returned by God, who went with them into exile, into the travail of history. Jews learned that the *Shechinah* (Divine Presence) is with them in eras of wandering as well as during the triumphant return to the Holy Land.

Their enemies called them "wandering Jews" and deemed it a curse. But the sukkah taught Jews that only those who journey know the value and limitations of a homeland. Wherever they went, God went with them. God is not just the God of Mount Moriah and Jerusalem but the God whose footstool is the Earth. No house could encompass the Lord but, in love, God could fit between the horns of the altar or into the modest dimensions of the sukkah.

The sukkah taught Jews that they could root deeply into particular cultures but that their faith was portable. Their enemies were baffled and accused them of being "rootless cosmopolitans." The term "cosmopolitan" was correct; "rootless" was the falsification. People who want fixed deities with controllable norms use "rootless" as a pejorative to lash out at those who march to the beat of a different drummer, people whose very presence undercuts uniformity.

Until the world is redeemed, Jews are on an Exodus journey; perforce, they are in, yet not totally of, the society and culture they inhabit. Jews can contribute without totally accepting the system. Jews can affirm, yet transform. The tremendous effort to participate in each political and moral stage led to Jewish integration and assimilation in the host culture. Then the sukkah reminded them to push on. There were miles to go, further along the Exodus way, and promises to keep —until the whole world becomes a Promised Land.

INSIDE THE SUKKAH

The sukkah is one of the few mitzvot into which one can throw oneself body and soul! One Chasidic master praised the greatness of this mitzvah precisely for this reason. To fulfill the mitzvah of living in the sukkah, people must put their entire selves into it.

Traditionally, living in the sukkah included eating any significant meal there. Jewish law defines a significant meal as one that includes water and bread, dishes made of the five basic grains—wheat, rye, spelt, barley, oats—or a main dish with meat or fish, eggs or cheese. Fruits or vegetables were not included in this definition. However, some traditional Jews will eat no food outside of the sukkah. When traveling and there is none available, one may eat outside of a sukkah.

Every time people eat in the sukkah they make the special blessing, *"leysheyv ba'sukkah,"* "to dwell (literally, to sit) in the sukkah." On the first night (in Diaspora, on the first two nights), people add the Shehecheyanu blessing of thanks to God "who has kept us alive to this season."

There is a special dimension of joy to the holiday of Sukkot. To underscore the pleasure principle, the obligation to dwell in the sukkah is suspended in a situation of discomfort. This is unique among commandments. The halacha does not recognize discomfort, inconvenience, or even financial loss as an excuse not to eat kosher or observe Shabbat. But joy is so central to the sukkah experience that if one carries out the mitzvah in pain or serious inconvenience it is not a fulfillment in the spirit of the holiday. If it rains on Sukkot, water drips onto the diners (remember that the s'chach is not permitted to be thick enough to keep out the rain); then one is exempt from the mitzvah of eating there. On the other hand, people were so determined to observe the mitzvah of eating in the sukkah on the first night that the tradition grew to wait even until midnight for the rain to end in the hope of getting a chance to eat in the booth. And in cases where rain prevented eating the full meal in the sukkah, people would hastily make kiddush (the blessing over wine) and hamotzi (the blessing over bread) in the sukkah before retreating indoors for the rest of the meal.

"To dwell" was also interpreted as sleeping in the sukkah. Some individuals and even whole families do sleep in the sukkah. In climates where sleeping outdoors would constitute a hardship, however, exemption from sleeping became the rule. Still, for families who are experienced in camping, overnight in the sukkah together is a treat.

Since sukkah is a fixed commandment that requires fulfillment at a specific time, it was not considered a mitzvah binding on women. Still, women fulfilled a mitzvah if they did eat or dwell in the sukkah. In our times, when women are making a historic move to assume full religious maturity, it is doubly important that they commit themselves to fulfill this mitzvah in every way.

BUILDING THE SUKKAH

Building can involve the whole family. Over the years people have shown great imagination in both construction and decoration of the sukkah. For those less handy, there are reasonable and attractive prefabricated models with easy directions for putting them together. Many prefabs come complete with bamboo stick s'chach. If there is no forest in your area, evergreen or perishable s'chach can be purchased from a nursery or landscape contractor. An evergreen roof will add welcome fragrance to the sukkah. When gathering s'chach in local forest or riverbank areas, one must be sure not to destroy public property and not to take s'chach belonging to a private person without permission. Jewish law rules that a mitzvah is not validly performed if goods used in its performance are stolen.

THE AGRICULTURAL DIMENSION

The Torah refers to Sukkot as *Chag HaAsif* (the festival of ingathering). Gratitude for the harvest, prayers for rain, and nature rituals fill the liturgy. Although Sukkot focuses on the paradigm of the journey— which would appear to point away from the settled character of agriculture—the festival focuses equally on the importance of nature, as no other Jewish holiday does. This contradiction underscores the divine genius of the Torah; it expresses its deepest values when it transforms a nature festival into a historical holiday.

In this we find a major characteristic of the Jewish religion, the shift from nature to history. This represents the movement from human passivity and acceptance of nature-as-destiny to a drive for liberation, which can be achieved only in history. As long as humans perceive nature as implacable and fate as immovable, they accept death, poverty, and oppression as their ineluctable condition. Humans celebrated—one is tempted to say bribed—nature to placate the gods who arbitrarily gave and withheld the staff of life, the rain and the harvest. But Judaism proclaimed that human beings, created in the image of God, are commanded to reshape the world, to conquer nature for the benefit of humanity. Nature is *not* God. The natural order is created by God to be used for human welfare.

Behind this biblical vision is an understanding of the universe that gave rise to science, technology, and medicine. Eastern religions, by and large, sought to discern the inner rhythms of nature and to guide humans to live in harmony with them. For the most part, Eastern religions sought to free people from the suffering and illusion of involvement with this world. Biblical revelation supplied the dynamic of Western civilization that sought to set humankind free.

Western culture has been a tremendous force in releasing humanity from grinding poverty and sickness. Yet, in that very drive, the West has often overridden the important insights of the East about living in harmony with nature and the rhythms of the body and soul. The price for this runaway technology has been growing pollution and an increase in diseases of disharmony—cancer, heart attacks, and the like. Judaism, refusing to accept a Hobson's choice between passivity and pathology, seeks both to intervene in the natural order and to prevent the negative side effects of that intervention. The Jewish strategy was to combine human activism and restraint, yoking mastery over nature with reverence for the natural order.

In the Sukkot rituals, human control over nature is balanced by deep sensitivity to its cycles and a sense of wonder at its rhythms. The human activity of agriculture is the harvest, a mitzvah, yet its fruit is celebrated as a divine gift. The liturgy sings of the need for roots and the acceptance of nature's gifts. There are controls over what can be done to nature. Halacha underscores the concept of limitation of intervention with its requirement that liturgical objects such as s'chach and first fruits cannot be "manufactured," that is, changed from their natural state. This is a striking counterpoint theme, considering that the holiday celebrates the produce of agriculture, which is a human process of manipulation of nature.

The Sukkot festival celebrates redemption, but the timing is set at the conclusion of the harvest season, when people moved into sukkot to complete the harvesting. Dwelling in the sukkah saved the travel back to the village where the farmers lived year-round. The halacha requires that the sukkah roof be open to the stars, so the experience of liberation is powerfully linked to being back in nature.

Two other Sukkot ceremonies, the water-drawing ceremony and the willow waving (see below), were carefully attuned to the coming rainy season. *Geshem*, the prayer for rain, was placed within the blessing for resurrection to make clear that agriculture is a human calling but rain is a miracle. The focus on rain was a reminder of the limits of human power; the Sukkot holiday repeatedly underscores the interaction of human initiative and nature's order.

This pattern is a theme echoed throughout the halacha. Eating bread—that product of human intervention and transformation of nature's grain—evokes the blessing of God "who brings forth bread from the earth." The first flower that blooms in the spring, thunder and lightning, the sight of special or beautiful creatures evoke a blessing of the God "who has withheld nothing from Your world," "whose strength and power fill the universe," "who has such creations in Your world."*

THE FOUR SPECIES

The central liturgical expression of the agricultural dimension of Sukkot was the mitzvah of bringing four agricultural species together and waving them in the Temple as a gratitude offering. "On the first day, you shall take the fruit of *hadar* (goodly) trees (an *etrog* or citron), branches of palm trees (*lulav*), boughs of leafy trees (*hadassim*) and myrtle, and willows of the brook (*aravot*), and you shall rejoice

---

*See these and various other blessings of enjoyment in *Daily Prayer Book* by Philip Birnbaum (New York: Hebrew Publishing Company, 1977) pp. 773–75.

before the Lord your God seven days" (Leviticus 23:40). The four species represent the beauty and bounty of the harvest of the land of Israel.

In the Hebrew text, the above verse can be interpreted literally as follows: "On the first day you shall take *for yourselves* the fruit" (Leviticus 23:40). The Rabbis derived from this that individuals must own their personal set of four species. The sets are available at reasonable prices in most cities. There are few more beautiful sights than a synagogue flooded with the four species; the fragrance, the color, the joyful processional around the synagogue are a delight. Local synagogues or Jewish bookstores may order sets for you. B'nei Akiva, a religious Zionist youth movement, has a special program whereby one can order Israeli *etrogim* at unusually reasonable prices; it is a mitzvah, in any event, to insist on the use of Israeli etrogim, thereby strengthening the land of Israel.

If one person owns the four species and a friend doesn't, the owner may make a gift to the other so that he or she may fulfill the obligation. The person given the etrog may then give it back to the other as a gift. (Who says Jewish legal minds can't figure out a way to have cake and eat it, too?) In our time, women should also own the four species, but thus far only a few women buy or carry them at services.

The myrtle and willow are inserted into a holder on the lulav (the holder is made of woven palm branch). Three myrtle branches are placed on the right and two willows on the left. With the lulav in the right hand and the etrog in the left hand, held close together, a blessing is recited and the whole is waved together. The waving motion consists of three times up, three times down, in all directions, east, south, west, north, up and down. This symbolizes God's universal presence. During the waving, the etrog is held with the stem down; purists hold the etrog wrong side up until after they recite the blessing so that the perfect waving is done *after* the blessing. Though the etrog is considered the most precious of the fruits, the whole act has come to be known as waving the lulav, obviously because the lulav is the tallest one and is eye-catching. Since the destruction of the Temple, the four species are brought and waved during the holiday in every synagogue (or home) in remembrance of this Temple ceremony.

Since the fruits represent the blessings of nature, they must be unspoiled. Jewish tradition further glorifies the fruit by seeking beautiful specimens to fulfill the mitzvah. The etrog is the crown of the set. The Torah calls it fruit of the hadar tree (*hadar* in Hebrew means beauty, pride, glory). It is considered a special mitzvah to get an aesthetically attractive etrog. The etrog is unfit if it is dried up, spotted, punctured, smaller than a walnut, or if its *pitum* (protuberance at the tip opposite the stem) has been broken off.

The myrtle branches are characterized by leaves that grow in clusters of three from the same point on the stem. The tips should not be dried up or broken, and the leaves should not be brittle. This latter regulation also holds true for willows, and the preferred length for both is eleven inches or more. True aravot have smooth leaf edges or obtuse (not acute) serrations. The lulav, generally at least two feet long, is unfit if its central spine is split most of its length. Since the lulav is a symbol of Jews, the message seems to be that a spineless Jew is not of much use.

The Rabbis noted that among the four species, the etrog has fragrance and taste, the lulav has taste but no fragrance, the myrtle has fragrance but no taste, and the aravot have neither fragrance nor taste. Say the Rabbis: Taste represents knowledge, and fragrance represents good deeds. Symbolically, the four species represent four kinds of Jews. Some know the tradition and do good deeds; some know but do not do enough; some do enough but do not know enough; some have neither knowledge nor good deeds. To fulfill the mitzvah, all four species must be waved together. This means that all Jews are united in destiny and all Jews are needed, even those who neither know nor do.

WATER DRAWING AND RAIN

The land of Israel is not rich in water resources; it has no river to give it basic fertility, as the Nile does for Egypt. For this reason a special prayer for rain was inserted in the holiday services. Since the Israeli rainy season starts approximately at the Sukkot holiday season, it was the appropriate time to pray for rain. (Jews are realists. One prays for rain during the rainy season, not during the dry summers. One walks across water by stepping on rocks. . . .) Since rain disrupts the mitzvah of sitting in the sukkah, however, it was decided to postpone the prayer for rain until the last day of the holiday.

In ancient times, there was a ceremony associated with water needs —a march around the Temple with water willows, concluding with a symbolic beating of the willows on the ground (to get the earth to come across with water?). This ceremony may well go back to pre-biblical days. Critics claim that its origins lie in sympathetic magic or fertility rites. The origins have long since been purged, and all that remains is the sound of people beating vigorously and grunting as they swing.

The classic water celebration, however, was the water-drawing ceremony. On the first night of Chol Hamoed (the intermediate weekday portion of Sukkot), a torchlight parade, including musicians, jugglers, and dancers, marched to the Temple where the first water of the new

season was drawn from Jerusalem's chief spring and poured as a liba-
tion. The Celebration of the Water Drawing (Simchat Bet Hashoeva)
was a happy, even ecstatic, occasion and symbolized the overflowing
joy when water was found in abundance.

The Talmud describes the event as follows: Jerusalem was lit up by
the light of gigantic menorahs. The lyres, cymbals, horns, and drums
played. The Rabbis entertained and clowned to add to the joy. Rabbi
Simeon ben Gamaliel (the head of the community!) did various gym-
nastic feats culminating in an incredible headstand. He also entertained by juggling flaming torches.

Not one day of Sukkot passes without festivities that celebrate the
happiness of the harvest and the joy of community and religious inspiration. The daily sojourn in the sukkah, the fragrance of the s'chach,
the fruit and vegetable decorations, dining under the stars—all give a
very strong sense of a deep connection to nature. The kiddush, the
complete Hallel, the Torah readings—all reiterate the message of redemption. The setting, the ceremonies, and the ritual objects together
celebrate the human as both creator and creature.

THE ZIONIST HOLIDAY

Because of its strong agricultural ties, Sukkot kept alive a strong identification with the land of Israel for Jews who were in exile. The Geshem (rain) prayer was chanted at the same time as it had been in the
land of Israel. This was the Jews' way of maintaining an unbroken tie,
a statement that as Jews they were living on Jerusalem Standard Time,
not Greenwich Meridian or Central Mountain Time.

Sukkot kept the folk connected to the land and to the dream of living in Israel again. When the first Zionist halutzim came to Israel, they
emphasized the renewal of Jewish life through the restoration of the
land. Early on, especially under the leadership of the late, great Chief
Rabbi Abraham Isaac Kook, etrogim became a prize cash crop that
helped support the new settlement. A controversy erupted in the last
century when the charge was made that Israeli etrogim were products
of forbidden grafting and breeding with other (non-citron) fruits. As a
result of that controversy, the Lubavitch-Chasidic group recommends
non-Israel etrogim to its followers. Religious Zionists feel that Lubavitch has erred in this case. Rabbi Kook fought for the religious supremacy of ritually proper Israeli etrogim precisely because he saw
how this mitzvah could support the reborn commonwealth of the Jewish people.

But there is a deeper Zionist dimension to the holiday. In this generation, the rebirth of the state represents the resumption of the Exodus

journey by the Jewish people. Creating the state was a bold affirmation of Exodus values—of the power of life and renewal—in the face of the greatest triumph of death in Jewish and world history. In many ways, the ability to manage the challenges of sovereignty will be the test of Jewish maturity and vitality in the next stage of the journey.

Increasing the productivity of the economy is essential to Israel's ability to hold its own population. Enjoying greater material well-being without loss of meaning and responsibility is critical, both to Israel's ability to attract world Jewish *aliya* and its capacity to serve as a model to the world. The ability to wrestle with day-to-day frustrations while not surrendering covenantal values will be crucial to the outcome.

In all candor, many Jews are not prepared for the constant demands and risks of power. Many who applauded and danced when Israel's independence was proclaimed and when it won a glorious victory in six days threw their hands up in despair because inflation ran rampant for a few years. There are internal divisions and external threats to Israel, so some people question the validity of the entire Zionist enterprise. Some Israelis grow intoxicated with the land, which leads to the absolutization of possessing territory. Some are willing to sacrifice peace prospects; others are ready to commit crimes.

All too many cannot deal with the results of Israel's freedom, namely, the anxieties of choice. Was a policy error made in Lebanon? (Actually, that is exactly what sovereignty is all about—policy choices.) In panic, some projected total collapse of support for Israel. If the government uses force to control the West Bank, some claim immediately that Fascism and apartheid have come to Israel, as if policy cannot be changed, as if any opening for peace would not change all the options.

After Israel's narrow escape from catastrophe in the Yom Kippur War, a leading rabbinic scholar would no longer recite the phrase, "the beginning of the growth of our redemption," in the prayer for the State of Israel. The war made him see the limits of Israel's power; he now saw the phrase as exaggerated and idolatrous. The Temple Mount is not the site of a rebuilt Holy Temple, so some traditional Jews rationalize that Jews cannot yet celebrate redemption. But the joy of redemption need not be postponed until the final consummation. True joy lies in the daily acts of planting the land, meeting the payroll, celebrating the Jewish calendar, yes, even deploying the Israeli army.

Those who give disillusioned reactions miss the whole point of Sukkot. In the desert, the people of Israel met their God at Sinai, ate the bread of heaven, and followed the pillar of fire. In that same desert, the Amalekites attacked, the water springs were bitter, the Israelites lusted after meat, the flocks were thirsty. Sukkot celebrates freedom's way—the risks, the failures, the boredom, the persistence, the responsibility. Sukkot is a celebration of the s'chach that falls into the soup, the rain that washes out a dinner, the frailty and persistence of human accomplishment. Like Sukkot, Israel is not a one-time event of liberation. Like Sukkot, Israel, with all its failings and risks, is the way contemporary Jews go toward liberation. In the twentieth century, reenactment moves from ritual to reality, and the covenantal way is renewed.

In the reestablishment of the State of Israel, the Jewish people are recreating the balance of vision and process, of rootedness and mobility, of possessions and sharing, of human mastery and restraint. The ability of Sukkot values to nurture the population will make or break the Jewishness of the State of Israel, just as Sukkot's capacity to lend insight for dealing with the journey's endless complications will quite possibly decide the state's levels of achievement.

SUKKOT: THE "MATERIALIST" DIMENSION OF JUDAISM

Most Jews still think that fasting is more righteous than feasting. Yet the Talmud suggests that in the world to come a person will have to stand judgment for every legitimate pleasure in this life that was renounced. The Nazirite—the person who gave up the pleasures of wine and family life to devote himself entirely to God—was called a sinner on the grounds that he gave up the joys of wine when the Torah did not require him to do so.

The perception that asceticism is superior to enjoyment is wrong. Many Jews who observe only one holiday a year make it Yom Kippur, a day of great deprivation since eating, drinking, washing, and sex are not permitted. Furthermore, Yom Kippur is a day of self-criticism, of repeated confession of sins, and even a day of Yizkor in which the memories of departed loved ones usually bring up a good deal of guilt. Since all this is hardly fun, presumably the one- or three-day observers feel that all this angst makes it the most holy day of the year. Sukkot gives the lie to this perception; because of its joys, it is known throughout the Talmudic period as Ha Chag, *the* holiday.

Rabbi Israel Salanter once wrote that to be a good Jew one has to have every human quality and its opposite. The Torah does not consecrate prohibition; it offers the full range of human emotion and behavior. There is "a time to cry and a time to laugh, a time to mourn and a time to dance" (Ecclesiastes 3:4). Correct behavior consists of when one does all these acts and *how*.

As a harvest festival, Sukkot incorporates frank recognition and celebration of material goods. Jewish tradition sees material possessions as
a necessary but not sufficient basis for spiritual fulfillment. As Maimonides writes: "The general purpose of the Torah is twofold: the
well-being of the soul and the well-being of the body. The well-being
of the soul is ranked first but . . . the well-being of the body comes
first." The well-being of the soul is more important, but the well-being
of the body comes first, for it is the context for spiritual development.
Thus, appreciation and enjoyment of material things is a legitimate
spiritual concern. It all depends on how it is done. Prosperity frees the
individual for personal development; but, worshiped or made absolute, wealth disrupts personal growth.

In many ways, Sukkot has become the model for this worldly enjoyment, which is why it is called *the* time of rejoicing. The depth of the
joy also grows out of its relationship to Yom Kippur. Sukkot comes just
four days after Yom Kippur, the most ascetic, self-denying, guilt-rid-
den, awesome holy day of the Jewish year. On the Day of Atonement,
Jews reenact their own death, only to be restored to life in the resolution of the day. Only those who know the fragility of life can truly
appreciate the full preciousness of every moment. The release from
Yom Kippur leads to the extraordinary outburst of life that is Sukkot.
On this holiday, Jews are commanded to eat, drink, be happy, dance,
and relish life to the fullest in celebrating the harvest and personal
wealth.

But making joy holy means being selective in the enjoyment of
God's gifts, not worshiping those gifts or those who own them. The
first and foremost expression of this insight is to *share* the bounty and
the joy. Gifts from the harvest were given to the poor: "You shall rejoice before the Lord. You, your son and daughter, manservant and
maid, the Levite . . . the stranger, the orphan, the widow in your
midst" (Deuteronomy 16:11).

A special holiday feature is the *ushpizin*, hospitality for honored
guests. By tradition, every night a different biblical personality is invited to visit the sukkah and join the company. A custom that has been
growing recently is to invite great matriarchs of the Jewish people as
well. Families invite stand-ins for these biblical figures—fellow human
beings, especially those who are needy or who need a sukkah in
which to eat. This mitzvah is especially important in contemporary
society; since bureaucracies and institutions take care of welfare and
medical coverage, people often forget the importance of personal acts
of *gemilut chasadim* (loving-kindness). The Rabbis say that such acts are
the foundations of the world because they are fundamental expressions of human solidarity and human contact in a largely impersonal
world.

The complete Hallel is recited on all eight days. On Passover, Jews diminish the songs of rejoicing because their deliverance meant that human beings had to be killed. But on Sukkot, the joy of redemption is at no one else's expense. The liturgy speaks of God's spreading a Sukkat Shalom—a Tabernacle of Peace—over all the world. Special prayers in the mussaf service carry on (in words, of course) a Temple tradition of offering seventy special sacrifices over the course of the holiday. The Rabbis understood the seventy sacrifices to constitute one offering for the welfare of each of seventy nations making up the known civilized world in biblical times. This messianist universalism, associated with Sukkot, is expressed in the prophet Zechariah's prediction that, at the end of days, all the families of the earth will celebrate Sukkot (see Zechariah 14:16, 17). Compassion for all people is consistent with the Jewish vision of the final perfection. Just as Passover/Exodus redemption will someday come to all the world, so will the Sukkot journey to freedom be taken by all of humanity. In the world's joy, Jewish joy will be complete; even as Jeremiah proclaimed that in the peace and prosperity of the nations among whom they live, Jews will find their peace and prosperity (see Jeremiah 19:7).

Tradition keeps pleasure balanced by interspersing corrective moves within the holiday to offset materialism. On the Shabbat of Sukkot, for instance, the scroll of Kohelet (Ecclesiastes) is read; its theme, "vanity of vanities, all is vanity," challenges the value of worldly living. On Hoshana Rabbah, the seventh day of Sukkot, Yom Kippur is summoned up again. By rabbinic interpretation, this is deemed to be the day on which the verdict of life and death, originally entered on the Day of Atonement, is finally sealed. The evocation of awe and the encounter with death challenges excessive materialism. A similar effect is implicit in reciting Yizkor memorial prayers for the dead on the last day. This counterpoint keeps Jews from seeing the good things, which they are encouraged to enjoy and celebrate, as absolute. The *balance* of pleasure and restraint is everything.

In time, the pleasures of the flesh were supplemented with intellectual delights. Hoshanah Rabbah, the final day of Sukkot, had been a special day of rejoicing in the Temple. On this day, the Temple was circled seven times instead of the usual once. Holding aloft the four fruits and the water willows, the celebrants sang: "Hoshanah (hosanna)—help us, please, O Lord!" with rain. Since there were many hosannas on this day, it became known as Hoshanah Rabbah (Great Hosannas). Connecting this day to the day of judgment increased its awesomeness: Yom Kippur spelled life and death for the individual; Sukkot spelled life and death for the economy. Then the tradition arose to cap the sealing of judgment with the learning of Torah, so the custom grew for people to stay up all night on Hoshanah Rabbah learning Torah. As on Shavuot, a special resource book was created with excerpts from the openings of various sections of the Bible and the Mishnah so that people could accomplish a summary review of the bulk of the Torah in one night.

There are deep subtle messages to be deciphered in the holiday of Sukkot. The goal of universal Exodus is far away. The tension of the lofty demand and the limited capacity for response is wearing. The day-to-day tasks of the journey are exhausting. From where can the people derive the strength to go farther down the endless road?

There is always the danger that the revolutionary spirit might turn ascetic. The visionary becomes angry at others for their indifference to the grand scheme of things. Out of frustration, the revolutionary is tempted to resent the rich and the powerful and then to extend that resentment to all riches and pleasure. To the revolutionary, the pleasures of daily life are bourgeois, if not counterrevolutionary. But in that contempt for the simple joy of ease, security, and dignity lies the seed of totalitarian oppression—a loss of sensitivity to human needs and normalcy. The pioneer who gives up all for a distant goal begins to resent those who live normal lives and enjoy the pleasures of the flesh. From there it is not a big jump to hate life, and this in the name of a mission to perfect life!

Judaism insists that *chessed* be the driving force of history and redemption. Chessed is a special kind of love, a love that accepts and treasures life *as it is*, even as it sees and embraces its potential for perfection. When love shrivels because of idealism, when sympathy dries up because of frustration, the outcome will be not redemption but a new "idealistic oppression." One fundamental criterion of a life well lived is love of life. It is terribly important, therefore, to enjoy life as it goes along. Joy cannot be postponed. Life *as is* is of infinite value.

There is another dimension to the focus on joy in this holiday. Those who serve out of obligation, such as those who are in servitude, do not find joy in their work. The joy of Sukkot reflects maturity. It is the happiness of the free person who chooses to live this way, who prefers this mission to all other alternatives. There is an inner joy even in the struggle against obstacles, the joy of choice and of anticipation of the goal.

Happiness also reinforces good behavior. It renews the will to go on even in cultures that accept Jews and sing siren songs of affluence and ease to them. A person who is suffering and deprived is likely to demand some *quid pro quo:* Let me be the only one who is right; let my enemies be humiliated and my exclusive righteousness be finally revealed! A person who feels burdened by an obligation is tempted to yield to ease when it finally comes. A person who is enjoying life and feels fulfilled does not need to cling. When reminded of the dream or after reliving the old drama of slavery and of liberation or when the cries of the needy come through, then that fulfilled person is able to pick up and move on. That is the Jewish theory.

Constant renewal of joy makes life on the Exodus road worthwhile in itself. Thence comes the strength to persist. The suffering self is, at some level, at war with itself and its biological—if not spiritual—need for satisfaction. The joyous self, properly fulfilled, can be unified in body and soul, and love God and humanity with the whole heart.

The entire Sukkot holiday is an object lesson in postmodern religious life. Nostalgia tends to romanticize poverty and the religious life of the old *shtetl*. But as affluence rises, the great religious calling is to learn to share the wealth and to learn how to consecrate it in enjoyment. Affluence and inherited wealth remove the "artificial" sources of purpose that most humans have faced throughout history: the need to earn enough to stay alive. Similarly, the high level of material well-being has removed the "artificial" source of values that most humans are confronted by: the constant need to choose and set priorities due to limited resources. When the imposed holiness of asceticism is removed, there is the challenge and the choice of finding the sacred amidst plenty and pleasure. It may be more difficult to do this religiously than to live properly in poverty. Thus, Sukkot is bound to be a major new focus of postmodern Jewish life.

CODA: PURE JOY

When the seven days of Sukkot end, the Bible decrees yet another holiday, the Eighth Day of Assembly. The Rabbis interpreted this as an encore. After the High Holy Days, after the intense seven days of Sukkot and pilgrimage, the Jewish people are about to leave, to scatter and return to their homes. God grows nostalgic, as it were, and pensive. The people of Israel will not come together again in such numbers until Passover six months hence. God will soon miss the sounds of music and pleasure and the unity of the people. The Torah decreed, therefore, an eighth day of assembly, a final feast/holy day. On this day Jews leave the sukkah to resume enjoying the comfort of solid, well built, well insulated homes. The lulav and etrog are put aside; this day, Shemini Atzeret, is a reprise of the celebration of Sukkot but without any of the rituals. The message is that all the rituals and symbolic language are important but ultimately they remain just symbols.

Over the course of history this day has evolved into the day of the rejoicing of the Torah (Simchat Torah). In Israel, Shemini Atzeret and Simchat Torah are celebrated together on one day. In the Diaspora

where an extra holy day is added (making a ninth day), Shemini Atzeret is followed by Simchat Torah on the ninth day. The rejoicing
makes a statement. Whatever the law denies to Jews, whatever suffering the people have undergone for upholding the covenant cannot
obscure the basic truth: The Torah affirms and enriches life. At the end
of this week of fulfillment, on this day of delight, all the scrolls are
taken out of the ark, and the Torah becomes the focus of rejoicing.

In many congregations the evening service mixes melodies of solemn days with melodies of modern music and frequently employs a
lay "cantor" and mock choir. Simchat Torah and its good humor puncture religious pomposity and overseriousness. At night, all the scrolls
are taken out of the ark and members of the congregation take turns
marching around the synagogue while holding the scrolls aloft. There
are seven circuits. At the completion of each circular procession (*hakafa*), songs and wordless melodies (*niggunim*) are sung, and people
dance with the Torah. All night, children march around the synagogue
carrying flags and accompanying the parade of Torahs. Candy and
gifts are showered on the children who escort the Torah and kiss it and
dance with it. The service is followed by a feast at home.

The holy pandemonium reaches a climax the following morning.
Again, there are seven hakafot. It is now a world-wide custom to go
outdoors for the seventh hakafa and dance in solidarity with Soviet
Jewry, which declared its renewed Jewishness publicly by dancing in
the streets of Moscow on Simchat Torah. As Jews spill out into full
public view, they declare the wonder and the glory of the eternal miracle: *Am Yisrael Chai!*—the people Israel lives! *Od Aveeynu Chai!*—our
Heavenly Father still lives! In traditional synagogues, mini-congrega-
tions are convened in various parts of the building. Thus, all present
(including women in liberal and egalitarian synagogues) have an opportunity to receive an aliyah (the honor of being called up to the
Torah) and recite the blessings of thanksgiving to God who chose
Israel "who gave us a Torah of truth and thus planted eternal life in
us."

As each person finishes the aliyah, it is traditional to pledge a contribution to charity. Then one makes kiddush over wine or liquor. With
each passing aliya the synagogue gets livelier and the happiness
higher (or is it that the synagogue gets higher and the happiness gets
livelier?).

For the final few aliyot, the entire congregation comes together
again for the special ceremonies. The first of these is called the *Kol
Ha'ne'arim* (all the children) aliya. The children under the age of twelve
or thirteen are gathered to the *bima*, the central podium where the
Torah is read. A group of adults hovers over the children, and a giant
canopy made up of large *talitot* (prayer shawls) held together by loving

human hands is stretched over the heads of the children. One adult takes the aliya and recites the blessing aloud with them. When the second blessing is finished, the classical blessing of Jacob is recited including the following: "Bless the children, and may my name and the name of my ancestors be called on them [that is, may they continue the line], and may they multiply and be fruitful in the midst of the land" (Genesis 48:16). With the shower of blessings comes a shower of candy and of song. The Jewish people have children, have life, have continuity. A generation ago the fate of cruelest death was decreed for every Jewish child and inflicted on more than one million of them. Today, they live, they grow, they laugh and dance, they rejoice to be Jewish, they are unafraid. Was there ever joy like this? Was there ever faith or power of life like this?

The final three aliyot evoke the classical symbols of marriage and covenant to extol the faithfulness of Jews to the Torah. The first is the *hattan Torah* (the groom of the Torah), an honor usually given to a person who exemplifies the love and practice of Torah. (In egalitarian settings, a *kallah* [bride] is sometimes substituted for any of the traditional *hattanim* [grooms.]). The hattan is called to the Torah with a special proclamation declaring his good deeds. In many synagogues the groom is escorted to the Torah under a *chuppah* (canopy) and with singing, dancing, and the throwing of candy and rice. In the good old days, in some central and eastern Europe congregations, people would light bonfires, leap over them, even shoot off gunpowder to add to the exhilaration of the "wedding."

The *hattan Torah* aliya completes the annual cycle of the reading of the entire Torah. The final portion of Deuteronomy is read. However, lest anyone think that the Torah reading is ever completed, the cycle is immediately begun anew by reading the first chapter of Genesis, the creation of the world.

This next aliya is called *hattan bereshit* (groom of Genesis). It is typically given to someone who has given outstanding service to the community of the people of Israel in the past year. As each day of the seven days of creation is read from Genesis, the congregation recites in joyous choral response to the reader: "And there was night and there was day, the first day . . . the second day," and so on. After each unit is completed, the assembled sing a *niggun* of rejoicing.

The last aliya is *maftir* (in some congregations it is now called *hattan maftir*—groom of the prophetic reading). Again, a person is chosen to be honored for appropriate service or exemplary living. The prophetic portion tells how Joshua succeeded to leadership when Moses died. Whoever may die, whatever leader or generation may perish, the circle goes on. Another Jew steps forward and says, "*Hineni*—here I am."

A joyous *mussaf* prayer is followed by a festive holiday meal at home. Community-wide visiting concludes this last day of Sukkot.

AFTERWORD

Many American Jews who have allowed their observance of tradition to diminish still observe Yom Kippur. This is a day of deprivation and denial, of guilt and self-flagellation. If Yom Kippur is their only contact with Judaism, one can only say: "O Lord, who is like your people, Israel?" What kind of devotion keeps people coming back year after year to a service that is long, exhausting, and solemn?

Russian Jews, totally cut off from tradition, had to rediscover Judaism or die. They chose life. With profound and prophetic understanding they chose to rediscover Simchat Torah first. What a way to recapture a religion! In song, in dance with or without understanding, with or without words, in the union of generations, in the voices of children blessing the Torah, in the love of adults blessing the children. It is a model way for all to rediscover the Torah.

"Whoever has not seen the *simchat beit ha shoevah* [the rejoicing of the water drawing] has not seen real joy in his life," says the Talmud.* The contemporary synagogue too often skimps on the heritage of uncontrolled elation. Could there be an experience that more profoundly unifies the generations than the rediscovery of how the family can celebrate together, of dance and joy in a house of sacredness, of nature for city dwellers, of religious purpose for the jaded, of concern for fellow Jews worldwide?

Says the Talmud: "The Shechinah (Divine Presence) comes upon us neither out of sadness nor out of raucous laughter . . . but out of the joy of mitzvah."† Perhaps this is why the prophet Zechariah predicted that in the end of days the whole world will come to celebrate Sukkot. It is in Jewish hands to bring that Presence into personal life and into the world at large in a deeper way than ever before in this generation, in rebuilding our land and our lives, in sharing and concern, out of enjoyment and love.

*Babylonian Talmud, Sukkah 51B.
†Babylonian Talmud, Pesachim 117A.

PART TWO:

Personal Life
Along the Way

THE PROMISE THAT UNIVERSAL PEACE can be reached and the earth turned into paradise is astounding. The demand to overcome sickness and poverty is revolutionary. Yet Judaism not only insists that these breakthroughs are possible but that they will develop in the context of normal human life. There will be a final redemption within human history—not beyond it. Judaism is not content to be a megavision of historical transformation. Nor would it simply deliver some cosmic revelation that dwarfs humans into insignificance with its gigantic purposes. The final perfection will come *through* humanity, not by rejection of or total transcendence of humanness. It follows that humans are the carriers of the divine message; the secular is the theater of religious action.

In pledging a covenantal partnership, the Infinite Source of Life has accepted humans, in all their finite and flawed nature, as the medium of divine activity. Human capacities will set the parameters and pace of *tikkun olam*. Human limitations are allowed for and human needs are met in the structure of Israel's redeeming faith. The Divine illuminates, orients, and instructs humans, but God does not and will not overwhelm them or destroy their dignity or integrity—not even to save them.

Pure ideological perfectionism would seek to create a fellowship only of believers. Kinship would be overridden by commitment. By contrast, Judaism is given to a family, and it makes the family the heart of its faith and religious life. The Divine thereby states the primacy of humanness over ideology. Relationship will not be dismissed. It would appear that there is a trade-off when religion is given to a family since the purity of the message is diluted by the loyalties and needs of families. But Judaism teaches that allowing such considerations does not represent a watering down. Incorporating family into religion upholds the dignity of humans. Family, relationships, and love are fundamental; they make the human being human. The Jewish mode of spiritual perfection, then, is to be achieved through family, not celibacy. The fulfillment of life is to come through directed and controlled pleasure, not through renunciation of the world.

If this religion is to be carried by a flesh-and-blood people, then, side by side with its call to perfect the world, Judaism has to offer a personal way through life. Two holiday clusters particularly address and nurture personal life; one is Shabbat, the other is the Days of Awe (Rosh Hashanah and Yom Kippur). These days were designed to orient the individual and the family toward redemption in their personal lives even as the pilgrimage holidays set the direction for the Jewish people collectively.

To the casual observer the notion of Shabbat as a day focused on personal life of the individual will come as a surprise. Shabbat is the classic communal day. Many of its special services, such as Torah reading, require a *minyan* (quorum) of ten. The creation of an *eruv* (enclosed domain) for Sabbath requires a community. Among contemporary Jews, other than the once or three times a year synagogue Jew, Shabbat is the day people are most likely to join other Jews in communal prayer and activities. The Shabbat service in the synagogue has always been the time and place for alerting Jews to the needs of worldwide Jewry.

More than any other holiday, Shabbat reflects the changing moods and concerns of *Clal Yisrael*, the total community of Israel. In the penitential season, Shabbat becomes Shabbat Shuva, the Sabbath of Return. In the weeks before Passover, four special Shabbat days prepare the communal agenda: Shabbat Shekalim, the occasion to give (or bear in memory) the annual gift to the national treasury for Temple sacrifices; Shabbat Zachor (Remember), a reminder of the Amalekite genocidal assault on Israel and of the ongoing dangers of anti-Semitism; Shabbat Parah (Red Heifer), the declaration of the need to purify in preparation for the Paschal lamb sacrifice and the central national feast; and Shabbat Hachodesh (the Month), an announcement of the arrival of the month of Passover, the new year of liberation. The Shabbat before Passover is Shabbat Hagadol (the Great Sabbath), the retelling of the great day when the Israelites sacrificed the lamb and joined the emancipation process. The three Shabbatot before Tisha B'Av are the three Sabbaths of Evil Tidings; the seven that follow are the Sabbaths of Consolation. The Shabbat before Tisha B'Av is Shabbat Hazon (Vision—full of the prophetic critique of Israel's behavior); the Shabbat after that fast day is Shabbat Nachamu (Console), full of consolation and comfort.

Yet, despite the tremendous communal dimension of the Shabbat, its outstanding impact and its focus remains the enrichment of personal life. In passing over from weekday to Shabbat, the individual enters a different world. The burdens of the world roll off one's back. In the phrase of a *zemirah* (Sabbath table song): "Anxiety and sighing flee." In the absence of business and work pressures, parents suddenly can listen better to children. In the absence of school and extracurricular pressures, children can hear their parents. Being is itself transformed. The state of inner well-being expands. As the Sabbath eve service text states: "The Lord ... blesses the seventh day and [thereby] bestows holy serenity on a people satiated with delight." The ability to reflect is set free. Creative thoughts long forgotten come back to mind. One's patience with life increases. The individual's capacity to cope is renewed.

Like Shabbat, the High Holy Days are not exclusively focused on personal life. Rosh Hashanah proclaims the rule of God; Yom Kippur speaks of grace and of divine mastery over the fate of nations and individuals. These days restore the cosmic frame to a religion that faces the temptation of zeroing in on the Jewish people and losing the perspective of universalism, thereby turning God into a tribal deity and Jewry into a private club.

Yet, above all, the High Holy Days nurture the power of renewal, of new birth. Without such renewal, the individual—indeed, the entire people—will become a burned-out case. Even redemption can become a cliché, a stale routine, a self-seeking ideology. In cutting through all the conventional self-flattering habits, in plumbing the depths of guilt and self-criticism, the Days of Awe remove the insulation that shields from pain but also deadens the heart. These days deepen the emotional life and extend the psychological range of the Jew, and enable the people to handle the whiplash and intensity of Judaism's dialectical moves.

Out of annual rebirth comes renewed vision. Out of Yom Kippur deprivations comes a new appreciation of pleasure. Sukkot follows Yom Kippur: "In the evening one lies down weeping; in the morning there is celebration [again]" (Psalms 30:6). Out of the yearly Days of Awe comes a release from self-centeredness that turns people to fresh consciousness of universal redemption again. Interconnected through the calendar, daily concerns and messianic tasks merge in the life of individuals, sustaining them through their personal odysseys. This occurs at the individual level even as the High Holy Days nurture, guide, and unify the entire people. As a result, the redemptive challenge need not kill individual concern or personal life. The individual's life, renewed, is strengthened sufficiently to sustain the burden of the national mission. The long march through history continues in every generation.

Judaism's central tactic to achieve tikkun olam is to create an experimental community—the children of Israel—seeking to care for its own. This would show an example, a human model, of how to move toward the final goal, step by step, without destroying the good that exists. In the community, no one would be abandoned. Shared memory, shared fate, and mutual responsibility would hold the people together and steady on course.

As Sukkot guides the community through the challenges along the covenantal way, so does Shabbat help the individual over the hurdles on the road to redemption. Shabbat is, quite simply, the dominant holy day of Judaism. Shabbat is celebrated fifty-two times a year, more days than all the other holidays combined. Thus, more than any other day, Shabbat sets the tone, inculcates the values, and teaches the message of Judaism. It is no accident that both Christianity and Islam, daughter religions of Judaism, took over the concept of a Sabbath although they shifted the day of the week in the process of differentiating themselves.

The first step in creating a living mechanism to cope with the challenge of the Jewish mission was to make the Exodus experience a motivating force and to keep its nurturing power continually present. The recreation of Exodus is not as total on Shabbat as it is on Passover or Sukkot, but the frequency of this day makes it an ideal way to keep the Exodus experience alive between one intense, searing reenactment and another. Every Shabbat day is a weekly release from labor that becomes a mini-Exodus experience.

On this day, every individual, including every servant, goes from the bondage of toil to freedom from work. Every seven days the Shabbat summons up the memory of liberation; the ritual and liturgy proclaim freedom for everyone. As for the total Jewish community, the practices and rules of Shabbat emancipate the people from the tyranny of the world and its judgments. At least in the private inner world of Jewry, sheltered in the Shabbat peace, Jews are dignified and free. Shabbat is living space when the world is too close.

The Shabbat is a vehicle of communal solidarity. Every week it is a theological reminder, a sign between Israel and God of the covenant that links them. The Shabbat has also played a practical role in segregating Jews from non-Jews while bringing Jews together in fellowship, prayer, eating, learning, and acts of mutual responsibility (*tzedakah*).

The very fact that there is a long way to the final goal poses certain risks: The people of Israel can lose sight of the goal and thereby distort the values of Judaism into self-righteousness or super-preservationism. There is a real human need to take the present moment seriously and to participate in it unselfconsciously. Yet that participation can cut off the connection to the beginning or the end. One little step, then another, minor adjustment by minor adjustment, can add up to a total deviation from the path. Shabbat reduces these risks. Freeing the people from the mass of contemporary experiences, Shabbat restores the root and the goal—the Exodus and the messianic vision—to the center of life. Through Shabbat, the vision of redemption is made concrete with food, song, family time, talk, and learning; thus it is infused into the masses.

No people could have carried the burden of the tension for millennia without being eaten up by the strain and guilt of the task unless they had extraordinary satisfactions along the way. What made Jewish continuity possible? The joy of Jewish living. The majority of Jews persisted because life was so good. Every Shabbat brought the family together with the necessary leisure to be one's self and to enter into deeper relationships. Each holiday had its own joys, its own sacred objects, decorations, and clothes to delight the mind and the heart. Life was with people. No Jew was alone; both God and fellow human beings cared. In the bosom of family and community, the challenges and strains of daily living and the existential anxieties of sickness, aging, and death could be met.

Even more than the collective, the individual needs nurturing. People cannot live just for tomorrow; they need a personal life along the way. No one should try to save the world without having an inner life; that way is an invitation to ant colony socialism. The halacha had to bring out the humanness in people so they would keep growing in a hundred different settings. Tradition had to develop an individual's love for life. How else could people embrace living with a full heart even as they yearned to improve it?

Embracing the vision creates an enormous tension in the individual because Judaism does not draw back from the present flawed reality. Judaism clings to life and at one and the same moment seeks to redeem it. Human cancer and divine concern are contradictory and irreconcilable, yet Judaism affirms the seriousness and the reality of both phenomena. The concept of redemption would appear to be a hopeless, almost insane affirmation, but the insanity is temporary; it is the madness of the one who sees the future now. Classical Judaism insists:

Do not be intimidated by the vast gap between ideal and reality. You have God's promise that the abyss will be overcome. You must develop the infinite wisdom to know that it can be done, the infinite love to want to do it, and the infinite patience to persist until it is done.

The key resource that gives individuals the ongoing strength to meet that challenge is the holy day of Shabbat. Recurring weekly, the Shabbat suffuses and guides every day of the week. Sabbath day supplies the most basic nurturing of selfhood and of family that Judaism provides. In its context, eating, sexuality, and relationship take on new richness. Shabbat incarnates the ultimate Jewish dream and makes it real. Weekly, it gives a taste of the final redemption and thus takes what would otherwise be a demanding, hopeless task, one that empties life of meaning, and fills it with life and joy. Shabbat is the most frequent Jewish holy day and the most present. Shabbat is the inexhaustible source that nurtures the people who carry the Divine Presence in the world—the people of the dream.

CHAPTER FIVE

The Dream and
How to Live It:
Shabbat

ISRAEL—THE PEOPLE OF THE DREAM

THE VERY FIRST CHAPTER of the Bible records a dream, a vision of the world in its perfect state, an Eden of order and beauty in which life emerges from the divine ground of existence. All life is related and intertwined, and the crown of physical creation is humankind. Every single human being, man and woman, shares the ultimate dignity of having been created in the image of God.

In the real world, however, poverty and deprivation are widespread, so human life is devalued. Every year children in the third world die from a critical loss of fluids and salt, a loss that could be stopped by the administration of sugar, salt, and water in the right proportions. The cost of this "miracle cure" is ten cents a dose. For want of that simple mixture, six million children die each year.

According to the Genesis account, this world originally was and is still meant to be a paradise. But only when there is peace, with abundant resources and an untrammeled right to live, will the world be structured to sustain the infinite value of the human being. This is the heart of Judaism, the dream.

Jewish existence without the dream is almost inconceivable. The drawing power of the vision has kept Jews faithful to their mission

127

over several millennia. Expulsion, persecution, and destruction have assaulted but never obliterated the dream. Jews have repeatedly given everything, including their very lives, to keep it alive. And when catastrophe shattered the vision, Jews spent their lives renewing it. The question is: From where can these people draw the strength to renew their dream again and again? The answer of Jewish tradition is: Give people just a foretaste of the fulfillment, and they will never give it up. The Shabbat is that taste.

Jews gained an extra measure of hope and optimism in the face of adversity thanks to the dream, but many dreamers have become soured and embittered by frustration because of the continuing lack of realization of their hope. How long can the Jews go on dreaming? How long can the Messiah tarry before the Jewish spirit will be embittered by the unrealized dream? What happens to a dream deferred? Will it dry up like a raisin in the sun?

Living with a dream is treacherous business. The dream gives and the dream takes away. Dreams can brighten an oppressive reality, or they can make the everyday appear drab and repellent. Dreams can give life purpose or rob it of value and meaning. Dealing with this double edge has been a major challenge for the Jewish people on their great trek through history toward redemption. In trying to live out a dream, Jews face a "Catch 22" situation. Without the dream it hardly seems worth living as a Jew. With it, everyday unredeemed life hardly seems worth living at all. In history, dreams have stimulated revolutionary ardor. They also have turned oppressed people into passive sufferers escaping into their fantasies instead of seeking to change their conditions. The question has been: Which tendency will win out in Jewish history? The Shabbat day is Judaism's central attempt to inject the dream into life while preventing its negative side effects.

Paradoxically, Judaism affirms both the dream and the reality, both the perfect, redeemed world to be brought into being by human effort and the imperfect, unredeemed world of today. However, it is extraordinarily difficult to live in the dialectical tension of the dream and the reality. The greater the power of the dream, the more it seizes the imagination. The more its fulfillment is postponed, the more it generates dissatisfactions that tear people apart.

The way to cope with the tension is to live dialectically, which is the biblical way. This means, first, to accept the world, affirm its sanctity, participate in it fully, and enjoy it. At the same time, the divine ideal prods the people to fundamental criticism of society's status quo. By living in the world while at the same time offering a testimony of hope to redeem it, the Jews have become the prophets of permanent dissent, demanding a messianic perfection and insisting that it is not yet here. In the rabbinic, halachic style, this permanent revolution moves in ceaseless steps toward justice, acting in the best way possible in each moment until the final goal is achieved.

Yet this dialectical way also has problems. Permanent dissent all too easily turns sour or cynical. There is no real enjoyment if the "not yet" robs every present moment of its intrinsic value. Long before the dream is realized, its pursuit may empty our waking life of significance. On the other hand, unrestrained affirmation of this life increases the risk of being absorbed into the status quo of society while the continual swing from participation to criticism continually raises the danger of overreaction and even of unleashing runaway, destructive utopianism.

Is humanity condemned, then, to oscillate continually between complacent surrender and radical nihilism? Have we really no choice other than to swallow this world whole or run away from it?

SHABBAT: THE RHYTHM OF PERFECTION

The classic Jewish answer to our dilemma is to set up a rhythm of perfection. The first movement is to plunge into this world as a participant. Then, just when there may be a danger of complete absorption into this world, there is an alternate reality to enter into: the Shabbat. Stepping outside the here and now, the community creates a world of perfection. Through total immersion in the Shabbat experience, Jews live the dream *now*.

The world of the Shabbat is totally different than the weekday universe: There is no work to do, no deprivation. On Shabbat, there is neither anxiety nor bad news. Since such a world does not yet exist in space, it is first created in time, on the seventh day of the week. Jews travel through time in order to enter a perfect world for a night and a day. The goal is to create a reality so complete and absorbing that these time travelers are caught up in its values and renewed.

The Shabbat is the foretaste of the messianic redemption. But even as this enclave of perfection is carved out in the realm of time, the world goes on as usual in the realm of surrounding space. This is why Shabbat needs a community in order to be credible. By an act of will, the community creates this sacred time and space, and agrees to live by its rules. For nineteen hundred years, before saying grace after meals on weekdays, Jews in the exile chanted Psalm 137: "By the rivers of Babylon, there we sat down and wept when we remembered Zion. . . . How can we sing the Lord's song in a strange land?" But on Shabbat, as the sun set and the power of evil was shut out, Jews were transported in their imagination to a perfect, rebuilt Jerusalem. It was so real to them that on this day, before saying grace, they sang Psalm 126: "When the Lord returned us to Zion, we lived as in a dream; then our mouths were filled with laughter and our tongue flowed with song."

The Shabbat comes to an end weekly, but it creates an appetite and a satisfaction that lasts through the week until it is renewed again.

The power of this rhythm of redemption is that it allows the fullest participation in the world as it is while giving recurrent fulfillment to the ultimate dreams of perfection. This periodic taste of fulfillment became the protection against the bitterness of gratification indefinitely postponed. Every seven days, the people of Israel were "married" again to the Divine Lover and to the beloved Shabbat queen. On Friday night, Jews sing a special Shabbat prayer-poem, Lecha Dodi: "Come my beloved to greet the bride, the Shabbat. . . ."* By this expression of weekly marriage and consummation with the Lord, the people Israel was protected from becoming the eternally pining lover whose capacity for real love shrivels up in a longing kept permanently within.

This partial consummation takes the frustration quotient out of the dream. It makes the dream too real to dismiss, too ecstatic to set aside even for the delights of the status quo. Yet Shabbat also allows the joy and affirmation of life-as-it-is to be full-hearted. It gives the revolutionary a sunniness that comes from joy realized; this mellows the puritanical fervor of the radical mission. Similarly, it injects a subversive, heady taste of what could be, even in those who are the beneficiaries of the status quo. It is a rhythm that gives strength to carry on the long-term calling of trying to realize the impossible dream. The vision, realized in such moments along the way, gives the strength to walk indefinitely through the unending corridors of history.

The Shabbat experience nurtures that special kind of love called chessed. Chessed embraces the world even in its grimmest reality. Because love accepts life totally, love is not discouraged by its flaws. Simultaneously, chessed affirms life's capacity to be perfected. By embracing all of being, chessed sets in motion the very process of becoming perfect. A person blessed with the wisdom of chessed knows that life is rooted in the infinite. Therefore, life can grow out of its fetters and flaws. Life can outgrow death by creating more life before death comes. Therefore, notwithstanding the universal power of death, life will overcome it.

*Philip Birnbaum, Daily Prayer Book (New York: Hebrew Publishing Company, 1977), pp. 245–47.

SHABBAT: THE ANTI-REALITY
WHOSE ESSENCE IS PERFECTION

Shabbat is the temporary anti-reality of perfection. For approximately twenty-five hours (Jews traditionally add some extra time to expand the realm of the good), all things are seen through the eyes of love, as if all of nature were perfect, in harmony with itself and with humanity. Normally, all the world conspires to persuade people that business cannot function without their personal presence, that great opportunities are being missed, that catastrophe looms, that crisis has struck and demands immediate attentiveness. For a day, Jews, dreaming, hear none of this. On Shabbat, it is not really that one is forbidden to work, it is that all is perfect, there is nothing to do.

Is this perfect day a fugue? An escape from reality? In the Shabbat itself, there is an exquisite dialectic that deals with this danger: The evil in the world is so durable and unyielding that a person seeking to uphold its perfection may be tempted to do violence to reality. The alternative is to live the Shabbat in trust and faith. Trust allows people to let go, to live in the realm of perfection without fear of their vulnerability or future disappointment. Faith is the commitment to live a life that is growing, to be so nurtured by chessed and the taste of Shabbat as to go out and transform the world.

The Rabbis say that in chanting the kiddush, the sanctification over wine at the beginning of the Shabbat evening meal, Jews give witness to the original perfection of divine creation. The prayer, as the day, is testimony to the ultimate truth of the final redemption. For six days a week, the Shabbat can only be testimony—a tale of what might be— until paradise is finally realized. But the pleasure in living it is so great that there is joy in giving the witness. "The world was meant to be perfect," says the Shabbat. "Experience that perfection. Now, go and make it happen!"

To be able to testify honestly (without resorting to avoidance or denial of reality), the witness must have a strong element of play and of humor. The world is flawed and full of suffering. To enter into the Shabbat spirit wholeheartedly, then, one must play with reality.

Shabbat is a day of imaginary boundaries. Put up a string around its neighborhoods and a vast city of millions becomes, in a halachic sense, a private domain, as if it were one's backyard. On this day the dream is so real that the world becomes the deviation. (Perhaps this is why it is a mitzvah to sleep on the Shabbat day.) On this day Jews are central to the drama of salvation instead of being the marginal outcast people of the weekday universe. All week long the ghetto Jew might have been a pariah pack-peddler. On this day he takes off the stained commoner's clothes, dons Shabbat finery, and reenacts his "true" role— that of cosmic royalty, the bearer of salvation.

This is the truth behind Ahad Ha'am's line, "The Sabbath kept the Jews more than the Jews kept the Sabbath."* After living in an atmosphere of demeaning images all week long, the Jew goes into a sabbatical hyperbaric chamber and breathes the pure air of redemption and dignity. In that breathing, the wholeness and integrity of self are restored. This is why, when the walls of the ghetto came down, Jews emerged with an ability to respond to every opportunity and calling. The Jews had not internalized the contempt of the outside world, nor had they been housebroken to the slave image. They had played with reality, had lived in an alternative world, until reality itself changed and they were off.

This is how the Zionist dream survived for two thousand years without becoming a bitter mockery of life. How can people cry out every year for nineteen hundred years, "Next year in Jerusalem," without becoming depressed by the fact that 365 days later they are still in exile, still calling out the slogan of hope? The answer is that on every Shabbat, Jews preenact the coming of messianic restoration. For a day, the sounds of joy and gladness, the voice of the groom and the bride, reverberate in the streets of a restored Zion. For twenty-five hours the heavenly Jerusalem exists on earth—in France and Poland, in Yemen and Bombay. No wonder that when the road to the earthly Jerusalem opened up, there were Jews who knew exactly what to do and where to go.

The weekly encounter with messianic perfection saves one from internalizing the indignity and injustice of the status quo. The taste of salvation gives new energy to resist the counsels of despair and to press on for higher levels of dignity and justice for all. It gives the Jew and all who benefit from the Sabbath the renewed strength to affirm with renewed credibility the classic proclamation: "I believe with perfect faith in the coming of the Messiah, and even though the Messiah tarry, I will continue to wait every day."†

And when the final deliverance comes, there will be those who will know what to do . . . where to go.

A DAY OF BEING: WORK

In Praise of Creation

Throughout history most people have lived as slaves to nature and were eventually broken on the wheel of time. To this day, most people

*Ahad Ha'am, *Al Parashat Derachim* (Tel Aviv: Dvir, 1946), vol. 3, p. 30.
†Philip Birnbaum, *Daily Prayer Book*, p. 155.

struggle to eke out a living and earn their bread at the cost of their lives. To dream of perfecting the world is to signal revolt against the fate of permanent deprivation.

Two components are necessary for liberation. One component is an activating vision of a better world. Most humans cut their self-respect to the measure of their reality; religions often affirm the appropriateness of this fate. Judaism injected the dream of perfection into the bloodstream of humanity. Once experienced and internalized, the dream leads to a challenge of the status quo. The other component is the development of the capacity to change the world: an end to human powerlessness. Perfection needs power. The greater the power, the greater the dignity. In the words of Rabbi Soloveitchik:

> The brute's existence is an undignified one because it is a helpless existence. . . . Men of old who could not fight disease and succumbed in multitudes to yellow fever or any other plague with degrading helplessness could not lay claim to dignity. Only the man who builds hospitals, discovers therapeutic techniques, and saves lives is blessed with dignity. Man of the seventeenth and eighteenth centuries who needed several days to travel from Boston to New York was less dignified than modern man who attempts to conquer space, boards a plane at the New York airport at midnight and takes, several hours later, a leisurely walk along the streets of London.*

The antithesis of the human as passive victim is the human responding to the biblical calling to "fill the earth and conquer it . . . to work it and protect it." The end product of human mastery of the earth will be a world that sustains the maximum of human dignity. Someday, when we make the earth a paradise, all will be on a permanent sabbatical so they can spend their lives creating rather than earning just to stay alive. Meanwhile, to improve the world, to increase productivity and bring us one step closer, is to respond to the covenantal imperatives; it is holy work.

Science and technology are commanded, consecrated work. In the words of Psalms, "You have made the human only a little lower than the angels and crowned him with glory and dignity. You set him to rule over your handiwork" (Psalm 8:6–7). "I shall *walk before the Lord* in the lands of the living" (Psalm 116:9). "This refers to walking and working in the marketplace," says the Talmud. To work, or to do business, is to stand before the Lord, because the material base of existence is basic to human dignity.

*Joseph B. Soloveitchik, "The Lonely Man of Faith," in *Tradition: A Journal of Orthodox Jewish Thought*, vol. 7, no. 21 (Summer 1965), pp. 14–15.

As the earth supports a higher level of worldly living, human dignity is enhanced. Human dignity is a category of holiness. To be holy is to be special and unique. The divine fullness of being and uniqueness is the ultimate holiness. Humans strive to come ever closer to this model and to shape a world in which this is manifest. The greater the margins of life and wealth, the more room there is for human perfection.

In the same spirit, the Rabbis taught that the human being is commanded to settle the earth. Creating civilization is a mitzvah called *lashevet*, to settle or civilize: "*Lo tohu bera-ah, lashevet yetzarah*" (Isaiah 45:18). "It [the universe] is not made to be void; it is created to be settled." The world is to be filled with creatures in the image of God. As they fill and perfect the universe, they make manifest the presence of God. The image of God testifies to its Master and Model. And as the world is improved it is revealed more manifestly as the divine sanctuary that it is.

The Shabbat begins, therefore, with the affirmation of human work. The most spiritual of days is built on the rock of material reality, on work and production. "Six days a week you shall work and do all your creative labor and the seventh day is Shabbat to the Lord your God." The very concept of work defined for purposes of Shabbat is modeled on creation, on God's work. This is to say that human creativity and production are forms of *imitatio Dei*, of being like God.

What is creation—God's work—like? There are thirty-nine categories of work in the Sabbath law, types of work that we are commanded to engage in all week and which are given up on Shabbat. Work is not measured by energy expended or effort involved. To work is to create something new; to work is to add something, some value or accomplishment that was not there before. The Rabbis used the term *melechet machshevet*, that is, work that involves the realization of thought, not mindless activity. It is labor guided by a plan, directed toward a goal. The result is not purely accidental or just an unintentional by-product of something else. It is constructive work, not destructive. Interestingly, if one spent twenty-four hours on Shabbat just being destructive, no matter how much effort was involved one would not be directly overriding the biblical Shabbat law, which defines work as constructive labor. Nonetheless, the Rabbis added a secondary prohibition of destructive labor, for they felt it runs counter to the spirit of Shabbat. Of course, sometimes one must destroy in order to build, for example, to clear away an old building in order to build a new one. In such a case, the work of destruction is considered part of construction.

Constructive work should be approached with the same care and awareness that characterizes religious activity. Indeed, there are many religious acts that serve as spiritual and mental preparation for constructive labor. One is a centuries-old Jewish tradition of washing the hands ritually upon rising in the morning. This mini-rebirth ceremony symbolizes the end of the cycle of sleep and the awakening to work in the world. Even as a priest pours water over his hands to remove the routine of his previous occupation in preparation for the service in the sanctuary, so the devout Jew awakens and pours water on his or her hands to cleanse them and dedicate them to labor in the divine sanctuary, that is, in the world itself. And just as ritual acts are to be done faithfully and exactly, down to the last detail, so, too, work is to be done honestly and meticulously.

The devaluation of business that exists even in American capitalist culture is due to the failure to see the redeeming character and significance of such work. Increased wealth alone is not redemptive, particularly if it is not distributed widely, but it supplies the infrastructure of care and health, the margin of existence that frees people from poverty and enables them to lead lives of greater dignity. Performing this capitalist function of increasing wealth is a fulfillment of the call to do good to others and participate in the work of redemption.

The thirty-ninth category of labor prohibited on the Sabbath (the ban on carrying items from one place to another) does not appear to meet the halachic test of being work that physically added or created something that was not there before. This classification of work might best be understood as the entrepreneurial category; it is an affirmation of the creative function of business and trade. To transfer oil from ten thousand feet below the surface or from a remote desert where it is unavailable for human use to the central terminals of industrial productivity; to change the level of utility of an area by developing value and usefulness where there was none before; and, by extension, to bring together borrower and lender, and through creative financing enable production or use of a raw material or product that could not be produced or otherwise used is to engage in the art of creation.

One can apply this concept of carrying or transfer to assay various forms of activity. Speculation in commodities, since it makes possible orderly protection for the manufacturers and processors of food, is the work of creation. Speculation in stocks as part of the formation of overall capital markets has the dignity of participating in creation. The markets are the mechanisms to pool savings and help finance the firms that create and produce. One might even be able to use this criterion as a relative measure of "holiness." Diverting money to a takeover (except where the takeover will lead to new productivity and increased efficiency) or other forms of activity that are primarily paper shuffling (perhaps a tax shelter that is purely for tax avoidance) would not be a mitzvah; it would certainly be less meritorious than using it for venture capital that opens up new productive possibilities.

This halachic entrepreneurial principle is not intended to give carte blanche to all forms of acquisition. Just as a mitzvah or ritual act cannot be based on stealing or exploitation, so labor or work cannot be sanctified if it is based on pure exploitation. The dividing line is suggested by the halacha itself which considers unfit to serve as witnesses those who are usurious lenders (those who take more interest than is justified or appropriate)* and professional gamblers (those who make a living by pure transfer of wealth from one to another through the mechanism of change where there is no economic productivity attached to the process). The major reason given for this disqualification is that such people "do not participate in the settling/civilizing of the world." Since nothing constructive comes out of their work, they are considered—like thieves—to be living off the exploitation of others. Such activity is a sin just as creativity and productive work are mitzvot. The sin is acting ungodlike; it is exploiting instead of creating.

Creating wealth is hardly the only form of dignified labor. In a world in which clerical work is often considered of low status, the halacha states that to write (to type) even two letters, that is, a word, a bit of communication, is work—an act of creation. In this light, work is not simply making a living; it is the expression of the divine, creative spirit within the human. Done right, work—dignity through labor—can be compared to the study of Torah or religious service. "One may do much or one may do little; it is all one, provided each directs his heart to Heaven."†

In this spirit, the thirty-nine categories of work prohibited on the Sabbath are directly modeled on the types of work done by the priests in the Temple. All work is classified in one of these categories. The message is that doing work in the world is holy work, just like doing work in the Holy Temple. Just as the priest served in the holy sanctuary built by humans, so does the human being working in the world serve in the holy sanctuary built by God. The universe *is* the divine sanctuary. In perfecting the world, the human being becomes co-creator with the Divine, "a partner in the work of Creation."

THE PATHOLOGIES OF POWER

Why must work be renounced on the Sabbath? Here again the dialectical nature of Judaism equips us to deal with polar truths. The mastery and productivity that the Torah celebrates bear within themselves the seeds

---

*Compare Psalms 15:5 and commentary of R. David Kimchi *ad. loc.* with Leviticus 25:35 and following, Deuteronomy 15:1–3, and commentary of the Abarbanel *ad. loc.*
†Babylonian Talmud, Berachot 17A.

of potential evil. Power can lead to the abuse of nature; production can lead to alienation. Both can lead to idolatry and slavery.

Science involves the desacralization of the world. We use nature and learn to treat it instrumentally. This treatment becomes mere manipulation, however, if the sense of reverence for nature is lost. As people are conditioned to analyze, to take things apart, they no longer see the world holistically. Once nature becomes pure object, pollution and abuse are not far behind.

So one day a week humans are called to enter a state of rest. "The Sabbath is the day of peace between man and nature"; work "is any kind of disturbance of the man/nature equilibrium."* In the state of sabbatical harmony, people relate to nature differently; they experience it as sacred and savor its mystery. From this perspective nature is endowed with intrinsic dignity independent of any instrumental usefulness. When the scientist returns to work on the weekday, the double vision of nature stays with him, protecting nature from exploitation.

Shabbat also saves people from becoming alienated from and oppressed by the fruits of their labor. Technology involves building and shaping the external world. It thus creates a solid existence outside of the human being. As Marx and others have suggested, the production machine is first reified, then absolutized, then worshiped. When value is projected onto the external product or machine, the human may be devalued.

Idolatry is not merely worship of stone and wood. Idolatry consists of giving absolute authority to something relative, that is, to anything other than the Divine. In degrading another human-in-the-image-of-God for the sake of achievement or profit, in sacrificing relationships for work, in wantonly destroying some part of the world for production, one sets up work as the ultimate authority and abides by its dictates. That is idolatry. The Sabbath is designed to take one out of such a framework.

All acts of abuse through work—be it an engineer producing an unsafe car, an industrialist dumping a carcinogen on the environment, or a businessman sacrificing ethics—tacitly give the profit goal an absolute status. To walk away from production and live the Sabbath is to renounce the absoluteness of the profit motive; it is intended to psychologically free the individual to impose moral values on his or her work as well.

There is grave danger in idolatry of wealth. If a person is located in a man-made universe of finite values, with work as the ultimate goal, the parameters of human value shrink. A society that worships wealth usually degrades the value of the poor or perhaps all humans. Net worth is confused with intrinsic worth.

*Erich Fromm, *The Forgotten Language* (New York: Rinehart & Co., 1951), p. 244.

Finally, as human involvement in work deepens, the labor in itself can become a form of slavery. The test of stopping short of servitude is the ability to stop working, to assert mastery over the work instead of succumbing to its lures and demands. This is the central function of Shabbat: "Six days [a week] you work/create; on the seventh day you rest/stop" (Exodus 34:21).

THE RHYTHM OF BEING AND DOING

The medicine for the pathologies of power/work is the same. Through Shabbat, Jewish tradition proposes a dialectical movement: to put aside the acts of creation and the products of work and to refocus on the sacredness of the human being. This is achieved by spending the entire day of Shabbat on being, not doing. It is a proclamation, "I am, not I do." If I could do nothing, I would still be me, a person of value. Thus, the individual reasserts the primacy of human value and the principle of the intrinsic worth of human existence, "unjustified" by productivity.

The inability to stop work is not always imposed by an outside oppressor; it may reflect a psychological enslavement of the individual. Workaholics abound who cannot ever relinquish work. Many people go to pieces on vacation or retirement. For the same reason holidays are, notoriously, periods of higher rates of depression and suicide. The ability to stop working is, therefore, an assertion of an inner freedom. In turn, the capacity for distancing enables one to resist absolute demands, even at work.

The exquisite dialectic of the Shabbat also seeks to break the classic tension between God's power and human power. In the Prometheus myth, the gods avenge themselves on the one who empowered humanity. In medieval religions the primary emphasis was away from worldliness and toward anticipation of the divine redeemer. This led to a suspicion of human power; powerlessness was the preferred theological mode because weakness made humankind dependent on God. No wonder, then, that modernizers who sought human liberation concluded that to free humanity, it was necessary to get free of God. This is the driving force in Marx's denunciation of religion as the "opium of the people" and in Freud's insistence that rejection of the illusion of a Heavenly Father is crucial to human maturation.

In contrast to these conceptions, Judaism offered the covenantal model—a partnership between God and man. In the initial phase, God is the initiator and driving force, but for the sake of human freedom and dignity, God self-limits. Humanity is to grow into ever greater responsibility. The scriptural passage on Shabbat states: "On it He rested from all His work which the loving God had created *la-asot*" (literally, to be made) (Genesis 2:3). Kabbalah and commentary interpret this verse to mean "the world which the Loving God had created to be made"; the world is left unfinished to be perfected by men and women.

However, as human power grows, it can easily lead to loss of perspective. Mastery leads to arrogance vis-à-vis creation. Power leads to making absolute the holder of power. The human forgets he is the image of God and thinks of himself as God. This idolatry is all the more credible because of the incredible power unleashed by modern technology. Totalitarian dreams have flourished in the modern period because unlimited power and control seem within grasp. This explosive expansion of potency raises the possibility of absolute power corrupting absolutely, for the shock of coming up against the limits tempts overweening tyrants to resort to unbridled use of force. The ultimate totalitarian outburst—the Nazi Holocaust—used overwhelming force to set up a world (Auschwitz) in which certain humans were God; they exercised the power of life and death. When mortals set themselves up as God, they create Hell. It is surely no accident that all the murderous fury of that Hell was turned on the Jews whose very existence gives witness to a Divine beyond human manipulation and control—a Divine, therefore, that serves as a check on absolute human claims.

Yet renunciation of power is not the solution to abuse of power. Renunciation would keep the human immature and condemn humanity to poverty and sickness. The Shabbat offers an alternative: a rhythm of work and abstinence, an alternation of creatorhood and creaturehood. In reciting the Kiddush, the Jew gives witness to creation. This is a statement that the human is a creature among creatures. Unlimited power is tempered by putting it aside temporarily and by affirming limits.

As they give testimony to creation, Jews witness to the covenantal partnership between God and man. The Shabbat rest does not express any divine weakness, nor does refraining from work on Shabbat express any human incapacity. The Shabbat rest teaches us that change is completed by peace, and action is enriched by contemplation. Since power is sometimes perfected by restraint, the overwhelming power of God is put aside to allow a truly equal partnership between God and humanity or between one human and another. Shabbat is the completion and celebration of that partnership.

A DAY OF BEING: ON BECOMING HUMAN

From Work to Self

The movement from weekday work to Shabbat rest is a move from acting outward to developing inward. The Shabbat is more than a day of being, it is a day of becoming. Rest is more than leisure from work, it is a state of inner discovery, tranquility, and unfolding. The ability to accept and affirm life in its own right frees me to become more than I am—through self-development and through intensified relationships with others. The Sabbath commandment is not just to stop working, it is actively to achieve *menuchah* (rest) through self-expression, transformation, and renewal. On this day humans are freed and commanded to explore themselves and their relationships until they attain the fullness of being.

In biblical teaching, the body and soul are intertwined in one continuum of life. The soul is a consciousness growing in the ground of soma, increasing in freedom and complexity as life grows upward toward its Creator. Deprivations of body shrink the soul, even as the soul's disturbances affect the body. The bodily self-denials commanded on Yom Kippur—not to eat, drink, wash, or anoint—are included under the rubric, "You shall torment (deny) your souls" (Leviticus 23:27). Caring for and pleasuring the body is a vital part of the re-souling process of the day. One welcomes the Sabbath by putting on good clothes. Clothes do not make the man, but they are part of an environment of expansiveness and self-affirmation. The Shabbat is ushered in with the lighting of candles (warmth and light expand the soul) and welcomed with a sanctification song, the Kiddush, celebrated over a cup of wine. A special Sabbath requirement is that there be an extra meal during this day. (Say the Rabbis: There is an "extra" soul in each person on Shabbat so there should be an extra meal.)

Hot food is to be served. Since cooking is a prohibited labor on Shabbat, *cholent* was invented—a dish that could be cooked before the Sabbath yet would stay on the stove for hours without spoiling, indeed, getting tastier all the while.

From Self to Relationship

Around the table, in the presence of family, the Sabbath meals overflow with conversation and catching up on family matters. As the joy unfolds, song wells up, naturally. A whole tradition of special Shabbat table songs (*zemirot*) developed to express the delight of the day. Since no one need rush off to business, the meal is extended with talk and words of Torah. The pressures of the week dissolve, and parents find time to relate to their children, exploring issues between them at leisure. Parents become the source of wisdom, the indispensable keepers of memory; learning together becomes a major activity of Shabbat. So important are relationships and intimacy that the Rabbis permitted a married woman to use certain cosmetics on Shabbat that were prohibited to single women.

One striking expression of this relationship enhancement is the tradition of celebrating Shabbat with sexual intercourse. It is a special Shabbat mitzvah to make love on Friday night. In biblical language, to have sexual intercourse is to *know* someone. It is the act that combines mutual understanding and physical attraction: Desire and relationship culminate in an act of union that touches the partners in body and soul. The lack of pressure and the leisure of Shabbat contribute to the possibility of a higher degree of intimacy and openness with each other. In turn, the union enriches and deepens the individual's sense of well-being and value. Thus, it strengthens the process of becoming more human on this day.

The changed environment also generates self-confrontation. In a different setting, the individual discovers talents and feelings that are not evident in the regular course of work. Removed from the routine preoccupations of the everyday, the individual cannot escape into busyness. The mindset of allowing things just to be is strengthened. Harvey Cox has compared this to the Buddhist concept of *sati*, or "mindfulness": "It is being fully aware of the apple tree but having no judgments, plans, or prospects for it.* The Shabbat clears the way for meditation, which becomes more than a reflection on the self. In Norman Lamm's words, it opens a personal inner silence "in which you make yourself available for a higher impression."† People who are too preoccupied for it to happen all week long may open up to the possibility of a spiritual experience.

This spirituality is an essential aspect of Judaism. In modern times, there has been a strong tendency to reduce Judaism to a system of universal ethics. Under this dispensation, to be a Jew is to be committed to social welfare. But this is a bowdlerized Judaism. Judaism is also a spiritual way that connects the individual and the nation to a divine ground. The Divine is the source of life and renewal. It is not that modern thinkers have totally falsified Judaism; there *is* a strong this-worldly ethical dynamic in Judaism: "Love your neighbor as yourself; I am the Lord" (Leviticus 19:18). Ritual acts serving as substitutes for ethics or performed by evildoers are offensive to God: "Even when you increase your prayers, I will not listen—because your hands are full of blood" (Isaiah 1:15). But life is rooted in the Divine and would die if it separated permanently from its source. Religious life is part of a healthy human culture. According to classical Judaism, ethics is the way to serve God; ritual is the way to connect to God. Shabbat unifies the two aspects in one experience.

Two major differences exist between Shabbat and other religious

---

*Harvey Cox, "Meditation and Sabbath," *Harvard Magazine*, September-October, 1977, p. 43.
†Norman Lamm, "Sabbath Rest," in *Yavneh Shiron*, Eugene Flink and Tom Ackerman, editors (New York: Yavneh, 1969), p. 43.

meditation disciplines, as Harvey Cox has pointed out. In most cultures, East and West, prayer and meditation are turned over to an elite. Shabbat, however, is given to all. All Jews are free to engage in spiritual disciplines, starting with prayer. The ethical dimension of Shabbat is reflected in a special concern that the weak, the poor, the slave also be granted rest. Cox suggests that such rest is mandatory in order to ensure the extension of its benefits to the poor and the powerless.* Furthermore, the Shabbat is extended to others through sharing. One act of preparation is to give to charity. (How many Jews tell of being trained for tzedakah by the weekly ritual of their mothers putting money into the Jewish National Fund "blue box" or a charity *pushke* [box] as the last preparatory act before lighting candles?) *Hachnassat orchim*, extending hospitality to guests who would otherwise have no adequate Shabbat meal, is considered an especially great mitzvah. "Extending hospitality [to guests] is greater than welcoming Shechina, the Divine Presence."† Jewish folklore tells how eagerly people vied for guests in synagogue on Friday night so that Shabbat would be properly celebrated in their homes. Whenever there was joy and feasting on holy days, the Torah instructed Jews to share with the widow, the orphan, the stranger, the poor.

From Self to Community

As consciousness expands, it moves beyond the self. Judaism views the self as the basis of human dignity, legitimately central in life yet incomplete of itself. "If I am not for myself, who will be? But when I am for myself [alone], what am I?" said Hillel. The complete self is rooted in both the ground of the transcendent and of the community.

On Shabbat, the regular prayer services are extended to incorporate more prayers because the pressures of the weekday are not driving people. Prayer lifts the earthbound soul and transfers its center of gravity from the mundane to the transcendent reality. On Shabbat, that spiritual reality is richer, more vivid, more attainable. The individual becomes aware of being part of a cosmic process, linked to a divine source of life. I am limited, but the infinite ground of Being upholds me; I will die, but the Absolute will embrace me. It is an oceanic feeling of connectedness and inner peace—a hint of the "flavor of immortality," say the mystics.

On Shabbat, the self also reaches out to community. Certain central

---

*Harvey Cox, "Meditation and Sabbath," p. 42.
†Babylonian Talmud, Shabbat 127A.

religious ceremonies, including the reading of the Torah, are possible only in the presence of a minyan (quorum of ten). However, reaching out also stems from the expanded consciousness one feels on the Sabbath. Many Jews who pray at home or not at all during the week come together on Shabbat in the *Beit HaKnesset*, the house of assembly, to share a communal experience of prayer. The community is linked horizontally with contemporary Israel by being gathered all over the world to pray on these days. The community is also linked vertically in time through the many prayers and words that were said by this community from the earliest days of its history. I pray as my ancestors did; in so doing, I become one with them.

At the center of the morning service is the reading and studying of Torah. The public parade of the scroll and the chanting of the weekly portion is a mini-reenactment of the original Revelation given to the Jews in community at Sinai. My soul is linked to the unbroken chain of generations that brought me here, gave me being, and shaped my values. Through many channels too hidden to describe or too mysterious to plumb, this community gave me a destiny to fulfill and a witness to bear. My consciousness expands to embrace the community and its concerns and experiences. I am multitudes.

From Shabbat to Life

By providing a sacred ground for existence, Shabbat enhances the sanctity of life. But what if Shabbat clashes with life itself? In biblical times, violation of the Shabbat was considered punishable by death because it is the holiest day. Since many acts of healing or military defense are types of labor not permitted on Shabbat, serious consideration was given as to whether one might violate the Shabbat even when one's life was at stake. The First Book of Maccabees tells of the Greeks attacking a band of Chasidim (pious fundamentalists of those days) on Shabbat. The group refused to fight; the Chasidim preferred to die rather than violate the law of God for which they had taken up arms in the first place. The Maccabees faced the same situation, but they chose to fight. In effect, the question was whether the Sabbath is an ultimate value. Is it better to die than betray it? Or is life the ultimate value of the tradition?

The question is not a simple one. It can be argued that the absolute sacredness of the Shabbat, whatever the cost in individual lives, is the best guarantor of human value. Only an absolute Shabbat, one that could never be overridden, would check both unlimited power and war that otherwise would destroy many more lives in the long run.

The Rabbis ruled that lifesaving overrides the Sabbath. Formulating the justifications for lifesaving on Shabbat, they drew on nuances of various verses. Rabbi Jonathan reasoned from the Exodus verse: "Keep my Sabbaths for it is holy unto you" (Exodus 31:14). "Unto you" meant given over "into your hands, you are not given over to it." Rabbi Simon tried to offer a quantitative argument: "Violate one Sabbath to save a life so that the person can live to observe many Sabbaths." Both interpretations need qualifiers; the first, that the life-enhancing quality of Shabbat lies in its ability to impose its values on otherwise unchecked human activity; the second, that saving a life is not merely a prudential calculation. Samuel gave the decisive answer (from Leviticus 18:5): "Observe my statutes and laws that a man shall do and live by them.... Live by them and do not die by them."* The Torah was given for life; therefore, saving lives takes precedence. One cannot build even the Holy Temple itself on Shabbat. Only one cause overrides the Shabbat: saving life.

In truth, when life is at stake, it is not a case of "permitted violation," it is a mitzvah, a fulfillment of the purpose of Shabbat. Indeed, even if there is only a possibility that a life is at stake, one must do whatever work is necessary to save it. In Maimonides' words (echoing the Talmud): "When these necessary things are done on Shabbat, they should not be done through Gentiles or children [not old enough to be considered violators of the Sabbath]...but by the greatest men of Israel and the Rabbis. It is forbidden to hesitate in any way to violate the Sabbath to save a [sick] person in danger of death for it says...live by them and not die by them. Thus, you learn that the laws of the Torah are not cruel or vengeful to the world but are [a source] of compassion, chessed, and shalom."†

OF HOLINESS AND TIME: ON BECOMING HOLY

The entire Torah can be read as a great midrash (poetic teaching) on the value of life. Life is the cutting edge of being, growing ever closer to the ultimate state of life—God. The Torah comes to nurture the plenitude of this life. That plenitude is known as holiness.

What is holiness? A quality of being special, but a specialness that is intrinsically good and oriented toward perfection. What are the elements that make up holiness? Life, growth, power, control, freedom, consciousness, uniqueness, and relationship. Add them together in their ultimate form, and you have a description of God. Add them together and develop them continuously, and you have a description

---

*This exchange is found in Babylonian Talmud, Yoma 85B.
†Maimonides, *Yad Hachazakah* (Mishnah Torah) (New York: Grossman Publishers, 1960), Sefer Zemanim, Hilchot Shabbat [Book of Seasons, Laws of the Sabbath], chapter 2, paragraph 3.

of a human being becoming more and more godlike, that is, holy.

God, the Holy Blessed One, *Hakadosh Baruch Hu*, is the most holy, that is to say, the most special Being, different from all else. God is unique because God is truly free. The Divine is not programmed. Therefore, God gives the appropriate response each time, sometimes hard, sometimes loving. God is neither male nor female. God is neither typed nor routinized. God is pure consciousness; nothing in the Divine is unaware. God is pure power capable of everything. God is, therefore, the ultimate source and model for holiness just as God is the source for life itself.

Attainment of holiness is one of the central goals of Judaism. Being holy is an imitation of God in its highest form. "The Lord spoke to Moses, saying: Speak to the community of Israel and tell them: Be holy, for I, God, your Lord am Holy" (Leviticus 19:1–2). In commanding Jews to become holy, the Torah calls them to serve as an avant-garde for humanity on its move toward holiness/perfection. Becoming holy means moving from a routine, homogenized existence to a life of distinctive, value-laden experience. This move is at once a recapitulation of the past history of life (for life has grown in the same direction) and a pacesetting breakthrough for humanity (which is going on that same path). Up to the human level, the development of life has been an unconscious process, driven by unseen forces although motivated by the Divine. Choosing to become holy means that humans now join —consciously, covenantally—in the process of perfecting life.

What is the history of life? Life itself can be seen as the expanding tip of the universe, that layer of being becoming more distinctive and unique, growing toward the ultimate One—the ground of holiness, the Divine. Initially, the world consisted of inorganic and inanimate matter. (Such matter is homogeneous.) But life emerged out of the ground of the Divine. Naturally, life absorbs and develops the infinite possibilities of its nurturing ground. Thus, as life grows upward, it becomes more and more distinctive. Life develops consciousness even as it develops somatic complexity. Even animals have soul qualities: "The righteous knows the soul of his animal" (Proverbs 12:10). The higher the animal, the more soul quality it has. The human being— the most distinctive, unique life of all the animals—is judged by the Torah to have crossed a threshold and become godlike (an image of God). Having reached this level, human life shares in the reverence and value that is associated with the Divine.

To treat something as sacred is to translate its holiness into a value or reverence that humans extend to it. The quality of holiness in something bestows sacredness on it; one must show concern for its feeling and reverence for its life. For this reason, Jewish tradition prohibited causing pain to animals (*tzaar baale chayim*). For the same reason, the

Torah's ideal is vegetarian (Genesis 1:29–30; Isaiah 11:26–7) because killing animal life weakens reverence for all life, including human life. On the other hand, human life is recognized as a holiness so highly developed that it overrides all other life, if necessary. Thus, animals may be sacrificed for human welfare, and from this stems the reluctant divine permission to eat meat.*

One of the great thrusts of modern science has been to homogenize reality. The once accepted notion that the heavens are of a different substance than earth has been overthrown by the universal application of physics to all of reality. This insight paved the way for the conquest and use of the physical world for human benefit. Similarly, modern science has brought the human body more and more within the parameters of genetic and hormonal control. Such physical processes define the human as less distinctive, more biologically determined and continuous with the rest of nature. This view of sociobiology is legitimate and even sanctifying; it underscores the close connection between human and animal life. There is a risk, however, that recognition of the biological factor might lead to the denial that humans are created in the image of God; therefore, the halacha seeks to imprint categories of holiness on the time and space that human beings inhabit. Human distinctiveness is sustained by unique experiences that bring out the textured quality of life.

The Shabbat is a primary source of the special experiences that nurture human holiness. By giving special texture to time, by emancipating human beings, by transforming perspectives on life, by enriching human activities, Shabbat brings out life's capacity for holiness. Similarly, the halacha applies holiness to the realm of space. Here (in Jerusalem), uniquely, the halacha says, is the Divine Presence. Here (at the Holy Temple), uniquely, memory associations and connections open humans to the Transcendent. Through elaborate rituals, awareness of this distinctive spot is nurtured. Therefore, there were stringent rules of ritual purity, ritual immersion and washing, special clothes, and elaborate orders of sacrifice for those who worked in or visited the Temple site.

In accordance with its covenantal partnership model, the halacha treats holiness sometimes as divinely imposed, sometimes as created primarily by human efforts. The Talmud rules that the holiness of the land of Israel was initially established by divine fiat but later confirmed through conquest by the Jews. However, that holiness was broken when the people of Israel were driven off the land by the Babylonians. When the Jews returned, they set about sanctifying the land again.

*Compare Genesis 9:1–7.

This time, because the sanctification was done through settlement and painstaking human effort, it could not be broken even by the later, more extended exile of the Jewish people. Thus, the Talmud seems to suggest that human-imposed holiness is more saturating and permanent.

Sanctification—the process of becoming holy—involves infusing reverence and specialness in all areas of life. When it comes to eating, food is divided into kosher and nonkosher. While all vegetables are kosher, eating meat is restricted so as to emphasize the hierarchical value of life itself. Methods of food preparation are regulated. Meat and milk may not be cooked or eaten together. Animals must be slaughtered in a prescribed manner. Ritual hand washing and blessing precede eating. Blessings are specific to different kinds of food and differing amounts. Thus, a homogenized biological act is placed within a grid of value and meaning, much as a gourmet seeks to heighten the eating experience through selection, preparation, and rituals of eating. To do this, the human being must go beyond the elemental need for nutrition and psychically choose to reshape the eating experience.

The same principle applies to sexuality. It is true that "in the dark all men/women look alike" and that hormones shape many sexual responses. Isolated from the total person, sexual acts involve male and female genitals that are relatively standard. Sexuality becomes holy only when it expresses a unique response to the other. Sexuality grows more human in a special time, a special place, out of a relationship in which the overall response to the partner affects the ability to relate sexually. The halacha seeks to orient the human being in this direction with its categories of permitted and prohibited sexuality, its focus on a covenantal partner in sexual intercourse, and its suggestions for a special time and special place. Growing out of these contexts, sexuality becomes a holy act. In turn, it confirms the human being in all of his or her uniqueness and dignity.

Time also has been homogenized by science and modern culture. Every hour has sixty minutes; each minute, sixty seconds; each of these intervals is split by a cesium clock into millionths of units. Measured by such machines, there is no distinctive time; there is only the steady linear flow of measured time. The combination of the endless natural order of days and the regularity of personal life and work can make existence routine, turning it into what Leo Baeck called a "mere succession of days." In the Shabbat, the Torah has created an antidote to this tendency; it is a framework to nurture holiness and to develop humanity's reverence toward nature and life. The Torah seeks to imbue time with this dimension of holiness so that the uniqueness of the human being will be sustained by the temporal reality.

The Shabbat is a response to routinization by creating a temporal counterculture, an island of special existence within the stream of time. Holiness involves a directional process, a shift from homogenized neutral reality to value-saturated reality. In becoming holy, the human being shifts from unexamined life to examined life, from instinctual existence to conscious being. To imbue every area of life with choice, levels of meaning, and value is to sanctify. At each step, the degree of psychic freedom must be raised, for unreflective life is determined by hormones or habits. Only one who is conscious of every moment can make choices or apply a hierarchy of values in every act of life. Thus, the detailed Sabbath ritual, which appears to prescribe everything by rigid rules, is really an assertion of consciousness and one's freedom to imbue every gesture and experience with value. It takes discipline and awareness to make these moves correctly. In this area, as in so many others, freedom grows in the womb of structure. And since every gesture is willed and directional, it is rich in meaning and statement. Every move on Shabbat is part of a dance of holiness.

The Shabbat experience can be evaded, of course, even by those who observe it. Some people use the Shabbat only for physical rest, sleeping through most of the twenty-four hours, hardly exchanging a word or emotion with others. But properly experienced, the Shabbat can be an overflowing source of holiness. Without distraction or outside involvement, one feels other humans becoming present with a vividness and fullness that reveal their image of God. The close family time gives a sense of rootedness and connection that enables the individual to embrace all of life with love. Out of the unmediated encounter with ideal perfection comes a sharp upsurge in eagerness to transform the world. Yet the serenity provided by relief from pressing concerns renews patience. Out of the springs of rest, life wells up with tremendous force and is renewed.

In the Talmudic view, there is a major distinction between the holiness of Shabbat and of the holidays. The dates for the holidays are set by events in Jewish history. The first day of each month was established by reports given to the Jewish high court of the sighting of the new moon. The decree of the Sanhedrin setting the start of a particular new month was binding. This decision fixed the dates of the holidays even if the court erred in setting them.

By contrast, Shabbat occurs regularly on the seventh day whether or not Jews recognize or acknowledge it. This day celebrates creation and a natural order that exists independent of human efforts. It is as if the Rabbis were trying to teach that holiness is an objective category and redemption is built into reality. Here, the typically dialectical approach of Judaism appears again. Holiness is not pure projection (which would make it a collective neurosis); it is the discovery of a depth dimension that underlies the material world. Nor is holiness purely cosmic. Jewish behavior on Shabbat makes it special. On this day it is a mitzvah to slow down, to take smaller steps and not to run. Through repeated acts of sanctification, the flavor of each minute is enhanced. Prayer, kiddush, candle-lighting, learning, eating, dressing, walking, making love—all operate in special ways on this day. A classic Sabbath prayer captures this dialectic: *"The people who sanctify the seventh day will all be satisfied and pleasured by Your goodness. You wanted and sanctified the seventh [day]; You called it the most desirable of days, a remembrance of cosmic creation."**

A DAY OF LIBERATION

Of all the holy days, the Shabbat alone is included in the Ten Commandments. The Ten Commandments are recorded not once but twice in the Torah. In the Book of Exodus, Shabbat is linked to the creation of the world and to the divine rest that completes it. In the book of Deuteronomy (5:12 and following), Shabbat is linked to Exodus. Here, Shabbat speaks for freedom and an end to oppression.

Jewish religion pursues "radical" ends by "conservative" means. The ultimate goal is equality and the total physical welfare of all people. To achieve that end, Judaism is prepared to legitimate profits, private property, and unequal wealth, and to compromise temporarily with a host of social evils. Nowhere is Judaism's dialectical nature as vividly manifest as in the social laws of the Torah— including Shabbat. Cultures that give high status to entrepreneurial skills and productivity tend to favor the wealthy and allow relatively unchecked economic primacy. By contrast, socialist, communist, or ascetic societies glorify control and state restriction of acquisitiveness but often generate an atmosphere hostile to productivity, wealth, and economic innovation.

Judaism refuses to fit into neat boxes or to allow unchecked dominance to any single set of values. Side by side with glorification of work and productivity, halacha insists on the sacred dignity of being. Along with an affirmation of the sanctity of private property, the tradition teaches that the land (and all property) belongs to the Lord: "The Earth and all that is in it is the Lord's" (Psalms 24:1). Even as it emphasizes going beyond materialism to perfection of the soul, Shabbat upholds the liberation of the poor.

The test of freedom is control over time. A slave must work all the

---

*My translation. The Hebrew text may be found in *Daily Prayer Book* by Philip Birnbaum, p. 399.

time or whenever the master orders it. A free man has the choice of not working. Shabbat gives this right to everyone, including slaves. In one sense, Shabbat is a spiritual affirmation of freedom that is oblivious to social classes. The master, too, can be inwardly enslaved to his work, and the Shabbat seeks to free the master as well. By releasing all people from work for a day, Shabbat insists that life is not a prison sentence of hard labor that must be served continually. However, the Shabbat commandment goes beyond spiritual dignity to make a statement for equality. The commandment specifically states: "You shall do no work; you, your male and female slaves, your ox, donkey, and all your animals, your stranger in your gates, in order that your male and female slaves shall rest just as you do (Deuteronomy 5:14). By equating slave and master, the Shabbat commandment objects to the very hierarchy that the Torah has temporarily accepted!

The truly subversive power of Shabbat is found in the command to stop the slave's work. By giving the slave equal freedom from work and prohibiting the master from ordering him to labor, the Torah ensures that on the Sabbath "servant and master meet as equals, as free human personalities." This disrupts the tendency for slave and master to internalize their status of inferior-superior relationship. Moreover, in giving the servant the taste of freedom for twenty-four hours while linking this rest to a reenactment of the Exodus, Shabbat communicates a message to the slave: You are entitled to freedom. By granting the slave the actual experience of liberty, the Torah plants the seed of rebellion against the status of slave that the Torah has temporarily accepted. Once the slave internalizes a new self-image—that of being entitled to freedom, then in tasting liberty—the appetite grows. Released from bondage on Shabbat, the slave, as the stranger, sees inferior status on a workday as a deviation, not a norm. A corner of life and privacy that cannot ever be invaded by the master gives the slave a margin of freedom and dignity that affords him some refuge from the cycle of psychic enslavement. Moses, the great liberator of Jewish history, was raised in the court of the Pharaoh where he had the freedom and margins to resist the enslavement process. A striking rabbinic midrash suggests that Aaron and the elders who supported Moses' demand for liberation were recruited from the Levites, the only tribe that enjoyed a day of Sabbath rest throughout the period of Egyptian slavery. Whatever the historical accuracy of this midrash, its psychological accuracy is exactly to the point.

Shabbat does not stop at the first step of freedom either. The ideal of equality is promoted by the character of Shabbat itself. On this day, commerce and transport and all the processes that create inequality of wealth are stopped. The prohibition of trade and of transfer ensures that there will be no change in social condition—at least not during this period. There is no earning on Shabbat. The prohibition of carrying and of handling money and financial instruments means that all people are equal—for a day. True, the wealthy can wear fur coats, gold, and diamonds that proclaim their status, but under the common prayer shawl in synagogue, even that difference is hidden. Moreover, in the command to help the poor to celebrate Shabbat and in the custom of dressing in one's best clothes for the day, the gap is further narrowed. An aura of equality is generated.

In a way—admittedly limited—the inability to draw upon the personal reserves of wealth equalizes the poor and the rich. The Torah thereby affirms that in a perfect world there would be a broader equality. The Torah has not imposed socialism or financial egalitarianism, perhaps due to its respect for human initiative and self-interest or to protect a greater individualism. But the Shabbat makes clear that its ideal includes overcoming the extremes of wealth. At the least, by the abolition of poverty, riches will no longer carry the clout they do now.

This point was driven home by an incident told to me several years ago. A wealthy Orthodox Jew collapsed and died on the street while walking home alone from synagogue on Shabbat. In accordance with Sabbath law, the dead man carried neither money nor any identification. He was also dressed quite modestly. The police who found the body were arranging for burial in a potter's field when the family finally tracked him down.

At first, I was staggered by the story. What a terrible fate for observing the Sabbath! Upon further reflection, however, it appeared to me that the incident captures the profound egalitarianism implicit in the Shabbat. By right, all people should be equal and indistinguishable by the external features that the world so admires: wealth, dress, the regalia of status. In relinquishing them on Shabbat, we voluntarily renounce the instant symbols of our standing. On Shabbat, we are all equal for a day so that personal being and relationships become the focus of our value.

Is there not a deeper implication in this aspect of Shabbat—that, ultimately, the fullest integrity of relationship can be achieved only when the people involved are equal? Whenever there is inequality, elements such as power, capacity to reward, and the impressiveness of wealth tend to distort the relationships between the weaker person and the stronger. A day like Shabbat, which focuses on the quality of human existence, eliminates these distortions. Its atmosphere of equality allows the full realization of the integrity of relationships. Of course, at this point equality is only conceptual, not actual. But creating it cognitively, even partially for one day a week, becomes an important statement of the basic value that informs all behavior.

Shabbat, therefore, creates a time in which freedom becomes the rule for all life. The earth is free from exploitation; servants and beasts are free from servitude; and workers are liberated from work. Then liberation radiates outward and grows. Freedom is a dynamic force; once unleashed, it is bound to spread. The mood of redemption gets stronger and stronger as the Shabbat wears on.

Thus, the theme of the Shabbat afternoon service (Minchah) is redemption. Both Minchah and the third meal (seudah shelishit) that follows it are identified with King David, the ancestor of the Messiah, the promised Redeemer. In the Havdalah (separation) ceremony at the conclusion of Shabbat, Jews sing of the coming of Elijah the Prophet, the herald of the Messiah.

Read one-sidedly, Judaism is a conservative, bourgeois religion. Private property, hierarchy, inequality, and slavery are all accepted. The primacy of self-interest, the right to help one's family and people first, and the pleasure of consumption are recognized and respected in the system. Yet here, in the Shabbat, lies a powerful counter thrust. There is no permanent legitimacy to slavery or unchecked validity to private property. The Torah is too realistic not to know that those in power and those who hold wealth cannot be automatically depended upon to live the Exodus way. The shepherds are as likely to clip the sheep—or pull the wool over their eyes—as to guard them from straying. Therefore, political and economic leadership is legitimate and necessary for society, but the halacha refuses to give this elite a normative monopoly. Leaders must be challenged in order to keep them honest and on the right path along the Exodus way. The prophet usually speaks for the poor because the prophet's task is to comfort the afflicted and (until the Messiah comes) afflict the comforted. In that role, the prophet imitates God who saves the poor "from one more powerful than him, [protects] the poor and needy from his despoiler" (Psalms 35:10).

Of course, taking the Shabbat as the economic norm is a one-sided reading of Judaism—as are the laws of slavery. In the social and political realms, as well as in the economic, Shabbat supplies the utopian and egalitarian impulses. Shabbat represents the messianic future, but it must be taken seriously now. In tandem with a committed work ethic and a morally realistic methodology, the Shabbat constantly moves society toward greater freedom and striving.

The dynamic of liberation and equality that Shabbat proclaims is extended in the sabbatical year. "The land shall keep a Sabbath unto the Lord.... It will be a Sabbath of solemn rest [Shabbat shabbaton] for the land, a Sabbath unto the Lord. Do not plant your field, do not prune your vineyard. Do not cut the after-growth of your harvest.... It is a year of sabbath rest for the Lord" (Leviticus 25:2–4). Through rest, the land is given back its original undisturbed state before man worked and exploited it. Here is the halachic dialectic again—reasserting reverence for nature and respect for its being, seeing it as subject and not just as object of human control. At the same time, the sabbatical liberates humans from working the land for the entire year, not just one day a week. Just as Shabbat is a day of being, so is the sabbatical year a year of being. Self-development and relationship are placed at the center of life. The messianic fantasy is acted out for a whole year. The radical assault of Shabbat theology on the moral compromises with inequality and private property is here multiplied fifty-fold. Coming every seven years, the sabbatical allows the compromising ways of the world to function but prevents them from becoming entrenched.

In the tradition of the Garden of Eden, that once and future paradise, human beings eat the produce of the land without effort or toil. All take what they need rather than what they can earn. The equality is extended by opening the yield of the land to all people—the poor and the landless first (Exodus 23:10–11) and the animals of the field as well. Private property, as it were, is suspended, and the primordial economic equality is recaptured. (Similarly, in the seventh year of servitude, the Hebrew slave goes free. This year is connected to the sabbatical year—see Deuteronomy 15). Moreover, at the end of the sabbatical year, all existing debts are cancelled. Debt was a major cause of loss of land and of enslavement in ancient times (see Leviticus 25:25–26) so the sabbatical year waiver-of-debt rule was a powerful attempt to ensure ongoing equality.

The climax of liberation from poverty and bondage is reached in the jubilee year (the fiftieth year), which is directly connected to the sabbatical year and, therefore, to the Sabbath. The jubilee year comes after counting seven cycles of seven years. In the fiftieth year, all slaves are released.

Originally, all the families of the nation were given a portion of land —a guaranteed source of income. Over the fifty-year cycle, despite the periodic abolition of debts and despite the Sabbath, some families became poor and lost their land. When land had to be sold, it was sold only until the jubilee year. Then, in that year, or once in a generation, redistribution of land was to take place—a powerful equalizer and a strong statement of the social ideal of equality. Thus, the liberation dynamic of Shabbat spread from a day to a year to a generation and "proclaimed liberty [and equality as well] throughout the land for all its inhabitants" (Leviticus 25:10).

The spread of liberation prefigures a messianic era when all humans will be free and equal. Each individual and each family will sit under "his vine and his own fig tree" (Micah 4:4). That era will be "a day [eon] which is entirely Shabbat" (Grace After Meals).

THE LIMITS OF THE DREAM

A dream without limits is an illusion. The Jewish dream is not an illusion, but neither is it reality yet. In offering hope of perfection, the Jewish tradition takes the countervailing evidence of reality fully into account. The party of hope fully admits the possibility of defeat but does not yield the dream. Rather, it offers a method to make the dream come true.

The Rabbis saw that as Shabbat progresses, a new danger emerges. Hope may grow out of control. With the practice of Shabbat, the idea of a perfect world becomes first vivid, then almost real. As the credibility of the dream grows, the risk grows that people will come to believe peace is the true condition of the world. Therefore, to take the Shabbat literally would be to turn the Jewish dream into an escape, a fantasy, and a deadly one at that.

As the Shabbat comes to a close, Jewish tradition moves to prevent hope from turning into illusion. A sobering note is introduced with the evening service (*Maariv*) in which a special blessing is recited, asking for the gift of intelligence to discriminate between ideal and reality, and for the strength to resist sin in the coming week. The Jewish tradition now makes another of its classic dialectical moves. Shabbat ends with a ritual that asserts the limits of the dreams—the *Havdalah* (separation) ceremony. The Havdalah offers a transition zone from the world of perfection back to reality.

Havdalah is no mere reversal of Shabbat. The ceremony itself holds in suspension the conflicting forces of ideal and real. In order to juggle dream and reality, one must draw a sharp line of distinction. That clear distinction, that drawing of lines is found in the Havdalah ceremony.

Havdalah is one of the liturgical successes of modern Judaism. It is so appealing because of its rich mixture of wine, fragrance, light, and group spirit that many people who do not observe Shabbat still participate in its ceremonies. But Havdalah's full power is best understood in its counterpoint to Shabbat.

Havdalah starts with consolation. Facing the reality of the week with its many problems, one might be driven to despair, especially by contrast to the joy and peace of Shabbat. The individual clings to the group or the family for strength. Many contemporary Jews follow the custom of forming a circle by interlocking arms or joining hands. The opening verses sing to us: Keep your spirits up! "Behold, here is my God of salvation. I will trust and will not fear." The verses climax with a joyous quote from the Book of Esther, sung first by the group and repeated in choral fashion by the chanter of Havdalah. "For the Jews, there was light and joy, gladness and honor . . . so may it be for us!" Before reciting the blessing over wine, the leader lifts the cup and says: "I will lift up the cup of redemption and call upon the name of the Lord."

The choice of wine is noteworthy itself. It is a cup of gladness. The heart is filled with regret at the end of the Sabbath; still, the Havdalah blessing is recited over a cup of wine, the same joyful symbol with which the Shabbat began. The difficulties of life should be taken on with joy because they are the hallmark of being alive. Only the dead are safe from anxiety and danger.

Perhaps there is another subtle image, too. Recited with the benediction over a cup of wine, Havdalah is implicitly not just the close of the Sabbath liturgy but a Kiddush that opens the weekdays. Just as Jews sanctify Shabbat over a Kiddush cup of wine and enter into its holy being, so Jews sanctify the weekday over a Havdalah cup of wine and enter into its holy doing. The week has a sacred calling: to work in and perfect the world. The one who recites Shabbat Kiddush witnesses to the divine creation of the world. The one who recites Havdalah witnesses to the human role perfecting and co-creating the world.

The second blessing of Havdalah, over fragrant spices, is really the last blessing of Shabbat. In symbolic language, the last memory of Shabbat should be a fragrant one so the soul will long for its return. The dream is gone, but the fragrance lingers on. The Rabbis stated that on Shabbat there is a symbolic "additional soul." Some commentators explain that the fragrance is for the departing additional soul, enticing it to come back next Shabbat. Others say the fragrance is meant to sustain the person who feels faint when the sense of loss deepens.

The third blessing, ". . . who creates the light of the fire," is really the first blessing of the new week. By tradition, the Havdalah candle has multi-wicks, which produce a powerful flame. After giving up work for twenty-four hours to focus on being and to enter into the Shabbat spirit, Jews immediately light a fire to reaffirm the dignity and sacredness of work. This act underscores the rejection of the Prometheus myth. The Sabbath command not to work does not reflect God's jealousy of human power and creativity. Not working is an assertion of creaturehood. To make this crystal clear, the first commanded deed after Shabbat is the creation of fire—the great act of human power and deliverance.

Fire freed humankind from subservience to nature, from fear of darkness, from enslavement to the round of seasons. Fire is the civilizing force that made possible cooked food and the regalia of civilization as well as human habitation in every clime on earth. Blessing the light celebrates human capability, our independence from nature and our capacity to reshape the world. The play of darkness and flame,

shadow and light, is mirrored and gazed at on the fingernails, symbolizing the ambiguities of the reality that we now reenter and attempt to
cope with. Perhaps there is another point, subtly made: Do not curse
the darkness, kindle the light.

The fourth and final blessing is that of separation. Thank God who
separates "between holy and profane, between light and darkness,
between the people of Israel and other nations, between the seventh
day and the six work days." Perhaps profane is too negative a translation; the Havdalah contrast is not that of the good versus the bad.
Rabbi Abraham Isaac Kook came closer to the spirit of Havdalah when
he said that there is the holy and the not yet holy (that is profane).
Shabbat is the *avant-garde* of the weekday. Someday all work will be
sacred calling. Similarly, Israel is the avant-garde of the nations. Its
commitment to live, model, and testify for the final perfection is not
against the nations but for them.

The sacred is the articulated realm of the holy. The secular is the
hidden, silent sector of holiness that awaits redemption and perfection. Judaism does not lump the two together. The differences are essential. Jews thank God for the capacity to distinguish. But these are
not two contradictory realities; they are part of a world waiting to be
unified and redeemed by human activity.

The play of being and doing, hope and reality, the juxtaposition of
the Shabbat concluded and the weekday emerging, lead to a final
messianic outburst. At the moment of setting the limits of the dream
comes an exultant—defiant!—affirmation of expecting the Redeemer
soon. By tradition, Jews now sing the song *"Eliyahu Hanavi"* ("Elijah
the Prophet"). The legendary harbinger of the Messiah "will come
speedily in our days with the Redeemer." This is one of the great
point-and-counterpoints of Jewish liturgy. The master stroke of realism
in the Havdalah is matched by the unbroken faith that the line of
David, the king of Israel, is alive and well.

This moment of fervent proclamation reveals again the balancing
nature of Judaism, its shrewd blend of romance and realism. After all,
according to tradition, the Messiah could come any day. Why then do
Jews sing out the call of "Elijah the Prophet" on Saturday night? The
answer is that even in dreaming one must consider the odds of success.
Since the Messiah theoretically could come any day in the week, the
odds that the Messiah will come on any particular weekday are seven to
one. However, the Rabbis calculated, if the Messiah did not come on
Thursday night, this Redeemer would surely not come on Friday night
either because that is the day of Shabbat rest. A Messiah destined to
come on Friday night or Saturday night would come on Saturday night.
In short, chances of the Messiah coming on Saturday night are two out of
seven—twice as good as any other weekday night.

By tradition, the good spirit of Havdalah is extended by singing other joyous songs written for this moment. Perhaps the most famous of these are "Do Not Fear, My Servant Jacob" and "Hamavdil"; which includes: "May the God who separated holy from secular forgive our sins, make our children and our wealth as numerous as the sands and as the stars of night."

Again it is the Jewish custom to increase the time of holiness and joy rather than break it off abruptly. Having asserted the limits, Jews now try to push them and extend them to incorporate more of reality. The Sabbath spirit is extended by more celebration. There is a Chasidic custom to add an outgoing feast—the Melaveh Malkah, escorting the Sabbath Queen on her way out—to keep the spirit going into the late hours of the night.

Sooner or later, of course, the Sabbath does end, but the dream goes on. The joy and fulfillment of the day gives us the strength to continue. Because Shabbat comes every week, it becomes, in Franz Rosenzweig's phrase, the "cornerstone of the year." The constant cycle of Shabbat prevents the everyday reality from becoming entrenched. The norms of the status quo are challenged and shaken up every seven days. The perfect is made credible and present.

Of all Jewish practices, Shabbat spread the furthest. Through Christianity and Islam it has entered world culture. True, it is found there in different forms, less intense and structured. But surely, in this day with its healing and rest for so many people, there is a paradigm of the final, total perfection that Judaism promises will be granted to everyone. Is it any wonder that the Sabbath, which the Rabbis called God's gift to Israel, is also called Israel's gift to humanity?

MAKING SHABBAT: PREENACTING THE MESSIANIC REDEMPTION

Shaping Time and Creating Shabbat

The central myth and model of the Shabbat rituals is the creation and preenactment of the messianic kingdom. The great theologian Abraham Joshua Heschel wrote that Judaism is "a religion of time aiming at the sanctification of time."* It is equally correct to say that Judaism seeks the transformation of time—the realm of history is to be perfected.

As Heschel described it, the Shabbat is an exercise in "orchestration

*Abraham Joshua Heschel, *The Sabbath* (Cleveland: World Publishing Company, 1963), p. 8.

of time," an attempt to shape a holy day—a day of special existence—
out of the endless, undifferentiated flow of time. For most people,
time, if it is confronted at all, is likely to be experienced in threatening
ways: as death moving closer, as quicksilver that can never be grasped
or held in control. Therefore, the Jewish attempt to create a special
realm in time and live within it is an exceptionally difficult undertaking. It is made all the more problematic by the need to recreate such an
intense experience once every seven days.

The language of Jewish faith is primarily action, that is, symbolic
statements. By association, by stylizing, by evoking past memories,
each gesture becomes part of the testimony that the Jewish experience
is credible and influential. The whole process must become so intense
that it breaks through the solid surface of reality and opens up new
encounters with existence. What follows is an attempt to describe the
actions of Shabbat living and their intended effects. The description
should be taken seriously but not too literally. As in every good play,
there must be a chemistry of players interacting with one another,
with the props and with the script, and even improvising until the
whole thing clicks.

For the purpose of Shabbat, an ideal world has to be created, in part
with props and in part by use of the imagination. It is a little bit like
having a Broadway opening every week. All in the family have assigned parts. Each person is his or her own producer. It takes preparation, memorizing the script, and ensemble playing to carry it off
successfully. The test of success is that the players develop the willingness to keep doing it and that the family and the others who are the
audience get the message.

STOP THE WORK

The first level of Shabbat's special state is the cessation of all work. In
seeking to define categories of prohibited work, the Rabbis used as a
master model of constructive work the activities performed for and
within the Holy Sanctuary. (Some hold that these are the labors involved in constructing the tabernacle/temple.) The Rabbis defined
thirty-nine categories of such work.

The main, overarching areas of labor are the provision of food
(beginning with growing it); clothing (including preparation of raw
materials), providing shelter, light and heat; writing (spiritual and
cultural work, and record-keeping activity); and transportation/carry-
ing (commerce and exchange activity). These are the general categories of work that provide the basic human needs. While the specific
categories are based on the agricultural society of biblical times, the

generic types of work apply to all societies and times.

The categories of labor are as follows:

(A) Growing and preparing food
1. Plowing (clearing land for cultivation)
2. Sowing (promoting growth)
3. Cutting/harvesting
4. Binding/gathering
5. Threshing
6. Winnowing
7. Selecting
8. Sifting (5, 6, 7, 8 all involve separating usable from useless)
9. Grinding (cutting a product into little pieces)
10. Kneading
11. Baking (preparing through use of fire or heat)

(B) Production and preparation of clothing (for priestly garments)
12. Shearing
13. Bleaching
14. Carding (reworking materials to be spun)
15. Dyeing
16. Spinning (twining into threads)
17. Inserting thread into a loom
18. Weaving (making fabric)
19. Taking off the finished product
20. Separating threads
21. Tying a knot
22. Untying a knot (in order to tie again)
23. Sewing (permanent joining together of two pieces of material with binding thread)
24. Tearing (for the sake of shaping, creating material, and so forth)

(C) Leather work (also preparing parchment) and writing
25. Catching game (bringing an animal under control)
26. Slaughtering
27. Skinning or flaying
28. Tanning (treating skin for leather)
29. Scraping (smoothing)
30. Marking out (marking with lines on a surface to prepare it for cutting or some other utilization)
31. Cutting (shaping)
32. Writing
33. Erasing (for the sake of writing again; erasing alone is destructive action, not creative labor)

(D) Providing shelter
   34. Building
   35. Demolition (for the sake of improvement of building)

(E) Providing fire
   36. Kindling
   37. Extinguishing (for positive purpose such as creating charcoal)

(F) Completion activity
   38. A [final] hammer blow (any act that completes or makes usable an unfinished product, as the final hammer blow makes the tool or shoe complete)

(G) Transportation/carrying
   39. Carrying from private into public domain or vice versa (transportation or transfer that changes the usability, ownership, or location of an object; this includes carrying in one's pocket or moving carriages from inside to outside, and so forth).

In all these categories, the Rabbis made great effort to define the necessary characteristics and minimum quantity of work that constituted a violation of Sabbath rest. Classical Christian theologians and modern thinkers have tended to dismiss this as soulless legalism or manifestations of rigid, obsessional behavior. But law versus spirit is not the correct analogy. It is more like seeking the ultimate experience of gourmet dining or music or art. The greater the understanding of connoisseurs, the subtler the variation that speaks to them and moves them.

The definition of forbidden labor is a statement about the significance of work. Once the characteristics of each type of labor are established, then all the work in the world—including all future innovations and technical breakthroughs—can be related to the holiness and purpose of labor that was once performed for the Sanctuary.

The Rabbis' definition of the minimum unit of labor (*melacha*) is an important statement on the nature of creation and achievement. "What is the minimum achievement that accomplishes enough to violate the Sabbath rest?" is another way of saying "What is the minimum attainment that constitutes a real accomplishment?" Achieving this much means that the life and labor spent on this work was not spent in vain. Stated this way, the rabbinic definition of labor is the equivalent of the byte in computers: the minimum amount of information that constitutes significant communication.

In the category of planting, the Rabbis hold that a seed or a cluster of seeds—enough to yield a plant—is sufficient. In harvesting, some say one row, and others say one plant is enough. In preparing food, the minimum is a mouthful or, in another view, an amount the size of an egg—enough to stop hunger. In writing, just inscribing two letters (in Hebrew this is the smallest word) is sufficient. When it comes to building, the Rabbis rule that *kol shehu*, any finite amount, is significant.

In a culture that overrates success and underestimates the difficulties of bettering the world, the halacha's categories constitute an important counter-testimony. Anyone who has tried to create—a building, an organization, a school, a society—knows that the difficulties are enormous. Even minute achievements represent a great effort and significant accomplishment. Creation starts small. Life comes out of a microscopic seed. The lesson is that any contribution that improves the world is a response to the divine mandate. In kabbalistic terms, it is a *tikkun*—an act of perfecting.

What constitutes an act of *tikkun olam?* How much achievement makes a human being a partner in creation? In essence, the answer is that each "bit" of constructive work is as significant as a divine creative act. Each and every act upgrading the universe is of cosmic significance because, bit by bit, is how the mosaic of perfection will be accomplished. During the week this minimum act makes a person a partner in God's Creation. On Shabbat, consciously choosing not to do it makes one a witness that the creation is God's. This testimony teaches that no one else owns the world. Everyone but God is a steward, not a master.

All the work in the world is classified by halacha as within these thirty-nine categories. In modern times, almost all halachists have proscribed electricity under the rubric of creating a fire. Contemporary nonobservant Jews have objected that it is no effort to flick a switch. Sometimes a permitted action that could be done easily by an electrical machine takes much more effort to accomplish by direct human activity. However, in the classic halachic tradition, creation—and not effort—is the criterion. Therefore, most halachists feel that it makes no difference whether you push a button to create fire and light or rub two sticks together tediously to obtain the same result.

A Different Environment

To create a totally different environment for living on this day, the Rabbis went beyond the prohibition of work. Since the Shabbat messianic atmosphere is highly vulnerable, the Rabbis instructed people to remove all objects associated with everyday reality; the presence of such objects could shatter the fragile air of Shabbat serenity. The Rabbis established a category of several kinds of *muktzeh* (literally, set aside, excluded). Objects that are used exclusively for labors prohibited on Shabbat or objects undesignated for human use on Shabbat that could only be made usable through prohibited labor are muktzeh. Since their only use would come through work inappropriate for the day, they were to be set aside and not even handled. Handling money is one example; another example is a tool that was not to be touched even if one did no actual work with it. The reason is that once it was handled, one might proceed to do work with it. Equally important: All of its associations are with prohibited labor, and, therefore, it will jar the mood of stopping work.

Another category set up was *sh'vut*. This involved extending the prohibited category beyond labor in order to ensure a true rest. For example, carrying in a nonpublic, nonprivate area is rabbinically prohibited although it does not involve transfer from public to private domain. Some Rabbis prohibited sports, even indoors. While many sports involve no work, the Rabbis felt that the involvement would interfere with the spiritual nature of Shabbat rest.

A third category was called *uvdin de'chol* (literally, activities of the secular), which means anything that is so associated with weekdays that it might disrupt the special character of Shabbat and give it a weekday tone. Thus, modern rabbis have prohibited watching television or using the telephone even when they can be turned on automatically and don't involve other technical violations of a labor category. The point is to avoid all association with the weekday world. Some scholars would not read books associated with their own weekday work, although reading is not prohibited on Shabbat. Counting one's possessions is prohibited for the same reason. Since this is an attempt to carry out the spirit of Shabbat, one's individual judgment as to what is "weekday" also comes into play.

The Power of Positive Shabbat Thinking

The Shabbat prohibitions aim to create a messianic ambience. Work (tikkun olam) stops when the world is made perfect. However, attainment of the messianic era involves more than the end of suffering. Social and political liberation is a necessary but not sufficient condition for perfection of life, for the human being is more than the sum of his or her living conditions. The highest state of redemption will be reached on the far side of social justice when the individual achieves forgiveness and love (meaning authentic relationships with fellow human beings), harmony with nature, and fulfillment of the spiritual capacities intrinsic in every human being (that is, mutual love with God).

Thus, there is a twofold purpose in the Shabbat rituals: The prohibitions of Shabbat remove the impediments to messianic living. The positive commandments of Shabbat bring out the fullness of the human spirit.

Were Shabbat observance to fixate at the level of prohibitions, Saturday could easily turn into a dark day of repression, a soul-constricting time. Instead, building on the foundation of no labor, the primary aim of Shabbat is to create an atmosphere of pleasure and fulfillment. Within this atmosphere, the self and the family are to be expanded and developed.

The two primary mitzvot of this type were derived by the Rabbis from a verse in Isaiah (58:13): "Call the Shabbat 'delight' (oneg); God's hallowed day 'honor.' " The Shabbat is *honored* by anticipation, preparation, special dress, cleaning, washing, and personally participating in the creation of the atmosphere. The *delight* of Shabbat is experienced through good food and drink, adequate meals, a joyful mood, communal song and dance, peace (no fighting on Shabbat), intimacy, and sexual relations. All cares should be put aside. Learning and liturgical experiences provide a spiritual dimension to "honor" and "delight."

To create a positive environment for Shabbat living, halacha permits the construction of an *eruv*. A public area is enclosed with string and posts, including existing wires. As a result of this symbolic action, an entire city or neighborhood is considered one private domain so that carrying is permitted within it. This legal fiction allows parents to take out babies in carriages and a host of other conveniences that make Shabbat observance more pleasant.

To those not familiar with the Shabbat laws, the detailed prohibitions may appear to be picayune or obsessional. To those who miss the forest for the trees, Shabbat may appear to be an orgy of food, dressing up, and prayers. Recalling the play analogy is helpful. A thousand details done to perfection with great discipline result in a great play or musical—a powerful story told with laughter and tears and song and dance. The story of creation and redemption, of the Jewish way, is the Shabbat drama. Paraphrasing Ahad Ha'am, one might say: The Jews created Shabbat even as Shabbat created the Jews.

PREPARATION

Preparation for the coming Shabbat begins on Sunday morning. Each day is related to the forthcoming Sabbath. In the traditional prayer service, a Psalm of the day is recited, the same Psalm that the Levites sang in the Holy Temple. (Again, note the symbolism that the individual's work in the world in daily life is parallel to the holy work of the sanctuary.) The Psalm is introduced with the formula: "Today is the first day of the Shabbat week."

The Torah says, "Remember the Sabbath day to make it holy." Traditional Jews fulfill this dictum by remembering Shabbat all the time.

Early in the week is a good time to invite guests for Shabbat. On Monday and Thursday, a small part of the Torah portion of the coming Shabbat is read in the traditional synagogue in anticipation of that great day. One can develop one's own variations all the week through: decorating for Shabbat, planning a menu, selecting a tablecloth, polishing silver, and preparing a *dvar Torah* (Torah teaching) for a Sabbath meal.

The anticipation of Shabbat strengthens from day to day but reaches its peak of intensity on Friday, otherwise known as *erev Shabbat* (the eve of the Sabbath). The house is decorated. The cooking, being done before Shabbat, fills the house with the aroma of food favorites. The table is set especially with the finest silver and china. Every member of the family should take part. Great Rabbis made it a practice to personally cut the vegetables or salt the fish in order to share in the mood of preparation. In many homes, and especially in Israel, it is customary to bring home flowers every Friday. Mystics draw the analogy between these actions and those of a groom eagerly preparing himself for a call on his bride-to-be. It is also customary to eat less on Friday in order to work up an appetite for the Shabbat meal.

Ideally, one should leave work early, go home, and get into the swing of preparation. Obviously, in a high-pressure, high-achievement society, leaving the job early poses problems. Richard Siegel has a solution: "Try to do as much work in half a day as you would normally do in a full day. This serves several purposes: It alleviates guilt at leaving work early, it emphasizes the difference between the work week and the Shabbat, and it exhausts the body and the mind so that you will welcome, even yearn for, the release and the relaxation that Shabbat offers."*

An extra measure of cleanliness is created for Shabbat: Rooms are straightened, linens are changed, showers are taken, and fresh clothing is donned. (Chasidim immerse themselves in the *mikvah*—ritual bath.) Dress is also changed totally for Shabbat.

Now is the time to slow down the pace deliberately, perhaps listen to music. Put some tzedakah in a tzedakah box before the candle lighting or write a check for charity. One of the strongest traditions in the Jewish religion is that days of joy and well-being must be shared with others who are less fortunate. This is also a time for a review of the week that was. Zalman Schachter emphasizes the value of this time for *teshuvah* (repentance). Seek out someone you've angered during the week and ask understanding (there's bound to be a family member whose feelings have been hurt lately).

*Richard Siegel, "Preparing for Shabbat," *Moment Magazine*, January, 1976, pp. 61–2.

Schachter also points out that there are two nervous systems in human beings: sympathetic and parasympathetic. The sympathetic system concerns itself with aggression and defense; it speeds up the heartbeat and acts out the more determined, less deliberate reactions. In the parasympathetic, people digest, eat, and sleep. The Shabbat mode is like the parasympathetic mode of being—it is a slower pace. The heart beats more slowly, one takes deeper, longer breaths, and all energies seem to flow to a center. However, whereas people normally sleep in the parasympathetic mode, on Shabbat they "learn to be awake parasympathetic."

These directions are not meant to intimidate. As one who works best under pressure and deadlines, I find that I often get some of my best work done on erev Shabbat. On occasion, this means that I am often on the go up to the last minute, having to wash, shave, and dress hastily in the few minutes just before candle-lighting time. Then I use the eighteen minutes before sunset for the meditation and slow movement that change the rhythm. There are countless ways to get into the mood. Each person is unique. Just getting home can be an achievement for some. In Shabbat, as in many other areas, the principle is that "the reward is commensurate with the effort." If a particular requirement is a problem, do not give up. Start slowly. Do it in stages. Grow into Shabbat.

ENTERING THE SHABBAT

Eighteen minutes before sundown, the women light candles—the Shabbat symbol of light and warmth. Despite the strong association of candle lighting as a woman's mitzvah, in truth it is a household requirement, which means that a man can do it too. If a man is away from home, the halacha rules that he should light candles wherever he is.

Candles are lit before sunset (when the new day actually begins in the Jewish calendar) on the principle that good should be done in extra measure. Starting Shabbat eighteen minutes early constitutes adding "from the realm of the weekday to the realm of the holy." The extension means that an extra slice of time is liberated from the realm of imperfection to the realm of perfection (only 143 hours and 42 minutes to go weekly for total redemption!). The Sabbath day is extended for the same reason; the Sabbath ends when the first stars come out. Traditionalists wait 42 minutes after sundown. Some, because they cannot get enough of a good thing, wait up to 72 minutes (which is in accordance with the minority view of a great medieval decisor, Rabbenu Tam).

At least two candles are lit. Some families light one for each member of the family, adding candles as the family grows. In kabbalistic circles some light seven candles, one for each day of the week. Others light ten, one for each commandment in the Decalogue.

The rewards of Shabbat begin now. The family gathers around for the lighting. Some mothers bless the children at this moment (à la *Fiddler on the Roof*!); though traditionally it is done later, at the meal. As the family exchanges kisses and talks quietly, one can probably feel the Shabbat peace begin to descend. A brave new time unfolds.

In most Orthodox homes, the male members of the family go off to synagogue at this point. Increasingly, more and more women also go, as women expand their participation in the spiritual life of the community. The walk to shul (or the release of pressure at home since work can't be done) creates wonderful opportunities for catching up on the week and with one another.

The Friday evening liturgy features an extra service—the *Kabbalat Shabbat* (welcoming the Sabbath). Established by the mystics in the sixteenth century, the service tries to deepen the Shabbat mood before the evening service begins. It features six Psalms, one for each day of the week, followed by a seventh prayer—Lecha Dodi (Come, My Beloved, to Greet the Bride, Shabbat), a joyous hymn written by a mystic almost four centuries ago to act out a ceremonial greeting of the incoming bride. On Friday night, the evening service inserts special verses proclaiming the Shabbat as the sign of the covenant and witness to creation.

To sustain the mood of total perfection and joy of the Shabbat, it is customary to act as if nothing tragic has happened. When a person has lost an immediate relative, he or she sits *shiva* (a week in mourning at home) and is visited and consoled by members of the community. On Shabbat, however, public expressions of grief cease, and the mourners come to synagogue where they are welcomed with a special greeting of consolation.

All week long, the heart of the Amidah (the central silent prayer uttered while standing in the peak moment of being in the presence of God) is a series of requests for personal needs: health, livelihood, forgiveness, and so forth. On the Sabbath, however, when a petitioner reaches the moment of intimacy with God, that person has everything. Since nothing is lacking, there is nothing to ask for. Instead of twelve blessings with requests, the middle section of the Shabbat Amidah contains one blessing—singing the praises of Shabbat!

In many traditional communities it is customary to recite a Mishnah, Bameh Madlikin (What oils do we use for the Sabbath lights?), just before the Maariv (evening) service. The original purpose of this recitation was to delay the Maariv service so that latecomers would not have to stay by themselves to finish their prayers. It was dangerous to walk home alone in those days because the synagogue was located *outside* the city, in the fields. Today, the customary recitation continues with unabated vigor; only now it is dangerous to walk home alone because the synagogue is located *in* the city.

Apparently this particular Mishnah text was chosen because it dealt with having fire, light, and heat in the house. Thus, it was a declaration against the view of the Karaites (from the tenth century on) who denied the oral law and allowed no fire in the home on Shabbat. The ultimate purpose of this practice, however, is study. On Shabbat, there is no time pressure, so the Rabbis inserted a study unit in every service. Today, many synagogues use this slot for study and teaching a wide variety of texts, often allowing lay people to participate through preparation and presentation of a dvar Torah.

Going to synagogue is important for the sake of reconnecting to the community and being kept informed of the needs of the Jewish people. Some families, however, in the process of growing into Shabbat, prefer to use this time for being at home together without interruption. Such a slice of life is rare in contemporary culture because everyone goes off in different directions. This had led to some backlash, both from rabbis and lay people, against late Friday night services. Havurah-type meals (small, intimate groups) and services in the home have grown in response. Many synagogues have encouraged these services as part of their program because people are reluctant to leave the house once the family, with or without friends, is together in a "shabbasdig" (sabbath-y) mood. On the other hand, while it is easy to dismiss the late service, many people have not been able to clear the time for a total Friday night experience. For them, the late service remains a serious expression of involvement in the experience of Shabbat and of the desire to pray with the community.

Our family spends the summers in Gloucester, Massachusetts, directly on the ocean. Since we do not drive on Shabbat, we perforce cannot go to synagogue. One of our most treasured times is the half hour of sitting together, looking out on the ocean, facing the sunset, and then praying. As darkness descends one can feel the presence of Shabbat "thickening" until it is almost palpably real.

If the family does choose to use the time in this private way, it is important to participate in some other synagogue service. The role of the synagogue in providing a connection to the Jewish people is essential. It would be a distortion of focus if family togetherness led to a loss of community. Part of the Shabbat spirit is to pray with a community. The Rabbis permitted Torah reading and certain other special prayers only in a community setting in order to "force" Jews, as it were, to join in the community. Judaism proclaims that authentic selfhood reaches out and shares in family and community. The self gives and thereby gets; it does not merely receive. One of the special joys of Jewishness that I always felt as a child was the experience of shaking hands with everyone on the way out of shul. For me, those hand-shakes played a powerful connecting role, especially when accompanied by the Yiddish greeting, "Gut Shabbos" (Good Shabbat), or the Hebrew, "Shabbat Shalom" (Sabbath peace be upon you).

Upon returning home, the family and guests join in the singing of "Shalom Aleichem" (each verse repeated three times in some Orthodox homes). The song evokes the angels of Sabbath peace who traditionally accompany people home on Shabbat. According to folklore, there are two angels, one good and one bad. If the home is Shabbat ready, radiant and peaceful, then the good angel blesses the family: "May the next Shabbat and the week be as beautiful"; the other angel is obliged to assent by answering, Amen. (Beware, however. Should the home be uninviting, with rancor and weekday divisiveness present, then the angel of bad tidings utters the prayer that it be the same next week, to which the first angel must answer, Amen.) In our home we have taken on an old custom of joining hands and moving about in a circle as we sing "Shalom Aleichem."

"Shalom Aleichem" is followed by the ceremony of blessing the children. There are separate blessings for boys and girls. In our home, both parents bless each child. Some years ago, the children decided to bless the parents back, and this has continued to this day. We add our own blessings and words to the traditional formulas. We often refer to recent special experiences or upcoming events in their lives. There has been an unspoken tacit psychological bargain that the time of this tradition not be invaded by any carry-over agendas. More than once, anger and "silent treatments" have evaporated in the close embrace and the good feeling of these shared blessings. We attribute to the power of this entrenched practice the good fortune that our young adult children continue to kiss us.

Following the blessing comes "Ayshet Chayil" (Woman of Valor) (Proverbs 31), sung by the father and, usually, by the children in honor of the mother. Some feminists have challenged the emphasis of this prayer—the wife as homemaker, praised for her value to her husband and children. Intellectual pursuits are not mentioned, though the hymn does have her engaging in handicrafts and commerce, and cites her leadership and compassion in helping the poor and in being God-fearing rather than a sex object. But in most traditional families, such as ours, this hymn is appreciated by the woman of the house for what it is, a song of love and appreciation for her goodness and many talents. As the experience of Marriage Encounter groups shows, it is important for people to say the obvious to one another: I love you; you are a wonderful person; I appreciate all that you do for me. A more recent twist in liberal Jewish households is to have the wife sing some verses in honor of the husband.

ONEG SHABBAT (THE JOY OF SHABBAT)

The family is now ready for kiddush. Red wine is preferred by Talmudic tradition. Connoisseurs find highly sweetened wines barbaric, of course. One suspects that Rashi, the great medieval commentator, who, according to folk tradition, was also a French-wine merchant, would be repelled by the popular Concords and Malagas. Some people are horrified at the thought of dry wines for Shabbat, feeling that this betrays their bubbe's and zayde's homemade, super-sweetened wines. Whatever one's personal taste, it is a mitzvah that the wine be an Israeli one, so that Shabbat observance does double mitzvah duty in supporting the State of Israel.

In Orthodox homes, the male head of the household generally recites the kiddush for everyone and pours out a bit of wine from his large cup for each one. Incidentally, this is one of those special occasions where the Talmud declares that the woman can perform the ritual for the man. However, it also states there that a curse will strike the man who allows this to happen. (Thus far there is no medical record of such having occurred. Perhaps God changed Her mind.) In some homes, each member of the family has his or her own cup and all recite kiddush, singly or together.

The main ritual function of kiddush is to give testimony. In the opening stanza, Jews give witness to the creation of the world, to its beauty, purpose, and order. The kiddush contains exactly seventy words—ten and seven are both perfection numbers in the Jewish tradition. Kiddush is, in part, an attempt to evoke "radical amazement" (Heschel) at the beauty of existence. It is, in part, an assertion of human creaturehood and limits. And it is, in part, a commitment to the covenant, to our role in perfecting the world. The Talmud says that whoever recites the kiddush becomes "a partner in the work of creation."

In ancient times, witnesses in Jewish court stood while they gave testimony, so some follow the custom of standing throughout the kiddush. Still others sit through the whole kiddush to underscore the fact that it is part of the meal to come. Still others follow the tradition of the Vilna Gaon (eighteenth-century scholar): standing for the first part, which is testimony, and sitting for the second, which thanks God for singling us out to be Jews. (This variety of practice supports the ancient folk dictum that two Jews between them have three views.)

The kiddush is followed by the ritual washing of hands with its special blessing. (In some homes of German Jewish background, the ritual washing takes place before the kiddush in order not to break the flow.) Tradition specifies that, for ritual washing, the water be poured over the hands by human agency, not by machine or faucet. The point is that awakening consciousness cannot be accomplished by mechanical means. Usually you pour water on your own hands (on the right hand first), but pouring can be done by someone else as a mark of love or friendship. It is also customary to be silent from the moment of washing until the challah is broken and eaten. The mind is concentrated, and consciousness focuses on the bread and the meal to follow.

The table is set with two whole challahs. These two loaves summon up the double portion of manna that the Jews were given in the desert on Friday so they would not have to gather any food on the Sabbath. By tradition, the two loaves are covered during kiddush because the Bible tells us that the manna was covered with dew above and below. Some commentators find an ethical teaching in this custom. Since the wine is given precedence in the kiddush, the challah is covered so it is not "shamed" by having been passed over for the wine. The lesson of this fanciful interpretation is an important model for treating humans. Rabbi Israel Salanter once was a guest in the home of a man who scolded his wife for not having the challahs set out properly for kiddush. Salanter took the man aside afterward and said, "If halacha instructed us to be so sensitive to the dignity and feeling of an inanimate challah, how much more sensitive must we be not to hurt another's feelings."

The two challahs are now uncovered, the hamotzi (the blessing over the bread) is recited, and the challah is cut. Again, customs vary. Some families give each person two small rolls to make the blessing for themselves; most use two large challahs for the whole group. Some people cut the bread and eat the first slice to connect the blessing to the act of eating; others first cut a slice of challah for everyone so the eating starts together. In the good old days, people would often tear the challah. Kabbalists introduced the custom of having children kiss their mother's hand after the breaking of the challah because she provided the festive meal.

There is a widespread tradition of sprinkling salt on the first piece of bread eaten (or dipping the bread in salt). The salt is used in accordance with the biblical tradition, "You shall offer salt with all your offerings" (Leviticus 2:13). Symbolically, this expresses the idea that a meal eaten in holiness is equivalent to a sacrifice brought into the holy sanctuary. The salt usage is associated with the covenant; just as salt preserves food, so the covenant commitment will be permanently preserved.

"Taste and see that God is good," says the psalmist. Weight watchers need not apply. Some people go off diets on Shabbat; others cut back during the week so they can live it up on Shabbat. Still others bring their diets with them into Shabbat to prove that until the Messiah comes nothing is perfect. Such fine points may appear to be excessively detailed. In a sense, they are. If the general spirit of Shabbat is successfully created, then these minutiae will hardly be noticed. In a deeper sense, however, these details reflect the artistic, dramatic nature of creating Shabbat. In a ballet, every detail, gesture, and pirouette expresses some nuance of plot or feeling. In the Shabbat ritual, every gesture—cutting, eating, standing or sitting—subtly expresses ideas and values; each movement tells a story through body language and by association.

The Shabbat meal is served. Every dish is saturated with theology as well as calories. *Item:* The popularity of fish as a Jewish food goes back to the sojourn in Egypt before the Exodus. There is a tradition that the Leviathan (a gigantic fish—whale?) will be served at the ultimate messianic feast in paradise. Since Shabbat is a foretaste of the age of redemption, fish dishes became *de rigueur.* In recent centuries, some halachists declared that separating bones from fish flesh was difficult to do without running afoul of halachic restrictions on the labor of sifting. Yet not to remove the bones could prove dangerous. To remove any possibility of violating Shabbat norms and/or of gagging on a bone, the creative Jewish wife developed a new form of preparation. The fish was ground up and stuffed back into its skin. Presto! Gefilte fish. In the past two centuries gefilte fish has become the favorite form of Shabbat fish. There are two versions: Litvack (from Lithuanian Jews), unsweetened, and Galitsayner (from Austrian or Galician Jews), sweetened.

Item: Chicken soup. This legendary food of great medicinal powers fulfilled the rabbinic injunction to eat hot food. The soup reflects Jewish poverty; chicken is cheaper than beef, and soup is cheaper than chicken. Vegetarians will find that squash- and turnip-based soups taste as rich as chicken, but of course they can't cure influenza.

Among the Sabbath delicacies are chopped herring, chopped egg and onion, chopped liver, tsimmes and carrot stew, potato kugel (pudding), helzl (stuffed neck skin), lokshen (noodle) kugel, and kishke (stuffed derma). Bucharian Jews serve bachsh (a rice cholent). Yemenite Jews serve a Sabbath pastry called ghininun, which is cooked overnight, sometimes with cottage cheese for dairy Sabbath meals. Other Sephardic Jews serve burekas (sesame-topped pastry). One could go on and on, as indeed many meals do.

As Rav Hiya bar Ashi said, even a modest meal, if prepared in honor of the sabbath, is a delight. The Talmud tells of a Roman emperor who was a guest at the house of Rabbi Judah the Prince for a Shabbat meal. The emperor was so taken by the delicious foods that he asked for and received the recipes. He was disgruntled when his own chefs served him the same food and he found it considerably flatter in taste. The rabbi explained to him that the missing ingredient was the flavor imparted by Shabbat itself.

The main feature of the Shabbat meal, however, is not what goes into the mouth but what comes out of it. To express the joy, *zemirot* (songs) and *niggunim* (melodies without words) by the thousands were developed. Many of the zemirot rehearse the laws of Shabbat or sing of its delight.

Telling words of Torah (dvar Torah) is another special feature of the Shabbat meal. During the week people might feel too rushed to linger at the table. Many families save special stories or items for sharing at these meals, and guests add spice to the conversations. The Shechinah or feminine aspect of God is greeted, according to kabbalistic teaching.

At the end of the meal, it is customary to say or sing the Birkat Hamazon (Grace After Meals). When there is a quorum of three people present, a special introductory call to the blessing is added. (If there are ten present, then the call is expanded a bit, adding the name of God. The more people present, then the more God's presence is felt!) Some follow the custom that the leader of the grace says it over a cup of wine, so rejoicing never stops. The blessing *after* the meal is linked to the biblical verse, "You shall eat, be satisfied, and give thanks to the Lord your God" (Deuteronomy 8:10).

Originally people improvised their own blessings for the Grace, expressing their special feelings. In time, a text became established and standardized, probably because people found it easier to have a fixed, familiar text. According to rabbinic tradition, the first blessing, for the food, was introduced by Moses when the manna was received; the second blessing, for the land, was introduced by Joshua at the original conquest of Israel; the third blessing was added by David and Solomon after the conquest of Jerusalem and the building of the Temple. The fourth blessing ("the Lord . . . who is good and does good") is associated with a more tragic moment. Some say it was introduced after the destruction of the Temple to fight despair and give hope that the Temple would be rebuilt. Others believe that the blessing originated when the Romans, quelling the Bar Kochba rebellion, refused to allow the Jewish dead to be buried. When permission was finally granted to pay last respects to the dead and to bury them, the Rabbis introduced this blessing in gratitude. A final segment of prayers that begin with the phrases, "May the All Merciful" were added later, in the time of the Geonim (ninth- to eleventh-century period). Today, it is a growing custom to say additional prayers of thanksgiving for the restoration of Israel, as well as prayers for the redemption of Soviet and other oppressed Jewries.

After the meal, especially in Conservative and Reform congregations, many families attend late Friday night services or an Oneg Shabbat program.

Kabbalists teach that on this evening the holy union of the Shechinah and the masculine aspect of God occurs. Its earthly counterpart is to make love out of the fullness, relaxation, and joy of Shabbat. (A friend once reported that in all his years in the rabbinate, he constantly criticized his congregants who failed to come to late Friday night services until he discovered the "mitzvah" of making love Friday night. "My God," he said, "all my Jews are home doing mitzvot! Let me stop pestering them." He and the board abolished the service. I am happy to report that in the next five years, the congregation doubled in size.)

The Shabbat morning services are the most elaborate of the week. The focus shifts from testimony-to-creation to encounter-with-Revelation. The mood is more reflective and intellectual as the initial flush of released emotion is succeeded by calm and awareness of the Eternal. The heart of the service is the Torah reading. Orthodox congregations and most Conservative ones divide the five books of Moses into fifty-two weekly portions. Many Reform, Reconstructionist, and some Conservative congregations follow a three-year cycle.

The Torah reading represents a mini-reenactment of the Sinai Revelation as the Torah is proclaimed to the congregation. It is also the occasion to learn and teach Torah. Instead of giving sermons, many rabbis today exchange views with their congregation or answer questions on the weekly Torah portion. The classic sermons also stem from the text. Shabbat leisure and the morning Torah study became the keystone of the extraordinary Jewish pattern of universal education and sharing of knowledge. Recovering this opportunity for learning is the key to overcoming Jewish illiteracy and educating Jewish lay persons, which is necessary to make Judaism a viable alternative in an open society.

After the Torah reading, traditional synagogues have a special Sabbath *Mussaf* (additional) service whose theme is historical. The Amidah (silent standing prayer) recalls the destroyed Temple and prays for restoration to Zion. In later years a prayer for the Jews martyred in the first crusades (eleventh century) was inserted. In this generation, some congregations include a prayer in memory of the Holocaust. More widespread is the practice of saying the prayer for the peace of the reborn state of Israel and a prayer for the United States (or whatever the home country is). In some congregations, there is the custom of having the entire congregation say, or stand at silent attention during, the recitation of the Kaddish after the concluding Aleynu prayer, in memory of the six million.

Another learning tradition that can be practiced easily is the study of the chapters of *Ethics of the Fathers*. This basic text of Jewish values and wisdom found in the Talmud was traditionally studied on Shabbat afternoons between Minchah and Maariv during the long spring and summer Shabbat days on a six-week rotation cycle, one chapter per week. The character and values of the entire people were profoundly shaped by the maxims of the Rabbis and by centuries of commentary and expansion of these ideas. The Talmud cites learning as one of the great joys of Shabbat: "Said Rabbi Berachyah: 'The Shabbat was only given for joy.' Said Rabbi Hagai: 'The Shabbat was only given for learning.' There is no disagreement between them. The joy is for scholars who work at learning all week and on Shabbat focus on [other] pleasures. The learning is for workers who all week long are occupied with work. On Shabbat, they come and take joy from learning."*

A Shabbat morning kiddush follows services. This is an opportunity for good fellowship in the synagogue and/or for visiting or having company at home. The Shabbat morning kiddush reiterates the Sabbath commandment; its text is taken directly from the Ten Commandments. Shabbat lunch has its own variety of foods, its own zemirot, its own words of Torah. Oftentimes one hears in the synagogue or through the rabbi's sermon the alarm about some Jewish concern. Lunch gives the opportunity to discuss it and decide what to do.

Shabbat afternoon splinters into a variety of experiences in traditional homes: It is a time to sleep for some, a learning session for others; or a nature walk or family time, with all sorts of heart-to-heart talks. For people newly come to Sabbath observance, conditioned to the constant work, travel, and being on the go, this is a hard period. The sense of being needed at work or at business or of missing entertainment can create an emotional crisis. But persistence yields deeper levels of calm and serenity.

As the Shabbat shadows lengthen, the mood of the day turns nostalgic, full of yearning. The sense of a human being's great potential for perfection grows. The Minchah service sings of the uniqueness of the Jewish people ("who is like your folk, Israel, one of a kind people in all the world") and of "the coming of the Redeemer of Zion." The third meal is more Spartan, its melodies slower and full of longing, but its thrust is more overtly messianic. One can almost feel the approach of the Redeemer. The Jew is taking off... which is why the Havdalah comes to separate Shabbat from the weekday and to restore a sense of

---

*Pesikta Rabbati, section on the Ten Commandments.

reality. Of course, reality is not a fact, it is a challenge. And the Shabbat gives the strength to take it on.

TOWARD A PLURALIST SHABBAT EXPERIENCE*

In every generation Shabbat has been celebrated as the ongoing center of Jewish living. It is a compendium of positive, touching, and moving experiences within Judaism. Historically, many of these effects grew out of the comprehensive, "wraparound" nature of Shabbat; total environment makes for a healing atmosphere of peace and joy. So comprehensive is Shabbat that on this day the tefillin (phylacteries) worn every day as a reminder and symbol of the covenant are not put on. As Heschel articulated the Talmudic principle, "Symbols are superfluous; the Sabbath itself is the symbol."†

I write as one whose life has been given a special dimension by the experience of the totality of a divinely commanded Shabbat. For example, people often ask whether our family finds the halachic prohibition of electricity (which means no telephone and no television on Shabbat) irksome and restrictive. On the contrary, we feel that Shabbat has protected a special private area of our lives together. We have found the same holds true in the concept of *uvdin d'chol*—weekday, mundane activities. A noted Israeli religious thinker once wrote that he would read only certain sacred texts on Shabbat, not the ones he studied professionally all week. To him, reading the texts that he studied would bring a weekday spirit to his Sabbath day! This total change is alien to most people, but it generates a sense of otherness on Shabbat that I find soul-renewing.

Yet the truth of my experience is the source of an aching dilemma. It is a fact that a substantial majority of Jews do not observe Shabbat in this traditional manner. Most of them seem to consider a change to this life-style impossible for them. Whether due to job and business patterns, psychological set, or whatever the reason, they turn off from the traditional Shabbat. I am torn by the cruel fact that many people I love are cut off from the day I love.

*I am indebted to Rabbi Haskell Bernat of Miami for the illuminating conversations, filled with his insights, that led to the formulation of the concepts and approaches used below. Indeed, I have included his commentary on my ideas. Rabbi Bernat sees his Shabbat practices as "beyond the strictures of the halacha—but with total reference to their inner meaning." The core values of halacha are internalized and applied by the person beyond the law. My personal hope is that once people achieve the level of Shabbat in these formulations they will find themselves closer to the possibility of taking on the halachic Shabbat experience. At the least, however, I believe that these suggestions will bring more of the power of Shabbat into more Jewish homes.

†Abraham Joshua Heschel, *The Sabbath*, p. 82.

There is, however, a growing interest in Shabbat on the part of many who seek rebirth as Jews, and after a century of moving away from classical Shabbat, Reform Judaism is seeking to deepen its liturgical and traditional life. Both groups repeatedly pose the questions: Is Shabbat all or nothing? Is there any partial experience that can bestow blessings of the day? The questions go deeper. Heretofore, all too often, nonobservant Orthodox, Conservative, Reform, and cultural Jews have kept a Shabbat day that was a compromise between the absolute demands of modern life and a residual traditionalism. Since modern values were usually dominant, the residual restrictions were often experienced as inconsistent and repressive even while their observance failed to bestow the benefits of a total Shabbat atmosphere.

Many people are willing now to let Jewish standards set the tone; they want a Sabbath day that is more than a day of leisure American-style. These people ask not what Judaism can do to meet modern criteria but what modern culture should do to meet Jewish norms. Yet often such a commitment goes hand in hand with a conviction that contemporary values and practices not provided for in the halacha may add a dimension of holiness. Can these values be integrated? Can there be pluralist experiences of Shabbat that might transform life? Can there be a Shabbat observance that does not operate by halachic measurements alone yet expresses a coherent commitment to its holiness principle?

To many Conservative and Reform Jews, these questions slight their practice. Is this not a challenge to their right to observe in accordance with their own denomination? To many Orthodox Jews the question may seem illegitimate. If people cannot observe Shabbat fully, that is one thing. The divinity of Shabbat remains, but the flesh is weak. Even the idea of doing whatever you can—observing Shabbat partially—is better than nothing but is a far cry from justifying any actions that violate halachic categories of Shabbat, the one holy day included in the Ten Commandments.

I mean no disrespect for anyone's standards. Indeed, I am reminded of the rabbi who responds to both litigants with the affirmation, "You are right." (And to you who point out that both sides can't be right, you are also right!)

Out of the belief that the human needs of Jews demand a Shabbat experience and that the sense of the sacred requires such nurture; out of the conviction that Jewish survival as a distinctive group demands the recovery of a distinctive Jewish time; out of the faith that after the Holocaust and rebirth of Israel we are living in an age of voluntary covenant and there will be plural standards even if one of them is imposed by the authority of the Divine; out of the affirmation that all who choose to live as Jews must be recognized as authentic carriers of the covenantal witness, the question must be addressed: Is there some integral model in the spirit of Shabbat?

We seek a model that can enrich life, that can serve as a guide for those who seek to grow into Shabbat even as they try it on for size. The right model should illuminate the traditional concept of Shabbat even as it varies in its own directions. If it works, it can give greater dignity and depth to various models of Shabbat even as it relates to the actual state of observance among Jews. Such a model is offered in the hope that it can bring Shabbat observance within the scope of more Jews without weakening the authority or undermining the halachic Shabbat experience of others.

A pluralist approach to Shabbat (one not bound to the categories and specific quantitative measurements of the halacha, yet shaped by the classical model of Shabbat) would be constructed on three levels. Shabbat is more than a day of leisure; *it is a shift in the mode of being*. The foundation of Shabbat is a negative commandment: to cease being manipulative on this day. Manipulation need not mean negative behavior. Even the appropriate use of society and the reshaping of the natural world create a utilitarian attitude toward people and things. People begin to rate themselves primarily in terms of efficiency and productivity. Shabbat is the day to step back and gain release from such activities and attitudes. On this day, one shifts from tampering, control, and aggression to harmonizing behavior. Being, friendship, and relationships become the central modes of existence. This is equivalent to the halachic stress on leaving the world in its original state of creation. This modal shift links behavior to the "remembrance of creation" even as the harmony and freedom of Sabbath link the day to "remembrance of the Exodus."

Bernat commentary: "Ideally, this means not working or even doing housework on Shabbat. However, acts of self-expression or in fulfillment of a relationship that would be prohibited by halacha would be affirmed by this criterion. Thus, one might drive to the country to see the trees in bloom but not pick apples from the trees. Calling and traveling to visit with friends or family would be an expression of Shabbat, but shopping would not. Some might accept mowing the lawn or other types of puttering around the house that have recreational effects as a shift of mode of being. Others might object to these activities as manipulative of nature, a tampering with creation. Playing or listening to music would be a valid expression of the fullness of being. The joy of music and art can intensify the pleasure and spiritual depth of Shabbat service and Shabbat rest.

"Notwithstanding the biblical ban on fire, smoking would be legitimate in terms of meditation, relaxation, and acceptance. Since smoking has been shown to be destructive of health, however, it would be unacceptable in this model because destructiveness is as much or more a violation of the integrity of nature as construction. In this model, shopping or working is not "shabbasdig." One would not call a broker to discuss stock purchases but might call that broker to catch up on his family or to share personal concerns. Furthermore, since Shabbat is a mode of being, one can revert to this mode once shopping or working has finished. Thus, keeping part of Shabbat would be an authentic fulfillment of Shabbat (during these periods).

"There is even a category of *shevut* in this model. The purpose of Shabbat leisure is to permit experience, not to destroy experience. Some music is so heavy and involving that listening to it leaves one exhausted; it does not allow any space for other experiences. The shevut prohibition applies to any experience in itself permitted that obliterates all other experiences instead of opening us up to experience of the world. Since such an activity leaves no room for Shabbat, it is incompatible with the spirit of the day."

The second level of Shabbat reflects the act of transcending—standing outside ourselves and our round of life. All other creatures live a self-evident, instinctive order of being and do not experience the pain of knowing choice and of their future nonbeing. This unique mode of human existence is affirmed on Shabbat as the source of upward striving and consciousness of the Divine. Of course, the capability of transcending exists in the human being all the time. On Shabbat, however, there is a heightened capacity. Thus, the Rabbis spoke of having an "extra soul" on Shabbat. One soul expresses the normal performance and involvement in our life. The "extra soul" is the transcending mode. By releasing people from the everyday round of life and by nurturing their souls, Shabbat makes possible and intensifies the examination of their lives from the perspective of eternity even as they are caught up in the process of living.

Abraham Joshua Heschel has written of the pathos whereby God empathetically shares human existence and the prophets share God's grief. Shabbat frees the vision and releases the soul qualities that enable people to identify with the Divine, to look at themselves *sub specie aeternitatis*, out of divine lenses, as if God were looking. This perspective checks the human tendency to arrogance and restores a profound sense of creaturehood. One of the central purposes of Shabbat is to remind people that all humans are creatures, linked in common creatureliness to all other things.

This Shabbat effect naturally makes the day a time for communion with God. Prayer is therefore an essential component of the Shabbat experience, both as communion with God and as a source of self-judgment. Communal prayer has the extra benefit of inspiring the community to judge its collective ways and policies as well. In this way, Shabbat is a time for different perspective and self-judgment, a time to look to God and to consider alternate ways of living. Despite this element of self-evaluation, Shabbat underscores divine acceptance, love for all creatures, and forgiveness for humanity with all its flaws. This very acceptance frees the individual to grow. Again, by this pluralist definition, activity to advance this process of self-judgment or to participate in worship becomes a positive expression of Shabbat.

Finally, at its highest level, Shabbat is a fantasy of perfection. In the imagination, reality is so perfect that there is nothing lacking. On this day, prayer consists of praise of God and thanksgiving but not request. Living out this fantasy taxes the powers of imagination and play, but the purpose is not to run away from reality. We live as if something were true in order to make it true. The Shabbat force flows into the week in the form of socially redemptive activity.

Bernat commentary: "Some might even hold that such redemptive activity is permitted on Shabbat as an expression of the spirit of the day. Others would argue that such activity should only be a last resort, for the gain involved should be balanced against the loss of perspective, self-judgment, and harmony. The erosion of these qualities might well lead to failure to reach the ultimate goal of a final perfection.

"If we look around us, we see that the cosmos is in order; it is marked by harmony, design, and beauty. However, human society is marked much more by conflict, oppression, and disorder. Shabbat is the restoration of internal harmony in the cosmos, in society, and in their alignment with each other. When cosmos and society are in tandem perfection, this is a messianic state. The Shabbat is, then, a forestate of the messianic era and of the world to come—when every day will be Shabbat."

Obviously this pluralist Shabbat model is not an easy model to live up to either. Business demands, ego involvement in work, and established routines of activity or shopping still combine to be a formidable obstacle to freeing one's self for a Shabbat experience. The homogenization of time is one of the most powerful of the assimilationist effects of the open American environment. The power of Shabbat is that it carves out a distinctive area of time that is Jewish time. Precisely for that reason, its rhythms may appear, initially, to be strange, its color or flavor insipid by comparison with pure leisure time. This is often true even of the Shabbat experience of observant Jews. It takes a conscious, ongoing process of Jewish liberation to undo the assimilated conditioning and develop a proper taste for Jewish modes. To move into this Shabbat mode, therefore, it will take an individual act of will or a major effort at spiritual rebirth or, at the least, seeing life in a fresh pattern.

Franz Rosenzweig, one of the great Jewish philosophers and baaleil teshuvah (returnees) of the twentieth century, is a superb model for such growth. Rosenzweig stressed the importance of growing into religious practice. When asked if he observed certain laws (which, in fact, he did not), he would not answer "no"; he would reply, "not yet." In many cases his explanation/prediction proved to be true.

When challenged as to how he could pick and choose among commanded laws, Rosenzweig drew a distinction. The law as commandment/norm but not yet integrated into his life-style was described by him as *gesetz* (law). Although he did not deny the law's divine nature, its very otherness placed it outside of his life. As he matured religiously and drew psychologically and philosophically closer to the practice, to the point where the law became near enough to reach for and to draw into his life, it became *gebot* (instruction, calling)—the law in a form "very close to you, in your mouth and your heart to observe it" (Deuteronomy 30:14).

Some novices might find it easier to grow into Shabbat in stages, starting first with Friday night and extending into the Saturday morning, then afternoon and evening. Others may find it easier to start on a monthly basis and then increase frequency. As in marriage therapy, it will take individual commitment, family interaction, and a collective decision to achieve changed patterns in order for those who do not observe now to enter into Shabbat living successfully.

Sometimes people will resist the behavior of a person who is subjectively observant more than that of someone they feel is bound by the halachic system. In a striking story, Rosenzweig tells of this additional difficulty in taking on the Shabbat in stages. Rosenzweig would write letters for the sake of friendship on Shabbat but not for business matters, not even those associated with his *lehrhaus* (academy for adult Jewish learning). A close friend was willing to respect Rosenzweig's refusal to write something down if he observed the total halachic prohibitions of Shabbat, but he could not accept Rosenzweig's fine distinctions between types of writing in the practice of his pluralist Shabbat. This incident led Rosenzweig to take on the halachic standard in this matter, although he continued to defend and respect other pluralist models of Shabbat.*

---

*See N. N. Glatzer, *Franz Rosenzweig: Life and Thought* (New York: Schocken Books, 2nd ed., 1972), pp. 356–57.

Working with others who are more experienced at keeping Shabbat can make the transitional growth phase not only easier but more interesting. (These same principles can be applied by those who already have the complete Shabbat but wish to renew its spiritual richness or deepen its effects on their personal lives.) Those who undertake this living pattern will find that once it is accomplished, however, the day is short and the reward is great.

In the words of the Hebrew prayer, the Sabbath is *chemdat hayamim*, "the most treasured (most desired) of days." On it, humans taste the ultimate peace, "a voluntary and loving rest, a truthful and faithful rest, a peaceful, serene, calm, and secure rest, a perfect rest."* Perhaps this is why Rabbi Yohanan said that if all Jews kept two Sabbath days properly, they would be instantly redeemed.†

---

*My translation of a passage in the Shabbat afternoon Amidah in *Daily Prayer Book* edited by Philip Birnbaum, p. 453.
†Babylonian Talmud, Shabbat 118B.

CHAPTER SIX

Rebirth and Renewal:
High Holy Days

THE HIGH HOLY DAYS:
A MATTER OF
LIFE AND DEATH

JUDAISM IS A RELIGION OF LIFE against death. Death negates redemption; it is the end of growth, of freedom. Death is so contradictory to liberation that a Talmudic sage exempts the mourner preparing for the funeral from the daily requirement of the central act of Jewish memory, remembering the Exodus. "That you remember the day you left Egypt all the days of your life—on days that you deal with life but not on the days when you deal with death."*

Death is a denial of dignity. Metaphorically, the Talmud tells that the great King David died on a holy day. Seeing the body lying there, unable to help itself, untreated (until after the holy day), decaying, Solomon burst out: "Even a live dog is better than a dead lion" (Ecclesiastes 9:4). What greater tragedy can there be for the living than the death of another loved human being? Someone of infinite value, someone irreplaceable has been snatched away. The power, the beauty, the uniqueness of that person is mocked by the inert, empty body that

---

*Jerusalem Talmud Berachot, chapter 3, halachah 1.

remains. In the presence of the unburied dead, the religious universe collapses into a void. "He whose dead one lies before him is exempt from the Sh'ma, from prayer [meaning Shmoneh Esrei], from tefillin, from all the commandments stated in the Torah."*

In a world growing toward life, death is a "contradiction" to God, who is pure life. In the end, therefore, death must be overcome. "God will destroy death forever. My Lord God will wipe the tears away from every face." (Isaiah 25:8). Judaism's ultimate dream, then, is to vanquish death totally. In fact, since God is all good and all life, ideally there should have been no death in God's creation in the first place. Classic Judaism therefore taught that when the ultimate redemption is achieved, when the Messiah comes, all those who have died will come to life again. Resurrection of the dead will nullify death retroactively.

Death is treated as the enemy. "Behold, I place before you today life and good, and death and evil. . . . Choose life" (Deuteronomy 30:19). In daily ritual, death is set up as the negative pole of contact with God. The human corpse was considered the most intense archetype of ritual impurity. No burials were allowed inside Jerusalem, the holy city. People who came in contact with the dead were not allowed to enter the Holy Temple without first going through an elaborate purification rite, including immersion in a body of living water, that is, a symbolic rebirth from the grip of death.

Yet, unlike Christian Science, Judaism does not deny the facts of death. When death strikes a family, the tradition prescribes unflinching recognition and acceptance rather than evasion. The proper response is to show love through caring treatment of the corpse and expression of grief and loss.

This is the concession Judaism makes to the universality of death. Otherwise, it is almost as if death is to be quarantined as a dangerous antagonist. Holiness, which is the fullness of life, is incompatible with death. Priests who were consecrated to the full-time service of God were not allowed to have any contact with the dead. They were prohibited from entering a graveyard or attending funerals, except for those of their closest relatives; in such a case, denial of attendance would be "inhuman."

Yet death is a fact of life. How one reacts to it can critically shape all of one's values. Buddha's encounter with death when he was a young prince turned him decisively away from worldly life as an illusion and snare. At Roman orgies, skulls were passed around to stimulate even more frantic excesses, with the admonition, "Eat, drink, and be merry! For tomorrow we die!" The American way of death has used euphemism to obscure the fact of mortality and cosmetic treatment to prettify the corpse.

*Babylonian Talmud, Shabbat 30B; Berachot 17B.

Judaism's general response to the fact of death is to fight back. Life is given the highest priority. All but three laws of the Torah are over-ruled to save a life from death. The physician is commanded to heal. Even partial triumphs—a sickness cured, some months of life snatched from the domain of death—constitute a fulfillment of the command. When someone dies, the mourner steps froward and, through recitation of the Kaddish, testifies that this family has not yielded to the crushing defeat. In effect, the survivors pledge to carry on, for the deceased as well as for themselves in the army of the Lord, among the soldiers of life. In essence, the Kaddish prayer affirms that God's kindom of total perfection and total life will be brought speedily into being, preferably in this very lifetime.

The one notable exception to the arm's-length treatment of death is the period of the High Holy Days. During this cluster of days, the tradition deliberately concentrates the individual's attention on death.

Human beings cannot be mature until they encompass a sense of their own mortality. To recognize the brevity of human existence gives urgency and significance to the totality of life. To confront death with-out being overwhelmed, driven to evasions or dulling the senses is to be given life again as a daily gift. People generally experience this gift through a trauma: an accident or a critical illness or the death of some-one close. Too often the encounter fades as the presence of death re-cedes and the round of normal life becomes routine reality. In the Jewish calendar, the Yamim Noraim (Days of Awe) structure the imagi-native encounter with death into an annual experience in the hope that the experience will recur to liberate life continually.

The Days of Awe are *Rosh Hashanah* (New Year) on Tishrei 1 and 2, *Yom Hakippurim* (Day of Atonement) on Tishrei 10, and the intervening days which all together are called the Aseret Yemai Teshuvah (Ten Days of Penitence). Unlike all the other Jewish holidays, neither Rosh Hashanah nor Yom Kippur is linked to remembrance of liberation or commemoration of catastrophe. This is the time for the individual to concentrate on mortality and the meaning of life.

Later tradition, uneasy with the absence of historical connections, did link these days to historical events. The forty days from Elul to Yom Kippur are the anniversary of the forty days that Moses spent on Sinai to receive the second set of tablets. Moses sought to win forgive-ness for the sin of the golden calf and to ensure continued life for the Jewish people. Yom Kippur thus becomes the anniversary of a day of forgiveness and reconciliation. Similarly, on Yom Kippur, Jews mourn for the lost Azazel (scapegoat ceremony) and the collective forgiveness it won. This loss becomes the paradigm of the national tragedy of exile.

Whatever the historical associations, however, they are marginal to the High Holy Days. There is no mistaking the "universalist" focus on Lord as Creator and Judge of mankind; year round the emphasis is much more on God who is known through Jewish history. Many prayers stress the hope that all humanity will come to know God. Yet the unique relationship of God and Israel is not scanted. (The marvelous dialectic of individual and community, of God of Israel and Lord of Mankind, that marks the High Holy Day liturgy is a standing rebuke to those theologies or secular views which insist that one cannot have both.) In this age, when the sense of Jewish group identity, historically shaped, has weakened among Jews, particularly in the Diaspora, these universalist- and individual-oriented themes have enabled these days to maintain their grip on the imagination and loyalty more powerfully than the other holy days. Still, the real power of the Days of Awe lies in the fact that they tap into the deep human feelings about death.

In the period of the High Holy Days, tradition guides the individual to take up the challenge of death on three levels. One is to deal with the constant gradual, partial encroachment of death in one's own life. Life is also a process of dying. Routine and stagnation are forms of death in life. People often stop growing long before they are recognized as dead. Such a "dead" person cannot be an agent of redemption. The tradition holds that the key to vital living is perpetual renewal of life; it seeks to attain that renewal by generating a continual process of examining life and constant rebirth. The awareness of being judged for life and death is a stimulus to stop living routinely.

The second level of the challenge is to deal with encountering abrupt, total death itself. Starting before and going through this period, the Jew focuses on the vulnerability of life and the limits of the human. People rediscover that "our entire life is God's mercy; by miracle we stand—but miracles may not happen every day."*

The encounter with nonexistence is set off by the awareness of creation. Whatever is born, dies. By tradition, Rosh Hashanah is the "birthday" of the world or of humanity. This birthday, that is, New Year's Day, is not the occasion for a party to wipe out the passage of time in the oblivion of celebration but a time for taking stock. The possibility of non-being leads one to the questions: What is it all worth? What has been accomplished? By what merit does it still stand?

The Rosh Hashanah and Yom Kippur liturgies focus on creation and on God as Creator and Ruler of the universe. "To say of the world that it is created is to say that it is not its own ground but proceeds from a will and a plan beyond itself. . . . [To say it is not created is to say that] the world at every moment is the last word about itself and measured

*Rabbi Israel Salanter, *Ohr Yisrael* (Vilna: n.p., 1874). Reprinted edition (New York: Friedman Press, n.d.), p. 44.

by nothing but itself."* In Jewish tradition, creation also implies the goodness of the world: "And God saw everything that God had made and, behold, it was very good" (Genesis 1:31). In other words, the controversy whether the world is created is less a theological argument than a moral one: The concept of creation teaches that this is a world of divine purpose, a universe of value and meaning. Human beings can be judged by the standard of creation. Are they acting in consonance with the fact that this is a universe with value, purpose and meaning?

From the combined themes of death and of judgment comes the central image underlying the Days of Awe: the trial. Jews envision a trial in which the individual stands before the One who knows all. One's life is placed on the balance scales. A thorough assessment is made: Is my life contributing to the balance of life? Or does the net effect of my actions tilt the scale toward death? My life is being weighed; I am on trial for my life. Who shall live and who shall die? This image jolts each person into a heightened awareness of the fragility of life. This question poses the deeper issue: If life ended now, would it have been worthwhile? Is one aware and grateful for the miracle of daily existence?

The trial image captures the sense of one's life being in someone else's hands. The *shofar* of Rosh Hashanah proclaims that the Judge before whom there is no hiding is now sitting on the bench. Sharpened self-awareness, candid self-judgment, and guilt are activated by the possibility that a death sentence may be handed down. Like standing before a firing squad, a trial for life wonderfully concentrates the mind.

Then, the High Holy Days move to meet the third challenge of mortality—to harness death into a force for life. On Yom Kippur, Jews enact death by denying themselves the normal human pleasures. It is not a morbid experience, however, because this encounter with death is in the service of life. The true goal is a new appreciation of life.

To know how fragile the shell of life is, is to learn to handle it with true grace and delicacy. Only one who realizes the vulnerability of loved ones can treasure every moment with them. The encounter with death turns the individual toward life. Death can only be opposed by life just as death-in-life can only be opposed by growing in life. Instead of standing there, letting death constantly invade life, Judaism strikes back by raiding the realm of death and turning this encounter into a spur to life.

The climax comes in living out death on Yom Kippur. On this day,

*Hans Jonas, *The Phenomenon of Life: Toward a Philosophical Biology* (New York: Harper and Row, 1966).

traditional Jews put on a *kittel*, a white robe similar to the shroud worn when one is buried. The life processes of eating, drinking, washing and sexuality are stopped for twenty-four hours. Guilt (in the form of confession), encounter with the dead (in Yizkor memorial prayers), and the final trial judgment dominate the days. But then relief from sin emerges on Yom Kippur. God forgives! "The Lord your God will open your heart and your children's hearts... for the sake of giving you life!" (Deuteronomy 30:6)

This is why the tone of the Days of Awe is basically hopeful, even joyful. This is why the liturgy bursts with life. "Remember us for life, King who loves life; write us in the book of life, for your sake, Lord of Life."*

This period seeks nothing less than the removal of sin and the renewal of love. Those who confront their own guilt and failure in human and divine relationships—in the context of community oneness and divine forgiveness—can correct errors, develop new patterns, and renew life. "For I do not desire the death of the wicked, but that he turn from his paths—and live." To turn is to be reborn. The people of Israel come out of Yom Kippur reborn. Forgiven and pure, at one with God.

One final comment should be made about the emotional mood of these days. Obviously in their focus on death, the High Holy Days are one-sided. The Torah seeks to present the full range of human emotion, from ecstatic joy to deepest depression. Life includes success as well as failure. There is a time for ambition and a time for sense of limit. Some experiences come only with unselfconscious living, others only out of self-criticism and guilt. The Yamim Noraim, then, are a "distortion" unless they are taken together with Sukkot and the rest of the Jewish tradition. In the sometimes delirious joy of Sukkot, with its celebration of harvest, of life-giving water, of goods and of the produce of the field, are the complementary experiences of affirmation of human pleasure and achievement. The days of Sukkot are the response to the denial and self-criticism of the High Holy Days. The two periods together give one the capacity to live through triumph and tragedy, aware that this, too, shall pass. Life in all its bewildering and uncontrollable variety becomes possible.

ELUL—THE MONTH PRECEDING
THE NEW YEAR

"My children, give me an opening of repentance no bigger than the eye of a needle, and I will widen it into an opening through

---

*From High Holy Days liturgy, opening blessing of Amidah.

which wagons and carriages will pass.*

The Rabbis taught that from time to time people must stop and assess their deeds and their spiritual condition and judge whether the balance sheet of the soul is showing a profit or deficit. The classic Jewish term *cheshbon hanefesh*—a reckoning with one's self—literally means accounting for the soul. Such moments are a time for penetrating questions and self-criticism; they pave the way for personal renewal.

Making a cheshbon hanefesh is appropriate all year round. But just as the month before the summer is the time when Americans go on crash diets, fearing how their bodies will look on the beach, so Elul, the month before Rosh Hashanah, became the time when Jews went on crash spiritual regimens, fearing how their souls would look when they stood naked before God.

Consciousness of going on trial always precedes the trial itself. So Elul reflects the awareness and anxiety of the trial. In the traditional synagogue, the shofar is blown every day in Elul to shake up people and remind them of the approaching trial. Understandably, Elul became a time for reconciliation with enemies (a trial for life is no time to fight other battles) and a time for resolutions ("If I get off, I'll never do it again!") and for heroic efforts to correct personal flaws ("Your Honor, I've turned over a new leaf!"). Rabbi Israel Salanter, the founder of the nineteenth-century Mussar (ethical revival) movement, annually undertook a forty-day silence from the beginning of Elul through Yom Kippur to review his past year's patterns of speaking, atone for wrongful speech, and recapture the awe and sacredness in every word uttered.

One should not exaggerate the tone of Elul. It is awe, not terror. There is a strong conviction that God is understanding, merciful, and loving. Sin, error, and failure are inescapable parts of human behavior. Judaism is not a religion of excessive guilt or of judgment standards that can never be met, but neither is it a religion of permissiveness. Through the self-criticism of Elul and the High Holy Days, Judaism keeps life from settling into deadening routine or evil habits.

Structuring cheshbon hanefesh into the yearly life cycle results in uplift and insight for the individual and a higher standard of behavior for the people. One might say that just as modern accounting has played a major role in creating a system of profits, so has the Jewish balance sheet of the soul yielded a high standard of moral living, a people of prophets.

The uplifting prophetic readings (*Haftarot*) of Elul keep people's optimism up through this trying period. These are the final four of the

---

Song of Songs Rabba, chapter 5, section 2.

seven prophetic portions of consolation that follow Tisha B'Av. They promise God's unfailing love and Israel's future joy.

As Rosh Hashanah approaches, the intensity of feeling rises. In the week before the New Year, traditional Jews gather for *Selichot*, penitential prayers. The first night's service is held at midnight; for the remainder of the week prayers are recited at dawn. The Selichot prayers orchestrate the themes of human guilt and God's forgiving nature. Some scholars suggest that each day of this week should be used to repent and correct for the particular day of the week throughout the year; Thursday is the day of reckoning for all Thursdays of the year, Wednesday for Wednesdays, and so forth.

Additional Psalms are recited this month, most notably Psalm 27 which refers to God's protection in days of trouble. Letters written during this period include the wish that people be written into and confirmed in the book of life. This led to the custom of sending New Year cards. Prayer, giving charity, and acts of repentance are also increased in Elul (call it life insurance—with the Rock of Ages). It is also customary to visit parents' graves, especially on the days between Rosh Hashanah and Yom Kippur. One also prays at the graves of righteous people on the day before Rosh Hashanah (we-can-use-all-the-help-we-can-get). Among other customs created to express the urgency of the season are fasting part of the day on the eve of Rosh Hashanah and spending the day in learning or asking forgiveness from people one has wronged.

Taking a haircut and dressing in new clothes are part of the preparation for Rosh Hashanah, as for other holidays. In spite of the awe of the moment, the joy of the holiday is not stilled. On the contrary, joy expresses confidence in God's forgiveness and love. Despite the fear and trembling, the trial is before a merciful Judge. If joy were suppressed, it would represent a failure to appreciate God's nature. This counterpoint of joy wells up even on Yom Kippur, when the anxiety of the trial reaches its peak.

Traditional Jews customarily annul oaths on the eve of Rosh Hashanah. One cannot annul business commitments or obligations but only customary practices or oaths of ritual observance that one does not wish to violate unintentionally (compare *Kol Nidre*). The ceremony, called *hatarat nedarim*, reflects the sacredness of the given word and the importance of fidelity to it in the religious economy of the Jew.

ROSH HASHANAH—NEW YEAR

According to the Talmudic analysis of the trial theme New Year's Day is the first day of court. Verdicts are handed down in open-and-shut cases, those concerning people who are one-sidedly good or bad. Many interpret the rest of the ten days as the time for appeals, rehearings, and applications for clemency. The peak of intensity is reached on Yom Kippur, when those whose records are mixed (like most people) receive their verdict.

In the trial, every act suddenly looms large, for every act is known to the Judge, and the whole verdict could turn on a hair. One of the most profound teachings of the Rosh Hashanah–Yom Kippur holidays is the cosmic significance of every single act.

Says Maimonides:

Everyone should regard himself throughout the years as exactly balanced between acquittal and guilt. So, too, he should consider the entire world as equally balanced between acquittal and guilt. If he commits one additional sin, he tilts down the scale of guilt against himself and the entire world and causes its destruction. If he performs one good deed, he swings himself and the whole world into the scale of merit and causes salvation and deliverance to himself and his fellow men.*

This truth applies throughout life, but most people are too self-indulgent to face the fact. There are those who earn their world in one act. The Talmud tells many such tales: of a Roman Senator who gave his life to annul an evil decree against the Jews; of a Roman executioner who died to release a rabbinic martyr from his suffering; of a Jewish man who bought a Jewish woman from captivity and prostitution and, having her in his control, voluntarily released her.

How many wasted lives have been redeemed by one heroic act? The most moving scene in Dickens' *A Tale of Two Cities* occurs when Sydney Carton pulls together an aimless and even squandered life and gives it transcendent significance by martyring himself for the happiness of the woman he loves.

In life as in tradition or literature, individual acts do have enormous effects. A man once came to visit Martin Buber. Buber was glowing inwardly from a personal, mystical experience, even as he sat and talked with the man. The friend subsequently came to a decision that led to his death. Reflecting afterward, Buber realized that while he had been amiable to the visitor, he was so focused on his own experiences that he had not been totally present and alert to the needs of his caller. He had failed to respond to the serious need for counsel; he had not

*Maimonides, *Yad Hachazakah* (Mishneh Torah) (New York: Grossman Publishers, 1960), Sefer Mada, Hilchot Teshuva, chapter 3, paragraph 4. After Babylonian Talmud, Kiddushin 40A, B.

offered the guidance that could have turned the young man's decision in a different direction.

Sometimes people hear the signals but hesitate to act. Many a night I have reflected on a similar experience. At a reception, I met a friend whom I had not seen for a while. He was passing through town for a week. In the conversation I detected a certain disturbance, perhaps even a bit of despair, so I tried to cheer him up. Dodging my efforts, he mocked me a bit. Several times during the week I reached for the phone to ask him to lunch, to talk things over and to follow up on a nagging feeling of concern. But I was busy and felt a bit embarrassed at pushing, since in the past he had made light of my attention or attempts to humor him. The days sped by; he left town.

Two months later a caller told me that the friend had died. In that moment I knew with crystal clarity what had happened. A thousand times since then I have felt moral revulsion at my self-indulgence that I had been too busy and had not detected the depths of my friend's needs. I knew that my rationalizations at the time were true, but I know that Maimonides' words were also true—I had not taken them seriously enough.

No act is too trivial. The Talmud lists acts "for which there is no measure," no minimum or maximum. Central among these are acts of loving-kindness. Sometimes an encouraging smile at the right time can change another person's life.

The decision to resist evil by one pastor, André Trocmé, in a southern French town led to an entire village's hiding, and thereby saving thousands of Jews from the Nazi Holocaust. Conversely, the shortsighted, taking-the-easy-way-out decision of a Von Papen in 1933 or Hindenburg in 1934 paved the way for the total domination of Germany and Europe by a monstrously evil man.

The sound of the shofar during the High Holy Days is meant to cut through the web of routine, rationalization, and indulgence; to wake up people and get them to take themselves and their actions as seriously as they deserve. One more cigarette—what differences does it make? Buckling a seat belt for a short trip—why bother? In the Talmud, Rabbi Eliezer suggests that people should live every day with the same moral intensity as they would if it were their last. Rosh Hashanah–Yom Kippur teach that we should perform every act as if our life depended on it because, in fact, it does.

THE LITURGY OF ROSH HASHANAH

On Rosh Hashanah, the trial opens, the Judge enters and takes the bench. The evidence is reviewed. Individual Jews hasten forward to plead their cases. The liturgy attempts to capture this mood. On Rosh

Hashanah, God as Creator and Ruler is the central focus of the prayer. The divine qualities of awesomeness and judgment stand out in the human mind. By the time of Yom Kippur the primary liturgical focus shifts to the trial itself and to God's mercy, which more than anything else sustains people in the process of the judgment. As the trial wears on, the initial panic or tension lightens and people relax enough to see that the Judge is not an impersonal authority who will be relentless but, rather (what good fortune!), a loving old friend who will do all to show mercy. Nachmanides suggested that in human experience Rosh Hashanah is a day of judgment with mercy; Yom Kippur is a day of mercy with judgment.

Special Prayers in the
Traditional Synagogue

Authentic prayer wells up from the overriding concerns of the individual petitioner. These concerns flow into the fixed prayers so that phrases reflecting the trial are inserted into the liturgy. The changes include the following:

l'eyla l'eyla mikal birchata v'sheerata (above and beyond any blessings or songs of praise) inserted into every Kaddish. It is as if the sense of God's transcendence is heightened when people focus on God as Creator and Judge.

hamelech ha-kadosh (holy King) instead of ha-eyl ha-kadosh (holy Lord) in the third Amidah blessing. This change in terminology stresses the experience of God as Ruler. It is a dialectical move, too. To speak of eyl (Lord; that is, God's mighty and impersonal aspect) would be to overly stress transcendence and remoteness too much. It is more than one could bear while on trial. People want the assurance that God is close at this time.

hamelech hamishpat (the King of Judgment) instead of melech ohayv tzedaka u'mishpat (King who desires righteousness and judgment) in the eleventh Amidah blessing. The reason is the same as above: God's close presence as Judge blots out everything else.

These liturgical changes are made throughout the ten days of penitence. To pray with the regular words is to be so oblivious to the spirit of the Days of Awe as to show that these are empty words, spoken without any feeling, without awareness of God's true nature. If one forgot to say the hamelech words, the prayer would not be considered authentic and would have to be repeated.

Special additional phrases reflecting the mood of the period and personal needs are inserted at key points in the Amidah. All year long requests are not inserted in these blessings, but during the Days of Awe the anxieties overrule the normal objections to such interpolations. Prayers for life include:

> Before the end of the first blessing: *zachraynu l'chayim, melech chafetz bachayim,* . . . (Remember us for life, King who loves life; write us into the book of life, for Your sake, Lord of life.)

> Before the end of the second blessing: *mi cha-mocha av harachamim,* . . . (Who is like You, Source of mercy; who mercifully remembers creatures for life.)

> Before the next-to-last blessing: *u'chtov l'chayim tovim,* . . . (Write in a good life for all Your covenant people.)

> In the last blessing: *b'sefer chayim,* . . . (In the book of life, blessing and peace, and good fortune, may we and all Your people Israel be remembered and inscribed for a good life and peace.)

In traditional congregations, the ending of the last blessing is changed to *oseh ha-shalom* (Who makes peace). This is meant to reassure people. God's judgment on evil could be perceived as a threat to human existence. No, says the liturgy, judging evil is a contribution to human dignity. Punishing the wicked makes peace possible—eventually.

When the Torah scroll is taken out of the ark, the congregation adds to its ceremony the prayer of the thirteen qualities of God that stresses God's loving-kindness and forgiveness of sin (compare Exodus 34:6–7). (This same prayer is added on the three pilgrimage holidays as well, but the resonance of its theme is considerably enhanced in the content of the High Holy Days.) The Torah itself is read on both Rosh Hashanah and Yom Kippur.

The special Torah readings echo the liturgical themes of the Days of Awe. Thus, the Rosh Hashanah portions tell of the birth of Isaac and of the Akedah, the binding of Isaac. These are classic examples of devotion to God and of God remembering and caring for Jews. By implication, hearing the past record of God's concern and of the merit of Abraham and Isaac should reassure and comfort contemporary Jews at this moment of high tension, the trial. Similarly, the Yom Kippur reading tells of the Yom Kippur Temple liturgy—as if to summon up the merit of those sacrifices and to underscore the Torah's promise that, on this day, atonement *will* be granted to the people of Israel.

Special Liturgical Customs for Home and Community

Judaism does not restrict its liturgy to the temple or the synagogue. The folk developed a number of additional customs and practices to strengthen the total ambience of the Days of Awe. Thus, during the ten days, a special greeting is spoken in conversations at home and on the street with other people. Like the Hebrew word, *shalom*, this salutation can come at the beginning or at the end of the conversation. From the beginning of Elul through the two days of Rosh Hashanah, people greet each other with *l'shanah tovah tikatevu v'taychataymu* (may you be written and sealed for a good year). After Rosh Hashanah, it is customary to omit the phrase "be written" anymore, since by tradition the righteous get their decision at once. Instead, people wish one another *"gmar chatimah tovah"* (may your good judgment be confirmed and sealed). To say otherwise would be to imply that the other person is not fully righteous and hence is still on trial. Thus, in classic Jewish fashion, an individual judges himself or herself to be on trial through Yom Kippur but not others. (The same response is true regarding suffering. One has the right to say that one personally is suffering for sins but has no right to say this about others. Correct Jewish behavior is to judge one's self more strictly than others.)

On Rosh Hashanah, a cluster of eating symbols has been developed to stress the hope for a good year. Round challahs are served (round = circle = endless, signifying a long life). The challah is dipped into honey instead of the customary salt, and the words "May it be a good and sweet year" are said upon eating it. A sweet apple is dipped in the honey and the same formula recited. In general, people avoid sour or bitter food on this holiday.

Some eat the head (may we be at the head this year) of the fish (may we be fruitful and multiply like fish) or lamb (reminding us and God of Isaac's sacrifice). The Talmud mentions eating vegetables whose names summon up positive associations. Folk imagination picked this up; for example, eating carrots; carrots in Yiddish is *mehren*, which also means increase (our children and our fortunes).

Blowing of the Shofar

The liturgical highlight of Rosh Hashanah is the shofar blowing. The shofar is sounded repeatedly throughout the service, a total of one hundred blasts in the traditional synagogue. This is based on the biblical verse: "In the seventh month, on the first day of the month, you shall observe a sacred occasion; you shall not work. You shall observe it as a day of sounding the horn" (Numbers 29:1). Although the Torah does not refer to Rosh Hashanah either by that name or as the Day of Judgment, it continually refers to this holiday as a day of sounding the shofar. But what is the symbolism or meaning of the blowing? And why on this day? The Torah gives no explanation.

The shofar, by tradition, is a curved instrument generally made from a ram's horn, although the horn of a goat, antelope, or gazelle is also permitted. It is one of the oldest musical instruments in human history still in use. Blowing the shofar predates Judaism. It is believed that pre-biblical use focused on the "magical" power of the horn. In ancient times, people believed that blasts from a horn drove away demons. It is striking that this association is picked up by the Talmud, which suggests that the shofar can drive away Satan and evil spirits. Hence, on Rosh Hashanah, the shofar blasts drive away the "prosecuting attorney," the angel who seeks to convict people when they are on trial for their lives. But the Bible gives no hint of any such function. What did the Torah have in mind by its commandment to sound the shofar? If the shofar's "power" is to drive away evil spirits, it would have lost all significance as belief in evil spirits declined.

The primary meaning of the shofar blast seems to be that of the coronation theme—a symbolic declaration of faith in God as Ruler of the world. "The Lord ascends [His throne] amidst a loud sound. God [rises] amidst the sound of the shofar" (Psalms 47:6). Some modern scholars argued that Rosh Hashanah is linked to the Canaanite annual divine coronation ceremonies at which the powers of the gods were "renewed" by sympathetic magic, assuring the Earth's fertility. But the Bible rejects the notion of humans giving power to God and/or a divine need for "renewal." However, the Bible does teach that human affirmation (especially in community and liturgy) makes the Divine present and effective on Earth in a greater way. In the Jewish context, the shofar blast represents the Jewish people's proclamation that the Lord is their King or Ruler.

In the Torah, Rosh Hashanah itself is not openly identified as the New Year Day. It took the oral law and rabbinic literature to articulate the full theme of the Jewish New Year, organized around the highly synthesized paradigm of the trial. All the observances were integrated into one educational whole. In the trial imagery, the shofar blast communicates: Oyez! Oyez! This court is in session! The Right Honorable Judge of the World presiding!

A Jew needed all the help he or she could get, so another association was summoned up. Abraham bound his son, Isaac, to the altar, prepared to make the ultimate sacrifice in faithfulness to God. A ram was substituted at the end; God wanted no human sacrifice. But the very willingness to sacrifice, both on Abraham's and Isaac's part, remained a merit that every Jew could draw upon. The binding is a classic symbol of Jewish faithfulness. In this interpretation, the shofar sound is a cry for mercy and forgiveness; it recollects the cries and tears of all Jewish martyrs from Isaac down to this day.

Akedat Yitzchak, the binding of Isaac, is referred to repeatedly in the liturgy of the High Holy Days. It constitutes the Torah reading on the second day of Rosh Hashanah. The Binding serves as a "vicarious atonement" mechanism, a credit to be called forth. At the annual trial, a Jew does not stand in the dock alone but is accompanied by the generations that have preceded. This generation is sustained by their sacrifices and merits. Thus, despite the focus on sin, the Yamim Noraim do not allow the Jew to become overwhelmed by guilt. The living community of Jewry that joins in the confession—and the past and future generations of Israel—stand together with the individual in a healing solidarity.

In the course of thousands of years, the shofar's meaning has been embroidered upon in many different ways. As Maimonides interpreted it: "Wake up from your deep sleep, you who are fast asleep, search your deeds and repent; remember your Creator... examine your souls, mend your ways and deeds. Let everyone give up his evil ways and bad purposes."*

The shofar recalls the Revelation at Sinai; there, too, a shofar was sounded. There are other meanings: to make people tremble in the awe of the day; to remind one of the words of the prophets; to arouse the Jews to save themselves; to remind them of war and its culmination in the destruction of the Temple; to pray for peace and restoration of the Temple. Still other themes include Judgment Day and the messianic dream, ingathering of the exiles, and resurrection. Different people and different generations focused on the elements of shofar that spoke most to their own situation. Chasidic tradition tells of the shofar blower who was so overwhelmed by all the meanings he intended to keep in mind during the ritual that he blanked out. Heartbroken, he burst into tears and then finally blew. "Never mind all the meanings," said the Baal Shem Tov, "your tears are the main message."

The Sound of the Shofar

The two primary sounds of the shofar capture the two major themes of Rosh Hashanah. The first, called *tekiah*, is a long, straight blast, nine beats long, a grand sound that was used for proclamation and coronation. The second sound is called *teruah*, three broken or wavering sounds. Two traditions of the teruah sound developed in different Jewish communities. One version held that teruah was a moaning sound, expressed in three broken sounds, each three beats long. They called this *shevarim* which means broken. The other version held that it was a sound of outcry, three times three or nine staccato, almost bleat-

---

*Maimonides, *Yad Hachazakah*, Sefer Mada, Hilchot Teshuva, chapter 3, paragraph 4.

ing sounds. They named this teruah which means alarm sound. This sound, in either version, is a cry for mercy invoking Isaac's sacrifice or alarm at the coming trial—or both. The tradition was to blow one straight blast, one broken blast, and again one straight sound, in sets of three together. The sounds are drawn out long enough to make an impression, say three to six seconds for a tekiah and three seconds for a teruah. After the destruction, Jews came together from communities with different versions of the teruah. To avoid splintering and dissension, Rabbi Abbahu of Caesarea ruled that a set of each sound version be blown and, for good measure, a third set incorporating both broken sounds together also be sounded. This became the practice down to today. Thus, the shofar sounds also point to the unity and pluralism of the Jewish people.

Isaac Arama (fifteenth century) interpreted the tekiah as the sound of joy, hope, and trust in future redemption, and the teruah as the sound of awe, fear, and trembling before present judgment. Characteristically, both aspects are combined in balance. In the same spirit, the tekiah is of equal length to the shevarim or the teruah. When the two broken sounds shevarim-teruah are blown together, the tekiah's length is extended.

After the Torah reading, the full range of shofar sound is blown (thirty blasts). The shofar blower recites two blessings: "Who sanctified us with commandments and instructed us to hear the sound of the shofar" and Shehecheyanu, "Who has kept us alive to this day." Note the language of the blessing is "instructed us to hear"; the primary commandment is to hear; the main concern is to affect the audience with the message. For this reason the Rabbis insisted on hearing the shofar directly and clearly—neither through an echo (nor through electronic media) nor a melange of different shofar sounds at one time.

The congregation participates in the blowing as if sounding the horn itself. The congregants answer amen to each blessing. The worshipers remain standing in awed silence. It is the absolute silence of the moment of coronation. Neither the shofar blower nor the congregation speak until the end of all the shofar sounding, as a sign that they are fully concentrating on the mitzvah.

The shofar can be blown all during the day ("a day of sounding the horn" [Numbers 29:1]). Originally it was blown as early as possible at sunrise or even at dawn. However, it was shifted to the middle of services, just before Mussaf, during a period of Roman persecutions when sounding the shofar was prohibited and spies checked to see that Jews did not blow the shofar. (In the good old days, the "secret police" were out checking only in the early morning hours, so the sounding ceremony was delayed until later.)

Rosh Hashanah Mussaf Amidah
(Additional Silent Standing Prayer)

In the traditional liturgy, the middle section of the Rosh Hashanah Mussaf Amidah is devoted to the testimony of the day. Instead of one middle blessing (for an Amidah total of seven) as on Shabbat and pilgrimage festivals, there are three blessings (for a total of nine). These comprise the three main themes: Malchuyot (God is King, Ruler), Zichronot (God remembers in merciful judgment), and Shofarot (the shofar evokes revelation and redemption). Each section consists primarily of ten biblical proof texts—three from Torah, three from Prophets, three from the later Writings, and a tenth verse from the Torah summarizing the theme. Proof texts and triplicating evidence are symbolic ways of asserting that something is definitively true. Each section concludes with a sounding of the shofar to confirm the theme. (The sounds are tekiah, shevarim, teruah, tekiah; tekiah, shevarim, tekiah; tekiah, teruah, tekiah.)

During the repetition of the Amidah in the traditional synagogue, the chazan kneels at the Aleinu prayer in remembrance of the kneeling in the Temple. The congregation does not join him at this time. However, during the Yom Kippur repetition when people "reenact" the moments of the actual Temple service, the entire congregation participates in the historical "happening" by kneeling. The kneeling tradition is a good example of the importance of avoiding glib generalizations about what is "Jewish" or what are Jewish modes of worship. Most contemporary people are convinced that Judaism, unlike Catholicism, *opposes* kneeling, presumably because it is "undemocratic" or "undignified." In fact, kneeling is a classic form of Jewish worship (compare the phrase in the Aleinu prayer: "We bow, kneel, and acknowledge before the King of Kings") that has been sharply limited out of respect for the destroyed Temple where it was widely used.

If the first day of Rosh Hashanah comes on a Sabbath, then both shofar blowing and Tashlich (see below) are postponed to the second day. In the Temple, the shofar was blown on Shabbat. After the destruction it was blown in Jerusalem on Shabbat. At Yavneh, the city of refuge and center of reconstruction after the destruction, Rabbi Yohanan ben Zakkai ruled that the shofar be blown on Shabbat, in the face of bitter opposition. Eventually, as central religious authority broke up, the tradition not to blow shofar anywhere on the Sabbath won out. The Rabbis prohibited sounding the shofar then for fear people would carry it into the public realm which is not permitted on the Sabbath.

After the Services

After the services on Rosh Hashanah, people go out of the synagogue in calm and good spirits, reflecting confidence in God's loving judgment. It is a mitzvah to eat a festive meal on this day to express the same confidence. On the other hand, "Hallel" is not sung on Rosh Hashanah and Yom Kippur. Full-scale, jubilant praise would not be authentic when life itself hangs in the balance.

Tashlich

After Minchah on the first day of Rosh Hashanah, the ceremony of Tashlich is performed. The custom was neglected by some in the course of modernizing the tradition, but it is attractive and moving enough to be reappropriated today. People go to rivers, oceans, or lakes (bodies of living waters) and symbolically cast their sins into the waters. Tashlich expresses the feeling of being freed from the burden of past sins by repentance and God's forgiveness.

The custom of Tashlich grew in medieval times. Many premodern rationalists (such as the Vilna Gaon) objected to it on the grounds that it was tinged with superstition. Others felt that the social nature of the event—people congregating at the site—led to new sins (such as telling evil reports, exchanging gossip, or boy-girl peccadilloes). On the other hand, one could argue that the mitzvah of *shadchanus* (arranging marriages) justifies Tashlich. Perhaps in our time we could add to its meaning a gentle reminder that societies should have unpolluted, living water.

During the Tashlich ceremony, various prayers are recited, including: "O may you cast all the sins of your people Israel into a place where they will not be remembered, nor counted nor ever again minded." The whole ritual is a symbol of the miracle of repentance and a pleasing reminder not to hold people responsible for past errors once they have turned from them. The sins are deep-sixed for good.

One special fact should be noted about the length of Rosh Hashanah. The custom of two days' observance goes far back in history. The second day of Rosh Hashanah, therefore, unlike other holidays, is not considered "an extra day of festival because we are in exile." Two days are also observed in Israel. The two days are called *yoma arichta*, that is, "one long day." For the same reason many Reform congregations observe the two days of Rosh Hashanah.

ASERET YEMAY TESHUVAH—
TEN DAYS OF REPENTANCE

The days between Rosh Hashanah and Yom Kippur move in two different directions, psychologically speaking. The sense of trial intensifies. Ordinary people whose lives are a mixture of good and evil have been held over to be judged on Yom Kippur. (Or, as some interpret it, the decision has been made for all, but a ten-day stay of sentence permits appeals and moves designed to reverse negative decisions.) Deeply aware of vulnerability, recognizing in rare candor the mixture of good and bad in one's self, the Jew intensifies efforts to undo the evil of his or her past. The descent into guilt and anxiety continues to its climax: twenty-four hours of living out "death" on Yom Kippur.

At the same time, a new mood surfaces. The individual experiences catharsis and reconciliation as God's love and forgiveness come into play. The link between these two directions—trial and forgiveness—is the human act of repentance which, with God's grace, brings forth a ruling of renewed life.

Three emphases mark this period: repentance, special prayers, and extra acts of goodness, especially charity. The ultimate goal is not to frighten people but to stimulate them to growth and improvement.

THE RELATIONSHIP OF
DEATH AND RENEWAL

The intense focus on death during the holiday period runs the risk of turning morbid. Since encounter with death evokes guilt, there is a risk that the High Holy Days will turn into a guilt trip; however, the goal of the Days of Awe is not merely repentance but renewal. It is a move toward an examined life, not masochistic self-flagellation.

It is not only physical death that threatens the humanness of life but a kind of death in life, a psychic numbing. Routinization, loss of responsiveness, and habituation deaden perception and concern. When we stop examining our lives, we lose the ability to give appropriate responses to the variety of experiences that life presents to us.

One definition of life is the capacity to respond. The direction of life's growth in the eyes of Jewish tradition is toward ever greater responsiveness. Inorganic matter does not respond. The higher up the evolutionary scale, the greater the movement from biological necessity to psychic freedom. The goal of the human in God's image is the fullness of life: to become more and more like God, Who responds out of the infinity of life, not in a pre-programmed fashion without necessity or determinism but uniquely and appropriately to each person and situation. The normal processes of routinization and numbing are the enemies of this growth.

Ordinary consciousness selects and filters from reality to construct a "stable" reality and consciousness. Human sensory systems have evolved to tune out everyday patterns and to respond primarily to *changes* in the environment. As people learn, the skills they acquire often become automatic; many personal movements no longer enter consciousness. People learn to numb responses and conscience in the face of cruelty, injustice, and death because these are traumatic, psychic-overload experiences that cause pain. Thus, in the daily normal process of living, the psyche begins to die. Even intense positive experiences such as love relationships eventually become routine and familiar. How, then, can individuals stay alive, intensely alive, psychically alive?

The answer given by Jewish tradition is that one cannot avoid death or death-in-life. The only way to overcome death is by rebirth. In the face of physical death and annihilation, human beings respond with the re-creation of life, the birth of children. To psychic death humans must respond with psychic rebirth. This is another goal of the High Holy Day season.

The power of sin—and of bad patterns—is that it convinces people that change is impossible. People despair of their ability to change and give up the capacity to grow or renew. The promise of repentance and the model of God challenge this hopelessness. There *is* a process of rebirth, but it needs attention, effort, and help.

The first step is to become conscious of one's life, to overcome the routines that block the capacity to evaluate, correct, and change. Setting aside time in Elul or during the High Holy Days is the beginning of liberation. It is a time for families to sit down together, for single individuals and for husbands and wives alike to do an inventory and accounting of the year that has passed in their lives. It is a time to express dissatisfaction and to weigh or gather the resources for change. If there has been no time for introspection all year, then it must be found in this period.

Here is where the consciousness of death plays a vital role. The shock of death reminds us that time is short, too short to waste, too short to let pride and despair trap one in a life pattern with little in it to savor or respect. The very awareness of mortality suddenly puts life into bold relief. No aspect of life can be taken for granted; no feature of one's personal way is either eternal or absolutely necessary. Thus, one can review, fine-tune, or alter with a new consciousness of alternatives.

The most dramatic expression of this concept is on Yom Kippur day when every possible occupation or distraction is suspended; even the life processes of eating and sexuality are stopped. It is as if all of life is stopped and now can be chosen anew.

The descent into death also energizes the life forces. Both the body and the psyche revolt against non-being by reasserting life. This is as true for community as it is for the psyche. It is no accident that the generation of the Holocaust is the same generation that established the State of Israel. Only those who have tasted degradation can fully savor the urgency of life and the goodness of dignity in this generation. And, like a blind person whose sight is restored, after the gloom of Yom Kippur people find the world a riot of color, an outburst of dazzling variety.

"The unexamined life is not worth living," said Socrates. "To live the unexamined life is not really living" would be the Torah's version. People stay alive by being reborn. When rebirth stops, the individual will soon be dead. If you are the same as you were last year, you have died a little in the interim.

The promise of divine help and the sustenance of a community of life that has been reborn repeatedly strengthen personal efforts to renew the self. In Jewish tradition, the concept of ritual impurity is identified with routinization. The ultimate impurity is death, which is the ultimate routine. Going to mikvah and the symbolic washing of hands are rituals that externalize the drive to be reborn. The Jewish tradition sees sin as the enemy of life. The despair of guilt is the evil force that tells people they cannot change or that they cannot perfect the world. Therefore, repentance is the process of these weeks, but rebirth and renewal are the substance.

REPENTANCE

"'Seek God when God is readily found,' these are the ten days from Rosh Hashanah to Yom Kippur." In Kabbalistic terms, this Talmudic teaching means that God is somehow closer during the High Holy Days. More rationalistically, it means that people are more apt to turn to God thanks to the mood of this period. In the face of death and trial, many self-deceptions fall away. People review acts of the previous year and try to correct their sins. Wrongs done to fellow humans are of particular concern. Yom Kippur does not bring forgiveness for them unless the injured person gets restitution and forgives the one who has sinned against him. Special time should be set aside both for self-evaluation and for seeking out people to make amends. During the year, typically, family members inflict more pain on one another than on any outsiders. Closeness means that it is easier to cause pain and that more opportunities for friction are present, so families should review basic relationships and living procedures and seek forgiveness, amendment, and reconciliation.

One of the blessings of Yom Kippur is that on this day forgiveness comes to us from a force beyond ourselves as well. As the Torah says: "On this day [God] will make atonement for you, to purify you from all your sins" (Leviticus 16:30). Yom Kippur was the day on which the mysterious scapegoat ritual took place. The High Priest confessed the sins of the children of Israel over the scapegoat, which symbolically carried the sins away into the desert. The ritual suggested that the community (with God's help) could purge guilt as no one person could. But while community could intensify the individual's experience of forgiveness, one day was hardly enough for any individual to change deeply integrated behavior. Over the years the Rabbis of the Talmud and later ethicists studied the process of change and tried to deepen it, especially after the destruction of the Temple when the scapegoat ritual was no longer available.

The process itself was called teshuvah—repentance or turning. The Rabbis pointed out that it was a *process*, not a single act. For most people, transformation takes time and occurs gradually. The time frame of repentance was expanded. The ten days beginning with Rosh Hashanah and ending with Yom Kippur were now perceived as an integral unit, the Ten Days of Repentance, a period in which individuals concentrated on self-criticism and self-correction. To set the mood and to strengthen the process, it was given a community setting through special Selichot (penitential prayers), public exhortations, and study, climaxing in prayer, confession, and the retelling of the scapegoat ritual on Yom Kippur. In later generations, the thirty days of Elul that preceded the High Holy Days were added to the period of self-analysis to give yet more time for the comprehensive process of turning.

Maimonides summed up the understanding of teshuvah. There are three key elements in achieving it; one could call them the "three Rs" of repentance.

The first is *Regret*. Maimonides places great stress on the role of confession; articulating the wrongful behavior provides relief from the guilt that traps people into continuing the pattern. Admission is perhaps the most difficult step in repentance, for there is an infinite human capacity for inertial evil and self-justification, and it is just plain painful to admit that one has done wrong. Psychologically, the sinner feels that he or she has gone on a road from which there is no turning back because one cannot "betray" what has already been done; because too much has been invested; because one will be shamed; and because one has gone too far. But God promises: "You [can and] shall return" (Deuteronomy 30:2). Making the admission openly represents a commitment not to back away from the liberating insight.

The second step is *Rejection*—to stop doing the wrong thing. No amount of regret will help if the sinning continues because action overwhelms intention. In Jewish tradition, actions speak louder than words.

The third is *Resolution*—a strong determination not to do it again. Habit is very powerful; even if one changes, it is all too easy to slip back into an old pattern. It takes resolution and ongoing effort to structure new behavior.

Repentance is not a momentary recoil or tiredness but a basic turning to a new way of life. It is an act of great merit to help people repent, to encourage them in their new ways. Thus, it is forbidden to remind a penitent of his sins. One should respond with forgiveness when a person who has sinned against us comes to ask for absolution. "Whose sin does God forgive?" He who forgives sins [against himself].* If, after repeated requests, a person still refuses to forgive, that person is considered a sinner. The Rabbis even set up procedures to make restitution easier than the law normally would allow, or even waived repayment, in order to help those who sought to return from a life of crime.

In Maimonides' view the penitent becomes almost a changed person. Regret deals with the past, nullifying conditioning by repelling it. Rejection deals with the present; not doing the sin keeps the present free and clear. Resolution deals with the future, preventing sin from coming into life again. Only when all three dimensions are in place will the full process of repentance occur.

In medieval times, all sorts of self-punishments were developed as acts of penitence. Later, Chasidim in particular protested that these developments led to depression (*atzvut*) and self-abasement, whereas God wants the service of joy. As the Gerer Rebbe once said, "He who thinks and thinks again about the evil that he did, his thoughts are full of the evil that he did . . . so he is completely sunk in the evil. . . . If you sweep dirt here or there, it always remains dirt. . . . Therefore, it is said: 'Leave evil and do good.' "†

Leave evil totally. Don't dwell on it, but do good. Grow away from guilt. Overcome it with new goodness in new life.

SPECIAL LITURGIES FOR THE TEN DAYS

The prayer Avinu Malkenu (Our Father, Our King), a list of many

*Babylonian Talmud, Rosh Hashanah 17A.
†Quoted in Martin Buber, *Tales of the Hasidim: The Later Masters* (New York: Schocken Books, 1945), pp. 306–7.

human requests and needs, and Selichot (penitential prayers) are recited every day (except Shabbat).

The first day after Rosh Hashanah, the third of Tishrei, is a traditional fast day, Tzom Gedaliah,* with special prayers and special Torah readings.

The Shabbat between Rosh Hashanah and Yom Kippur is called Shabbat Shuva (after the first word of the prophetic portion Shuva, which deals with repentance) or Shabbat Teshuvah (repentance). Traditionally, a leading figure in the community reads the prophetic portion to underscore its importance. Even in the days when Rabbis did not give sermons on the Shabbat, it was customary to give a special talk to arouse the community to repentance or to the spirit of the period.

In time, this simple motive was obscured by rabbinic displays of scholarship. Not unusually, a Rabbi would talk for hours on erudite themes to which crowds would come and listen in perfect silence— and utter incomprehension. The Ropshitzer Rabbi once suggested that the purpose of the discourse was to give the innocent, other-worldly Rabbi of those days a chance to sin by too much talk and torturing his congregation through boredom so he could have something to repent for on Yom Kippur. (The funny thing is that people seemed to be deeply affected by these discourses anyway and repented. Perhaps this proved that what the speaker and audience shared in background and values was more crucial than what was spoken or heard between them.)

It is customary to increase charity, perform good deeds, and increase observance during this ten-day period. In one sense, such responses represent foxhole conversions (people usually go back to normal after Yom Kippur), but the acts are still considered worthy. Kabbalists stressed that after excluding the two days of Rosh Hashanah and the one day of Yom Kippur there are seven days, one for every day of the week. By doing things right, one sets up a model of the ideal Sunday, Monday, and so forth, to live by the rest of the year.

EREV YOM KIPPUR—
THE EVE OF JUDGMENT DAY

The dread and hope of the Ten Days of Repentance approach a peak on Erev Yom Kippur. It is a time to prepare for "death," and the Seudah Mafseket (pre-fast meal) has overtones of the prisoner's last meal. (The sense of imminent death is so strong that traditional Jews recite the Viddui, the deathbed confession of sins, during Minchah before

---

*Tzom Gedaliah, see p. 532.

the meal, lest they die during the meal and not make it to Yom Kippur.)

Yet at this very moment, the halacha elicits another classic dialectical move. Buoyed by their trust in God's love, the people of Israel turn this pre-fast meal into a festive and rich repast meant to offset the torment of the Day of Atonement. Thus, the day before Yom Kippur balances the inherent asceticism of the sacred day. The message is that there is no intrinsic religious superiority in deprivation. Denial is only a technique for concentration on spiritual matters. "One who eats and drinks on the ninth of Tishrei, the Torah considers it as if one fasted on the ninth and tenth of Tishrei."* People sanctify life through eating and drinking on the ninth as they sanctify it through fasting on the tenth. As Rabbi Israel Salanter once said, "What a wise man can accomplish by spiritually eating and drinking on Erev Yom Kippur, a fool cannot achieve fasting on Yom Kippur."†

In Geonic times (eighth and ninth centuries), a custom known as *kapparot* was added to the day. Families purchased a live fowl and waved it as "exchange" over the head of family members, then it was slaughtered and given to the poor. This custom is undoubtedly a folk attempt to substitute for the scapegoat ceremony of biblical times. For those who will settle for nothing less than the original biblical scapegoat, or those whose supply of fresh birds is low or whose rationalism quotient is high, money is usually substituted for the live creature. The money is given to charity.

This is almost the last chance to ask the forgiveness of people one has hurt; it is a time for giving restitution to those we have wronged and forgiving those who have hurt us. One should forgive freely, with a full heart. The way of Israelites is to be slow to anger and quick to be pacified.

Some traditional Jews immerse in the mikvah on this day. The removal of ritual impurity is a symbolic statement of removing the stain of sin (death). Special candles are lit to light up the house ("for mitzvah is a candle and the Torah is light" [Proverbs 6:23]) and in memory of departed parents as well. Sabbath clothes are put on before Minchah. During Minchah, the confession of sins is recited, and it is customary to give to charity.

On Yom Kippur an extra effort is made to avoid conspicuous display of jewelry or wealth; ostentation is out. There is a widespread custom to wear white clothes as a symbol of purity and hope that even "if your sins are red as scarlet, they will be made white as snow" (Isaiah 1:18). Many Orthodox Jews wear a kittel, a shroudlike white cloak.

*Babylonian Talmud, Yoma 81B.
†See Dov Katz, *Tenuat Hamussar* (Tel Aviv: Beitan Hasefer, 1952), volume 1, pp. 302–3.

The kittel captures the sense of dread and the confrontation with death even as its whiteness expresses the sense of purity and forgiveness. It also creates equality of dress on a day when all humans stand equally before judgment.

In the last act before the Day of Atonement, the parents bless their children, praying for their long life and expressing the love that unites the family.

YOM KIPPUR—
THE DAY OF ATONEMENT

Yom Kippur is liberation day: It brings freedom from the crushing isolation of guilt. "You will be purified from all your sins, before God" (Leviticus 16:30). But Yom Kippur does more than lift the burden of evil. Forgiveness alone would leave the individual still alienated. This is the day of atonement, which means restoration to the wholeness of community and roots. It means a new reconciliation and a new unification of impulses and values, of individual and community, and of God and the human.

Yom Kippur is a day of dazzling paradoxes. Israel stands before God, united as a community of sinners, publicly admitting the universal evil in all yet expecting and experiencing forgiveness and the purging of guilt through confession and mutual acceptance. Giving themselves over to the realm of death, which knows no eating, drinking, or sexuality, Jews emerge with renewed meaning in life. All day is spent in prayer and fasting, yet the Haftarah's theme is that God wants no prayer or fasting unless it leads to justice, to freeing the oppressed and feeding the hungry. In their trial, the people finally drop all their defenses and excuses and throw themselves on the mercy of the court, yet the same people never lose the conviction that they will be pardoned. This atonement is by divine grace; it is above and beyond the individual's own effort or merit.

Many Jews assume that only Christianity focuses on grace and on the merits of another's sacrifice for their behavior, but in biblical times, Temple worship had strong sacramental overtones. God's grace was the underlying principle of the scapegoat and Avodah service in the Temple. After the destruction of the Temple, the liturgical balance shifted toward a focus on individual acts rather than on sacramental forces. This reflects the Rabbis' teaching that God had called Israel to greater participation in the covenant. The individualization tendency is all to the good. Still, Maimonides affirms that this sacramental power of grace and atonement still emanates from the community of Israel. Modern Jews would do well to recover the sense of grace that brings us forgiveness even when we do not earn it for ourselves. With the setting of the sun at the end of Yom Kippur, the catharsis from sin of the people of Israel will be completed. They will stand forgiven, beloved, and at one in life before their Maker and Covenant Partner.

WITHDRAWAL FROM LIFE

"On the tenth day of the seventh month, you shall afflict your souls" (Leviticus 16:29 and 23:27; Numbers 29:7). On Yom Kippur day, the ritual trial reaches its conclusion. Jews experience what a death sentence would mean by living as if dead for a day, giving up the fundamentals of dignified life: eating, drinking, washing, using cosmetic lotions, having sex. Also, leather shoes are not worn; this means giving up the pleasure of proper support and comfort for the foot. The Sabbath work prohibitions apply to Yom Kippur as well. In fact, Yom Kippur is called the Sabbath's Sabbath.

On the Day of Atonement, denial is an act of strength. The individual asserts control over the body and voluntarily undergoes death in order to be reborn into life. On Yom Kippur one puts aside the assumption that one's well-being and dignity is dependent on these normal acts. This makes clear that in an ultimate sense, well-being and dignity transcend the presence of everyday material pleasures. Playing dead gives one a perspective on the vanity of conventional life.

Certain people are exempt by Jewish law from restrictions to eat or drink. They include the dangerously sick (when there is a potential threat to life) and pregnant women, seized by an irresistible urge to eat, whose denial could be dangerous. In such cases, regular blessings over food are said and the *yaaleh v'yavo* prayer for Yom Kippur is inserted in the grace after meals.

Many Orthodox rabbis urge that when feeding is necessary, it be done in smaller than legal size portions. I follow Rabbi Chayim Brisker's ruling in favor of normal feeding for the dangerously sick. As he used to say, "I am not treating Yom Kippur lightly, I am treating lifesaving seriously." In 1848, during a cholera epidemic, Rabbi Israel Salanter instructed the *entire* community of Vilna to eat. Folk tradition tells that he publicly ate first to show the way, for fear the plague would spread to people in weakened condition from fasting. It was later deemed one of his greatest moments of religious leadership.

Cosmetic washing for pleasure's sake is given up. An exception is made for a newly married bride, who washes her face so she will not appear unsightly to her husband and be repellent to him. (Ah, that romantic Jewish law!) Sexuality is so basic to human nature that giving up sex is considered an "affliction of the soul."

The liturgy is the vehicle through which the Yom Kippur miracle of transmutation takes place. It produces awe and a feeling of *kavana* (concentration and dedication); what comes through above all in the liturgy is the sense of devotion and closeness that unites the congregation of Israel. On this day there is also a camaraderie of the congregants that reassures and breaks the tension.

Before Kol Nidre, there are beautiful traditions: of accepting the commandment to "love thy neighbor as thyself" and of committing one's self to be "mochel," that is, to forgive all those who have sinned against us. The congregation recites the legal formula that we are permitted to pray with all Israel, with sinners and saints alike. Tonight we are one. Kol Nidre concludes with the Shehecheyanu, a blessing expressing gratitude to the Lord who has kept us alive to this day. Judgment threatens, but it also makes life possible. Many special *piyutim* (liturgical inserts) follow; they focus on forgiveness and God's power as shaper of human destiny.

GUILT, CONFESSION, AND REPENTANCE

Of course, the closeness of the end of the trial tremendously heightens consciousness of one's sins, faults, and failures on Yom Kippur. Still, after having gone through so much guilt and self-criticism for ten to forty days, what can one do for an encore? The answer is plunge into death itself and come out again to new life. There are two important insights that Yom Kippur's encounter with death gives beyond the experience of Rosh Hashanah or the Days of Penitence. One is the discovery that a broken heart or faith or love is stronger than a never-broken one. With this insight Judaism checks its own high standards and prevents them from oppressing life. This is an essential move; without it, Judaism would be an unlivable guilt trip.

Judaism is a religion of perfection, but perfectionism can be dangerous to your health. Leo Rotan, a psychiatric social worker, made a study of the maxims believed in by men who had heart attacks and matched them to control subjects who did not. The heart patients believed "be ye therefore perfect" and demanded perfection of themselves; the healthy ones believed "little strokes fell great oaks" and were more accepting of failure.

Those who have internalized Judaism's drive for perfection find it difficult to admit their imperfections, so how can they obtain forgiveness? This is why Maimonides asserts that the indispensable but most difficult first step in repentance is to admit the flaw or sin. The confirmed sinner is afraid to turn back; the sinner lives in dread that once he or she lets go and admits the failure, his or her whole life will fall apart. Many also fear that once there has been a serious breakdown, even atonement cannot restore the original wholeness. I once had a congregant who had a brief affair, which he broke off. The guilt preyed on his mind. One day, seeking relief, he confessed to me and asked what to do. I asked whether he considered telling his wife, or did he doubt that she would forgive him? He thought she would be angry but truly believed she would forgive; however, he feared that once she knew, their relationship would never be as whole and as trusting again. Here, I explained to him the rabbinic concept of Yom Kippur.

In the fantasy of perfection, once a flaw or break is discovered, things will never be perfect again. In the Arthurian epic of the Holy Grail, only Galahad could find the talisman because he was pure and faultless. Lancelot could not bring in the cup of salvation because he had sinned with Guinevere and had stained his sword with blood. In the Rabbis' view, this is a superhuman—therefore, inhuman—conception of redemption. Yom Kippur teaches that humans inevitably fail or sin: "There is no righteous person in the earth who does only good and never sins" (Ecclesiastes 7:20). But when people turn, they come out stronger. In a relationship between two people love based on the assumption of perfection on both sides is vulnerable to the almost inevitable crack in the mirror. Each person probably falsifies the other's image to avoid reality. Once flaws are acknowledged and accepted, love becomes genuinely unconditional. It may be tested by inescapable failures, but it overcomes and becomes truly whole.

Rabbinic tradition claims that Moses broke the tablets of the Ten Commandments on the tenth of Tishrei, that is, on Yom Kippur. The original tablets of the Ten Commandments were fashioned by the Divine, untouched by human flaws, but when the people of Israel sinned and created a Golden Calf, God despaired and wanted to get rid of them. Moses was so distressed that he smashed the tablets. It was almost as if the tablets were too pure to be left in human hands. Then came forty days of working through the heartbreak. Reconciliation and catharsis were followed by forty days of Moses' labor fashioning new tablets. This set of tablets—the product of hard-won repentance built on realism, forgiveness, and acceptance of others' limitations—would guide the Israelites for centuries to come. Such tablets express the spirit of Yom Kippur when out of our brokenness we become stronger than when we claimed to be whole. (Today, many people are shocked by the suggestion that the Holocaust broke the covenant. They fear that faith will be weakened by such a statement. They fail to understand that this broken covenant is even more powerful, having been renewed by the Jewish people and their Covenant Partner.)

In Hebrew, *selichah* is the word for forgiveness. The term is used heavily in the Yom Kippur liturgy and terminology; it means wiping out sin but not necessarily an inner change. For example, greed leads to stealing, then one repents and makes restitution, and the theft is forgiven. But the conflict between greed and ethics remains.

The word *kippur* derives from the Hebrew *kapparah* and is translated as atonement rather than forgiveness. Kapparah means that a person's inner drives, previously acted out in sinful fashion, are redirected for good. A passion for possession is redirected to helping others. The drive that once expressed itself in theft now expresses itself naturally in giving. In this case one has achieved the level of *kippur/kapparah*. The split between desire and conscience has been overcome, and the person has achieved at-one-ment.

In the twentieth century, Rabbi Joseph B. Soloveitchik has made an extraordinary further contribution to analysis of the concept of teshuvah. Soloveitchik points out that on Yom Kippur more is at stake than forgiveness of sin. He cites the biblical phrase, "You shall be purified before the Lord." Yom Kippur means not only the removal of stain but purification, a change in essence, a redirection of the inner person. The extremity of the Yom Kippur "death and resurrection" experience is able to transform the person.

In Soloveitchik's view, *teshuvah* goes beyond elimination of sin to renewal of the individual. Habit and conditioning often combine with the structures of individual life to keep the person torn between evil and ethic, between apathy and ideal, between inertia and desire for improvement. Against these powerful forces which proclaim that humans cannot change, Yom Kippur teaches that there is capacity for renewal and unification of life.

The Torah's vision of the good person is that of a mature *baal teshuvah* (returnee). Such a person is truly free. Having other real alternatives, he or she has chosen the Torah, thereby choosing life. To choose life, using all the human drives, is a triumph of life. Through confession Yom Kippur seeks to turn the sinner from the routine of evil. Through encounter with death, life is shaken up and healed again. Finally, through purification, the power of evil is turned toward the goal of good and all those energies are redirected toward redemption and life.

In recent times, there has been much notice of the *baal teshuvah* phenomenon, that is, Jews who make a radical break with their past and live a completely traditional life, often in the Lubavitch or Yeshiva community. This is a salutary development because it is an additional way of fighting assimilation.

A broader concept of renewal should also be recognized: Teshuvah means not just rejecting the past but also using it in a powerful new way. Many Jews do not so much desire to leave their past as to bring it into a Jewish way of life. The capacities of autonomy, self-expression, and identification with humanity that currently lead people away from Judaism can be redirected to the service of God and the Jewish people. In this approach, teshuvah is a growth process. Instead of staying "dead" Jewishly, one grows into Jewish life. Increased observance nurtures human talents and shapes them with Jewish values. In the broadest understanding of repentance, a baal teshuvah is a "growing Jew." Baalei teshuvah are Jews who unify their secular and Jewish lives in a continual process of at-one-ment.

THE LITURGY OF REPENTANCE

In a culture striving for permissiveness, the self-critical mood of Yom Kippur strikes a note of jarring counterpoint. The tradition's answer is that guilt in its right time and place is healthy; it is crucial to conscience. Moral maturity lies in a willingness to recognize one's own sins, not to lay upon oneself a universal or destructive guilt, a guilt that cripples all and focuses on nothing specific. Concrete acts can be corrected; bad patterns can be overcome.

Against the brokenness of guilt and the isolation of sin, Yom Kippur offers the wholeness of living, the oneness of community. To this end there is repeated confession of sins on Yom Kippur. The sins are listed alphabetically to cover the range of human behavior and to jog memory. Compassionately enough, the confessions are in the plural form (*we* have sinned). Everyone confesses all the sins, and each individual applies the appropriate category to herself or himself.

The sins range from violence or cheating or slandering of others to arrogance or unfairness in word and deed. The range is staggering: There are sins you have committed, sins you would never think of doing, (even sins that sound so exciting you wish you *had* done them). A number of congregations have updated the confession by inserting contemporary possibilities of sin. The focus should be on what the individual can change in personal life, not just on the sins of society. People dredge up their sins, but in a way they are glad to do so because the sins remembered and repented for, are all forgiven. (In the case of sins against fellow humans, one must give restitution and ask forgiveness before God will forgive.)

Thus, Yom Kippur is both a fierce jolt and a great relief. The theme that threads through the night and is repeated by day and especially in the Neilah, the closing prayer, is "the Lord sitting on the throne of mercy" is preeminently gracious, loving, and forgiving.

Classically, one of the emotional peaks of the service is the Mussaf Avodah section in which the ancient Temple scapegoat and atonement service was retold and verbally reenacted. Many wept at the recollection of the lost Temple but those tears were shed as much for the living reality of the Exile, in which persecution, and powerlessness was the fate of the Jewish people. Today, this part of the service has lost some of its emotional force, but for those free of modern hangups, it gives a glimpse of the raw power and the sacramental experience of unmerited grace that characterized Temple worship.

Adding to the emotional peak was the prayer which told the tale of the Ten Rabbinic Martyrs of the Roman persecution. In a way, the ten Rabbis, like Isaac, were invoked for the sake of vicarious atonement; the merit of their devotion and martyrdom should win forgiveness for their descendants, the living people of Israel. In this generation, readings and prayers on the Holocaust are added (most appropriate are readings from the writings of martyrs or survivors of the Holocaust). Further, no trial in Jewish liturgy can be authentic without including the trial of God as well, the *din Torah mit dem Ribbono shel Olam*. The awe and seriousness of the Yamim Noraim demand this integrity from us.*

Yizkor is also recited on Yom Kippur because the memory of the dead deepens guilt and solemnity and summons up the merits of the departed. Giving charity is a crucial fulfillment both of Yizkor remembrance and of the day. Hallel is not recited, despite the festival overtone, because the awe of judgment paralyzes the capacity for happy songs of praise.

In the morning, six people are called to the Torah (seven if Yom Kippur falls on Shabbat) to read the Yom Kippur tabernacle ritual. (On this day in Jerusalem the High Priest entered the Holy of Holies, the inner sanctum, to ask forgiveness for his people.) Another person is called to read the prophetic portion, the Haftarah, with its critique of mere ritual and its demand for justice. In the afternoon, three are called to the Torah to read about permitted and forbidden marriages (because in ancient times, after the scapegoat ritual was completed and atonement obtained, celebration and marriage-arranging went on). At Minchah, the regular year-round tune is used for the Torah reading. The congregation is already anticipating the return to normal life.

The third aliyah at Minchah reads the Haftarah, which is the book of Jonah. It encompasses the many themes of the day: repentance, confrontation with death and, above all, God's love for all creatures. The theme is universal: God wants the people to turn to life. Jonah is a prophet to the Gentiles, and they set an impressive example of repentance for Jews. In Chasidic circles, Minchah particularly ends on a

---

*Compare Elie Wiesel's *Night* (New York: Avon, 1969), chapter 5.

happy, even triumphant note. The community feels that it is going to make it. Forgiveness is very close. People are emerging from the shadow of death to light and life.

A special service, Neilah (the closing), is inserted at twilight, and it lasts until the stars come out. The day is ending, and in a kind of runner's second wind, Jews are inspired to a new burst of prayer. Many stand through the entire service. The image that weaves through the prayer is that the gates are closing—the gates of heaven, of prayers, of the courthouse. The congregation tries to get its prayers in before the closing; each person hopes to enter within the gates of life. Neilah's final prayer is "Our Father, Our King" (Avinu Malkenu). This prayer, normally not recited on Shabbat, is recited on Yom Kippur even if the day coincides with Shabbat because this final and most urgent pleading for human concerns overrides the normal consideration of not asking for needs on Shabbat.

The prophet says, "Those who trust in the Lord shall exchange strength [for weariness]" (Isaiah 40:31). Neilah ends with a crescendo. The congregation cries out: Sh'ma Yisrael! Hear, O Israel! It utters the pledge of loyalty of the Jewish people, for the Lord of judgment is their God; Baruch shem kvod—the call for God's kingdom and redemption. In the clear light of Yom Kippur, Jews have considered the normal idolatries to which they give their lives, and now they know their emptiness, so they give the final triumphant cry, seven times repeated: God is the Lord! There is one long, loud blast on the shofar, which evokes the cry: L'shanah ha'baah b'yerushalayim!—Next year in Jerusalem! Next year redemption!

MOTZAI YOM KIPPUR: THE HAPPINESS OF THE LONG-DISTANCE RUNNER

Like the good long-distance runner, the Jew's prayer does not stop at the finish line but keeps going until it runs down. The first things one does after Yom Kippur are additional mitzvot. Maariv is prayed. Havdalah is chanted. Those who did not bless the new moon before Yom Kippur do it now.

The aesthetic anticlimax of this and most Jewish prayer services, which never end at the emotional peak, has led Rabbi Joseph B. Soloveitchik to suggest that this is a conscious dramatic image. To take leave immediately after Neilah prayers, having made the best argument for one's case, would be to act in full self-possession. But the underlying image, Rabbi Soloveitchik suggests, is that of people who, suddenly released from the mesmerism of closeness to God, come to the realization that they stand in the presence of an overwhelming transcendent Being. Suddenly conscious of the chutzpah of the requests and demands, and covered with confusion, the people awkwardly retreat and stumble out, "making fools of themselves" because of the awe of the One to whom people have been speaking all this time.

After Yom Kippur, Jews eat, drink, and rejoice. The Midrash says, "A [heavenly] voice declares on this night: 'Go and eat your bread joyfully, drink your wine in good spirit, for the Lord has accepted your efforts'" (Ecclesiastes 9:7). Here again is a dialectical move of the tradition. Since Judaism seeks the triumph of life, it strives to generate a continual process of examining life and of death and resurrection in daily life. The core of this process is the season of the High Holy Days. Death can be opposed only by life; death-in-life can be opposed only by growing in life. Therefore, one must go on from Yom Kippur to live more intensely. Many start building the sukkah that very night. The vitality of Sukkot will counterbalance the asceticism of Yom Kippur.

Joy is more powerful than sorrow or denial. In the sukkah and its joy, even children can participate. This is why the final sealing of the judgment is connected by rabbinic tradition to Hoshana Rabba—the seventh day of Sukkot. In the words of a midrash: "A city revolted against its ruler. The King set forth to subdue and punish it, and the city hastened to request a pardon. At a distance from the city, the elders and great men came and begged forgiveness. 'For your sake,' the King said, 'I forgive one-half the guilt.' At the gates of the city, the masses turned out and pleaded for mercy. 'For your sake,' the King said, 'I forgive half the guilt that is left.' When he entered the city and found all the little children gathered with song and dance and joy to appear before him, he exclaimed: 'For your sake, I forgive everything!' —and joined in their celebration." So it is with Israel and God. In Elul, the righteous repent and plead for forgiveness, and God forgives partially. By Rosh Hashanah and Yom Kippur, the mass of people appear, and God forgives more. But when on Sukkot even the children appear, dancing with joy, for their sake all is forgiven and the Shechinah (Divine Presence) joins in with them.

PART THREE

Walking the Way—
Through Jewish History

THREE HOLIDAYS (Passover, Shavuot, and Sukkot) formulate the core message of Judaism: Exodus, Covenant, and the Way. Shabbat and the Rosh Hashanah–Yom Kippur cluster nurture personal life along the way. All these holidays are instructed in the Torah, the Five Books of Moses (the Pentateuch) that constitute the fundamental text of the Jewish tradition.

Later Jewish generations applied the term Torah (meaning teaching) generically to the entire Jewish tradition, but they accepted the Five Books as uniquely authoritative. Sinai was the greatest of revelations: "From the day that the Lord created the human on earth and from one end of the heaven to the other—has anything as great as this ever happened, has anything like it even been heard of? Has a people heard the voice of God speaking out of the fire as you heard—and lived?" (Deuteronomy 4:32) Moses was the greatest of prophets: "Never again did a prophet like Moses arise in Israel, one whom God knew face to face" (Deuteronomy 34:10).

When seeking the meaning of later events and behavior, the leadership turned to the primary Torah models. Joshua attributed the successful conquest of the Promised Land to the faithful following of the Torah of Moses. The Prophets understood themselves not as innovators but as messengers of God calling for a return to the sacred principles of the founding Torah.

Nevertheless, the Jewish message of redemption is future-oriented. Even though the Exodus is the shaping event of Jewish history, the liberation itself would not be complete until the Promised Land was reached. Then the blessings and the possession of the land promised to Abraham would be realized. The concept of covenant imputes a key role to later generations. The later generations, in turn, concluded that the covenant would not be fulfilled until the end of days; then all the nations would flock to Zion; no nation would lift up sword against nation.

Through its message of redemption, then Judaism is committed to be open to history. Great historical events revealed the will of God and the direction of history, and set the Jewish people in motion on the Jewish way. History itself is open and directional; so the people look to further events to illuminate and "justify God's ways to man."

The Torah teaches that the Jewish people are the carriers of the divine message and that the promised perfection will occur in this world. Serious defeats for Jewry cannot simply be dismissed, therefore; they challenge the credibility of the redemption promise. Great disasters that endanger the survival of the Jewish people threaten the transmission of the Exodus vision. Destruction of the Jewish people would wipe out belief in God's power, and so catastrophes of Jewish history have brought great turmoil and crises of faith. The tradition could not go on without addressing the question of meaning in light of these occurrences. Leadership quickly lost its following unless it could convincingly harmonize new events with the classic Jewish way.

But tragedy is not the only threat to Jewish existence. The land of Israel was never totally insulated from outside culture. Acceptance by others opened Jews up to hearing the messages of others. Whenever the persuasiveness of the Jewish teaching was undermined by a rise in the credibility of alternative ways of life, Jews were likely to drop out. Jewry had to compete culturally for the commitments of Jews. Thus, both ease and persecution could weaken Judaism's hold on Jews.

The ongoing Jewish way of life is guided by the events and crystallized models of the past. Normally, the paradigm of Exodus-Covenant-Way was able to interpret and account for all the data of Jewish history. But over the centuries three major experiences had such an impact on Jewry that they affected Jewish self-understanding; they became major orienting events in their own right.

The classic method of incorporating events and their lessons into Jewish life is through the holidays. Over the course of six to seven centuries, three new holy days were created and then absorbed into the Jewish calendar: the holy days of Purim, Hanukkah, and Tisha B'Av.

Purim marks the Jews' narrow escape from an attempted genocide of the Jewish people in the Persian empire. Their enemies were crushed, and Jews were elevated to senior leadership in the empire. The date for this occurrence is in controversy. Due to the absence of corroborating Persian records and the offbeat character of the holiday, many critical scholars have challenged the historicity of the Purim event. I believed that, on this one, the critical scholars have been misled by their methods. Purim eludes easy categories; it doesn't fit many traditional norms either. Purim mocks all orthodoxies, including those of critical scholars. And for those for whom biblical authority is not enough and for whom my deep faith in Jewish tradition is not an answer either, I would invoke Elie Wiesel's dictum: Some stories are true although they never occurred, while other events happened but are not true. By this standard as well, Purim is real.

Hanukkah celebrates a victory of the Hasmoneans and their allies over the Jewish Hellenists and Greeks in the second century B.C.E. The Hasmonean wars lasted for decades, but one particular victory enabled the loyalists to capture the Temple, expel the idolatrous cult that had been set up there, and purify and rededicate the Temple. That rededication of the Temple in the year 164 B.C.E. gives its name to the holiday. Hanukkah means dedication.

Tisha B'Av is a fast day of commemoration and mourning for the destruction of the Second Temple in the year 70 C.E. and the crushing of Bethar, the last major redoubt of the Bar Kochba rebellion against Rome on that same day in 135 C.E. Actually, Tisha B'Av and its auxiliary fast days had a preexisting model—the fast days marking the first Temple's destruction.

Each new holy day reflects a different challenge to Jewish understanding. Purim reflects the challenge of Diaspora living. When Jews were exiled to Babylonia and Persia and other points in the beginning of the sixth century B.C.E., they saw their fate as expulsion from rootedness and direct access to the Divine. For a religion like Judaism, heavily focused on land and family, this fate seemed like the end of dignified existence. When the population of the kingdom of Israel was exiled in 721 B.C.E., their religious and cultural life disintegrated. They eventually disappeared (the Ten Lost Tribes). Yet in Persia, the refugees from the Kingdom of Judah achieved remarkable financial and political gains. In fact, they won great social acceptance and developed new positive relationships with Gentiles. Then, suddenly, Jews experienced a devastating reversal—a raw encounter with genocidal anti-Semitism.

What kind of world is this when innocent men, women, and children can be marked for destruction by the rise of a new minister and a casting of lots? And why were *all* the Jews singled out for destruction? What does this do to the relationship between Jews and Gentiles? Can non-Jews ever again be trusted? Can there be permanent Jewish life outside of Israel? Since the operating model of Judaism is the Jewish way through history, then the Torah should be livable under circumstances other than in the land of Israel—or shouldn't it? These are the questions to which Purim addresses itself. The holiday offers a rip-roaring, hilarious, heartbreaking paradoxical answer to the riddle of Diaspora existence.

Hanukkah grows out of a different matrix of existence, a moment in history when a fascinating, sophisticated culture—Hellenism—gradually began to permeate and then to dominate Jewish life. The simple version of Hanukkah is that of Jews struggling against Greeks. But, in fact, Hanukkah grows out of a split in the Jewish soul. In most of the battles in that extended war, Jews fought among themselves as soldiers in the armies on both sides. There were Jews committed to hellenization who called in Seleucid kings to control Jerusalem and get rid of the traditional opposition. There were Jews so traditional that they would make peace with the Greeks and abandon Judah Maccabee as long as they were left alone in their cultural withdrawal.

The most important group was the one in the middle, Jews who had imbibed Hellenistic ideas but were not totally assimilated. Many such Jews were in the leadership of both armies, but victory in arms alone could never resolve the conflict of values and cultural models. One side used Hellenistic ideas to shuck off the traditions of the ancestors; another side used them to deepen the power of the traditions of the ancestors. The ultra-traditionalists were critical of both views. In the crunch, some Hellenizers went with the traditionalists because they couldn't bear to kill fellow Jews for the benefit of a foreign people.

Finally, when the smaller Jewish group defeated the larger Seleucid-led coalition long enough to consecrate the Temple and to buy time for spiritual rearmament. They struggled to place their experience within the framework of Jewish history and tradition. Was their victory even worthy of being marked by holy days and observances? The Maccabees acted immediately to answer this question by creating Hanukkah. But because the Hasmonean dynasty proceeded to confirm some of the worst fears of the pious traditionalists, the holiday suffered guilt by association with the Hasmonean dynasty. Thus, the Rabbis were cool to the new holiday initially. In fact, Hanukkah never received the final pedagogical shaping from the Rabbis that the other holy days did.

The destruction of the Temple which is commemorated on Tisha B'Av posed the sharpest challenge to the viability of the Jewish covenantal way (although one can argue that a clear-cut threat of destruction may be easier to handle than the complex threat of being accepted, loved, and competed to death by a thousand compromises and acts of assimilation). The catastrophe was so overwhelming that it threatened the structures of meaning in Judaism. The old channels of grace and communication with God were cut off by the fires of Tisha B'Av. In the course of dealing with the crisis, one older layer of leadership—the Sadducee nobles—fell away, unable to meet the Jewish people's need for meaning.

The Pharisees' successor leadership, the Rabbis, emerged from a relatively limited role to the front-and-center direction of the Jewish community. In the course of that rise to power, they shaped understanding, institutions, and practices that kept the Jewish people emotionally and spiritually healthy through almost two millennia of persecution and pariah status. In Tisha B'Av, they created a holy day so powerful it was able to explain and absorb the later catastrophes of the Jewish people for eighteen hundred years and keep the Jews firmly on the road to redemption—until the Holocaust.

Over the course of centuries, the Rabbis' heritage of oral law, their interpretation of the human covenantal role, and their own brilliant pedagogy enabled them to develop the central liturgical model for all the holidays—that of reenactment of the event. But the initial development of these three holy days took place in an improvised and struggling fashion against sharply divergent backgrounds.

In chronological occurrence, the order of the holidays is Purim (fourth century B.C.E.), Hanukkah (second century B.C.E.) and Tisha B'Av (70 and 135 C.E.). Purim occurred under the Persian empire which was then a world power; Hanukkah developed in the context of Greek, then Hellenist, world domination; and Tisha B'Av was reinstituted under the impact of a crushing defeat at the hands of the great Roman empire. Purim celebrates an escape from death; Hanukkah honors a fragile, temporary victory; and Tisha B'Av commemorates a monumental disaster.

The net balance of these days is closer to tragedy than triumph; yet so powerful has the structure of Jewish life been—as mediated in the holidays—that the Jewish people have outlived all three world powers by two millennia. The three empires suffered defeat and sank into the ruins of history; the minuscule people were strengthened in their inner calling by tragedy and persisted in their lives. In the twentieth century, the successor states to the ancient empires struggle to find their way, a way that is almost totally sundered from those ancient glory years of world power. In the twentieth century, the Jewish people, although more modernized than the others, still observe these holy days and relive those experiences. Indeed, those events are still of such moment that Jews fight over their lessons for today. Who mourns the sack of Rome? Who fights over the implications of Homer?

CHAPTER SEVEN

Confronting
Jewish Destiny:
Purim

PURIM: THE HOLIDAY OF THE DIASPORA

Purim is deceptively simple. On the surface, Megillat Esther (the Purim scroll) is a charming melodrama: We have Hardhearted Haman, the wicked vizier; simple, Addlepated Ahashverosh, the dotty banker/king who "sells the mortgage" to the scheming villain; sweet Excellent Esther, the beauty (and her family), menaced by Haman's advances; Mild-mannered Mordecai, the good hero who finally saves the old homestead. No wonder the atmosphere of synagogue and the community on this day is all fun and games, masquerade and mummers, drinking, partying, and gift-giving.

Yet appearances can be deceptive. Purim, which supports enormous theological freight, may well be the darkest, most depressing holiday of the Jewish calendar. Its laughter is Pagliacci's—a hair's breadth away from despair. While Purim's authenticity as history has been challenged, it is really the holiday that grew out of Jewish history. More than anything else, it is *the* holiday of the Diaspora; it reflects and affirms the experience of the Jewish people living as a minority outside the land of Israel. In its own way, it offers a special guide to Jews who plan to continue living in Diaspora despite the fact that, after two thousand years, the road to Jerusalem is open to any and every Jew who wants to go there.

When the first Jew, Abraham, was initiated into the Jewish covenant, he was addressed: "I am the Lord who brought you out from Ur of the Chaldees to give you this land as a possession" (Genesis 15:7). The Exodus promise that Moses brought to the Hebrew slaves in Egypt said, "I will bring you to the Land . . . and I will give it to you as an inheritance" (Exodus 6:8). Throughout the Bible, the land is the embodiment of the covenant, the place where God is close. There were countless commandments that could be fulfilled only in the land of Israel. Good deeds (honoring parents, teaching children Torah, observance of the laws) are rewarded by longer life on the land. And when the Israelites pollute the land by murder and by sexual immorality, the land vomits them out. When Israel fails to free the slaves, to observe the sabbatical year, or is idolatrous and betrays the covenant, then "the Lord uproots them from their soil in anger and fury" and blasts the land.

Exile is a punishment for sins, more like a jail sentence than a state of living. Exile is a curse, a location where Jews are "a disgrace, and a proverb, a byword and a curse [that is, a proverbial example of how bad things are] in all the places to which I banish them" (Jeremiah 24:9). God is so manifest in the land that expulsion from it is like expulsion from God. So says David to Saul, complaining that he has been driven out of Israel. Attachment to the land bespeaks the fundamental Jewish concept that the human is rooted in the natural life. Exile is unnatural, a sign of brokenness. Restoration to the land is the hallmark of the reconciliation of God with the people, a sign that the covenant is still valid.

The first exile to Babylonia and the East was a devastating experience. Had God rejected the people and the covenant? Why else would God allow God's home to be destroyed? Many Judeans gave up and assimilated, but those who remained steadfast became even more faithful, determined to win forgiveness and be reconciled with God. They were sustained by the hope that God would bring a new Exodus and bring them back to the Promised Land.

When the Jews actually settled in the lands of Diaspora, theology and reality did not quite mesh. The Israelites adjusted well. Many of the deportees had belonged to the urban population of Palestine. In the words of Salo W. Baron:

> To till the foreign soil was a great change, and it is no wonder that many poured into the larger cities, such as Nippur. . . . Here they entered the active industrial and commercial life of the country. . . . They may have pioneered, therefore, in the development of a banking system based on loans granted on the security of real estate mortgages and pawns. . . . They were a significant factor in accelerating the "progress" of Babylonia's and Persia's semicapitalist

economies.... There hardly was any important vocation where Jews ...were not represented.... [In Babylonia] Jews apparently belonged to the large middle class.... Within this class...Jews lived on the basis of perfect equality. Those who had amassed great wealth or who possessed some personal merit achieved prominence at the King's court in Babylon, and to an even greater extent in Susa, the Persian capital.... Neither the Babylonian nor the Persian government seems to have hostilely interfered with the inner life of the Jewish community.*

As their wealth grew and the exile lengthened, the exiles followed Jeremiah's advice to "build homes...plant gardens...take wives, beget sons and daughters... [to] multiply there" (Jeremiah 29:5–6). In accordance with Jeremiah's instructions, they sought the welfare of the city to which God had exiled them, and in its prosperity, they prospered. No wonder that when the Israelites were called to return and build Jerusalem, a goodly number returned but most did not. It is hard to uproot the family when things are going well.

The people who returned were poor and not very well organized. When the temple was rebuilt by the year 515 B.C.E., those who dedicated it wept at the contrast of this poor building and the grandeur of the First Temple. The Jews in the Exile were better off than the needy, struggling community that had returned to the ruined, run-down Holy Land. When Nehemiah, a courtier of the Persian king, heard a report of the poor condition of the restored community, he wept and was in mourning for days. Nehemiah decided to obtain the king's backing, go to Jerusalem and revitalize the community. Persian Jews sent money and, occasionally, high-quality people such as Ezra and Nehemia, but they stayed put.

Meanwhile, back in Susa and throughout Persia, the Jews were doing famously. This is the context of the Purim episode.

YOU NEVER HAD IT SO GOOD

The Book of Esther opens in Shushan, capital city of Persia, celebrating the peace and prosperity of King Ahashverosh's rule. All the inhabitants of the capital were invited to the party. A Jewish community was concentrated in that city. Jews, then as now, were finding economic opportunity and social acceptance in the post-destruction period; they, too, were invited.

---

*Salo W. Baron, *Social and Religious History of Jews* (Philadelphia: Jewish Publication Society, 1952), vol. 1, pp. 108–10, 115–17.

Of course, there were old-fashioned, "fanatic" Jews who kept to themselves. (As Haman later said to the king: "There is a people scattered and *separated* among the nations whose religion is different") [Esther 3:8].) But the Talmud portrays the Jews of Shushan eating, drinking, and carousing along with all the others. They were more Persian than Jewish, which is why they were so shocked when Haman turned his murderous fury not just against the "fanatic" Jews who wouldn't bow down, but against all of them.

Today, Purim is a quintessential Jewish holiday. To every little boy and girl who masquerades on Purim, Mordecai and Esther are archheroes of Jewishness. But a good case can be made that Mordecai and Esther, too, may have been quite integrated in Persian life and that Purim is the holiday brought to you by assimilated Jews.

What kind of Jews were Mordecai and Esther? Obviously, the answer has to be a speculation, and their record of saving the Jews speaks for itself. Still . . .

First, there is the matter of their names. Esther's name probably is derived from Ishtar, a Babylonian goddess, and Mordecai's name from Marduk, a Babylonian god. Equivalent names today might well be Mary and Christopher. Of course, committed Jews in open societies also adopted Gentile names. My parents, Orthodox Jews, wanted an Anglo-Saxon WASP name for their little son, Yitzchak—so they named me Irving. But Christopher!

Then there is that Miss Persia contest. Esther was entered into a competition to become queen by marrying a Gentile king. Imagine that the president of the United States gets divorced and there is a nationwide beauty contest whose prize is marriage to the president. What kind of Jewish women would enter? Not likely Chasidic girls or Stern College graduates. The Megillah tells us that, at Mordecai's instruction, Esther did not reveal her people or her origins while she lived at the king's court. What did she eat? Did she go to the mikvah? The Rabbis of the Talmud recognized the problem, and while some claim Esther had secret arrangements to keep Shabbat and kashrut, others conclude that she did not act very Jewishly.

It is also interesting that neither Mordecai nor Esther had any family, at least as far as the Megillah reveals. (A midrash suggests that they were married to each other, but that is another story.) One of the "crazy" reversals of the Purim story is that the Jewish characters seem to be living alone while the Haman types had the strong family ties.

Adaptation was the key to a Jew's ability to rise, and often it was the price of admission. Thus, the "court Jews" (to whom the community turned, over the later course of Jewish history, to intercede with the ruling powers when Jews were in trouble) were typically half-Gentile in their ways of living. When Mordecai asked Esther to plead with the king, she vacillated at first—just the reaction one would expect from a marginal Jew who was reluctant to lose her place in society.

Mordecai did stand up to Haman, but his refusal to bow does not make him a traditional Jew. "Non-Jewish Jews" such as Spinoza, Freud, and Marx used their outsider status as a source of creative insight to become critics of the Establishment. It is equally plausible that, like Leon Blum of France and Benjamin Disraeli of England, whose marginal Jewishness led them to work for a new political order, Mordecai also opposed Haman's emerging tyranny. When the resentment he generated focused not on the issues but on the Jews, the anti-Semitism-induced "shock of recognition" followed. At that point there was one of three choices: to be craven and yield, to ignore the Jewish issue, or to accept one's Jewishness as a decisive fact and take up Jewish cause and fate.

Mordecai and, after some initial hesitation, Esther responded not only by defending their principles but by reaching out to all Jews and rallying the community to self-defense and self-affirmation. They saved the Jewish people and wrote a glorious page in Jewish history. Perhaps it is no accident that the Purim holiday they and the folk fashioned is offbeat. These "born-again" Jews contributed a vital new element to the total Jewish religion and celebration.

The above analysis is deliberately provocative, even overstated. On balance, the evidence points to Mordecai's and Esther's being devoted Jews; usually it takes that type to risk their lives to save their people. The rabbinic tradition very strongly insists that they were observant Jews. Note that when Esther was in trouble, she asked the Jews to fast and pray. Esther's Jewish name is Hadassah; she possibly lived in two worlds, with the name Esther on her diploma and the family calling her Hadassah at home.

Still, even if Mordecai and Esther weren't assimilated, many of their friends and allies in the war against Haman were, as the Rabbis indeed set forth.

The point of this exercise is to underscore one of the deep lessons of Purim: Never write off assimilated Jews. They come out of the historical closet in the greatest crises and when they are least expected. After the Holocaust and in defense of Israel, thousands of hitherto marginal Jews rallied to fight for Jewish survival. I once heard the late Jacob Herzog tell of a key mission in a banana republic, trying to buy weapons for Israel in 1948. He ran into strong resistance. All appeared lost, when suddenly he obtained desperately needed arms through the intercession of a general. Afterward, the general secretly revealed to him that he was a Jew whose family had "passed" to get into the aristocracy.

THE REVERSAL

In any event, it seems that the Jews—observant and nonobservant alike—were doing well and living it up in Persia. Then onto this complacent scene came a new prime minister called Haman. He was glorified by everyone except Mordecai the Jew, who refused to bow down to him. In a fit of fury (perhaps it was paranoia or megalomania), Haman determined to kill not only Mordecai but his entire people. He obtained the king's authorization, cast lots to pick a day for the genocide, and set the wheels of destruction in motion.

"And the city of Shushan was bewildered," says the Megillah. One can imagine the Jews' confusion, their inability to understand and believe all this. Jews have tended to believe in the goodness of human nature. Who would willfully decide to kill an entire people, an innocent people—men, women, and children? Almost two millennia later, Alexander Donat explained in his chronicle of the Warsaw ghetto why the Jews did not resort to armed resistance initially: "We could not now believe that the Third Reich was a government of gangsters embarked on a program of genocide 'to solve the Jewish problem in Europe.' We fell victim to our faith in mankind."[*]

The Jews of Persia thus experienced a capricious, almost incredible reversal. Nothing could more clearly demonstrate the built-in vulnerability of Jews in the Diaspora. One minute they were highly integrated, loyal citizens of Persia, basking in their acceptance, invited and fully present at great civic moments of Persian life like the king's feast. Mordecai sat at the gate of the king's palace, and a Jewish girl even became queen. In the next moment, a prime minister went berserk and took out all his jealousy and anger in a murderous rage at the Jews. And the king casually, almost unthinkingly, removed his ring and gave it to Haman, condemning the entire Jewish people to death in that slight gesture.

The initial reaction of the Jews of Persia was that "it can't happen here." This is Persia, tolerant, pluralist Persia; Haman's a Johnny-come-lately upstart. The true Persians will never tolerate this kind of behavior. The whole thing didn't make sense. Why pick on the Jews who prayed for the welfare of the city, who developed a banking system that charged little or no interest in a society where twenty percent-plus interest rates were the norm,[†] and who stimulated the

---

[*]Alexander Donat, *The Holocaust Kingdom: A Memoir* (New York: Holt, Rinehart and Winston, 1963), p. 103.
[†]Compare Salo W. Baron, *Social and Religious History,* vol. 1, p. 115.

economy and created jobs for all Persians? Be angry at Mordecai for his defiance, but why hate all the Jews?

The question of Jew hatred is one of the great moral conundrums. By now, anti-Semitism is one of the longest running, most widely adapted social pathologies in history. For some, the explanation is social. The Jews meet the perennial need for a scapegoat. Middleman merchant groups serving rural populations who are very different in culture, dress, skin color, and background particularly have lent themselves to the scapegoat role in many cultures: the Chinese in Malaysia and Vietnam, the Indians in Uganda and South Africa, the Jews in Persia, and later in medieval Europe and Eastern Europe. Such eruptions are particularly likely to happen when the host groups develop their own middle class, which begins to compete for the middleman role and finds xenophobia a handy weapon to dispatch the competition.

Rabbinic tradition suggests that Haman had no aristocratic lineage. He had insinuated himself into power by advancing the cause of Ahashverosh, himself an upstart who had seized the throne. Clearly, the king's crown did not sit lightly on his head. There were plots that reached into the king's own court in the form of the courtiers Bigtan and Teresh, executed for conspiracy against the king (Esther 2:21–23). By this line of reasoning, Haman, equally insecure and determined to crush any possible opposition, was threatened when Mordecai defied his bid for absolute power.

Some scholars argue that anti-Semitism, in general, is a product of social unrest in a society, especially when the political institutions have weak legitimacy. Jews do best in stable societies; the unraveling of the social fabric generates a need for scapegoats and leaves the Jews vulnerable to assault. Other analysts focus on Jewish visibility in the role of outsider as the key element in the growth of anti-Semitism. All societies and people prefer their "own kind." By remaining different and by being identifiable as a distinct group, Jews draw repulsion down upon themselves. Some anti-Semites have put the responsibility for anti-Semitism on the Jews, arguing that Jewish visibility, particularly when it is associated with improper behavior, is to blame for the antagonism to them. There is much truth to the argument that Jewish otherness is a lightning rod for hostility, particularly if this view is used to judge the intolerance level of society rather than to blame the victims for the crime of being themselves. This argument does not account, however, for the fact that anti-Semitism is directed as much —if not more—against Jews who assimilate as against Jews who are clearly different. In *Mein Kampf*, Hitler described the westernized assimilating Jews as a greater "threat" because they were harder to distinguish. Nor does this analysis explain why anti-Semitism continues so strongly in East European or Arab countries in which Jews are no longer present, or in Japan where Jews hardly ever were present; nor does it account for Haman's decision to wipe out all the Jews. Hatred is one thing; genocide is another.

The truth is that Jewish behavior has little to do with anti-Semitism or its degree of virulence. As the Purim account hints, there are two additional elements that play a role in spreading this hatred over so wide an area.

Anti-Semitism has appeared in ancient, medieval, and modern societies; it has been spread under tyrannies and democracies, by reactionary nationalists and by radical universalists; it has been practiced by Christians and pagans, liberals and conservatives, capitalists and communists. There is something in common in all these cases, and it is not in the Jews! Not *all* capitalists or *all* communists, not *all* Christians or *all* pagans have been anti-Semites. It is the *absolutists* among these groups who have been anti-Semitic. Those Christians who believe that the Messiah has come and that Christianity is the final answer, the perfect religion for all people, resent the continuing Jewish insistence that redemption is not here yet. Those Christians who believe there is salvation outside the Church and that there is room for many mansions in God's house have no problem with Jews. Liberals who are pluralist, tolerant, and aware of liberalism's own limitations have been leaders in giving Jews equal rights and full dignity. But liberals who are absolute universalists, who feel that since liberalism has given everyone freedom, the Jews should show their gratitude by giving up their benighted distinctiveness, show anti-Semitic resentment when the Jews demur.

Jewish difference stubbornly defies those who insist that everyone join together and stop holding back the ultimate truth. Thereby, Jewish distinctive existence continues to be a very sensitive litmus test of the capacity of human groups and isms to accept their own limitations and respect the dignity of others. The fact that Jews exist and are different poses a challenge to all who make absolute claims for themselves. The absolutist character of their claims shows in their assumption that those other than themselves are *ipso facto* illegitimate for being different.

The issue can be translated into theological language. The Bible insists that Jews are witnesses to the Divine Presence in the world and carriers of the message that a final redemption is coming. By now, after millennia in this role, the message is associated with the existence of all or any Jews, whether or not they consciously avow it. The message is that only God is absolute; by implication, this makes all other messages *relative.*

Any totalistic view is challenged and feels threatened by the Jewish message that only God is absolute. Jewish existence constitutes a witness that the Messiah and/or the final perfection is not yet here. If it were here, the Jews would be one with humanity, that is, would disappear. Premature messianists, in whatever form, are angered by the persistence of the Jew who thereby gives the lie to their presumptions. Idolatry is tempted to make the Jews disappear and thereby clear the way for its own uncontested dominance.

The twentieth century has made the matter even clearer. *Whosoever would be God must destroy the Jews totally.* As long as one Jew is alive, the Jewish denial of all but God remains. The twentieth century has unleashed such gigantic and total power that the temptation to become God is overwhelming; therefore, a plan to murder every last Jew became conceivable—and doable.

Rabbi Joseph B. Soloveitchik calls attention to this special aspect of the Purim story: The Megillah identifies Haman as the Agagite, a descendant of Amalek, the arch-enemy of Israel. In Jewish tradition, Amalek is no longer the original Bedouin tribe but rather symbolizes evil incarnate, a force seeking to wipe out the Jews. Amalek represents a total claim, a human absolute that sees itself "contradicted" or challenged by the existence of the Jew. Although the Jews protest and try to reason with the aggressor, Amalek's unrelenting slogan is, "Come, let us wipe them out from the nations so that the name of Israel will not be remembered" (Psalms 83:4). To quote Rabbi Soloveitchik:

> Suddenly, the Persian Jew discovered that he is hated. No one hates the United States or France, though particular policies may be vehemently decried. The mere existence of a Jew, however, irritates Amalek, and his hatred can erupt suddenly and violently and be translated into mass murder. The very presence of a Mordecai arouses . . . Haman; he just can't bear him. As Haman clearly declared: "Yet all this [honor] is worth nothing to me, as long as I see Mordecai, the Jew, sitting at the King's gate" (Esther 5:13).*

Whether Amalek is Fascist (Hitler), Communist (Stalin), absolute capitalist, radical terrorist, or even American super-patriot, the Jew becomes the target of his irrational and total hatred. Although Jews as liberals have been uncomfortable with the idea, the tradition has insisted that as long as an Amalek exists, the Jews are unsafe. God's rule cannot be completed until Amalek is no more.

---

*Abraham Besdin, editor, *Hashkafah Lessons* (New York: Rabbinical Council of America, n.d.).

CONFRONTING JEWISH DESTINY

Perhaps some assimilated Jews saw the dangers of Haman's self-inflating tendencies, but they looked the other way and hoped to fade into the landscape. They were confident they had nothing to do with "Mordecai, the Jew" types who would not go along with Persian rules. It was a rude awakening to discover that Haman designated all Jews as his target. Even more shocking was the discovery that the respectable Ahashverosh, who would never kill Jews (some of his best friends were Jews), passed the ring to Haman without hesitation and was ready to stand by indifferently while the mass murder proceeded. Jews discovered the bitter lessons of the Diaspora: It *can* happen here, and we *are* one.

The Talmud says ironically: "That removal of Ahashverosh's ring accomplished more than [all] forty-eight prophets and seven prophetesses who prophesied to the Jews [in the First Temple period]. The prophets failed to get the Jews to turn to good, but the ring removal turned them around."* During the years of the First Temple, the Jews had been divided into two kingdoms, Judah and Israel. The Judeans and the Israelites were like two peoples, and they even went to war with each other. Now, in exile, they learned that they all were the same; they were one people—the Yehudim, the Jews. Later, when Esther hesitated to face the king and ask for mercy (for fear she would jeopardize her own life), Mordecai said simply, "Do not think that you will escape from all the Jews [and their fate] into the king's house" (Esther 4:13). Esther, in turn, asked Mordecai to gather "all the Jews" in Shushan to fast and pray for her. The principle of common destiny that was to rule Jewish life penetrated the Jewish mind in the Exile, where its truth became self-evident. But it took the Hamans (and the Hitlers) to teach the lesson, to jolt the Jews into a new sense of peoplehood and culture.

The Jewish response to the threat of genocide in the Book of Esther reflects stereotypically *galut* (exile) mentality. First, there is perplexity and divided counsel. Some Jews, like Mordecai, wept. Some, like Esther, initially denied the problem. Then the process of redemption begins, first with Mordecai, who wears sackcloth and ashes publicly and demands action.

One good deed leads to another, says the Talmud. Courage is contagious. Esther, who has been quibbling and hesitating ("Don't make

*Babylonian Talmud, Megillah 13A.

trouble; don't stand out") now joins in. Esther invites the king and Haman together to a wine feast. When the king offers her whatever she wants, she starts to speak but then holds off and invites them to another party the next day. This hesitation may have been tactical—overnight the king remembered Mordecai's past good services to him. Yet an alternative reading suggests that Esther started to speak the first day but pulled back in fear. Indeed, her appeal to the king on the second day is a classic of galut mentality. "*If* I found favor in your eyes, O king, and *if* it pleases the king, let my life be given to me at my request, and my people [spared] at my pleading: For we are sold, I and my people, to be destroyed, slain, annihilated. *If only we were sold to be male and female slaves, I would have been silent because for merely this kind of suffering, I would not have wanted to cause damage to the king*" (Esther 7:3–4). [The translation and emphasis are the author's, after Ibn Ezra's commentary.] This is the language of the Jew, totally dependent on the good will of the other, currying favor, pleading, unable to make demands.

Even after Haman is hanged, Esther must beg that the decree of genocide be revoked. Again, the language is that of self-abasement: "If it pleases the king, and if I have found favor in his eyes . . . then let the decree of Haman be repealed!" One cannot read these texts today, after the Holocaust, without moral nausea and anger, not at Esther but at the vulnerability of the Jew: to have to plead so self-belittlingly for release from genocide! Here is the overwhelming, absolute ethical and moral need for an end to Jewish dependency. Of course, Purim took place before the Holocaust. Then one could still live with the hope or illusion that dependency is a workable policy as long as Jews can win the goodwill of the king/czar/pope/president. Then the galut appeared tenable as long as Jews could either "know [or bribe] the right people" or could escape to the next country or kingdom.

Part of the dizzying paradox of Purim is the extraordinary and capricious reversals it reflects. Vashti is deposed as queen for showing modesty. Esther wins favor for the queenship because of her modesty. The depths are the Jews condemned and Esther on her knees pleading to be spared for the fate of slavery, if that is the king's pleasure. Yet in an instant the Jews are reprieved. Then they arm and are totally triumphant over their sworn enemies. Mordecai, in one day, is raised from gallows candidate to prime minister. The very name of the holiday—Purim (meaning lottery)—suggests the absurdity and vulnerability of historical events when a turn of the wheel, a night's insomnia, a moment of jealousy on the part of a drunken king spells the difference between degradation and exaltation, between genocide and survival. It reminds one of Alexander Solzhenitsyn's *Gulag Archipelago:* If Stalin had lived another few months, would not all the Jews of Russia have been killed and/or deported to Siberian concentration camps? Is it exaggeration, then, to see in the celebration of Purim a substratum of despair? Eat, drink, and be merry, for tomorrow Mordecai may hang and a new Haman may be enthroned.

The Rabbis speak of the Book of Esther as the book of the hiding God. God's name is not mentioned;* the redemption is brought about by flawed human effort. The meaning is "hidden" beneath the surface. This may account for the masks and masquerades of Purim. As one scholar put it, "Wear masks, get drunk, for meaning is hidden beneath the visible."†

LIVING ON IN THE DIASPORA

Even after they were saved from genocide, the Jews had to come to grips with existence in the Diaspora. Could they go on living that good life without an inner gnawing of anxiety: How long can this last? When will the next reversal come? Once Jews learn that "it can happen here," can any life lived in Diaspora be other than a hollow, dissembling one? Can any enlightened Diaspora patriotism be other than a civic deception? Should we not condemn citizenship to be a fruit "good to the taste, desirable to the eyes" with a canker at the core?

True, Haman and his cohorts were wiped out. But what about Ahashverosh and the governors who so casually cooperated with the plan for destruction? What about all the good Gentiles who looked away? Is the whole experience not a confirmation of Balaam's dictum that "this is a people that dwells alone"? Is not the message that, in the showdown, Jews can depend only on Jews?

The questions bite deep. They suggest another question: Is the proper observance of the Purim victory a celebration or a mourning day? Would assimilated Jews use Purim to celebrate Persian virtues and Jewish citizenship, and repress the troubling problematics of what happened? Would committed Jews deny the day or treat it as a day of anxiety and alienation from society, one that proves that incipient treachery lurks behind every friendly Persian gesture?

In general, Jews of the day were conflicted in trying to assess the Purim salvation. To a people living with the messianic hopes so eloquently expressed in the Book of Isaiah, the Purim victory had to be only borderline meaningful. Here was an expectation so powerful that Cyrus could be called "my [God's] anointed." Isaiah dreamed of a

---

*Only one other book of the Bible, *Song of Songs*, fails to mention God's name outright.
†Elliot Yagod, "Chanukah and Purim: Two Models of Jewish History," unpublished.

New Exodus, with a broad road paved through the desert for a triumphant march back to Israel. A new era was to dawn: The nations would carry the Jews homeward in triumph; kings and nobles would carry the Jews as gently as nurses carry infants. What pitiful contrasts: the vision of Cyrus, God's anointed, sweeping the world and using that power to be Israel's shepherd, versus the reality of Ahashverosh, the besotted buffoon from whom permission for every act of Jewish self-defense must be wheedlingly coaxed. How unromantic is a vulnerable existence in Diaspora, making a living every day, compared to being in a restored Jerusalem whose streets are to be paved in sapphires, whose battlements would be made of rubies, whose gates would be of precious stones.

In its resolution of these alternatives, the Book of Esther represents a striking maturation of political and theological judgment. The remarkable, albeit limited, victory of Persian Jewry is sufficient cause for affirmation and celebration.

Sure, it would be nice if the Jews were totally restored, to sit every man under his own vine and under his own fig tree *"and none shall make them afraid"* (Micah 4:4) (italics supplied). The redemption of Purim left the Jews far more insecure. After the victory, the basic Diaspora conditions remain; no one can give assurances that such absurd changes in people and national moods will not happen again. Rather, the celebration of Purim grows out of a wise acceptance of vulnerability. The truth is that all of life is deeply vulnerable. Health, success, children can be snatched away overnight. The sweetness of life should be savored today, for that is all one really has for sure.

Purim affirms that the choice is not between a totally transformed reality brought about by God's Redeemer or life in a hollow, inauthentic status quo. Just as Shabbat gives the pure taste of the final messianic perfection to free the Jew to participate with a full heart in the partial, flawed daily reality, so the temporary victories of a Haman defeated or a Mordecai elected prime minister should not be robbed of significance by the infinite dream not yet realized. The holiday of Purim's dialectical resolution of the tension between dream and reality is to celebrate the victory while poking fun at it, to enjoy it fully while appreciating its limitations.

The most remarkable contribution of Purim and the scroll of Esther is to present the transformation of Persian Jewry not as a product of either blind chance or human effort alone but, in true covenantal fashion, as a result of God's working in history. It is not chance (*pur*) but Providence that ultimately accounts for the reversal of Esther's fortunes and, because of her, of Israel's as well. Thus, the Book of Esther brings the Diaspora into the great pattern of redemption history.

The Persian Jewish community, as reflected in the Book of Esther, responded to the entire episode with a determination to survive as Jews and with a discerning reaffirmation of its Jewishness in relation to Gentiles. Nowhere is there a hint that all Gentiles were like Haman. Jews attacked people because they were unjustified enemies intent on murder not because they were Gentiles. Gentiles who helped were neither censured nor criticized. The Jews avoided blind affirmation of the victory and naive praise of Jewish-Gentile cooperation.

Purim celebrated the ability of the Jew to live and cope with an imperfect world where shrewd use of power and opportunity often spelled the difference between destruction and survival. It celebrated (and admitted!) the narrow margin by which Jews snatched meaning from the jaws of tragedy and absurdity in history. The humor, mockery, and tongue-in-cheek tone of the Book of Esther and of the holiday is a perfect way to express the ambiguities and reversals built into the occasion. The way to deal with reversals is to *play* with them; humor can be the key to sanity. It is the only healthy way to combine affirmation with ongoing doubt.

Although the Bible uses humor to mock the pretensions of God's adversaries, the application of satire in a holy day was unprecedented. No wonder established thinkers hesitated or resisted; adoption of the Purim holiday came from the folk, which expressed itself in a rollicking (to scholars, "unseemly") way. It took time for the religious authorities to confirm the holiday, and it took centuries for the Book of Esther to be fully accepted as worthy of inclusion in the Bible.

Persian Jews gave up neither on the Diaspora nor on their Jewishness. Despite the narrow margin of their salvation, they remained committed and involved in Persia. The scroll of Esther describes their remarkable transformation from a condemned, vulnerable minority to a powerful, confident community. Thanks to Jewish self-assertion and the *hidden* grace of God, the mourning, fasting, weeping, and lamenting are turned into "light, joy, gladness, and honor" for the Jews. Purim "reruns" the Exodus story. This time its result is not a happy ending in the Promised Land but peace and prosperity in the Diaspora.

By expanding the history of Jewish redemption to include Diaspora experiences, the Book of Esther opened up Judaism to the world. Once the Megillah made clear that God's redemption operates in diaspora as well, Judaism became an option for those who never lived or have no intention of living in the land of Israel. The Book of Esther tells that many of the peoples of the land became Jews or passed themselves off as Jews. While the obvious motive for this behavior was fear of the new Jewish power, the result was that people now saw Jews as a religious community that all could join and not just a tribe living in a certain land.

The Book of Esther communicates a new sense of triumph, of an optimistic, self-confident Jewish Diaspora that can boast of one of its own as prime minister, a community fully able to defend the Jews from further attack. Yet in its narrative the scroll reminds Jews that they are permanently vulnerable in Diaspora. (Perhaps one should say that as long as the world is unredeemed, Jews are vulnerable; for today even the rebuilt land of Israel is also not totally secure.)

Persian Jewry can serve as a model for a Diaspora Jewry that strives to be powerful yet live without illusions, one which enjoys prosperity and freedom yet is aware of the risks of history. To affirm the centrality of Zion and the unity of the Jewish people while living one's own good life and striving to maintain Jewish loyalty is not easy, although the Book of Esther suggests that it is possible. But those who choose this way should never forget the Talmud's wistful comment: Had all the Jews returned to Israel from the first Exile, the Jews could never have been thrown off the land again.

EGYPT AND PERSIA: OR, THE HUMAN ROLE IN REDEMPTION

There are two classic experiences of Jewish exile found in the Bible—one in Egypt and one in Persia. Both experiences started off well (Jews fleeing from trouble were well received); both took an ugly turn for the worse (tyrants arose to threaten their very existence). In each case there was a happy ending. The people of Israel were redeemed and the tyrants overthrown. In each case the climax was an acceptance of the covenant of Israel—the commitment to live a special life as a chosen people. In each case both the suffering and the salvation are remembered because both aspects offer lessons for life. One lesson that both experiences teach is the critical role humans must play in their own redemption.

Every tragedy in exile throws the entire covenant into question. When crisis looms, the fundamental promise and hope of Judaism hang in the balance. Will redemption come? Will the covenant hold true and Israel escape destruction? The answer given in Egypt and Persia is yes. However, there is a closely connected question that still must be clarified. Who will save the Jews when danger looms? The answer given in Egypt and Persia is that it takes the decisions and actions of human beings to bring redemption.

In Egypt, when the Jews were no more than the unpaid work gangs of Pharaoh and were facing genocide, the process of resistance started in one act of saying no. Two midwives refused to participate in the killing of male children. Their act led to another heroic step. "And a man of the tribe of Levi went and took a daughter of the house of

Levi . . ." (Exodus 2:1), and she became pregnant and bore a son. With no hope of hiding the child, this anonymous couple floated him in a basket rather than yield him to death. Their act of faith and hope led to an act of Gentile kindness: The Egyptian princess saved the boy and raised him at the king's court.

Moses grew up and elected not to live the life of an indulged Egyptian prince but "to go out to his brothers and see their suffering." Had he decided to live in the oblivion of the royal palace, Israel's slavery would have endured. Had he remained silent, there would have been no Exodus. Seeing an Egyptian taskmaster beating a Hebrew slave, Moses stepped forward, took responsibility, and struck down the Egyptian. Moses fled. Had he forgotten his people, there would have been no liberation. Only after these human actions did the Divine Partner intervene and send Moses on his mission.

In Persia, the twist of fortune brought the Jewish community to the brink of destruction. The initial act of saying no to Haman's absolutism—Mordecai's refusal to bow—brought great danger to the Jews. When catastrophe loomed, Mordecai's inner reaction was to identify with their destiny. When his people mourned and wept at hearing the decree of genocide, he screamed in their pain. The next stage of resistance was his decision to reveal himself publicly.

By the time of the Persian empire, the Jews knew their faith did not guarantee invincibility. God's presence had undergone self-limitation; direct access to God seemed to be over. Mordecai made no claim of direct revelation, nor was he called as was Moses. The Megillah reports Mordecai's election with subtle understatement: "And Mordecai knew all that had happened" (Esther 4:1).

In a moment of insight, Mordecai grasped the whole situation: the effects of his action, the danger to the Jewish people, the need to take responsibility, and the providential nature of Esther's ascent to the queenship. Without divine signs and miracles,* without the prophetic certainty, Mordecai recognized his destiny and embraced it. He could not send miraculous messengers to Esther to convince her, but he was absolutely firm in pressing forward his plan. Human responsibility is not lessened for being the product of the leader's best judgment rather than unequivocal divine instruction.

This scene is one of Mordecai's finest moments, as he combines insight and responsibility with imaginative planning and decisive action. Since royal decrees cannot be reversed, Mordecai knows that the king must issue a new policy directive to stop the genocide. Since only Esther can reach the king, Mordecai instructs her to approach him and plead her people's cause.

---

*Contrast Exodus 3 and 4.

But Esther is a woman in Persian society; she is not accustomed to taking initiative. It has been a month since she was called to the king. Isolated in the palace, fearful of her fate, she hesitates. She will never gain an audience with the king, she thinks, and if she does get in, what will she say? Can she argue with Haman, who rides high and holds the king in the palm of his hand? Even if she could argue, would the king—who deposed Vashti for fear her independence would give Persian women rebellious ideas—listen to a mere woman speaking against his own decree, especially one initiated by the powerful prime minister?

Lashed by Mordecai's words (that she would betray her people if she did not approach the king), Esther agrees to go, though she is convinced the scheme will not work. The king who issued a decree that wives be properly submissive is not going to welcome a visit by his wife for the purpose of opposing a royal policy decision. Haman keeps the king under his sway by playing on Ahashverosh's fear of being overthrown. Esther, living in the court, understands the atmosphere. In such an atmosphere, those who stand up to object are not listened to; they disappear. In truth, she feels the cause is lost and her life forfeit ("As I am lost, I am lost" [Esther 4:16]), but she will do it for her uncle and her people's sake.

For Esther, these days are the long night of the soul. All around her in the court she sees the sharpening of the knives. Since people do not know that she is Jewish, they talk freely of the coming bloodbath and gleefully anticipate the rich spoils of the dead Jews. She cannot trust anyone, nor dare she betray her own tremendous anxiety for her people. So she must sit with fixed smile while the courtiers roar with laughter, anticipating how the cowardly, helpless Jews will run around like drugged cockroaches in a bottle.

Esther feels Mordecai's disapproval of her delay. She is surrounded by dangers. She is not used to thinking on her own. Who is she to take the responsibility for Jewish fate into her own hands? The king steadfastly ignores her. She feels abandoned. There is almost a self-destructive element or some ritual preenactment of her own death in the decision to fast for three days before going to the king. (The one thing Esther has going for her is her beauty; fasting is not what the beautician ordered.) But in those three days Esther learns a lot. She learns to trust in a higher power. She learns that death is not the worst: "All who have gone down to the dust shall bend the knee before God, for the Victor restores to life."* She learns that Providence has chosen her, a woman, and not Mordecai to be the redeemer of the Jewish people.

---

*Psalms 22:30, after Mitchell Dahood translation in Psalms I, Anchor Bible (Garden City: Doubleday, 1965). See Babylonian Talmud, Yoma 26A, Megillah 15B.

This means that she has to use whatever resources being a woman and a queen give her to effect the rescue. She learns that in her hesitation lies a disagreement with Mordecai. The strategy of going to the king is right. The tactic of pleading is wrong. In her judgment, knowing the king as she does, it will not work. So Esther works out her own plan. (There is no evidence in the text that she informed Mordecai of her strategy.) She will turn the tables on Haman by showing, somehow, that Haman is disloyal, that he is the real plotter. Esther approaches the king, exuding all the sexuality the king finds so magnetic. Then she responds to the king's invitation to request anything she wants by asking only that the king and Haman come to her special feast.

One can imagine what an atmosphere of desirability Esther created, what glances, what sweetmeats she lavished on both men, what message she communicated when she asked that the king and Haman come back—alone—for another such feast on the morrow. Haman went home so swollen with anticipation and so heady with power that he decided to wait no longer. He slept blissfully and rose up early in the morning to go and ask the king to dispatch Mordecai at once. But, while Haman had slept the sleep of the sated, the king had spent a sleepless night. What went through his mind that he asked to read the chronicles and, as it turned out, the records of the conspiracy of Bigtan and Teresh to destroy the king?

Then the king asked: What reward had Mordecai received for saving the King's life? The answer was: Nothing was done for him. Suddenly there was a loss of confidence in Haman. With so many enemies around, shouldn't someone who uncovered a plot have been richly rewarded? Who is in the court? Haman. Why was he loitering around the court at this early morning hour? When the king instructed Haman to honor Mordecai with the signs of royalty, he must have noticed Haman's shock, fear, and conflict. Can Haman have been in sympathy with the plotters? And why were the queen and Haman so obviously close? What surprise did she—did they—have in mind for tomorrow's feast where, at her insistence, they would be alone together?

When Ahashverosh reiterated that Haman should shower every honor he conceived on Mordecai—"Omit nothing of what you have proposed"—was this not a semi-hysterical request for reassurance that Haman was loyal and trustworthy? Ahashverosh was suddenly swamped with suspicion that at the heart of his network to control society there was treason.

This was the most dangerous aspect of Esther's plan. She walked the narrow line of arousing the king while stimulating his jealousy and fear. She hoped that his lust and pride of possession would win out over his anger at her forwardness. She hoped to set him against Haman. But one step too many, one moment of anxiety too high, and

she and Haman—she more likely than Haman—would be condemned to death, and the fate of the Jews would be seven times
sealed.

It was a risky plan, unsavory in many ways. If Esther failed, she
would be denied the dignity of death as a martyr. She would die as a
courtesan. What would Mordecai think when he learned that the
queen had died for the crime of sexual infidelity with Haman? Was this
why she had held back from going to the king when he asked?

Esther understood that just as there were no simple, easy-to-read
directions from God anymore, there were no guarantees of salvation
either. Esther's use of feminine wiles was only the first step in redemption. Her tactic worked. Then she and Mordecai won the right of
self-defense for the Jews. In a bloody showdown, the Jews' genocidal
enemies were destroyed.

Bedroom politics, revenge, murder. Some twenty centuries later,
Martin Luther wanted to drop the Book of Esther from the Bible because it lacked piety and "spirituality." Yet these actions—fallible,
open to question, morally ambiguous—were acts of responsibility that
interacted with the forces of history and brought forth salvation. A
woman's daring saved the people of Israel.

Perhaps this is the point of the traditional concept of a *personal*
Messiah. Modern people are embarrassed by this concept and prefer
to speak of a messianic age or the triumph of the forces of progress.
The Purim story, like the Passover story, emphasizes that one cannot
pass the buck to forces of history. The concept of the personal Messiah should not represent some *deus ex machina*, some divine intervention that will relieve humanity of its responsibility or of the
consequences of its folly. Rather, it is meant to underscore that, in
the final analysis, humans must take responsibility for their own
fate: The final liberator will be a human redeemer. Then all our
limited strides forward will become part of the way to the realization
of the grand design.

PURIM: THE REENACTMENT

Celebrating Purim

The holiday of Purim is marked not as "sacred time" but as a time of
secularity and natural joy. There are no restrictions on creative labor
such as there are in the pentateuchal sacred days (that is, Shabbat, first
and last days of Passover, first and last days of Sukkot, Rosh Hashanah, and Yom Kippur). All men, women, and children are commanded to celebrate. Women are obligated to hear the Megillah

reading. The Talmud adds that since they are obligated to hear, they may fulfill the mitzvah to read the Megillah for others, including men. It is a rare if unexercised religious role for women found in the traditional sources.

One has to love the Purim holiday. At what other time can one eat, drink (even get drunk!), send and receive gifts, make jokes and kid around, even have the rabbi *encourage* everyone to make noise in the synagogue (at the proper time, of course), and get mitzvah points for doing this!

Still, the core religious model of Purim observance is the classic mode of reenactment. Jews relive the entire event, from the depths of despair and looming genocide to the delirious exaltation of deliverance, revenge, and victory.

Purim opens on a somber note. Haman is identified as the descendant of Amalek, whose people attacked Israel in the desert, the symbol of cruelty to the weak. Before celebrating the defeat of the wicked, one must remember that God (as well as God's people) has a war with the Amalekites and will not be at ease until the Amalekites are blotted out. Jews are pledged to work for the end of oppression of the weak everywhere; a temporary, partial victory should not blind one to the persistence of evil in the world. On the Sabbath before Purim, the portion of the Torah dealing with Amalek is read. This day is called Shabbat Zachor, the Sabbath of Remembrance. It is a special mitzvah of the Torah to hear the reading and thus remember.

Zachor is a mitzvah that has made modern Jews uncomfortable. The natural desire to forget and be happy collides with the ongoing pain of memory and analysis. When asked why President Ronald Reagan in 1985 initially declined to visit the Dachau concentration camp, a presidential aide explained that the President was an "up" type of person and did not like to "grovel in a grisly thing."

Modern people who are future-oriented stress the need to forgive. They argue that there will be no reconciliation as long as the memories of the cruelties and atrocities of the past are preserved and thrown in the face of those involved. "Forget and forgive" becomes the slogan. This argument can even take the form of an attack on the victims for keeping the memory alive. In May 1985, a storm of opposition arose against President Reagan's visit to the Bitburg, Germany military cemetery because the ceremony involved paying homage and laying a wreath in a cemetery with graves of S.S. soldiers. During the uproar, one German parliamentarian attacked the Jews for their unchristian-like refusal to forget the past!

The primary lesson of Parshat (Torah reading) Zachor is that true reconciliation comes through repentance and remembrance. Confronting the evils of the past is the most powerful generator of moral cleansing and fundamental reconciliation. Repentance is the key to overcoming the evils of the past. When people recognize injustice, they can correct the wrongdoing and the conditions that lead to it. In the twentieth century, repentance has liberated many Christians from past stereotyping and hatred of Jews, thus beginning to transform Christianity into a gospel of love—which it seeks to be.

Remembrance is the key to preventing recurrence. Goaded by the memory of the failures of the 1930s, the indifference toward Jewish refugees, the American government in 1979 organized a worldwide absorption program for two million boat people. Goaded by memory, America's Jews and Israel responded to the crisis of Soviet Jewry and, belatedly, of Ethiopian Jewry.

Naivete and amnesia always favor the aggressors, the Amalekites in particular. The Amalekites wanted to wipe out an entire people, memory and all; amnesia completes that undone job. Ingenuousness leads to lowering the guard, which encourages attempts at repetition. One of the classic evasions undergirding naivete is the claim that Amalek is long since gone. Only "primitive" people are so cruel; only madmen or people controlled by a Svengali/Hitler type would do such terrible things. The mitzvah of Zachor is a stern reminder that Amalek lives and must be fought.

Through Zachor one learns to distinguish types and levels of evil. Not every evil is Amalek, but the ultimate evil must be destroyed. King Saul had a chance to wipe out Amalek but in pity he spared Agag, the king. Centuries later, Haman the Agagite, the descendant of Agag, plotted the mass extermination of Jews (Esther 3:1). Says the Talmud: "Whoever is compassionate to those who deserve cruelty ends up being cruel to those who deserve compassion."*

Having recalled the forces of evil, the Jew now proceeds to recall the bitter memory of the helplessness and the terror of innocents suddenly condemned to death without rhyme or reason. This mood is actually part of the story of the Megillah, but it would be almost impossible to capture in the midst of Purim exultation. Therefore, the day before Purim was established in the rabbinic period as a fast day, the fast of Esther.

Again, the Rabbis show the strong halachic preference for dialectical experiences that reinforce one another. Here, fasting is just as important to holiness as feasting. The fast day of Esther corrects the excesses in Purim. To the sense of triumph and mastery over fate celebrated on Purim, the fast of Esther responds with a reminder of the powerlessness that preceded the day. Before the merrymaking and dulling of

---

*Midrash Tanhuma Metzora (Jerusalem Eshkol, 1971), section 1.

one's senses through drunkenness begin, the fast day offers the intro-spection and meditations of penitential prayers and Avinu Malkenu (Our Father, our King, we have sinned before You). As against the sense of triumph over enemies celebrated by booing Haman (it could easily turn into arrogance), the fast of Esther holds up the teaching of vulnerability.

As dusk falls, the Jewish people make the dramatic transition from sorrow to *simcha*. Men, women, and children gather together—as they would have been gathered together for destruction—to hear the story retold. This is one of the four mitzvot that the Rabbis established to communicate the spirit of the day.

First, a special parchment Megillah containing the Book of Esther is folded and laid out; it is read forth as if it were a letter just received from our relative, Queen Esther. Before the Megillah is read to its own special melody, three blessings are sung by the reader. The blessings are for the commandment to read the Megillah, gratitude for the mira-cles done for our ancestors, and Shehecheyanu—the words, "who has kept us alive to this day" carry special resonance on this night. The overall liturgical goal is to reenact the story in all its gripping power. However, to capture the spirit correctly, one must grasp the humor, absurdity, happiness, and emotional rollercoaster of the event. Thus, in many congregations, people come dressed in costumes and primed with groggers (noisemakers) to drown out Amalek's name; this gives a manic tone to the evening from the very beginning.

Each chapter is read like another installment of the Perils of Pauline. The Jewish heart spends half the time in its throat, the other half bursting for joy. Chapter 1 ends on a note of buffoonery—the drunken king and councillors have deposed the queen to assert their male su-premacy but have shown only what fools they are. Chapter 2 is "up"—Esther wins the contest and Mordecai saves the king. Chapter 3 is a total reversal: Wicked Haman comes to power; Mordecai arouses his anger; the Jews are swiftly condemned to death; the city of Shu-shan is in total turmoil. In Chapter 4, Mordecai revives and pushes Esther to remonstrate. Will she or won't she? Chapter 5 is a downer: It ends with Haman building the gallows to hang Mordecai. Chapter 6 is another lightning reversal: The king remembers Mordecai; Haman is forced to honor him; Haman staggers home, bowed and grieving, but is whisked away to the party. Chapter 7 contains the climactic roll of the dice by Esther. She describes the terrible state of the Jews, con-fesses that they are her people, and throws herself and them on the mercy of the king. The queen wins; Haman is terrified; by royal de-cree, Haman is hanged on the very gallows he prepared for Mordecai —and so it goes.

At each revelation of Haman's viciousness—indeed, of his presence

—the congregation explodes into a cacophony of angry booing, hissing, and demonstrating. The community, delighted by Mordecai's rise, exultantly chants aloud the verses of his rise to power at every stage: from his initial appearance as a refugee immigrant from Jerusalem and Babylonia (Esther 2:5) to his first appearance as prime minister amidst the shouts of joy of the inhabitants of Shushan (Esther 8:15–16), to the fadeout with the "full account of the greatness of Mordecai" (Esther 10:2,3).

The synagogue atmosphere can be compared to that of an old true-blue "meller-drammer." Haman is booed whenever he is mentioned (by clacking groggers, blowing horns, firing cap pistols, stamping feet, and so forth). Mordecai is saluted. Some have developed the custom of reading the Megillah with appropriate voices—a snarling basso for Haman (ha! ha! me proud beauty, I've come to foreclose the mortgage), a sweet soprano for Esther, a beamish baritone for Mordecai, and so on. Some insert mock melodies that satirize the action.

Purim certainly challenges the uptight approach to religion. On this day, no fasting is permitted, no eulogies are given, no penitential prayers are recited. The Rabbis were so determined to make this point that they instructed people to drink—at least to the stage when they could no longer tell the difference between blessed Mordecai and accursed Haman. (Those who can't tell the difference all year long are excused on Purim.)

Other elements of celebration have been added, such as "Purim nussach" (musical mode). The evening service is chanted with a medley of melodies taken from the more solemn holidays, which holidays are, in effect, being satirized here. Some use popular and folk melodies for the prayers to create a humorous musical effect. People teach "Purim Torah" in which learning and scholarship are burlesqued. A sample: The Megillah tells us that on 15 Adar the Jews found relief from their enemies (Esther 9:16—*v'noah may—oyvehem*). In Hebrew, this phrase can be read literally as: And Noah was from their enemies. *Question:* What was Noah—a "good man" (see Genesis 6:9)—doing amidst their enemies? He should have been on the side of the Jews! *Answer:* The Rabbis command us to drink on Purim until one cannot tell the difference between Mordecai and Haman. Noah, that old rapscallion and drunkard, was only too glad to get blotto on Purim, and then, not knowing the difference, joined Haman's side by error.

Purim Kiddush is recited; its text consists of bits and pieces of various other prayers and verses strung together in nonsense meanings. Verses run into each other. A sample: *Aleynu leshabeach la-adon/Adon olam asher malach beterem Kol/Kol od baleyvav pnimah (Hatikvah)*. Thus, the tradition satirizes its own pretensions, affirming yet recognizing the contradictions to its own fundamentals.

FUN AND PLEASURE

Over the years the Jewish community has developed Purim carnivals and Purim masquerades. Note the role of costumes in the Megillah: Mordecai dons sackcloth and ashes to symbolize the looming genocide; he is clothed in royal robes by Haman in a foreshadowing of the coming reversal; he is dressed as the actual prime minister at the moment of triumph. On this one day, in Eastern Europe, Jews were permitted to dress as Gentiles (Haman, Ahashverosh). In fact, men were permitted to dress as women (Esther, Vashti, and others) and women as men, something that normally was strictly forbidden.

There seemed to have been a practice in Eastern Europe of snatching food from one another and hitting one another on the holiday. The legal codes rule that these actions on Purim do not constitute violations of the prohibitions against stealing and assault.* The actions add to the topsy-turvy tone of the day. On the actual Purim day then, Jews did *not* take spoil from Gentiles (Esther 9, 10:15–16). In a reversal, on Purim day now, they do take spoil from Jews.

There is a double vision throughout the day, strengthened by the spoofing that enables one to play a role and yet be an observer at the same time. The double vision reflects the contrast of blind fate or chance (Purim means casting lots), as against a hidden Providence. It also stems from the split in the Diaspora Jew's life between Esther and Hadassah; her two names, her two personalities and lives are paradigms of the bifurcation in the soul of the Jew living outside of the land of Israel.

Then there are the Purim-shpielers, Purim players circulating through the community, visiting homes and putting on skits. They are rewarded with coins for charity. In the yeshivot, it became a tradition to satirize the Rabbis and *Roshei yeshiva* (heads of the yeshiva), their personalities and styles of learning. Thus, an act of *lèse majesté* year-round became part of the fun of Purim.

The centerpiece of the day is the Purim *seudah* (Purim feast). Since on Purim the Jewish body was to be destroyed, the celebration must stuff the Jewish body for joy. Since the entire family was exposed to danger, the entire family is to be brought together for the feast. As the meal is eaten, the exaltation and relief of the day sinks in, overcoming

*Monford Harris, "Purim: The Celebration of Dis-Order," *Judaism*, volume 26, number 4, Fall 1977, pp. 161–70.

the residue of sadness that tinged the evening. The seudah is eaten by day to underscore that it is part of the celebration of the holiday itself. The prayer of thanksgiving, Al Hanissim ("we thank You for the miracles") is recited during the Birkat Hamazon (Grace After Meals) as well as during the three prayer services of the day.

Since there is a commandment to eat, drink, and be joyful, a variety of Purim foods have been created to highlight the occasion. Among Ashkenazic Jews, three-cornered cakes filled with poppy seeds, called hamentashen (Haman's pockets), are eaten. Folk tradition makes this a reminder of the three-cornered hat supposedly worn by Haman when he was the prime minister. Among Italian Jews, three-cornered dough pockets filled with chopped meat and called *orechi di Aman* (Haman's ears) were served on Purim. In some communities, *kreplach* (triangular pieces of dough filled with ground meat) are served. The two layers (outward, dough; inward, meat) represent the double vision of Purim; thus, food expresses the same experience as the masks and costumes. In some communities, special cookies with the names of Vashti and Zeresh (Haman's wife) written on them were baked and eaten. Thus, Jews "devoured" their enemies.

The Megillah tells that in the city of Shushan, Jews continued to fight their foes for a second day. Therefore, in another act of historical verisimilitude, 15 Adar is celebrated as an extra Purim day (known as Shushan Purim). By halachic ruling, all cities in Shushan's class, that is, walled cities with fortifications going back to the days of the conquest of the land of Israel (Joshua bin Nun's time), observe the second day of Purim. Thus, Jews in Jerusalem (but not Tel Aviv) celebrate the second day as a holiday.

No true Jewish simcha is complete unless it is shared with friends and with the needy. Accordingly, the Rabbis instituted two other Purim commandments:

Shalach manot (gift-sending): On Purim day, two portions or gifts (traditionally of ready-to-eat food) are sent to at least one friend. Spending time making up the gifts and then going around with the children to deliver them became a special family activity on the day. The pleasure is redoubled as others bring their offerings to your family. Behind the acts of friendship is the dreaded memory of the isolation, of being set aside for destruction and suddenly finding that people avoid those who are condemned. Only the friendship and solidarity of fellow Jews or special friends gave the strength to go on; that solidarity is ritually expressed in the shalach manot.

Matanot la'evyonim (gifts to the needy): The memory of past suffering should sensitize people to the needs of others, particularly the poor. The Rabbis established a separate and special mitzvah to give money or food to at least *two* poor persons on the day of Purim. An ideal way to fulfill this mitzvah is to give a contribution to synagogue funds for food to be given directly to the poor. It is a mitzvah to give as much as possible; no personal joy is complete unless others share it.

Similarly, before the reading of the Megillah, on the night of Purim, it is customary for all people over the age of twenty to donate three half dollars to the synagogue in remembrance of the half shekel given in ancient times to the Temple. These are used for charity.

In sum: Although reenactment is the primary model for celebrating the festivals, Jewish tradition particularly stresses the actual and total retelling of the story of two holidays, Passover and Purim. Contemporary Jews who have lived through a period in which genocide was successfully carried out can especially appreciate the delirium with which Jews greet the defeat of the Persian evil decree. The joy of Purim is occasionally a bit too boisterous and loud, but that is because the people know how close it all came to successful genocide. All in all, Purim is a marvelous holiday: joyful, secular yet religious, and full of humor, gifts, charity, friendship, and family. It is a classic example of how to serve God in affluence and pleasure, just as Jews once served primarily in poverty. It is noteworthy that the solidarity that the Jews created among themselves in the moment of despair lasted into the days of triumph.

PURIM: A NEW STAGE OF REVELATION

The holiday of Purim represents a great step forward in the history of Revelation and in the sophistication of Jewish religious understanding. Unlike the earlier traditions of Exodus, where the redemption from Egypt was accompanied by phenomena of a miraculous nature, and unlike even the later victory of Hanukkah, which had at least one extraordinary sign attached to it (the oil that burned for eight days), Purim appears to be a purely natural, human-made phenomenon. It was achieved by court intrigue and bedroom machinations. In the plain sense of the text its heroine is presented not as a God-intoxicated superhuman "saint" but as "the girl next door," frightened, lonely, using feminine wiles, an "ordinary" person.

Like all achievements in the real world, Purim was an admixture of moral ideal and moral compromise, which upsets perfectionists and religious purists. Fundamentalists objected that the holiday was not given in the Torah. It lacked the overtly supernatural; it was flawed by evil and human frailty and its victory was achieved by morally ambiguous methods. It would have been easy to dismiss Purim as secular, as not sanctioned by God, or to explain it away as accident. This is expressed in the absence of God's name in the scroll. However, by their acceptance of the Purim holiday, the people and ultimately the Rabbis, showed their grasp of the way to understand how God acts in history in the postprophetic age. They realized that God operated not as the force crashing into history from outside but in the center of life as the One who is present in the "natural" and in the redemptive process in which the human is co-partner.

In the tractate of Shabbat (88A) the Talmud tells a story that captures that transformation in the character of redemption and of covenant. The Talmud says that when the Israelites came out of Egypt to Sinai, God held the mountain over their heads and said: Accept my Torah or I will bury you right here. To which a scholar, Raba, comments: Then we can plead "acceptance under duress" (as extenuating circumstances if we fail to live up to the covenant). Not so, responds the Talmud, in the Book of Esther, for it states that "The Jews accepted and upheld [the Purim holiday]," (Esther 9:27). This means that the Jews, by freely accepting Purim, upheld (reinstituted) the original covenant acceptance of Sinai.

In hindsight, the Rabbis perceived the Exodus model of Revelation as "flawed" in that the saved humans were overawed, "coerced" into accepting God's revelation and commandments. On Purim, however, the mature Jewish people, rejecting the need for audiovisual fireworks, discerned God's presence in their history. This understanding enabled them to encounter God in the reality of natural, or partially redeemed, history. They concluded that, after all, in Shushan, flawed human beings had been the carriers of divine redemption. The lesson may be generalized: moral ambiguity dilutes but does not negate the triumph of good.

Living after the Destruction, they noted that the Divine had ceased to intervene in manifest fashion. Therefore, in retrospect, the overt divine salvation that backed the Sinai offer of covenant was perceived as coercive, if for no other reason than the gratitude in the heart of the people saved from slavery obligated them to accept. The recognition of the hidden divine hand in Purim was the insight that showed that the Jews had come of age. They had reaccepted the covenant of Sinai on the "new" terms, knowing that destruction can take place, that the sea will not be split for them, that the Divine had self-limited. They took on the additional responsibilities for the covenant, maturely and bravely.

If one takes the Talmudic story to its ultimate logic, it is even bolder. It says that were Jews living only from the covenantal acceptance at Sinai, the Torah would not have been fully binding after the Destruction. Post-destruction Jews are living under the command of the Torah by dint of the reacceptance of the Torah at Purim time. The covenant of

Purim is also a covenant of redemption, but it is built around a core event that is brought about by a more hidden Divine Presence acting in partnership with human messengers. Yet the covenant of Purim does not replace Sinai; it renews it. Purim confirms that the road to redemption continues even though we live in a world where the mighty, manifest acts of God are not available.

The Talmud finds the biblical source for Esther in Deuteronomy 31:18: *Anochi haster asteer*—"I will hide my face on that day." (*Asteer* is a Hebrew pun on Esther.) Esther's and Mordecai's covenantal roles are rooted in the hiddenness of God. The lesson of Purim is that in an age of "eclipse of God," look for divine redemption in the triumph of the good, even if that victory does not meet preset notions of purity and perfection. To pass that up is to ask to be back in the ruddy youth of religion when the answers are crystal clear and miraculous, and redemption is untouched by human hands. By the will of God, that world is no longer. If people insist on having extraterrestrial redeemers, they will perceive themselves as living in a world abandoned by God, when in fact God is the Divine Redeeming Presence encountered in the partial, flawed actions of humans. The truth of this salvation eludes both those who explain everything away as coincidence or random occurrence and those who insist on "out of this world" revelation.

Purim is the holiday for the post-Holocaust world; it is a model for the experience of redemption in the rebirth of Israel. In this era, too, the redemption is flawed—by the narrow escape, by the great loss of life, by the officially "irreligious" nature of the leadership, by the mixed motives and characters of those who carried it out, by the human suffering it brought in its wake, and by the less-than-perfect society of Israel. In our time, too, the "purists" wait for a "supernatural" miracle. Some object because of the religiously nonobservant element; others are crushed by the morally disturbing Arab refugee problem. Just as doctrinaire feminists get hung up on the "feminine" techniques of Esther, so are ideologues put off by the moral compromises involved in Israel's alliances and by the fact that it now gets support from the Establishment. People preoccupied with the equivocal details miss the overriding validity of the Purim and Israel events, events which occurred when the moral condition of the world needed such redemption, almost at all costs. Similarly, the Martin Luthers of the world are embarrassed by religious miracles that cost blood, so they question the fundamental validity of any divine but all too human redemption. The people, Israel, knew then and now better. In an imperfect world, one must be grateful for partial redemption. Celebration inspires the people to perfect that redemption.

In fact, there is a way in which the contemporary Redemption outranks Purim. Purim left Jews in exile; their fundamental position of powerlessness was unaffected. The Talmud suggests this is why "Hallel" is sung on Hanukkah but not on Purim. Yom Ha'Atzmaut (Israel Independence Day) brought independence and a decisive shift in the ability of Jews to protect themselves. In this way, Yom Ha'Atzmaut is closer to Hanukkah, which upheld Jewish self-government. Of course, Israel's independence lacked one thing Hanukkah did not: discovery of a supply of oil. I have been convinced for years that if only Israel discovered a large supply of oil, the whole world would recognize it as a miracle, vote to uphold it, and sing "Hallel" over it. In the absence of that "miracle," Israel awaits maturation of religious insight to bestow on it the central dignity it deserves.

PURIM: HOW TO SPEAK OF GOD TODAY

There is another important model in the holiday of Purim: how to speak of God today. A process of profound secularization has occurred in recent centuries. The growth of a scientific mind-set, of the sense of natural law and the tendency to reductionism that denies all transcendence, has made the use of religious language problematic. Some would deny the possibility of religious experience. But this is cultural imperialism that makes absolute a certain literal cast of mind and seeks to deny any alternative models of reality. Such arrogant secular claims are increasingly disputed by sophisticated philosophers. After the Holocaust one must challenge the absolute claims of a secular culture that created the matrix out of which such a catastrophe could grow. It is all the more urgent to bridle runaway secularism in light of the warning that comes to us out of the concentration camp universe. That world constituted an attempt at a total kingdom of man where God was excluded and humans assigned themselves the role of God. The result was the devil's work: total degradation and hell.

One way to check the excesses of secularization is to continue speaking in the same old way, i.e., the language of human helplessness and easy miracle. The resurgence of fundamentalism in the world is, in part, a dialectical corrective to the abuses of secularism. However, using premodern language means being out of place in this civilization; it almost suggests that the Torah can flourish only in certain limited cultures. So the question remains: How can a Jew speak of God today?

Other problems deepen the question. The rise of pluralism in an open society has created a sense of embarrassment and loss of credibility with the language of absolute demand. How can one speak of the absolute in such a setting? The rise of affluence and hedonism has created a new ethic and search for expression in pleasure. Yet many of the classic religious models are focused on denial, control, and restriction of pleasure. How can one express religious values in the pleasures of the body?

Then there is the excruciatingly intense problem of theodicy—the problem of evil, which looms larger than ever because of the monstrous evils inflicted in this time. In *The Brothers Karamazov*, Ivan dramatically underscores the difficulty of speaking of God after an innocent child has been brutalized and torn to death by dogs. Then what shall be spoken in a generation when thousands went by dogs and by fire, when over a million innocent children were savagely killed? No statement, theological or otherwise, should be made that would not be credible in the presence of burning children. Any easy affirmation of God would appear to mock the burning children. Any easy denial of God would appear to turn the children's deaths into a gigantic travesty. A simple denial of God would appear to deny the reality of redemption in our time and the validation of biblical promise by contemporary fulfillment. How then can one speak of God with integrity?

The holiday of Purim is a good guide as to how one can affirm. The answer is: humorously, tentatively, humanistically. Purim teaches how to speak subtly, admitting the alternatives yet knowing the reality of meaningfulness. Purim speaks of "chance" (lots), yet hiding between forms of chance is the Divine Presence. Vashti's recalcitrance enabled Esther to assume the throne; the king's insomnia raised Mordecai to greatness. These are "random" incidents that, decoded, spell out a pattern of redemption. These are natural events that point beyond themselves to a greater meaning.

Such speech about God also torments, of course. What kind of world is this, where a king authorizes mass murder and, a short time later, does not even remember the incident! When Esther tells him of the Jews' tragic fate, he asks her: Who is this who has dared to do this? What kind of world is this, where genocide is narrowly averted by flirty tea parties, by currying favor and appealing to male chauvinism? Yet by that margin the Jews are saved. The promise endures. The people of Israel live. One recognizes the implication: Our Father still lives.

No wonder Purim speaks in the language of party, feast, and drinking. Celebrate the vulnerability of life. Eat, drink, and be merry, for today the good win! Tomorrow the turn of the wheel may endanger it all. Do not despair or sulk! Admit your vulnerability and share your wealth with the poor, your friends, your family. In this way, pleasure expresses religious value. The material embodies the spiritual hope and affirmation.

HUMOR: THE LANGUAGE OF FAITH

On Purim, the laughter reaches surprising heights. This forces some consideration of the role of humor in religion in general. Purim is a put-on in many ways: witness the broad caricature of the Megillah and the raucousness of the celebration. The humor carries a religious message, however. Humor expresses transcendence of unredeemed reality, and it takes sanctity itself with a sense of limits. Satire prevents us from making the sacred absolute (only God is absolute). The unchecked tendency to respect religion all too often leads to deifying the ritual and the outward form of God. If people take the sacred too solemnly, they are confusing their religious expression—which is relative and limited in truth—with the infinite God whom they really seek to serve.

There is another element involved, an element one can appreciate a bit more in the generation after the Holocaust. The humor is in part a defiance and an outcry. In a sense, is it not absurd that the genocide came so close? That a tyrant was enraged and a whole nation was condemned? That a drunken, fatuous king casually agreed (a week later he didn't remember) and a whole people's doom was sealed? Is it not ridiculous that but for Esther's tricks and by that narrow margin Jews were barely saved from total savagery? Does this momentary confrontation with mass death not strip the veil of rationality from reality, exposing its tragic and outrageous nature?

One can only respond with laughter and mockery and put-on, satirizing God and the bitter joke this world threatens to become. It is enough to drive a person to drink! (Jews act this out.) But as the hilarity reaches its climax, Jews move beyond bitterness to humor. In laughing at religious forms and at reality, one admits the fallibility of religious hopes but one also affirms them. In satire and humor, the pretensions of the moment are punctured. Through the humor, Jews project themselves into future redeemed reality that transcends the moment. Thus, hope is kept alive and the Messiah remains possible.

Ultimately, laughter is a unique reflection of Judaism's conception of life and reality. One of the Torah's central positive teachings is that there is no other God. If one believes in the infinite One God, then everything else is relative. No other deity, no other value source, no other power has the right to claim absolute status.

Therefore, Jews not only teach monotheism, they teach against idolatry. To be a Jew is to fight idolatry. The *midrashim* about Abraham's earliest years describe him as a child smashing the idols in his father's shop; this is his introduction to becoming a Jew. But how should one fight idolatry? One of the real dangers is that in trying to refute the absolute claims of the idols, the very argument gives them significance. The presumptuousness of the demand for absolute loyalty on the part of human systems is best undermined by mockery and laughter, which puncture pretensions without giving weight to the pretender.

The Book of Exodus describes how the awesome all-powerful Pharaoh, the tyrant who claimed to be the embodiment of the Divine, was undermined by a plague—a profusion of frogs that crawled out of his shelves, his closets, his very bed. One can imagine the queen or the king climbing into the royal four-poster and sliding under the sheets with all the arrogance of dynasty, only to jump out in fright at the little frogs. Similarly, the Torah describes how the Egyptian wise men, who claimed they controlled the powers of the universe, were undermined by crawling, swarming, and biting little bugs. One can picture in the mind's eye how they scratched desperately and in vain until they had to retreat before Moses, the representative of the slaves and of the Infinite One whom they were trying to dismiss.

The same satiric approach is captured by Isaiah, who describes a naive bumpkin shaping and worshiping idols. The idolator carved half his wood into an awesome god before whom he bowed down and to whom he sacrificed everything. The other half—the broken pieces of wood and shavings—were thrown into a fire on which he cooked his food, and the bumpkin sat there and said, "Ahhh." The Psalms poke fun at idols who have eyes but see not; ears but hear not; and legs but walk not.

Just as idolators absolutize their deities, so do people tend to give infinite weight to their own contemporary situation. People are obedient to the norms of their society; they stand in awe of the authority that addresses them in their own lives. In a way, this is contemporary idolatry. When people sacrifice all ethics for the sake of making money, money has become their god. When people kill or drop all their values because of a totalitarian system that demands it, this is contemporary idolatry. Humor comes to the rescue by debunking the present situation, by revealing that this structure of the world is not absolute; there is something beyond it.

One of the amazing things about the record of the shoah is how Jews were able to use humor in the face of the most absolute evil of all time in order to reassert their human values. They told the story in the Warsaw ghetto, during the bitter mass roundups in which thousands of children were deported. An S.S. officer invaded one home and was about to take away a woman's only child. She pleaded and wept so piteously that the Nazi hesitated for a moment. Then, to make cruel sport with her, he said, "I will give you one chance to save your child.

I have one glass eye. It is so perfectly matched that it is indistinguishable from my normal eye. If you can pick out which one is the glass eye, I will spare your child." The woman looked deeply into his eyes for a moment and without hesitation said, "It is the one on the left." The Nazi was taken aback. "You are right," he said. "But how did you know?" The woman's answer: "The left eye is softer and more compassionate than the other one."

In Auschwitz, they told the story of a band of slowly freezing Jewish prisoners being marched up and down in the coldest winter. Their guard had them maintain military precision as they walked exhausted on the muddy, swamplike paths that passed for streets in Auschwitz. Taunting them, he ordered them to repeat after him and call out with military smartness the location they were at. They marched down one path. The guard called out, "Goering Strasse!" The prisoners replied, calling, "Goering Strasse!" On the next path, the guard called out, "Goebbels Allee!" The prisoners replied, "Goebbels Allee!" They reached the open field where they stood for roll call, and the guard shouted out, "Hitler Platz!" (meaning square, but also meaning, in Yiddish, drop dead!). The prisoners replied, "Amen!"

This relativization of the absolute authority of humans is an affirmation that every Jew, even the most secular and atheist, can make. The Talmud says that if one denies idolatry, it is equivalent to affirming the whole Torah. Thus, even in that hell when man was god over life and death, humor denied the absolute pretensions of the evil idolators.

But why on Purim do Jews satirize their own traditions and not just those of the evil ones? The answer is that the ultimate Jewish claims of faith are truly dissonant with the world as humans know it. Judaism affirms that this is a world in which life will overcome death, yet people die. Judaism affirms that the ultimate truth is justice and human dignity, yet now people perish from hunger and oppression and sickness and neglect. Judaism affirms that God has created a good world, and someday this will be manifest in every aspect of life, yet in this interim world there is cancer and persecution and slavery.

By what right, then, do Jews make their affirmations? The Jewish answer is that religious statements are expressions of faith. Faith is a vision of a truth that will come into being, backed by a commitment to make it happen. Faith is trust in the divine promise that this is not a quixotic mission but that the situation of redemption can be attained and realized in this world. Humor is the most appropriate way to express this faith—by simultaneously affirming and admitting the present limitations. True faith is neither oblivious to the facts that contradict nor afraid to affirm that the vision will finally triumph. Humor makes statements of faith credible without being insensitive to present states of suffering. Through humorous affirmation, Jews admit that they follow God not because their hopes have been realized but because they have trust in the Divine.

Purim is the balance to Passover; it is the humor that admits that the Shabbat is still a dream. To act as if Shabbat and the final redemption are fact would be insane; but not to affirm the totality of hope would be a sellout. Purim offers an alternative: humorous affirmation. Thus, Purim's laughter preserves integrity and sanity together. This is Purim's remarkable role in Jewish history.

CHAPTER EIGHT

Assimilation, Acculturation, and Jewish Survival: *Hanukkah*

THE CHALLENGE OF HELLENISM

The story of Hanukkah really begins in the fourth century B.C.E., with Alexander the Great's invasion of the Middle East and Asia. This conquest paved the way for the blend of Greek culture and Eastern traditions that became known as Hellenism.

Hellenistic culture was the most developed civilization that part of the world had ever known. Art, sculpture, and architecture flourished, as did poetry, satire, biography, and history. Philosophy prospered; science attained peaks that were not matched for more than a thousand years.

The spread of Hellenism tore down barriers between peoples; in the process, many traditional beliefs and ways of living proved vulnerable. The rise of sophisticated criticism went hand in hand with the decay of pagan idolatry, leaving a void that was filled by skepticism, mystery religion, superstition and, later, even Judaism and Christianity. The cosmopolitanism of Hellenistic culture and its vision of the individual, supported and associated with political power, proved irresistible to the wealthier educated and ruling groups throughout the East and Palestine.

Alexander's successors established Greek city-states throughout

Asia and Africa. The *polis* or city-state, with its council and assembly, civic cult, gymnasium, temple, and public buildings, was a living center of Greek ideas, values, and institutions.

The empire that Alexander made possible was split into three fragments: the Macedonian kingdom in Europe; Asia (including Syria, Mesopotamia, and Persia), ruled by the Seleucids; and Egypt, ruled by the Ptolemies. Hellenic cities were established in Palestine, and the settlers there intensified the diffusion of the foreign culture as never before. The result was a Greek-speaking, culturally Hellenistic Jewry in the Diaspora and an assimilating upper class in Palestine.

In the generation after Alexander's death, Palestine fell into Ptolemaic hands. A century later Antiochus III, the Seleucid king of Syria, captured the country. Antiochus issued a charter giving a series of privileges and projects of assistance to the Jews, including help in rebuilding Jerusalem, money for supplying the Temple with sacrifices, wine, and other items, and a grant of permission to live according to their ancestral laws.

As the Jerusalem aristocracy and priests drew closer to the Seleucids, the Jewish religion became a state religion. The priests' wealth and power were linked to commerce and tax collection. Wealthy Jewish tax farmers (who paid a fixed fee to the king and then collected the taxes) became part of the ruling class. Exploitation of poor Jews and of Gentiles caused resentment. Still, the initial period of Antiochus' rule confirmed the lesson of the Ptolemaic Jewish experience: Israel, the Lord's chosen people, had little to fear as long as it observed the Lord's commandments.

But by the second century B.C.E., the cumulative effect of Jewish exposure to Hellenism was beginning to affect the internal life of the Jews. Their traditions of separation and distinctiveness seemed increasingly parochial, old-fashioned, and embarrassing to well-to-do Jews. Hellenism ruled the world, and the elite everywhere joined it. Thus, each local culture faced the challenge of adopting Hellenism or losing its elite. But Jewish law prohibited intermarriage, and Jewish dietary laws prevented social contact. Soon, says the Book of Maccabees, a group of Jews arose who favored aggressive assimilation.

Had the process of Hellenization continued gradually and peacefully, it might well have taken over the Jewish people. The brightest and the best, the richest and the most powerful were increasingly attracted to it. The flow of authority and cultural superiority toward the Hellenists seemed irresistible. There was resistance to the process, but it came from the less sophisticated in Jerusalem, those who were not philosophers. It came from the farmers, the poorer classes, the less educated, the people who did not mix much with Greeks. Like country people who come to the big city and are horrified by its fleshpots and sinfulness, so the farmers of Judea were outraged and offended by the nakedness, the "bohemian," *avant-garde* air of Hellenism. In their boorishness and provincialism, in their "reactionary" attitudes, the farmers seemed laughable and backward (we would say old-fashioned) to the Jewish Hellenizers.

Then a new Seleucid king, Antiochus IV, came into the picture. He needed money for his plan to conquer Egypt. The Tobiads, a Jewish tax farmer family, gave Antiochus a substantial payment to replace the high priest, Onias III, with his younger, Hellenized brother Jason, plus an additional major sum for two privileges: the honor of founding a gymnasium and a Hellenist school, and the prerogative of drawing up a list of people to be citizens of a *polis* within Jerusalem to be established by Antiochus. The citizens would be called Antiochenes in Jerusalem, the polis name honoring the King. Under the existing confirmation of ancestral laws, any Jew who departed from the laws of Moses could be punished by the theocratic government. Under the special citizenship, Jews who became apostate in order to fulfill their Antiochene citizenship obligations would be untouchable.

Antiochus was setting up such poleis throughout his empire in the hope of stimulating voluntary Hellenization, and the money offered was far more tribute than Judea had ever given. Jason was appointed high priest. (One measure of Jason's fitness for the position was that under his leadership the priests increasingly neglected the Temple service for the newfangled Greek games. One measure of Jason's piety is that as high priest he sent an offering of three hundred drachmas of silver to the festival of Heracles at Tyre.) Armed with Antiochus' permission, the Hellenizers built a gymnasium in Jerusalem. According to 1 Maccabees, "They even submitted themselves to uncircumcision [a painful operation to remove the marks of circumcision] and repudiated the Holy Covenant."

However, once the precedent was set that the high priest was an appointee of the king (not merely confirmed by the king), the game could be played twice. After three years of Jason's rule, the Tobiads determined to replace him with someone even closer to them, a layman named Menelaus. Menelaus offered Antiochus a sum far larger than Jason's; he was duly appointed. Jason would not easily surrender his position, however. A split developed between his followers and Menelaus' group. Antiochus backed his second appointee, Menelaus. When Antiochus left on an Egyptian campaign, a false rumor spread that the king had died. Jason attempted to overthrow Menelaus. Antiochus returned, reinstated Menelaus, interpreted the fighting as resistance to him, and resolved to punish Jerusalem severely. He sacked the holy Temple.

Throughout Judea there were groups of pious Jews—called Pietists

(Chasidim)—who were most unhappy with the Hellenizing pressures of Antiochus and of the followers of Jason and Menelaus. The Chasidim believed, however, that they were bound by the Torah not to revolt against any foreign king who ruled over them. The foreign king was the "rod of God's anger," and Jews must accept their fate. If they repented, God would redeem them. If the king exceeded his role and harmed Jews excessively, God alone could and would punish him.

The sack of the Temple stunned the Chasidim. The First Temple was destroyed at God's will because of Jewish sinfulness. This second sack could only mean that the Lord was angered at Jewish Hellenizing apostasy and at the failure of pious Jews to do something about it. Some of the Pietists began to attack and harass the "wicked" Antiochenes in Jerusalem.

To Antiochus, the turmoil in Jerusalem brought a long-standing concern to a head. He was seeking to unify the world. Yet here were the stubborn, rebellious Jews refusing to worship with the citizens of the empire and harassing those Jews who were responsive to the new universal dispensation. Antiochus decided that the obstreperous fanatics must go; Judaism must be "purified" to be a conforming citizen religion of the great Seleucid empire. And so he issued a series of edicts. On penalty of death, all Jews must cease observing the Torah; instead they must follow an imposed, "purified" Judaism. An Athenian expert was sent in to direct the practices of the "purified," that is, universalized Judaism. Monthly sacrifices to the gods were begun. Sacred prostitution was set up in the Temple. A statue of Zeus was erected, and Zeus' name was associated with the Temple. The offering included the sacrifice of pigs on the altar. The laws of purity of the Temple were systematically violated.

It should be noted that Antiochus was not imposing his own faith in these decrees. He seems to have concluded that this is what pure Judaism would have been, had it been truly a religion with decent respect for the opinion of mankind. It was neither the first nor the last time in Jewish history that a "universalist," determined to straighten out the Jews and/or Judaism, showed gross ignorance of the faith, condition, and integrity of the Jews.

Had these "recalcitrant" traditional Jews been prone to philosophize, they might have argued that it was important for Judaism not to disappear, but since they were untutored city folk and farmers, they could not articulate a philosophic defense of their position. They only knew the old ways and clung to them passionately, outragedly, doggedly. The Hellenists smiled condescendingly.

Backed by the power of the king and the growing religious indifference of the elite, the rituals of Zeus worship and pig sacrifice were extended widely and successfully throughout Judea. Hellenization seemed unstoppable. The few who resisted were arrested, punished, and slain. The king's order proscribing the Torah was enforced with a vengeance. Sabbath observers and those who practiced circumcision were condemned to death.

In their simple faith, the Pietists believed that as long as Jews were faithful to God they were under divine protection, yet obedience to God's commandments had become a crime punishable by extreme severity. They also believed that it was sinful to revolt against the king. As more and more innocents were put to death, a significant fraction of the Chasidim concluded that the only resistance possible was to remain faithful and die for God's commandments. And so the concept of martyrdom developed into an ideal. The stature of the prophet and the martyr became merged into one: the highest stage of serving God.

The willingness to make this greatest of sacrifices, to die rather than to deny the Lord, became central in Jewish (and later Christian) testimony in the following centuries. Immortality and resurrection—ideas that heretofore had hardly played a role in Judaism—became central in Chasidic thinking. The promise of eternal life and rebirth undergirded the strength of Chasidic faith. This devotion should have warned the Syrians and their Hellenizing collaborators of stiffening resistance.

Yet martyrdom alone could not have stopped the massed power of the Seleucids and Hellenizers. In Chasidic reasoning, apocalypse was the only hope left. Indeed, had the Chasidim survived the persecution and won out within the Jewish community, the religion would have been decisively turned onto a path of pacifism, apocalyptic expectation, and denigration of secular life and human activity. The classic dialectic that moored Judaism in daily life would have been decisively broken.

THE MACCABEE REVOLT

In 167, in the town of Modiin, the new sacrificial cult was introduced. The resentment at the forced paganization and the desecration of the altar with the unclean pig boiled over in an act of rebellion. Mattathias, a priest of Modiin, stabbed a Jew who sacrificed in the new cult, killed the king's agent, and pulled down the sacrilegious altar.

Mattathias' social position made him the natural person to lead a revolt. He was a priest of a small town—not Jerusalem. He combined in himself enough aristocratic status and exposure to Hellenism to be a leader. At the same time he was a "country" man who shared the conservative party's position and was detached enough and rival enough to fight the Jerusalem priests and their policies. It is also revealing that his five sons were named Yochanan, Simon, Judah, Eliezer, and Jonathan. These biblical names contrasted with the Hellenist names, such as Jason and Menelaus, that abounded among the Jewish assimilating elite.

Elias Bickerman, a noted scholar, has pointed out that Mattathias did not demand the right of freedom of religion, nor did he fight for individual conscience. This was "a conflict between earthly power and the law of the state of God"—opposition to a King's order that was at variance with the commandments of God.

Mattathias shared the Pietists' faithfulness to Judaism. Where, then, did he find sanction to revolt against the king in defiance of what appeared to be the prophets' repeated strictures that the children of Israel not revolt against kings "whom the Lord had placed over them."* Mattathias justified his act by analogy with Phineas' act of zealotry in the desert, striking down Zimri, the son of Salu, and his paramour. That act—unjustified by law and in contradiction to the priestly role—was validated after the fact by God's blessing (Numbers 25:6–13). Mattathias dared to assert that a king who commanded the violation of the Torah could not rule Jews by divine right. In effect, Mattathias was operating out of a covenantal model in which humans could not "leave it all to God" but had to initiate some action to save the Torah and the Jews. In some Chasidim's conception, God did everything; humans only observed, repented, persisted, and waited on the Lord for deliverance. Significant numbers of Chasidim were highly critical of Mattathias' action as impious.

This split is not a simple case of Maccabees versus Chasidim. The controversy between Mattathias and the main wing of the Pietists was over how to properly apply their shared values. Mattathias and his men were saying that God had given a significant role to humans, including the authority to apply the principles of the tradition creatively. As for the passive, passionate Pietists, theirs was not to question why, theirs was but to do or die.

Mattathias and his five sons fled to the mountains to escape the government's punishment for their act of political terrorism. They were joined by other Jews, among whom were militant Chasidim who came over to Mattathias' view of the right to fight. The group was too weak to clash head-on with the Syrians; farmers, after all, are not well-trained soldiers.

And so Mattathias' band began a guerrilla war that depended on

---

*Compare Nehemiah 9:36–37, Daniel 1–6 and cp. Jeremiah 21, 24:1–25:29, 27:1–29:19; Ezekiel 17; 2 Kings 24:18–25:21. See especially Jonathan Goldstein's commentary on 2 Maccabees 1:7 and 15:10–17.

mobility and superior knowledge of the terrain. (The mountains granted them inaccessibility and allowed strategic maneuvering.) This tactic proved crucial in the unfolding of the revolt. Mattathias died shortly after the uprising began, and his son, Judah Maccabee, took over the leadership. As the Hasmoneans fought, the basic resistance of the masses to Hellenization gave the guerrillas a sympathetic local population. Hellenist settlers rallied to the Syrian government's side, eager to settle scores with their Jewish competitors.

THE MACCABEE COALITION

The entire process forced a choice on many Jews who had been drifting into Hellenism. In the crunch, seeing their Jewish brothers defending their home soil, seeing the destruction of local Jewish populations to advance the interests of Syrians made many people decide that they were primordially Jews, not Hellenists. Judah and his band might never have succeeded but for the shift of moderate Hellenizers to the side of the revolt. Thus, what started as a revolt of the fundamentalists became a viable coalition of simple traditionalism and moderate Hellenization.

The Chasidim's simple faith was their great strength, but their non-analytic obedience to the law made them vulnerable. The First Book of Maccabees tells how a band of Chasidim was trapped in a cave on the Sabbath by a Syrian/Hellenizer army. The Jews, refusing to fight or even to wall up the caves on the holy day, were killed without offering resistance.

Mattathias and his band, however, resolved to defend themselves if attacked on the Sabbath. The Rabbis formulated this principle: "You shall observe my statutes and laws that a man shall do and *live by them* and not die by them.... From this we learn that life saving overrides the Sabbath."* Ultimately, this principle was generalized in the ruling that every commandment of Torah except three—idolatry, murder, and certain sexual immoralities—can be overridden to save life.†

Unlike the Chasidim, who left everything to God, the Maccabees drew upon the covenantal model in which humans were called to take action *and* to make judgments about the appropriateness of that action. It is not that the Hasmoneans did not believe in the divinity of the commandments; it is that they were able to ask different questions of the Torah: Is there a goal to be reached? Is there a priority when princi-

---

*Babylonian Talmud, Yoma 85A, B.
†Babylonian Talmud, Sanhedrin 74A.

ples conflict? Is there a role for human judgment and action in executing the covenant?

The development by the Maccabees of a hierarchy of value—which in this case expressed itself in priority for life—reflects a philosophical influence. The concept of a fundamental principle that expresses itself in all commandments and that guides the resolution of conflicts of values, draws upon philosophic, literary, and rhetorical analysis of texts and their relationships. Exposure to Hellenist modes of thinking and philosophy evoked greater depth and sensitivity to such thinking in the Maccabean and later leadership—just as contact with more developed literary and philosophic models enriched traditional rabbis' capacity for halachic and narrative thinking in the past two centuries. Such thinking became a hallmark of the Maccabees and the later rabbis. They responded respectfully to Hellenism's ideas and methods, but only where they could enrich and be assimilated compatibly with the tradition. In short, without fundamentalism there would have been no Maccabean revolt; without moderate Hellenization the revolt would not have succeeded. The differences between these allies led to significant splits later on and to errors on both sides. Yet, without the coalition, the Maccabean Jews very likely would have been destroyed.

There was another important bonus in this decision to fight on the Sabbath. Authority to govern and to give religious rulings had been vested in the high priest and his council. The assumption of the power to give such rulings confirmed the authority and leadership of Mattathias. The lesson, then, is obvious: Authority flows from the ruling, not the ruling from the authority. It is a lesson that modern-day religious leadership must still learn.

THE MACCABEAN VICTORY

At first, Judah defeated the Seleucid auxiliary armies because the government was preoccupied elsewhere. By 165, he had cut off Jerusalem. Then a major Syrian army was sent to fight, and it became expedient for the rebel Jews to settle the war in the face of so serious a military threat. Menelaus, the high priest, served as mediator, and the agreement reached was a triumph for the Maccabees. The king gave amnesty to the rebels and granted the Jews the right to use their own food and to observe their own laws as of old.

However, Menelaus and his group still maintained control of the city and the Temple, and Judah's Chasidic fighters soon melted away. They were satisfied with the grant of freedom to worship and were relatively uninterested in the concerns of a national government. Later in the year the Syrian army was called away to another war. Judah gathered his followers and struck, capturing Jerusalem and driving Menelaus out of the priesthood.

The Temple was now in Maccabee hands, but nothing happened for months. Apparently the Pietists believed that the fulfillment of the apocalyptic prophecies in the Book of Daniel and elsewhere was imminent. The Seleucid empire would come to an end, and the eternal kingdom of the saints would be ushered in with the resurrection. But these prophecies mentioned no *human* acts of restoration. It would be presumptuous for humans to restore the Temple when God was about to do it. According to the Pietists, God would act at the beginning of the sabbatical year, coming in Tishrei 164/3. Out of respect for this Chasidic view (fear of being accused of impiety?) Judah waited. Tishrei came and went, and no miraculous intervention took place. However, it was argued that the current calendar was imperfect. It was short two intercalary months; the calendar had not been intercalated during the period that the aggressive Hellenists had controlled the Temple. Therefore, one should wait at least these two months.

In his brilliant commentary on the Books of 1 and 2 Maccabees,* Professor Jonathan Goldstein argues that Judah waited to meet the Pietists' objections but that two steps were taken in the interim. The idol installed in the Temple, known as the Abomination of Desolation, was destroyed on the opening of the New Year. This destruction was an act of zeal for God that could not be interpreted as a permanent substitution of human action for God's work. Then the Temple altar which had been utilized in the imposed cult was moved out. Some Pietists argued that the altar remained sacred even if desecrated. Human action cannot transform a divinely sanctified object; therefore, no Hellenist abuse could remove the original sanctity of this altar and no human could dismantle it now. ("Tear down their altars.... You shall not do so unto the Lord your God" [Deuteronomy 12:3–4].) Judah's decision was to interpret "not do so" as "not to do the same" to this divine altar. The altar was not smashed as a pagan altar would have been; but it was taken apart and put away.

The new altar may have been ready before the Feast of Tabernacles, ready for the possible fulfillment of Zechariah's prophecy that all those nations that did not come and celebrate the eschatological Sukkot would be denied rain. Judah and his group waited through the twenty-second day, that is, through the end of Sukkot. Again, no miracle. At this point, 23 Mar Heshvan (eighth month), they removed the

*Anchor Bible (Garden City: Doubleday & Company, 1976 and 1983).

latticework used in the sacred prostitution rites of the imposed cult.

The Maccabees again waited through the twenty-third day of the ninth month. When nothing happened then, there was no reason to wait anymore. There was a natural date to target for completion of the Restoration—25 Kislev; this was the third anniversary of the imposed cult's desecrating sacrifices. What more appropriate day to dedicate the purified Temple?

By his actions, Judah had accepted the idea that, after the first destruction, the age of prophecy and miracles was over. (The return of prophecy and of miracles would happen only just before God's ultimate victory.) In the interim, a human victory, helped by God, was an adequate basis for renewing the Temple. All these conclusions were arrived at without benefit of prophetic guidance or direct inspiration. Indeed, every day that the miraculous divine intervention did not occur was a crushing disappointment. Every step of Judah's policy constituted an act of covenantal responsibility-taking, probably done in the teeth of bitter criticism from other Pietists who wanted only a divine intervention. One can only wonder at the courage and un-quenchable hope that kept Judah and the Maccabees going.

What model should they now follow for the dedication? Moses had dedicated the tabernacle for eight days.* Solomon also had dedicated the Temple in connection with Sukkot; that dedication extended eight days (or so it is understood from 1 Kings 8:66). It was decided that this time, too, eight days of dedicatory ceremonies and sacrifices would be held. The Maccabees also may have hoped that this rededication would be graced with a miraculous fire from heaven when the sacrifice was offered, as both Moses' and Solomon's dedications had been favored.†

The first dedication act was done on the eve of 25 Kislev. The absence of fire from heaven was one of the great traumas of the Second Temple history (TB Yoma 21B). (Heavenly fire was one of the casualties of entering the post-prophetic period, but this is a hindsight observation.) Instead, the Maccabees focused their liturgy on the menorah lighting. They brought the Temple candelabrum and kindled the lights, even as they brought the incense and the showbread. This was a natural highlight for the dedication. First, the light of the menorah was a symbol of the Divine Presence. Second, finding any oil undefiled by the Greeks was in itself a miracle. This candle lighting was the main symbol referred to in the prayer of thanksgiving, Al Hanissim ("for the miracles").

*Compare Leviticus 8, especially 33–36, and 9:1.
†Compare Leviticus 9 with 2 Chronicles 7:1–3.

However, lighting a light was a ritual that could be carried on in homes so the idea caught on with the masses. In Josephus, the festival is known as the Holiday of Lights (Hag HaUrim).

Feeling their way as to an authentic model for the dedication holiday, uncertain as to the appropriate symbols for such a dedication, concerned by the question as to what (or whether a) human authority can decree an eight-day dedication holiday, Judah and his men proceeded in accordance with their own best judgment. They may have relied on a possible interpretation of the account in 1 Kings 8: 2 and 65. The verses imply that in dedicating the First Temple, Solomon extended the Sukkot holiday an additional seven days, running into the eighth day. That dedication festival went for eight days (Sukkot plus one), so let the same be done again. Following that model also suggested the use of Sukkot symbols during the dedication. Indeed, an account of Hanukkah (2 Maccabees 10:6-8) reports that they "held an eight-day celebration after the pattern of Sukkot" and sang hymns of praise and marched around carrying lulavim and etrogim, or at least some fruits and branches (associated with the harvest?), around the Temple. The strong associations with Sukkot led some Jews initially to call the dedication holiday the Days of Sukkot in the Month of Kislev.

Everyone was struggling to understand the significance and religious dimensions of the Hasmonean victory. The various interpretations turned on one primary question: Was there a significant role for humans as active agents in the covenantal redemption process? If there was, then the Maccabee revolt had been pioneering, visionary, and necessary. On the other hand, if the proper response to suffering was "let him put his mouth in the dust. . . . Let him give the cheek to the one that smites him" (Lamentations 3:30), then Chasidic martyrdom was the only valid response.

One can sense the deep debate within the community of the committed in the texts of 1 and 2 Maccabees. The first book repeatedly glorifies the Hasmoneans and their destiny; they were called by God to rule and to deliver the Jewish people. That book suggests the uselessness, if not destructiveness, of the Pietists' martyrdom. The second book, which ends with Judah's victory, stresses the martyrs' role in opening up God's renewed love and concern to save Israel. The same struggle is mirrored in the conflict over observing and defining the holiday that marks the Maccabee victory—Hanukkah.

One of the ironic results of the struggle was that neither 1 Maccabees, with its somewhat propagandistic treatment of the Hasmonean revolt, nor 2 Maccabees, with its strong quietist, supernaturalist bias, was able to attain recognition as revelation. Neither became definitive.

Ironically, Jews put these books aside, but the two continued to circulate among the early Christians. The martyrdom stories were powerfully relevant to Christians groaning under Roman persecutions. These Jewish books ended up incorporated in the Christian Bible but essentially lost to the Jewish community.

In a way, Hanukkah is the least developed of the holidays, but it was the most difficult accomplishment. The presence of the Chasidim as coalition partners, with their overwhelming expectation of divine signs and their devaluation of human initiative in sacred matters, put enormous pressure on the Maccabees, who themselves were uncertain of what was appropriate ritual and liturgy. At the religious officials' level, it was axiomatic that a holiday had to have a miracle associated with it, that is, an overt miracle reflecting the presence of the manifest God and/or biblical authorization. Passover was marked by the Exodus, Sukkot by the clouds of glory, Shavuot by the Sinai theophany. Hanukkah incorporated no miraculous victory comparable to the splitting of the Red Sea. Even a vial of oil that lasts longer is not much on the scale of wonders and plagues that mark the Exodus.

In the end, the Maccabees did not lose their nerve. They were neither crushed nor intimidated into yielding the holiday by the absence of a massive divine manifestation. The Al Hanissim prayer thanks God "for the miracles, for the redemption, for the mighty deeds and triumphs, and for the battles which You performed.... You delivered the strong into the hands of the weak, the many into the hands of the few."* Voting to trust their own experience as worthy and significant, the Maccabees decreed that Hanukkah, the dedication holiday, be celebrated annually for eight days, starting with 25 Kislev. The decision was all the more courageous in light of the fact that the Hasmonean wars were far from over.

A year after the rededication of the Temple, the Hellenizers, led by a Greek general named Lysias, defeated Judah's men and besieged them on Mount Zion. Judah's cause appeared lost. Suddenly word came to Lysias that, before his death, Antiochus had appointed a new regent to his Kingdom, a general named Philip, and that he was about to seize the kingdom of Antioch for himself. Lysias hastily negotiated an agreement with Judah that granted Jews the right to live undisturbed; it stipulated that the Jews would regain the Temple and be permitted "to live after the manner of their ancestors." The Torah became the obligatory law of the land. The triumph of traditional Judaism appeared to be complete.

*Philip Birnbaum, Daily Prayer Book (New York: Hebrew Publishing Company, 1977), pp. 91–4.

AFTER THE MACCABEAN VICTORY

Once again, however, the limitations of Judah's followers became apparent. The apolitical Chasidim, as long as they were not bothered religiously, were content to let the Syrian government rule. Thus, when the government appointed a new high priest, Jakum, who Hellenized his name to Alcimus, the Chasidim were the first to accept his authority. Judah, however, withdrew to the mountains.

When Antiochus V was overthrown in Antioch, Judah sought to exclude Alcimus from the priesthood on the grounds that he had tainted himself by joining in pagan worship during the time of persecutions. The majority stood by Alcimus, and bitter war followed. Once again brother fought brother. In a gallant last stand, Judah was killed. In two years Judah's forces had gone from triumph to tragedy. Large numbers of Maccabean followers were executed, and Judah's surviving brothers fled to the wilderness.

In 152 B.C.E., another revolt broke out against the Seleucid King, Demetrius I, the man who had conquered Judah. He desperately needed military allies, and the Jews were known to be excellent fighters. Demetrius realized that only Judah's brother Jonathan could organize an army for him, so he quickly negotiated a deal that allowed Jonathan to occupy Jerusalem in return for his military help. The pretender to the Syrian throne now made a counteroffer and appointed Jonathan high priest! This incredible reversal of fortunes restored the Maccabean dynasty. For twenty years the brothers Jonathan and Simon played politics back and forth between reigning kings and contenders for the Seleucid throne.

After the Maccabees came to power, the ultratraditionalist Chasidim dropped out of the coalition. They felt that any government would have to make political deals, compromise with Hellenism, and allow its cultural influence. The Chasidim were right, but the alternative was worse. The committed Jewish majority saw that without a state and some acculturation, the Jewish people and eventually Judaism, too, would be suppressed.

The Hasmoneans, who were priests, now insisted on taking over the kingship as well as the Temple priesthood. The Pharisee elements in the coalition opposed this unification of political and religious power in one group. With a deep historical wisdom they realized that some moral and religious compromises were inescapable in the process of government and struggle for survival. But when religion and state are totally identified, compromises turn into corruption because there is no independent channel of criticism and renewal. The Pharisees also wanted state help to strengthen religion. But they foresaw that moral and religious contamination was the inevitable result of the union of priesthood and kingship. Religious concerns would inevitably be mixed up with the pure political interests of the ruling group, to the detriment of both religion and government.

The Maccabees went ahead and united both powers. The Pharisees did not drop out, but they soon were involved in continual political and religious conflicts with the government. The worst years came with King Alexander Janneus (103–76 B.C.E.). The Pharisees challenged his legitimacy as well as his right to combine the roles of high priest and king. The result was a bitter fight. Alexander attacked and even massacred Pharisees. Eventually, the successor Rabbis were so alienated that they all but cut the Hasmoneans out of the Talmud.

The justification of the holiday that the Rabbis offer is the classic tale of the miracle of the Temple oil, which lasted eight days instead of one. Later, as Roman oppression grew, the longing for independence focused on dreams of a new Hasmonean to throw off the hated foreign yoke. Then the holiday of Hanukkah became the focus of hope that a new restoration was on its way. Hanukkah became a popular holiday among the masses. However, its ritual and liturgical structure is probably the least developed of all the holidays because unlike the others it was never pedagogically refined by the Rabbis.

Despite the later religious decline of the Hasmonean rulers, the work of the Maccabees was essentially a success. Had the revolt not taken place, the combination of political backing and Hellenistic cultural imperialism might have overwhelmed Judaism. Thanks to the uprising, the basic rule of Torah was assured. Hellenization continued. However, a strengthened Judaism now possessed the inner capacity to assimilate some new elements and yet remain a vital religion. The triumph of the Pharisees was made possible by the temporary respite won by the Maccabean revolt. In turn, their theological power led to the fullest development of the Oral Law. Thanks to the Pharisees, the values of individualism and the sacred dignity of the human were deepened within Judaism.

History is rarely neat. The liberators became tainted. The Chasidim's disillusionment with government only intensified the assimilation and alienation that separated the Hasmonean rulers from the people. The moderate Hellenizers saved the revolt, yet Hellenization led to moral and political deterioration of the rulers that followed. Following generations were embarrassed at the deviations and ambiguities of the actual historical record and of the movements through which God saved the people and the faith, so they idealized the holiday. Even the stress on the miracle of the oil was one-sided in that it scanted the miracle of the tenuous military triumph and of the coalition that saved Judaism.*

*Maimonides, *Yad Hachazakah* (Mishneh Torah) (New York: Grossman Publishers, 1960) Sefer Zemanim, Hilchot Hanukkah, Chapter 3, paragraphs 1, 2.

Still, the ultimate gift the Maccabees have given later generations may well be the holiday of Hanukkah itself. It took great spiritual courage to recognize that marginal, sharply contested victory as the decisive redemption that it actually was. It took even greater courage to apply the classical model of Exodus to the event. The Hasmoneans believed that just as God had led the people Israel out of Egypt, so God had redeemed the people in their generation. The Maccabees therefore decreed a holiday celebrating God's new redemption, even though it was achieved through human agency. On this humanly instituted holiday, one recites a blessing to the Lord "who... commanded us to light the Hanukkah candle" and "who performed miracles for our fathers in those days at this time."

HANUKKAH CELEBRATION

Because of its checkered history, the reenactment pattern of Hanukkah is poorly developed. It is the only significant historical holiday for which there is no book in the Bible.

Later, the Rabbis had to ponder the central significance of Hanukkah. They concluded that the primary lesson was the power of the spirit, the ability of God's people to live by the divine light. The Greeks sought to coerce Jews to forget the Torah and abandon the commandments. But God had fought the Jewish battles, handing over the many to the few, the evil to the righteous, the wicked to those who occupied themselves with God's Torah. For the main prophetic reading of Hanukkah, the Rabbis chose the prophecy of Zechariah, which ends, "not by might, nor by power but by My spirit, saith the Lord" (Zechariah 4:6).

Hanukkah's central symbol, the menorah, carries the same message. The light of the menorah is the symbol of the light of God. The fact that the light burned even when it appeared that no supply was left is a perfect symbol of the eternity of God's word. At the heart of the Hanukkah celebration, the Rabbis fixed not a retelling of the saga of revolt and renewal but the relatively passive experience of the overt divine miracle of oil. In a way, this rabbinic decision curtailed the central liturgical action of the Hanukkah holiday. One can reenact slavery and a voyage to freedom; the discovery of miraculous oil, while it can be proclaimed, does not lend itself to human reenactment.

Unlike the biblical holidays (except for Purim), the days of Hanukkah are not considered sacred time in which work is prohibited. The eight days are marked by prayers of thanksgiving (Hallel). A special song of praise, "Al Hanissim" ("for all the miracles and the redemption," etc.), is added to the Shmoneh Esrei (the central silent prayer) three times a day and to the Grace After Meals.

The major ritual ceremony of the holiday is the lighting of the Hanukkah menorah. The Maccabees' initial edict prescribed no specific liturgy for Hanukkah, merely calling for celebration "with mirth and gladness." The grass roots began the custom of kindling lights on Hanukkah. The purpose of the lighting is to "publicize the miracle" of Hanukkah. The Talmud emphasizes as the cruse of untainted oil that burned for eight days instead of one. On the other hand, Maimonides and other codifiers (as the ancient prayer of Al Hanissim itself) make clear that the original, primary miracle was the military and diplomatic triumph of the few over the many, so that memory did not totally disappear over the centuries.

The school of Hillel ruled that one candle should be lit on the first night and one additional light be added every subsequent night. The school of Shammai suggested starting with eight candles the first night and decreasing one every night. This is in imitation of the miracle in which the supply of oil was progressively used up. The tradition of adding lights each night won out, on the grounds that holiness and sanctity should always increase. On the first day, one candle is lit and placed on the right side (generally the preferred side in Jewish ritual). One additional candle is added every night (light two on the second night, three on the third night, and so forth). The candles are added from right to left on the menorah. The newest candle is lit first so that the actual lighting ceremony is conducted from left to right.

Since the original lighting in the Temple was done with oil, a reenactment model would seek to recreate that effect, so the tradition preferred to light menorahs using oil and wicks. Beautiful multicolored Israeli-made candles are available for those who use candle menorahs. Traditional rabbinic opinion has leaned toward using electric menorahs only as supplements to a regular menorah.

Since the object of the lighting is to publicize the miracle, the candles are placed near the windows; thus, they can be seen by passers-by who will be reminded of the holiday and the redemption. If one lives in a high-rise apartment (over the eyesight line of pedestrians), the custom is to consider the family the passer-by and to place the menorah where family members can best see it. One tradition is to place the menorah near the door, opposite the mezuzah, so that a person entering the apartment is surrounded by mitzvot.

It is customary to light the candles right after sundown, but if working parents come home at a later time, the lights may be lit at any hour of the evening—as soon as possible. On Friday evenings, the candle is lit before the Sabbath has begun, that is, before lighting the Sabbath candles. (Traditional law requires that the candles burn for a half hour after "sunset," and the Sabbath candles are lit almost an hour before that time, so it is best to check the local calendar or rabbi for proper lighting times. Many traditional Jews use larger candles on Friday to last for the extra period.)

Over the years the idea of a candelabra for the home developed naturally out of the lighting ceremony. The vessel was modeled on the Temple menorah. Out of respect for the Temple, the candelabra could not be a seven-branched one—thus the eight-branched Hanukkah menorah.

The first menorah was a central biblical sacred object, the seven-branched candelabra used in the tabernacle and, later, in the Jerusalem Holy Temple. Carved out of one ingot of gold, it had six branches, three on each side, curved upward from the menorah's central shaft. The seven lights were lit every night and burned from evening until morning. It was called a *ner tamid*, a perpetual lamp symbolizing the Divine Presence.

After the destruction of the Temple, the menorah became *the* most important Jewish pictorial motif; what had been a holy implement became the symbol of Judaism. Some of the menorah's appeal undoubtedly stemmed from longing for the lost glory of sovereignty and Temple. To preserve the awe of its sanctity, the Talmud ruled that it was forbidden to make an exact copy of the seven-branched menorah.

And so the Hanukkah lamp has been multiplied in form and size in every generation and every culture. The menorah may be of almost any shape as long as it keeps the lights distinct, although the straight line menorah is preferred. Since the lights are devoted to the commandment of publicizing the miracle, they are not used for any other purpose (such as illuminating the room for reading or to light other candles). It is customary to use a special candle (the *shamash*, servant) to light the others; this is more elegant than matches. Generally, the shamash is put on a different level or place to make clear it is not one of the candles burning in celebration of the day of Hanukkah.

One menorah may be lit for the entire family, but a beautiful tradition has developed for each member of the family, even children, to light his or her own menorah. On the first night, three blessings are said over the light: *l'hadlik ner shel Hanukkah* (to light the Hanukkah candle); *she'asah nissim* (who performed miracles for our fathers in those days and at this time); and *shehecheyanu*. For the rest of the holiday, only the first two blessings are said.

The lighting provides a wonderful opportunity for the family to sing the traditional Hanukkah songs together: "Hanerot Halalu" (these are sanctified candles), "Maoz Tzur" (fortress rock of my redemption), "Al Hanissim," and other songs of thanksgiving. It is a good time for telling the story of Hanukkah and discussing its fine points because the ceremony is always such a warm family occasion.

It is customary to light candles wherever one is, even away from home. If one is a guest at another's home and has no access to a menorah or lights, it is considered meritorious to contribute a token amount toward the cost of the candles so as to be truly a partner in the mitzvah. If one cannot light candles, one can make the blessing on seeing a lit menorah, omitting only the first blessing, *l'hadlik ner* (to light the Hanukkah candle).

WOMEN AND HANUKKAH

There are special traditions associating women with the Hanukkah miracle. The most famous is that of Judith and Holofernes. During the Maccabean wars, Judith's hometown of Betulia was beseiged by a Greek army led by Holofernes. The military situation appeared to be hopeless. Despite the fact that she was a modest, shy widow, Judith volunteered to go on a dangerous mission to save the town. Dressed stunningly, she went to seek out Holofernes. The general, besotted with lust, invited her to his tent and remained alone with her. She plied him with wine and good food. When he was overcome with sleep, she cut off his head and escaped. When the Greeks discovered Holofernes' death, they fled in panic and the town was saved.

Since a woman had been the primary agent of a Hanukkah redemption, the Talmud ruled that women are included in the obligation to light candles (although normally they are excused from time-fixed positive commandments). Since women are obligated to light, they can halachically fulfill the mitzvah and light candles on behalf of others as well.

The involvement of a woman in the redemption created two other traditions. The first is the custom that women not work during the period the candles are burning; the second is to serve that gastronomic delight of Hanukkah, latkes (ground potatoes fried in oil). Tradition has it that Judith prepared a dairy meal for Holofernes to make him very thirsty. It became customary to serve an elegant dairy meal in reenactment of that event. Latkes are, after all, an elegant preparation of the inelegant potato. (If the latka is heavy and hard rather than light and heavenly, one has not fulfilled the mitzvah!)

THE JOY OF HANUKKAH

Jewish tradition sought to embellish these days of joy. Since joy overflows, it is customary not to fast or mourn during this period. It became the practice to have festive meals for the eight days, and in addition to latkes, jelly doughnuts fried in oil became popular. (Both summon up the miracle by the use of oil.)

It is striking, however, that whereas the festive meal of Purim is central to the holiday, Hanukkah feasting is more marginal. "Hallel," the spiritual songs of praise, stand out in this holiday. Commentators have suggested that this difference reflects a deliberate religious strategy. On Purim, the Jewish people's physical existence was threatened; therefore, the body should get special treatment to underscore its importance. On Hanukkah, the religious and spiritual existence of the Jews was challenged. If the Jews had yielded their religious principles and assimilated, the Greeks would not have attacked them. Therefore, the soul and the spiritual should be the focus of this holiday.

Hallel prayers are said on Hanukkah although they are not said on Purim. The difference is that Purim was a temporary reprieve. After the Purim victory, the Jews remained dependent on the goodwill of the government and society in which Jews were, at best, a tolerated minority. Hanukkah is marked by Hallel because it celebrates a fundamental solution: This victory gave Jews some independence and a measure of control over their fate.

Other popular sources of joy, especially for the recipients, are Hanukkah gifts and Hanukkah *gelt* (money). Those who would like to part quickly with their gelt—Hanukkah and otherwise—play the game of dreydel (spinning top) during Hanukkah. On the dreydel are written the Hebrew letters: nuhn, gimmel, hey, and shin, symbolizing "*nes gadol hayah sham*—a great miracle occurred there." Each player puts money into "the pot," then the dreydel is spun. If it falls on a nuhn, it means nothing happens. Gimmel means "ganz" (winner takes all). Hey means "halb" (winner takes half). Shin means "shtell" or put in money.

The Rabbis, not surprisingly, opposed these gambling games, but the folk adored them. Because the Rabbis considered gamblers' earnings as akin to taking someone's property without real consent, it became customary to give dreydel money to charity.

In olden days the gelt tradition was pennies. In America, the gift-giving has escalated as Jewish parents seek to assure their children that they are not missing anything by being Jewish. This is turning Hanukkah into Christmas times eight. On the one hand, Judaism should be a source of gratification and joy, and on the other hand, it is hopeless and wasteful to think one can "offset" Christmas by lavishing gifts.

Some scholars have sought to connect the lights of Hanukkah and the Christmas celebration to a winter solstice festival celebrating the passing of the shortest day of the year. If the connection were correct, Hanukkah would be another example of how Jewish tradition takes a natural phenomenon (such as spring or harvest) and transmutes it into a festival of history (such as Passover). This symbolizes the movement from necessity and physical dependence on the world toward human freedom and striving to redeem the world. However, there is little convincing in the solstice theory.

In the case of Hanukkah, the theory ignores the fact that an actual historical event—purification and rededication of the Temple—occurred and its date is attested to by contemporary accounts. Furthermore, the dedication anniversary was marked every year, and the date is far from a literary (or anthropological) convention. Moreover, 25 Kislev in the year 164 coincides with December 6, not even close to the solstice day. One can never stop people from exegesis of holidays—or even eisegesis. That this theory is dignified with the label "critical" or scientific while more traditional stories are dismissed or treated with skepticism is distressing. It only proves that midrash varies from culture to culture. In this culture, science is a more accepted form of literary fantasy than is tradition.

HANUKKAH NOW

Not as tightly knit in paradigm, theme, and practice as the other holidays, Hanukkah lends itself to being a type of holy day Rorschach test. Every community and generation has interpreted Hanukkah in its own image, speaking to its own needs.

When the Rabbis asked, "What is Hanukkah?" their answer focused on the purification of the Temple and the miracle of the oil that burned for eight days. As a new spiritual leadership dealing with the religious challenge of Jewry's survival after the loss of sovereignty and power, the Rabbis stressed the divine miracle to the exclusion of military and diplomatic acts and the sovereignty exercised by the Maccabees. Similarly, medieval Jews focused on the divine miraculous activity in Hanukkah, projecting their own sense of helplessness and their longing for the messianic redeemer to do it all for them.

By contrast, modern Zionists saw in Hanukkah a reflection of *their* agenda; they celebrated the Maccabee military prowess and political achievement. An early secular Zionist song proclaimed that "a miracle did *not* happen to us, we found no cruse of oil." To these Zionists, the Maccabee state building was the eternal message of the holiday.

For modern liberal Jews, Hanukkah became the holiday of religious freedom. The Maccabee fight was presented as the uprising of a religious community against suppression; the Festival of Lights was a victory for, and a living model of, the religious tolerance that Jews sought in the modern world. To uphold this view, liberals had to filter out the fact that while the Hasmoneans fought for the right to practice their own religion, they were hardly pluralist. In fact, the Maccabees fought Hellenizing Jews to the death and suppressed them as soon as they achieved power.

Similarly, American Jews have turned Hanukkah into the great gift holiday. Other than children's games and very modest Hanukkah gelt, there was not much in the tradition of the holiday that supported the idea of an eight-day orgy of giving presents. But Christmas is so pervasive in America and the children's sense of being shut out was so fierce that Hanukkah was rededicated as the season for giving.

The question is: What model of Hanukkah can speak to this generation? Several important issues in Hanukkah's origins remain central in contemporary culture. One theme is the clash of the universal with the particular. Hellenism saw itself as the universal human culture, open to all. But Mattathias, Judah Maccabee, and the brave people who saved Judaism were not fighting for a pluralist Judea. They were fighting against the state's enforcement of Hellenist worship because they believed it was a betrayal of Israel's covenant with God. When, after decades of fighting, they liberated Jerusalem and purified the Temple, they established a state in which Jews could worship God in the right way—not in just any way. Hanukkah is not a model for total separation of church and state. On the other hand, the Maccabee victory saved particularist Judaism. It preserved the stubborn Jewish insistence on "doing their own thing" religiously; never mind the claims of universalism that only if all are citizens of one world and one faith will there truly be one humanity. By not disappearing, Jews have continued to force the world—down to this day—to accept the limits of centralization. Jewish existence has been a continued stumbling block to whatever political philosophy, religion, or economic system has claimed the right to abolish all distinctions for "the higher good of humanity." Since the centralizing forces often turned oppressive or obliterated local cultures and dignity, this Jewish resistance to homogenization has been a blessing to humanity and a continuing source of religious pluralism for everybody, not just the Jews.

In this time, too, many universal cultures—Marxism and Communism, triumphalist Christianity, certain forms of liberalism and radicalism, fascism, even monolithic Americanism—have demanded that Jews dissolve and become part of humankind. All these philosophies have claimed that Jews can depend on their principles and structures to provide for Jewish rights. The Maccabee revolution made clear that a universalism that denies the rights of the particular to exist is inherently totalitarian and will end up oppressing people in the name of one humanity. Universalism must surrender its overweening demands and accept the universalism of pluralism. Only when the world admits that oneness comes out of particular existences, linked through over-arching unities, will it escape the inner dynamics of conformity that lead to repression and cruelty.

Those stubborn Chasidim raised a subtle issue of political existence and religious truth that is only coming into its own in the twentieth century. Ultimately, the touchstone of human survival will be the ability of people with passionately held beliefs and absolute commitments to allow for pluralism. National peace will turn on the capacity of groups organized around values to allow the inherent dignity of the other into their own structures. How to achieve this respect without surrendering to indifference or group selfishness is the great challenge. On Hanukkah, Jews celebrate that challenge and affirm the Jewish determination never again to let universal rhetoric ("to make the world safe for...") cripple the Jews' right to defend themselves. On Hanukkah, Jews urge humankind to take responsibility for the varieties and multiforms of human life. Hanukkah is also a profoundly Zionist holiday, for it asserts the right of politically self-determined existence for each group.

Hanukkah is a paradigm of the relationship between acculturation and assimilation. The final victory of Hanukkah was set in motion by the resistance of the most traditional elements—many of them "square" country folk—to the growing encroachment of Hellenistic values. In many ways, the rebels were in greater conflict with their fellow Hellenizing Jews than with the Hellenes. The arrogant universalism in Hellenism demanded that Jews give up their distinctive religious ways for the greater good. Many Jews agreed, but the Pietists did not.

Hanukkah dramatizes the positive strength of Pietism, of Chasidism's unquestioning loyalty to Judaism. It challenges modern Jews to review their own easy acceptance of cosmopolitanism and sophisticated culture as superior to the sentiment and tribal feeling of being Jews. It asks whether, consciously or unconsciously, modern Jews are part of the Hellenizing, assimilating majority. Like the crisis of the Holocaust and threats to Israel, it forces people to face up to the issue: Are they ultimately Jews? In an ultimate crisis of loyalties, would one choose Jewish survival?

People who would never consider a Hebrew day school for their child because what is American comes first are making Judaism a secondary loyalty. People who would be more upset if their child married an Orthodox Jew than if their child married a Gentile have really made a determination of primary loyalty. The lesson of Hanukkah is that a strong priority to being Jewish is the key to right choices in Jewish history. Sometimes one should not reason. There has to be a primordial will to Jewishness first or to Israel's survival first. The reasoning and the willingness to negotiate some issues come second.

At the same time, it is not enough to be stubborn or to ignore the surrounding culture. This tactic works only when Jews are isolated. It was not working in the big cities of Judea in the second century B.C.E., and it will not likely work well in the highly magnetic culture/society of today.

The Chasidim of those days could not have won the battle alone. In the conflict, many Hellenizing Jews decided to stand by their fellow Jews rather than by the Greeks. A coalition won the victory of Hanukkah—the traditionalists united with acculturating Jews who decided to come down on the Jewish side. Even as they fought the cultural battle, the Maccabees and, later, the Pharisees did not simply reject Hellenism. They were profoundly touched by its individualism, its methods of analysis, literary rhetoric, and its theological concepts. They absorbed a great deal, but they gave a distinctively Jewish cast to the outside ideas and rejected many others.

The paradigm of the Jewish way implies passing through a wide variety of historical situations and cultures on the road to redemption. No one section is indispensable; the Jewish community can always sit out one particular stretch of the road. But in general, the Jewish way implies the need and willingness to go into and through many cultures—participating, learning, filtering, incorporating, handling. Exposure and integration are the keys to coping, although overexposure can lead to a blank or totally dark record.

The Rabbis deepened Judaism to cope with a dynamic civilization, one with more highly developed cultural models. In that response, Judaism rose to new heights of competence and developed the ability to swim in the sea of Hellenism. The present host culture of Jewry is even more developed, magnetic, and challenging. Jews and Judaism will have to master the field. Properly done, acculturation (modernizing) is an alternative to assimilation. Since no one group can offer all the answers for all the life situations or cope with all the options in society, it becomes very important to form coalitions to cover the field, to correct one another, to give Jewry the strength of variety and numbers.

The further lesson of Hanukkah (as Purim) is not to write off assimilating Jews. In a showdown (as in 1967 and 1973), many more Jews will be with the cause of Jewish survival than appears on the surface. A coalition of traditional, acculturating, and assimilating Jews pulled off the Maccabee miracle. What is needed is a coalition and symbiosis of traditional Jews, modernizing Jews, and those assimilating Jews who can still be reached. The real task is to begin the "guerrilla warfare" that weans people from their excessive absorption in the status quo and liberates them for authentic Jewish existence.

Hanukkah points to the fragility of historical redemption and the ambiguity of its messengers and leaders. Salvation does not come from one group or through pure angelic leaders. Redemption comes out of a mixture of self-interest, ideas, class and social conflicts; out of governmental errors and human miscalculation. One should not be put off by the all-too-human frailties and shortcomings of Jewish leaders and organizations. The faults should be challenged and worked on, but the ultimate validity of the cause is not destroyed by such flaws. There are those who insist on perfect religious frameworks or absolute victories; they grow disillusioned with the ambiguous victories of Israel or the Jewish community. There are those who grow weary that the victories of 1967 and 1973 are not final. Hanukkah shows that spirit can persist.

By the same token, there are religious Jews who insist that this generation does not have the spiritual authority to create Yom Ha'Atzmaut as a religious holiday or to develop Jewish law to respond fully to the valid needs of the Jewish state. The lesson of the Maccabees' rulings is that authority in Jewish law flows from the community of Israel (standing before its God and its commandments) and not necessarily from official rulings. Those who persevere in the historical task will live to celebrate the flowering of the victory. Those who insist on perfection or nothing will surrender the world to evil, making possible the triumph of evil. That is the punishment for simplemindedness.

This confirms Rabbi Israel Salanter's argument that to be a good Jew one must have every human quality and its opposite. There was a point in the Hasmonean revolt where martyrdom was the only option that could deter the enemy and rally Jewish faithfulness. There was another point where the insistence on martyrdom meant handing over control of the everyday world to the wicked. Some used resurrection and immortality—two of the greatest teachings of Judaism and of all religion—as an anodyne. These teachings softened the pain of martyrdom but also removed the Chasidim from the world of historical responsibility where a new, modest, but vital redemption was being won in the hills of Judea. For others, resurrection and immortality were the burning moral necessities that spurred them on to fearless acts of courage and liberation.

The Jewish way calls on every human quality and every skill known to humanity. The past culture demanded fortitude and long-suffering, tolerating powerlessness and persecution without internalizing them. The present culture demands active responsibility, handling affluence, acceptance and power without absolutizing them. The battle of Hanukkah is being fought again, not in military engagements but through creating family ties, competing educationally, communicating values and messages, holding and deepening loyalties. It can only be won by partial solutions, visionary persistence, and realistic dreams.

Pessimists and assimilationists have more than once informed Jews that there is no more oil left to burn. As long as Hanukkah is studied and remembered, Jews will not surrender to the night. The proper response, as Hanukkah teaches, is not to curse the darkness but to light a candle.

CHAPTER NINE

Destruction and Response:
Tisha B'Av

DESTRUCTION

On THE NINTH AND TENTH DAYS of the month of Av in the year 70, the Roman legions in Jerusalem smashed through the fortress tower of Antonia into the Holy Temple and set it afire. In the blackened remains of the sanctuary lay more than the ruins of the great Jewish revolt for political independence. To many Jews, it appeared that Judaism itself was shattered beyond repair.

Out of approximately four to five million Jews in the world, over a million died in that abortive war for independence. Many died of starvation, others by fire and crucifixion. So many Jews were sold into slavery and given over to the gladiatorial arenas and circuses that the price of slaves dropped precipitously, fulfilling the ancient curse: "There you will be offered for sale as slaves, and there will be no one willing to buy" (Deuteronomy 26:68).

The destruction was preceded by events so devastating that they read like scenes out of the Holocaust. Hear the words of the ancient Jewish historian, Josephus:

Famine: "Famine overcomes all other passions and is destructive of modesty. . . . Wives pulled the morsels that their husbands were eating out of their very mouths and children did the same to their fathers, and so did mothers to their infants, and when those that were most dear to them were perishing in their hands, they were not ashamed to take from them the very last drops of food that might have preserved their lives. . . ."

Carnage: on the ninth day of Av: "One would have thought that the hill itself, on which the Temple stood, was seething hot from its base, it was so full of fire on every side; and yet the blood was larger in quantity than the fire, and those that were slain were more in number than those that slew them. For the ground was nowhere visible for the dead bodies that lay on it."

Civil war between Jews: "The shouts of those [Jews] who were fighting [one another] were incessant both by day and night, but the continual lamentations of those who mourned were even more dreadful. Nor was any regard paid by relatives for those who were still alive. Nor was any care taken for the burial of those who were dead. The reason was that everyone despaired about himself."

The exhaustion from all-out sacrifice of lives and fighting in vain was in itself debilitating, but the religious crisis was even worse. God's own sanctuary, restored after the return to Zion in the sixth century B.C.E., the symbol of the unbroken covenant of Israel and God, was destroyed. This cast doubt on the very relationship of the people and their Lord. Had God rejected the covenant with Israel?

The Temple was central to Jewish religious life in a way that is hard to recapture today. Many Jews believed that sin itself could be overcome only by bringing a sin offering in the Temple. Without such forgiveness, the sinner was condemned to alienation from God, which is equivalent to estrangement from valid existence. But the channel of sacrifice was now cut off.

For many Jews, the whole experience of Judaism was sacramental. The Priests served; the ignorant masses watched; their religious lives were illuminated only by those extraordinary moments when multitudes gathered in Jerusalem. There, in the awe of a Paschal sacrifice or at the Yom Kippur atonement ritual, they felt an emanation of divine force that showered grace and blessing on the people and made the Lord's power a stunning presence. For these people, after the destruction there was only emptiness.

Some people were carried away from Jewry by the shock wave of the Destruction (including Jews driven into exile or sold into slavery) and adopted the culture and religion of the masters or of other slaves.

Some Jews concluded that Judaism was finished. Among them were the marginal Jews, people already moving into the cultural orbit of

Hellenism, because they found Judaism increasingly narrow and irrelevant; the event of Destruction thrust them further in that direction. Precisely because of the agony, the cries of the Jewish faith community became more anguished, perhaps more parochial and inwardly oriented. So these cries became less and less appealing to assimilating "universal" Jews—until these people were absorbed into the world around them; they dropped out as Jews and disappeared.

Others gave up out of despair and loss of faith. In the absence of effort and will, they sank out of sight, into the sea of Hellenism. It does not necessarily take a conscious act of abandonment of Judaism to assimilate. The Jewish way has always meant swimming against the tide of majority culture and the realities of history. So whenever there is an erosion of knowledge and loyalty, when disaster or moral exhaustion weaken the will, people need only stop trying in order to be swept into oblivion as Jews. There should be no illusions on this score. Over the years this group was probably the largest in number in Jewish life.

At least one other small group of Jews concluded that Judaism was finished following the Destruction. Christian Jews until then had operated within the covenant of Judaism, praying in synagogues and regarding Jesus as the fulfillment of the messianic promises within Judaism. The polarizing effect of the Roman wars, the spread of Christianity primarily among Gentiles but not Jews, and the Destruction of the Temple convinced them that they had misread the signs. The razing of the sanctuary convinced them that the old channels of atonement and connection to God, which they initially thought were being extended through Jesus, were in fact blotted out by the Destruction. They concluded that Jesus was not a continuation of the Jewish way but a new channel of salvation. The Gospels were a *new* testament, not a section of the old; Jesus' sacrifice must have been the inauguration of a *new covenant*, one that would live on and provide salvation even as Judaism disappeared.

Paradoxically, these Christian Jews were using traditional Jewish categories in this response. They accepted the events of Jewish history as normative—as the Bible and the tradition taught that they were. Initially, they continued to observe the Jewish holidays, perhaps adding some new interpretive level in light of Jesus' life. As the force of the Destruction sank in, it seemed to them to be a message from God, a message of rejection of Jewry. However, they could not believe that God had abandoned humanity totally. Once they perceived the Destruction as a sign of the end of the Jewish covenant, then Jewish revolts to reestablish the Temple could only alienate them further. The logic of the new situation, as they saw it through the eyes of their faith, turned them on to a new road; they went out to the world as a separate religion. Rejecting some Jewish beliefs, spiritualizing the old promises by transferring their focus from the land and people of Israel to personal salvation, yet preaching the basic religious love and consolation of Judaism to the world, they created Christianity.

The majority of the Jews refused to quit. One element in this community reacted with overwhelming despair. The Talmud speaks of "mourners of Zion," who would neither eat meat nor drink wine. They rejected any possibility of normal life and chose not to marry or have children. Simple human activities—having a child, getting married, doing acts of kindness in a community—are sustained only by enormous levels of faith and life affirmation, and trust in ultimate meaning. Considering the tragedy and the threat that still hung over the Jewish community, these people felt they simply could not go on with life as usual. Yet by refusing to live normally, they harnessed despair into a force for action: to make an all-out effort to restore the Temple. Only rebuilding the sanctuary could reduce the terrible angst and restore life to normal.

The two major remaining sects, the Pharisees and the Sadducees, shared a common conviction that the Temple must be rebuilt, although the Sadducees, who included the court nobility and priests, were particularly unable to envision Judaism without a Temple. This consensus drove people to drastic action. In the years 115 to 117 C.E., there were widespread rebellions by Diaspora Jewry, which were bloodily suppressed. In 132 C.E., the remaining population of Judea revolted, led by Simon Bar Kochba. But again, the overwhelming might of Rome was brought to bear. Bar Kochba and his troops were destroyed, and the remaining population of Judea was deported. With this defeat, hopes for an immediate restoration of the Temple were set back indefinitely.

THE PARADIGM OF RESPONSE

For the Jews who continued to walk the Jewish way, the main direction was supplied by Rabbi Yohanan ben Zakkai and the circle around him. In an age of death and destruction, Rabbi Yohanan taught that a fundamental religious response was to increase loving-kindness and multiply life itself. Smuggling himself out of the capital, Yohanan obtained Roman permission to create a new seat of life and learning in the settlement of Yavneh (Jamnia).

Ben Zakkai had faith that neither the Jews nor Judaism was finished. The hope was unchanged. The end goal was the same: the dream of a messianic fulfillment for the entire world. The destruction of the Temple could only mean a call to serve in a new way. Over the next stretch of the road, new resources would be needed.

The schools of Rabbi Yohanan and other Rabbis developed primarily out of the Pharisaic fellowship's commitment to live "the holy life among profane and ordinary men." This world outlook had been evolving even before the Destruction. In their view, every Jew should eat every meal in the same state of ritual purity as the priest in the Temple. Every Jew could take up the charge of holiness; every table and home would be the table of the Lord. Ultimately, one would feel that every act of life was being carried out in the presence of God. But to be able to live up to this standard, every Jew would have to learn and know Torah.

The Rabbis' fundamental theological breakthrough was a "secularization" insight. God was becoming less visible, more hidden. The Destruction was a signal that *manifest* divine activity was being curtailed. God would not stop the Romans or save the Temple (even though God had destroyed the Egyptians at the Red Sea). Still the covenant was not being disowned; it was being renewed.

The rabbinic interpretation was that the Jewish people, the passive partners in the biblical covenant, were being urged by their divine counterpart to take a higher level of responsibility for the outcome of the covenantal way. Divine Presence was becoming more hidden so that the Jewish people could become true partners with God. Although the covenant concept is two-sided, the word "partner" does not appear in the Bible; it is, however, one of the great *leitmotif* words in rabbinic literature. Thus, the people of Israel and the individual Jew became partners of God through religious activity. The Jewish people had to be educated to see the holiness hidden everywhere. Blessings to express gratitude and the awareness of God were articulated for every moment of life, from awakening to going to sleep, from feeling or flexing muscles to urination. Blessings helped the individual to discover the Divine Presence that is hidden in the everyday "secular" reality.

A world in which God is more hidden is a more secular one. Paradoxically, this secularization made possible the emergence of the synagogue as the central place of Jewish worship. In the Temple, God was manifest. Visible holiness was concentrated in one place. A more hidden God could be encountered everywhere, but one had to seek and find. The manifest presence of God in the Temple gave a sacramental quality to the cultic life of the sanctuary. Through the high priest's ministrations and the scapegoat ceremony, the national sins were forgiven and a year of rain and prosperity assured. In the synagogue, the community's prayers are more powerful and elaborate than the individual's, but the primary effect of the prayers grows out of the individual's own merits and efforts. The human-Divine dialogue goes on through human address to God. Prayer, viewed today as a visibly sacred activity, was, by contrast with Temple worship, a more "secular" act. Though prayer existed long before the Destruction, it became the central religious act because of the silence of God.

The Rabbis were a more secular leadership than priests or prophets. Priests were born to holiness and were bound to ritually circumscribed lives. The Rabbis won their status through learning; unlike the priests, they were not bound to sacramental requirements different from the average Jew. Prophets spoke the unmediated word of God: "Thus saith the Lord. . . ." In contrast, the Rabbi exercised the best human judgment, guided by knowledge of the past record of God's instruction—biblical models and legal precedents—to interpret what does God want from the people now. The Rabbis came to see that in calling humans to use their judgment, God was allowing them significant autonomy. When two Rabbis disagreed, "both views were the words of the Living God." (For the purpose of decision making, one followed the rabbinic majority vote in such contested cases.) The sum of the Rabbis' educational and halachic efforts was that participation in religious life was democratized.

Rabbi Yohanan's response to the destruction of the Temple was: Extend learning to as wide a group as possible. "If you have learned much Torah, do not congratulate yourself, for this very purpose you were created."* If the direct connection to the Temple was lost, then Torah study would verbally recreate the destroyed cult while enabling every Jew—not just priests—to participate. Learning would lead to internalization of the teachings and values of God's way. Study was glorified as the ultimate mitzvah: "Talmud Torah [study of Torah] equals them all" that is, all the commandments.† The Beit Knesset (House of Assembly/Synagogue) was broadened into a Beit Midrash (House of Study). Opportunities for study were built into the services and home liturgies. All aspects of life could be suffused with Jewish values and the meanings taught through actions and words. Through learning, all Jews could participate in unfolding the covenantal way. The result was an extraordinary increase and application of covenantal principles to every aspect of life.

The cumulative result of the Rabbis' work was the transformation of biblical Judaism into rabbinic Judaism. Of course, there was fundamental continuity between the two stages. The Rabbis attached every detail of their work to Scriptures and paid repeated homage to the divinity and absolute nature of the Bible. Yet, when all was said and done, the Rabbis' work represented a profound discovery: The covenant was being renewed. The original covenant remained, but

---

*Babylonian Talmud, Avot, chapter 2, Mishnah 8.
†Babylonian Talmud, Peah, chapter 1, Mishnah 1.

humans became more active and responsible. The Destruction was a call from God for a fundamental shift in the paradigm of the human role in the covenant. The Rabbis' faithfulness showed itself in following God, not just form; theirs was the continuity of metamorphosis.

Whence came the Rabbis' authority to carry out so fundamental a transformation of the covenantal process? Their underlying model was the Jewish way through history. Just as redemptive events set the Jewish people in motion and just as later redemptive events shed light on the direction, so could an event of Destruction illuminate comprehension of the Exodus way by testing, challenging and, ultimately, redirecting understanding.

To go on with the same religious way of life would have been a contradiction of the model of revelation in history. Covenantal thinking demands that catastrophe be taken seriously in order for Judaism to make credible—not merely pious—statements. This historical model of revelation also explained the Rabbis' powerful sense of their own continuity with the Bible.

Some contemporary scholarship tends to treat the Rabbis as cynics or liars, or at best simpletons, when they spoke of continuity or the absolute authority of the Torah since, clearly, the Rabbis themselves were changing the style, tone, and development of biblical religion. These dismissive interpretations sell the Rabbis short.

A classic rabbinic story tells that Moses came back to visit the yeshiva of Rabbi Akiva. There he heard Akiva expounding the Torah, Moses' own teaching. Yet Moses didn't understand a word. Feeling quite badly, Moses became faint from his own embarrassment and shame at not understanding. Then a student raised his hand and asked Rabbi Akiva how he knew the particular law he was expounding. Rabbi Akiva answered, "It is *halacha l'moshe misinai*. We know it by tradition from Moses at Sinai." At this, the rabbinic story assures us, Moses was greatly relieved and cheered.*

It is not that the Rabbis failed to see that their own work had incorporated into the Torah rulings and practices which Moses himself did not "understand"; that is precisely the point of the story. But we are doing what Moses has taught us, say the Rabbis—applying the Exodus model in our time as he applied it in his. Following God into the new theological/historical situation is true covenant loyalty and is continuous with Moses' teaching.

As it turned out, the Temple was not rebuilt nor was Jerusalem freed. The interpretation offered by Yohanan ben Zakkai triumphed

---

*Babylonian Talmud, Menachot 29B.

completely and became the main continuous form of Judaism. Indeed, it became a covenant renewal that flourished, brought forth many fruits, and bore up well under the repeated whirlwinds of exilic history.

RESPONSE

The classic Jewish response to catastrophe is to renew life. Every major Jewish catastrophe has led to the falling away of some Jews as they lost faith, but every major tragedy has also led to revival, as other Jews strove harder to match tragedy with hope.

After the Destruction, Yohanan ben Zakkai tried to dampen apocalyptic expectations by shifting the Judean community's efforts to a realistic rebuilding of life. Said Rabbi Yohanan, "If you are planting a tree and they tell you that the Redeemer is coming, first plant the tree, then go to greet the Messiah."

Rabbi Yohanan and his colleagues provided a theological key to interpret the Destruction as a further stage on the Jewish covenantal way. The average Jew was still devastated by the catastrophe. The immediate dangers lay in a sorrow so overwhelming that it might destroy life's livability, in a continuing religious dependency on the Temple, in a community unable to function without it, and in the blatant contradiction between the hope of redemption and the present triumph of the evil Romans.

Here, the Rabbis made another of their brilliant moves. The best way to diffuse grief is to express it, so special prayers of mourning were inserted in various liturgies. Special petitions for the restoration of the Temple were added in the daily services. The actual order of the Temple sacrifices was recounted daily. But while grief and mourning prayers were being added, the message was: thus far and no further. To a group of grieving Jews who proposed to stop normal life, Rabbi Joshua said, "Not to mourn at all is impossible because the evil decree [the destruction blow] had fallen. But to mourn too much is also impossible because the majority of the community cannot live this way."*

The Rabbis created a string of mourning rituals. They ordained that a glass be broken at every wedding in empathetic grief to the catastrophe, but weddings were not to be stopped. Life, family, children must go on. They instructed that a portion of every newly built home be left unfinished. Let every feast or party be less than complete. Let every full-course banquet omit a food item or two. In each case, the

*Babylonian Talmud, Baba Rathra 60B.

mourning ritual stylized—and thereby limited—grief, while moving life forward toward normalcy again.

Rabbi Yohanan ben Zakkai placed the restoration of the Temple at the heart of the prayers in the synagogue, but in so doing enabled the Jews to go on living without the Temple. Similarly, by placing mourning rituals at the heart of Jewish life, the Rabbis enabled the Jews to go on living with exile.

The very depth of the defeat made it necessary to make a counter statement of hope. The prophet Zechariah had promised that, in the future, the four days of fasting and weeping, established after the first Destruction, would be turned into happy holidays. Similarly, the Rabbis asserted that the day of the destruction of the Temple was the birthday of the Messiah. Above all, the inherited four fast days became the vehicles of a dialectical move—release of grief and reaffirmation of hope as one. In the Rabbis' view, incorporating the fast days into the Jewish calendar would strengthen the credibility of Jewish promises of restoration. After all, Jewish tradition had always asserted that the hope of faith and the joy of living with God does not blot out the reality of tragedy in life. Until a final redemption occurs, the awareness of defeat and destruction must be incorporated into faith, thereby becoming a learning experience. The days of mourning would demonstrate that Jewish affirmations are not Pollyanna statements untempered by hard reality but rather are made in the face of tragedy.

The days of sorrow served another function by reminding Jews of their unfinished business: No matter how well off they were individually, the world was still unredeemed. Continued grieving affirms that no consolation would be accepted; only a reversal of fate could relieve the mourning. Thanks to Jewish memory and Jewish eternity, these defeats would not be final after all.

The ninth of Av was set as the commemoration day for three destructions. The Second Temple primarily burned down on the tenth day of Av, although the fire started on the ninth. Still, the Rabbis chose to commemorate the Temple tragedy on the ninth because that day marked Bethar's fall in 135 C.E. as well. In setting 9 Av as the major fast day, the Rabbis fixed the religious calendar from the past to reflect the living experience of their own generation. How to do this is the primary issue in the present conflict over whether to commemorate the Holocaust through its own day (Yom Hashoah) or through Tisha B'Av. (See below.)

Jewish tradition and legend went on to add more tragedies to each of these four fast days. On Shivah Asar B'Tammuz (the seventeenth day of Tammuz), Moses broke the first set of tablets (see Exodus 34); the daily sacrifices in the first Temple ended due to the siege, and

Apostomus, a first-century Roman governor, burned the Torah after placing an idolatrous statue in the Temple.

On Tisha B'Av, the Jews of the Exodus generation were condemned to die in the desert. On the same date in 136 C.E., Tineius Rufus, the Roman procurator, plowed up the Temple area to signify its final destruction.

As the memories of temporal sovereignty faded, the Temples and their spiritual realities became the focal point of yearning in Jewish culture and religion. The brokenness of the world was reflected in the abandoned, wasted state of Jerusalem and the Temple Mount. Later generations saw in the Destruction and Exile the symbol of ongoing Jewish suffering and oppression. Later tragedies were incorporated into this day. Repeated destructions were goads to greater commemoration and increased observance.

In 1492, Spanish Jewry was expelled from Spain—on the ninth day of Av. In the aftermath of this great disaster, a new form of mysticism, Lurianic Kabbalah, developed and spread throughout Jewry. Tisha B'Av became an even more central day in the calendar, but the sorrow was channeled into raising the standard of religious and communal behavior. The Jewish people were called to reenact the divine exile and to perfect the world by faithfulness. Every halachic gesture, every child born, was an act of cosmic tikkun (perfection), a step toward tikkun olam (total repair of the world).

Some Kabbalists went up to Israel and generated a great flowering of mysticism in the city of Safed. Around the world, a new wave of religious observance spread throughout the Jewish community. The practice of arising at midnight for special mourning rites for the Temple was established. Prayers were increased and infused with mystical intentions. Mysticism—heretofore an elitist, esoteric doctrine—became the possession of the masses and was applied to everyday behavior. Later, this popular mysticism paved the way for an explosive messianic movement led by Shabbetai Zevi in the 1660s and, still later, for the extraordinary spread of Chasidism. The force behind Jewish survival has hardly been the strength of victory; the secret of survival has been in the incredible capacity of Jews to use the memory of tragedy to spur themselves to come back again and again after defeat.

In time, the days of mourning were expanded into an entire three-week period of sorrow, stretching from the seventeenth of Tammuz to the ninth of Av. The Omer period also became a period of semi-mourning. Fasting and mourning were a way of turning people to repentance. After the Holocaust, many find it impossible to accept the idea that punishment for sins is the explanation for all Jewish suffering; however, these days retain their power as calls to action and repentance.

History has treated the Jews cruelly on Tisha B'Av, each generation adding its dirges to the chronicles of suffering. On Tisha B'Av, communities were destroyed during the Crusades; the Talmud was burned in Paris in 1242; the deportation from the Warsaw ghetto to Treblinka in 1942 started on Tisha B'Av. Next to Yom Kippur, it is the most total fast day in the traditional Jewish calendar.

In accordance with rabbinic religious conceptions, the dominant model of the fast days is to reenact past tragedies. Reliving and remembering these sorrows is the key to overcoming history's setbacks. The memory of the martyrs is kept alive; their sacrifices gain meaning. By experiencing the tragedy afresh each year, Jews can never become reconciled neither to the destruction of the Temple nor to the Exile. Through reenactment, every year it is as if the tragedy has "just occurred" and the shock is still fresh. So Jews taste the dregs of defeat and suffering even when they experience success and peace in their daily lives. Thus, they become more sensitive to those who still suffer and those who need help. This is the messianic spirit, the faith that builds on the sands of despair, the faith that knows death and fights it. This people, overthrown many times, has rebuilt the ruins and lived on. Today, the hope that Jews can avoid becoming drunk with the power of sovereignty and evolving into unfeeling conquerors lies in the retention of the memory of being victims and losers in the past. The key to that accomplishment is the continuing power of reliving the past.

TISHA B'AV (NINTH DAY OF AV): THE REENACTMENT

In classic Jewish style, the fundamental model of Tisha B'Av is a reenactment of that tragic historical orienting event. In going through the four historical fast days, Jews relive the stages of destruction of the First and Second Temples as well as the loss of Jewish sovereignty. (It is interesting, in light of the role that food plays in Jewish culture, that intense grief and guilt are expressed by giving up food!)

While the primary model is reenactment, the halacha also draws upon its imagery of grief for a dead member of the immediate family. There is this difference, however, between grief over death of a loved one and mourning an historical tragedy: In the case of a death in the family, the shock of loss sets in motion the sorrow and mourning that come pouring out in the *shiva*, the seven days of mourning that come after the death and burial. When reliving historical tragedy, one knows the outcome at the outset. Thus, the sense of doom and grief builds up *before* the day actually arrives. The day of Destruction is a culmination of the grief, but immediately thereafter—since nothing can be done to prevent the tragedy from happening—the psychological balance shifts toward the renewal of life.

The first fast day in the sequence is the tenth day of Tevet, the day on which the siege of Jerusalem began in 586 B.C.E. However, since the day occurs more than six months before the date of the actual Destruction, the pang of recollection on this day has not had so much resonance. The same can be said of the last day in the sequence, the Fast of Gedaliah, occurring the third of Tishrei. Coming two months after Tisha B'Av and dwarfed by the propinquity of Yom Kippur, the Fast of Gedaliah has had a limited impact. Both of these fast days begin at dawn, whereas Tisha B'Av starts at sundown on the previous night. On Tisha B'Av, the sorrow is so total that it goes beyond fasting to giving up such other pleasures as washing, cosmetic anointing of the body, and sexual relations. Not so the other three fast days, on which deprivation is limited to fasting.

In modern times, when the temperament of the culture is unsympathetic to denial, observance of all the fast days has declined. The tenth of Tevet, segregated from the other days, has particularly lost ground. This led the Israeli rabbinate to an unfortunate attempt to shore up the day by declaring it the day of saying Kaddish for the millions in the Holocaust whose dates of death are not known. The artificial stimulant did not resuscitate the tenth of Tevet. There was no organic connection between this day and the Holocaust. Besides, the rabbinate's proposal was too transparently an attempt to use the great catastrophe to revive a minor fast day.

The primary liturgy of grief for the Destruction is acted out in the three-week period between the seventeenth day of Tammuz and the ninth of Av. It should be noted that these two days antedate the Talmud. When the Rabbis brought the two days together in a choreography of grief reenactment, the three weeks were gradually filled in, to help the mourners recreate the rising crescendo of destruction. The halacha structured the entire period into five stages of grief, corresponding to the imminence of catastrophe. The underlying experience that the individual should live through is that of a first-century Jerusalem defender who goes through the siege from inception to becoming a prisoner of the Romans at the climax.

Stage 1: 17 Tammuz—the wall of Jerusalem has been penetrated by the Romans, a clear signal that the end is coming. Jews, feeling the shock of forthcoming destruction, do not eat from sunrise to sunset. Penitential prayers are recited, summoning up the many terrible occurrences on this day.

Stage 2: After this day, the intensity drops as people settle in for the terminal state of siege. The final part of the siege is reenacted during the three weeks between the two terminal days (17 Tammuz to 9 Av). While the city of Jerusalem is gradually reduced, Jews correspondingly intensify their grief and anxiety. Weddings are prohibited because the joy of marriage is incompatible with the mood of sorrow. Engagements are permitted for fear that by postponement they may be lost, though engagement parties are not held.

There are other grief rituals during the three weeks: taking no hair-cuts (in ancient times, letting hair grow long was a sign of mourning) and performing no acts that would inspire a blessing of Shehecheyanu (the blessing for something new and joyful), such as buying new clothes, a new home, a new car, or eating a new fruit for the first time in a year. (If the fruit will no longer be available after Tisha B'Av, this restriction is waived on Shabbat because on the Sabbath the fantasy of a perfect world still operates). The symbolic statement in these self-denials is: Who has the faith to go out and buy new things or plan for the future? Who has the heart to try to look good when the end is clearly drawing near?

Throughout the three weeks, prophetic portions that proclaim Israel's sin and the forthcoming destruction are read in the synagogue. The last of these prophetic phillipics, Chazon Yeshayahu, the Vision of Isaiah (Isaiah 1), is a devastating critique of the sin and corruption of Israel. In anticipation of sorrow, the portion is sung in the melody of Eichah, the Lamentations of Tisha B'Av. Chazon is always read on the Shabbat preceding the ninth of Av; that Shabbat has become known as Shabbat Chazon (vision).

Stage 3: From the beginning of the month of Av, there is a count-down of nine days to Destruction. The grief intensifies. In the initial Talmudic phase, the most intense mourning rituals were observed during the week in which Tisha B'Av itself occurred. Over the years, however, the entire nine days have become a unit of mourning among Ashkenazic Jews. Sephardic Jews generally restrict these deprivations to the immediate week in which Tisha B'Av occurs.

A folk saying goes, "When Av begins, cut back joy." Home construction or painting is held off (with exile imminent, who would build or improve his home?). Orthodox practice prohibits the eating of meat and the drinking of wine. (Symbolically, "The anxiety is crippling my capacity for enjoying life"; "I'm losing my appetite.") Interestingly, these deprivations are also rituals of an *onen* (that is, one who has lost an immediate family member but has not yet buried him.). It is as if people know the Temple is doomed but have not yet reached the full acceptance symbolized by burial.

Fresh clothes are a source of pleasure, so laundering and dry clean-ing are postponed (diapers are exempted). Total bathing is given up except for Shabbat, hence there is no swimming in that period, according to the orthodox tradition.* Symbolically, the noise of the Roman armies approaching disrupts the ease and order of daily life.

Stage 4: The last meal on the day before Tisha B'Av—the Seudah Mafseket, the meal that separates eating from fasting—is highly restricted. It is as if Jews already feel the grief of the survivor or the severe loss of appetite felt by a war prisoner. Since people want to be able to fast well, lunch is generally a full meal, but in the late afternoon, a simple meal is eaten without multiple courses. In many families people even eat separately to avoid the festive aspect of a *mezuman* (a trio for grace). Some people eat eggs and/or beans (the food of mourners because their circularity evokes the idea of the wheel of fate and of silent mourning). Some eat only bread and water, even dipping a piece of bread in ashes before eating. In Jewish ritual, mourners give up wearing leather shoes because they are comfortable. Besides, those who have just experienced the powerful loss of death do not want to wear something manufactured from animal skin, that is, something derived from death of another. Therefore, shoes are exchanged for canvas sneakers or sandals before sundown (unless the day preceding Tisha B'Av is Shabbat, in which case public display of mourning is inappropriate; in such a case, sneakers are not put on until after Shabbat ends).

Stage 5: For approximately twenty-four hours (adding on—as is usual with Jewish sacred time), Jews act out total grief on Tisha B'Av. The symbolic acts draw from the rituals of a mourner sitting shiva, but the powerful paradigm is that of an overwhelmed defender of Jerusalem, now a Roman prisoner of war. From sundown to sundown, traditional Jews neither eat nor drink nor wash nor anoint themselves (recall the scenes of Jews in the Holocaust, kept sitting in the open squares all day without food or water). In the same spirit, they give up sexual relations that night. The story of the Destruction is retold vividly by reading the Book of Lamentations. Unshaven, unwashed, hungry, people reexperience the tragedy of the Destruction.

THE TISHA B'Av, LITURGY

For the night service of Tisha B'Av, the ark curtain is removed. The synagogue is kept in semidarkness. All this suggests that in this event there was a *Hester Panim* (literally, the hiding of God's face). In disas-

---

*In actual practice, many modern Orthodox Rabbis permit showers (especially relatively cold showers) on the grounds that not bathing is an excessive hardship in this society, particularly in the summer.

ter, humans experience "the eclipse of God" and live in a void and empty universe. It is as if the Divine Presence had abandoned the physical Temple. Only an empty building remained, and destruction followed. After Maariv, the Book of Lamentations is read, followed by Kinot (mourning prayers). In some synagogues the book is read by the light of candles. To heighten the discomfort it is customary in traditional synagogues to sit on the floor, or on hard benches, or on seats that have been turned on their sides. The effect of gloom created can be overwhelming.

There is an anti-Exodus structure to the day. The Exodus led Jews from slavery to freedom. It is celebrated with light, good clothes, good food, and family celebration at home. The Destruction led Jews from freedom to slavery. It is relived with darkness, poor clothes, no food, and an undifferentiated mass of Jews jammed into a synagogue. The Exodus feast (the seder) is marked by Jews reclining on soft pillows in comfort as free people do. The captivity fast is marked by people sitting on hard benches or overturned chairs on the bare floor. The Exodus is a harbinger of hope, proof of God's presence in the world. The Destruction is a declaration of doom, witness to God's absence.

The Book of Lamentations is an intricate set of dirges and descriptions of Jerusalem under siege and of the destruction of the First Temple. The elegy bewails Jerusalem, once teeming with life and now sitting abandoned and alone like a solitary widow. It captures the horror of the siege: children pleading for water and bread in vain; cannibalism on the part of hunger-maddened mothers ("those who died by the sword were better off than those who perished by hunger"); nobles hanged; women raped; priests defiled. The prophet basically blames Jewish immorality and idolatry for the tragedy. Yet there is a fascinating outburst in Chapter 3 in which the believer, as it were, accuses God of being the enemy—like a lion lying in ambush to destroy his victim. The prophet comes close to losing his faith ("I thought my strength and hope in the Lord had perished") before the memory of God's past kindnesses restores it—barely.

The Book of Lamentations is read softly at first. The volume of the reader's voice builds to the climax which is sung aloud by the entire congregation: "Turn us to you, O Lord, and we will return. Renew our days as of old."

The Kaddish that is recited at night and in the morning omits the standard phrase "tiskabbal": "May the prayers and requests of all the House of Israel be accepted by our Father in Heaven and say, Amen." This omission is normally made in the house of a mourner. Here, too, the omission expresses the Jews' sense of rejection, the feeling that God did not hear Jewish prayers, since, in fact, the Destruction did take place.

Some mourners sleep on the ground on Tisha B'Av night or with less mattress and padding than usual. (Again, compare the experience of a refugee or war prisoner.)

At the morning prayer, tefillin and tallit are not worn. These are glorious symbols, and all glory has been stripped from Jews on this day. Again, it is the experience of an onen; the burial has not yet occurred, and one cannot carry out these mitzvot. Only when the burial is over—by afternoon, when the finality of the Destruction has sunk in—are the tefillin put on. During the repetition of the Amidah, the cantor intones the prayer Anenu—"Answer us, Lord, on our fast day." The blessing of the priests is omitted. One feels no spirit of blessing now; the Temple, the classic locus of this blessing, is being burnt down at this very moment. A special prayer, Nachem, is inserted in the Amidah; it is a plea to God to comfort desolate Zion and her grief-stricken mourners. Following the Shmoneh Esrei, in another of those remarkable dialectical moves of the halacha, the traditional service omits Tachanun, the penitential sorrow prayer, because at this point Tisha B'Av is referred to as "moed," an assembly day, hence a holiday. The point is that whenever the balance seems to be tilting to total despair or defeat, Jews make the countervailing move. In the depths of defeat, anticipate rebirth and triumph. In a noteworthy parallelism, the folk tradition decided that Av had been so bad a month in Jewish history, it should be cheered up. The folk colloquially call the month Menachem (Comfort) Av ("Cheer Up Av").

On Tisha B'Av morning, the Torah reading refers to exile and despair as well as to the fact that the Jews will return to God and to the land. Three people are called up to the Torah. The third reads the prophetic portion, a dirge that ends with hope. Then the book of Kinot is chanted. This book encompasses a variety of laments covering many of the tragedies of Jewish history. No one generation's grief, as central as it was, could be the sole focus of this day. Each generation was better able to empathize with past grief by projection out of its own sorrow.

All during Tisha B'Av, the only portions of the Torah studied are those that deal with destruction, tragedy, and mourning. All other Torah learning is so pleasurable, it is inappropriate for this day of grief. The classic text for Torah study on Tisha B'Av became the story of Jewish internecine fighting and divided counsels portrayed in the Babylonian Talmud Tractate Gittin. The reason for this is instructive.

The first Destruction was interpreted by the prophets as punishment for Israel's sins, especially those of idolatry, sexual immorality and murder. The revolt, which brought on the first Destruction, was opposed by Jeremiah, who warned that no good would come of it. In a way, that Destruction was easier to take because it made sense in the context of covenantal responsibility. As the prophets saw it, God had willed the Destruction as rebuke to Jewish infidelity; therefore, the destruction "proved" God's might. As Ezekiel proclaimed (in the famous vision of the chariot of chapter 1), the Divine Presence had left the Temple long before the enemy had entered its courtyard.

The second Destruction, however, was the end result of a major national religious revival. The "crime" of the Jews was excessive enthusiasm and determination that only God would rule over them. The crushing defeat was all the more devastating. How could it be rationalized? The Rabbis sought to assert that Israel's sins were responsible for the Destruction—again. But what were the sins? Interestingly, the Rabbis focused on Jewish divisiveness. Unjustified hatred among the people had invited the tragedy; indeed, the catastrophe was hastened by the civil war between the guerrilla groups. Instead of uniting to oppose the Romans, they spent much time and energy assaulting one another.

As mourners are too grief-stricken to recognize or greet people, so traditional Jews do not greet people with a "good morning" or "good day" on Tisha B'Av. This acts out the withdrawn, depressive state of a captive. If someone who is not aware of this custom extends a greeting, one replies softly so as not to embarrass or reject the other person.

Work and business activity are generally restricted, at least until Tisha B'Av afternoon, unless it is something urgent that might be lost if delayed. Ceremonies of mitzvah such as circumcision are postponed until after the Kinot are completed; the associated festive meals are put off until after the fast day.

At Minchah, as adjustment to the new reality grows, the tallit and tefillin are put on, and the various prayers that had been omitted in the morning are now recited. During the Shmoneh Esrei, the prayers Nachem and Anenu are inserted, in the Jerusalem blessing and the Sh'ma Koleynu respectively. Two amended versions of Nachem are circulating today, one by the chief rabbinate of the Israeli army and one by Ha Kibbutz HaDati (Religious Kibbutz Movement). Both take into account the reunification of Jerusalem in 1967. For the first time in nineteen hundred years, Jerusalem is entirely under Jewish rule. In the chief rabbinate's judgment, saying the old words of grief as if nothing has changed would make light of the prayers uttered when Jerusalem was in ruins and under foreign domination.

When the day ends, if the moon is shining, the ceremony of the sanctification of the new moon is recited. The kabbalistic meaning of this ceremony is the hope for the Messiah and the prayer that all of nature and history will be restored to wholeness and perfection. The encounter with degradation always unleashes the hope of total redemption. As is customary in Jewish practice, the reenactment does not end abruptly but rather tapers off. The mourning practices of the nine days, such as not eating meat, are carried into the night of the tenth. (This is, in part, due to the memory that the Second Temple burned down mostly on the tenth of Av.)

TO REMEMBER THE DESTRUCTION

The crises of the destruction of the Temple, the death of a million Jews, and the loss of sovereignty and exile were so great that they threatened the religious meaning and physical survival of Jewry. The Rabbis responded to these events with faithfulness and hope for restoration built around a renewed national religious life. Still, the whole tragedy was too great to be dismissed. It had to be incorporated into the sacred round of Jewish life. Like the mourner who cannot have full-hearted joy in the first year after the loss of parents, so acts of mourning shadow the joyful occasions of Jews. Inasmuch as the tragedy recurs each year, Jews are always in the first year of mourning. In this way, one never forgets, in fulfillment of the verse, "If I forget thee, O Jerusalem, may my right hand lose its strength" (Psalms 137:5). Due to the constantly renewed pain of going into exile, the Jews never fully reconciled themselves to exile existence. This incredible tenacity made possible the Zionist restoration almost two thousand years later.

When reviewing the observance of Tisha B'Av, one is struck by the responsibility to do no less for the greatest destruction in all history, the Holocaust. To fail to develop mourning practices for the Holocaust is to strike at the integrity of all Jewish mourning observances and to create weakness and irrelevance in the halachic process of our time. "The death of one righteous man is equal in weight to the destruction of the Temple," says the Talmud. To what, then, can we compare the death of six million?

TISHA B'AV AFTER THE RESTORATION
OF ISRAEL AND JERUSALEM

Now, in this lifetime, Jewry's period of exile and powerlessness is coming to an end. The Holocaust and the rebirth of the State of Israel have brought that about. Tisha B'Av cannot be unaffected by the miracle of Israel and the reunification of Jerusalem. The prophet Zechariah revealed to Israel God's promise that, after the return, Tisha B'Av and the other three fasts would become days of celebration. While it is too early to claim that messianic fulfillment is here, the process of redemption now underway is discernible. The three-week mourning of Tisha B'Av should be balanced by awareness of the approach of redemption.

It is incongruous for people in the diaspora to mourn excessively for the ancient loss of Israel. Past generations wept and prayed for the return because they could not go up to Israel. Today, if you are depressed over being in exile, a few hundred dollars for a ticket on El Al will end your state of misery. Simple traditionalism in observance of Tisha B'Av mocks the genuine agony of our ancestors.

What happens to Tisha B'Av in an age of fundamental reorientation, when the tide of Jewish history turns from exile to rootedness, from sorrow to increased rejoicing? Is there still meaning to days of remembered grief and defeat? In actual practice, the bulk of the Jewish people have given up the four fast days. Many do not even know of these days; others no longer identify with this tragic aspect of the past. Reform, Reconstructionist, and most Conservative Jews consider sacrifice and the Temple era finished. (The Conservative movement does, however, officially commemorate these days.) The tone of modern culture is set by the pursuit of pleasure; there is little room in our lives for deprivation. This mindset may be an important factor in both the achievement of and the besetting dissatisfaction with modern life. People today are hardly accepting of disappointment and frustration, let alone tragedy. But Judaism would be emotionally impoverished by the removal of its darker, more tragic side. The loss of a more powerful sense of the past is a loss to Jewish identity and religion. Therefore, one should fight for recovery of memory rather than yield to the modernizing trend.

The solution of the traditional Orthodox and of some nationalists has been to affirm that Tisha B'Av be observed and its emotional relevance be restored by incorporating the great catastrophe of our time, the Holocaust, into this day. For two thousand years it has been the practice to incorporate each generation's sadness into the roster of Tisha B'Av commemorations so that Tisha B'Av has become the record of these millennia of exile. The Holocaust appropriately folds into this day, but . . .

This well-intentioned and plausible approach does not do full justice to the Holocaust or to the dynamics of Tisha B'Av. The Holocaust was an event so overwhelming that it calls for its own special day and framework in order to be authentically encompassed. Those who see the Holocaust incorporated into classical interpretation of punishment for sins wish to fuse its memory with that of other past destructions. But the very idea that this catastrophe was inflicted as divine punishment is both morally and religiously wounding.

Immediately after World War II there might have been a serious attempt to commemorate the Holocaust on Tisha B'Av. The rabbinate did not grasp that moment, however. Surely it is providential and a tribute to the inspired sense of history that dwells in Knesset Yisrael (the General Community of the People Israel) that Yom Hashoah emerged instead. More than thirty years later it is clear that a fundamental reorientation of Jewish history and faith is underway. No less than a third great cycle of Jewish destiny is emerging. As the Rabbis memorialized the Destruction with Tisha B'Av, so should our generation incorporate this moment into the calendar in a living way. The goal is not to "save" Tisha B'Av; it is to encounter, apply, and struggle with the implications of the Holocaust. (See Chapter 11.)

But Tisha B'Av should be taken seriously in its own right. With the loss of the land of Israel, the whole tone of Judaism became more somber and sorrowful. One simple indicator was that before the exile all the holidays were days of rejoicing. There were no extended periods of sorrow in the biblical calendar. Throughout the rabbinic period, whole periods of grief and mourning were added to the sacred calendar, as if the cosmos were in mourning. As Exodus and the conquest of the land had created an ever-expanding beachhead of liberation, so the exile reflected a shrinking of the liberated areas. Thus, Tisha B'Av became the major focus of a mood of grief that covered and darkened but did not obliterate the peaks of redemption and joy in the Jewish calendar.

In this lifetime, the ultimate enslavement and moral chaos was inflicted in the Holocaust. Surely this was the climax of the rollback of redemption, threatening to destroy redemption itself. However, at that point, the Jewish people did not yield to the triumph of nihilism and despair. With an incredible lightning strike, they created a new, indeed unparalleled beachhead of redemption, the reborn state of Israel. Despite all assaults and attempts to crush it, that beachhead has steadily widened with the years.

With the rebirth of Israel we must recognize that the concrete tragedy that Tisha B'Av commemorates is being overcome. While exile is not yet over (Israel remains vulnerable and Jews in Russia, Syria, and Ethiopia are still too much at the mercy of oppressors), liberation has grown. Incorporating the Holocaust into Tisha B'Av would incorrectly obscure this process of liberation as well as deny the integrity of past sorrow and loss. The wound of exile *is* being healed. As it heals, so the day and period around it must be healed and gradually turned into renewed joy.

Premature abandonment of Tisha B'Av runs the risk of insensitivity to suffering and of Jews becoming unselfconscious sovereigns and conquerors. On the other hand, failure to begin to heal the day is a failure of recognition and gratitude felt. Now that the Jewish people seek to recapture an authentic Jewish life-style, it behooves those who have not known these fast days to recover them, while those who have kept these days must begin to reshape them.

After two millennia, the tide of history has shifted decisively as the sector of joy and redemption expands. It is a mitzvah to liberate even more days in the Jewish calendar from the grip of grief. This is the generation that has been privileged to be there at the fulfillment of the prophet Isaiah's words: "Comfort ye, comfort ye, my people, saith your Lord. Speak to the heart of Jerusalem and call out to her: Her time [of mourning] is up" (Isaiah 40:1–2) [my translation]. "Make Jerusalem happy and rejoice in her all who love her; celebrate celebrations with her all who mourned for her" (Isaiah 66:10).

Until final fulfillment is at hand, the sorrow and memory must be mixed with exultation as Jews experience the overcoming of exile and the resurrection of the "dead loved one" for whom the people symbolically mourned for almost two thousand years. With joy, one must give and receive the testimony in our time that God is faithful to God's promise.

PART FOUR

Unfolding the Way: Jewish Holidays in Our Time

For EIGHTEEN CENTURIES the structures of Jewish faith, especially as mediated through the Jewish holidays, guided and contained the Jewish historical experience. After the Bar Kochba revolt was suppressed, hope for a speedy restoration of Temple and sovereignty were dealt a devastating blow, but only with the passage of time was it established that exile and dependency had become a "permanent" Jewish condition. For the first two centuries Judaism competed aggressively with Christianity as a missionary religion. However, when the Roman emperor Constantine the Great established Christianity as the official religion of the empire in 325 C.E., he set the seal on a downward spiral for Jewish existence that was only sporadically checked until the modern age.

During this cycle of rabbinic Judaism—almost two thousand years long—the mainstream of Jewish settlement moved from the Middle East to North Africa, to Spain, to western Europe, to eastern Europe, and to the Western Hemisphere; ancillary waves of settlement moved to the Arabian peninsula and Asia. In all of these settings, until the modern age, Jews existed as an outsider minority. At times they came by invitation, at times by their own initiative. Sooner or later their standard condition became life on the edge—tolerated acceptance or imposed subservience, occasionally degradation. Often, Jews either moved on or were forced to leave.

Despite recurrent tragedies, Judaism did not yield its messianic hope. Despite the drastic shifts in geography and culture, Jewry did not yield its conviction that it was central to the final outcome of history. The Jewish way of life became an ethic of powerlessness that sustained faith and values under circumstances of incredible adversity.

That ethic is one of the great triumphs of the human spirit. The Jews should have become a battered people, affected by the classic syndrome that the abused, in turn, abuse their own spouses and children. Instead, the halacha developed within Jewry extraordinary levels of communal responsibility through consciousness of solidarity, institutions of philanthropy (tzedakah), and acts of loving-kindness (gemilut chasadim). Family life was sustained above all by the holidays and Shabbat time and celebrations. By keeping the vision of final redemption vividly alive, the holy days sustained the conviction that all these disasters were temporary setbacks; Jewish outsider status was not a reflection of intrinsic worthlessness. Christians taught that Jews were a cursed "wandering" people; the halacha and the holidays reassured Jews that they were still God's chosen vehicle of blessing for humanity, walking the way toward the ultimate redemption of the world.

Of course, the vulnerability and the repeated disasters had an impact on Judaism. Exile became a central condition; powerlessness was elevated to a principle. The hope of redemption focused increasingly on a miraculous divine action. Passivity grew. The prayers for restoration became petitions for intervention, not blueprints for action. Judaism itself, without yielding its ultimate hope, took on a darker, more tragic tone.

Certain tragic events "forced" their way into the holy days. By tradition, mourners were not to manifest their mourning openly on Shabbat and holy days, and therefore public memorial prayers were not recited. But then the Jewish communities of the Rhine (Mayence, Worms, and Speyer) were decimated, first by the savage assault of wandering Crusader armies and then by their own choice of suicide rather than forced conversion. At that point, the urgency of public commemoration of their ultimate devotion overrode all halachic objections. At first, the Yizkor (memorial prayer) for the martyred communities was recited on the Shabbat before Shavuot, that is, at the anniversary season of their devastation. Then the Yizkor was moved to Shavuot, not only because it was an anniversary but also because on such a day even larger groups of Jews would come together to mark the occasion.

From this entry point, Yizkor spread to become the memorial prayer for all the dead, not only the martyrs, and to be recited at all the major holiday seasons, not just on Shavuot. Only a deeper sense of sadness that soaked the entire religious ground of Judaism would have allowed such a widespread insertion of mourning into these days of joy. Perhaps the spread is also silent witness that all Jews—or at least a large percentage—were martyrs, in whole or in part, for their faith. This fact became the norm as the Exile lengthened and the suffering stretched out interminably.

One cannot help but feel that as the historical experience of powerlessness extended itself, as the persecutions became more overwhelming, the Jewish sense of unworthiness grew. The Jews did not accept the Gentiles' judgment of contempt for them, but they transposed that sense of disgrace to their relationship with God. The Exile was long because the roll of Jewish merit was short. The community clung to the merit and martyrdom of the ancestors, almost as if its own record was worthless. Therefore, one did not create new days to commemorate the grief and mourning of the community; one included it all under the rubric of Tisha B'Av.

The fundamental attitude was that creating new days of mourning was "presumptuous." How could a new tragedy compare to the cosmic proportioned destruction of the Temple that sent God, as well as the people of Israel, into exile? Moreover, each generation increasingly felt unworthy or lacking in authority to add new days to the calendar. It was as if, from now on, all Jews were epigones, living through pale reflections of the Ur-redemptions and catastrophes of the Jewish way. The conclusion was to consolidate all the expression of woe into Tisha B'Av.

Perhaps it was just as well that this conclusion was reached, for otherwise the Jewish calendar might have become one mass of never-healing wounds, each day sporting the stigmata of yet another community massacred, another collective martyrdom. Still, the net result was that the rabbinic tradition that had so powerfully articulated a partnership model for covenantal living had now turned into an ethic of theological as well as historical powerlessness.

One historical tragedy was of such magnitude that it threatened to stress the system beyond its capacity to absorb. The expulsion of Spanish Jewry in 1492 was so total a disaster that the foundations of the bridge of meaning, laboriously built by past covenantal generations, tottered and seemed close to crumbling into the abyss of historical death and destruction. Judaism could not go on with business as usual. The challenge to meaning and hope was too strong; the gap between Jewish faithfulness and suffering was too great. Into the void came a powerful expansion of the mystical tradition, as reformulated in Lurianic Kabbalah.

New observances were sought to channel the overwhelming spiritual search for repair and to hasten the redemption. Some mystics went to Israel to prepare the ground for the reunion of God with perfection, of the Jewish people with their home source. These same Pietists sought to perform every act mystically; even sexual union was to be timed (Friday night at midnight when the male principle of deity seeks union with the female principle so as to restore the cosmic unity) and practiced with such mystical intentions as to uphold the divine process of repair and unification. Those same mystics added a Kabbalat Shabbat (welcoming the Sabbath) service to deepen the preparation for Shabbat and the meaning of prayer on Shabbat. Special midnight prayers and acts of penitence, denial, and mourning for the Temple were established to intensify the sharing of the divine fate and hasten the process of overcoming the exile. Every existing observance was interpreted and invested with cosmic effect.

Additional holy days of special observance were developed by the mystics. The new moon (Rosh Chodesh), the first day of the Hebrew month, a biblical holy day that had diminished significance in later times, was invested with new sacredness through mystical meaning. A related ceremony, Kiddush Levanah (sanctification of the moon), prayers of praise combined with a dance on the occasion of the reappearance of the new moon, was intensified and given new meaning. The moon's miniature size compared to the sun was a sign of the cosmic world gone awry; the Kiddush Levanah expressed the yearning for the "restoration" of the world to perfection. The day preceding the new moon was converted into Yom Kippur Katan (miniature Day of Atonement), a day of special fasting, meditation, self-judgment, penitential prayers, and repentance. Tu B'Shvat, the fifteenth day of the eleventh Hebrew month (referred to in the Talmud as a New Year's Day for trees, that is, the day on which the fate of the trees was decided for the year), was given a mystical interpretation. A haggadah and ceremony of celebration were elaborated for the day. With the combination of additional days, systematic expansion and elaboration of the standing holy days, and a powerful mystical reinterpretation of all the festivals, the search for meaning was finally contained within the existing structures.

Then came the challenge of sweeping changes created by modern culture. The arrival of political and economic liberation and redemptive ideologies of all stripes overwhelmed Jews. The appeal of citizenship, the end of pariah status, and the opportunity for upward mobility intensified the powerful magnetism of liberalism, socialism, universal brotherhood, and other secular ideologies. Add to the above the extraordinary productivity of modern industrial society as well as its incredible scientific achievements in overcoming sickness and liberating people from poverty, and you have little trouble understanding why Jews flocked to modernism.

In the course of entering this culture during the past two centuries, many Jews lost confidence in the Jewish way. Redemption seemed more likely to come through science or socialism. Secularism spread, eroding faith and undercutting the very notion of sacred time. Assimilation weakened the will to continue living in distinctively Jewish patterns. To many, Judaism seemed passé. Jewish values were now universal; the best way to advance them was to join humanity and end tribal divisions. The Jewish way appeared to be coming to its end.

If modern culture or some part thereof was the Messiah, then some Jews followed its call (as they understood it) to dissolve into universal humanity as the appropriate response. In so doing, they acted out a traditional theme: At the end of days, the whole world would be one. It is not surprising that many of those Jews who joined certain absolute forms of liberalism accepted the demand that they prove their loyalty to humanity by giving up their practices and holidays.

Understandably, also, the holidays were modified or reinterpreted in the spirit of modern culture. Passover became the holiday of freedom and equality. Hanukkah celebrated religious freedom and separation of church and state. A much loosened Shabbat became the symbol of liberty and leisure. Sukkot simply faded; it and other holidays were deemed to be inconvenient, unable to generate a meaningful message in the modern context.

Among some more aggressive secularists—particularly some radical Jews of East European background—a conscious attempt was made to reverse classical models and thus express rejection of traditional or "bourgeois" Jewish values. There were those who organized Yom Kippur balls, engaging in festivities and feasting in conscious defiance of the traditional solemnity, fasting and, indeed, awesomeness of the day. To carry out such programs one had to be sufficiently knowledgeable and rooted in the tradition to know the classical models and be sufficiently exposed to modern culture to want to reverse them.

These developments could have led to a transformation of the classical system but for the fact that the Jews generally split into polarized groups. Those who were exposed strongly to modern culture tended to drift away from observance altogether; they therefore showed less involvement in adapting Jewish tradition to the new reality. Similarly, there were Jews who brought Christmas trees into their homes as symbols of their modernity, but these cases tended to be self-limiting as assimilation carried such people away from the Jewish community. Jews who were strongly sheltered from modern culture wanted to keep it at bay. For such Jews, the tradition was to be kept as it was at all costs.

For these reasons, while modern values led to sweeping reinterpretations of the holidays and significant shifts in levels of observance, they did not generate new holidays or transform the inherited system.

It all added up to a remarkable display of stability for almost two millennia.

In this century, however, in this generation, there have been two historical events of such magnitude that they test the Jewish way to its limit. One, the Holocaust, encompassed a destruction of such proportions that it came close to destroying the Jewish people totally. (That was, of course, the intended goal of those who carried out the process.) Because of its success in wiping out major centers of Jewish culture and values, the Holocaust challenged the credibility of the Jewish redemptive hope and of the God who is the partner and guarantor of the classic covenant. It is clear that Judaism cannot go on credibly with its message of final perfection without confronting and incorporating this event.

Shattering the assumption that perfection was nigh, mocking the perception of Jewish acceptance, the Holocaust radically challenged the norms of modernity as well. In fact, most surviving traditional Jews regrouped and recreated the classic modes of observance and learning. It is striking that the response "God is dead" and other despairing responses to the catastrophe have had little impact on the Jewish community. If one is to judge by the numbers of people changing their life-styles and priorities, then the primary effect of the Holocaust has been to release Jews from the iron grip of modern culture and reopen them to the tradition or, at least, to the primacy of Jewish destiny.

There was a widespread new willingness on the part of all Jews to assert Jewish priorities. But although the impact of the Holocaust often translated into support for traditional Jews and their institutions, it did not necessarily follow that Jews became individually more observant. Many more became newly involved in the institutions and observances that were directly related to the Holocaust and to Israel. Thus, tzedakah (philanthropy) and political action to help Israel or the oppressed Jews of Russia and Syria picked up enormous levels of support. (The Nazis made Jewish life cheap; we can make it dear again by giving. Jewish fate is indivisible. Israeli lives are on the line; we can march, lobby, make a trip to, and so forth.)

The other transforming event of this century stands in stark contrast to the first: It is a modern exodus, the recreation of the State of Israel. Not since the founding experience of Jewish peoplehood had a redemptive event of this scope occurred in Jewish history. Not since then has the condition of the Jewish people been transformed so rapidly and so totally from slavery to freedom, from dependence to independence. In many ways, the State of Israel is the dialectical response to the Holocaust. If the experience of Auschwitz symbolizes that we are cut off from God and hope . . . then the experience of Jerusalem symbolizes that God's promises are faithful and God's people live on. If Treblinka makes human hope an illusion, then the Western Wall asserts that human dreams are more real than force and facts.

Historical events of this magnitude classically have been incorporated into the Jewish way of life, particularly through holidays. The record of the past suggests that a move to create new holidays is the likely outcome of such historic shocks. In truth, there is no historical choice; the system must respond or it is over. As long as Judaism's hope is alive, it responds to great catastrophes or great triumphs in order to assert or to calibrate the credibility of its message. "No response" implies that no one cares anymore or that Judaism has surrendered history to the "other side." Yet the way of Judaism still has great power to move people, and the covenantal goal will evoke response even among Jews who do not acknowledge the classic sources of its authority. In all these circles, a response has begun.

Haltingly, in fragmentary fashion, in fits and starts, two major new holy days are being added to the Jewish calender: Yom Hashoah (Holocaust Remembrance Day) and Yom Ha'Atzmaut (Israel Independence Day). In consonance with the past, the challenge of these two events will not be met without transformations in the human and divine roles in the covenant. This development is best described as an unfolding of the covenant. In "unfolding," the historical experience peels away one level of meaning of the term covenant and reveals another dimension of the concept.

As the post-prophetic experience of Jewish history suggests, there is not likely to be a revelation to instruct this generation or the next as to how to live out these holy days. Nor does it appear that the rabbinate or any formal religious leadership is taking the lead in creating models. We are all peering intently into the dimness of future history, seeking to make out nascent form. Any attempt to formulate these days can be only a speculation. The formulator is *ipso facto* guilty of chutzpah. In trying to encompass events of such magnitude, whose judgments can be sufficient or even worthy? Yet there is no other choice but abandonment of responsibility and deafness to the call. Better to risk and err than to betray the covenantal mission by hardheartedness and business as usual.

Therefore, the chapters that follow will not only describe the practices that already exist, commemorating these two days. In the light of past models and following the currents set in motion by the theological cunning of the Jewish people, I will attempt to outline what are the future patterns.

CHAPTER TEN

The Shattered Paradigm:

Yom Hashoah

WHEN THE NAZIS CAME to power in 1933, they began a devastating assault on the Jewish people. As other nations and peoples failed to resist, the attack broadened. Between 1939 and 1945, almost six million Jews were killed in the Holocaust, one-third of the world Jewish population in 1939.

The Holocaust was more than an attack on the Jewish people, more than a decision to kill every last Jew in the world for the crime of being. Nazi mass murder was a systematic assault on the values that the Jewish people and the Jewish way represent. It is one thing to forcibly deport millions of people to their deaths. It is another thing to offer an *Ausweis* (exemption card) to a man supporting a wife and a mother with only *one exemption* to force him to send one away. It is one thing to murder millions of people in killing camps; it is another thing to number them, degrade them, turn them into *Mussulmen*, that is, "an anonymous mass . . . of non-men who march and labor in silence, the divine spark dead within them, already too empty to really suffer. One hesitates to call them living: one hesitates to call their death death, in the face of which they have no fear, as they are too tired to understand . . . their faceless presences . . . emaciated . . . with head dropped and shoulders curved, on whose face and in whose eyes not a trace of a thought is to be seen."*

It is one thing to gas people; it is another thing to burn the body and use the ashes to strew the roads for traction in winter, for fertilizer, for soap. At that point, a theological statement is being made. A human being—or, at least, a Jewish human being—is *not* an image of God but a *thing;* not free but owned; not unique but numbered. A Jewish life belongs to Germans to be used up and then converted into usable end products.

Nazism had a profoundly theological dimension; one should not be distracted from that truth by the fact that it was the theology of the devil. Uri Tal and other scholars have documented the search for wholeness, for secularized salvation that supplied enormous dynamic to the Nazi movement. The Fuhrer is at once the Messiah and the god of the movement, the source of the standard of good and evil. Hitler's dream of stopping at nothing to realize perfection reflected a yearning for human absolutes. The dream could not be realized without totally eliminating the Jewish people, who represent the presence of a God who is not controllable. As Hitler complained, the Jews were a source of conscience and judgment that he felt was irksomely restrictive and repressive of the natural pagan man. Jewish existence was a statement of "not yet" to all messianic pretensions. As long as one Jew remains alive, there can be no triumph, no monopoly, for anyone's absolute claims. The Jews had to be totally annihilated; their witness must not live on.

So began the most total assault of death on the people who teach that life will triumph. The process was death for death's sake, death defying the rational needs of wartime productivity, of economic profit, of military strategic priorities. Starvation, disease, terror, deportation, airless crouching boxes, chemical poisoning, medical experiments, freezing, burning, beating, whipping, burial alive, bayoneting, smashing heads, shooting squads, gassing—the kingdom of night, the triumph of death.

As the attack developed, Jewish rabbis, scholars, and teachers were special targets, mercilessly hunted down. Thirty percent of world Jewry alive in 1939 was dead by 1945; eighty percent of the rabbis and full-time students of Talmud were gone by then. Jewish holy days were violated with specially scheduled roundups. The Warsaw ghetto was enclosed on Yom Kippur 1940. Deportations from Warsaw to Treblinka at the rate of six thousand a day were begun on Tisha B'Av

*Primo Levi, *Survival in Auschwitz* (New York: Collier Books, 1961), p. 82.

1942. The final destruction of the Ghetto was scheduled for Passover 1943. Josef Mengele scheduled special selections for Yom Kippur in Auschwitz so that *he* would decide "who shall live and who shall die." In yet other camps, special food, rich soup and soft noodles, was served on the Day of Atonement, to mock that day when even many nonobservant Jews fasted.

Public prayer was prohibited in Warsaw in 1940. Keeping the Sabbath became impossible because forced labor was required on that day. Kosher slaughter was banned. Education was forbidden; newspapers were closed; libraries were confiscated. A food ration of eight hundred calories per day was established in the ghettoes, in a climate where working people needed three thousand calories a day. But the amount of food needed to supply the official caloric standard was never delivered. Every mother who did not abandon her children or who fed them knew that whatever she gave them was taken out of her chance to survive.

Jews were pressed into service to round up other Jews for transport. The alternative was being killed or being sent themselves. Parents were pitted against children and children against parents for survival. There were special actions against children; parents could let their children go, or go with them. Sometimes the targets were old people. Every child who did not abandon a parent on a death march or in the camps knew that the weight of the parent was dragging the child down to death.

An early Nazi analysis concluded that by working prisoners to death in an average of nine months, the profit per prisoner (keeping clothing and food costs infinitesimally low) was 1,431 marks, plus "income from an effective utilization of the corpse: (1) gold from the teeth, (2) clothes, (3) valuables, (4) money less the cost of burning [the corpse]," which added 200 marks additional profit "to which must be added income from utilization of the bones and the ashes."[*]

Shooting squads were used to kill more than 1.5 million Jews. Then this method was deemed too costly, too slow, too problematic. The search for cheaper, swifter methods of killing led to use of Zyklon B gas, an insecticide, in the Auschwitz gas chambers. Zyklon B causes death by internal asphyxiation, with damage to the centers of respiration, accompanied by feelings of fear, dizziness, and vomiting. In the summer of 1944, the amount of gas used in each chamberload was halved. This cut the price of killing in half—to less than one-half cent per person—but doubled the time of agonizing death.

Life was hated. On February 5, 1942, the Gestapo summoned two

---

[*]Jacob Robinson, *And the Crooked Shall Be Made Straight* (Philadelphia: Jewish Publication Society, 1965), p. 285.

members of the Vilna Judenrat and notified them that "from that day on no more Jewish children were to be born." In Kovno, pregnancy was prohibited on pain of death. In Treblinka and Auschwitz, children were automatically selected for gassing on arrival (except for some twins and others chosen for medical experimentation). Mothers who accompanied children were sent with them to the crematorium, as were pregnant women. One Mrs. Eliaz testified in a hearing about Josef Mengele that he did not at first detect her pregnancy. Angered that she had thus escaped the gas chambers, Mengele ordered her to give birth to the baby. Once it was born, he forced her to cover her breasts with tape. "The child grew thinner and thinner, weaker and weaker. Every day Mengele would come and look at it," Mrs. Eliaz recalled. Mengele thus studied how long a baby could live without food. After some days, a nurse stole some morphine and a syringe and told Mrs. Eliaz to put her baby out of its misery. After more days of seeing the infant's suffering, the mother finally acted. "I murdered my own child," she testified.

As the killing frenzy intensified, thousands of Jewish children were thrown directly into the crematoria or into the burning pits alive.* This is the most radical countertestimony possible to the Jewish covenant of life. Elie Wiesel has stated it most profoundly: "Never shall I forget the little faces of the children, whose bodies I saw turned into wreaths of smoke beneath a silent blue sky. Never shall I forget those flames which consumed my faith forever. Never shall I forget these things, even if I am condemned to live as long as God Himself. Never."† The cruelty and the killing raise the question whether those who continue to believe after such an event dare *talk* about God's love and care lest they be charged with mocking those who suffered.

Since there can be no covenant without the covenant people, is not the covenant shattered in this event? In Wiesel's words: "The Jewish people entered into a covenant with God. We were to protect His Torah, and He in turn assumes responsibility for Jewish presence in the world. . . . Well, it seems, for the first time in history, this very covenant is broken."**

In the course of the war against the Jews, the traditional vision of perfection was not the only paradigm that was shattered. The modern paradigm was also devastated. It cracked in the very same spot where Wiesel's faith was murdered, shattered on the rock of the burning children. When Wiesel arrived in Auschwitz with his father, they were

*Testimony of S. Szmaglewska in *Trial of the Major War Criminals Before the International Military Tribunal* (Nuremburg: 1947–49), vol. 8, pp. 319–20.
†Elie Wiesel, *Night* (New York: Hill and Wang, 1960), pp. 43–4.
**Elie Wiesel, "Jewish Values in a Post-Holocaust Future," *Judaism*, vol. 16, no. 3, p. 281.

stunned by the nightmarish scenes of shooting flames, of emaciated prisoners who looked like skeletons. Terrified by the screams of panic, the dogs, the whips, the guns, Wiesel turned to a prisoner and asked what was going on. The prisoner harshly replied: "... You're going to be burned... turned into ashes."* Wiesel simply refused to believe this. He thought, "We are living in the twentieth century, after all."†

Standing one hundred yards away from the pits where children were being burned alive, Wiesel and his father could not believe the killing process was going on—because this was the twentieth century! So powerful was the paradigm of moral progress, of perfection being ushered in by science and human reason, that the victims could deny what was happening to them—out of the certitude of faith in modernity.

No assessment of modern culture can ignore the fact that science and technology—the accepted flower and glory of modernity—had climaxed in the factories of death. Germany was one of the most "advanced" Western countries—at the heart of the academic, scientific, and technological enterprise. One of the most striking characteristics of the Einsatzgruppen (shooting squad) leadership was that seventeen of the top twenty-four leaders had higher education; they were professionals, especially lawyers, Ph.D.'s and, yes, even a clergyman. In the shadow of unparalleled genocide, the entire structure of autonomous logic and sovereign human reason now takes on a sinister character.

The indifference of the democracies strengthened the will of the murderers to carry out the genocide. The ideology of universalism ("this is a war to make the world safe for democracy") was used as an excuse not to bomb the rail lines to Auschwitz and not to make special efforts to save the Jews. And the acceptance of modern values in Western Jewry, the strong consciousness of being an American Jew or an English Jew, meant that those communities did not adequately see their fate as indivisible from that of the European Jews who fell into Hitler's hands.

Highly valued norms of modern culture are deeply implicated in creating the background for a pursuit of mass murder. Such cruel slaughter was made possible only by colossal human and moral failure. And, as George Steiner points out in *Language and Silence*, culture and cold-blooded murder were not mutually exclusive. Germans cried when they listened to Mozart, Haydn, and Beethoven at the classical concerts in Auschwitz, but quite unemotionally they shot and gassed women and children. The moral light shed by the Holocaust on the

*Elie Wiesel, *Night*, p. 41.
†Elie Wiesel, *Legends of Our Time* (New York: Holt, Rinehart and Winston, 1968), p. 176.

nature of Western culture validates skepticism toward contemporary claims of cultural superiority, moral progress, and methodological supremacy over the past. On the rock of Auschwitz, the classic assumptions of modern culture are broken.

How does one respond to the new condition? Richard Rubenstein has written: "We learned in the crisis that we were totally and nakedly alone, that we could expect neither support nor succor from God nor from our fellow creatures."* For Rubenstein, the authentic response to the brutal truth of the Holocaust is that it obliterated hope. The covenant is revealed as illusion. The only Messiah is death.

Armed by the conviction that the covenant cannot be finished, and strengthened by the correct perception that most Jews have not lost hope, many traditional Jews have insisted that the covenant was not damaged at all. In the extreme version of the argument, the covenant was upheld by the Holocaust because the catastrophe was a classic case of God's punishment of Israel for its sins. The right-wing Orthodox who uphold this view are split. One group identifies assimilation as the sin for which Israel has been chastised. The other group, the Satmar Chasidim, hold that Zionism is to blame. Jewish impiety— taking autonomous action to redeem history instead of waiting for the Divine Redeemer—has brought the Holocaust down upon the Jews by arousing the Gentiles and offending God.

There is an alternate interpretation of the impact of the Holocaust. Jewish ongoing covenant faithfulness is too real to dismiss the covenant as finished.

The Jews had every right to reject the covenant. Instead, countless assimilated Jews, seeing that modernity's messianic claim was premature and that the Jewish witness of "not yet" was still needed, have turned around and become more Jewish. Committed Jews have increased tzedakah and responsibility for other Jews to the highest levels in Jewish history. Observant Jews—backed and in some cases joined by nonobservant Jews—have recreated yeshivot and the study of Torah so that more people study Talmud today full-time than ever before in Jewish history. Indeed, right-wing Orthodoxy has had magnificent resurgence with the active and generous support of nonobservant Jewry.

The bulk of Jews, traditional and modernist, religious and secular alike, acted together to recreate the great biblical covenantal symbol, the State of Israel. Israeli and Diaspora Jewry alike responded to the Holocaust with what could be called a frenzy for life and renewal. On the other hand, the magnitude of the destruction and the sheer gravity

*Richard Rubenstein, *After Auschwitz: Radical Theology and Contemporary Judaism* (Indianapolis: Bobbs-Merrill Company, 1966), p. 128.

of six million dead witnesses against redemption make it impossible to act as if nothing happened.

What then happened to the covenant? Could it be that the covenant was broken, but the Jewish people, deeply committed to the partnership, chose voluntarily to take it on again? Not just those observant Jews who heard commandments from Sinai but the vast majority of Jews who heard no commandments but were still so in love with the dream of redemption that they volunteered to carry on the mission. They were all so committed to the triumph of life that they would brave the threat of limitless death again. Samuel Bak, who portrays the Holocaust in powerful images of broken tablets, writes as follows: "Throughout their long history of violation and abuse, the Tablets have maintained their eternal power to reemerge as a guide for those who choose to accept their covenant. Their power cannot be totally annihilated: Out of their fragments new Tablets are being created."*

When the Jewish people originally accepted the covenant, they had no way of knowing what the cost might be. Under the impact of the incredible blows of the Holocaust, the Jews might well have withdrawn to cut their losses. In fact, their faithfulness proved unlimited. The Jewish covenant is a commitment, out of faith, to achieve a final perfection of being. True faith sees the risks but knows that without them the goals will never be achieved. In the generation after the Holocaust, the staggering costs were never clearer, yet the Jewish people did not yield their dream.

If the covenant is not over, then what does the Holocaust reveal about the nature of the covenant? One can try to learn from the model of the Rabbis. The message of the destruction of the Temple was that God had hidden to call the Jews to greater responsibility. In the Holocaust, then, God was even more hidden, and the catastrophe was a more drastic call for total Jewish responsibility for the covenant. After the destruction of the Temple, the people of Israel moved from partial participant to full partner in the covenant. After the Holocaust, the Jewish people were called upon to become the executive partner in the mission of redemption.

Following the Rabbis' insight, when God is hidden, God is even more present (but must be discerned). To the question, "Where was God at Auschwitz?" the answer is: God was there—starving, broken, humiliated, gassed and burned alive, sharing the infinite pain as only an infinite capacity for pain can share it. What is the message in the Divine Presence's not stopping the Holocaust despite the most desper-

---

*Quoted in David G. Roskies' *Against the Apocalypse:* Response and Catastrophe in Modern Jewish Culture (Cambridge: Harvard University Press, 1984), p. 303.

ate pleas? In effect, God was saying to humans: you stop the Holocaust.... True, the world did not respond adequately; even the Jews of the world failed to meet their responsibility. But, finally, the Jewish people heard the call and responded by taking responsibility and creating the State of Israel. Thereby, the Jewish people has undertaken to stop another Holocaust as best it can.

If this is a correct application of the Talmudic model, the Jewish people are at the beginning of a new stage of relationship to the covenant and to God. This is the beginning of the third great cycle of Jewish history. In this cycle, God is more hidden, which means that God is more present. The Rabbis used this insight to discern God's presence in the home and in the worldwide synagogue. The equivalent today would be the simultaneous expansion and secular application of the halacha. Secularization is necessary because in an age of divine hiddenness, manifest statements are less powerful than intimations and signals. Just as prophecy became no longer appropriate after the destruction of the Temple, sacramental and formalistic statements are less likely to be heard today. Expansion is necessary because in an age of extreme hiddenness God must be discovered everywhere—in business, in medicine, in political life, in the army, in social work, in learning. Wherever people pursue the covenantal way, there God is present.

The primary religious act is to recreate the image of God. In an age of divine hiddenness, the most credible statement about God is the creation of an image of God which, silently but powerfully, points to the God whose image it is. There is a quantitative dimension to this call: to increase the number of Jews, to increase the presence of life in the world. There is also a qualitative dimension to this commitment: to treat a person as a being of infinite value. To feed a starving child, to heal a sick person, to nurture the uniqueness of a wife or husband are in themselves all sacred acts.

Ritual plays an indispensable role in sensitizing people to the Divine Presence, to the covenantal way, to the goals of Judaism. In an age of staggering power force, rootedness in the Divine and a strong sense of covenant are moral essentials, literally life-saving. Rituals and the holidays have the power to connect people to the Divine and to implant covenantal consciousness in humans. Learning Torah is essential to mastery of the new situation. One cannot properly discern the sacred dimensions of life without the models, tools, and records of past precedents that learning alone can supply. Learning is the way to develop religious receptors in people.

The other great religious act is taking power. This is a response to the divine call to assume responsibility to achieve the goals of the covenant. To advance freedom, to perfect life, to prevent Holocaust—all will take enormous amounts of power. A sense of devotion to the covenantal way holds out the promise that the power will not create arrogance or be used for destructive, degrading purposes. Here again, one notes that power passes for secular activity, precisely the place to look for religious action in this third era of Jewish history.

This interpretation of the present Jewish condition can lead to deeper understanding of the covenant. One cannot blink away the fact that the Holocaust wounded the covenant and its carriers. But the broken covenant still exercises a powerful magnetism—witness its renewal by the Jewish people. Paradoxically enough, the brokenness is also testimony to the profound bond between the covenant and the Jewish people. The covenant shares Jewish fate, as God does. The Torah is not insulated from Jewish suffering. Its very brokenness makes the covenant relate more closely to the Jewish people and to the human condition. This is a reason for its extraordinary pull on this generation of Jews.

Note that the first tablets given at Sinai, divinely made and perfect, proved impossible to carry, once the people sinned with the golden calf, and they were broken. The second set, carved by Moses in the search for forgiveness, was able to stay among the Jews and escort them wherever they went. Recall Rabbi Nachman of Bratslav's famous dictum that "nothing is so whole as a broken heart." Then after the Holocaust, "no faith is so whole as a broken faith." By this logic, no covenant is so complete as a broken covenant.

The shattering of the paradigm suggests that at the heart of the world is a crack; reality is fundamentally flawed. Perhaps this is what the Lurianic Kabbalah was driving at in its notion of *shvirat ha-kelim* (the cracking of the vessels), that the basic receptacles of reality were overwhelmed and damaged in the initial infusion of divinity into the world.

The Exodus event revealed that perfection in the universe is a model toward which history is moving, a standard that all models and categories try to approximate. The Holocaust reveals that behind the flux of history is an ideal paradigm that is fragmentary, broken. If the central normative models are "flawed" or "cracked," then the criteria of systemic adequacy used by most people—i.e., wholeness, completeness or even being perfect—may be fundamentally erroneous. No belief system or philosophy can be perfect if it seeks to deal with or grow out of reality. The discovery of failure, the critique of a system, is the key to reconciling it with reality and making it capable of coping. Those models that perceive themselves as perfect are fundamentally misguided; they even pose a danger. Those categories that recognize themselves as fragmentary are more congruent with the ultimate and more capable of guiding and interpreting life correctly. Even correct theories are not one hundred percent so; they must allow for—indeed, welcome—criticism that illuminates the exceptions and the elements of reality that are beyond itself.

This insight frees all religions and all ideologies to build in self-critique and to welcome criticism as a sign of greater health and spiritual vitality. Those who claim that they have the whole truth and nothing but the truth and there is nothing to correct prove thereby how false and how ineffective their religious viewpoint is. This insight is the key to a legitimate pluralism growing out of religions and ideologies that are fully committed to absolutes and not just out of toleration or indifferentism. Pluralism grows out of the recognition of their limits by *valid*, even revealed, systems. This also paves the way for correcting imperfections in systems that are divine.

As long as traditional Judaism upholds its own position univocally and fails to see the flaw in the paradigm, it is driven to defend and uphold injustices to women, to the handicapped, to Gentiles. When the "cracks" are accepted as a recognizable aspect of divinely given as well as human paradigms, Judaism will be freed to work on healing the imperfections and moving itself and the world closer to redemption. Similarly, only a chastened modernism, severely self-critical, ready to break up the absolute claims of science, reason, and human power, can overcome the cancerous tendencies of power and the idolatrous trend of human self-affirmation. Only thus can modern culture restore itself as a safe vehicle of human liberation and dignity.

Now which interpretation of Judaism is the appropriate response to the Holocaust? The failed/replaced paradigm, the shattered paradigm, or the unscathed paradigm of perfection? Each of these models has profound consequences for the future of Jewish religion, for Jewish self-understanding, and for the kind of holy day that Yom Hashoah, as a commemoration day for the Holocaust, should be. In the absence of revelation and in the absence of sufficient time to gain perspective, it is hard to prove anything. Yet faith cannot wait generations for an interpretation, nor can policy wait a century until the matter is clarified. When the Torah tells the Israelites how to discern between two contradictory oracles as to who is the false prophet, it says that the one whose prophecy does not come true is the false prophet. But the decision as to which prophet to follow is to be made now!

There is, however, a straw in the wind, perhaps two. Both the unreconstructed traditional view (for our sins we are punished) and the radical view (the covenant is finished; it was an illusion) have resolved the incredible tension between the Holocaust experience and the Jewish covenantal way. One (by obedience) and one (by despair) have released the dialectical spring that throws us back and forth in tension between faith and doubt, hope and despair, triumph of life and victory of death. Evoking the broken paradigm image, one can argue that both views err because they account for everything. Both views give a definitive interpretation of the Holocaust that subsumes it under known classical categories. But neither classical theism nor atheism is adequate to incorporate the Holocaust; neither is credible alone—not in the presence of burning children. Richard Rubenstein argues that no statements about the God of history can be persuasive anymore. But it is not so much that affirmations (and denials) cannot be made but that they can be authentic only if they are made after working through the impact of the Holocaust, which is ceaselessly tormenting and dialectical. In the same sense, the relationship to the God of the covenant cannot be unaffected.

Another indicator of where the spirit is blowing is the response of the Jewish people. Only a handful have chosen the way of pagan stoicism and despair of the covenant. A larger group has affirmed the fullness and absolute adequacy of the tradition; their ranks have been swelled by the *baalai teshuvah* (returnees) movement, reflecting a significant turn from modernity toward tradition.

By far the largest group response has been the cluster of behavior identified with a broken and renewed covenant paradigm. This has been the direction of building the State of Israel and focusing much of Jewish life and learning around it or in it; stopping or slowing assimilation; getting involved in the creation of Jewish power and in political action for Jews; and building the Israeli army and Jewish capacity to prevent another Holocaust. People of all three views have been deeply involved in the re-creation of Jewish life via family; but here the palm must go to the most traditional sector.

All these activities are partial, subject to human error and often derided as falling short of the old standards of ideal morality or as lacking divine assurances of perfection. Yet these are the deepest expressions of covenantal continuity. Their partial character and brokenness only reveal their close affinity to the covenant. True, there is great openness to the tradition; however, other than in the traditional group, there is great confusion about the relationship of these activities and priorities to the inherited traditions and observances of the Jews. Part of the confusion lies in the failure to connect the traditions to the contemporary great events; part stems from the presentation of the classic observances in "sacramental" or divinely "dictated" forms cognitively dissonant with the spirit of post-Holocaust hiddenness of God; part stems from the ongoing power of assimilation. Deeper understanding is needed to help us articulate the true covenantal rootedness of the Jewish people's behavior.

If one does not think of religion purely as a source of meaning for the individual (which interpretation reflects a high degree of assimilation to Western values), and if one maintains the classic Jewish emphasis on the covenantal way, the number of Jews responding to the new orienting events is highly significant. However, the statement is essentially behavioral; for the most part, people have not articulated what they are doing, even to themselves. (Theology is not a high-priority in the Jewish community.) Since rituals are formulations of the beliefs and values that undergird the covenantal way, this void is particularly problematic in trying to formulate a model of Yom Hashoah, a holy day for the Holocaust. Still, one can venture some general theoretical guidelines for such a new holy day.

It is reported that Hitler hated the holiday of Purim. To him it symbolized the absolute opposition of Jew and Gentile. Either Mordecai hung on the tree or Haman did—the two could not coexist. The Jewish victory that Purim marks was the antithesis of Hitler's visions. And so ghetto humor told of Hitler's announcing a series of harsh decrees to a straggly Jewish community, standing before him flinching under the repeated blows. One Jew, however, stands tall and the smile on his face grows wider with every additional decree. Finally, Hitler breaks off and angrily demands to know why the man continues to smile. The Jew replies, "I am thinking of Haman and his terrible decrees. What a wonderful holiday we have because he was overthrown—there is laughter, feasting, drinking. I am thinking of what an incredible holiday we will have after *you* are overthrown."

Despite the defeat of Hitler, there is not going to be that kind of holiday. This time the genocide was not averted. Yom Hashoah will be a lot closer to Tisha B'Av than it will be to Purim. The question is whether the Tisha B'Av model or the day itself can contain a catastrophe so great, a tragedy so shattering. Tisha B'Av is a day of mourning and loss, a secular day yet a holy day, a day whose structure expresses the rabbinic reinterpretation of the covenant in light of the Destruction and Exile. Yom Hashoah is likely to incorporate similar elements. The day will have to be one of hiddenness—the hiddenness of God, the loneliness and abandonment of the victims, the absence of the Allies, even the equivocal nature of survival and liberation, including D.P. status, exclusion from Israel (then Palestine), and "shame" of survival. Like Purim, there will be an awareness of how arbitrary and meaningless history and survival can be. Unlike Purim, the hiddenness can hardly come through masks or humor.

But neither can Yom Hashoah be a day solely of destruction. Such an exclusive focus on defeat would ignore the revelations of strength, human greatness, and even messianic affirmation in the Holocaust, as well as the fact that the catastrophe evoked an extraordinary response: the re-creation of the State of Israel. It may be that, in accordance with the Tisha B'Av precedent, the day will start with desolation and commemoration at night and go on to some dialectical redemptive moves by day.

Yom Hashoah will have to find its expression institutionally; existing sacred institutions are too manifestly religious to contain all of the event. A new institution, the Holocaust Memorial Center, is now spreading in America. After a generation in which Yad Vashem and a handful of memorial centers around the world stood alone, the concept of a dedicated, total-environment memorial is gaining acceptance. Major centers are being developed in Washington, D.C., and New York City; other important centers have sprung up in a dozen American cities. This is the birth of a historic new institution to express the claims of memory and values after the Holocaust. Like the synagogue after the destruction of the Temple, this new center appears to be "secularized" compared to its predecessor institution. But like the synagogue in that time, the memorial center is really holy space in a new guise. Here the orienting event is encountered, studied, and related to the past and future of the Jewish way. Of course, the final shape of Yom Hashoah will be linked to the need to bring Holocaust memory into the home—the home being the secular sacred place, the primary victim of the destruction, the source and focus of life response.

Finally, this will be a day of secular tone and acts. Any attempt simply to fit the Holocaust into classic modes of prayer, ritual, and affirmation must confront the radical countertestimony to hope and faith in the Holocaust. It is questionable whether any traditional system can tolerate such tensions. On the other hand, it would be another victory for Hitler to have the Holocaust destroy the traditional Jewish prayer service or synagogue. How to orchestrate the tension between these insights is a major aspect of the unfolding third cycle of Jewish history.

THE EVOLUTION OF A HOLY DAY

Not until World War II came to an end did the total dimensions of the Holocaust become apparent. The six million dead constituted one-third of the estimated world Jewish population, but they were fifty percent of European Jewry and ninety percent of the two major Jewish communities of the world: Poland, and western Russia and the Baltic states. These were the core communities of Yiddish-speaking Jews, secular and religious, and the biological and religious heartland of Orthodox Jewry. The two communities had been the main center of Zionist Jews as well.

Whole communities had been wiped out; cultural institutions by the thousands were destroyed. The creative and cultural world of east European Jewry was in rubble. Yet the surviving Jews of the world had to come to grips with the event. How could they commemorate a catastrophe whose traumatic effects they carried with them every day? How could the victims' relatives memorialize their lost families? And how could the State of Israel, as the guardian of Jewish continuity, contribute to a solution?

There were three primary sources of the call to memory. One was the Zionist leadership. In addition to their personal losses, they saw themselves as the "inheritors" of European Jewry as well as of the mantle of historical leadership of the Jewish people. They were not unaware of the Zionist implications of the Holocaust, so this was extra incentive to keep the memory alive.

One of the central figures who emerged to take leadership in this area was Ben Zion Dinur. Dinur was a Labor Zionist with a Lithuanian Yeshiva background. By 1948, he was professor of Jewish history at the Hebrew University. According to Dinur's philosophy of Jewish history, the moving idea of that history was the fluctuation of the Jewish psyche and community structure between establishment in Diaspora and yearning for Eretz Yisrael, the homeland. For Dinur, the Holocaust was the crushing, final proof that the end goal of Jewish history —and its appropriate focus—was the reestablishment of Jewry on its land. He moved early to ensure that the Holocaust and its lessons would be centrally commemorated in the State of Israel. In 1948, Dinur, by then the minister of education and culture, proposed setting up a memorial commission for the Holocaust. It was to be located on a mountain next to Mount Herzl, that is, next to the national embodiment of Zionist history and values.

But there was also some ambivalence about commemoration among Zionist leaders. For most, the highest priority was building the state. Some—like David Ben-Gurion—felt a need to distance themselves from the Holocaust. Ben-Gurion thought that the Jews in Israel should concentrate on new life and creation; energy focused on commemoration and death would divert people from the central goal.

There was another problem as well. One of the incredible aftereffects of the catastrophe was a widespread sense of "shame." Why did those Jews go "as sheep to the slaughter"? In effect, the victims were blamed for the weakness that permitted their victimization. It was as if contact with their memory would rub off the same attitude—and fate —on the new *yishuv* (community) in Israel. To Ben-Gurion, the Holocaust was a negative model; the Israeli, the Sabra, the new Jew would be different. Ben-Gurion was not for amnesia. He was too Jewish and historically minded for that. But the Jews in Israel would do better to give the Holocaust less attention; it was more important to focus on the challenge of the state.

More than one hundred and fifty thousand survivors finally settled in Israel. They were the second potential source of pressure for commemoration. However, many of them were preoccupied with the struggle to adjust to a new country, to rebuild their lives and families, to fight in the War of Independence, to make a living, and to stay alive. For many survivors it was all that they could do to resume normal lives. There was not a good deal of energy left to campaign for national commemoration of the Holocaust. Indeed, for many, putting aside those terrible memories was a *sine qua non* of their ability to function at all. They were not in a position to open the old wounds by expressing memory or seeking to ensure that others would.

Furthermore, many of the survivors carried the stigmata of Holocaust "guilt." Yes, guilt! Unbelievable as it may be, disgraceful as it was, there was a powerful widespread feeling—sometimes shared by survivors—that there was something guilty in the state of survival. (One of the harrowing truths about the Shoah is that the event was so extreme and unprecedented that comprehension failed. During and after the Holocaust, people made colossal misjudgments, especially when they made conventional judgments about matters that defied all categorization. The innocent victims, abandoned and betrayed during the Shoah, were blamed afterwards for not being heroic fighters. The survivors who were living martyrs should have been gathered up lovingly and nursed back into life. Instead they were kept at arms' length, surrounded by silence, judged out of context, and made to feel guilty.) The survivors soon learned that one should not talk much about one's experiences in the Holocaust; it wasn't welcome in polite company— too much of a downer. Besides, if a survivor talked about it, the questions soon followed, typically whispered off in the corner: Why did *you* survive? *How* did you survive? Why didn't *they* fight?

The truth is that many survivors lived with those questions constantly, whispered by them or their loved ones (alive or dead) in the silence of the night or the heart. As Rivka Yosselevska, one of the few living survivors of an actual *Einsatzgruppen* mass shooting, testified at Adolf Eichmann's trial, these were her words as she lay next to the mass grave of her family and community: "I cried out to my mother, to my father. 'Why did they not kill me? What was my sin?' I saw them all being killed. Why was I spared?"* Social scientists now call it survivor guilt.

A third group instinctively understood there must be commemoration for the Holocaust: the religious Jews. They had the sense of Jewish fate and family; they had suffered some of the most grievous losses in numbers; they had a strong tradition of days of memory; they even

*Quoted in *Documents of Destruction*, edited by Raul Hilberg (Chicago: Quadrangle Books, 1971), p. 66.

had models for memorial commemoration. But there was also ambivalence about the Holocaust among the Orthodox. The event was a great shock to religious faith; given the very high losses among the most religious Jews (eighty percent of Chasidim), memory might become a source of doubt and of questioning the divine justice. The Holocaust was a particularly great challenge to those groups that had fought modern Zionism relentlessly—as a rebellion against God. The tragedy could be interpreted as proof that this policy had been a grave error. (The extremist ultra-Orthodox leadership eventually resolved this danger by insisting that Zionism was the cause of divine [and Gentile] wrath that brought the Holocaust down on the head of Jewry.)

There was a strong tradition that all great tragedies were to be incorporated into the sacred round of Judaism. The great question was: What day should be used? From the beginning, one of the deep issues in dealing with the Holocaust has been the issue of continuity or discontinuity. Given the totality of the tragedy, was this event something unique or just another in the long list of tribulations, expulsions, disasters that mark Jewish history?

Classically, tradition tried to choose a day connected to the event, preferably an anniversary date such as Passover, Hanukkah, or Tisha B'Av. But what could be the anniversary of the Holocaust? This was no one-time affair; it went on year-round for years. Perhaps a period of the year should be set aside, but when?

So massive was the scale of the Holocaust killing and so reckless its speed that for most of the dead there was no firm knowledge of the *Yahrzeit*, the actual date of death. Indeed, for many of the dead there were no survivors of the immediate family to say *Kaddish*. Finally, in 1948, after some earlier incidents and rulings crystallized the question, the Israeli rabbinate proposed a Yom Kaddish Klali, a general Day of Kaddish to be said for all those for whom there were relatives to say the prayer but no known date of death, and for those for whom there was no relative to say Kaddish but others would say it for them. Given the high number of victims in the above two categories, the rabbinate also proposed that this general (or communal) Kaddish day be the day of Holocaust commemoration. The day chosen was Asarah B'Tevet, the tenth day of the tenth month of the Hebrew calendar. This is a fast day that traditionally marks the beginning of the siege of Jerusalem which led to the destruction of the Temple.

The choice of the tenth of Tevet is worth consideration. Clearly, its selection reflects the idea of incorporating the newest tragedy into the chain of tradition without introducing any halachic innovation. This decision affirmed that the destruction of the Temple remains the paradigm and acme of Jewish tragedy. But why not incorporate this event into the ninth of Av, as most of the medieval tragedies had been?

The answer is instructive. Of the four days of mourning for the Temple, Tisha B'Av was the strongest in terms of participation by the Jewish people. Shivah Asar B'Tammuz was far less observed. The third fast day, Tzom Gedaliah, was more neglected yet. Of all the fast days, however, the tenth of Tevet was by far the weakest. Isolated from other holy days, far removed on the calendar from the climactic destruction whose inception it commemorates, the day had dwindled to a marginal existence except in the most traditional circles. This day could benefit most from an injection of ceremony and from connection to a new constituency. In short, the choice of the tenth of Tevet for a Holocaust commemoration day was designed to shore up the dwindling fortunes of the day. In other words, far from coming to grips with the awesome emotional, historical, and theological weight of the Holocaust, the rabbinate still was operating under the sign of the destruction of the Temple. For it, that was the catastrophe of record. Far from considering that the Holocaust was a novum or at least was too massive to be subsumed within existing rubrics, far from confronting the Holocaust as a category-shattering event, the rabbinate sought to incorporate this *churban* within an existing (minor) halachic pattern in order to strengthen that pattern.

The rabbinate's ruling fell totally flat. There was no intrinsic connection between the Holocaust and the chosen day. The lack of fundamental thinking implicit in the decision reflected itself in the absence of any other proposed rituals. The ruling left the Labor left wing, the nonobservant Zionist, and the ghetto fighter groups totally dissatisfied. The proposal never caught on with religious Jews either. The Holocaust could not be used to save the tenth of Tevet. The choice of a memorial day that sought maximum continuity with the past was a nonstarter. That fact is a powerful statement of the theological common sense of the Jewish people.

The final and critical source of a push for commemoration came from a group of ex-ghetto fighters, partisans, members of the underground resistance to the Nazis. During the Holocaust, Zionist youth groups had been particularly active in armed resistance. A number of these fighters had come to Israel and had been absorbed into the Labor establishment. It is ironic, of course, that this group took the lead in pressing for Holocaust commemoration. In effect, this was deemed the one group that had no apologies to make—because it had fought! These leaders had brought no "shame" on Zionist ideals; they represented no negative model that might "contaminate" Sabras.

Under this leadership, the campaign for a memorial authority soon built armed resistance centrally into the theme. The authority was to memorialize *Hashoah Ve Hagevurah*, the Holocaust and the Heroism. For the ghetto fighters, there was only one day worthy of being a memorial anniversary for the Holocaust—April 19, the beginning day of the Warsaw ghetto revolt, the greatest revolt of them all, the uprising that had held the Nazis at bay for a longer period than the great French army.

The Zionists living in Israel objected to the solar calendar date, insisting that the day be marked on the Hebrew lunar calendar. That date was totally objectionable to the Orthodox Jews: It was the fifteenth of Nissan; the Warsaw revolt had broken out on the first night of Passover. The revolt began then because the Nazis, determined to wipe out the ghetto totally, had scheduled their attack on that day. The Nazis hoped to accomplish two additional objectives in choosing that date for the final assault: one was shattering and trampling the Jewish Passover holiday; the other was completely mopping up in one day, in time to offer the final solution of the Warsaw ghetto problem to Adolf Hitler as a present for his birthday, which was April 20.

In hindsight, one shudders to think about what would have happened had the Orthodox Jews not been opposed and the date of 15 Nissan or the immediate days of Passover following been chosen as the day of commemoration. This would have constituted a decision to permanently incorporate unspoken disdain for the vast majority of the six million dead into the official Holocaust commemoration. All the arrogance of those outside the Holocaust—those who had never known hunger beyond endurance, terror beyond imagination, family obligations under conditions of grave peril—would have been crystallized in this statement. The Western macho tradition would have won out over some sense of the heroism of mother love, of the courage of educating children in the shadow of death, of the humaneness of thousands of self-help tenant committees, of the quiet dignity of people who (as a Sonderkommando survivor testified) even when standing before the gas chambers never crawled begging for their lives.

As it turned out, the Orthodox Jews would have none of it. Yom Hashoah would necessarily be a day of mourning, sadness and destruction. Passover was a happy day, full of food, family, and assurance of faith. To impose Yom Hashoah on such a day or the festival days following, would utterly negate its character; it would cripple the holiday that was the very heart of Judaism. The Orthodox were ready to accede to a day dedicated totally to the memory of the Holocaust, but they would not allow that day to destroy Passover.

For two years, in the Knesset, the two main antagonists over the commemoration bill blocked each other. The turning point came in late 1950 when earnest bargaining began. The ghetto fighters and their allies wanted a special day, as close to 14–15 Nissan as possible. Their *terminus ad quem* was May 16, the date on which Jurgen Stroop, the German general, declared that the ghetto was totally destroyed. The

Orthodox wanted to push the date as far back as possible from Passover—at the least, into the next month of Iyar (the second Hebrew
month) so as not to infringe on the prohibitions of mourning and eulogies in the month of Nissan. If the date could be deferred to the
month of Iyar, it would fall within the Sefirat Ha'Omer mourning period, which would make it less troublingly "innovative" to the current
mindset of the halachic authorities.

As the parties jockeyed back and forth, the Orthodox representatives, hoping for some leeway, privately sought out the leading *posek*
(halachic decisor) of the Orthodox right, a man of towering stature, the
Chazon Ish. But the Chazon Ish was unyielding; it was prohibited to
disrupt the joy of Nissan with any such public mourning. In effect, the
Chazon Ish ruled that not the slightest hair on the head of tradition
could be touched for the sake of remembering the Holocaust. The inherited practice was unaffected by historical experience; the halacha—
and Judaism—remained outside of history, untouched by the flux of
time or the sledgehammer blows of the Holocaust.

The Labor Zionist establishment provided the "swing" vote that decided the outcome. They agreed with the Orthodox that Passover
should be spared and they felt that Holocaust Commemoration Day
should precede Israel Independence Day, which occurred on the fifth
of Iyar.

Finally, after much negotiating and sparring, the deal was struck
(there were even rumors of job trading and other "payoffs" to obtain
the necessary agreement, although a number of the key negotiators
deny that story to this day). As close to Passover as possible turned
out to be 27 Nissan. For the Orthodox, this was a breach of the unmiti-
gated joyfulness of the month. Setting this date for mourning directly
violated a halachic tradition, albeit a minor one. Indeed, the right-wing
Orthodox were so unhappy that they have never accepted this date.*
There could be no "compromise" of a jot or tittle of the halacha. To
somewhat assuage their feelings, the Orthodox were granted a further
concession: If the memorial date fell on Friday or Saturday, it would be
postponed until Sunday.

To this day there have been abortive attempts to find an alternative
date. As late as 1984, Rabbi Pinchas Teitz, a member of the presidium
of the Agudat HaRabbanim (the European-trained, right-wing Orthodox Rabbis of America), proposed that an alternative date, which
would avoid the month of Nissan entirely, be set: the anniversary of
Hitler's *death*. Teitz urged that the seventeenth day of Iyar, the day of
Hitler's suicide, be set aside to commemorate the destruction. The day

---

*In the late 1980s, elements of the Chasidic and Agudas Israel communities began to partici-
pate in Yom Hashoah commemorations in New York City.

should be a fast day and a day of study and remembrance. The mood of the day should change gradually to one of rejoicing that the Jews survived. That night, the eighteenth of Iyar, is Lag B'Omer (the thirty-third day of the counting in the Sefirah—see chapter 3), which is already a day of semirejoicing, breaking the gloom of the Omer period.

No one was satisfied with the outcome. The Orthodox were un-happy because they had been forced to accept an official day that in-corporated a violation of the halacha. The fighters were unhappy because the commemoration was not on the day of the uprising. There was no significant event or special association with 27 Nissan, and thanks to the Shabbat protection, the memorial day was not even fixed on the same date every year. But the overall pressures to create a me-morial day could no longer be denied. On April 12, 1951, the Knesset declared 27 Nissan as Yom Hashoah U'Mered HaGetaot (Holocaust and Ghetto Revolt Remembrance Day). The day was soon referred to as Yom Hashoah Ve Hagevurah (Devastation and Heroism Day). In 1953, the memorial authority was established and named *Reshut Zik-karon Yad Vashem* (Memory and Memorial Authority).

Behind the various proposals to locate Yom Hashoah on the Jewish calendar was a clash of values. Given the differing interpretations of the meaning of the Holocaust, it was hardly surprising that groups disagreed on the proper date and methods of memorializing the Shoah. To have allowed any one interested group to determine the specific date of Yom Hashoah would have meant overriding the others' models. To have accepted from any of the groups the date required by their own reckoning, would be equivalent to saying that their para-digm of interpreting the Holocaust was one hundred percent correct. But was any one group's vision of Judaism totally correct and un-scathed by the Shoah? No such perfect model exists; perfection is least of all possible when it comes to dealing with the Holocaust. Instead, the pluralism and give and take of democracy led to an outcome in which each group was partly upheld and partially defeated. This is the equivalent of a broken paradigm. As I will argue below, adoption of any one of the groups' dates would have brought very unfortunate side effects with it. Only a "broken" date (drawn from a broken para-digm) could be appropriate for Yom Hashoah.

The truth is that all through the fifties the day was neglected. Not until 1959 did the Knesset legislate a national public commemoration of the day; two years later it passed a law closing all public entertain-ment on that day.

Meanwhile, by the late 1950s, David Ben-Gurion became convinced that he had erred in his treatment of the Holocaust. Too many Israelis had a sense of discomfort over the "passivity" of the victims. Too many citizens failed to understand the moral urgency of the state and why Jewish power was absolutely necessary. He saw the danger of chauvinism and mindless power lurking in the distancing from the weak, powerless Diaspora Jews. Determined to educate the Israeli public, Ben-Gurion set in motion the capture and trial of Adolf Eichmann. The trial proved to be a stunning breakthrough in public understanding. The "curtain of shame" was lifted and the enormity of the Holocaust revealed. The public, out of new empathy generated by the vivid testimony, suddenly grasped the heroism of daily life in the Holocaust. From that time on, the remarkable spread of Holocaust consciousness began.

Then came the Six-Day War, preceded by a "rerun" of the Holocaust. Israel stood alone while the threat of genocide seemed overwhelming, except this time the Holocaust did not repeat. This time, it was Exodus again! Analysts have speculated that the triumphant resolution of the Six-Day War overcame, in a way, the barrier erected by the tragic conclusion of the Holocaust. People had not been able to confront the story of the Holocaust because the ending was always so devastating. Now there was a "reenactment" that ended with a miraculous deliverance. This psychologial breakthrough cleared the way for a new rise in consciousness and an enormous expansion of observance of Yom Hashoah in Israel and America. It was also noteworthy that increasingly the day was referred to as Yom Hashoah—leaving off ve hagevurah; the need for apologetics had declined sharply.

By 1979, the President's Commission on the Holocaust was established in the United States to recommend a national policy of commemorating the Holocaust. An initial bill to set up an American national memorial day was introduced by Senator John Danforth (Republican–Missouri). Danforth proposed observing the dates of April 24–25, the day the American armed forces liberated Dachau. Had that date been adopted, what kind of day would American Jewry and the entire American people be commemorating now? In 1985, a survivor who ended the war in Dachau gave an account of that day.*

The Americans entered Dachau and discovered the horrific scenes that have burned themselves into the memories of the world. The armies brought in photographers to take pictures of the atrocities, then they left the camp as they had found it—with the dead bodies left in their discovered places. The soldiers locked the gates to prevent the erstwhile prisoners from spreading infection and disease to the German population and the Allied soldiers. The survivors were mostly too sick and too weak to bury the bodies. Within a week's time they were

---

*Interview with Josef Gutman, survivor, March 15, 1987.

dying in great numbers from the contagions they caught from the dead and from the cumulative weakness of their systems.

When the D.P.s came down with typhus and dysentery (the two most widespread diseases), they were taken to a special barracks; it was surrounded by barbed wire, and there were almost no nurses, healthy prisoners, or trained personnel to take care of them. In its high-fever stage, typhus leaves the patient too weak and sick to feed him or herself. Many D.P.s died from this neglect.

The Allied soldiers were not totally insensitive to the plight of the survivors. They brought with them their own supplies of food and rations, which they freely gave to the D.P.s, but the foods were fat and rich, too fat and rich for the survivors' digestive systems. After extended starvation, the body must be built up again gradually. In a colossal medical misfeasance that compounded the tragedy of the Holocaust, thousands of prisoners died from food that was too rich for their weakened digestive systems.

Senator Danforth's original dates were chosen out of goodwill yet also out of ignorance of what actually happened at the liberation. By 1979, the entire liberation experience was covered with a haze of romantic nostalgia and selective memory by the survivors, who had a deep desire to identify with the American people and government. For their part, the American people were showing genuine desire to remember and commemorate the Holocaust. That goodwill enabled the commission to persuade Senator Danforth, the major sponsor, to shift the commemoration date to Yom Hashoah.

The United States follows a solar calendar; the decision to observe Yom Hashoah meant that the day of observance would shift every year (a source of confusion in the United States). But the commission concluded that Yom Hashoah had emerged as the crystallized date; there was no acceptable alternative day. Of Yom Hashoah one can say that no one accepted it but the people, but when they decided, it was decisive.

After Menachem Begin was elected Prime Minister of Israel in 1977, there was one last effort to shift the date of Yom Hashoah. In an attempt to remove the 27th of Nissan, the rabbinate proposed that Tisha B'Av be designated as the day for Holocaust commemoration; mourning for the Shoah would be incorporated into the order of that day. Begin was a nationalist with great respect for Jewish tradition. In his mind, this was a chance to uphold tradition and associate the Holocaust with all the other tragedies of Jewish history. Begin was strengthened in this approach by the active encouragement of Rabbi Joseph B. Soloveitchik, the revered leader of American modern Orthodoxy.

Rabbi Soloveitchik believed that the new memorial day would never amount to anything, especially since it was being resisted by the Orthodox. Convinced that the day would disappear in another generation (when the living survivors were gone) and fearful that the memory of the Holocaust would sink into historical oblivion with the day, Soloveitchik urged that Yom Hashoah be shifted to Tisha B'Av. In his proposal, the rabbinate would give up the Asarah B'Tevet concept, the "secularists" would give up 27 Nissan and the eternal memory of the Holocaust would be assured.

The proposal failed to be adopted. First, Soloveitchik could not deliver the right-wing Orthodox or assure that there would be important liturgical additions to Tisha B'Av that would do justice to the memory of the Shoah. Second, the organized survivors and ex-partisans were a solid phalanx against the shift. Although they were unhappy with the 27th day of Nissan, they grasped the central point: The Holocaust should not be subsumed under the rubric of the tragedies that preceded it. It was too momentous for that; it needed its own day and liturgy.

The most important factor of all was that, under the unseeing gaze of the traditional leadership, commemoration of Yom Hashoah had spread significantly in the previous decade. Holocaust consciousness was spreading in America through subterranean channels and word of mouth. In Israel, the shock of the Yom Kippur war, the experience of Israel facing the threat of destruction and (temporarily) unable to help itself, brought a new humility to Israeli self-understanding. The gap between the self-assured "super-Jew" Israeli and the passive, sheep-like Holocaust victims suddenly narrowed. Many Sabras now embraced the martyrs of the Holocaust with a new understanding of the agony and the loneliness. A new appreciation of the limits of self-help and of the courage of being a Jew blossomed. There was a surge in study of the Holocaust and commemoration of Yom Hashoah.

Had the rabbinate suggested that Tisha B'Av be the commemoration day for the Holocaust right after the war—perhaps that date might have won out. By 1977, history had passed this possibility by. Indeed, observance of Yom Hashoah among the Orthodox grew significantly in the ten years that followed. It would appear that Rabbi Soloveitchik, the master of halacha, was correct in insisting that memory must be incorporated into ritual and liturgy in order to become permanent. He only overlooked that the halacha was being shaped and was growing within the bosom of the Jewish people, without asking permission from the halachists. Yom Hashoah, like Hanukkah and Purim, seems to show that when Clal Yisrael acts properly, the halacha will eventually confim the truth.

The entire struggle over Holocaust commemoration was fought out in behavioral terms (what day shall be marked) rather than in theological terms. If one looks at the emergence of the day through a theological lens, however, a striking truth emerges: The day itself is a classic expression—I would say, proof—of the thesis of the emergence of a new cycle of Jewish history, one in which the human role in the covenant becomes even more responsible, while God becomes at once more hidden and more present. A new holy day has been added to the Jewish calendar. Most of the rabbis—the established "sacred" authority—had failed to grasp the idea of a sacred mourning day that would articulate this epoch-making event. The additional holy day was legislated by the Knesset, a "secular" institution acting under the cross-purposes of different groups, many of them secular and subject to political argument and even manipulation. The day thus came into being with few classic religious associations; it emerges as a totally "hidden" holy day, perceived as secular.

To those who grasp the context of the new cycle, Yom Hashoah fits the parameters of a holy day perfectly. The flaws and the all-too-human admixtures provide the necessary "cover" to enable the day to make a credible, persuasive statement about history, God, covenant, and meaning. A more visibly sacred day would have sharply limited credibility in the present cultural context. A formal holy day could not be accepted by many Jews. The non-observant would feel excluded by the halachic/sacred dimension; secularists would lump it into the category of fairy tale, which is their conception of religion; the Orthodox would be misled into assimilating this tragedy into the earlier ones as if nothing has been changed by the Holocaust.

Why is 27 Nissan the right day for Yom Hashoah? Had the fighters/partisans gotten their way and 15 Nissan been chosen for the commemoration, this coincidence would have negated the Passover holiday; the joy of Exodus, as it were, would have been buried under the ashes of Auschwitz. Impressing the total experience of destruction on the very day of national liberation would constitute a statement that hope is overwhelmed; redemption has been defeated by catastrophe. In effect, the Nazis would have gained a posthumous victory; their assault on Passover finally would have succeeded. Furthermore, the message would have been that identification should be made only with the fighters; all the other Jews in the Holocaust were a source of shame, their deaths best played down or forgotten. The implication would have been that the overwhelming might of the Nazis that crushed the victims and killed them beyond their capacity to resist or respond had robbed their deaths of dignity and meaning. This judgment would have been a triumph of Western values over the classic Jewish concepts of Kiddush HaShem (sanctification of God's name) through martyrdom. The idea that death is meaningful only through resistance is a plausible one but it had already been judged during the Holocaust to be wrong.

As the full extent of the Holocaust revealed itself to the captive Jews of Europe, many recognized that the concept of Kiddush HaShem, martyrdom for God's sake, might lose its significance. In the Middle Ages, Jewish martyrs had the choice of converting to Christianity and saving their lives or of consciously offering their lives rather than abandoning their God and Torah. In many cases, they had the chance to publicly witness their faithfulness and to state their defiance of those who sought to intimidate them into betrayal. During the Holocaust, however, the Nazis gave *no* choice. All Jews were killed whatever their intention, practice, or desire. Assimilated Jews and even Jews converted to Christianity were killed. Then what possible connection could there be between the nobility of martyrdom and involuntary death for a cause one does not believe in? Can this be the Nazis' final triumph, that mass death robs all death of meaning? These questions were posed to Rabbi Menachem Ziemba of Warsaw and to other rabbis.

Rabbi Ziemba and the other rabbis knew better. They ruled that any Jew who was killed because he or she was Jewish was considered to have performed Kiddush HaShem. The truth underlying this ruling is that every Jew carries the covenant in his or her very existence. Whatever the religious behavior or commitment, a Jew's existence alone is witness to God and covenant. As long as one Jew is alive, all the associations and testimony of the tradition are summoned up: One God, Messiah-is-not-yet-come, ultimately-we-shall-see-the-triumph-of-life. For this reason, the Nazis sought to destroy every last Jew. Therefore, chosen or not, each death was a statement fraught with meaning. The very need to kill the Jews is, in a way, a statement of how powerful is the message they still radiate.

A commemoration day on 15 Nissan, defined by armed resistance, would have been a betrayal of this truth of Jewish existence and death in the Holocaust. Pushed off for two weeks, the connection to armed revolt attenuated and obscured, Yom Hashoah became a day of mourning for *all* Jews who died. The modern bias for intentionality notwithstanding, despite the demand for overtly expressed defiance, all Jews who died in the Holocaust are martyrs; all witnessed with their lives and deaths. In fact, the Holocaust is increasingly revealed as the fundamental watershed in Jewish and human history after which nothing will ever be the same. It is one of those reorienting moments of Jewish history and religion when basic conceptions of God, of humanity, and of Jewish destiny shift.

As the commemoration day now stands, Passover joy is shadowed by Yom Hashoah. In effect, Passover is wounded but not destroyed, which is the truth witnessed by Jewish life after the catastrophe. (Wounding but not destroying Passover is another way of saying the covenant is broken but not defeated or replaced.)

Had the Orthodox gotten their way in the final negotiations, Yom Hashoah would have been deferred to the month of Iyar or beyond. Had that happened, there would have been no connection between Yom Hashoah and Yom Ha'Atzmaut. But, in fact, Yom Ha'Atzmaut is the fundamental response to Yom Hashoah. Now Yom Hashoah occurs one week away from Yom Ha'Atzmaut, and nothing could more profoundly capture the fundamental relationship of Holocaust and Israel than that positioning. The State of Israel is not a reward or a product or an exchange for the Holocaust; it is a response. The Jewish people responded to the total assault of death by an incredible outpouring of life. The survivors came and rebuilt their lives. Jewish life was made precious again. The great biblical symbol that, according to the prophets, would some day prove that the covenant had endured is the reestablishment and repopulation of the land of Israel.

The Jewish people moved to take power to be able to prevent a recurrence. When on July 4, 1976, at Entebbe, Jews were separated from others and taken by hijackers, set aside by their enemies to experience isolation and destruction like the European Jews, the statement of "Never again!" was made. That statement was prepared decades earlier by Jews who made the correct response to the Holocaust. When ten thousand Ethiopian Jews were rescued from hunger and sickness and death and flown to Israel in Operation Moses in 1984, the seeds of that Exodus were sown in the decision that, after the Holocaust, the Jewish people would not wait any longer to have their own state.

Yom Ha'Atzmaut is neither recompense for nor resolution of the Holocaust. The two orienting events confront each other in unrelieved dialectical tension. As long as memory and faith exist, they will continue to cast their shadow and duel for dominant effect in the mind and heart of Jewry and of the world. The two days are forever twinned, without softening the tension between destruction and redemption and without betraying the character of either event. It could not have been better orchestrated by Providence than it was.

YOM HASHOAH:
THE "BROKEN" REENACTMENT

If Yom Hashoah were to follow tradition, the classic model for historical commemoration would be reenactment of the event. But the very term reenactment illustrates the problematic nature of Yom Hashoah. Given the extremity of the Holocaust, what form of reenactment would not constitute trivialization and betrayal?

On Monday, September 7, 1942, during the Great Deportation, the Jewish workers at Army Supply II shop had to march by S.S. officers for a selection. Since only able-bodied workers were eligible to be spared to live, no children could pass muster. Indeed, "to be accompanied by a child was a sentence of death." Alexander Donat described the following scene:

> With them was Samek and his wife, and they had given their two-year-old Miriam a sedative and put her in a knapsack slung over Samek's shoulder. The column advanced slowly while up ahead the S.S. officer grandly dispensed life and death, *left* and *right, links und rechts.* In the tense silence the wails of a baby suddenly rose. The S.S. officer froze, and a thousand men and women held their breaths. A Ukranian guard ran out, plunged his bayonet several times into the knapsack from which the criminal sounds had come. In seconds the knapsack was a blood-soaked rag. *"Du dreckiger Schweinehund,"* the S.S. officer shouted indignantly, bringing his riding crop down on the ashen face of the father who had dared to try smuggling his child past. Mercifully, the Ukranian's bullet put an end to the father's ordeal, then and there . . .
>
> Adek, Samek, and their wives were only three ranks away from the S.S. men at that point. All the blood drained from Samek's face, but his wife was stronger at that moment. . . . "Take off the knapsack!" she hissed. As if in a trance, he did so and without losing his place in the ranks, he . . . edged over to the end of the row of marchers and carefully deposited the knapsack on the curb. It took no more than a fraction of a minute. Then he went back to his original place, eyes vacant.*

What reenactment could do justice to that scene?

Like a force field that reorients everything in its range, the Holocaust forces us to admit the inadequacies of standard judgment categories— our framework of comprehension is shattered.

Given the impossibility of proper reenactment, the liturgical model must accept its limitations and strive for modest, partial encounter with the event—a broken reenactment, if you will. There have been suggestions for an evening service of total silence or even a "speech fast day"—total silence for an entire twenty-four hours. Thus far, how-

*Alexander Donat, *Holocaust Kingdom: A Memoir* (New York: Holt, Rinehart and Winston, 1963), p. 91.

ever, the community has felt a need for words, prayers, and songs. A fragmentary retelling of the story seems to be the most appropriate form for a broken reenactment.

Most of the commemoration programs have taken place by day. In America, in the past, this has led to shifting the day to the nearest Sunday because it is difficult for people to miss work during the week. But as observance of the day has strengthened, the practice of shifting has been increasingly challenged. Offsetting this "loss" of Sunday has been a growth in observance of the Shabbat that precedes Yom Hashoah as a second Shabbat Zachor—a Shabbat of Remembrance. Shabbat Zachor II is more than a check to the mood of freedom and euphoria of the month of Nissan; it turns the Jewish mind toward moral realism, tough policy analysis, and confrontation with the evil unleashed as well as the heavy losses brought about by the Holocaust.

Most Yom Hashoah ceremonies in the United States have been held in the late afternoon, after work; however, many synagogues hold services the night before in accordance with the Hebrew calendar in which night precedes day. For some Orthodox synagogues, the form follows the regular evening prayer service, adding perhaps a Psalm such as Psalm 83 ("Lord, do not be silent . . . for your enemies rage. . . . They say let us go and wipe them out as a people, that the name Israel not be remembered anymore"). This is followed by a lecture or film on the Holocaust. Other synagogues have found the tension between a traditional service and the annihilation of life in the Holocaust too great to bear and have avoided any traditional service.

Nor is there an agreed division of the tone of the evening and of the day: Should the mood be the same? Or should an attempt be made to capture two different facets of memory at different times? Some have suggested that the night program focus on the tragedy and the day on the response of resistance and re-creation of life. One problem with the division is that, except for Orthodox Jews, most people are not accustomed to attending full-day holy day commemorations. To divide the memory is to risk the likelihood that some will encounter only one-half of the experiences that Yom Hashoah seeks to communicate and would be left with a one-sided, even distorted, experience.

THE RITUALS OF MEMORY

The single most widespread ritual observance is the lighting of memorial candles for the six million. This practice is well–nigh universal. Candles have a long history as memorial lights and as symbols of life. In a day that started with no inherited form, how powerful is the religious spirit that instantly picked out a symbol so totally rooted in tradition yet so contemporary. In most ceremonies, six candles are lit, one for each million. Survivors, when present, are asked to do the lighting.

In some communities, seven candles are lit, thereby linking up to the ancient menorah symbolism. The seventh candle has been designated differently in various communities. Some have honored righteous Gentiles who died in the Shoah trying to help Jews; some paid tribute to the righteous Gentiles whether or not they died; some have lit the light in memory of non-Jewish victims (for example, gypsies and Poles killed in Auschwitz). Inclusion of non-Jewish victims has been criticized as a dilution of the Jewish character of the Holocaust, an attempt to evade the uniqueness of the Nazis' demonic decision to wipe out every last Jew. The critics point out that mass killings of other groups were connected to "rational" objectives (killing of political opposition, annihilation of Russian POWs, genocide of Polish intelligentsia). In this view, the evil of such crimes should not be mitigated but they should not be lumped together with the "final solution" of the Jewish problem, whose total nature defied logic, economic advantage, and even military need.

The matter is complicated and highly emotional. There is a danger of so stressing the uniqueness of the Holocaust that it is turned into a solipsistic event with no consequences or meanings for others. Excess in interpretation can even turn talk of the Shoah into a covert claim of superiority (I suffer, therefore I am better than you). On balance, legitimate use of analogies and comparisons to other events is possible, although the distinctions must be kept clear, perhaps even underscored, at such moments.

When the President's Commission on the Holocaust created the first American national civic commemoration of the Holocaust in the rotunda of the Capitol in 1979, Yom Hashoah that year occurred on the same date as the communal day of mourning for the Armenian victims of Turkish genocide in 1915–17. The coincidence of this date appeared to the commission staff as providential, especially since the Turkish government has continued to vigorously deny the crime even as a growing number of so-called revisionists have sought to deny the facticity of the Shoah. The rotunda ceremony used a traditional seven-branch menorah; six candles were lit by survivors in memory of the six million, while "Ani Maamin" —the melody of faith widely sung in the ghettoes—was sung. This followed such program elements as Kaddish, the singing of the "Partisans' Hymn," and words about Jewish fate in the Holocaust. At the end of the ceremony, an Armenian minister was invited to light a seventh candle in memory of other victims of the Nazis and of other victims of genocide around the world. He also recited a traditional Armenian prayer for the dead. Elie Wiesel's closing words then followed: "Let us remember the heroes of Warsaw, the martyrs of Treblinka, the children of Auschwitz. They fought alone, they suffered alone, but they did not die alone, for something in all of us died with them."

To the commission staff, the seventh candle was an appropriately distinguished analogy, particularly since the end result was a seven-branched fully lit menorah. Lessons were drawn from the Holocaust as to the need for human solidarity and the indivisibility of responsibility, lest the bystander be guilty of complicity. Thus, the Holocaust, a uniquely Jewish tragedy, shed a penetrating if baleful light on the moral condition of humanity and, hopefully, moved people to responsibility. Thus the Holocaust was at once particularly Jewish and universal in its implications. However, the inclusion and associations were sharply criticized by a number of figures important in Holocaust commemoration in the State of Israel. The issues of universality and particularity in the Holocaust remain unresolved—as they should—since the two polar positions are in dynamic tension within Judaism itself.

MENORAH

Any time there are multiple candles in a lighting ceremony, the situation calls for a menorah. Scholars believe that the biblical menorah is a stylized tree in tandem with fire; it can be compared to a burning bush. What could be a more appropriate symbol for suffering, dying, and yet persisting than a "bush burning in the flames, yet the bush is not consumed"?

Both continuity and discontinuity with past liturgical/theological models are present in the emerging Yom Hashoah liturgies. It is too early to tell which approach will emerge as the dominant one. History points to the suitability of the menorah as a vehicle of such conflict and development.

Originally, the menorah was a religious appurtenance in the Tabernacle and in the Temple. When the first Temple was destroyed, the relics of the candelabra were almost lost. The prophet Ezekiel appears to have despaired that there would ever again be a menorah, for he omits it from his Third Temple prophecy. The menorah was rebuilt in the Second Temple, but then candle lighting was all but extirpated when the Greeks took over. After the Maccabee triumph, the menorah was revived. Later, the menorah was extended in the form of an eight-branched candelabra and used to light the candles of the Hanukkah victory.

The precedent of Jewish history suggests that a menorah to hold the lights of Yom Hashoah will emerge. The candelabra will probably be different, presumably six rather than eight branches. Forty years ago, Yad Vashem leadership sought to commission a menorah for the home and for public display. Because the resultant design was both aesthetically disappointing and impractical, the model chosen for the home totally failed in acceptance. It had only one light and could not accommodate the universal preference for six memorial lights. It used a special oil that was messy and hard to get. Not surprisingly, this ungainly menorah simply disappeared.

The leadership of Yad Vashem should have admitted their aesthetic limitations and released the concept of a menorah for the Shoah as a challenge to the legendary creative talents of the Jewish people. Aesthetic freedom paved the way for the incredible variety and ubiquitous presence of Hanukkah menorahs in Jewish homes. Instead, the leadership has continued to insist that its own patented communal model be used everywhere, thus more or less writing off the home as a locus for commemoration. Yet the home is typically the most important setting for deep Jewish experiences; there, even simple ceremonies carry great resonance. (In one Israeli kibbutz, people cut six flowers from their gardens and placed them in a vase to make a simple but moving statement of loss and memory.)

Some years ago the Holocaust Liturgy Project of Zachor (the Holocaust commemoration center of CLAL) proposed an international contest for the creation of an appropriate menorah for the home. One member of the project task force was Abba Kovner, the legendary organizer of the Vilna ghetto uprising who went to Israel after World War II. During his life in Israel, Kovner played a unique role as a poet, philosopher, and educator in the areas of Jewish history and values with particular reference to the Holocaust. At Kovner's suggestion, the project was redefined as the creation of a ritual object for commemoration in the home, thus leaving open the possibility that someone might create not a menorah but some other appropriate symbol. Kovner himself raised the possibility of a quasi-mezuzah. Just as a mezuzah is placed on a doorpost in traditional homes, so perhaps some object could be created to be placed on the door. Alternatively, the object could be placed in that spot in every home that the Rabbis proposed be left unfinished in memory of the destruction of the Temple.

As Yom Hashoah grows in acceptance, the new menorah awaits its creator, one who will design a model that will take its rightful place in every Jewish home and public place. When that menorah comes, it will be a reaffirmation of the Rabbi Israel Salanter's dictum: When darkness surrounds one, it cannot be fought; but even a little bit of light drives off darkness.

EVENING SERVICE:
TOWARD A MEGILLAH
FOR THE SHOAH

Beyond the candle lighting, the model of the evening commemoration has not yet been set. There have been two published attempts to create a major text that could serve as a Megillah, a scroll to retell the story, paralleling the Lamentations scroll that is read on Tisha B'Av. The first was created in 1971 by David Roskies (at the age of twenty-three!). It is called *Night Words* and was presented as "a midrash on the Holocaust" rather than as a scroll.* It might better be described as an order of service for the evening of Yom Hashoah. However, the material is drawn with such scope, integrity, and power that it can serve as a Megillah. *Night Words* requires a quorum of thirty-six men and women as readers. Of the thirty-six, three roles are extensive enough to require preparation. As participants enter, they line up in a row and relinquish their shoes to the ushers. Participants sit on the floor, and roles are distributed at random by the ushers. Then a stunning palimpsest is unfolded: excerpts from the Bible, modern Hebrew and Yiddish poetry, material culled from sources that include Kafka, Kazantzakis, and Kierkegaard, as well as a central, striking selection of Holocaust accounts.

The entire service is marked by extraordinary moments. Examples are the Ritual of the Number, in which one person inscribes numbers from A81173 to A81209 on the left arms of the participants—these are taken from the first thirty-six numbered prisoners sent to their deaths on March 19, 1945, in Auschwitz; the Reading of the Scroll, in which an account adapted from the chronicle of the Chemielnitsky massacres of the seventeenth century is almost seamlessly intertwined with accounts of Einsatzgruppen activity, underscoring the continuity of Jewish tragedy; the Ritual of Tearing, in which the *hazan* (cantor) rips an article of clothing, as is customary when mourning the dead; an "Amidah" prayer in which eighteen counter-blessings illuminate the shattering effect of the Holocaust on traditional affirmations; and the Halitsah, the Ritual of the Shoes, in which ancient sacred acts and rituals race after Holocaust events in a phantasmagoric parade of scenes that include the shoes of the victims by the thousands.

The effects of *Night Words* are frequently achieved by juxtaposition of a classical source and a Holocaust testimony that reverses—or deepens—the traditional model. Thus, the Akedah, Binding of Isaac, as hauntingly retold by Kierkegaard, is recited contrapuntally with the testimony of a nurse who survived the Einsatzgruppen shootings outside of Vilna, until the Akedah is finally overwhelmed by the account of the massacre at Ponar. In a section called "Mattan Torah: Revelation," the incomprehensibility and the cruelty of evil are revealed as the selection platform in Auschwitz is built (in words of testimony) to oppose the construction of the Tabernacle/Holy Temple. *Night Words* ends with a roll call of labor and death camps and ghettoes in counterpoint to classical praises of God and, significantly, a final Kaddish.

*David Roskies, *Night Words: A Midrash on the Holocaust* (Washington, D.C.; B'nai Brith Hillel Foundations, 1971).

The ending is significant because Kaddish is at once a prayer for the dead and a prayer for God's kingdom. It is an affirmation of hope and, by implication, of resurrection—even as it summons up the reality of death. The Kaddish is really a survivor's prayer; the one who lives on states that he or she has not yielded to this victory of death and will carry on for those who have fallen with the goal unreached. Out of fear that a prayer overcoming death is too "easy" and perhaps premature or superficial, Rabbi Ichiel Poupko has proposed that the Kaddish not be recited altogether. Poupko has thought deeply about Holocaust liturgy. However, his theologically profound views have been overruled by Clal Yisrael, which determined that all Jews are survivors who must say Kaddish for their lost, near and dear relatives.

The main weakness of Night Words is that it has not been widely adopted. Part of the reason may be lack of sponsorship. Another factor might be that the midrash takes an hour and a half to read. While the Orthodox night service for Tisha B'Av runs close to that length, many Jews today are impatient at any service of that duration. Night Words incorporates both Yiddish and Hebrew, which is difficult for some people, and its surrealistic style may be hard on those who are used to a more literal mode. One guesses that its polarities and tensions, although authentic to the mood of Holocaust memory, may be too jarring for most.

The other major effort, *Megillat Hashoah* (Scroll of the Holocaust), was compiled in 1976 by Albert H. Friedlander. Directly modeled on the scroll of Eicha (Lamentations), Megillat Hashoah seeks to follow the Tisha B'Av model. The book is five chapters long, as is Lamentations. As in Eicha, there is no narrative line, only a series of laments and vignettes, mostly drawn from personal accounts of the Holocaust. Among the memorable scenes are Elie Wiesel's unforgettable portrait of the hanging of the little child in Auschwitz and Alexander Donat's heartbreaking account of the child who skipped away from his mother and fell into the roundup for Treblinka. Each chapter opens and closes with a verse from one of the five biblical scrolls; these verses are correlated to the rest of the accounts quoted in that chapter. Since Rabbi Friedlander lives in England, this piece has been used primarily in that country. Megillat Hashoah has some very powerful excerpts but lacks the extraordinary tensions and shrieks that make Night Words so riveting and devastating. The antiphonal readings, alternating between congregation and reader, are more conventional in structure, and the chapters include many poems. (While the liturgy chooses from the very best poems written about the catastrophe, one is reminded of Theodor Adorno's protest that there can be no more poetry after Auschwitz.)

As this book is being written, two major new attempts to create a fundamental document for recounting the Holocaust are under way.

The first is *Megillot Ha-Edut* (Scrolls of Testimony), an extraordinary retelling of the story of the Holocaust. The Megillot were written by Abba Kovner and substantially edited by him before his untimely death. While there are some incomplete sections and Kovner's extensive commentary on the text (in the shape of a Talmud) was not totally realized, the Megillot are a liturgical masterpiece.*

Kovner did not specify how he intended Megillot Ha-Edut to be used. They are labeled "a reader . . . for the individual, the family, the community." Clearly he sought to write a foundation work for the liturgy and ritual of remembering the Holocaust. Kovner was so suffused with the texts, language, and models of the tradition that he was able to evoke past paradigms of liturgy and memory in the process of writing a chronicle of the greatest tragedy in Jewish history. Yet the anthology is too long to be read in its entirety in any normal service. Possibly he intended that sections be read aloud during Yom Hashoah services and the entire text be studied over the course of the year or read during extended study sessions such as *layl shimurim*—all-night seminars (see below).

The Megillot Ha-Edut brilliantly solve a number of conundrums that tax the capacity to commemorate the Holocaust appropriately. As Gershom Scholem has pointed out: In the past, historical events in themselves have not shaped Jewish values and liturgy as much as the midrashic or folk representation of these events. One of the great moments of the classic Yom Kippur liturgy—the Ten Martyrs, which makes up the martyrology section—is a legendary account of the death of ten of the greatest Rabbis of the Mishnah. The killings are telescoped, interwoven with the legend, and brought together for dramatic unity—as if all the Rabbis were executed at the same time and by a coherent plan. Another version of the Ten Martyrs story is a highlight of the Tisha B'Av Kinot. Even though the two stories differ on the facts of what happened, both have been taken to heart by the folk; both play central roles in the liturgical life of their respective holy days.

However, in dealing with the Holocaust, embellishment is offensive. To try to make the burning of children into the stuff of edifying drama would be morally repugnant; to accomplish it, the writer would have to achieve a clinical detachment more appropriate for cold-blooded, indifferent bystanders.

Any attempt to turn the nakedness of defenseless mothers into emotional currency would more likely end up in exploitation and sleaze than in transfiguration. Imaginary scenes from the Holocaust have already been used for purposes of pornography or to give

---

*The Hebrew text of Megillot Ha-Edut will be published by Mossad Bialik in Israel in 1989.

pseudo-depth to standard literature. As it is, anti-Semites, unrepentant Nazis, and revisionists driven by hatred wait in the wings to deny the factual truth of the most demonically planned and most heavily documented crime of history. Any imaginative addition to the facts, even if well intentioned, could be "refuted" and then used to undercut the credibility of the actual record.

On the other hand, objectivity is a misleading category in dealing with the Holocaust. The testimony of survivors during and after the Holocaust, which is normally the most reliable source, must be translated and transposed. Survivors' testimony is not only necessarily limited by their partial view of what happened, it is also biased, colored by their own perceived guilt. These innocent victims, the survivors, feel guilty for having survived, whereas many murderers or indifferent bystanders are girded with a sense of their own "innocence." This paradoxical fact colors all accounts of the Shoah. Since most of the records and the pictures of the Holocaust were kept by the Nazis and their allies, anyone who presents the actual historical record as it has been received may be presenting the Nazis' approved version. What the Nazis left out may be part of their total war on the Jews. Thus, Raul Hilberg's masterwork on the killing process, *The Destruction of the European Jews*, based on the Nazi records, understates the actual record of Jewish resistance and dignity during the Holocaust. Furthermore, some historical treatments convert these events—so powerful that to touch them is to risk emotional electrocution—into a routine recounting that domesticates the radical cruelty and betrays the actual suffering. Sometimes the net effect of a conventional study is to make these awful behaviors more acceptable and more doable.

The decision to write five Megillot clearly reflects the fact that there are altogether five Megillot in the Hebrew Bible. Of the biblical scrolls, only one, *Eicha*, is focused on destruction, namely, the destruction of the First Temple. The implicit message is that the Holocaust goes beyond the destruction of the Temple in its vastness, intensity, and implications. Unlike Albert H. Friedlander's *Megillat Hashoah*, whose five-chapter structure imitates Eicha, Kovner's account parallels all five scrolls in extent but none of them in structure. (Note also that Kovner's title is Megillot Ha-Edut—Scrolls of Testimony; less is more.) Just as the Shoah is at once overwhelmingly continuous and totally distinctive from past tragedies, so are the Megillot Ha-Edut in relation to the ages-old historical narratives that make up Jewish sacred literature. In literary sophistication and narrative technique, in the portraits of individuals, in unrelenting impact, the Megillot are inescapably modern and post-modern; in unadorned account, in fablelike simplicity, in the elements of witness and testimony, they come right out of the ancient world of saga in whose midst the Bible record emerged and in whose nimbus it speaks. The Megillot beg to be read aloud, to be chanted, to be encountered, to have Midrashim written about them.

Since the scrolls have not yet been published or even made available to the Jewish people or its liturgists, it is too early to speculate how they will be used or what standing they will achieve. One encouraging sign is that they were commissioned by the Memorial Foundation for Jewish Culture whose endowment was created out of reparations payments for victims of the Shoah; its board represents one of the broadest cross-sections of organizations and communities in Jewish life. The foundation was established to support the re-creation of Jewish cultural life as well as Holocaust scholarship and commemoration. Morally, then, this is an appropriate auspice for an attempt at creating a post-Holocaust, post-modern sacred scripture.

On the other hand, can any primary national chronicle of such a catastrophe, cosmic and transforming in its implications, carry anyone's personal signature? The prophets who were seen as pure channels of divine communication were allowed to have their names on the books of their collected works. But post-Pentateuchal Scriptural narratives of tragedy and triumph in history are presented anonymously as chronicles. Then what individual can be associated by name with the "canonical" account of the experience of the people who incarnate the divine presence in history?

The Megillot Ha-Edut

One cannot plunge *in media res* the world of Auschwitz any more than one can stand before the soaring flames of Sinai again without being gradually ushered in. Therefore, the first Megillah begins with an *Akdamot* (introductory poem), to be spoken silently before reading the Megillah.

Thus says the author:
This Megillah is different from all other Megillot. In all other Megillot
   we draw up memory from the well of what
occurred to our ancestor in generations of old,
This megillah brings forth that which occurred to our
   fathers and to us in the generation of Auschwitz.

*Thus says the murdered Jewish people, whether by silence or by speech, to
the living Jewish people:*
You who were not able to save us, bend your ear and heart
to our testimony; it is the remnant of life:
Try to understand what destruction is, and these were

the things that strengthened
our spirit in moments of separation;

. . .

Thus says the Megillah to the reader:
Do not view this testimony as inspiration to hatred. By the waters of
    Europe
there we sat and we wept on our queue to be murdered.
    At the feet of the crematoria chimneys

e v e n   t h e r e

we snatched at scorched fragments of time and we reflected
    on the future
as we thought of you.

Do you have a free moment of time to think of us, we who are
innocent of crime and free of shame?

The introduction that follows asserts that in every generation, humanity's evil urges burst forth. History is full of mass murders, from ancient tribal enmities to the Mongol massacres, from medieval holy wars to extirpation of the Indians and the Armenian genocide. All the rivers of blood run to the sea, and the sea of death flows around the Old World and the New World, the evangelistic world and the third world, and flows back again. Yet the Holocaust is an organized annihilation whose equal the human race has not seen. This was neither the rampage of rabble nor the desperate revenge of the oppressed; this was no atrocity driven by religious frenzy or revolutionary fervor that would stop at nothing. This was total extermination of a people undertaken by government decision, pursued day and night without pause for holy day or exception for age or gender or health or locale. This was carried out as a policy overriding all other considerations in the high noon of the twentieth century.

The last introduction is written and laid out in a style that evokes the Book of Esther. Its enumeration of the hunting groups:—"The S.S. and the S.A. and the S.D. and the Gestapo. And the Einsatzgruppen and the Hitler Jugend. And the Wehrmacht... and the 'blue' police of the Poles... and the Lithuanian Fatingas... and the Vichyites in France; and the Nazis in Austria and Mussolini's Fascists in Italy... and in Rumania... Iron Guard... and in Hungary... Arrow Cross; and the Ustashis..."—at once summons up the ten sons of Haman and the list of unclean birds of prey in Leviticus.

The preface tells the story of the Holocaust as a historical chronicle from the beginning of Hitler's reign through segregation and exclusion; from mass shootings to ghettoization and roundups; from forced labor and gassings to pulling gold teeth and burning bodies; from mass transports in cattle cars to death marches. Jewish response is portrayed: from the self-deceptive patriotism of German and Italian Jews to the denials of reality by Hungarian and Polish Jews arriving at the gates of Auschwitz; from the persistence of teachers who taught children in the face of death to the tenacity of those who collected and wrote down accounts of life in the face of oblivion.

The Scrolls of Testimony then turn to the telling of the tale. The first Megillah is called Introductions: Counting Retrospectively, or the Corridor of Lost Choices. This Megillah focuses on Jews of Germany and the Baltic states. In a *parshah* [portion] entitled: The Man Who Is Being Beheaded Continues to Hope, a German-Jewish father writes to his son abroad. In a series of letters, the father, who runs the Jewish orphans' home in Dinslachen, describes the deterioration of the Jewish condition, culminating in the Kristallnacht pogrom. The burning of the synagogue and roundup of Jews being shipped to Dachau climaxes in a humiliating beating of one Hugo Cohn, a distinguished veteran of World War I. Before the Nazi era, Cohn was given a place of honor at all patriotic public occasions since he is the only possessor of the Iron Cross, First Class, in Dinslachen. "Jew swine! Where did you steal this medal of honor?" swears the S.S. man who sets upon him for daring to wear this cross when the Jews are paraded through the streets on the way to the trains.

The second and third Megillot, entitled "By the Rivers of the Four Lands," capture the experience of Jews in Poland and Lithuania. These scrolls include two unforgettable portraits. One *parshah*, "The Journeys of Devorah from Kalisch," tells of a young woman whose wanderings take her from refugee flight to love and life in Warsaw, and a fighting death in the Warsaw ghetto uprising. The other portrait, of a young man named Saul, contains not a little of Kovner's own experiences. Saul recalls many things: scenes from a childhood in a living Jewish community, memories of everyday life suffused with the glow of holiness, and nostalgia of hairbreadth escapes from Nazis and service with partisans. His reveries are full of searing images: months of living hidden in a convent, narrow escapes accompanied by death on all sides, survival in the merciless forest, first amid hostile anti-Semitic partisans and then among fellow Jewish fighters.

The fourth Megillah, "Does Birkenau Exist?" includes a cluster of personal accounts by a group of prisoners in the seventh block at Auschwitz. Block Seven was the last step before the gas chambers, yet these inmates have retained their humanity and Jewish dignity. They include Rafael Habib, rabbi of Solonika, Greece, who survived the original selection by passing as a stevedore; Gundar Redlich, a Czechoslovakian halutz who set up children's schools in Theresienstadt;

and Natan Cassuto, member of the traditionalist branch of an aristocratic, assimilating Italian Jewish family. He is an ophthalmologist who
turned to serving as a rabbi after he was expelled from the government
clinic in which he worked. Each life portrait is indelibly etched. They are
paradigmatic of the entire Jewish experience, yet they have the rawness
and textured quality of life rather than of literary artifice. One gets a
sense of the overflowing tide of evil and the infinite sands of suffering,
the countless daily acts of love and heroism, and the abandonments and
despair that make up the mosaic of existence in the Holocaust. The
Megillot tackle incredibly difficult themes with feeling and dignity.

One major section of the fifth Megillah, "The Death March," was
planned, but the pen was thrust from Abba's hand by death before he
could write it. The final *parshah* captures life with the Jewish partisans
without romanticizing; it even projects the postwar *bricha* (illegal immigration) to Israel (then Palestine) and the cruel British war against
the survivors and their deportation to Cyprus.

While no account of these Megillot can do justice to them, three
remarkable characteristics must be cited. The first is the use of words
as recurrent, narrative themes. Studded through the verses of the Megillot are hundreds of motif words that summon up biblical or other
classic texts. Each association refracts the light and mirrors meanings
back and forth between the present text and the classic source. This
word method is used in the Hebrew Bible to give multivalent meanings and interpretive interactions among many different narratives
in the Tanach (Hebrew Scriptures). Rabbinic Midrash and modern Hebrew literature have also walked in these footsteps. In the Scrolls of
Testimony, such words give depth to the field of vision in each scene
and add layers of historical meaning to every event. Thus, the language depicts the uniqueness of the moment and simultaneously reveals it to be the enactment of a repetitive scene from Jewish history.

Because the Hebrew language uniquely carries these overtones, it is
almost impossible to capture this effect in translation. A few examples
may give an inkling: In a reverie by a partisan on Jewish isolation:
"Scholars will research and retroactive wise men will ask: *how solitary
sits the people between the walls, crying out in her blood and she has none to
hear her?"* (Compare Lamentations 1, 1.) Describing a party guided by
a youthful Italian informer, about to seize Natan Cassuto: "The Italian
officer, Mario Gezini, Schurer Von Maria (?), a German officer and a
little Fascist child leads them." (Compare the classic messianic scene in
Isaiah 11: 6.)

In a scene depicting the life-endangering lashing of a prisoner for
the "crime" of wearing tefillin in Auschwitz, the beating count is represented as follows: *one and two, one and three, one and four*—evoking
the classic liturgical retelling of the High Priest's repeated sprinklings

during the Yom Kippur purification rite in the Holy of Holies. A Jewish woman, reflecting on the unceasing evils visited on the head of Lithuanian Jewry, recites a reverse dayyenu (the Seder prayer that recounts God's overflowing miracles): "If only my daughter was in captivity among the Lithuanians but this war had not come upon us, dayyenu! (It were enough!) If only the war had come upon us and the wicked Polish government had been pushed aside, but the Soviet tyranny had not come unto us, dayyenu! If only the Soviet tyranny had come but our big and beautiful house had not been burned down, dayyenu!" Hundreds of such passages in the five Megillot are weaved into a seamless web with the classic sources of the past.

The second characteristic is the Megillot's incorporation of a torrent of unforgettable vignettes so overwhelming in their repeated impact as to suddenly make real the classic Jewish outcry *in extremis*, "The waters have risen to [the point of drowning] the soul!" In every aspect of the Holocaust, Kovner has found the telling detail that releases the flood of our emotions; hear the story of Big Leo, a defiant Jewish orphan in Dinslachen. When an anti-Semitic teacher enters for the first time, the Nazi pompously introduces himself: "My name is Lewin, but I am not of the Mosaic race." Big Leo (in a stage whisper): "Thank God that until now we had no ass in this class." The teacher calls him up and slaps his face. Without hesitation, Big Leo returns the teacher's slap forcefully. After Kristallnacht, he is sent to the camps. The Megillot portrays the constant search for the right category to protect from selection and the constant German shifts and reversals: "Every detail of personal data seemed to be absolutely fateful—age, gender, profession, refugee status, or being a son of Germany. But no one really knew which detail would decree his fate on the day of judgment."

The text continually reveals the shattering event that breaks down all routine, smashes defenses, and breaks the heart. A thousand scenes haunt the mind:

the Italian Jews, facing a roundup, who know that "it can't happen here";

two Jewish children, accepted and hidden in a convent on condition that they not make trouble, who refuse to eat pork or deny their name;

Berel Lopatin, the Judenrat head who refuses to send one hundred Jews to an unknown—but really known—fate . . . and the Nazis back down;

Berel Lopatin sent to the shooting pits with his people;

a devoted Jewish father, suddenly destroyed by the announcement that two hundred able-bodied men including him will be spared but the other six thousand ghetto Jews will be selected, ignores the permission to go home and walks on to the line of life without going to say good-bye to his wife and family;

a starving young girl hides the body of her four-year-old brother (who died of hunger) under her bed for a week so she can use his ration card—until she is felled by the smell;

a father pulls out his own gold-crowned teeth to barter for life-giving medicine for his son;

the Germans save the lives of a couple who have slashed their own wrists and then send them to the shooting pits—to establish the principle that the Germans decide when Jews live and when Jews die;

the inebriated feeling of the Vilna ghetto group that has just decided to organize and fight;

the feelings of guilt and betrayal that assail those who must leave their parents behind to go to the forest to fight;

the boy, sentenced to a few lashes for performing a religious act, who refuses to cry out, so the blows are heaped on, up to fifty lashes; afterward, close to death, he wearily says: It was worth it;

a prisoner in Block Seven who sings an El Maleh Rachamim— prayer for the dead—that at once defies humans and God;

two brothers working as a team are caught smuggling an extra piece of bread; each vies to convince the sadistic S.S. supervisor that *he* is the one who did it; the officer scornfully kills them both for daring to have courage at such a moment.

If divine inspiration is proven by power rather than by sponsorship, then this is holy writ.

Finally, an authentic Megillah for the Holocaust should capture the experience of every kind of Jew. Only then can it speak to and for Clal Yisrael—the unity and totality of the Jewish people. Megillah Ha-Edut is marked by a sensitive understanding of the existential unity of the Jews, a oneness rooted in their common fate. Just such awareness appears as a thread that runs through all the portions of the scrolls.

From the historical introduction: "As one they were marched on the roads, bare heads* and shtraimel-wearers,† those that fastened their kaputas** with three buttons and those that took pains that they not lack, God forbid, the fourth button required by yet another [Chasidic] court. When suddenly they were joined by those who recently arrived, hat wearers from Amsterdam and among the deportees from Budapest even a real top hat bobbed up, they neither laughed nor were surprised; for, after all, they saw the general pile to which all the hats and caps and berets go." Scenes:

An observant family takes four young road-weary, dirty, blood-

---

*Secular Jews normally go with head uncovered.
†Chasidim wear a special circular fur hat called a shtraimel.
**A kaputa is a special long black frock worn by Chasidic and some other ultra-Orthodox groups.

stained secular halutzim into their Sabbath meal without asking any questions:

Samuel, a halutz on the way to Palestine, walks from Warsaw to Kovel where he faints from exhaustion, and the religious family that rescues him finds that he has wrapped a Zionist flag around himself under his shirt in order to save it from the Nazi. "Some carry tzitzit (fringes) on their body and some carry a flag," says the father. "These and those sanctify God's name," whispers the mother;

The orphans' home in Cracow was an "institution, to our regret, where they taught equally, in the two languages of the Jews, Yiddish and Hebrew; they even sang together 'Kinneret,'* and 'Oifn Pripit-chuk't and no one was harmed";

Dolek, a Zionist underground movement leader, "organizes" and trades for wax to provide Sabbath candles for a group of his erstwhile women comrades who hold an Oneg Shabbat (Sabbath celebration ceremony) every Friday night in Auschwitz; Dolek is taken to his death; for weeks, Elli, a young fair-haired assimilated boy from Paris whom Dolek has befriended, trades his own bread to provide the candles for these women he has never met, until his own death;

Two children of a deported Italian rabbi are placed in a convent and absorbed into its life; during the battle for liberation of the area, one of the boys, nine years old, is sent to get water; dodging bullets, he bumps into Eliyahu Klatzkin, a member of Hashmer Hatzair and a hard-core secularist serving in the British army; the boy sees the Star of David on Eliyahu's dog tag and whispers, "Shma Yisrael"; Eliyahu recovers the two orphans and returns them to their family;

Rudy, the assimilated communist Jew, organizes the underground in Buchenwald; he steals food and medicine for the newly arrived Polish Jews and rallies their spirits "with the exact same words that Natan Cassuto, the rabbi of Florence, used to raise morale at Auschwitz: not to surrender. Jews are forbidden to yield to the evil. Victory will come"; Rudy is executed, and that night his comrades mourn him, singing the "Red Flag" hymn. When the head of the cell asks if someone knows how to say Kaddish, a youngster from the Hiechalutz Halochem (The Fighting Halutz) from Cracow is the only one who knows how, so he recites it.

There is an incredible level of empathy in the Megillot which enables Kovner, with the wisdom of years, to present every experience with an understanding that surpasses understanding. Time and time again the Megillot pass up the easy victory of hindsight to see the deeper dignity of those who lived in the reality of that planet, Shoah. How easy it

---

*A popular Zionist song of longing for the Lake of Galilee.
†A popular Yiddish folk song about the alphabet.

would have been to mock the patriotism of Hugo Cohn who marches to the train for Dachau wearing his Iron Cross. But even as he described the rain of blows on Cohn's head, Kovner captures the majesty of the man: "But he continued to march head high; this was, as it were, the final military parade." Kovner, who in his youth authored the famous stinging critique, "Do not go as sheep to the slaughter," designed to goad the ghetto into resistance, now can tell a tale of those Judenrasts with compassionate understanding. "It is not one of the easy tasks to be the leader of the Jews at such a time. A person awakens in the morning and finds that he is the representative of the Jews before Nazis and representative of the Nazis before his brothers, his people." In these pages, thousands go on death marches, thousands walk to the gas chambers. We are so deeply within their world that we live it and understand it and embrace it; we are not able to step outside of that world and falsely judge it. Nor are there any easy escapes into blaming it all on modernity. Nor is there any explaining away of the Holocaust as an atavistic reversion to barbarism. "Explain to me, how did it happen? In enlightened Europe in the high noon of the twentieth century, how could it happen?" asks one person. "It happened because we did not believe it could happen," answers his friend.

The account of the Megillot ends with the Israeli captain of an illegal immigration ship lecturing the passengers about the dangers of the forthcoming journey into a hostile sea filled with blockading enemy ships. He offers them a last chance to debark and seek asylum in another land.

Do we not read here Kovner's prophetic call to the Jewish people who have now embarked on a historic voyage to freedom and power over the stormy seas of history? Sailing in waters as uncharted and unknown as the oceans were to the pioneering discoverers of new worlds in the fifteenth and sixteenth centuries, facing trackless seas filled with monsters more dangerous than the feverish imaginations of medieval superstition could have conjured up, can this people successfully pursue the goal of creating life overflowing and a just society without being crushed by evil or warped by hatred and arrogance along the way?

The last words are those of Leo the Younger, a survivor of Germany and Eastern Europe and the forest and the camps. He turns to Saul and says: "Tell your friend there is no need to frighten us. Simply, we are Jews who are not afraid anymore. Tell him, excuse me, tell him. Please."

The author's epilogue concludes: Here end but are not completed the Scrolls of Witness. More than I read before you—is written here!" (Mishnah, Yoma, 7).*

---

*TB Yoma 68B.

The Six Days of Destruction

Another work of extraordinary promise has now been written by Elie Wiesel with Rabbi Albert H. Friedlander. Published in the United States by the American Reform movement, *The Six Days of Destruction: Meditations Toward Hope* (Paulist Press, 1988), is an attempt to create a Megillah of the Holocaust for the ages. To make it more useful for Yom Hashoah, the volume incorporates a set of liturgies developed by Rabbi Friedlander and others for Jewish and Christian communities. The liturgies are of a wide range of quality and content.

The *Six Days of Destruction* starts with one weakness and one strength that grow directly out of the fact that the text was written in Diaspora. The scroll is written in English. While some passages evoke famous biblical verses in translation and while it incorporates classic phrases and verses in Hebrew (transliteration), an English text simply cannot embody the extraordinary layers of association, memory and meaning that a Hebrew text does. Perhaps this is as it should be: By deepening impact, by summoning up the entire Jewish way at every step, the Hebrew language protects the centrality of Israel and Tanach in Jewish religion and culture.

On the other hand, the Diaspora setting means that Gentiles are "significant others" to Jews; in the State of Israel, Gentile judgments are more marginal in their impact. As a result, most Diaspora Jewish religious statements are made in the context of non-Jewish audiences as well. *Six Days* speaks directly to Gentiles and this is a real strength. In this new era, Jewish history is inescapably intertwined with general events. Jews are constantly aware that the Holocaust, so uniquely a Jewish tragedy, is nevertheless momentous in its consequences for humanity at large. In particular, many Christians have begun to wrestle with the implications of the Shoah. This includes dealing with the question of Christian responsibility for centuries of teaching contempt for Jews (those teachings which created the context of anti-Semitism which the Nazis exploited) and with the theological challenges of the catastrophe. Increasing numbers of Christians seek to incorporate Yom Hashoah or some Holocaust liturgy into the spiritual life of the church. This effort is necessary and even noble; yet it treads a path through spiritual minefields, risking dilution of the uniqueness of the Holocaust and too easy forgiveness. At its worst, it leads to religious syncretism and betrayal of the spiritual vision and solitude of the victims.

To its credit, American Reform—the Jewish movement most sensitive to interfaith concerns—has tackled this challenge head on in creating this Megillah. By choosing Elie Wiesel to write the scrolls, the movement insured that the search for universality would in no way lead to blurring the distinctive fate of the Jews or the particularity of

Judaism and its religious values. Still, the book comes complete with endorsement from such outstanding Christians as Joseph Cardinal Bernardin, the head of the National Conference of Catholic Bishops at the time that *Six Days* went to press. This very inclusion, including the joint liturgies, has the effect of placing the relationship with Christians ahead of the relationship with Orthodox Jews.* The American edition is even more denominational and less likely to be adopted by traditional Jews and by most Israelis. This is one of two question marks that loom over this extraordinary Megillah (see below).

The Megillah is structured around a classic biblical framework—the Six Days of Creation. As the account unfolds the pitiless tale of the Kingdom of Night, the face of reality peels back, revealing a world in moral reverse. In the beginning, there was life and order and beauty; but in six days the world is returned to chaos and void and darkness over the surface of the deep (see Genesis 1:2). Each day opens with verses of creation from Genesis. Each day, a prayer rises up for mercy, for life, for breathing space from the suffocating grip of death. Yet, each day we are led deeper into that realm from whose bounds no traveler emerges unscathed. Each day the truth becomes clearer and more unbearable: In this universe, death is the essential medium which all inhabit; night, not day, is the state of permanent equilibrium. One suspects that, in some future Yom Hashoah liturgy, each day's reading will wrest from the depth of each listener's soul, an unwilling but unquenchable cry that hideously parodies the biblical account and Simchat Torah's liturgical chorus—"it was day and it was night, one night."

On Day 1, in the 1930s, we meet Hava—whose name is also Bracha and Leah and Sheindl and Rosa and Feigele—who begs her husband to leave Kreinsdorf, Germany. She is afraid . . . But Baruch—whose name is also Zelig and Yaakov and Leon—has the wisdom of roots and habits, and possessions, and standing, and friends, and familiar language, and two millennia of Jewish experience. Baruch replies: "We have been afraid for two thousand years. As long as a Jew is alive and as long as he is a Jew, he is filled with fear. Is that reason enough for him to leave everything and rush into the unknown?"

Throughout the course of the account, Wiesel's insights pierce. "In those days one had to be a pessimist to survive. . . . In those days, one had to surrender to extreme despair. . . . A community does not voluntarily uproot itself overnight . . . there must be a sign, an unmistakable portent—. . . . Unfortunately, Death came far too slowly [for that]. . . . "

---

*Out of concern for this problem, Rabbi Albert H. Friedlander incorporated a letter of introduction, written by Orthodox Chief Rabbi Immanuel Jakobovits, in the English edition. Unfortunately, the letter is equivocal about the significance of the Holocaust and is unlikely to offset the sectarian atmosphere that surrounds the publication.

Daily, the noose grew tighter. "Decrees, persecution, brutality. Burned: sanctuaries, books, holy scrolls. Humiliated... Expelled... Outlawed... [Then] the Night of the Broken Glass... Organized madness. Mass arrests. Unending queues at the consulates...."

Gradually, the gates were closed. "'Where can we go?' Baruch asks himself. 'I would go anywhere.'" Wiesel's ironic counterpoint eviscerates: "Unhappily in the accursed world, there was no place with that name. No one was interested in the Jews—except the executioner."

On Day 2, through the phantasmagoric, confused reveries of a woman called Sarah, we hear the account of one family; we relive the life of a nameless ghetto and its now deported Jewish population. Sarah, wife of Romtche, mother of Berenyou, Perele, and Srelenyou, is lying in the darkness of a dugout cellar. She cannot grasp the fact that her family is gone. When the ghetto was deported, they had hidden out in this bunker, dug by a Jewish "big dealer." After five days of hiding in terror and immobility, hearing the footsteps and laughing and drinking and snoring of the Germans installed in the apartment overhead, the dealer had taken the opportunity to go out for air—for one hour. He was sighted and denounced. The Nazi assault followed swiftly. Shots... explosions... in Sarah's mind it is all blurred.

> The date of her wedding coincides with that of the birth of her first-born which coincides with the day the Germans came.... Sarah and her family celebrate the Seder with songs yet it is not Passover but Purim and the Jews are all assembled in the big square and an officer talks to them in a monotonous and murderous voice: he speaks and Death responds Amen.

As Sarah hallucinates, we experience the original relief of concentration in a Jewish ghetto with Jewish officials, Jewish authority, Jewish discipline, Jewish police, Jewish atmosphere. We feel the constriction of four families living in one miserable hovel; of Sarah, who detested immodesty, learning "to swallow it, to hold her tongue, to stare into space." Everyone changes. Berenyou, the oldest, the shy one, becomes a resourceful, aggressive food gatherer. Srelenyou, the wild daring one, full of charm, withdraws and spends his nights reading Psalms. Perele, the twelve-year-old sheltered girl, becomes active in a Zionist youth movement; she brings home advance warning of the liquidation of the ghetto.

Only Romtche, gentle, kind, thoughtful Romtche, who asked her to promise only one thing on their wedding day—"that in our house beggars will feel at ease"—is unchanged. "But lately Romtche thought only of the Messiah. He talked about him endlessly." People shook their heads; he is losing his mind, they said. Sarah defends him. "Why mad?

Because he believes in God? Because he wants to hasten Redemption? But then, good people, his madness is better than your sanity."

People lived; children studied; old men told their tales; young people flirted and made plans: to escape, to get married, to have a career. The rich got richer; the people with power had other thoughts than the mass of Jews. Finally, the family hid with the big dealer and with "Milou the fool," a real madman who shared Romtche's passion for the Messiah. In the end "Death has a thousand eyes. It is hard to deceive, hard to avoid. Death scents life, sniffs it out, draws it up and inhales it the better to snuff it out." Sarah lies in her solitude, too weak to move, pressed down under the weight of the dead "in the ghetto [which] was their communal cemetery."

On Day 3, we hear the story of a candle and of Itzikl who guarded it all his life, at the instruction of the Tzaddik of Gorobetz, of blessed memory, that it was destined to be used only for "a special occasion."

Itzikl lives in hope. "When everything seems lost forever, . . . it is then that we Jews must sanctify our hope and proclaim it in the sight of the world." When he and the neighbors are deeply shocked by an account of a mass shooting from the mouth of one who survived and returned alone, Itzikl still hopes. "Look . . . I have kept this candle to light in His honor and to illumine the way. I promise you we shall see it shine some day. . . . " And the people do believe. "As long as the candle was there, nothing would happen to them."

In the end, Itzikl and Mirele and their six hungry and exhausted children are swept up in the mass of people, pushed by the soldiers toward that place which is nameless but we know is called Ponary, Rumboli, Ninth Fort, Babi Yar . . . There: the Rabbi says Vidui (the death confession), and is rebuked by another for confessing to acting falsely when "we have not been false to God or to His Law"; the Rabbi seems to agree, yet continues to confess. There: one does not rebel because "one does not rebel against the laws of creation . . . [and] Heaven is far away." There: men removed their clothes; women, too. Whoever refused was beaten. There: Itzikl remembers, opens his tallit and tephillin bag, finds the candle, tries to light it. By the time that the last child has fallen into the pit, the candle is finally lit . . . truly a special occasion.

On Day 4, we accompany Rachel and Yekel and their family on an endless three-day train ride to that place where "Jews from Hungary and Poland, Czechoslovakia and Germany, Lithuania and France, Belgium and Holland, Norway, Estonia and Austria: all reached their destination." A whole community of Israel was in that railway carriage with Rachel. We overlook and overhear every step and every thought on their final road: from the illusions and hopes to the expectations and certainties, from those who threw messages through the skylight of the car whose protest is swallowed in the wind, to the mother who had packed her child in a parcel and dropped it out at a point when the train slowed down. We taste the hunger and thirst; we hear the outcries of terror—and the silence of Rachel lest she communicate her terror to the children. Mesmerized, we cannot look away, not even from the sea of light created by the gigantic flames leaping out of factory chimneys. We hear everything, even the cry of victory of Death.

On the fifth day, we meet twenty-year-old Yehuda and the first dozen young Jews gathered to plan the first civilian uprising against the Nazis in all of occupied Europe. We recognize that only the death of family, friends, teachers, of hope for life itself, has freed them to fight. Yet, even here, thoughts of future generations, of the Jewish past, of eternity, still drive their decision. Here, young fighters rebuke Yehuda for claiming that fighting is the only source of dignity. As Wiesel warns, "Even the heroes perished as victims, even the victims were heroes."

On the sixth day, there is "total, absolute, enveloping darkness: the darkness of Final Parting." Birkenau, Treblinka, Sobibor: selections, a turn to left or right that signaled life or death; or to put it more accurately, a turn that signaled death or life-and-death. On this day, we are reminded of the forced labor and the roll calls, the public floggings, the hangings, the fixed gaze of the Musselmen. Yet, we are warned that even the survivors' account is a failure. On this day, Wiesel remembers a Dutch lawyer who gave "the most wonderful address of his career," a comic speech to entertain and distract when there was a selection. He was taken that next day; we share the narrator's shame that we cannot remember the talk. We remember a father who shared moldy bread with his son and a son who took the blows meant for his father. We swallow the victims' bitter torment when the killers mock them and warn that no one will believe the survivors.

There is not a little of Wiesel's own direct experience in this day. At the end, his experience bursts through his writer's discipline (as it must! portraying the Holocaust is not art) and leads him to address us and all humanity. He lashes us with the solitude, the indifference. He tortures us with the prayers of the tortured which tortured God. He implores people "to join us as Allies.... Together, we can face the killers..." In the end he pleads for memory. He begs us not to weep—"That would be too easy"—Instead "listen to their tears which flow in us without a sound, without the slightest sound."

In sum, any piece created by Elie Wiesel has both assured power and instant credibility with the Jewish people. What could be more appropriate than that one who lived through the unspeakable be the witness to the event and a voice for the dead? One is reminded that Jeremiah, the traditional author of Lamentations, was an actual survivor of the siege and destruction of Jerusalem.

Yet there are two problems with this project. The first is, here again, whether any Megillah that seeks to do liturgical justice to the memory of the Holocaust can come with names attached. Instinctively, one feels that before the awfulness of the event, only an anonymous text will be acceptable. On this matter, however, one cannot make rulings. History and the response of a Jewish people and their covenantal partner will decide. However, the other major problem is more regrettable and should have been avoided. The scroll was commissioned and is to be distributed by the Reform movement. This almost certainly ensures its rejection by the Orthodox and probably that the Conservative and Reconstructionist denominations will commission their own as well. Yet any service that seeks to be the central liturgical vehicle for Holocaust commemoration must transcend sectarianism. If there is one lesson of the Holocaust, it is the unity in fate of the Jewish people. No authentic expression of the catastrophe should be perceived as the product of one denomination. It would be a great pity if a masterwork by Elie Wiesel and the creative, good intentions of the Reform movement are defeated by the denominational politics that grow out of the dominance of modern—really pre-Holocaust—values.

Evening Service (Continued)

One other attempt to create some order of service for Yom Hashoah should be mentioned: "Holocaust Commemoration for Days of Remembrance," a publication edited by the author and David Roskies, and designed to be a "secular" sacred service. It was widely distributed by the United States Holocaust Memorial Council in two editions, 1981 and 1982, with a substitution of one excerpt in 1982 because some survivors found the initial source too brutal.

The pamphlet offers two alternative orders of service, both based on primary accounts from the Holocaust. Both orders of service are fifteen to twenty minutes in length, which is much closer to traditional weekday prayer-service length and to the human capacity to absorb. (Each order is followed by an appropriate eyewitness account, lecture or film as dramatic presentation.)

The first order starts with the lighting of six candles and goes on to focus on the interacting fates of parents and children, surely the most heartbreaking aspect of the Holocaust. It portrays the nadir of human suffering—the Mussulmen—and the role of bystanders. It incorporates the Song of the Partisans, Ani Maamin, El Maleh Rachamim, and the late poet Aharon Zeitlin's variation on the Kaddish. Along with the lighting of candles, the two hymns and El Maleh Rachamin and Kaddish are probably the most widely disseminated rituals of Holocaust remembrance.

The second order is based entirely on sources from the Vilna ghetto on the theory that in remembering the Holocaust one must concretize. Remembering one individual or recreating one city is a more powerful triumph of memory than partial accounts that touch upon various lives and communities fleetingly. The service starts with a lullaby from the ghetto, followed by the lighting of the six candles and a poem of despair written by Abraham Sutzkever, a poet who lived through the Vilna experience and wrote about it with unique poetic fire. Next Zelig Kalmanovitch's account of a Passover talk on "what is a Jew and who is a Jew" is read. There follows another Sutzkever poem, an attempt to pray that can only yield babbling. The order of service concludes with El Maleh Rachamim and Kaddish are said.

ZACHOR—WITNESS

Both orders of service recommend use of a film to communicate significant aspects of the Holocaust; both orders list a talk by a survivor as a key component of the service. This points to a feature that some day will be incorporated in all future Holocaust commemoration. Call this section "Zachor—Remember" or "Witness." This incredible crime and the entire *univers concentrationnaire* were documented, photographed, and filmed as few events in history have been. Since the classic Jewish model of remembrance is reenactment, then documentary films, pictures, and survivors' testimony are appropriate and moving enclosures in such a service. When no more survivors in the flesh are left, film clips will be used in all commemorations to bring the immediacy of witness to the attention of all. (The parallel would be a film clip of Moses or of a Jew who went through the desert being played at every seder!)

Ideally, a commemoration should reach out and bring Jews of every background together. In the Holocaust, there are no differences between religious or secular, assimilated or committed Jews. The unity of Jewish destiny should be a given in all remembrances. Any Holocaust liturgy should avoid total affirmation or resolution. This tragedy, too destructive to be overcome lightly or swiftly, poses radical questions to all humanity. Nor should the mood be one of total defeat and despair; that would not do justice either to those who remained faithful even in the moments of greatest agony or to the incredible renewal of life that survivors exhibited after the war.

In light of the inability to express the inexpressible, prayers preferably should be taken from the actual writings and testimony of those who went through the Holocaust. Similarly, most commemorations incorporate music from the camps and ghettoes. The various languages of the Jewish people also should be included. One must fight Hitler by refusing to yield cultural heritage to destruction.

A service should conclude with the traditional mourners' prayer, the Kaddish. Traditionally, when someone dies without leaving immediate family, the nearest relative recites the Kaddish. For millions in the Holocaust, the entire family, with all its branches, was wiped out; now all Jews are the nearest living relatives; the entire congregation can appropriately join in saying Kaddish. For those who have religious or other reservations, however, the alternative is that the entire group stand together while some recite the words. Those who feel they should not recite the Kaddish should stand in silence, which, after all, may be the only authentic liturgical response to the Holocaust.

LAYL SHIMURIM— A NIGHT'S VIGIL

One other order of commemoration has been created, developed by Abba Kovner. Kovner's model has not been restricted to Yom Hashoah; in fact, it has been used mostly throughout the year. It is called *Layl Shimurium*, A Night's Vigil.* These programs generally run all night until the dawn (as did the original Exodus night from whence the title is borrowed). Typically, the program starts with a film or lecture on "the world that was," which seeks to communicate the incredible richness of Jewish life in Europe, the life that was destroyed. Then various presentations portray life in the ghettoes and camps, including the music, culture, religion, and writings expressed during the Holocaust. Most often, survivors speak, teach, answer questions, and seek to communicate the actual experience of living through the catastrophe. The program generally concludes with music of the Jews in the Holocaust and, often, a memorial prayer or ceremony. Sometimes a particular community is chosen, and all aspects of its culture, history, and existence before and during the Holocaust are studied. The total immersion and the re-creation of the life that was lost, as well as the sheer range of types of learning make this a very powerful experience.

FOOD AND DRESS

Should one fast on Yom Hashoah? Fasting is strongly associated with historical mourning days. Rabbi Avi Weiss argues that fasting on this day would have extra resonance precisely because, until the Shoah,

---

*Compare Exodus 12:42.

fasting was considered halachically inappropriate in these days of Nissan, the month of liberation and rejoicing. On the other hand, perhaps
a fast is an inadequate response. A well-fed, well-clothed, warm, and
safe American or Israeli Jew would find this too easy. A one-day fast
could turn too lightly into a needed loss of a pound or two, and dull
the sense of how really bad perpetual hunger is.

An alternative way to grasp the event might be to eat a scant, unfill-
ing meal that includes rotting food: breads dried up, just short of
mold; potato peelings; turnips rather than meat; flat coffee. The
prophet Ezekiel was instructed to undergo a series of symbolic acts
that would re-create, for the Babylonian Jews, the slaughter of the
Judean Jews and the destruction of the Temple. One of the instructions
specifically involved preparing and eating a scanty amount of coarse
bread made out of a motley mixture of grains and baked with cow
dung fuel so that it was ritually impure. Ezekiel's model is particularly
evocative because his task was to communicate to a people who had
been spectators at the Destruction what it had been like to be inside
the whirlwind.* The halacha requires that people neither wash nor
anoint themselves with cosmetics or lotions on Tisha B'Av. For mod-
erns, who are used to daily hygiene and washing, this discomfort is
particularly telling and would appear to be appropriate for Yom Hashoah. However, here, too, some have objected that in this case more
is less; the deprivation gives too much satisfaction ("righteous suffering") without the substance. Surviving accounts consistently talk of
the overwhelming excremental odor in the barracks caused by the
combination of no soap, inadequate washing, no towels, and widespread dysentery.

Similarly, there are traditions of special dress for various holy days.
Roskies' ritual evokes the memory of the huge mounds of shoes in the
Auschwitz storerooms, mute reminders of the millions who were
stripped of everything before being killed. But it also reminds one of
another halachic practice involving shoes: On Tisha B'Av, traditional
Jews do not wear leather shoes, either as a form of deprivation (leather
being luxurious) or, secondarily, as obedience to a commandment not
to kill animals for their leather—a sanctification of life as a response to
the many deaths in the destruction. Both motives would be appropriate for Yom Hashoah.

Two other special dress practices have been proposed for Yom Hashoah. One is to wear yellow "Jude" armbands all day, thus commemorating the "mark of Cain" that every Jew had to wear. The other is to
wear a Jewish star sewn on the front or back of coat or jacket, the

*Shalom Carmy, written communication, March 31, 1988.

telltale mark of a Jew during the Holocaust. I know of one survivor who saved his prisoner's ragged uniform; he puts it on every Yom Hashoah to remind his children and himself what it was like.

NAMES AND LIVES

One of the most powerful rituals of Yom Hashoah commemoration was developed by the late Shragai Arian, a Jewish educator. Students collected thousands of names of Holocaust victims. Then, for an entire twenty-four hours, they read the names in relays. As Roskies writes in Night Words (page 48): "Count by ones to six million, a number each second. 1, 2, 3, 4, 5, 6, 7.... You will be here [for four months]...8, 9, 10, 11, 12.... Not even naming names, each person a number...13, 14, 15, 16, 17, 18, 19, 20, 21, 22...." The litany of names, all so evanescent, doing so little justice to the total life behind those brief words, is a stunning reminder of the dimensions of the Holocaust. A variation on this memorial ritual has been collecting the names of all the relatives lost in that community or known to the group. The names are printed and circulated to the congregation or posted on the walls, even as the names of countless Czech Jews sent to their deaths are permanently posted on the walls of the synagogue in Prague.

The late Louis Weinberg of Flushing, New York, created yet another ritual of memory and names. He instructed that his own tombstone incorporate the names of relatives who died in the Holocaust without trace or record.

Yom Hashoah is a day when one must strike back at death by remembering the life that was, and by creating new life in response. After the Shoah, the D.P. camps were marked by one of the highest birth rates in the world. Against pure hatred and death, one must offer urgent life and love. In response to the triumph of killing, one must reply with the immediate creation of life. After the expulsion from Spain, Lurianic Kabbalah placed great stress on tikkun (perfecting the cosmos) through sacral performance of the acts of daily life. Citing this precedent, a Kabbalistic scholar once suggested that the time would come when it would indeed be a mitzvah to make love on the night of Yom Hashoah; better still would be to make love and create a new life on that night. (Many have proposed that each Jewish family should have an extra child, one more than planned, to begin to rebuild the shattered body of the Jewish people.)

One should not underestimate the psychological difficulty of thinking about love after exposure to the brutality and sadness generated by the Holocaust. This would be a heroic response—but ordinary humans are heroic. It is a known demographic fact, worldwide, that people have more children during and after a war. Of course, part of the reason is that people seek comfort and companionship after experiencing the loss of dear ones. On the deeper level, however, this is a human way of making a statement that love rather than hatred is the cosmic principle. Creating life after the Shoah bespeaks the power of chessed—which is the driving force of the messianic hope. The Talmud says that the Messiah will be born on Tisha B'Av. A Talmud written in our time would state that the Messiah will be conceived on Yom Hashoah.

THE SERVICE OF THE DAY

What of the day of Yom Hashoah itself? One suggestion is not to put on tefillin in the morning service, following the Tisha B'Av custom. The omission of tefillin expresses one's state when a loved one is dead but not yet buried. In this condition the mourner is exempted from many positive commandments in the halacha. Some say the exemption is to enable the mourner to prepare the burial. Rabbi Joseph B. Soloveitchik has suggested that the release reflects the collapse of meaning in the presence of death; it speaks subtly of an inability to pray or act authentically piously under conditions that are in absolute contradiction to classic Jewish covenantal claims. The same should apply to Yom Hashoah.

The more appropriate religious act would be, as it were, to put on God's tefillin. According to the Talmud, God also puts on tefillin. In the Jews' tefillin are verses such as Sh'ma and others that describe God's mighty acts of liberation in the Exodus. In God's tefillin, says the Talmud, is a hymn of praise to the Jewish people for its faithfulness to the covenant.* "Who is like Your people, Israel, a unique nation on earth?" (Chronicles 17:21). My father, of blessed memory, once rebuked an overweening expression of religious one-upmanship on my part when I was a teenager. I had put down the Jewish people for not being observant enough to suit my purist taste. "So," he said, "you glorify God and demean the Jewish people? Who should be more ashamed of their behavior in the past two decades? Who has shown more faithfulness to the covenant? Your task," my father concluded, "is to find the merit of the Jewish people and to defend it." On Yom Hashoah morning one should put on God's tefillin for God and praise the Jewish people for its ultimate covenant loyalty, its faithfulness and display of "a love that is as fierce as death" (Song of Songs 8:6).

* Babylonian Talmud, Berachot 6A.

A friend once told me that on Yom Hashoah he finds it almost impossible to pray formally. Instead, he steeps himself in learning and rereading sources from that world of the Holocaust and thus finds closeness to the presence of God in the midst of the fires and the pain. In a way, not putting on tefillin is a recognition of the fire and smoke that blocked the heavens over Auschwitz; it quietly acknowledges the break in the covenant that total destruction represents. Then again, by analogy to the Minchah service of Tisha B'Av, on Yom Hashoah at Minchah one can put on the tefillin. The wrapping of the thongs around the finger and the recitation of the classic covenantal formula ("I betroth you to me forever; I betroth you to me through righteousness and justice, with loving-kindness and compassion; I betroth you to me in faithfulness, and you shall know the Lord") becomes the symbolic renewal of the covenant, a re-creation that constitutes the voluntary re-acceptance of the covenant.

PUBLIC COMMEMORATION

In the United States, the day of Yom Hashoah has been the occasion for the special ceremonies of public and governmental remembrance of the Holocaust. At the national level, typically, the chairman of the U.S. Holocaust Memorial Council as well as the president of the United States or some other major public figure speak to the occasion. At the state level, governors or senators often give speeches drawing the lessons of the Holocaust for all. Here, too, ceremonies include survivors or witnesses, Jewish and non-Jewish clergy participation, and music of the ghettoes and camps.

In Israel, the night ceremony is the occasion for presidential or prime ministerial participation in the national commemoration ceremony at Yad Vashem. By day, the most impressive moment comes at 11 A.M., when a long whistle blast pierces the air in every city of Israel. All work, traffic, and broadcasts cease; people stop and get out of cars to stand at quiet attention. A moment of national silence follows, a moment that is in many ways more awesome than the full-scale broadcasting of the Holocaust record and the speeches that surround the day.

One other ritual of memory could be of special meaning on Yom Hashoah. There is a need for an almanac of the Holocaust. Almost every day in the year, a different community was invaded and/or destroyed by the Nazis. A calendar listing each community, its fate, and the date and major incidents of the final solution would not only preserve the memory but also give the opportunity to reclaim the life and distinctiveness of each locale. Through such an almanac, understanding of the Holocaust would be re-directed from a global sense of the Destruction to the concrete events of each day and period, each with its own locus, community fate, and response. Simon Wiesenthal has created an almanac of Jewish historical suffering that partly fills this need. His book deals with the entire breadth of Jewish tragedy throughout the ages; however, it borders on excess. We need a focused almanac that would list all the communities destroyed in the Holocaust on the appropriate days. A candle can be lit for a community on its day of doom as well as on Yom Hashoah. Most survivors and families of Holocaust victims light *yahrzeit* memorial candles on Yom Hashoah as well as on the actual anniversary, if it is known.

Rabbi Ichiel Poupko has proposed that every holiday be marked by the lash of the Holocaust. At one Shabbat meal, matzah could be served instead of challah to commemorate the bread-of-affliction ration in the Holocaust. Since God is also put on trial on Rosh Hashanah, selections from the Book of Job or from Levi Yitzchak of Berditchev's "Trial with God" can be used. For Sukkot, Poupko suggests that one wall of the Sukkah be left unfinished, thus invoking the memory of decrepit barracks in which Jewish prisoners subsisted and died. For Passover, along with matzah on the Seder plate there could be a moldy, inedible piece of bread representing Auschwitz. Poupko suggests, finally, that every synagogue and Jewish institution choose by lottery from a list of all the destroyed communities of Europe. The name drawn would become part of the synagogue's name. Each synagogue would concentrate its memorial and remembrance on that community, its life and death. The endless possibilities are a challenge to collective conscience, memory, and religious responsiveness.

TZEDAKAH

One of the classic traditions of every Jewish holy day is that it has its own special form of tzedakah (philanthropy/righteousness). Tzedakah means taking responsibility for life. One shares one's own possessions in order to take responsibility for the needs of others because life is indivisible. My life cannot be whole while others' lives are not. Therefore, every happy and holy occasion must be shared with the widow, the orphan, the stranger, the poor.

On Passover, one invites the hungry to the seder, in preparation for the holiday, a special *Maos Chitim* fund is raised. Purim has its *matanot la'evyonim* (gifts to the poor), and Shavuot its *bikkurim* (first fruits) brought to the Temple and shared with the priests even as the tithe is shared with the poor. Rosh Hashanah–Yom Kippur are marked by special tzedakah designed to "prevent" a death sentence. On Sukkot, *matnot aneeyim* (the agricultural portions for the poor) are left in the field for the needy. For many the charity of choice for Tisha B'Av, the day of the destruction of the Temple, is the Jewish National Fund which plants trees and rehabilitates the land inside Israel.

One of the key elements in creating Yom Hashoah would be to establish its characteristic tzedakah. Indeed, one can say that a proper Yom Hashoah would be unthinkable without tzedakah. In the light of the Shoah, it is revealed that giving tzedakah is not a matter of money, fund raising or communal activity. Giving tzedakah is the answer that one gives to the question: Do you still affirm the image of God? In the face of the total assault on life in the Shoah, one cannot be a bystander. One must be for God/for life, or for Satan/for death. Given the starkness of the reduction in human dignity inflicted in the camps, one must respond without equivocation. All Jews are sworn into the witness box before a world that asks if the image of God itself has been gassed to death, or whether hope itself has been cremated. The answer comes with deeds not words. The deposition starts with acts of human kindness and taking responsibility for fellow human beings— starting with one's own family. Giving tzedakah is a statement of belief in the perfectibility of the world; it is testimony to the value of life given with actions.

The finger of history points to the United Jewish Appeal as the appropriate tzedakah for Yom Hashoah. U.J.A. itself is the product of a response to the Holocaust. Through the 1920s and early 1930s, there were two major Jewish philanthropic appeals— the Joint Distribution Committee (J.D.C.) which was non-Zionist and the United States Palestine Appeal, a Zionist organization. On November 9, 1938, after a couple of years of partial association, the executive committee of the J.D.C. turned down a proposal for a joint campaign with the Palestine Appeal. On November 10, the Nazis savaged German Jewry on Kristallnacht, dispelling illusions that Nazi persecution would fade. A wave of grass roots demands in America forced reversal of the J.D.C. decision. A major relief effort was needed. Disunity over Zionism was no longer an acceptable reason for division; relief and life saving were more important. In one month's time, the United Jewish Appeal was set up. Relief activities rose sharply in 1939, and $15 million, twice the 1938 figure, was raised.

The central Nazi assault was on the value of Jewish life—the Nazis killed without mercy; but before killing, they steadily reduced the value of Jewish life. Through scientific planning, the cost of killing was brought down to less than one-half a penny per person.

The primary countertestimony to such pure evil is to reestablish the value of life.

It is particularly urgent that the bystanders respond in this way. A major factor in the colossal moral failures which made the Shoah possible was the nonresponse of the bystanders. In February 1943, Romania offered to release (that is, sell) seventy thousand Jews for fifty dollars each. The British and American governments blocked the program. Himmler offered in 1944 to spare the last Jews left in Europe for a payment of several million dollars. There was no response.

Under orders, Adolf Eichmann—who bitterly resented the command—finally sent Joel Brand of the Hungarian Zionist Federation abroad to the British with a final offer. Deportation of Hungarian Jewry would be stayed temporarily. One million Jews could be saved for a payment of ten thousand trucks and two hundred tons each of tea and coffee plus some strategic metals. The trucks would only be used on the Russian front. The whole package would cost $10 million —$10 per Jew. Brand was arrested by the British; no response was offered. So five hundred thousand Hungarian Jews were killed in the summer of 1944. The Allies adamantly refused to give money to the enemy in wartime.

Since 1938, U.J.A. has become the central vehicle for this monetary witness as to what life is worth. In 1946, American Jewry responded to the sight of the survivors and the D.P. camps by raising $131 million— compared to $15 million in 1939. In 1948, the year the State of Israel was declared, a peak amount of $205 million was given. In 1967, when the threat of genocide loomed over Israel seeking to stamp out the reborn life of Jewry, American Jews pledged an unprecedented $322 million. In the course of this evolution, philanthropic giving stopped being a favor and became a privilege and a duty. Every time death has threatened to overwhelm hope, Jewry has escalated its commitment to life.

Beyond the response to the Holocaust and Israel, the other powerful force in the U.J.A.'s appeal is the fact that it is united. By bringing together Jews of every type, the U.J.A. expresses the unity of Jewish fate, intuitively recognized by any person who responds to the Holocaust. The U.J.A. campaign goes on all year long; but just as Yom Hashoah makes manifest and focuses the memory of the catastrophe that went on year-round, so it should spotlight the response of giving and uniting that goes on all year. The proper culmination of a day of memory would be an act of support for the value of Jewish life in Israel, the United States, and around the world.

Of course, the specific charity one chooses to commemorate Yom Hashoah is not as important as the principle itself. Thus, another extraordinary expression of the relationship of Yom Hashoah and tzedakah has been created by Beth Tzedec congregation of Toronto, Canada.

In conjunction with Yom Hashoah, there is a special fund-raising campaign that climaxes with a special program on Yom Hashoah, whose proceeds go to the Fund for Oppressed Jewry. The money is used directly to ransom Jews from lands of oppression such as Syria and Ethiopia. One generation after Jewish life was worthless and all sorts of excuses were offered not to ransom Jews, here is the countertestimony.

In Jewish tradition, the mourner is asked to say the Kaddish, the prayer for the speedy coming of the messianic redemption. If a person who has just experienced absurdity and deep loss through death and who is in the despair of mourning can nevertheless express the hope of final perfection, that is incredibly powerful testimony. It means that life is strong enough to overcome death and that the Jewish hope is no illusion. This generation of limitless death and grief is saying Kaddish through its tzedakah and acts of chessed (loving-kindness).

The overwhelming response of this generation, outstripping the worst that death can do, renews the hope of redemption. Perhaps this is what the Talmud meant when it told us, as Rabbi Judah says:

> Great is tzedakah (charity), in that it brings the redemption nearer. . . . He also used to say: Ten hard things have been created in the world. Rock is hard, but iron cleaves it. Iron is hard, but fire softens it. Fire is hard, but water quenches it. . . . Death is the hardest thing of all, but tzedakah overcomes death.*

*Babylonian Talmud, Baba Batra 10A.

CHAPTER 11

Resurrection and Redemption:
Yom Ha'Atzmaut

THE NEW EXODUS

Zionism: Ancient and Modern Beginnings

Zionism began with the first Jew who searched and yearned for an unknown land whose very name he did not know. Abraham knew only that he had a promise that in this destined land, his family would develop into a great nation, a blessing to the entire world.

In Judaism, the natural is the seat of the eternal. Human beings, in their finitude, are the carriers of the infinite. By living everyday life with a dimension of depth, people become at once more human and more holy. There are no two separate realms of the sacred and the secular. Making a living and making life holy become a joint venture. Improving the world and perfecting it go hand in hand.

To exemplify the Bible's message, the Jews should be a people rooted in their land (a place overflowing with the bounty of nature) and pursuing a life of justice and loving-kindness, at peace with neighbors—a living witness to the infinite possibilities of finite existence. Therefore, the central political concern of the Bible was Israelite

373

sovereignty and independence in the land. Possession of the land became a classic sign of the faithfulness of the people, the concern of the Lord, and the viability of the covenant. When the Lord and the people were in Zion, all was well with the world.

The extended Exile that began in the first century C.E. uprooted the people of Israel from the land and made them outsiders, at the mercy of the policies and whims of others. For eighteen hundred years, Jews lived on the margin of society. By creating a cohesive internal culture and life, the people survived without a homeland as a nation within a nation.

Amazingly, this humiliated people—often subject to drastic persecution and expulsion—never internalized the degradation. The Exile was an expiation of past sin and a test of their faithfulness. They were still God's beloved people and the key to the outcome of history. Zion became the ever more shining symbol of a future state of blessing. Though exile became its prevailing condition, the Jewish people never totally adapted to it. Even when generations were born, reared, and died in the same country, Jews never lost the feeling of being strangers in a foreign land.

The Exile lengthened; the suffering deepened; Jewish numbers declined; the margin of survival narrowed. Defenseless, without military or political recourse, the people increasingly threw themselves on the mercy of the Lord to preserve them through history. In time, the religious balance shifted from this world to that of the world to come. Judaism became more ascetic and more passive. Jews settled in to wait for the Messiah who would redeem them when God finally saw fit. Piety came to mean passivity; human power was arrogance, *goyishe nachas*; waiting and hope replaced action to transform Jewish fate; prayer, not power, held the key to release Israel from the prison of Diaspora. Theirs was not to do and die, theirs was but to hope and cry.

In the nineteenth century, modern culture and emancipation had fundamentally changed the Jewish people. Modernity's message was power, human power. It was time for humanity to take charge of its destiny and create a brave new world. Many Jews, drawn by the siren song of liberation, left the community altogether. Most became patriots of the countries that admitted them to citizenship; they dismissed talk of returning to Israel as unnecessary or disruptive of their *Drang Nach* integration. Others, imbued with the new spirit of activism, turned to Zion with a commitment to act for its restoration.

Most traditional religious leaders were repelled by the powerful assimilating force of modernity. In their view, Zionism was manifestly modern and Zionists were guilty of the sin of rebellion. What need was there for a human state? God would, in time, miraculously restore Jewry to Israel. As leadership of the Zionist movement passed to secularist or modernizing Jews, the religious hierarchy convicted Zionists of another heinous sin—trafficking with the (secular, nonobservant) enemy. However, other Jews, equally rooted in the tradition, gradually absorbed the new messages of human power and self-help; this smaller group began to translate prayers into action. Rabbi Yehuda Alkalai (1798–1878) said that the redemption would begin with efforts by the Jews themselves; they must organize and unite, choose leaders, and leave the land of exile.

Given the opposition of the majority of the Orthodox and the influence of modern culture and politics in shaping Zionism, the soul of modern Zionists was divided from the beginning. Some envisioned the movement as a decisive break from the traditions of eighteen hundred years of exile, while others defined it as the culmination of a long-delayed but never abandoned hope. Both sides grasped the truth that reclaiming the land was bound to transform the people. "We have come to the land... to build and to be built in it" sang the *haluzim* (pioneers).

Fired by the vision of a Jewish homeland, thousands left hearth and home and chose a life of personal sacrifice, a life of hard work and bitter struggle, to restore the neglected, ruined land. By the turn of the twentieth century, modern political Zionism was born. The Aliya* came primarily from Eastern Europe where Jews resented their outsider, poverty-stricken status. Yet, even there, most of the poor preferred to go to the New World with its lure of streets paved with gold.

By the thirties, the decisive fact was that the growth of Palestinian Jewry was not yet sufficient to change the basic Jewish condition. In 1930, the population of Jewish Palestine constituted little more than one percent of world Jewry. For most Zionists, the goal of statehood remained a long-term pious wish. Those who saw sovereignty as a near-term concrete possibility were considerably fewer in number even in Palestine itself.

CRISIS AND TRANSFORMATION

The Nazi assault changed the conditions and priorities of Jewish life. Up to the thirties, the dominant reaction of westernized Jews was that Zionism was a threat to Jewish acceptance because it "confirmed" the assertion of anti-Semites that Jews were foreigners in the countries they inhabited. Robert Weltsch, a German-Jewish journalist, wrote in April 1933: "The Jews did not want to know that a Jewish question exists; they believed that it was only important not to be recognized as a Jew."† The shock of recognition that one could not *escape* being Jew-

---

*Used here to mean a wave of settlement; literally it means going up (to Israel).
†Reprinted in *Out of the Whirlwind* by Albert H. Friedlander (Garden City: Doubleday & Company, 1968), p. 121.

ish set off developments that were to turn Zionism into the acknowledged central historical process of the Jewish people.

The first result of Nazi persecution was the largest wave of aliya yet. Two hundred and sixty-five thousand went to Palestine between 1932 and 1939, most of them from Germany or from the lands where Nazism had penetrated. The population of Palestine more than doubled, and investment surged as well. Talk of statehood grew, but so did Arab opposition to Jewish immigration, let alone statehood.

By 1941, Hitler unleashed all-out war on Jewry; this raised the salience of Zionism for many Jews, but the true dimensions of the onslaught were not yet clear. As the death camps were liberated, the full significance of the Holocaust emerged. Of more than three million Polish Jews, less than one hundred thousand survived. Of their highly integrated peers, five hundred thousand German Jews, only twelve thousand remained alive in Europe. A credibility crisis grew in the primary substitute faiths that modern Jews had embraced—modernity, universalism, and naive liberalism. Freed of that anodyne, Jewry entered a much deeper crisis of faith and will to live.

The extent and extremity of the attack became clearer with every survivor's tale. The Shoah was a gigantic triumph of death, of cruelty, of despair. The Holocaust threw down the gage to every hope and affirmation in Judaism. It made a mockery of Jewish millennial faithfulness.

In light of such a successful assault, would anyone want to continue living as a Jew? After the war, fifteen thousand French Jews converted to Catholicism to spare their children a possible future repetition. What would be the reaction of the other Jews?

All Jews entered into a crisis of faith. Tradition was shaken by God's inaction. Modernity was challenged by evil and human inaction. "Normalizing" Zionists were shocked by Jewish aloneness. To carry on, Jewish people had to answer the most fundamental questions: Do we still believe? Is the covenant still valid? Does the dream of redemption still move anyone?

This time, belief in the Exodus could not be simply affirmed. This time, in Europe, no Moses had been saved from the drowning. On this Purim, the decree had not been averted; it had been carried out. Hope could not be affirmed without a new Exodus to confirm it. Jewish powerlessness had to be ended at once, or it would end the Jewish people.

To go on living, the Jewish people had to decide to live. Evil and death had played their highest cards. The Jewish people had to raise their bid on life. To bring home the survivors and to end dependence on a world that did not care, the Jews would have to win a state. To do that, they would have to venture what was left, including the six hundred thousand souls who constituted the Yishuv, that is, the Zionist settlement. A decision to establish a state would place at risk the Jews living in Palestine. They would become independent or die. This was the conclusion—first of a handful, then of the masses. The restored Jewish state, the long-term goal of Zionism, could no longer be postponed.

THE NEW EXODUS

Arising from the beds on which they had slept with death, two hundred and fifty thousand survivors chose life. They set about marrying and having children. They applied to countries for admission to start new lives. Overwhelmingly, they chose to go on living as Jews. Even more remarkably, over one hundred thousand D.P.s determined not to accept any other haven but Palestine. The decision not to go to America or back home meant being condemned to an indefinite number of years in limbo in a D.P. camp, or it meant having to board leaky, suffocatingly crowded tramp steamers to run a British blockade, and most likely end up in another prison camp in Cyprus until further notice. Yet by their refusal to go elsewhere, by placing their bodies as hostages and subjecting their spirit to torment, the survivors held world conscience, against its will, captive to the demand for a Jewish state.

To create the new commonwealth, Jews knew they would have to establish sovereignty on the land. What else can account for the steady flow of Jewish public opinion in the Yishuv toward statehood now, even though the threat of Arab war on such a state grew daily? In November 1947, when fighting began, the available fighting force of the Haganah (Jewish Defense Forces) consisted of the Palmach, made up of three thousand fighters, one thousand of them women. Yet the Haganah's military leaders, who knew how weak the Jewish settlers were, supported the decision to go ahead. At the price of scattering the thin line of fighting men and equipment even further, they followed a policy not to yield a single settlement to the invading Arab armies.

Even Zionists, who dreamt that the Jewish nation would become like all the others, understood that this state could not wait for normal political process. (As Ben-Gurion put it, in Israel, if you do not believe in miracles, you are not a realist.) How else can one account for the determination to declare the state in the face of the conventional wisdom that the Yishuv didn't have a prayer?

Religious Zionists came to see that faith in God could be expressed only in action. They understood that the crisis of faith could be overcome only by a new redemption, even as they recognized that the state could not meet their hopes for a religious Israel. After the establishment of the state, the first Chief Rabbi of Israel, Isaac Halevy Herzog, was roundly challenged for endorsing the establishment of a state that he knew would have to operate in violation of Jewish law in many areas of political and economic life. Herzog's honest answer was that the criticisms were correct, but he knew only one big truth—that after the Holocaust, the Jewish people could not go on living and believing without some great redemption. The deeper truth was that Israel's faith in the God of history demands that an unprecedented event of destruction be matched by an unprecedented act of redemption. World Jewry bent its energies to see to it that this now happened.

And so, in the words of Rabbi Joseph B. Soloveitchik,

In the heart of a night of terror, full of the horrors of Maidanek, Treblinka, and Buchenwald, in the night of gas chambers and crematoria, a night of Absolute Hiddenness [of God], in the night of the reign of the Satan of Doubts and Apostasy...a night of ceaseless search...when the people of Israel lay inundated with sorrow, and faint, tossing and turning in its bed amidst death agonies and the torments of hell, [came a knock on the door of Jewish history].*

The knock on the door was a new exodus made possible by no less than six reversals which in biblical times would have been called miracles:

Political: The United States and the Soviet Union were bitterly competing in the Cold War; they were divided and sought to undermine each other's position. Yet they changed course for one brief period and came together *on this issue only,* agreeing to the creation of the Jewish state.

Military: The nascent state was launched without proper arms. It had no armored force whatsoever. The only planes in Israeli possession were of the Tiger Moth (Piper Cub) type, single engine flying machines primarily good for crop dusting. Hamstrung by the British who openly favored the Arabs and supplied arms and ammunition to the Arab armies, the embattled, mostly amateur army fought off heavily armed units of Egyptian, Syrian, Iraqi, Lebanese, Arab Legion (British-led Jordanian), and Arab irregulars grouped in the Arab Liberation Army.

*Joseph B. Soloveitchik, "Kol Dodi Dofek," in *Torah U'Meluchah,* Simon Federbush (Jerusalem: Mossad Harav Kook, 1961), p. 21

Theological: The Jewish people, persecuted as "wandering Jews," repeatedly told that the biblical prophecies of a Promised Land had been spiritualized and transferred to an international, landless Christianity, retook possession of the actual land of Israel.

Cultural: Jews hell-bent on assimilation, suffused with the illusion of blending in among the nations, were seized by the drama of the particularity of the Jewish return to Israel and rallied to its support and to reaffirmation of their Jewishness. How many "assimilated" Jewish ex-U.S. Army pilots volunteered to fly planes into and for Israel? How many "forgotten" Jews remembered their origins or birth and stepped forward to fight for Israel or recruited support for the state?

Value of Life: Jewish blood had been spilled recklessly in the decade before. Jewish life that had not been worth anything in the Shoah was precious again. The losses in the War of Independence were staggering. But with every death the Israelis bought freedom, security, and the assurance that Jewish blood could not be spilled with impunity ever again. Thanks to the Jewish state, Jewish blood is no longer cheap.

Citizenship: For centuries, Jews were expelled and wandered the face of the earth, often with no refuge. How many Jews might have been saved had the doors of the Jewish state been open in the early years of the Holocaust? Now, Jews from Arab lands, from eastern Europe and the Soviet Union, from Ethiopia and Iran—wherever Jews were put at risk—found guaranteed admission to the land of Israel.

Rabbi Soloveitchik pointed to a seventh knock on the door as well: The land of Israel remained faithful to the Jews. It gave temporary shelter to Crusaders and other conquerors; it gave actual settlement to individuals and groups in modern times, not least to the Arabs who settled Palestine extensively. But it never recovered its ancient fertility and full greenness. The bulk of the land remained desert and untilled until the return of the people of Israel.

To Rabbi Soloveitchik's spiritually inspired vision, the religious signature of the state was manifest. But this restoration took place in modern times, participated in—indeed, carried out—by countless Jews who no longer shared Soloveitchik's religious assumptions. A majority of self-styled secularists led the State of Israel, fought in its armies, tilled its soil. In the eyes of many secular and religious Jews, any state so obviously brought into being by human activity, a state often not observant of Jewish traditional practices, a state manifestly vulnerable and full of flaws, could not define itself as a fulfillment of Judaism's millennial hope.

When writing a prayer for the newborn society, even the chief rabbinate, deeply committed to the Zionist enterprise, could summon only a modest, tentative, almost apologetic description of the state;

it was "the beginning of the growth of our redemption." Yet just as the original Exodus was the core of Jewish faith and covenant, and possession of the land the basis of Jewish life and hope, so was the new exodus a major event of renewal of life, of hope, of faith, of covenant.

In 1973, an Israeli father from a secularist kibbutz, burying his son killed in the Yom Kippur War, stepped forward to say Kaddish. He explained that he had not been able to bring himself to say Kaddish for his own father who had died at Auschwitz. He now understood that his son's death—and life—was the act of upholding Jewish life. In retrospect, it was a response and continuation of his father's.

The creation of the state was a deeply human act, flawed in a thousand ways: by deaths of the innocent in battle; by military miscalculations that led Jews to blow up a ship full of blockade-running Jews, drowning hundreds accidentally; by sending untrained survivors fresh off the boat into battle where they were mowed down by the hundreds; by the creation of hundreds of thousands of Arab refugees; by the expulsion of hundreds of thousands of Jews from Arab lands. Such flaws are inescapable wherever humans operate. To take on responsibility is to take the guilt of redemption. The alternative (not to act) is to take the guilt of irresponsibility or apathy. The flaws only confirm the humanness of the participants. They do not repudiate the transcendent nature of the miracle, they only conceal it.

The creation of the state was an act of redemption of biblical stature. The numbers of Jews involved—six hundred thousand in Israel; one hundred and fifty thousand D.P.s; six hundred thousand Jews from Oriental lands—dwarf, in their total, the number who were redeemed from Egypt. The sweep from the degradation of slavery in Egypt to the heights of Sinai and the Promised Land had a shorter arc than the swing from the depths of Auschwitz to the heights of Jerusalem. If ever such a swing were necessary to reassert the claim that history is the scene where God's love and redemption is manifest, it was in the 1940s, after Auschwitz. The redemption then was nothing less than renewed witness in a world where all transcendence seemed to have collapsed.

The Bible insists that the human role in redemption in no way reduces the divine intentionality and responsibility for the outcome of events. This is implicit in the meaning of covenant. In the case of the State of Israel, however, the human role in redemption is dominant and self-assertive. This secularism should not be confused with atheism or celebration of the death of God. The claims of absolute secular human power were shattered in the Holocaust. No one knows better than the Jewish people that total human power leads to idolatry and mass murder—of Jews first. Rather, as argued above, the creation of the State of Israel takes place in the context of a new era in Jewish history.

In this new era, God becomes even more hidden, the circumstances of redemption even more ambiguous. This ambiguity serves a twofold function: It allows those who prefer to interpret the activity as purely secular to do so, and it permits the religious soul to recognize the divine role out of mature understanding and free will rather than out of "coerced" yielding to divine *force majeure*.

The ambiguity allows each group to admit—without admitting—the deeper truth that each senses and fears, namely, that their fundamental assumptions have been "broken" by the new historical reality which they have brought into being by their own efforts. Under cover of the ambiguity, secular Jews can build a state in which, in the words of Paul van Buren, "the whole [biblical way] story suddenly becomes modern. . . . The existence of this state with Jerusalem as its capital reawakens the whole possibility that this [way] is not all in the past. Maybe God is not as dead as we thought? . . . This rings a note in the subconscious of even the most secular."* Conversely, behind the shield of ambiguity, religious Jews can build a state in which the covenantal way is being carried on by secularists, raising the real possibility that religion will no longer be understood or controlled by the religious.

The alternative approach for each group would have been to acknowledge the fundamental change and affirm it humorously à la Purim. But neither group could admit even that much to itself openly. On the other hand, to give both groups credit, there is a deeper integrity in going ahead without admitting the truth of what one is doing, for the alternative to ambiguity would have been paralysis.

On May 14, 1948, as Israel's Declaration of Independence was being drawn, agreement on the text was held up by an intense battle over the inclusion of an overt reference to the God of Israel. The Sabbath was fast approaching. If no agreement could be found, the declaration would have to be postponed. With the Arabs invading and the United States and Great Britain seeking to delay and even to shelve partition, who knows if the state might not have been seriously set back by any postponement?

A clear reference to God's intervention in the declaration would have had two ideological flaws: It would have imposed religious definition on secularists, and it would have sounded as if this redemption was self-evidently of divine origin like the original Exodus. This would have falsely removed the ambiguities of history and the hiddenness of

---

*Quoted in "The Focus on Israel" by Thomas A. Friedman, *New York Times Magazine*, February 1, 1987, pp. 17–18.

God in the new era. A clear elimination of reference to the Divine also would have had two philosophical flaws: It would have imposed a secular definition on religious Jews, and it could have sounded as if secularist understanding was fully adequate to the mystery of Jewish rebirth and renewal.

Compromise wording was worked out: "With trust in the rock (strength) of Israel, we sign with our own hand as witnesses to this Declaration in a session of the Acting National Council, on the soil of the homeland, in the city of Tel Aviv, today, the eve of Sabbath, 5 Iyar 5708, May 14, 1948." Secularists read it "rock (strength) of Israel"; religionists read it "Rock (Strength) of Israel"—the Hebrew language does not have capital letters. Thus, the interchange and political compromises of the conflicting groups led to the precisely ambiguous interpretation and divine hiddenness that characterizes post-Holocaust redemption.

Ambiguity also serves another positive function: It undercuts the natural tendency to absolutize the state. Humans tend to conflate the notion of a divine role in history with the principle of *Gott Mit Uns*, that is, that God endorses every act, evil or otherwise, inflicted by the group on others. Some of the greatest crimes in history have been committed in the name of the Lord; when the believers experience direct revelation, they tend to silence their critical faculties and confuse their will and God's. Ambiguity challenges this tendency and constantly raises doubt: Maybe this is your willfulness rather than the divine will? This sense of the unfathomable ways of the Lord and the fallibility of human interpretation of divine action in history, combined with deep trust in the Divine Presence, informed Abraham Lincoln. This perspective led Lincoln to tell ministers who assured him God was on his side that his main concern was that he should be on God's side.

In our time, God hides in the dark cloud of ambiguity and human errors. But the hiddenness makes possible a situation in which God is closer, and more present, just as the secularist victory and sacrifices make God and covenant more credible. In truth, when it comes to Israel, as to the Holocaust, the terms "religious" and "secular" are undone.

INGATHERING OF THE EXILES

One of the strongest biblical dimensions of the redemption was that it led to the ingathering of the exiles. The first paragraph of Israel's Declaration of Independence, after proclaiming the state, announced: "The State of Israel will be open for the aliya of the Jews and the ingathering of the exiles." The *olim* understood this. They expressed their feelings in such ships' names as *Exodus 1947* and *She'ar Yashuv* (A

Remnant Shall Return). On April 7, 1947, Yehuda Arazi of the Mossad arranged a sailing from Boliasco, Italy. The site was the former Gestapo headquarters for northern Italy. A seder was held first. In answer to the question, "Why is this night different from all other nights?" Arazi answered because tonight they would leave Italy and sail for the land of Israel. The immigrants finished the seder on the ship taking them to freedom.

Fulfillment of the promise of ingathering was clear to Jews of the Arab lands. A wave of messianic fervor swept Yemenite Jewry when they heard of Israel's Declaration of Independence. They left their homes and wandered to Aden, where planes came to airlift them to Israel. Sephardic Jews evoked the old Sinaitic verse, "I carried you on eagle's wings and brought you to me" (Exodus 19:4). Sophisticated modern Jews smiled at the invocation of the verse. Was it the simpleness of Yemenite Jews or ours?

One eyewitness described the arrival at the transition camp of

fifteen trucks full of 313 [Yemenite] people, fully or partially naked because of the heat or habit or sheer lack of clothing. Cramped, dirty, full of sores... it is hard to get them to speak—either because of exhaustion (they tell of fifteen days' nonstop travel) or because of apathy and fatalism or fear of what they are going toward.... They step down... in absolute silence... twelve thousand people were packed into the camp which was supposed to hold five hundred. Many simply lay down in the sands of the desert, without shelter or tent.*

Joseph Zadok reported:

The sight of the shining white "Skymaster" airplane aroused joy in the hearts of the *olim.* They look at it from afar and their eyes light up for joy. They will fly for eight hours and reach the land on the "flying horse" of the Messiah.... Two thousand years they waited and prayed for this moment. What a great privilege is theirs. Neither fathers nor grandfathers had the privilege for they died in exile with their souls longing for redemption.†

Of course, there were agents of the Jewish Agency to reenact and organize this "messianic airlift." Of course, many poor Yemenite Jews

---

*Quoted in *1949: Hayisraelim Harishonim* by Tom Segev (Jerusalem: Domino Press, 1984), page 177 (my translation).
†Ibid., pp. 177–78.

left to escape poverty and persecution, as Moroccan Jews left in masses after a pogrom in Oujda, and as Iraqi Jews were driven out by Arab hostility that reached flash point *because* the State of Israel had been declared. There, in the mixture of motives, at the inter-action point of reality and dreams, is where modern miracles take place.

This was a messianic yet human moment. Since the Jewish people returned to history, the Jewish messianic hope also was drawn into all the processes that reality demands. All the great accomplishments that resulted from this process would inevitably be scarred with the flaws to which human flesh and human will fall prey. The redemption of Sephardic Jews was replete with such flaws. Some Israelis complained of the "low cultural level" of Oriental Jews. The Oriental Jews were packed into overcrowded camps in Israel. Many lived in shantytowns in shacks of corrugated metal and worse. The very same parents who understood the millennial dimensions of their aliya experienced deep personal and cultural wounds in the uprooting and loss of parental authority. They were consigned to a lifetime of struggle in a society where they were second-class citizens. Many of their children were deliberately cut loose from religious moorings because Labor politi-cians feared that the children would vote for the religious parties when they grew up. Many other children followed suit in repudiating par-ental religious and ethnic culture as they sought to emulate the exter-nals of the new society.

So this ingathering of the exiles is no immaculately conceived heav-enly redemption untouched by dirty human hands. Yet it remains a stunning statement of the faithfulness of the divine promise: "From the East I will bring your children; from the West I will gather you. I will instruct the North 'Give back!' and tell Yemen [South] 'Do not withhold.' Bring my sons from afar; my daughters from the ends of the Earth" (Isaiah 43: 5–6).

THE END OF GALUT
(EXILIC) JUDAISM

The Holocaust made manifest a fundamental shift in the balance of power between victims and aggressors. Thanks to the extraordinary concentrations of power made possible by modern cultural technol-ogy and science, forces of evil have unlimited power available to carry out their designs. Death now has the capacity to stamp out life.

The lesson of the Holocaust was that in the face of overwhelming concentration of power, acts of self-sacrifice and spiritual demonstration had little or no effect on the murderers. Classic moral traditions—martyrdom in Judaism, satyagraha in Hinduism, the cross and turning the other cheek in Christianity—were shattered in the Holocaust. Nor did the norms developed by modern society—humanitarianism, liberalism, universal rights, rule of law—protect the Jews. Nor did established sources of aid to victims (religion, taboos on killing) prove any more capable of blunting the force of the Nazis' murderous fury. Only the transfer of power to potential victims—power enough to defend themselves—can correct the new imbalance of power. Other than surrendering their values, those committed to life and morality had only one choice left: to take power sufficient to protect those values. Covenant, dreams of perfection, and commitments to life could not remain dreams. Either they took on flesh and blood form in a human community with the power to defend themselves, or they would be crushed.

Thus, the Holocaust brought to an end the period of Galut Judaism. The Jewish ethic of powerlessness had given dignity and ethical direction for almost two thousand years in Diaspora. Emancipation had begun to erode that tradition. The messages of self-help and human power had caught up many Jews and had begun to transform their traditional values. The Holocaust made it clear that the old accommodation was now impossible, both physically and morally. Physically, the capacity and the will to kill all the Jews had already been demonstrated. Morally, powerlessness tempts the anti-Semites into evil behavior. There had to be Jewish power now; the only way to accomplish that was by creating a nation for Jews.

The State of Israel was designed to place power in the hands of Jews to shape their own destiny and to affect or even control the lives of others. Creating the state meant that Jews took on major responsibility for saving their own lives. With this decision, use of prayer alone or Torah study alone—heretofore the pillars of authentic Jewish response—henceforth became an evasion of covenantal responsibility. If one seeks out one moment that symbolizes the transition, it might well be the Haganah drafting able-bodied males in Meah Shearim (a community populated by Jews opposed to Zionism, waiting for the Messiah) to build defenses for the Old City in the battle for Jerusalem in 1948.

Taking power and the costs of power in human lives and resources have become central concerns of the Jewish people. Inescapably, Jewish hands become dirtied with blood and guilt as they operate in the real world. The classic Jewish self-image—the innocent, sinned-against sufferer whose moral superiority sustained self-respect—is being tested and eroded. Ethical muscles not flexed for centuries are now used; sometimes they are stiff and sore. A rabbinate not accustomed to politics is often jingoistic or chauvinistic. Generals and soldiers have become national heroes after centuries of judging such occupations as improper jobs for good Jewish boys.

There is still some disagreement as to whether the assumption of power is a basic change in the Jewish condition. Some scholars argue that far from ending the threat to Jews, the State of Israel itself is isolated and threatened continually by Arab aggression and Communist-bloc hostility. But this only proves that the margin of power of life over death is not yet great enough. However, there is already a fundamental difference from the past. In the past, a threatened Jewish community in Diaspora could hope only to sustain bearable losses and to live on by sufferance or flight. Israel has—and, through it, all Jews have—a major voice in its own fate. In the past, when Jews were destroyed, their wealth and achievement enriched their enemies. While Israel's wartime losses have been devastating, with their lives the Israelis have bought freedom and a measure of security for Jews everywhere.

Since no nation in the world today has power enough to absolutely ensure its own safety, these accomplishments of Israel are noteworthy. It is a basic measure of human dignity that my life is not cheap, that I choose for whom it shall be given, that my family, not my enemies, inherit me. Thus, the power created by the state upholds the covenantal statement of human dignity and the sacredness of life.

Creating the state applies these principles not just to the choices of death but to the priorities of life. In Israel, the priorities of Jewish fate and purpose determine everything from national park preserves and museums to phone systems and garbage dumps. Decades of building the land of Israel have created a remarkable Jewish infrastructure of life: schools teaching Judaism and Jewish history; media, art, literature, and scholarship in Hebrew; a national system of industrial and agricultural productivity. All these are taxed and utilized for the benefit of Jewish life all over the world.

The assumption of power—and therefore support of the State of Israel—has become central to Jewish life everywhere. Driven by the will to live, survivalist Jews have become overwhelmingly Zionist, even if they have no intention of ever living in Israel. After two decades of living vicariously through Israel, American Jews came to see that they must also take responsibility for Jewish power. As a result, they and other Jews of the world have arrayed themselves for political activity and to influence the foreign policies of their national states in support of Israel. Thus, Galut Judaism is coming to an end—even in Galut!

One might add that the decision to create the state and take power also constitutes a commitment to end the martyrdom tradition of Jewish history. Since martyrdom means the risk of total annihilation, it is no longer acceptable.

In August 1942, Rabbi Menachem Ziemba of Warsaw was asked if the Jews should resort to armed revolt in the face of the deportations. He ruled that they should not endanger the entire community by revolting. If Jews waited and trusted, God would not allow the people of Israel to be entirely destroyed. By January 1943, when the totality of the decision to kill Jews was clear, Ziemba was asked the same question. He ruled as follows:

> Of necessity, we must resist the enemy on all fronts.... Sanctification of the Divine Name manifests itself in varied ways. Indeed, its special form is a product of the times we live in. Under the sway of the first crusade, at the end of the eleventh century, halacha—as an echo of political events of the times—had determined one way of reacting to the distress of the French-German Jews whereas in the middle of the twentieth century, during the onrushing liquidation of the Jews in Poland, halacha prompts us to react in an entirely different manner. In the past, during religious persecution, we were required by the law "to give up our lives even for the least essential practice." In the present when we are faced by an arch foe, whose unparalleled ruthlessness and total annihilation purposes know no bounds, halacha demands that we fight and resist to the very end with unequalled determination and valor for the sake of the Sanctification of the Divine Name.*

The call to power was perceived by Jews everywhere as a call to end the tradition of suffering, to serve God in the joy of victory. The declaration of the state itself was a decision to reverse the trend of history, which steadily added days of woe and memorial to the Jewish calendar. Yet, since victory and joy are purchased at the cost of sacrifice and struggle, this could not be translated into a simple-minded hedonism or Pollyanna spirit. In the creation of Yom Ha'Atzmaut (Israel Independence Day), Jews had to confront the basic question: How does one commemorate the new exodus? What rituals, reenactments, ceremonies can do justice to the magnitude of the new redemption?

As a newly established state, Israel found it only natural to imitate the practices of European nationalism and declare the national day of

---

*Menachem Ziemba, *Chiddushay Garmaz* (n.p., 1980); See Samuel Rothstein, Rabbi Menachem Ziemba: Chayav U'Peulotav (Tel Aviv: Netzach, 1948), pp. 98–101.

independence a national holiday. It seemed proper that the Knesset create the holiday. And so it did: Yom Ha'Atzmaut was voted to be 5 Iyar (the Hebrew anniversary of May 15, 1948). However, all the unresolved issues of religious authority, multiple sources of norms, and the basic ambiguity of religious and secular definitions of Zionism all came to bear on the unfolding character of the day.

YOM HA'ATZMAUT: THE NEW REENACTMENT

The Knesset established the date but not the character of Independence Day. No one was quite sure what should be the appropriate content of the day. After all, as David Ben-Gurion pointed out in his own message for the occasion, this was the first new holiday to be added to the Jewish calendar in over two thousand years.

The joy of the year of freedom was mixed with pain. The Yishuv had suffered heavy losses in the War for Independence; hardly a family was spared. The government proclamation focused more on the memory of the fallen soldiers—"heroes of the nation, who put their lives in mortal danger in the battle lines, and with their precious, pure, courageous young lives bought freedom for their people"—than on the celebration. The official resolution said only: "On this day, let all labor cease.... Let the people gather in families and settlements for rejoicing and gladness, for memorial and thanksgiving, for unity and inspiration, for on this day Israel will celebrate its new holiday of independence.*

How to celebrate? One leading educator, Yom Tov Lewinski, proposed that the holiday be modeled on the Sabbath. In Lewinski's view, Yom Ha'Atzmaut should begin the evening before in accordance with Hebrew calendrical practice. Work should cease before sundown; traffic should stop, stores close, and the "Sabbath of the State" begin. Lewinski proposed lighting candles, as on Friday night, but placing them in the window to "publicize the miracle," as on Hanukkah. After services, families should gather for a festival meal, including blessing the day over a cup of wine. Lewinski assumed that synagogues would follow classic festival models—for example, chant the "Hallel," recite the *yaaleh v'yavo* prayer, and read portions from the Torah and prophets topically related to the day. This was "a folk holiday, a holy festival, in remembrance of our exodus from slavery to redemption."†

---

*Published and distributed as a broadside, this is quoted in Yom Tov Lewinski's *Sefer Hamoadim*, vol. 8, *Y'mai Moed V'Zikaron* (Tel Aviv: Dvir, 1956), p. 486.
†Yom Tov Lewinski, "B'Fros Chag Haatzmaut Harishon BaMedinah," *Davar*, Nissan 20, 5709 (April 19, 1949).

Years later, upon assuming the role of minister of education and culture, Professor Ben Zion Dinur also offered liturgical guidelines. In Dinur's judgment, the holiday should be focused on the home and family. He proposed filling the house with candles and lights (symbolic of an exodus "from slavery to freedom and from darkness to light" [Haggadah]) and decorating with greens, especially olive branches. The greens represented the renewal of the land; the olive branch, the search for peace. Dinur called for a festive family meal—possibly inviting neighbors and friends as well—at which the Declaration of Independence would be read liturgically.

Despite the various efforts to direct observances, the population of Israel did not turn to any one source for guidance. Improvisation, experimentation, and grassroots initiatives were the order of the day. Year by year new features were developed. Some spread rapidly; some fell into desuetude; some remained local initiatives.

In the first year's Yom Ha'Atzmaut, a cornerstone was laid in Jerusalem as a memorial to those who fell in the defense of the city. The ceremony, in the presence of bereaved parents and families, was one of a number of memorials that were to emerge as a constant feature of the holiday. Festive lighting in the streets, folk dancing, and youth group marches marked the occasion in Tel Aviv.

In synagogues, there was little to distinguish the day. Some held special services incorporating the Hallel prayers, but many others, especially the less formal shuls, had regular daily prayers. Some people objected to any commemoration on the grounds that the day occurs during the Sefirah (Counting the Omer) semi-mourning period. The ultra-Orthodox fasted and even mourned the sacrilegious human initiative, the state.

The twentieth of Tammuz, the yahrzeit of Theodor Herzl (the founder of modern political Zionism), had been scheduled to be a day of military parades. A last-minute decision was made to shift the parades to Independence Day. Fourteen military parades were held around the country, from Eilat in the southern tip to Nahariya on the northern coast; such parades became a central feature of the holiday.

On the second Yom Ha'Atzmaut, another custom emerged that was to become a permanent feature of the day. In fulfillment of Theodor Herzl's dream, his bones were brought from Vienna and buried on the mountain in Jerusalem that became a national shrine, named in his honor. On this night, torches were lit on Mount Herzl, recapitulating an ancient rite that signaled the new month. A relay of torches was lit on a string of mountains over Israel, in response to the beacon of light from Jerusalem. Torchlight parades thus became a standard feature of Independence Day celebrations.

Another innovation of the second year was a marathon race (Independence Run) from Yafo to Jerusalem. The eighty-three-kilometer distance was divided into six sections, and teams of relay runners competed. In future years the marathon distance was shortened and turned into a race among individuals.

YOM HAZIKARON
(REMEMBRANCE DAY)

By the third Yom Ha'Atzmaut, commemorating the fallen soldiers had become so widespread a practice that it was emotionally dominating the day. It was decided, therefore, to set aside the day before Independence Day as a permanent Yom Hazikaron (Remembrance Day) for the dead of Israel's wars. (In Nathan Alterman's immortal poem, the fallen soldiers speak: "We are the 'silver tray' on which the Jewish state was served.")* A public ceremony of lighting a remembrance flame on Mount Zion was matched by the lighting of "soul candles," a yizkor candle, in all the military encampments in Israel, while flags flew at half-mast.

The first year, an extended whistle blast was sounded nationwide to begin Remembrance Day. That night the whistles blew again to signal the end of the day. All traffic stopped, and the population of Israel stood silent for two minutes. In that lightning moment, the Yishuv went over to the celebration of Yom Ha'Atzmaut, beginning with the torch lighting on Mount Herzl and continuing with relays of torch lighting around the country. In a remarkable statement of theological continuity, the liturgy established by the secular Knesset recapitulated the classic dialectical move of Jewish tradition from sadness to celebration, from mourning to joy, from death to life, in the wink of an eye. As Purim's orgiastic joy was preceded by the Fast Day of Esther, with its burden of woe and vulnerability, as Passover's celebration was preceded by the ominous Fast of the Firstborn, as Sukkot's celebration followed the sackcloth and denial of Yom Kippur, so Yom Ha'Atzmaut would follow on the heels of loss evoked by communing with the memory of the fallen soldiers.

Thus, the seven days before the anniversary of independence—between Yom Hashoah at the beginning and Yom Hazikaron at the end —became a week marked by deep and reflective sadness. Visiting graves in the military cemeteries, with row upon row of stones, most of them marking young lives cut off in their teens and twenties, placing flowers, saying commemorative prayers, and lighting yizkor can-

*Nathan Alterman, "Magash Hakessef" in Shirim (Givatayim-Ramat Gan: Ministry of Defense, 1974), pp. 314–15.

dles set a powerful chord of grief reverberating through the entire population. Over the years many have complained that the contrast was too powerful, the swift transition too difficult to bear. During these four decades many of the celebratory features of Yom Ha'Atzmaut have been shifted to the day and the following night to relieve some of the tension.

One guesses that the pain is at its peak in this generation when the living parents and families of the fallen summon up not some past tragic events but the never-closing wound of a lost child, husband, or brother. Future generations with a stylized, ritualized grief will find the sudden shift less tormenting. Someone must pay the price of the time it takes for a holy day to become a vicarious memento of the past reenacted rather than one's own literal experience. Yet, notwithstanding pain and protests, Yom Hazikaron and Yom Ha'Atzmaut have not been separated. On one level, this is testimony to the classic Jewish insistence that the fullness of freedom cannot be appreciated without the taste of slavery or the fullness of life without the encounter with death.

The juxtaposition works as well on another level: The acute initial experience of loss prevents the glorification of war in the later celebrations. There is no consolation in victory that can overcome the pain of death.

Most powerfully of all, the intensity of loss summoned up when the dead are recalled to memory makes clear the necessity of the ultimate Jewish hope—resurrection. Nothing—not peace, not victory, not present children—can stand in for the unique, irreplaceable lost one. This is the power of the doctrine of resurrection. It makes clear that the loss of the concrete, deeply beloved individual cannot be offset by generic life or happiness. This one, lost, finite person is of infinite value to me. No substitute can be accepted.

In experiencing again the fatal wounds of war, one is led to reflect: How can we achieve the ultimate Jewish dream which is to overcome death? The answer is that in the present state of things, we cannot undo the death of the individual. But life can overcome death if people carry on an all-out renewal of life. Death is constantly winning individual battles, but as long as life keeps renewing and reproducing, it can outrun death itself. When life creation stops, then the second law of thermodynamics takes over and the physical universe degrades toward death.

When the Nazis overwhelmed the biological capacity of Jews to reproduce and nurture the children, then their death machine inevitably won its battle with life. Israel represents the renewal of the life creation processes of Jewry. It incarnates the power of resurrection within the Jewish people. The Talmud compares a day of rain, giving life to grass and harvest, to the day of the giving of the Torah and the day of resurrection. All three represent the power to respond to the irreplaceable loss of life with the fathomless vigor of generativity and growth. This is the only power of resurrection available to humans now. Re-creation cannot overcome the pain of loss, but it can assure the eventual triumph of life. It continues the chain of life until the covenantal, longed-for resurrection can occur.

THE EVENING OF
YOM HA'ATZMAUT

In the classic tradition, the night of Yom Ha'Atzmaut should be a family night, but it hasn't worked out that way. One major constituency for a family holiday—the Orthodox community—has proven to be religiously ambivalent about Independence Day and recalcitrant in developing its character. The official Israeli rabbinate developed no seder or haggadah for the home. Even in the synagogue, the rabbinate called for Hallel but then split on the question of whether to say a blessing beforehand.

Since no halachic authority would object, one can recite any of the Psalms that constitute the Hallel anytime; Tehillim (Psalms) are often read as an act of daily piety. The central issue is: Does one trust the redemptive experience? If one does, then reciting the blessing is an acknowledgment that a miraculous redemption equivalent to Passover and Hanukkah has occurred again in this time. If Israel's birth is no miraculous redemption, then by making the blessing one is guilty of saying a blessing (and, therefore, God's name) in vain. The real question is not a logical one. The question would be better put as: Do you experience the miracle deeply enough, despite its ambiguity, so that a blessing of thanksgiving wells up unavoidably? In the words of Rabbi Tsvi Yehuda Kook, the son of the first great Chief Rabbi of Zion and spiritual father of the Gush Emunim (Bloc of the Faithful): "What is lacking is an element in our soul. The key question is how to strengthen this true faith [in the miracle]. One can [properly] judge the halachic situation only if there will be a true recognition of the matter, of the true state of affairs that we find ourselves in Israel... for the moment we have lost the trust [faith].*

Most Orthodox rabbis do not recite the blessing. The same hesitation has crippled the development of a seder or haggadah for the day by its natural constituency, the modern Orthodox Jews. As a re-

*Quoted in Y'mai Moed V'Zikaron by Yom Tov Lewinski, p. 471.

sult, the evening of Independence Day itself is not home- and family-centered; people go outside to enact and enjoy the celebration.

Rabbi Tsvi Yehuda Kook has defined joy and rejoicing as the fundamental religious response to the day: "They speak of the 'beginning of the redemption.' In my view, it is already the middle of the redemption."* The increase of joy becomes the celebration of the miracle. In this matter, the folk have ruled in accordance with the opinion of Rabbi Kook. Merrymaking, fireworks, folk dancing, street partying, pageants, carnivals, and Luna Parks (temporary fairs with kiddie rides and thrills) grow from year to year. The folk differ with Kook only in their hermeneutic of suspicion of the messianic claims of his students and Gush Emunim. For most people, the redemption is too hidden to lend itself to unrestrained messianism. Israel is still too fragile to dismiss considerations of security or democracy out of conviction that the eschaton is near.

Professor Eliezer Schweid, a leading Israeli philosopher, has argued that the present joyful celebration of Yom Ha'Atzmaut bespeaks an attitude of hedonism/pleasure and not the joy of mitzvah. Schweid is correct in thinking that the sense of being commanded (which stimulates home and family joy) is weak, but it is not true that there is no higher purpose than hedonism behind the joy. Israel represents a people's reaffirmation of the body after centuries of abstraction and after a decade of extermination. The appropriate gladness is the pleasure of the body. Compare Purim's hedonistic tone (a reaction to Haman's and Ahashverosh's threat to destroy the Jewish body) with Hanukkah's more spiritual flavor (the Hellenists endangered the spiritual traditions, not the people's existence).

In this same spirit, Schweid finds fault with a folk prank performed by many on Yom Ha'Atzmaut. Little plastic "hammers" are widely sold for the holiday. People run through the teeming masses on the streets and "bop" unsuspecting passersby on the head or shoulders. The plastic is harmless, but it makes a pinging sound much like a cluck or a bleat. The recipient of the blow feels a bit foolish. Then the prankster runs on, too swift for the riposte. Schweid judges this custom to represent masked hostility brought on by anomie, the anonymity of the mass, and frustration at the lack of sense of community and conviction of this evening.†

This is a rather sweeping judgment. It can be argued that, on the contrary, Purim is the model for this behavior. In a small way, a prank that punctures complacency and provides laughter is particularly appropriate in light of the "farcical" level of forces that pulled off this

---

*Ibid.
†Schweid argues his views in *Sefer Machzor Hazemanim* (Tel Aviv: Am Oved, 1984), chapter 11, especially page 230.

miracle of the War of Independence. (Silliness is also an antidote for the virus of militarism.)

The joy of Yom Ha'Atzmaut is not yet as full-spirited as is the joy of Purim. Perhaps this gap is inevitable in the generation that lives the restoration and recognizes that the shift from dependence to sovereignty is not as idyllic as one dreamed. You can liken this to the unceasing internal criticism of Israeli society, lamenting its limitations. In 1954, Professor Joseph Klausner suggested that the unrelenting criticism go on 364 days a year—appropriate in a democracy compounded by a citizenry that is Jewish with an insatiable lust for perfection. However, said Klausner, let Yom Ha'Atzmaut be the one day a year that people speak only in praise of the state and its accomplishments. Klausner's proposal fell on deaf ears; the torrent of self-criticism flows on.

Most of the suggested models for Yom Ha'Atzmaut celebrations are derived from the paradigm of Passover. Having a seder and reading a haggadah are at the heart of many of the services developed for family night. Some haggadot totally eliminate references to the Divine; some are suffused with traditional faith. Almost all express the shift from genocide to rebirth through narrative, songs, and even foods. One can visualize eating foods in remembrance of the suffering that preceded the state, even as maror, the bitter herb, summons up the memory of slavery on Passover. One survivor's child tells that at his family seder, his parents served potato peelings as the food of bitter memory, explaining that these were luxury, fattening foods in Bergen-Belsen.

The population has been slow in responding to the suggestion to eat certain foods as ritual foods. Matzah appears to be an ancient, exotic food steeped in the lore of history. But 3,250 years ago, it was a daily bread. Due to the patina of antiquity with which religion has been overlaid, there is resistance to seeing that today such Israeli foods as tehina (sesame paste), hummus (chick-pea paste), and pita (bread) are the breads of freedom. Eating falafel (little fried balls of chick-peas and flour, highly spiced), then, bespeaks the faith reenactment of the redemption of the Jewish people. As one wag put it, one must show great faith and courage to eat Israeli falafel.

No one haggadah has won broad acceptance since 1948. The traditionalist-secularist split leads to veto by one side for haggadot written for Yom Ha'Atzmaut by the other or for any haggadah written by one group exclusively. There is no religious/cultural instrumentality that could force the two sides to put their heads together and create a compromise that is ambiguous enough to do justice to the truth of both positions. In the absence of such a compromise document, the folk in its wisdom rejects all one-sided interpretations of the redemption. (It should be noted that there is still resistance on the part of the partisans of Labor Zionism to give full credit to the Revisionist-sponsored Irgun Zvai Leumi (National Military Organization) for its role in starting the revolt against Britain. When Menachem Begin, the former head of the Irgun, came to power as prime minister, he showed some reluctance to give full credit to the Haganah for its role. Such conflicts as to which is the legitimate historical tradition also block the consensus needed to create a liturgical tradition.)

Of course, there may be a deeper wisdom involved in the failure of any haggadah to win universal acceptance. With a haggadah being written in the twentieth century, perhaps the tale should be told in film and tape and not just by the book traditions of the past. Imagine how the genius of the Rabbis would have used actual documentary film (such as Haim Gouri's *The Last Sea* and Israeli TV's *Pillar of Fire* series) to make the reenactment even more vivid. Then again, maybe not. Maybe actual film is too literal and earthbound. Maybe movies allow the participants to watch passively and distance themselves instead of actively immersing themselves in the ritual summoning up of the great events. For the moment, a current ruling on this question is premature. The centrifuge of the passage of the years must yet separate out the liturgical cream from skim milk solids.

THE DAY OF YOM HA'ATZMAUT

The day of Yom Ha'Atzmaut is not marked by any restrictions of labor or food, so the joy is at once secular and relatively unrestrained. Halachically, the absence of a prohibition on labor reflects the fact that this is a post-Pentateuchal holiday. At a deeper level, however, secularity and the call to power are at the heart of the day. There is where the holiness that is hidden is expressed in this age.

The Rabbis established the practice of reciting Hallel on Hanukkah in gratitude for the miracles and redemption—but not on Purim. The Talmud explains that the deliverance of Purim was not a complete one—the Jews remained in the Diaspora. This left them still enslaved, dependent on Ahashverosh. Hallel is appropriate only for a full-hearted celebration of independence. This talmudic logic makes the case for Hallel on Yom Ha'Atzmaut overwhelming.

In most Israeli synagogues, the joy of the day is expressed in the fact that prayers of contrition and mourning (Tachanun) are omitted. The Israeli rabbinate also established a reading from the prophets in honor of the day, but not a Torah reading. The prophetic portion includes the classic messianic prophecy of universal peace in which the wolf and the lamb shall dwell together and "nothing evil or destructive will be done, for the earth shall be filled with devotion to the Lord as water covers the sea" (Isaiah 11:9). This portion is also the Haftarah of the last day of Passover. Thus, the rabbinate draws an implicit parallel between Passover and the creation of Israel. Then, as now, a great military triumph confirmed the liberation of the Jews and upheld faith in God. Then, as now, the limited deliverance of Israel points to a greater final redemption for all the world.

To uphold its commitment to redemption, the religious kibbutz movement established Torah reading. The movement also recites the blessings of the Hallel. Significantly, the religious leadership of Ha-Kibbutz Hadati is relatively shielded from the peer judgments of the haredi (ultra-Orthodox) world that appear to play an intimidating role in the rabbinate's decisions. One of the unfortunate side effects of this controversy is that the religious groups have little influence on the development of the day or on the search to fill the day with values and content.

During the first few decades of the state's existence, the outstanding feature of Yom Ha'Atzmaut celebration has been the military parade, both in national and local events. Considering the absence of a military tradition, this is surprising. Diaspora Jews who still live with the ideals and illusions of powerlessness are often embarrassed by this phenomenon. Yet a military parade is a most appropriate symbol for an era whose central theme, set in motion by the Holocaust and the creation of the state, is the emergence of the Jews from powerlessness.

If attaining power is a major concern, then wielding power must be appreciated and honored. An ethic of power incorporates the value of creating an army. Disapproval of the parade on the grounds of opposition to militarism is morally inappropriate. The plain truth is that without the Israeli armed forces there would have been no state and the survivors would have been held in limbo. Without the army there would have been another Holocaust. To obfuscate this truth is not a moral act but an evasion of reality.

In going for power, the Jewish people are again the *avant-garde* of humanity and morality. People everywhere are in revolt against the fates of poverty, suffering, and death to which they have been sentenced by birth. People have grasped the ancient Jewish vision that human destiny is not blind fate. Life can be perfected, but people must take sufficient power to accomplish the goal.

The ethic of power means that every aspect of morality and life is transformed by the facts of power. The prayer of the powerful is different from that of the powerless. The prayer of the powerful is more properly focused on self-judgment. We ask God not to save us from our fate but to strengthen our good tendencies and accompany us as Friend, Partner, and Judge in our use of power. When there is power, then prayer also takes the form of action—proper action. A military parade, then, is an act of celebration, prayer, and self-judgment.

Over the course of history, the step from military parades to parading militarism has been a notoriously easy one to take; however, the religio-moral depth of the Jewish people has come through to block this possibility. The army is not a separate cadre of people on a different plane, idolized by a passive citizenry. Israel's is a citizen army, deeply connected to its civilian population. The closeness shows up in elements of informality and lack of pretentiousness in the military displays.

Often, army units are interspersed with other groups. In one year's parade, the Golani Brigade, liberators of Jerusalem, were followed by a group of Japanese Jewish sympathizers dressed in blue and gold kimonos with the Star of David on their fronts. The contrast of the Israeli Sabras and the diminutive, flowery, "exotic" Japanese in itself cut through the military air, bringing widespread laughter and applause. Then came marching children's groups, young scouts, and *gadna* youth settlement contingents. Despite the awesome power in the tanks and planes, the entire parade took on the air of a homely, improvised presentation rather than a display of awesome force that people could objectify and worship. In other countries, police barriers keep people on their side of the line, in a strictly enforced separation from the soldiers. Here, children darted in and out; civilians wandered across the line; soldiers slouched. The entire affair was a family party, with bantering interchange between soldiers and civilians. Thus, even the children experienced an army on a human scale, not a majestic monolith.

Behind the use of force is the concept of taking responsibility for Jewish fate. Many soldiers—especially women—are used as teachers in development towns or as supplementary farmers, and they march accordingly. The local military parades frequently have been interspersed with groups of people whose civilian lives represent taking responsibility for society. It has been suggested that the parade be turned into a march by the various peoples whose contribution make Israeli life tick: transportation workers, industrial workers, social workers, and so forth.

In recent years, a countermovement to the centralization of display and the focus on public ceremony has grown. More and more families have reasserted the private character of the day, not so much by ceremonies at home as by going on family picnics. They often combine the picnic with exploration of the land and its nooks and crannies. In this approach, the day is a celebration of the earthly concreteness of Jewish existence on a specific land. Building the state is a reaffirmation of the earthly Jerusalem, an actual society in which Jews live and carry on life functions. The good food and drink on a picnic is another way of treasuring the body.

Other expressions of love for the earthly Jerusalem have grown popular in recent years, such as walks to Jerusalem and hikes all over the country. For centuries, Diaspora Jews idolized Eretz (the land of) Israel. "Everyone who walks a distance of four cubits [six feet] in the land of Israel is guaranteed a share in the world to come. . . . All his sins are forgiven," said the Talmud.* It was a special merit to be buried with some earth from the land of Israel thrown into the grave. In a gesture going back to Talmudic times, travelers would, upon arrival in Israel, bow down and kiss the ground. But those beautiful expressions of affection reflected, like the chivalric love code, the love of a man for the unattainable, rarely seen woman of his dreams. Hikes and picnics express the tangible love of flesh and blood people for their beloved whose essence they have touched and smelled, whose foibles they know, whose particularity they embrace and cherish. Exploration of the land, archaeology, the Society for the Protection of Nature bespeak a new, intimate, living bond between a people and its soil—truly a fulfillment of the psalmists' verse: "Your servants delight in [Zion's] stones and cherish its dust" (Psalms 102:15). Yom Ha'Atzmaut is thus experienced as the wedding anniversary of a people recovenanted to its land.

Still another emerging feature of happiness on Yom Ha'Atzmaut is the slowly growing number of weddings celebrated on that day. The fifth of Iyar occurs during the semi-mourning Sefirat Ha'Omer period when weddings were not permitted. In joyful response to the creation of the state, the Israeli rabbinate ruled that weddings and joyous occasions are permitted on this day. Thus, the joy of Israel reborn begins to vanquish centuries of grief induced by the Exile.

This is not to say that Yom Ha'Atzmaut is the only time for rejoicing with Israel, any more than birthdays are the only time to be happy with a child. Every day is a celebration of the life of Israel. A Zionist friend precedes the grace after meals every day with Psalm 126: "When the Lord returned the returnees of Zion, we were as dreamers; then our mouths were filled with laughter and our tongues with songs of joy. . . ." His logic is that throughout the years of exile, weekday grace was preceded by Psalm 137: "By the waters of Babylon we sat and wept. . . ." He feels that to recite that Psalm daily would be equivalent to ingratitude for the restoration. On the other hand, on Shabbat, Psalm 126 was sung because Jews fantasized the perfection of the world—with the people, Israel, back in its home. Now, the fantasy is

---

*Babylonian Talmud, Ketubot 111A.

real every day, so he sings its joy every day. Some Jews mark their homes with Israeli art objects, as traditional Jews mark them with mezuzahs. Others fill their homes with Israeli music, which bubbles with the liveliness of a restored land and people.

In tandem with these developments, Yom Ha'Atzmaut becomes the climax of a year-long celebration.

THE RELATIONSHIP OF DIASPORA AND ISRAEL

Early Zionists thought the end of diaspora would come with the renewal of Israel. The leadership of the Yishuv was not prepared for the possibility that Israel would be born and grow mightily while the Diaspora would flourish as well. Therefore, no attempt was made to build some connection to Diaspora into Yom Ha'Atzmaut. Aside from extra tourists arriving in Jerusalem and Israel for Independence Day and some growing celebration of the holiday among Diaspora Jews, there has been little or no special effort by world Jewry to think through the day.

Jewish holidays have always been important expressions of the relationship between diaspora and Israel. The three core holidays—Passover, Shavuot, and Sukkot—were days of pilgrimage to Jerusalem. Admittedly, the farther away people were, the less often they came, but still the holidays served to focus attention on Zion. Jews in faraway lands prayed for rain when the Israeli rainy season began on Sukkot. The summer harvest was celebrated when Israel brought it in on Shavuot. During the period of Exile, Shabbat and holidays were the time to pray for and raise funds for the building of Israel.

In all the holidays, the relationship of Israel and diaspora is secondary to the overrall theme of the festival. But precisely because Yom Ha'Atzmaut focuses on renewed Jewish sovereignty and power, this is the day to articulate the relationship of Diaspora Jews to the Jewish state. Therefore, Herschel Blumberg, a major American Jewish communal leader has suggested that Israel and Diaspora communities ought to look at the paradigms of the first conquest and the first Jewish commonwealth in the land of Israel for models of developing Yom Ha'Atzmaut in terms of their interrelationship. After Joshua led the Israelites across the Jordan, five symbolic actions were taken. Blumberg proposes that all be utilized today, metaphorically if not literally, to build a relationship between Zion and world Jewry.

First, twelve stones were taken up from the Jordan by individual representatives of the twelve tribes and set aside as an everlasting witness. Another twelve stones were set in the Jordan to commemorate the miracle of the passage into Israel. Blumberg calls for a ceremony to be held at the Jordan, celebrating the passage of Jewry from stateless-ness to sovereignty. The communities (the contemporary tribes of Israel) from throughout the world would send representative delega-tions to participate. Stones from the Jordan would be set up as a per-manent witness to the unity of world Jewry around Israel. (Stones would be added every year, or there could be one permanent monu-ment.) Pointing out that the Jordan River constitutes a mikvah, Blum-berg suggests that if in any year there is a major influx to Israel of Jews from a particular country, a representative of that community could undergo immersion in the Jordan, together with representatives of all the other communities, to symbolize their rebirth as an indivisible part of the Jewish people. There has been a bitter controversy over the acceptance of Ethiopian Jewry as a rediscovered tribe of Jewry. The Israeli rabbinate has sought to require immersion of Ethiopian Jews as a formal completion of rebirth as Jews. The Ethiopians object, consid-ering this requirement as singling them out unfairly and as a denial of their legitimacy. Blumberg suggests that representatives of all Jewry enter into this mikvah together with Ethiopian Jews.* This would af-firm the equality of Ethiopian Jews and the unity of fate and status of all Jews, even as it would meet the rabbinate's request and remove an obstacle to the oneness of all Jews.

The Bible recounts that when the Israelites entered the land, those males born in the desert who were not circumcised throughout the forty years of wandering in the desert were now ushered into the cov-enant of Abraham. Yom Ha'Atzmaut could be the day when Jews who have come from lands of oppression where circumcision was not al-lowed or available would be circumcised and welcomed into the fel-lowship of Israel. Yom Ha'Atzmaut could also become the time for mass conversions. By timing this ceremony to coincide with Yom Ha'Atzmaut, converts would be stating their recognition of their re-sponsibility for Jewish destiny.

After making the first major conquest within Israel (Jericho), Joshua built an altar. This was in gratitude for divine help, designed to re-mind people of the higher purposes to which Israel was dedicated. The contemporary counterpart would be dedicating a synagogue or groundbreaking for a synagogue or even completing the physical re-furbishing of a house of worship. The dedication of other institutions (a university, yeshiva, concert hall, or art center) is also appropriate for this day. Diaspora Jews have endowed many such structures. Yom

---

*Normally, people who immerse remove all their clothes to achieve total immersion and to enter in and come out as on the day they were born, for this is a rebirth ceremony. Some-times, in places where no private mikvahs exist, rabbis have to use living bodies of water (such as lakes, oceans, or rivers) for this purpose. Under these circumstances, Orthodox rabbis have permitted wearing loose-fitting bathing suits which allow all parts of the body to be directly in contact with the water while preserving modesty.

Ha'Atzmaut would thus become the occasion for a twin declaration: of the reciprocal dedication of world Jewry and Israel, and the common recognition that Israel does not live by bread alone.

Joshua performed two other symbolic actions after completing the initial stage of possessing the land. He inscribed on the altar stones a copy of the Teaching (the covenantal instructions of the Torah) that Moses had written for the Israelites. Then, in the presence of all Israel, he read forth the Torah. Clearly, this was a renewal-of-the-covenant ceremony.

The counterpart today would be a national renewal-of-the-covenant ceremony. Representatives of Diaspora Jewry and Israel would exchange "ratifications" and pledges of mutual help. Or they could together renew the commitment of the Jewish people to the final redemption of the world. The president of Israel or the prime minister and heads of government could read sections of the Bible over radio and television.

Since the secular-religious split in Israel might make such a ceremony too controversial, more modest variations are possible. People may undertake to study the Five Books of the Torah or the entire Bible over the course of a year (or years), with the conclusion to be studied and celebrated on Yom Ha'Atzmaut. Torah scrolls could be written over the course of the year with the completion on this day. Copies of the Pentateuch or Bible—could be given as gifts on this day.

The people of Israel have already anticipated Blumberg's suggestion in a particular way. On Yom Ha'Atzmaut, the finals of the World Bible Contest are held. Jewish children from all over the world compete in answering questions derived from biblical sources. The contests have become major media events in Israel and a focus of communal life in the Diaspora. Thus, contemporary media and technology underscore the fact that Jews are still the people of the book, while, at the same time, deepening ties between Diaspora and Israel. Another example also comes to mind. In almost prophetic anticipation of the multiple sources of values in this most secular holiday, the government of Israel has made it the occasion for granting the Israel prize for outstanding accomplishment to leading Jewish cultural and spiritual figures.

Finally, no Jewish holiday is complete without some acts of tzedakah. The profile of the appropriate charity for Yom Ha'Atzmaut is clear: It should focus on self-help and taking power, while strengthening relations between Israel and Diaspora. Maimonides says:

> A great level of tzedakah—there is none higher—is to uphold a Jew in need by giving a gift or loan or making a partnership with him or finding employment for him in order to strengthen his hand so that he will not need to ask assistance from others. Our Scripture says:

"You shall strengthen him, whether stranger or settler, he shall live with you" (Leviticus 25:35); in other words, uphold him *before* he falls and needs help.*

No matter how kind and loving the help extended to someone who is failing, that very help creates dependency and loss of self-esteem. Therefore, the highest form of tzedakah is that which enables the person to become self-supporting. A loan that creates a business or a job is higher than welfare help because it paves the way for independence of the beneficiary.

The most appropriate tzedakah for Yom Ha'Atzmaut is, therefore, Israel bonds or investing in Israeli companies' stocks and bonds. The proceeds create the infrastructure of the Israeli economy, providing jobs for people who would otherwise be on welfare. The investment creates an economic base for Israel's military and political strength. More and more American Jews have become aware that investment in Israel or buying Israeli products may be healthier for Israel's economy than outright gifts. In many communities, Israeli fairs featuring displays of Israeli products and technology, and bringing numbers of Jews and non-Jews in touch with Israeli goods or services, have become annual events. Holding such fairs in the Diaspora is a particularly appropriate way to celebrate Yom Ha'Atzmaut.

The deepest meaning of tzedakah may be the obligation to create a society in which people do not need kindness because of dependency or weakness but rather to obtain and give love out of equality and dignity. Economic justice through productivity and jobs means that the ultimate tzedakah is the one that makes tzedakah obsolete.

YOM YERUSHALAYIM (JERUSALEM DAY)

Modern Zionism was born in the 1880s. While the new Yishuv grew slowly and steadily, it was at the center of Jewish life until the shock of the Holocaust made Jews aware of the urgency of statehood. In somewhat analogous fashion, the State of Israel came into being in 1948, then grew slowly but steadily more important in the hearts of Jews everywhere. But Israel did not occupy an unequivocal, towering position in Jewish life until the threat of losing it jolted Jews into new awareness that they could not live without it.

May 15, 1948, caught the rabbinate unprepared for the full signifi-

---

*Maimonides, *Yad Hachazakah* (Mishneh Torah). (New York: Grossman Publishers, 1960), Sefer Zeraim, Hilchot Matnot Aneeyim, chapter 10, halacha 7.

cance of the state, which explains the ambivalence toward Yom Ha'Atzmaut as well. Many Jews around the world responded to Israel but many others went on politically and spiritually with business as usual.

The Six-Day War of 1967 gave Israel to the Jewish people for a second time. In the anxious months of April and May 1967, Diaspora Jewry and even many Israelis saw another Holocaust looming. Israel was surrounded by enemies openly proclaiming their intention to destroy her; she was abandoned by her friends in the free world. For many Jews this situation opened the floodgates of Holocaust emotion. Then when Israel was not snatched away, when Israel triumphed overwhelmingly, it struck many as a second coming of the State of Israel.

Swept along by a wave of enthusiasm and religious uplift, the rabbinate declared Yom Yerushalayim (Jerusalem Day) a joyous national holiday. The ruling of the day included reciting Hallel with a blessing, offering special prayers, celebration, and performing marriages. This holiday was established on the day of the liberation of Jerusalem, despite the fact that it occurs in the middle of the Sefirah period.

Since 1967, the euphoria of the Six-Day War has subsided. Winning back Jerusalem did not resolve the political and spiritual problems of the past. As a result, Yom Yerushalayim observance has languished. In Israel, marathon hikes to Jerusalem became popular, but the holiday is generally poorly developed. The critical question—and the true obstacle to acceptance of Yom Yerushalayim—is the lack of clarity about the meaning and the new pattern of Jewish history.

For nineteen hundred years, as the role of Jewish suffering unfolded, the Jewish calendar expanded with days of sadness. Grief so dominated the calendar (three weeks in the summer; several weeks of Sefirah in the spring; Monday and Thursday in the fall; the eve of the new moon every month; the four fast days) that there was fear additional days might tip the balance of the year into excessive mourning.

The climax of these nineteen hundred years of growing gloom and pain came in the Holocaust. Jewish suffering could go no further without ending the very existence of the Jewish people. The sheer magnitude of the Holocaust dictated the inclusion of another mourning day, Yom Hashoah. But the bulk of the Jewish people declared that Jewish suffering should go no further. "Never again!" meant no more permanent grief days as well. In Israel's War of Independence an aroused Jewry beat back the invaders by the narrowest of margins. The victory upheld the state, and the celebration of that redemption added Yom Ha'Atzmaut—a happy day—to the calendar. Since Independence Day fell during the Sefirah period, the modern Exodus reclaimed one day from the ranks of the days of sorrow and added it to the days of joy.

But a question remained: Was this merely a respite, a short-term upturn from an unchanged long-term trend of oppressive sorrow, or was this the beginning of a major reversal of historic proportions from sorrow to joy? This question was answered in the Six-Day War. By a far greater margin, would-be destruction was turned back. The margin of victory made clear the incredible accomplishment of two decades of state-building. The perfect symbol of this joyful discovery was an add-on to the achievement of statehood, that is, the reunification of Jerusalem. After two thousand years of being deprived of the focus of Jewish spirituality and hope, the circle was closed by the recovery of the Temple Mount. This event was recognized as the confirmation of a turn in Jewish history. A second day of celebration was added—Yom Yerushalayim.

Since Jerusalem Day occurs in the Sefirah period, another calendar day was shifted from the side of sorrow to the side of joy. As the security and peace of Israel's establishment sinks in, one can project a pattern: In time, the day of concluding the peace treaty of Camp David (and the day of the signing of the final total peace) will be added to the holidays of celebration. Eventually, the three weeks between Yom Ha'Atzmaut and Yom Yerushalayim will be filled in as days of joy and celebration.

One devout Jew no longer recites the daily *tachanun* (penitential prayers) because every day that Israel exists is a happy day. (Traditionally, one does not say these grief-filled prayers on celebration days.) Now he says tachanun only when there are special anniversaries of grief or destruction. Step by step, victory by victory, the Jewish people are reversing the tide of Jewish history from mourning to celebration, from death to life.

Israel's right to exist is still challenged, of course. Attempts are made to inflict defeat on the Jewish people. But Jewish fate is in Jewish hands and, from year to year, the people get stronger and stronger. The hope grows that indeed an age of life and redemption has begun. We can envision that the memories of pain and grief will fade as the habits of peace and happiness grow. We can anticipate the fulfillment of the prophetic promise that "the [four fast days] will become days of joy and rejoicing and good festivals for the House of Judah; so love truth and peace . . ."(Zechariah 8:19).

Afterword

IN THE CREATION OF ISRAEL, one sees the greatness of dreams and of those who have the courage to pursue them through time when "realists"—people of lesser faith and stamina—give up. For eighteen hundred years, Jews proclaimed the vision of going back to Jerusalem. They could not act on this hope, but because the dream was kept alive, when a window of opportunity to go back opened in the nineteenth century, there were Jews ready and able to act.

For decades, the Zionist settlers struggled to build the infrastructure of a new society. They were pitifully few in number, even by the scale of Jewish history. When modern Zionists started their work, they could hardly have anticipated the emergency caused by the Holocaust. Yet, when the catastrophe struck and a Jewish state was an absolute necessity, they and their handiwork were in place to provide the base for the new sovereignty.

Modern Zionism was a classic reprise of the experience of the primordial Jew setting out on a journey toward a destination "that I will show thee." The conclusion of Zionism one could neither know in advance nor wait for, but only those who set out could be there to realize the goal. The miracle of 1948 could only be accomplished by those who had banged their heads against history's wall since the 1880s.

The Zionist pioneers were not a random sample of the Jewish people in the nineteenth century. Perhaps five percent of the Jewish world was socialist/secularist in the 1880s. But since the pioneers drew heavily from that group, this sector made up forty to fifty percent of the population that founded the state. And the religious minority in Israel was overwhelmingly Modern Orthodox. Breaking through the barriers of belief and observance that separated these two groups from each other, defying both the assimilating westernizers and the great rabbinic scholars who were still opposed to the state, they united in a historic alliance to pull off a miracle—a new redemption.

After World War II, in response to the historical emergency, a Jewish consensus emerged for statehood now. That decision forced each particular Jewish group to go beyond some of its basic values, to create a real-life situation that would strain, if not undermine, some of its most cherished assumptions. The Zionist "normalizers" almost complacently expected a peaceful, conventional relationship with the neighboring Arabs and their states. The decision for statehood in the face of an Arab world not ready to accept it meant the creation of an island of Jews, proudly sovereign and expecting equal rights, in a sea of Islamic culture that could accept Jews only as *dhimmi*, permanently inferior wards of the Arab state. The action guaranteed that Israel would be in a "permanent" state of siege as an outpost of westernism in a Middle East frontier swept by a growing frenzy of fundamentalism and xenophobia. The *Sitz im Leben* ensured that the state would not likely survive if life within it ever became normal. The new condition made the normalizers dependent on all the religious and other groups in Palestine that were imbued with the conviction that Israel had a divine calling or philosophical or political mandate to be special.

The religious groups, in turn, found themselves forced to push for a state whose majority governing group would be nonobservant and often even antagonistic to the common tradition and memory. Thanks to religious Zionists' support, their atheist and nonobservant allies would become heroes and role models for the national culture. Every day religionists and their children would see men and women, openly manifesting their conviction that religion was outdated and doomed to disappear, play the leading roles as the shakers and movers of the state for which religious Jews had prayed and dreamed for centuries. The agents of the divine redemption—which the religious saw in messianic terms—would be ignorant of Talmud, hostile to halacha.

Rabbi Y. L. Maimon, a leader of the religious Zionists, once said to his son-in-law, Yitzchak Raphael, "Were it not for Ben-Gurion, it is highly doubtful that we would have been worthy of the privilege of a state in our time." To which Raphael replied, "We believe that this state is bestowed on us by God. Did God choose for Himself, as his agent, a Sabbath violator? A Jew who does not observe the commandments of the Torah?" Maimon brooded deeply and finally responded, "It is a miracle that Ben-Gurion is not an observant Jew. Were he perfect [that is, observant], people would mistakenly believe that he is the Messiah—but the Messiah has not yet come."

True . . . but what a painful, "lame" excuse to offer to the critics from the religious right. The ultras insisted that it was the religious Zionist approval that made people such as Ben-Gurion the lords and masters of the state, from whom one had to beg crumbs such as an open reference to God in the Declaration of Independence (declined), an army mess that was kosher (granted). And the embattled, isolated condition of the state meant that the religious would be permanently dependent on the goodwill of the others for whatever concessions to religious sensibilities they would grant. One would have to live with secularists even when they used their power to wean children from tradition or reward the nonobservant minority institutions with the plums of statehood support.

The historic emergency meant that the secular Zionists who defined Israel's specialness as a bastion of Western progressivism and scientific leadership would have to preside over a mass infusion of hundreds of thousands of Oriental Jews (slurred as Levantine) into the population of the state. This new group would reinforce the traditional sector and sharply dilute the image of an elitist Western state. Each group wished—or expected—that the other would disappear. Yet creation of the state made each group more likely to sustain itself. And none of the groups could live or the state survive without the other's full participation.

The irony of Jewish history has assured a state of inescapable cooperation and permanent tension between the conflicting views and groups of modern and traditional Jewry. The result often is cooperation in action but deep conflict in interpretation of the meaning of actions. Another result was the almost miraculous creation of a democratic system with rule of law among people who had not exercised political power in millennia. Yet because of conflicts in basic values, the two sides could not agree to a common constitution or fundamental law. The new balance of power forces a constant attempt to define a satisfactory status quo which, by its nature, has to have built-in dissatisfaction for all groups. And the status quo is inherently unstable as the fortunes and inner dynamics of each group wax and wane.

The alliance of the conflicting groups, undertaken for the sake of the greater truth of the state and historic redemption, imposed a permanent set of compromises and conflicts, lies, and forced interpretations on each of the groups. The inherited positions carved out under the impact of modernity were in constant tension and spiritual torment due to the demands of statehood and sovereignty. Except for moments of crisis and absolute danger, the sacred occasions of the state, when the societies seek to express their unity, are condemned to be the occasions of conflicting interpretations and symbols and ambiguous meanings.

To their great credit, the majority rose to the historic occasion; they put the state and the demands of reality ahead of ideology. As the Talmud might have stated it, "It was a time to do for the Lord—so they violated your Torahs" (Psalm 119:126). The deeper truth was that Judaism was alive, generating new responses and facts. By admitting the inadequacy of their categories, Jews were allowing something new to be born. The Rabbis of the Talmud would have described this triumph of historical intuition over the objections of partisan reason as proof that the holy spirit still has not abandoned the Jewish people or forsaken its judgment.

All these built-in interactons are tensions that operate in the context of unparalleled freedom and power for Jews. In Israel, Jews have taken command of responsibility for Jewish fate. That freedom and power can be used to create the greatest Jewish society of all time, one that carries the covenantal mission to new heights of justice and exemplary behavior in full view of the nations. Yet that same choice and force can be applied abusively to Jews and Arabs alike.

Struggling with the dialectic of secular and religious understandings can lead to a higher synthesis, a third-era Judaism, exquisitely reconciling the universal and particular in the covenant. It can also create internecine warfare, leaving Israel more vulnerable to external enemies or leading to a social rupture that could result in mass emigration and a residual chauvinist population. Sometimes it appears that all of the above possibilities are being realized.

Given the extraordinary range of adaptation and survival reflected in the record of the Jewish holidays, given the incredible force of redemption and faithfulness exhibited along the Jewish way, one has a right to increase hope. But the outcome is open. Decisions being made now or to be made in the future will decisively shape the final result. Anyone who chooses to share in Jewish destiny can come forward and be a partner in the process. All the resources developed along the way can be drawn on to sustain Israel and humanity along the next stretch of the road. The risk is high. It is hard to conceive that the Jewish witness could survive failure or disaster here. The potential is equally high. The Jewish people can become teacher, model, and co-worker with all of humanity on a biblical scale. And this could be an era of breakthrough for all humankind.

This generation is living in the most exciting period of Jewish history. The redemption of Israel restores the paradigm of the Jewish way from Exodus to final redemption. As Rabbi Abraham Isaac Kook once said, this is the generation furthest from the miracles of Exodus and Sinai but closest to the messianic age.

There is a danger, of course, that this messianic vision could overpower judgment and draw the Jew into a pursuit of fantasy that undermines the state. Among some Israelis, renascent messianism stimulates a grandiosity that dismisses considerations of military and diplomatic feasibility when making policy judgments. Yehoshafat Harkabi, former head of Israeli military intelligence, warns that messianism can lead again, as it did in the first century, to loss of contact with reality. But this is not the messianism that lies at the heart of the State of Israel. Not magic but the sweat, blood, and tears of pioneers brought the miracle to pass. The mature Messiah to be brought by Israel will not be a *deus ex machina* on a white donkey. Rather, the Messiah's reign will be the product of infinite, painstaking construction of a better world. As Maimonides wrote:

> Do not think that the messianic ruler need perform signs and miracles or create a new state of the world or resurrect the dead and the like. Not so. . . . If a ruler arises . . . meditating on the Torah and performing commandments . . . in accordance with the written and oral Torah and moves all Israel to work in its ways and to strengthen and fight the wars of the Torah, this one is presumed to be the Messiah. If the Messiah acts and succeeds and builds the Temple on its place and brings together the scattered people of Israel, then you can be sure this is the Messiah. And the Messiah will perfect the whole world to worship the Lord together.*

Israel today represents with others the thrust for redemption out of the matrix of ordering natural life. It brings testimony—which grows every day—to the power of life over death, to the ability of a land and a people to come to life again. The work is unfinished, of course. Many Sephardic Jews and Arabs hardly have a full life of equality and dignity. The uprising of the Palestinians tests Israel's power and conscience at once. The Palestinians assault Israel's right to exist; yet only a people determined to take its destiny into its own hands can develop an indigenous leadership capable of making peace. Some Jews grow weary; some grow impatient; some lash out in anger. The record of the past three millennia gives hope and strength as well. "Those who trust in the Lord will renew their strength; they will run and not grow tired; they will work and not grow weary" (Isaiah 40:31).

There are no guarantees but the future is open. The obstacles and

---

*Ibid., Sefer Shofetim, Hilchot Melachim, Chapter 11, halacha 3–4.

forces of evil are strong. There are those who malign, who exploit, who wreck. But Jewish fate and human destiny are in our hands. Israel is a light unto the nations as Jews have not been in centuries.

Israel's actions are put before the worldwide public through media coverage that is without equal for a nation of its size. The coverage itself is quiet witness to the paradigm role that the world expects and Israelis assume even as they grumble at the burden. Not since the Hebrew Bible's instruction was spread to the rest of humanity have Jewish teaching and behavior been as closely studied and influential as they are today. When Israel discovers drip irrigation or how to store grain in low-cost tents so that it will not rot or how to bring people from primitive environments into the modern world in one generation while preserving their values, it becomes a model for humanity. Sometimes Israel's behavior makes one shrink because it falls short of classic moral ideals, but that, too, is part of the human model of the state that is not—cannot be—perfect. The holidays, including Yom Ha'Atzmaut, will have to develop sufficiently to be able to sustain the people's capacity to carry the covenantal burden without collapsing or betraying the mission.

The fundamental truth is that once you create a new exodus and incarnate it in a state, then "future exodus" is also possible. Life breeds life; rescue generates rescue. Iraqi Jews, Russians, Ethiopians —they continue to come unexpectedly, and they bring with them new problems and new hope for the world. The accomplishment of Israel is nothing less than a decisive sign for suffering humanity that love is stronger than hatred, that life will overcome death.

A time will come, says Maimonides, "when there will be no more hunger nor war, no jealousy and fierce competition. Goodness will be overflowing and all manner of delicacies as common as sand and the primary occupation of the entire world will be only to know God."* This is the measure of how much more there is left to do. To live the Jewish way is to be pledged to go and do it.

*Ibid., Chapter 12, halacha 5.

Two "Minor" Festivals:
Rosh Hodesh and *Tu B'Shvat*

Two semi-festivals on the Jewish liturgical calendar are not treated in the body of this book primarily because they do not encapsulate the historical way of the Jewish people as do the other holidays. These two holy days are generally regarded as minor even by observant Jews. They are Rosh Hodesh (literally, the head of the month, that is, the first day of each month) and Tu B'Shvat (the fifteenth day of the eleventh Hebrew month) which is described in the Talmud as the New Year for trees. Perhaps the "minor" festival status of these days proves the thesis of this book. Those holy days that express the great events, conflicts, and issues of Jewish historical experience become central holidays even if they are born later in history. Those holidays that do not have historical salience fade even if they are Biblical in origin.

ROSH HODESH:
ITS DATE AND EFFECT
ON THE HEBREW CALENDAR

The Hebrew calendar is primarily based on the lunar cycle. As the moon circles the earth, there is a moment when the moon is directly between the Earth and the sun (but not in the same plane, for that would create a solar eclipse). At that time, which is the conjunction of the moon with the sun, the moon is invisible. Then it makes its reappearance. This moment is called the Molad ("birth" of the moon and, hence, of the new month). A month represents the passage of time from the beginning of one cycle—the appearance of the moon, its waxing, waning, and "disappearance," until the next reappearance. The mean lunar month is twenty-nine days, twelve hours, forty-four minutes, and three and one-third seconds.

The cycle of twelve lunar months adds up to approximately 354⅓ days. The solar year (in which the Earth completes one cycle around the sun) adds up to approximately 365¼ days. Since the lunar year is about eleven days shorter than the solar year, Jewish holidays set in an unadjusted lunar cycle year would occur eleven days earlier on the solar calendar every year. Thus, the holidays would wander through the solar year. But the Torah fixes certain holidays in the seasons according to the solar year. Passover is to be a spring holiday and Sukkot a fall harvest festival (see chapters 3 and 5). Therefore, the lunar calendar is adjusted to the solar by the insertion of an extra lunar month seven times in every nineteen years. (This makes the Hebrew calendar a luni-solar one.) This process, known as intercalation, roughly synchronizes the two calendars. Over nineteen years there is a gap of about 209 days, which is approximately equivalent to seven lunar months. In post-Temple times, the intercalated months were fixed for years 3, 6, 8, 11, 14, 17, and 19 of the nineteen-year cycle. The extra month is known as Adar Sheni (Adar the Second) because it is always inserted after the twelfth month, Adar, and before the month of Nissan, the month of spring and the Exodus.

The lunar month is about twenty-nine and a half days long. For calendar purposes, the Hebrew day, which is keyed to the moon, begins at night. It would be inconsistent and inconvenient to have the new month start on a half day and in daylight every other month. Therefore, the beginning day of the month is rotated. In some months, the new month begins on the thirtieth day. (This makes the previous month twenty-nine days long, and it is categorized as "less than full" [Heb. *haser*].) In the other months, the new month begins on the thirty-first day (which makes the previous month thirty days long, and it is described as "full" [Heb. *malei*]).

In biblical and early talmudic times, the new month was not fixed by astronomical calculations. The members of the high court gathered in Jerusalem, and witnesses came to testify that they had sighted the new appearance of the moon. The court then proclaimed and sanctified the new moon. (A residual echo of this practice may be found in the traditional synagogue. The date of the forthcoming new month is proclaimed on the Sabbath preceding the new moon. At that time a prayer is said that the coming month be one of life, health, prosperity, and spiritual fulfillment. This Sabbath is known as Shabbat Mevarchim [the Sabbath on Which They Bless the New Month].)

If the moon was not sighted on the thirtieth day, then the new moon was automatically celebrated on the thirty-first day. A string of beacon lights was lit from Jerusalem's Mount of Olives across Israel and into parts of the diaspora to signal the beginning of the month. The system was later rendered inoperative; one factor was the determination of a rival religious group, the Samaritans, to sabotage the process. The Samaritans kindled "counterfeit" beacons on the wrong days to mislead the Jews into observing their holidays at the wrong time. From then on, messengers were sent to inform distant communities of the correct date in place of using the beacon fires as a notification system. The custom developed that those Jewish communities situated great distances from Jerusalem automatically celebrated the thirtieth day of the month as the new moon (Rosh Hodesh). If and when they were notified by the messengers that the new month had been postponed to the thirty-first day, they also observed the second day as the new moon. That second day became day one of the new month; the first day of Rosh Hodesh became, retroactively, day thirty of the previous month.

The shift to a messenger system meant that diaspora communities at a great distance from Jerusalem could not be notified in timely fashion as to which day (thirty or thirty-one) was day one of the new month. This meant that people living in these communities could not be sure of the exact day of the sacred holidays of that month. For example, the date of Passover (15 Nissan) or the date of Sukkot (15 Tishrei) could occur a day earlier (if the new moon was on the thirtieth day of the previous month) or a day later (if it was on the thirty-first day). Since the first and last days of the biblical festivals were sacred, that is, labor was prohibited on these days, one could not work normally on either day for fear of violating the prohibition. Thus, the tradition developed to add a second sacred day at the beginning and end of the major biblical festivals. The extra days were called Yom Tov Sheni Shel Galuyot (the Second Festival Day of the Diasporas), for they were observed only in Diaspora communities. By rabbinic ordination these extra days were observed essentially in the same manner as the biblical sacred days. This procedure was followed initially out of doubt as to which day was the actual sacred day of the holiday, but eventually the practice became entrenched. Even when the calendar was fixed and set by astronomical calculations so that all knew the exact dates, the tradition of Yom Tov Sheni Shel Galuyot was retained. To this day special rituals and prayers including mussaf services are performed on these days as on the biblical holy days.

This arrangement means that there are extra sacred days as follows: in Passover, the first and second and seventh and eighth days instead of just the first and seventh; Shavuot is two days instead of one; and in Sukkot, the first, second, eighth, and ninth days are prohibited in labor instead of just the first and eighth. In the diaspora, this practice doubled the number of days in each holiday when labor and business were prohibited. This was no small economic burden. It should be added that since Rosh Hashanah is the only major Jewish holiday that starts on the first day of the month, Rosh Hashanah was celebrated for two days from early times on, out of uncertainty as to which day the moon would be witnessed. Thus, Rosh Hashanah is observed for two days *even in Israel*. Logically, there should also be two days of Yom Kippur. However, except for a trace of such a practice in limited areas in medieval times, it appears that this was not done, probably due to the problematic nature of a two-day total cessation of food, drink, sexual activity, work, and so forth. Such a total fast would have jeopardized people's health and likely would have distracted from the spiritual search or even disrupted the deep religious impact of Yom Kippur.

Retention of the extra days made life in the diaspora more onerous. It constantly reminded Jews that no matter how comfortable the exile, they were not at home. In the early days of emancipation, Reform Judaism dropped Yom Tov Sheni. In the late twentieth century, the halachic leadership of American

Conservative Judaism ruled that observing the extra days is optional. These shifts were based partly on the argument that the calendar was astronomically fixed and securely established so that the extra days' observance was no longer necessary. The shifts also reflect the fact that liberal Jews feel more at home in diaspora, and they also find the extra day an economic and social burden. In Orthodox Judaism's consensus view, authority is lacking to make this change. Furthermore, Orthodox Jews are more likely to feel that, despite acceptance by Gentiles, they are still in a state of exile. Also, the Orthodox community is less attuned to the idea that economic considerations should affect religious behavior.

ROSH HODESH:
SIGNIFICANCE AND STANDING

The Torah seems to place Rosh Hodesh on a par with the other festivals. In the Book of Numbers (28:11–15), the additional (mussaf) sacrifices for Rosh Hodesh are listed alongside the other shabbat and holy festival mussaf offerings. The Rosh Hodesh sacrifices are identical in number and kind with those of Passover and Shavuot. (In post-Temple times, a mussaf prayer service was established for this day, as for all holy days on which there had been a mussaf sacrifice.)

Rosh Hodesh day was marked by many festive elements. There was a celebratory meal, and family gatherings were a natural for such occasions (see 1 Samuel 20:18–42). (Over the course of later history, by association, the day was considered especially appropriate for housewarmings, dedications, wearing new clothes, saying Shehechiyanu over new fruit; it was also called the Day of Good Beginnings.) The joyous spirit of the day, in biblical times, is suggested by two references. It states in the Pentateuch: "And on your joyous occasions—your fixed festivals and new moon days—you shall sound the trumpets" (Numbers 10:10). The prophet Hosea, projecting a future catastrophe to be inflicted on sinful Israel, warned that ". . . I (God) will end all her rejoicing: Her festivals, new moons and Sabbaths." The tradition of joy persists down to today in the halachic prohibition of fasting on the new moon and in the custom of cutting short funeral services and not eulogizing on the day.

Nevertheless, unlike the other biblical holy days, the new moon is not described as a sacred day on which all labor is prohibited. There may have been some restrictions on commerce; the prophet Amos, denouncing some greedy, exploitative businessmen, portrays them as saying: ". . . if only the new moon were over so that we could sell grain [and cheat the poor]" (Amos 8:5). The Talmud rules that work is permitted on the new moon but describes a tradition that women abstain from work on the day. Later sources explain that on this semi-festival, partial abstention from labor was a reward to the righteous women who refused to surrender their jewelry for the creation of the Golden Calf.* One wonders whether this tradition may not reflect a special wom-

---

*TB Rosh Hashanah 23A, Tosafot s.v. Mishum. Compare also Pirke de Rabbi Eliezer, chapter 45.

en's affinity for this day, a connection that has been revived in recent times.

Rosh Hodesh was celebrated only eleven times a year. In Tishrei, Rosh Hashanah coincides with Rosh Hodesh; to this day, the new month of Tishrei is not proclaimed in advance in traditional synagogues; the new year rather than the new moon is dominant liturgically. In the same spirit Rosh Hashanah celebration takes precedence over Rosh Hodesh.

Rosh Hodesh obviously lost some of its import with the destruction of the Temple and the end of sacrifices. Unlike the other festivals that carried or incorporated major historical events and their lessons, this day retained only a nature (that is, astronomical) connection. Given the dominant and growing historical dimension of Judaism and the holidays, Rosh Hodesh naturally suffered attrition in importance. In the course of centuries, the liturgical impact of the day shrank. In the Orthodox synagogue, a special set of prayers is recited on the Shabbat preceding the new moon, and the date of the coming Rosh Hodesh (as well as the name of the month) is proclaimed. On the day itself, the Hatzi (partial) Hallel, the *yaaleh v'yavo* prayer, and an extra (mussaf) service are added. In Yemenite and other Sephardic customs, a candle is lit for the day both in the synagogue and home. Beyond these practices the day hardly makes a ripple.

In one way the new moon did develop a tie to history. Through the Kabbala, Rosh Hodesh developed a special mystical meaning that reflects the suffering and tragedy of Jewish history.

From early days a special relationship and analogy between the moon and the Jewish people was discerned. One obvious connection is the Jewish calendar, which follows the lunar system whereas most Gentile calendars were solar. Then, too, the waning and waxing of the moon, its disappearance and rebirth, appeared to parallel the vicissitudes of Jewish history. The moon's stubborn reappearance after every disappearance became identified, in the mind of the Jews, with this people's power of rebirth after every catastrophe.

Rabbinic Midrash ultimately led, through kabbalistic development, to a theological/mystical ceremony and special attitude toward the moon. The creation chapter (Genesis 1:16) states that "God made the two great lights, the greater light [sun] to dominate the day and the lesser light [moon] to dominate the night." The Rabbis noted that the phrase "two great lights" could be interpreted as referring to two heavenly light sources of equal size, whereas the sun is the greater light and the moon is the lesser.

Rabbinic Midrash imaginatively projected that in primeval creation the two luminary bodies were of equal size, but the moon was later reduced to a lesser status. The moon's smaller size became a symbol of the inequality and imperfection that mar the world at present. Therefore, the moon's diminutive stature and periodic waning become visible signs, as it were, of the fragmented, flawed world that humanity inhabits. This reality is far short of the perfection that a divinely created world should possess. In the Rabbis' fancy, then, some day the moon will be restored to its full size and permanent equal stature—a hallmark of the final stage of worldwide messianic perfection!

In Second Temple times, a ceremony "blessing the moon" (Birkat Halevanah), sometimes called "sanctification of the moon" (Kiddush Levanah), was developed. Recited from the third evening of the reappearance of the moon (when the moon is clearly visible) up until the fifteenth day of the month (as long as the moon is waxing), the prayer quickly became associated with the messianic hope. The plea that God would readjust the moon's size and the prayer for the restoration of David and his line, the once and future messianic rule, became part of the ceremony. ("David, King of Israel, is alive and present," which became a modern halutzic as well as a religious messianic song, is recited three times in the Kiddush Levanah.) The ceremony is warm and upbeat. Each participant chants Shalom Aleichem (Peace to you! Greetings!) to three different participants; those addressed reply: Aleichem Shalom! (To you, peace! Greetings!)

In later kabbalistic development, the moon's size became a classic symbol of the *shevirat hakelim* (the breaking of the divine vessels, the primordial rupture in creation that left the universe flawed and full of evil). The present state in which evil is intermixed throughout existence must be overcome in order that the world be perfected. By this association, Rosh Hodesh took on greater importance to the kabbalists. They worked up spiritual exercises in anticipation of this day on which they sought to achieve liturgical messianic breakthroughs. They developed a day of preparation, the day before Rosh Hodesh, as a day of fasting and repentance. (Note again the classic Jewish liturgical move from sadness and solemnity to joy and triumph.) The day was called Yom Kippur Katan (a mini Day of Atonement); as if God were passing judgment on the world and its messianic future. Nevertheless, this kabbalistic exegesis was not popular enough—or historical enough—to sweep the masses into its spirit; Rosh Hodesh did not recapture its biblical era stature.

In the 1970s Rosh Hodesh was rediscovered by a group of feminists seeking to find liturgical models for women.[*] Since the major festivals were associated with male leadership and religious expression, the search for women's rituals led to the recovery of distinctive women's connections to Rosh Hodesh.

The medieval source Or Zaruah had suggested that Rosh Hodesh, which marked the cycle of the moon's renewal, is a referential symbol to the monthly cycle after which women renew themselves through immersion. A rabbinic midrash stated that righteous women would be rewarded "in the next world in that they are destined to be renewed like the new moons."[†] In the feminist interpretation this suggested that as the moon would be restored to its primeval equality with the sun in the messianic era, so would women be restored to their primordial equality without becoming identical with men.

In the following decades a wide range of women's groups have developed special celebrations of Rosh Hodesh. Such celebrations take place, regularly or sporadically, in the major cities of the United States as well as in Jerusalem, Montreal, Toronto, and in England. Rosh Hodesh liturgies have spread to many college campuses since these are places where interest in both feminism and spiritual creativity is high. Many halachically observant women are in-

[*]The seminal article articulating this connection is Arlene Agus's "This Month is for You: Observing Rosh Hodesh as A Women's Holiday," in *The Jewish Woman: New Perspectives*, edited by Elizabeth Koltun (New York: Schocken Books, 1986), pp. 84–93. The author is indebted to Arlene Agus for much of the information in the following section of this appendix.
[†]Pirke de Rabbi Eliezer, chapter 45.

volved because they are particularly moved by and interested in religious ceremonial expression. Apparently the absence of a highly structured observance pattern and the relative "secularity" of the day allow greater freedom for such creativity. In some yeshiva high school settings, male and female students participate. Interestingly, some secular women have joined in the creation and celebration of these ceremonies. Thus, through feminist motivation, some secular Jews have been led to the recovery of sacred time and religious observance.

The most widely used type of Rosh Hodesh ceremony will be described here. It should be stressed, however, that the matter is in the full throes of exploration and discovery, and the liturgical situation is highly fluid. The ceremony celebrates divine creation and three qualities of existence that feminists particularly associate with the feminine: the life cycle, rebirth, and renewal. Since Rosh Hodesh is associated with the woman's monthly cycle, the ceremony focuses on such symbols as water, sphere, and circle, representing purification and rebirth in the mikvah, the shape of the moon, and the cycles of life. Foods containing the seeds of life are also appropriate for the celebration. Traditional elements of the Rosh Hodesh commemoration are also included, such as lighting a candle, eating a festive meal, giving charity, and reciting the Rosh Hodesh prayers.

The group comes together dressed in holiday clothing or in new clothes saved for the occasion. Many give tzedakah before the ceremony. A candle is lit to burn for twenty-four hours. Some use a floating light because it resembles the moon floating in the sky. A prayer is read. Also widely used is a poem, "Create Me Anew," written by Hillel Zeitlin, the martyred religious poet and philosopher of the Warsaw ghetto. Among its verses are:

> O great and holy Father of all mankind
> You create the world, Your child, every instant.
> If for an instant You withdrew
> The loving gift of Your creation
> —All would be nothingness. . . .
>
> . . . You create everything anew
> Father, please, create me, Your child, anew.
> Breathe into me of Your spirit
> That I may begin a new life.

The new month is honored typically by a presentation on a Jewish holiday occurring that month (or study of its laws and practices) or by commemorating a historical event or a yahrzeit (anniversary of death) that occurred during the month. Many forms of Jewish study are built into the order, here or later in the ceremony. Torah study is a central observance of Judaism; the admission of women to advanced Torah study is one of the great accomplishments of the late twentieth century and is particularly appropriate for women's religious expression.

Some groups incorporate a kiddush text—possibly reading an excerpt from the Kiddush Levanah or biblical verses dealing with the moon, followed by a blessing over a cup of wine. The ceremony concludes with a Rosh Hodesh feast. As on the Sabbath or festivals, two rolls or challahs are served; they are round or crescent shaped, preferably, thus invoking the shape of the moon. A new fruit will be sought for the menu for the sake of making a Shehecheyanu. The egg soup, traditionally served at the seder, is often included as a symbol of the seed of life immersed in liquid. A quiche of circular shape or a nut loaf, with its seed content, are popular choices for the menu. During the meal, zemirot such as verses from the Hallel or special Rosh Hodesh songs are sung.

Despite the growth of Rosh Hodesh celebration groups as well as the movement for Jewish women's religious expression, the numbers involved in these special liturgies are still quite small. They are certainly marginal to the total number of halachically observant Jews. Nevertheless, this development would appear to be the main hope—short of restoration of the Temple—that Rosh Hodesh will become more than a minor festival with limited liturgical elements. Since the proper response to great destruction is to achieve messianic breakthroughs for life and toward redemption, then we all should pray for the "restoration" of the moon and for a Jewish liturgical flowering in which the Rosh Hodesh festival would blossom again.

Perhaps through women's efforts, Rosh Hodesh can be restored as part of a great thrust toward perfection. Then Isaiah's vision would be fulfilled: ". . . as the new heaven and a new earth which I will make will endure . . . so shall your seed and your name . . . and from new moon to new moon and Sabbath after Sabbath, all flesh shall come before me to worship, says the Lord" (Isaiah 66:22–23).

TU B'SHVAT:
VARIATIONS ON AN
AGRICULTURAL THEME

The other minor festival, Tu B'Shvat, never achieved even the currency of Rosh Hodesh. There is no trace of the festival in the Bible. The origins of the day may lie in the ancient custom of celebrating the first day of each season. A talmudic passage describes the year as divided into six seasons. From 15 Shvat to 15 Nissan is the season of *kor* (cold) which comes after the season of *choref* (winter) and before the season of *katzir* (reaping, harvesting).

In the Talmud, the school of Beit Hillel rules that 15 Shvat rather than 1 Shvat is to be considered the New Year's Day for trees. Rabbi Elazar explains that Shvat was chosen because in Israel most of the annual rain falls by that date.* Another explanation offered is that 15 Shvat is the day when the trees have, by and large, used up the water from the earlier year's rainfall and begin absorbing the water of the new year. Therefore, the fruit of those trees that blossom after this date are considered produce of the coming year for purposes of tithing and also for purposes of *orlah*. (In the first three years of fruit bearing, a tree's fruit is defined as *orlah*; that fruit is set aside for God and is

*TB Rosh Hashanah 14A.

prohibited for human consumption or utilization. This constitutes a symbolic recognition that the land really belongs to God and not to its human masters.)

Because of the strong association with Israel, Tu B'Shvat was observed in Diaspora as a reminder and expression of attachment to the land of Israel. In some Ashkenazic communities, a custom arose to eat fifteen types of fruit on this day. Special efforts were made to obtain fruits of Israel—especially of the seven types of fruit and grain that, in the Torah, represent the fertility of land of Israel (Deuteronomy 8:8). It was considered especially meritorious to obtain such produce directly from Israel, if possible. Psalm 104 (a creation psalm) and the fifteen psalms of ascent (originally chanted by pilgrims going up to the Temple) were chanted. It was customary not to recite *tachanum* penitential prayers on this day for these prayers were too sad to be appropriately said on a semi-festival.

The custom of giving students the day off from traditional Torah studies also spread widely, despite critics' complaints that the teachers were cheating on the Lord's work. In defiance of such puritanical carping, a book of customs of the German community of Worms in the seventeenth century included a frolicsome requirement: Teachers of Torah had to supply their students with whiskey and good cake at the teachers' own expense when the students left synagogue in the morning to take the day off.

After the expulsion from Spain and the spread of Lurīanic Kabbalah, there was a major expansion of halachic practice. Kabbalists sought to intensify the cosmic process of *tikkun* (perfection) through liturgy. The kabbalists who went to Israel and who gathered in Safed and the Galilee developed a special ritual including a seder for Tu B'Shvat. The Tu B'Shvat liturgy was modeled on the Passover seder; it followed a prescribed order of eating, and four cups of wine were drunk.

The seder was as follows: The group gathered at nightfall in a study hall or private home, well lit with candles and tables bedecked with white tablecloths, garlands of flowers, and fragrant greens of all sorts. Pitchers of white and red wine were placed on the table. The kabbalists believed that white represented the forces of hibernation and exfoliation, the cumulative loss of life's power due to the shrinking sunlight—for the hours of sunshine had been declining all these months from the summertime peak. Red represented the forthcoming reawakening of nature's life force and the coming seasonal strengthening of the sun. It was as if the forces of life and death, sunlight and darkness, awakening and hibernation, were locked in final battle. With the triumph of the red, spring would not be far behind. This ascendancy of the red was liturgically preenacted and fostered through the seder.

Thirteen biblical passages, referring to the plants and produce of the land, were read. Passages from the Talmud and the Book of Zohar dealing with grains, plants, and agriculture were studied. A prayer for renewed growth followed. The first glass, consisting entirely of white wine, was poured. Wheat (in the form of cookies or "pasta" type foods), olives, dates, and grapes were blessed one by one and eaten. Then the first cup was blessed and drunk.

Now a second cup of wine was poured; this cup consisted mostly of white wine with a small portion of red wine blended in. Four more fruits of Israel were served one by one: figs, pomegranates, citrons (etrogim), and apples. All of these fruits have kabbalistic referents, but in the spirit of kabbalistic esotericism I won't explain them here. Then the second cup of wine was blessed and drunk.

The third cup, consisting of half white wine and half red wine, was now poured. Walnuts, almonds, carob fruit, and pears were blessed and eaten. Again, appropriate passages of the Talmud and Zohar were studied before each food was eaten. With toasts to a fruitful year, a good and blessed year, the third cup was downed.

The fourth cup, mostly red wine with a bit of white wine mixed in, was now poured. Crab apples, quinces, cherries, sunflower seeds, peanuts, plums, and chestnuts were presented and eaten. Thistle and lupine were served as "chasers" or dessert. Some kabbalists even proposed that thirty types of fruit be eaten: ten consisting of fruits such as apples and grapes that could be eaten wholly; ten of such types as walnuts and peanuts whose shell is thrown away and the inside meat eaten; and ten such as olives and plums whose inside core is inedible but whose outer flesh is eaten. Thus, the mystics identified with the fertility of the land of Israel, celebrated with its produce, and sought to strengthen its life-giving forces. Finally, the fourth cup of wine was drunk and the seder was completed.

In modern times, Tu B'Shvat was commemorated in the renewed agricultural settlements of the land of Israel in various ways. The Jewish National Fund, which replanted the denuded hillsides of Israel with forests, has made this a special day for tree planting. The day was widely presented as a "Jewish Arbor Day." In diaspora, the day also has become a time for picnics and outings and identification with nature as well as with the land of Israel. Still, in the absence of historical significance, the day remains a minor semi-festival.

APPENDIX B

Passover—
Prayer for the Seder

*A special prayer to be inserted into the Passover Seder
before opening the door for Elijah*

THE FIFTH CHILD
The One Who Cannot Ask
שֶׁאֵינוֹ יָכוֹל לִשְׁאוֹל

On this night, we remember a fifth child.

This is a child of the Shoah (Holocaust), who did not survive to ask.

Therefore, we ask for that child— Why?

We are like the simple child. We have no answer.

We can only follow the footsteps of Rabbi Elazar ben Azariah,

who could not bring himself to mention the Exodus at night

כְּנֶגֶד בֵּן חֲמִישִׁי מְדַבֶּרֶת כְּנֶסֶת יִשְׂרָאֵל:
בֵּן הַשּׁוֹאָה שֶׁנִּסְפָּה וְאֵינוֹ יָכוֹל לִשְׁאוֹל

לְפִיכָךְ אָנוּ שׁוֹאֲלִין בַּעֲדוֹ, "מַדּוּעַ?"

כְּבֵן הַתָּם אֲנַחְנוּ. וּמָה נֹאמַר, מָה
נְדַבֵּר, מָה נִצְטַדָּק? אֵין לָנוּ אֶלָּא לָלֶכֶת
אַחֲרֵי רַבִּי אֶלְעָזָר בֶּן עֲזַרְיָה שֶׁאָמַר,
לֹא זָכִיתִי שֶׁתֵּאָמֵר יְצִיאַת מִצְרַיִם
בַּלֵּילוֹת עַד שֶׁדְּרָשָׁהּ בֶּן זוֹמָא

421

until Ben Zoma explained it to him
through the verse:

*In order that you REMEMBER the
day of your going out
from Egypt, all the days of your life.*
(Deuteronomy 16:3)

"לְמַעַן תִּזְכֹּר אֶת־יוֹם צֵאתְךָ מֵאֶרֶץ
מִצְרַיִם כָּל יְמֵי חַיֶּיךָ (דְּבָרִים טז)

"The days of your life" indicates the
daylight and the goodness
of life. **"All the days of your
life"** means even in the darkest
nights when we have lost *our*
firstborn, we must remember
the Exodus.

"יְמֵי חַיֶּיךָ" — יְמֵי הָאוֹר וְהַטּוֹב;
"כָּל יְמֵי חַיֶּיךָ" — הַלֵּילוֹת שֶׁבָּהֶם
אָבְדוּ לָנוּ בְּכוֹרֵינוּ וְלֹא בְּכָרֵינוּ בִּלְבָד.
וְחַיָּבִין אָנוּ לִזְכּוֹר אֶת יְצִיאַת מִצְרַיִם.

We answer that child's question with
silence.
In silence, we remember that dark
time.
In silence, we remember that Jews
preserved their image
of God in the struggle for life.
In silence, we remember the seder
nights spent in the forests,
ghettoes, and camps; we remember
that seder night when
the Warsaw ghetto rose in revolt.

וּכְנֶגֶד שְׁאֵלָתוֹ אָנוּ יוֹשְׁבִין וְדוֹמְמִין.
יוֹשְׁבִין וְדוֹמְמִין וְזוֹכְרִין אֶת הַחֹשֶׁךְ.
יוֹשְׁבִין וְדוֹמְמִין וְזוֹכְרִין שֶׁקִּיְּמוּ בְּנֵי
עַמֵּנוּ צֶלֶם אֱ-לֹ-הִים בְּמַאֲבַק הַחַיִּים.
יוֹשְׁבִין וְדוֹמְמִין וְזוֹכְרִין אָנוּ אֶת לֵילוֹת
הַפֶּסַח. בַּיַּעַר, בַּגֶּטוֹ, וּבַמַּחֲנֶה.
אָנוּ זוֹכְרִין אֶת לֵיל הַסֵּדֶר שֶׁבּוֹ קָמוּ
וּמָרְדוּ בְּגֶטוֹ וַרְשָׁא.

(lift the cup of Elijah)

(lift the cup of Elijah)

In silence, let us pass the cup of Elijah,
the cup of the final
redemption yet-to-be. We remember
our people's return to the
land of Israel, the beginning of that
redemption. Let us each fill
Elijah's cup with some of our wine,
expressing the hope that
through our efforts, we will help
bring closer that redemption.

יוֹשְׁבִין וְדוֹמְמִין אָנוּ וּמַעֲבִירִין מִיָּד לְיָד
כּוֹס הַגְּאֻלָּה, כּוֹסוֹ שֶׁל אֵלִיָּהוּ.
אָנוּ מַזְכִּירִין אֶת שִׁיבַת בְּנֵי עַמֵּנוּ לְצִיּוֹן
רֵאשִׁית צְמִיחַת גְּאוּלָתֵנוּ.
אָנוּ מוֹזְגִין אֶת הַכּוֹס בִּתְקַנָּה שֶׁבִּזְכוּת
מַעֲשֵׂינוּ תְּקָרֵב שְׁעַת גְּאוּלָתֵנוּ.

We rise now and open our door to
invite Elijah, the forerunner
of the future which will bring an end
to the nights of our people.
We sing as they did:

נַעֲמֹד וְנִפְתַּח אֶת הַדֶּלֶת וְנַזְמִין אֶת
אֵלִיָּהוּ שֶׁיָּבִיא קֵץ לְלֵילוֹת עַמֵּנוּ. נָשִׁיר
כְּמוֹתָם: אֲנִי מַאֲמִין

*Ani maamin b'emunah shleimah, beviat
Hamashiah,
V'af al pi she yitmameah, im kol zeh ani
maamin.*
For I firmly believe in the coming of the
Messiah, and even though the Messiah
may tarry, in spite of this, I still believe.

אֲנִי מַאֲמִין בֶּאֱמוּנָה שְׁלֵמָה בְּבִיאַת
הַמָּשִׁיחַ; וְאַף עַל פִּי שֶׁיִּתְמַהְמֵהַּ, עִם
כָּל זֶה אֲנִי מַאֲמִין!

Alternate prayers and songs may be found in the anthology on the Holocaust, *Out of the Whirlwind*, by Albert A. Friedlander (New York: Doubleday & Co., 1968), especially pages 264–82, or you may choose your own from the pages of Holocaust literature. A number of the modern haggadahs listed in the bibliography incorporate readings about the Holocaust.

PRAYERS FOR OPPRESSED JEWRY

Set aside a special matzah and say:

This matzah which our ancestors ate in Egypt in slavery, they later ate and we eat in freedom.
We have fellow Jews in Syria, Ethiopia, and Russia who are not free.
We promise not to forget them. May we yet eat the matzah as one whole Jewish people. This year, some are bondsmen of fear; next year may all be as free men. This year we eat where we are; next year in Jerusalem.

The above ritual refers to the outstanding oppressed Jewries of the world. The Soviet Jewry movement has developed a ritual for this special matzah focused on Soviet Jewry. The matzah is called the matzah of hope and the following text is used:

This matzah, which we set aside as a symbol of hope for the Jews of the Soviet Union, reminds us of the indestructible links that exist between us.

מַצָּה זוֹ, שֶׁאָנוּ מְיַחֲדִים, עַל שׁוּם מָה?

עַל שׁוּם הַתִּקְוָה שֶׁיֵּשׁ לְאַחֵינוּ בְּנֵי יִשְׂרָאֵל, יְהוּדֵי בְּרִית-הַמּוֹעֲצוֹת. מַצָּה זוֹ מַעֲלָה עַל לִבֵּנוּ אֶת הַקֶּשֶׁר בֵּינֵינוּ לְבֵינָם אֲשֶׁר בַּל יִנָּתֵק לְעוֹלָם.

As we observe this festival of freedom, we recall that Soviet Jews are not free to leave without harassment; to learn of their past; to pass on their religious traditions; to learn the language of their fathers; to train teachers and rabbis of future generations.

עַתָּה, בְּחַג הַפֶּסַח שֶׁהוּא זְמַן חֵרוּתֵנוּ, נִזְכֹּר שֶׁיְּהוּדֵי בְּרִית-הַמּוֹעֲצוֹת אֵינָם בְּנֵי חוֹרִין.

אֵינָם בְּנֵי חוֹרִין לָצֵאת וְלַעֲלוֹת צִיּוֹנָה. אֵינָם בְּנֵי חוֹרִין לִלְמֹד מָסֹרֶת אֲבוֹתֵינוּ וּלְשׁוֹנָם. אֵינָם בְּנֵי חוֹרִין לְהַכְשִׁיר מוֹרִים וְרַבָּנִים לַדּוֹרוֹת הַבָּאִים.

We will stand with them in their struggle until the light of freedom and redemption shines forth.

אָנוּ עוֹמְדִים בְּצִדָּם, וְנַעֲמֹד יַחַד אִתָּם עַד שֶׁיֵּרָאוּ אֶת הָאוֹר הַגָּדוֹל — אוֹר הַפְּדוּת וְהַגְּאֻלָּה.

The most appropriate place for this ceremony would be at the very beginning of the haggadah recital, after the leader points to the three matzot and says: "Hah Lachm Anya . . ." "This is the bread of affliction which our fathers ate in the land of Egypt," etc.

PRAYER FOR ISRAEL

The recreation of the State of Israel, the modern-day exodus experience of the Jewish people, should also be included in the seder. The following prayer, modeled on the popular dayenu celebration of the Exodus from Egypt, is recommended. It can be inserted after the original dayenu or recited in conjunction with the extra cup of wine (see: "The Fifth Cup," page 56).

"IT WOULD HAVE BEEN ENOUGH..."

דַּיֵּינוּ

Had God upheld us throughout two thousand years of Dispersion But not preserved our hope for return

Dayenu!

אֵלּוּ קִיְּמָנוּ שְׁנוֹת אֲלָפַּיִם בַּגָּלוּת
וְלֹא שָׁמַר בָּנוּ אֶת תִּקְוַת
שׁוּבֵנוּ   דַּיֵּינוּ

Had God preserved our hope for return But not sent us leaders to make the dream a reality

Dayenu!

אֵלּוּ שָׁמַר בָּנוּ אֶת תִּקְוַת שׁוּבֵנוּ
וְלֹא שָׁלַח לָנוּ מַנְהִיגִים
לְהַגְשִׁימָהּ   דַּיֵּינוּ

Had God sent us leaders to make the dream a reality But not given us success in the U.N. vote

Dayenu!

אֵלּוּ שָׁלַח לָנוּ מַנְהִיגִים לְהַגְשִׁימָהּ
וְלֹא זָכָנוּ בְּהַצְבָּעַת הָאוּ"ם   דַּיֵּינוּ

Had God given us success in the U.N. vote But not defeated our attackers in 1948

Dayenu!

אֵלּוּ זָכָנוּ בְּהַצְבָּעַת הָאוּ"ם
וְלֹא נִצַּח אֶת רוֹדְפֵינוּ בְּתש"ח דַּיֵּינוּ

Had God defeated our attackers in 1948 But not unified Jerusalem

Dayenu!

אֵלּוּ נִצַּח אֶת רוֹדְפֵינוּ בְּתש"ח
וְלֹא אִחֵד אֶת יְרוּשָׁלַיִם   דַּיֵּינוּ

Had God unified Jerusalem But not led us toward peace with Egypt

Dayenu!

אֵלּוּ אִחֵד אֶת יְרוּשָׁלַיִם
וְלֹא הוֹלִיכֵנוּ לִקְרַאת שָׁלוֹם עִם
מִצְרַיִם   דַּיֵּינוּ

Had God returned us to the land of our ancestors But not filled it with our children

Dayenu!

אֵלּוּ הֶחֱזִירָנוּ לְאֶרֶץ אֲבוֹתֵינוּ
וְלֹא הִרְבָּה בָּהּ יְלָדֵנוּ וְטַפֵּנוּ   דַּיֵּינוּ

Had God filled it with our children But not caused the desert to bloom

Dayenu!

אֵלּוּ הִרְבָּה בָּהּ יְלָדֵנוּ וְטַפֵּנוּ
וְלֹא הִפְרִיחַ אֶת הַמִּדְבָּר   דַּיֵּינוּ

Had God caused the desert to bloom But not built for us cities and towns Dayenu!	אֵלוּ הִפְרִיחַ אֶת הַמִּדְבָּר וְלֹא בָּנָה לָנוּ עִיר וּכְפָר דַּיֵּנוּ
Had God rescued our remnants from the Holocaust's flames But not brought our brothers from Arab lands Dayenu!	אֵלוּ הִצִּיל אֶת שְׂרִידֵינוּ מֵאֵשׁ הַשּׁוֹאָה וְלֹא קִבֵּץ אֶת אַחֵינוּ מִתְּפוּצוֹת עֲרָב דַּיֵּנוּ
Had God brought our brothers from Arab lands But not opened the gate for Russia's Jews Dayenu!	אֵלוּ קִבֵּץ אֶת אַחֵינוּ מִתְּפוּצוֹת עֲרָב וְלֹא פָּתַח שַׁעַר לִיהוּדֵי רוּסְיָה דַּיֵּנוּ
Had God opened the gate for Russia's Jews But not redeemed our people from Ethiopia Dayenu!	אֵלוּ פָּתַח שַׁעַר לִיהוּדֵי רוּסְיָה וְלֹא גָּאַל אֶת אַחֵינוּ מֵאֶרֶץ כּוּשׁ דַּיֵּנוּ
Had God redeemed our people from Ethiopia But not strengthened our hands throughout forty years of statehood* Dayenu!	אֵלוּ גָּאַל אֶת אַחֵינוּ מֵאֶרֶץ כּוּשׁ וְלֹא הֶחֱזִיק אֶת יָדֵינוּ בַּמְּדִינָה אַרְבָּעִים שָׁנָה דַּיֵּנוּ
Had God strengthened our hands throughout forty years of statehood But not planted in our hearts a covenant of one people Dayenu!	אֵלוּ הֶחֱזִיק אֶת יָדֵינוּ בַּמְּדִינָה אַרְבָּעִים שָׁנָה וְלֹא נָטַע בְּלִבֵּנוּ בְּרִית עַם אֶחָד דַּיֵּנוּ
Had God planted in our hearts a covenant of one people But not sustained in our souls a vision of a perfected world Dayenu!	אֵלוּ נָטַע בְּלִבֵּנוּ בְּרִית עַם אֶחָד וְלֹא קִיֵּם בְּנַפְשֵׁנוּ חֲזוֹן תִּקּוּן עוֹלָם דַּיֵּנוּ

This prayer was written by Rabbis Steven Greenberg and David Nelson for CLAL. However, it is being circulated anonymously in the hope that this will remove one obstacle to its being adopted by Clal Yisrael.

*Change the year number appropriately every year.

APPENDIX C

FOR STUDY AND DISCUSSION

Passover is the central Jewish holiday because the Exodus is the central core of Judaism. Below is a list of the laws that the Torah identifies directly with the imitation of the Exodus (that is, making it the norm of life).

Laws of the Exodus Pattern

Exodus is the fruit of the covenant, the agreement between God and Israel, and the creator of the covenant between God and the people (Exodus 6:208); (Deuteronomy 4:37).

I am the Lord your God who took you out of Egypt (Exodus 20:2).
God loved you and your fathers so he took you out of Egypt and kept His promise (Deuteronomy 9:8).
Do not violate My (God's) Holy Name because I took you out of Egypt to be your God (Leviticus 22:32–33).
The Exodus sets Israel to be God's people (Deuteronomy 4:20).
God took you in the desert and fed you to teach you man does not live by bread alone (Deuteronomy 8:2 and following).
God spared Israel and did not destroy them for the sake of the Exodus (Deuteronomy 9:26–29).
Israel should follow God's ways: love God; be kind—in gratitude for God's taking them out of Egypt (Deuteronomy 10:12–22; Deuteronomy 11:1–9).

Ethical

1. Hebrew slaves became servants instead of slaves. They get good treatment and go free after six years (Exodus 21:2 and following; Leviticus 25:39–55).
2. Do not oppress the stranger. You were strangers in Egypt (Exodus 23:9).
3. Sexual morality is defined (partially) by not doing what the Egyptians did when you were in Egypt (Leviticus 18:3 and following).
4. Treat a stranger right. Treat the alien (stranger) as you treat your

native citizen; love him as yourself, for you were aliens (strangers), too, in the land of Egypt (Leviticus 19:33–34).

5. You should act justly in law of measures and weights. You should have honest weights, measures, and scales—for I am the Lord who took you out of Egypt (Leviticus 19:35–36).

6. Help the poor; do not take interest on loans to the poor—because I (the Lord) took you out of Egypt to give you the land and to be your God (Leviticus 25:35–38).

7. Give servants (slaves) extra payments when they go free. You remember you were a slave in the land of Egypt and the Lord your God redeemed you (Deuteronomy 15:13–15).

8. Take care of the widow, orphan, Levite; rejoice with your family—remember you were slaves in Egypt (Deuteronomy 16:11–12).

9. Do not hate Egyptians—for you were once strangers in their land (Deuteronomy 22:8).

10. Do not pervert justice for stranger and orphan or use widow's coat for collateral—because I (the Lord) took you out of Egypt (Deuteronomy 23:17–18).

11. Leave part of your crops in the field for stranger, orphan, widow—remember, you were slaves in Egypt (Deuteronomy 23:21–23).

Ritual

1. Passover (Exodus) is celebrated and reenacted every year (Exodus 23:15).

2. Paschal lamb sacrificed; eaten in the family feast; no leavened bread; reenactment of Exodus (Exodus 12:3–11; 14–20; 25–27; 43–49).

3. Firstborn are sanctified (Exodus 13) to serve God (Numbers 8:16–18) in response to the Exodus.

4. Sacrifices and the tabernacle are reminders of Exodus (Exodus 29:46).

5. Pilgrimage to the Temple in commemoration of Exodus (Exodus 23:15).

6. Kashrut (permitted foods) is to be observed because I took you out of Egypt to be your Lord—you be holy because I am holy (Leviticus 16:44–45).

7. Live in tabernacles (Sukkot) so you will know that Israel lived in them when they came out of Egypt (reenactment) (Leviticus 23:42–43).

8. Wear tzitzis (fringe) to be holy and remember and to know that God took you out of Egypt (Numbers 15:37–41).

9. The Shabbat commemorates the Exodus—freeing of the slaves (Deuteronomy 5:14–15).

10. Bring the first fruits to the Temple in gratitude and evoke the memory of the Exodus (Deuteronomy 26:1–11).

Theological

1. Keep (all) the laws as commandments of the God who took us out of Egypt (Deuteronomy 6:20–25).
2. Thank God and be grateful for all the goods that you have—they are the gift of God who took you out of Egypt (Deuteronomy 8:10–13, 14–18).
3. The sin of idolatry is betrayal of the God who took you out of Egypt (Deuteronomy 13:5–12).
4. Keep the covenant in gratitude for Exodus (Deuteronomy 29:1–8) or God may send you back to Egypt (Deuteronomy 28:68–69).

Bibliography

A would-be convert to Judaism asked the great Talmudic teacher Hillel to teach him the entire Torah in a nutshell—while he stood on one foot, in the idiom of the Talmud. Said Hillel: "Do not do anything to others that you would not want the others to do to you." Then Hillel added: "That is the entire Torah. The rest is a commentary [on this principle].... Now, *go and study* the rest" (Babylonian Talmud, Shabbat 31A).

This book is intended to serve as a summary "on one foot" of the way of life of the Jewish holidays. In the hope that the reader will want to "go and study" more, the following very personal bibliography is included. This is not a comprehensive listing but essentially a list of the books and articles that have been useful to me or influential in shaping my thinking about the holidays. Unfortunately, many important central sources are available only in Hebrew. I have included some of them for readers who have command of Hebrew.

The primary and best source for understanding holidays is the biblical account, but not all holidays have such. Passover, Shavuot, and Sukkot are grounded in the narrative of the Exodus. The Exodus is the core event and message of Judaism, and its story is told in the Five Books of Moses (Pentateuch), especially the books of Exodus and Numbers. The most important source for the holiday of Purim is the biblical Book of Esther, otherwise known as the Megillah (Scroll) or Megillat Esther (the Scroll of Esther). For Tisha B'Av, the Book of 2 Kings, especially chapters 20 to 25, covers the destruction of the First Temple with important parallel material in the Book of 2 Chronicles and Jeremiah, Ezekiel, and other prophets. For the destruction of the Second Temple, the shaping texts for the halacha are the various talmudic accounts; see especially Babylonian Talmud, Gittin 55B, and following pages. The two most important sources for the holiday of Hanukkah, the Books of 1 Maccabees and 2 Maccabees, were not included in the Hebrew Bible. The newly emerging holidays of Yom Hashoah and Yom Ha'Atzmaut do not have central primary sources yet.

The halacha, the laws and practices of classic Judaism, has given form to the Jewish experience of the holidays. As Rabbi Joseph B. Soloveitchik has shown us, the laws form the frame of understanding that shapes both the philosophy and emotional core of the holidays. In turn, the vision and philosophy (and the emotional experience) guide the development of the law, as I have tried to show in this book.

The primary halachic source books are Rabbi Joseph Caro, *Shulchan Aruch* (The Set Table), which became the definitive code in later rabbinic Judaism. (My personal library holding was published in New York by L. Reinman in 1951, but there are countless editions.) The laws of the holidays are found in the Orach Chayim section, with the chapters as follows: Shabbat, sections 242–416; general laws of Holy Days procedures, sections 495–548; Passover, sections 429–93; Shavuot, section 494; Sukkot, sections 625–69; Rosh Hashanah and Yom Kippur, sections 581–624; Purim, sections 685–97; Hanukkah, sections 670–84; Tisha B'Av, sections 549–61; some general laws of fast days, found in sections 562–80; and Rosh Chodesh (New Moon), sections 417–28.

An equally significant source that is enlivened by more philosophical reflections and articulated religious insight is Maimonides' *Code of Jewish Law,* known as the *Yad Hachazakah* or *Mishneh Torah* (New York: Shulsinger Brothers, 1947; this is my favorite edition, but there are countless editions). Most of the material is found in the Zemanim (Seasons) volume under the names of the individual holy days or under the rubric of major observances associated with the holiday, such as Laws of Shofar (Rosh Hashanah), Laws of Megillah (Purim), Laws of Sanctifying the Month (Rosh Chodesh). In the case of the Days of Awe, one should also look at Hilchot Teshuvah (Laws of Repentance) found in the Mada (knowledge/wisdom) volume.

There are many modern digests and also volumes on individual holy days and explications of the laws, but none are as comprehensive and useful as the Caro and Maimonides codes. One twentieth-century multivolume work comes close to the *Shulchan Aruch,* but it is probably too scholarly for most people: Ichiel Michal Epstein's *Aruch Hashulchan* (Arrange the Table) (New York: Halacha Publishing, n.d.), which quotes the Shulchan Aruch and expands upon it by giving the sources, logic, and alternative rulings as well.

While the Shulchan Aruch presupposes an Orthodox way of life, I believe that all Jews can find meaning, fulfillment, and life enrichment in halachic practices. It would be well to read these sources with an open mind and incorporate into one's life what one is able to absorb. (Keep in mind that the capacity for absorbing more will grow with every absorption.) Liberal Judaism should not be confused, not even by its own practitioners, with rejection of the practice of halacha in principle. Liberal Jews want more out of their Jewish lives; halacha has much to offer them. This guide to the holidays should help make connections. This book shows how much I have learned from liberal Judaism. I hope Liberal Jews will be open to learn from traditional Judaism.

Those who wish directions specifically designed for liberal Jewish observance will find an outstanding and definitive statement of Conservative practice in Isaac Klein's *A Guide to Jewish Religious Practice* (New York: Jewish Theological Seminary of America, 1979). Chapters 4 to 18 deal with the Sabbath and holidays. (In all fairness it should be said that the differences between Orthodox and Conservative observance at this official level are, in the larger picture, minuscule.)

After a historical period of defining itself against the tradition, the mainstream of Reform Judaism has now turned in the direction of tradition and observance—albeit on a selective basis guided by autonomy and Reform values. Such Reform guides to practice as Peter Knobel's *Gates of the Seasons* (New York: Central Conference of American Rabbis, 1983) and *The Shabbat Manual*, edited by W. Gunther Plaut (New York: Central Conference of American Rabbis, 1972), express this trend. These volumes are official publications of the Reform movement. Similarly, the Reconstructionist movement is about to reprint a manual for observance: *Toward a Guide for Ritual Jewish Usage* by A. Elihu Michaelson (New York: Jewish Reconstructionist Foundation, 1941).

Another central source that communicates the values and attitudes of the faith is the prayer book. There are special prayers associated with each holiday. The High Holy Days prayers are so expanded that a separate prayer book called a Machzor (Prayer Cycle) was developed (see below). In America, each of the movements has developed its own official prayer book except for Orthodoxy. Since there are neither changes nor a central authority in Orthodoxy that could serve as a basis for establishing one authoritative edition, there are various editions of the inherited classic Siddur (see below).

On the Hebrew calendar, see the treatment in the *Encyclopedia Judaica* (Jerusalem: Keter Publishing House Ltd., 1972) and the introductory and afterword material in Arthur Spier's *The Comprehensive Hebrew Calendar* (New York: Behrman House, 1952). Two recent books on time are eye-opening, fresh, full of lore and insight into the Hebrew calendar and are highly recommended: Eviatar Zerubavel's *Hidden Rhythms* (Chicago: Free Press, 1981) and *The Seven Day Circle* (Chicago: Free Press, 1985).

Over the years the Jewish Publication Society of America has published a series of individual volumes on the holidays (except for the two emergent holy days). The volumes include sources, observances, explanations, folklore, art, music, and literature. I have found them all useful. In parallel to the chapters in this book they are: Philip Goodman, *The Passover Anthology* (Philadelphia: 1973); Philip Goodman, *The Shavuot Anthology* (Philadelphia: 1974); Philip Goodman, *The Sukkot Anthology* (Philadelphia: 1973); Abraham E. Millgrom, *Sabbath: The Day of Delight* (Philadelphia: 1965); Philip Goodman, *The Rosh Hashanah Anthology* (Philadelphia: 1970); Philip Goodman, *The Yom Kippur Anthology* (Philadelphia: 1971); Philip Goodman, *The Purim Anthology* (Philadelphia: 1970); Emily Solis Cohen, *Hanukkah: The Feast of Lights* (Philadelphia: 1951).

In recent years, a number of publications have presented the entire range of the Jewish holidays in the context of a book on Jewish living or on the holidays. I consider the best one-volume presentation in the English language to be Blu Greenberg's *How to Run a Traditional Jewish Household* (New York: Simon & Shuster, 1984). (In accordance with the laws of full disclosure, I should state that I am married to the author of that volume. However, I believe the comment is objectively true.) Among the volumes on Jewish living that incorporate holiday material, I have found most useful: Hayim Halevy Donin's *To Be A Jew* (New York: Basic Books, 1972); Eliyahu Kitov's *The Book of Our Heritage* (Jerusalem: "A" Publishers, 1968), and Leo Trepp's *The Complete Book of Jewish Observance* (West Orange, New Jersey: Behrman House, 1980). In the comprehensive volumes on the holidays, I have found the following to be helpful and informative from a wide variety of perspectives: Michael Strassfeld, *The Jewish Holidays* (New York: Harper & Row, 1985); Arthur Waskow, *Seasons of Our Joy* (New York: Bantam Books, 1982); Theodore Gaster, *Festivals of the Jewish Year* (New York: William Morrow & Co., 1952); and Arlene Rossen Cardozo, *Jewish Family Celebrations* (New York: St. Martin's Press, 1982).

Among Hebrew-language treatments of the holidays, I have found the following books useful:

Eliezer Schweid, *Sefer Machzor Hazemanim* (The Book of the Cycles of the Seasons) (Tel Aviv: Am Oved, 1984). This is the most sophisticated and philosophical work on the holidays in the Hebrew language. It is all the more interesting for having been written by a scholar outside of the rabbinic tradition's perspective.

The *Sefer Hamoadim* (Book of Holidays) series (Tel Aviv: Dvir, 1952) is comparable to the Jewish Publication Society series but is somewhat richer in material. The series includes:

Y.L. Baruch, *Rosh Hashanah and Yom Kippur*

Yom Tov Lewinski, *Pesach*

Yom Tov Lewinski, *Shavuot*

Yom Tov Lewinski, *Sukkot*

Yom Tov Lewinski, *Ymai Moed V'zikkaron* (Days of Assembly and Memory) (Rosh Chodesh, Hanukkah, 15 Shevat, Purim, Lag B'Omer)

Yom Tov Lewinski, *Ymai Moed V'zikkaron* (Days of Assembly and Memory) (Churban and Geulah) (Destruction and Redemption)

See also: Y.L. Baruch, *Sefer Hashabbat* (The Book of the Sabbath), listed in section 6 of the Shabbat bibliography.

Shlomo Zevin, *Hamoadim BaHalacha* (The Holidays in Jewish Law) (Tel Aviv: Avraham Zioni Publishing, 1956). Features superb and fascinating disquisitions on the halachic concepts and features of each holiday. This book has been translated into English and published in the Art Scroll series, but it has been "censored" in the process so only the Hebrew edition is recommended.

Shlomo Goren, *Torat Hamoadim* (The Seasons) (Tel Aviv: Avraham Zioni Publishing, 1964).

Y. L. Maimon, *Chagim Umoadim* (Holidays and Seasons) (Jerusalem: Rav Kook Institute, 1952).

Nahum Wahrmann, *Chagei Yisrael Umoadav* (The Holidays and Convocations of Israel) (Tel Aviv: Achiasaf Publishing, 1961).

Z. Ariel, *Sefer Hachag Vehamoed* (Tel Aviv: Am Oved, 1985). An excellent one-volume collection of source material, analyses, and popular scholarly articles edited by a nontraditional Jew. Rabbi Samuel and Devora Avidor-Cohen have written a new series on the holidays called *Chagim U'Moadim* (Jerusalem: Keter, 1981). It is rich in traditional material and approaches written from a contemporary Israeli religious viewpoint and on the popular level.

INDIVIDUAL HOLIDAYS:

The experience and understanding of the individual holidays will be enriched by the following:

PASSOVER

The Haggadah (narrative/retelling) is the central text. Thousands of haggadahs have been published over the years. They can be drawn upon for enrichment materials for your own seder. For a survey of many editions, see Yosef Yerushalmi's *Haggadah and History* (Philadelphia: Jewish Publication Society, 1975).

My favorites in Hebrew are as follows:

M.D. Eisenstein, *Ozar Perushim we-Ziyurim al Haggadah shel Pesach* (New York: 1917; reprinted in Israel, 1969).

Daniel Goldschmidt, *Haggadah shel Pesach* (Jerusalem: Mossad Bialik, 1960). (Nahum Glatzer has edited an English abridged version of this haggadah, *The Passover Haggadah* (New York: Schocken Books, 1979).

M. M. Kasher, *Haggadah Shelaymah* (Jerusalem: Machon Torah Shelaymah, 1961).

Benno Rothenberg, editor, *Haggadah shel Pesach, Archaeologit/Historit* (Tel Aviv: Lewin Epstein, n.d.). Has superb archaeological illustrations.

Over the years, the American denominations have developed their own haggadahs:

Philip Birnbaum, editor, *Haggadah* (New York: Hebrew Publishing Company, 1976). Orthodox, although not officially adopted by the movement.

Michael Strassfeld, editor, *A Passover Haggadah* (New York: Rabbinical Assembly, 1979). Conservative.

Mordecai Kaplan, editor, *The New Haggadah* (New York: Jewish Reconstructionist Foundation, 1978). Reconstructionist.

Herbert Bronstein, editor, *A Passover Haggadah* (New York: Central Conference of American Rabbis, 1974). Reform. See also Chaim Stern, *Gates of Freedom* (Chappaqua, New York: Rossel Books, 1981).

Rabbi Joseph Elias, editor, *The (Artscroll) Haggadah* (New York: Mesorah Publications, 1977). Has achieved wide currency among traditionalist Orthodox. The Shalom Seder, *Three Haggadahs* (New York: New Jewish Agenda, 1986) has achieved similar status among many liberal and radical Jews.

Aviva Cantor, editor, *An Egalitarian Haggadah* (New York: Lilith Publications, 1982). Has attained similar standing among many feminists. See also Ms. Cantor's comments on the origins of this haggadah in Elizabeth Koltun, ed., *The Jewish Woman: New Perspectives* (New York: Schocken Books, 1976), pp., 94–102.

Of course, individual commentary haggadahs may appeal to you, depending on which wavelength you and the commentator are on. Numerous haggadahs with English translations exist, some with commentary. Among those that I have enjoyed particularly are the following:

Reuven P. Bulka, editor, *The Haggadah for Pesach* (Jerusalem: Machon Pri Ha'aretz, 1985).

Shlomo Riskin, *The Passover Haggadah* (New York: Ktav Publishing, 1983).

David J. Derovan and Moshe Berliner, editors, *The Passover Haggadah* (New York: Student Organization of Yeshiva, 1974).

Steven F. Cohen and Kenneth Brander, *The Yeshiva University Haggadah* (New York: Student Organization of Yeshiva, 1985).

Jack Schuldenfrei and Joel Harris, editors, *The 4th World Haggadah* (London: World Union of Jewish Students, 1970).

The Orphan Hospital Ward of Israel has reproduced paperback copies of old or rare haggadahs from Prague, China, India, and other places. Unfortunately, the editions are not of good quality. For a small donation you may secure copies from their office at 1 West 20th Street, New York, New York 10010. More and more first-class reproductions are coming on the market.

A superb exploration of the Exodus theme and the Haggadah is found in Chaim Raphael's *A Feast of History* (New York: Simon and Schuster).

A magnificent work of art, possibly the most beautiful Haggadah of all time, David Moss' Haggadah has been reproduced in a collectors' facsimile limited edition: *A Song of David* (Rochester: Noralpha Associates, 1987).

SHABBAT

Over the years, Shabbat is the one holy day that has had the benefit of an extraordinary number and quality of full-scale treatments from many different perspectives. This is a testimony to the evocative power of Shabbat as well as to its centrality in Jewish living. People considering taking on Jewish tradition and living will want to focus especially on the Sabbath. Since seven is a perfection number by biblical convention (the Sabbath itself is the seventh day), I offer a seven-fold selection of seven types of writings in tribute to this extraordinary literature.

1. *Seven favorite essays on the meaning of Shabbat:*

Saul Berman, "The Extended Notion of the Sabbath," *Judaism*, volume 22, number 3 (Summer 1973): 342–350.

Samuel Dresner, *The Sabbath* (New York: Burning Bush Press, 1970).

Erich Fromm, "The Sabbath Ritual," in *The Forgotten Language* (New York: Holt, Rinehart and Winston, 1951).

Isidor Grunfeld, *The Sabbath: A Guide to Its Understanding and Observance* (New York: Feldheim, 1959).

Abraham J. Heschel, *The Sabbath* (New York: Jewish Publication Society, 1963).

Abraham Millgram, *Sabbath: The Day of Delight* (Philadelphia: Jewish Publication Society, 1947). Includes a potpourri of material.

Emanuel Rackman, "Sabbath and Festivals in the Modern Age," in *Studies in Torah Judaism*, edited by Leon D. Stitskin (New York: Ktav, 1969).

Note: Yavneh Shiron, edited by Eugene Flink and Tom Ackerman (New York: Yavneh, 1969), contains several outstanding essays. I would call particular attention to the essays by Norman Lamm, "Sabbath Rest," and Zalman Schachter, "Living the Sabbath."

2. *Seven "how to" books dealing with Shabbat:*

Hayim H. Donin, *To Be a Jew* (New York: Basic Books, 1972).

Blu Greenberg, *How to Run a Traditional Jewish Household* (New York: Simon and Schuster, 1984).

The liberal denominations have begun to develop their own basic books. The following "how to" books focus on Shabbat observance from the Conservative and Reform perspectives:

Isaac Klein, *A Guide to Jewish Religious Practice* (New York: Jewish Theological Seminary of America, 1979). W. Gunther Plaut edited *A Shabbat Manual* (New York: Central Conference of American Rabbis, 1972). Chaim Stern edited *Gates of the House* (New York: Central Conference of American Rabbis, 1977) for the Reform movement. This prayer book for the home includes material for Shabbat and holidays.

Shiron (New York: National Jewish Resource Center, 1980). Songs, practices, and liturgy. Has Hebrew, transliteration, and translation. The *Yavneh Shiron* also contains many songs of Shabbat.

Richard Siegel and Michael and Sharon Strassfeld, editors, *The Jewish Catalog*, vol. I (Philadelphia: Jewish Publication Society, 1973).

Michael Strassfeld, editor, *A Shabbat Haggadah* (New York: American Jewish Committee, 1981).

Leo Trepp, *The Complete Book of Jewish Observance* (New York: Behrman House, 1980).

3. *Seven insightful articles on aspects of Shabbat:*

Harvey Cox, "Meditation and Sabbath" in *Harvard Magazine*, September–October 1977, pp. 39–43. With this suggestive article, Cox does a bit of *teshuvah* for his cruel caricature of Judaism in his best-selling book, *The Secular City.*

Encyclopedia Judaica, article on Shabbat, volume 14 (Jerusalem: Keter Publishing, 1971).

Norman Frimer, "Law as Living Discipline: The Sabbath as Paradigm," in *Tradition and Contemporary Experience* edited by Alfred Jospe (New York: Schocken, 1970), pp.257–268. Gives the flavor of Jewish philosophy in action.

Samson Raphael Hirsch, "Prohibition of Work on Sabbath," in *Edoth,* section 2, subsection 21 of *Horeb: A Philosophy of Jewish Laws and Observances,* translated by Isidor Grunfeld (London: English Soncino Press, 1962), pp. 61–78. The best succinct definition in the English language of the halachic prohibition of work and its detailed categories.

Gunther Plaut, *The Sabbath as Protest: Work and Leisure in an Automated Society* (Syracuse: Syracuse University Press).

Alvin Reines, "Shabbat as a State of Being," *CCAR Journal,* January 1967, pp. 28–38. A Reform paradigm of Shabbat that challenges fixed models of observance.

Joseph B. Soloveitchik, "The Lonely Man of Faith," in *Tradition,* vol. 7, no. 2 (Summer 1965), pp. 5–66. The article does not deal directly with the Shabbat, but its exposition of human power and submission profoundly influences my treatment of the Shabbat.

4. Seven major traditional sourcebooks on Shabbat (for those who can read Hebrew):

Babylonian Talmud, Tractate Shabbat (London: Soncino, 1971). Available with English translation.

Menachem Kasher, editor, *Torah Sheleymah,* vol. 2 (New York: n.p., 1952). Collected rabbinic commentary on the Genesis Sabbath verses.

Maimonides, *Yad Hachazakah (Mishneh Torah),* vol. 3, *Zemanim (Seasons), Hilchot Shabbat (Laws of the Sabbath)* (New York: Grossman Publishers, 1960).

Yosef Karo, *Shulchan Aruch (The Set Table), Orach Chayim (Way of Life),* sections 242–416—*Laws of Shabbat* (New York: L. Reinman, 1961).

Solomon Ganzfried, *Code of Jewish Law,* edited and translated by Hyman Golden (New York: Hebrew Publishing Company, 1961). A new standard digest of the *Shulchan Aruch.*

Siddur (Prayer Book):

Philip Birnbaum, editor and translator, *Daily Prayer Book* (New York: Hebrew Publishing Company, 1949), pp. 221–565. The traditional Sabbath liturgy.

Jules Harlow, editor, *Siddur Sim Shalom: A Prayer Book for Shabbat, Festival and Weekdays* (New York: The Rabbinical Assembly, The United Synagogue of America, 1985). The New Conservative Prayer Book with important insertions and modifications of the traditional text.

Chaim Stern, editor, *Gates of Prayer: The New Union Prayer Book (Reform)* (New York: Central Conference of American Rabbis, 1975). This New

Reform prayer book is a striking mix of traditional and innovative materials.

Mordecai M. Kaplan and Eugene Cohen, editors, assisted by Ira Eisenstein and Milton Steinberg, *Sabbath Prayer Book* (New York: Jewish Reconstructionist Foundation, 1965). The revised edition of the Reconstructionist prayer book with its distinctive revisions and recasting of the traditional liturgies. The Reconstructionist movement has also published a festivals machzor: Eugene Kohn, editor, *Festival Prayer Book* (New York: Jewish Reconstructionist Foundation, 1958).

The process of liturgy is dynamic, as exemplified in all four prayer books above, in different ways. The liberal prayer books are the official ones of their movements. The Rabbinical Council of America (Orthodox) sought to create an "official" Orthodox prayer book—*The Traditional Prayer Book*, edited by David de Sola Pool (New York: Behrman House, 1960)—but the Birnbaum prayer book seems to have achieved wider currency in American Orthodox synagogues. Lacking the resources to do a new Siddur, the Rabbinical Council is now using a special reprint of the non-Zionist Art Scroll series, *Complete Art Scroll Siddur* (New York: Mesorah Publications, n.d.), a lamentable sign of the weakening of modern Orthodoxy in recent decades. All four movements' Siddurim have extensive Shabbat prayers, liturgies, and readings.

Chayim I. Lipkin, editor, *Taryag Mitzvot B'Halacha V'Aggadah* (613 Commandments in Law and Lore), vol. 2. (B'nai Brak: Netzach Publishers, 1963). Contains many well selected sources.

5. Seven books on Judaism that deal with Shabbat in illuminating fashion:

Leo Baeck, *This People Israel: The Meaning of Jewish Existence*, translated by Albert Friedlander (New York: Union of American Hebrew Congregations, 1964). See also Leo Baeck, "Mystery and Commandment" in *Contemporary Jewish Thought*, edited by Simon Noveck (New York: B'nai Brith, 1963).

Joseph Blau, editor, *Reform Judaism: A Historical Perspective* (New York: Ktav, 1973). See the Plaut article. For a comparison see *Tradition and Change: The Development of Conservative Judaism* edited by Mordecai Waxman (New York: Burning Bush Press, 1958). See the Jewish law section.

Martin Buber, *Moses: The Revelation and the Covenant* (New York: Harper Torchbooks, 1958).

Hermann Cohen, *Religion of Reason*, translated by Simon Kaplan (New York: Ungar Publishing Company, 1972).

Mordecai M. Kaplan, *Judaism as a Civilization* (New York; Schocken Books, 1967).

Franz Rosenzweig, *The Star of Redemption*, translated by William W. Hallo (New York: Holt, Rinehart and Winston, 1970).

Herman Wouk, *This Is My God: The Jewish Way of Life* (New York: Pocket Books, 1974).

6. Seven truly useful Hebrew-language volumes on Shabbat:

Menachem Cohen and Benny Don Yahia, editors, *Shalom Levo Shabbat* (Welcome the Coming of Shabbat) (Tel Aviv: Don Publishing, 1977). Songs and Shabbat zemirot, customs, and tidbits from rabbinic sources for the Sabbath. Beautifully illustrated.

Meir Hovav, *Zeh Hashulchan* (This Is the Table) (Jerusalem: World Zionist Organization, 1975). Compilation and commentary on the Shabbat zemirot.

Isachar Jacobson, *Binah Bamikra* (Meditations on the Torah) (Tel Aviv: Sinai, 1952).

————, *Hazon Hamikra* (The Vision of the Scriptures) (Tel Aviv: Sinai, n.d.). Not books on Shabbat but two volumes of classic studies on the weekly Torah portion and prophetic readings for every Sabbath of the year. Gives a good idea of how people study the meaning of the Bible every Shabbat.

Yehoshua Y. Neuwirth, *Shemirat Shabbat K'Hilchata* (Observing the Sabbath Properly) (Jerusalem: Feldheim, 1964). Comprehensive coverage of detailed halachic requirements of Orthodox Sabbath observance. English translation of the first twenty-two chapters (Jerusalem: Feldheim, 1984).

Moshe H. Schlanger, *Yesodot Hilchot Shabbat* (Foundations of Sabbath Law) (Jerusalem: Harry Fischel Institute, 1969).

A. I. Sperling, *Taamei Haminhagim U'Mekoray Hadinim* (The Rationale of Customs and Sources of Law), reprint (Jerusalem: Eshkol, 1971). Traditional explanations for hundreds of Shabbat practices.

7. Seven historico-critical books that offer insight into the Sabbath:

Peter R. Ackroyd, *Exile and Restoration: A Study of Hebrew Thought of the Sixth Century B.C.* (Philadelphia: Westminster Press, 1968).

Niels-Erik A. Andreasen, *The Old Testament Sabbath* (Society for Biblical Literature Dissertation Series #7, 1972). Truly outstanding, rich in insight and scholarship.

Roger D. Congdon, *Sabbatic Theology*. Unpublished Ph.D. thesis, Dallas Theological Seminary, 1949.

Roland De Vaux, "Ancient Israel," vol. 2, *Religious Institutions* (New York: McGraw-Hill, 1965).

Theodor H. Gaster, *Festivals of the Jewish Year* (New York: William Morrow, 1974).

William A. Heidel, *The Day of Yahweh: A Study of Sacred Days and Ritual Forms in the Ancient Near East* (New York: Century, 1929).

Johannes Pedersen, *Israel: Its Life and Culture*, 4 volumes, reprint (London: Oxford University Press, 1973). A classic study of Biblical religion.

ROSH HASHANAH–YOM KIPPUR

The laws of Rosh Hashanah through Yom Kippur are collected in Rabbi Joseph Caro's *Shulchan Aruch, Orach Chayim, Simanim*, sections 581 to 624, and parallel chapters in Rabbi Jacob ben Asher's *Tur Shulchan Aruch, Orach Chayim*.

From these volumes and their commentaries and bibliographical aids, as well as from Rabbi Yehiel M. Epstein's *Aruch HaShulchan, Orach Chayim*, parallel chapters (that is, sections 581 to 624), one can explore these laws in greater detail and check the sources on more complex issues. This guide is meant only as a capsule summary of the laws and an explanation of the spirit underlying them and the effect they are designed to achieve or create.

For further readings in the spirit of the holidays, I recommend Shmuel Yosel Agnon's superb anthology, *Yamim Noraim* (Jerusalem: Schocken Publishers), called *Days of Awe*, in its abridged English version.

Maimonides' important halachic material is scattered through various sections of his *Yad Hachazakah (Mishneh Torah)*, including *hilchot teshuvah, hilchot shevitat asor, hilchot shofar, hilchot avodat yom hakippurim*, and other sources. The material in the Talmud is even more widely scattered, but the biggest concentrations are found in the *Babylonian Talmud (TB) Rosh Hashanah* and *Yoma* (this last volume deals primarily with Yom Kippur).

Of course, the other great sources of the spirit of this period are the *machzor* (prayer book) and the *selichot* (penitential prayers). The traditional selichot are available in the *Authorized Selichot for the Whole Year* translated and annotated by Abraham Rosenfeld (New York: Judaica Press, 1979). The Reform service for selichot is published in *Gates of Forgiveness* edited by Chaim Stern (New York: Central Conference of American Rabbis, 1980).

The most widely used Orthodox machzor is Philip Birnbaum's *High Holiday Prayer Book* (New York: Hebrew Publishing Company, 1951). The use of the Art Scroll series machzorim for Rosh Hashanah and Yom Kippur, edited by Nosson Scherman and Meir Zlotowitz (New York: Mesorah Publications, 1986), is growing—especially among traditionalist Orthodox Jews. For the Conservative movement, Jules Harlow reedited *Machzor for Rosh Hashanah and Yom Kippur* (New York: Rabbinical Assembly, 1972). The Reform movement's revised machzor, edited by Chaim Stern, is called *Gates of Repentance; The New Union Prayer Book for the Days of Awe* (New York: Central Conference of American Rabbis, 1978). The Reconstructionist movement machzor edited by Mordecai M. Kaplan, Eugene Kohn, and Ira Eisenstein, is *High Holy Days Prayer Book*, 2 volumes (New York: Jewish Reconstructionist Foundation, 1948).

PURIM

In addition to the standard classical commentaries on the Book of Esther, I would recommend for further reading two sources that have deeply shaped my understanding of the holiday of Purim. One is Rabbi Joseph B. Soloveitchik's extraordinary analysis of the holiday, found in three talks summarized by Rabbi Abraham Besdin and entitled "In the Days of Mordecai and Esther," "Galus Egypt and Galus Persia," and "The Megillah Is Both Praise and Petition," circulated in Hashkafah Lessons edited by Abraham Besdin (New York: Rabbinical Council of America). The sections in my chapter called "The Reversal," "Confronting Jewish Destiny," with its comments on Esther's "sexual strategy" and "Egypt and Purim" are particularly based on or directly follow the arguments in Rabbi Soloveitchik's talks. An acknowledgment of Rabbi

Soloveitchik's influence throughout this book is found in the Preface.

The other source is Jon Levenson's brilliant article, "The Scroll of Esther in Ecumenical Perspective," published in the *Journal of Ecumenical Studies*, volume 13, number 3 (Summer 1976), pages 440–52. The section of this chapter, "Purim: The Holiday of the Diaspora," was suggested by Levenson's article. Beyond the quotations cited, the section, "Living On in the Diaspora," is deeply influenced by Levenson's article, as indeed my whole conception of Purim is. Levenson's work, in general, is a remarkable blend of originality, critical scholarship, and theological insight that deserves the widest possible attention.

I am also indebted to Monford Harris's highly original and illuminating essay, "Purim: The Celebration of Dis-Order," published in *Judaism*, volume 26, number 4, Fall 1977, pages 161–70, and to Elliot Yagod's insightful "Chanukah and Purim: Two Models of Jewish History" (unpublished).

HANUKKAH

Professor Jonathan Goldstein's remarkable commentary and brilliant historical treatment of the Books of 1 and 2 Maccabees in the *Anchor Bible* (Garden City: Doubleday & Company, 1976 and 1983) has given us a new understanding of the holiday, its origins and the internal Jewish conflicts that it reflects. Although Goldstein's work is the object of scholarly controversy, I find his arguments totally persuasive, and the chapter on Hanukkah in this book was rewritten under his influence. Professor Goldstein's scholarship is another rare combination of textual insight, theological sophistication, and critical historical discoveries. Goldstein's work "dates" many existing scholarly treatments, but Professor Elias Bickerman's work especially continues to illuminate understanding. For a general introduction to Bickerman's approach, see his *From Ezra to the Last of the Maccabees* (New York: Schocken, 1962).

TISHA B'AV

Rabbi Soloveitchik's insights into the nature of mourning and the expression of grief on Tisha B'Av are articulated in his talk comparing communal and private mourning, given at a convention of the Rabbinical Council of America (and written up and circulated by Rabbi Abraham N. Besdin), and in two talks, "Sitting Shiva Is Doing Teshuvah" and "From Negation to Affirmation" (written up by Rabbi Besdin and published in *Conspectus* [New York: Student Organization of Yeshiva, n.d.]). Peter R. Ackroyd's work, *Exile and Restoration* (Philadelphia: Westminster Press, 1968), on the impact of the destruction of the First Temple, and Jacob Neusner's paradigm of responses to the destruction of the Second Temple have helped shape my thinking on the rabbinic response to destruction and exile. Neusner's scholarly output is overwhelming and beyond listing here. For an early Neusner popular article that gives some of the flavor of his views, see his "Emergent Rabbinic Judaism in a Time of Crisis: Four Responses to the Destruction of the Second Temple," in *Ju-*

daism, volume xii, number 3, 1972, pages 313–27, reprinted in Jacob Neusner, *Early Rabbinic Judaism* (Leiden: E. J. Brill, 1975). The whole book is an introduction to Neusner's work. See also Irving Greenberg, "Crossroads of Destiny" (New York: CLAL, 1984), "The Third Great Cycle of Jewish History" (New York: CLAL, 1980), and "Voluntary Covenant" (New York: CLAL, 1982). A major source is the Book of Kinot (elegies) that is read on the day; it includes threnodies for more than a millennium of historical tragedies. A good English edition is *Tisha B'Av Compendium: Tephilot and Kinot*, translated and annotated by Abraham Rosenfeld (New York: Judaica Press, 1983). See also the works of the great ancient Jewish historian, Josephus, especially *Wars of the Jews* (Lynn: Hendrickson Publishing, 1982), volumes 5 and 6.

YOM HASHOAH AND YOM HA'ATZMAUT

There is little published literature dealing directly with these days, a testimony to the fact that they are in the early stages of unfolding. Astrophysicists study quasars and supernova with particular fascination because analysis of the development of these bodies sheds light on the origins of the universe—a process to which we have very little access otherwise. Similarly, one can study the process of formation of Yom Hashoah and Yom Ha'Atzmaut and thus obtain insight as to how new holy days originate. The impact of those days and their reception also give fresh perspective on the development of the overall holiday cycle.

The relative neglect of these days reflects the fact that the secularists who are playing an active role in developing them do not think in terms of holy days, while the official halachists are in a defensive mode and are striving to preserve what is, rather than trying to incorporate new days into the calendar. In the English language there have been no extended (one might say, serious) discussions of Yom Hashoah and Yom Ha'Atzmaut. In Hebrew, Yom Tov Lewinski's *Sefer Ha'Moadim*, volume 8: *Yemai Moed V'Zikkaron* (Tel Aviv: Dvir, 1957), is the best collection of materials on the days, but there is little analysis in it. Eliezer Schweid's *Sefer Machzor Hazemanim* (Tel Aviv: Am Oved, 1984) contains the most extended analysis of the two days attempted heretofore.

The theology underlying chapters 11 and 12 is spelled out in greater detail in two personal essays, "The Third Great Cycle of Jewish History" and "Voluntary Covenant," listed above, and an essay tentatively called "Dialectic Thinking and Living," which will appear in the Festschrift for Elie Wiesel's sixtieth birthday being edited by Carol Rittner. Much of the data underlying these chapters is derived from personal conversations with survivors and public figures in Israel over the course of three decades.

Three other volumes in Hebrew have rich materials on Yom Ha'Atzmaut: Nahum Arieli and Shlomo Levin, *Asufah L'Yom Ha'Atzmaut* (Anthology for Israel Independence Day) (Jerusalem: Department of Torah Education and Culture, 1971); Menachem M. Kasher, *Hatekufah Hagedolah* (The Great Epoch) (Jerusalem: Machon Torah Sheleymah, 1969); and Nahum Rakover, editor, *Hilchot Yom Ha'Atzmaut V'Yom Yerushalayim* (Laws of Israel Independence Day and Jerusalem Day) (Jerusalem: Misrad Hadatot, 1973).

Glossary of Names

Abbahu of Caesarea, Rabbi (ca. third century). Third-generation amora (teacher in Talmud) in Israel, head of Yeshiva and judge.

Adorno, Theodor (1903–1969). Leading German social scientist, refugee from Hitler.

Akiva ben Joseph, Rabbi (ca. 50–135 C.E.). One of the central rabbinic figures of the Talmud, both for his teaching and his life and martyrdom.

Alkalai, Rabbi Yehuda (1798–1878). Orthodox rabbi. Early Zionist thinker and pioneer of practical Zionist efforts.

Arama, Isaac (1420–1494). Author of *Akedat Yitzchak,* commentary on the Bible.

Arazi, Yehuda (1907–1959). A leading figure in the Aliya Bet ("illegal" immigration of Jews) to the land of Israel from 1945 to 1948.

Baal Shem Tov, Israel (ca. 1700–1760). Mystic and wonder worker; founder of Chasidism, the most influential Jewish religious revival movement of the eighteenth and nineteenth centuries.

Baeck, Leo (1873–1956). Major rabbinic figure of German Reform and author of important philosophical works; survivor of Theresienstadt in the Holocaust.

Bak, Samuel (1933–). Sculptor with important pieces on the Holocaust.

Baron, Salo W. (1895–). Premier Jewish historian of the past generation.

B.C.E. and C.E. Events in Jewish history are also dated according to the world calendar which, by convention, dates everything in relation to the birth of Jesus. However, rather than use the Christian referents of B.C. and A.D., Jews use the letters B.C.E. (Before the Common Era) and C.E. (Common Era).

Ben-Gurion, David (1886–1973). First prime minister and primary architect of the State of Israel.

Bernat, Rabbi Haskell (1935–). A leading American Reform Rabbi with particular interest in Reform approaches to the tradition.

Bickerman, Elias (1897–1981). Leading Jewish studies scholar with particular expertise in Second Temple and Hellenistic periods of Jewish history.

Blumberg, Herschel (1924–). A leading American Jewish communal figure, past chairman of the National United Jewish Appeal and CLAL (National Jewish Center for Learning and Leadership); author of concepts of commemorating Yom Ha' Atzmaut (see chapter 12).

Brand, Joel (1906–1964). Leader of Hungarian Jewry in the Holocaust; tried in vain to work out a rescue/exchange for Hungarian Jewry.

Buber, Martin (1878–1965). Major existentialist, personalist religious thinker; perhaps the most influential Jewish philosopher of the twentieth century in non-Jewish religious circles. Author of *I and Thou* and many other writings.

Cox, Harvey (1929–). Harvard University professor, theologian, and cultural analyst; author of *The Secular City* and other works.

Dinur, Ben Zion (1884–1973). Leading Jewish historian and Zionist leader, cabinet minister in Israel, and founder of Yad Vashem.

Donat, Alexander (1905–1984). Survivor of the Holocaust; author of *The Holocaust Kingdom*, one of the best memoirs of the Holocaust; founder of the Holocaust Library.

Eichmann, Adolf (1906–1962). S.S. officer in charge of execution of the Nazis' Final Solution of the Jewish problem.

Eliaz, Mrs. Survivor of Auschwitz; witness in the Jerusalem hearings on Josef Mengele in 1985.

Eliezer ben Hyrcanus, Rabbi (end of first, beginning of second centuries). One of the leading talmudic scholars of the period immediately after the destruction of the Temple.

Elijah of Vilna, Rabbi (Vilna Gaon) (ca. 1742–1821). A major scholarly figure of classic rabbinic tradition in Eastern Europe who attained legendary stature; chief opponent of Chasidism.

Friedlander, Albert H. (1927–). Reform rabbi in England; editor of Holocaust literature and liturgy.

Fromm, Erich (1900–1980). Important psychoanalyst and cultural analyst; author of *Escape from Freedom* and other works.

Goldstein, Jonathan A. (1929–). Professor of history and classes at the University of Iowa; author of commentary on 1 and 2 Maccabees (*Anchor Bible* series).

Gouri, Haim (1923–). Israeli writer, poet, and educator; has written and created films on the implications of Holocaust and Israel.

Ha'am, Ahad (1856–1927). Pen name for Asher Ginsberg, leading Zionist thinker of early twentieth century.

Harris, Rabbi Monford (1920–). Jewish studies academic scholar, now teaching at Spertus College and Judaica in Chicago, has written on the philosophy of Judaism and Jewish values.

Herzl, Theodor (1860–1904). Founder and principal figure of modern Zionism.

Herzog, Rabbi Isaac Halevy (1888–1959). First chief rabbi of the State of Israel; scholar of Jewish legal institutions.

Heschel, Rabbi Abraham Joshua (1907–1972). A leading philosopher, theologian, and activist for justice and peace in America; author of *God in Search of Man* and other works.

Hillel (end of first century B.C.E., beginning of first century C.E.). One of the great figures of the Mishnah (primary portion of the Talmud); influential teachings and life.

Himmler, Heinrich (1900–1945). Head of the S.S. and principal official responsible for the final solution of the Jewish problem.

Hitler, Adolf (1889–1945). The greatest and most savage anti-Semite of all time; central figure of Nazism; the German dictator under whose leadership the Holocaust was conceived and carried out.

Hirsch, Rabbi Samson Raphael (1808–1888). Biblical commentator and Jewish educator; a leading figure in development of German modern Orthodoxy with philosophy of *Torah im derekh eretz* (Torah with secular culture).

Hiya bar Ashi, Rav (ca. 3rd century C.E.). Second-generation Babylonian Amora; disciple of Rav; known for ascetic piety.

Isaac Alter of Gur, Rabbi (1789–1866). Founder of the Gur Hasidic dynasty, a leading community of Chasidim located not far from Warsaw, Poland, and later in the land of Israel.

Jacob ben Asher (1270–1340). Author of important legal codes and commentaries, including the Tur Shulchan Aruch (4 volumes).

Jonas, Hans (1903–). Major philosopher and one of the extraordinary scholars who came to America in flight from Hitler.

Jonathan ben Joseph, Rabbi (ca. 2nd century). Fourth-generation Tanna (teacher) of the Mishnah.

Judah the Prince, Rabbi (latter half of second century C.E., beginning of third century C.E.). Head of the Jewish community in Israel, chief editor and compiler of the Mishnah.

Kagan, Rabbi Israel Meir HaCohen (1838–1933). Known as the Chafetz Chayim; a saintly scholar, leading figure in ultra-Orthodox world, and a founder of Agudat Israel, the anti-Zionist Orthodox movement.

Kasher, Rabbi Menachem M. (1895–1983). Israeli rabbi and scholar; editor and initiator of major encyclopedia of Biblical interpretation, *Torah Shelaymah.*

Klausner, Professor Joseph (1874–1958). A leading Jewish historian of previous generation; author of *History of the Second Temple Period* and many other works.

Kook, Rabbi Abraham Ha Cohen Isaac (1865–1935). First chief rabbi of the Yishuv (Zionist settlement and community that preceded the State of Israel); a major mystic and theologian known for his charismatic outreach efforts to nonobservant Jews.

Kook, Rabbi Tsvi Yehuda (1891–1982). Son of Abraham Isaac Kook; head of Mercaz Harav Kook, the yeshiva founded by his father. Central figure in Gush Emunim (Bloc of the Faithful), the Israeli religious nationalist movement that grew after 1967.

Kovner, Abba (1918–1987). Survivor and partisan; extraordinary spiritual leader, poet, and educator; spiritual architect of Beit Hatefutsot (Museum of the Diaspora).

Kuhn, Thomas S. (1922–). Professor, intellectual historian, and author of the influential book, *The Structure of Scientific Revolutions*, and other writings on the development of science and culture.

Lamm, Norman (1929–). President of Yeshiva University, leading Modern Orthodox institution in America.

Levi, Primo (1920–1987). Survivor of Auschwitz; wrote some of the most important memoirs of the Holocaust period; author of *Survival in Auschwitz* and other works.

Levi Yitzchak of Berditchev (1740–1810). One of the great charismatic Rebbe figures of Chasidism, known particularly for defending the Jewish people— even if it involved challenging God.

Lewinski, Yom Tov (1899–1973). Scholar, editor, co-worker of Hayyim Nachman Bialik, a leader in making Jewish tradition available to secular Jews in the land of Israel.

Maimon, Rabbi Yehuda Leib (1875–1962). Rabbi and scholar; Orthodox Zionist leader; one of the signers of the Israeli Declaration of Independence.

Maimonides (1135–1204). The leading Jewish philosopher of the Middle Ages and the great codifier of Jewish law.

Mengele, Dr. Josef (1911–1979). Doctor and chief selector of the victims at Auschwitz.

Moyne, Lord (1880–1944). British lord high commissioner of Egypt during World War II, declined to try to save Hungarian Jewry; assassinated in 1947 by Jewish underground.

Nachman of Bratzlav, Rabbi (1772–1810). Chasidic Rebbe, founder of Bratzlav Chasidism, with unique mystical philosophy and messianic strivings.

Raphael, Yitzchak (1914–). Orthodox Zionist leader, member of Knesset, former Cabinet minister, and head of Mossad HaRav Kook publishing house.

Rashi, Rabbi Shlomo Yitzhaki (1040–1105). Medieval French rabbi and scholar; author of *the* classic and most widely used commentaries on the Torah and on the Talmud.

Rav and Samuel (end of second century to mid-third century). Transitional Babylonian rabbinic figures from Tannaim (teachers) of the Mishneh (senior portion of the Talmud) to the Amoraim (teachers) of the Gemara (the latter portion of the Talmud, which expands and applies the mishnaic teachings); heads of yeshivas (academies).

Robinson, Jacob (1889–1977). Jewish legal expert and historian; scholar of the Holocaust.

Rosenzweig, Franz (1886–1929). Major twentieth-century philosopher of Judaism, particularly influential because of his personal model of turning back from assimilation (in his case, potential conversion to Christianity) to an ever-deepening involvement in Judaism; author of *The Star of Redemption* and other writings.

Roskies, David (1948–). Professor of Yiddish literature; founder-editor of *Prooftexts,* a magazine of literary criticism and history; author of *Against the Apocalypse: Jewish Responses to Catastrophe* and *Night Words* (see chapter 11).

Rotan, Leo. Psychiatric social worker.

Rubenstein, Richard (1924–). Professor of religion at University of Florida-Tallahassee; in response to the Holocaust became a leading death-of-God theologian and cultural analyst; author of *After Auschwitz* and other works.

Salanter, Rabbi Israel (1810–1883). Founder of the Mussar movement, an ethical-religious renewal movement in nineteenth-century East European Jewry; a psychologist-thinker of extraordinary insight.

Schacht, Dr. Hjalmar (1877–1970). Financial wizard and important Nazi government official.

Schachter, Zalman (1924–). Founder of *B'nai Or,* a spiritual renewal movement; has worked on the frontier of Jewish and ecumenical liturgical development; author of *Fragments of a Future Scroll* and other writings.

Schweid, Professor Eliezer (1929–). Leading Israeli philosopher; has written extensively on tradition's relevance to modern, non-Orthodox Jews in Israel; author of *Israel at the Crossroads* and many other works.

Shabbetai, Zevi (1626–1676). Was proclaimed Messiah and followed widely in the world Jewish community in the 1660s. His career and thought grew out of the mysticism that suffused the Jewish world after the expulsion of Spanish Jewry in 1492; however, he could not bring the redemption and instead converted to Islam under duress.

Siegel, Richard (1947–). Co-editor of *The Jewish Catalog,* an important expression of the Havurah (fellowship) and countercultural Jewish religious revival groups of the 1960s and 1970s.

Simeon ben Gamaliel, Rabbi (first century C.E.). Nasi (head) of the Jewish community after the destruction of the Temple.

Simon ben Menasya, Rabbi (*ca.* end of the second century, beginning of the third century). Fifth-generation Tanna (teacher) of the Mishnah; contemporary of Rabbi Judah the Prince.

Soloveitchik, Rabbi Hayyim (Brisker) (1853–1918). Chief rabbi of Brest-Litovsk, Russia; founder of the Brisker method of Talmudic study using more conceptual methods and categories.

Soloveitchik, Rabbi Joseph B. (1903–). The leading halachist/theologian and teacher of Modern Orthodoxy in America, author of *Halachic Man* and other works.

Solzhenitsyn, Alexander (1918–). Major contemporary Russian novelist; dissident opponent of the Communist regime exiled for his moral critique of the system; author of *The Gulag Archipelago* and other works.

Steiner, George (1929–). Scholar and cultural analyst; has written important reflections on the Holocaust, including *Language and Silence.*

Stern College. The undergraduate college for women of Yeshiva University. Offers Jewish religious as well as general studies. Yeshiva is the central institution of American modern Orthodoxy.

Sutzkever, Abraham (1913–). Leading Yiddish poet in prewar Vilna, Lithuania, and postwar Israel.

Szmaglewska, S. Polish woman guard in Auschwitz; witness at Nuremberg crimes trial.

Tal, Professor Uri (1926–1984). A leading Jewish studies scholar particularly noted for his studies of Jews and Germans in the nineteenth century and of Nazi "theology" in the twentieth century.

Talmud—The authoritative body of post-biblical law and lore, containing the primary documents of the Oral Law which interprets and applies the biblical tradition. Its earliest stratum, the Mishneh, includes the teachings of scholars (called Tannaim) up to (circa) 200 C.E. and is the primary reflection (albeit, an indirect one) of rabbinic response to the destruction of the Temple. The later, larger part is called Gemara (teaching) and contains the teachings of scholars (called amoraim) up to (circa) the seventh century.

Tanach—an acronym for Torah (Five Books of Moses), Neviim (Prophets) and Ketubim (Writings) which together constitute the canon of Hebrew Scriptures.

Teitz, Rabbi Pinchas (1908–). Chief Orthodox Rabbi of Elizabeth, New Jersey; leader of Agudas Ha-Rabbonim, old-line Orthodox rabbis with strong European roots.

Van Buren, Paul (1924–). Leading Christian theologian on the frontier of Christian theology with special reference to Jews and Judaism; author of *A Theology of the Jewish Christian Reality* and other works.

Weinberg, Louis (1905–1980). A lover of Yiddish and the Jewish people.

Weiss, Rabbi Avraham (Avi) (1944–). A leading modern Orthodox Rabbi and activist especially for Soviet Jewry and women's tefillah (prayer) issues.

Weissmandl, Rabbi Dov Ber (d. 1957). Leading Czechoslovakian rabbi, Holocaust survivor; tried in vain to arrange ransom to stop the destruction; author of *Min HaMeytzar,* important letters and an account of his attempts to get the Jews rescued.

Weltsch, Robert (1891–1982). Editor of *Juedische Rundschau,* a German Jewish Zionist publication; author of famous editorial response to initial Nazi persecutions, "Wear the Yellow Badge Proudly."

Wiesel, Elie (1928–). Nobel Peace Prize laureate; his prophetic voice has grown out of his unique role as lifelong writer and witness to the Holocaust.

Yad Vashem. Founded in 1953, a major archive and leading Holocaust memorial center in the world; created by the State of Israel to memorialize the Holocaust.

Yochanan, Rabbi (ca. 180–*ca.* 279). Palestinian amora whose teachings are central to Palestinian Talmud.

Yohanan ben Zakki, Rabbi (first century C.E.). Primary architect of post-Destruction rabbinic response which rebuilt Jewish life.

Yosselevska, Rivka. Holocaust survivor; witness at Eichmann trial on experience of surviving an Einsatzgruppen operation.

Ziemba, Rabbi Menachem (1883–1943). A leading scholar and Orthodox rabbi in prewar Warsaw, Poland; declined to be evacuated and saved by himself; killed in the Warsaw Ghetto.

INDEX